SEVENTH-D

International Bible Commentary

GENESIS

Jacques B. Doukhan

PACIFIC PRESS
REVIEW & HERALD

GENESIS

SEVENTH-DAY ADVENTIST

International
Bible Commentary

Designed by Bryan Gray

Cover photo © Thinkstock

Copyright © 2016 by Pacific Press® Publishing Association

Published by Pacific Press® Publishing Association and Review and Herald® Publishing Association

Printed in the United States of America

The author assumes full responsibility for the accuracy of all facts and quotations as cited in this book.

Unless otherwise marked, Bible texts quoted in this book are from the New King James Version®. Copyright © 1982 by Thomas Nelson. Used by permission. All rights reserved.

Scriptures marked ASV are from the American Standard Version.

Scriptures marked CJB are from the Complete Jewish Bible, copyright © 1998 by David H. Stern. All rights reserved.

Scriptures marked DBY are from the Darby Bible, by John Nelson Darby, 1890.

Scriptures marked ESV are from The Holy Bible, English Standard Version®, copyright © 2001 by Crossway, a publishing ministry of Good News Publishers. ESV® Text Edition: 2011. All rights reserved.

Scriptures marked ISV are from The Holy Bible: International Standard Version. Copyright © 1995-2014 by ISV Foundation. ALL RIGHTS RESERVED INTERNATIONALLY. Used by permission of Davidson Press, LLC.

Scriptures marked JPS are from the Jewish Publication Society Tanakh, copyright © Jewish Publication Society, 1917.

Scriptures marked KJV are from the King James Version.

Scriptures marked NAB from The New American Bible, copyright © 1970, by the Confraternity of Christian Doctrine, Washington, D.C., and are used by permission of copyright owner.

Scriptures marked NASB are from the NEW AMERICAN STANDARD BIBLE®, copyright © 1960, 1962, 1963, 1968, 1971, 1972, 1973, 1975, 1977, 1995 by The Lockman Foundation. Used by permission.

Scriptures marked NET are from the NET Bible®, copyright © 1996–2006 by Biblical Studies Press, LLC. All rights reserved.

Scriptures marked NIV are from THE HOLY BIBLE, NEW INTERNATIONAL VERSION®, NIV®. Copyright © 1973, 1978, 1984, 2011 by Biblica, Inc®. Used by permission. All rights reserved worldwide.

Scriptures marked NJB are from The New Jerusalem Bible, copyright © 1985 by Darton, Longman & Todd, Ltd. and Doubleday, a division of Random House, Inc. Reprinted by Permission.

Scriptures marked NJPS are from the New JPS Jewish Bible: Tanakh. Copyright © 1985 by the Jewish Publication Society. All rights reserved.

Scriptures marked NRSV are from the New Revised Standard Version Bible, copyright © 1989 the Division of Christian Education of the National Council of the Churches of Christ in the United States of America. Used by permission. All rights reserved.

Scriptures marked REB are from The Revised English Bible, copyright © Oxford University Press and Cambridge University Press, 1989. Reprinted by permission.

Scriptures marked RSV are from the Revised Standard Version of the Bible, copyright © 1946, 1952, and 1971 the Division of Christian Education of the National Council of the Churches of Christ in the United States of America. Used by permission. All rights reserved.

Scriptures marked TNK are from the Tanakh: The New JPS Translation of the Holy Scriptures, copyright © 1985, the Jewish Publication Society. All rights reserved.

Scriptures marked YLT are from Young's Literal Translation, copyright © 1989 by Robert Young.

ISBN 978-0-8163-6248-6

August 2016

TABLE OF CONTENTS

3. FROM BABEL TO THE PROMISED LAND: ABRAHAM

GENESIS 12–22:19

4. FROM THE PROMISED LAND TO EGYPT: ISAAC-JACOB-JOSEPH

GENESIS 22:20–48:22

5. PROSPECT OF THE PROMISED LAND: THE PEOPLE OF ISRAEL

GENESIS 49–50:26

SELECTED ANNOTATED BIBLIOGRAPHY
SUGGESTIONS FOR FURTHER READING OR CONSULTATION

EDITORS' PREFACE

The title "Seventh-day Adventist International Bible Commentary" (SDAIBC) is meant to mark more than just a confessional identity. This name points both to the beginning and the end of the canonical Scriptures. "Seventh-day" refers to the first page of the Bible, with the Sabbath that crowned God's creation and started human history. "Adventist" refers to the last page of the Bible, with the "Advent" of the Lord that will conclude human history and bring the life, glory, and peace of God's presence. Carrying the two poles of Scriptures the name of "Seventh-day Adventist" is a testimony to the totality of Scriptures and to its profound unifying message. At the same time, the name reminds us that the interaction with these Scriptures does not stop with the written page but also points to the presence of God in the reality of our personal existence and in the history of humankind. As for the word "International," it testifies to the global identity of its writers as well as to the world church it is designed for.

Because the classic "Seventh-day Adventist Bible Commentary" (SDABC) was produced some seventy years ago, it has become increasingly more urgent to prepare a new commentary. Among the various reasons, three stand out. First, our world has changed dramatically and the men and women of today are facing unprecedented philosophical and spiritual challenges. Secondly, our knowledge of the Scriptures has improved. New information and technical skills have provided us with new findings that illuminate and enrich our reading of Scripture. And finally, the church has changed. From an overwhelming American majority, it has now grown into an international community. For the first time in history, the Adventist Church is benefiting from the contributions of a growing number of biblical and theological scholars across the globe who are proficient in every area of expertise.

Concerning the intended audience, the present commentary has been prepared with two kinds of readers in mind. The first group consists of pastors and seminary students as well as theologians and Bible teachers who explain and expound the lessons of Scripture in the church or classroom. The second group includes every other person who is seeking to understand the biblical text at a deeper level.

It is important to note that although the commentary has been worked out on the basis of the original Hebrew and Greek texts, it has been written so as to be read and understood without any previous knowledge of these ancient languages. However, when a reference to the original language is needed to make an argument, transliteration of the Hebrew or Greek word is provided. The authors of this commentary have tried, as far as possible, to make their presentations simple and clear in order to facilitate their readers' ability to follow their explanations and arguments. For readers interested in more technical details, we have included additional discussions in the footnotes, along with any relevant bibliographical information. The authors have also sought to integrate theological and spiritual lessons, along with their practical applications, into the flow of the textual commentary.

The method followed in this commentary is that of the "close reading" of the biblical text. This means that we have given careful attention to the biblical text, to the way it speaks, involving a study of its words, its meaning and its grammar, its literary forms, its literary structure, and its theology. This approach arises out of the conviction that God has acted in history to inspire the Biblical writers to convey His message through their own human words and literary expressions. Thus, the text is studied against its historical background, not to determine the context out of which the text arouse, but rather to understand the context within which God communicated His message.

This quest for the meaning of the text from within the particular passage under study is accompanied by the quest for further illumination from the entire biblical context (Old Testament and New Testament). Where other commentators are quoted, or noted in the footnotes, this is done to give the obligatory acknowledgment to a piece of carefully investigated biblical research, or to appreciate a particularly well-worded statement of a truth, and does not represent an endorsement or reliance on everything that author may have written. The speculations and philosophical presuppositions of the historical-critical method and its derived theories have been strictly avoided.

The writers of this commentary are not under any illusion of having arrived at a complete and infallible interpretation of the text. It is not the last word on Scripture. Rather it is the *next* word on Scripture, advancing the ongoing conversation as believers study and seek to understand God's Word. It is our hope that the reading of this commentary will not only bring more information and clarification on a given problem or passage, but that it will be an incentive to go further in the exploration of the biblical Scriptures. More importantly, it is our prayer that the consultation of these commentaries will empower the life of the reader and bring him or her nearer to our Lord, the invincible Hero of the ancient events recounted in this book, the very One who inspired its writing and continues to appeal to us today. As Ellen White urges: "study God's word prayerfully. That word presents before you, in the law of God and the life of Christ, the great principles of holiness, without which 'no man shall see the Lord.' Hebrews 12:14. It convinces of sin; it plainly reveals the way of salvation. Give heed to it as the voice of God speaking to your soul."[1]

The Editors of the SDAIBC

---

1   Ellen G. White, SC 35.

HOW TO READ THE SDAIBC

The Bible commentary is primarily a tool to aid in the understanding of the Scriptures. While its reading may be at times easy and interesting, at other times the difficulty level will increase and demand more careful attention. As the SDABC stated, "A Commentary is not a storybook, which may be read for idle diversion and with no concentration of mind. A commentary worth the name is a sober, serious work, very literally a textbook" (SDABC 1:19). Some may use this commentary in the classroom as a textbook and read it from the first page to the last. Most will use it as a reference work and consult it to address specific problems or because they are interested in particular biblical passages. To help the reader get the maximum profit from the commentary, we suggest the following guidelines:

1. Before consulting the commentary on a passage, take time to read the biblical text in your preferred version in a slow, careful, intelligent, and prayerful manner. Pay attention to the words, flow of thought, and the literary style. Appreciate the beauty of the presentation. The truth in the text is often expressed through its poetic forms. Read with ethical sympathy and love (we should not read the Bible with prejudices *against* other people but rather to find the truth). Use your reason and intelligence with humility to understand the Word of God, and be open to new and surprising meanings of the text. Confront your own understanding of the text with that of your fellow believers. Ask God for the Holy Spirit to help you in this exercise of receiving His Word.

2. Remember that your Bible is only a translation of the original Hebrew (or Aramaic) Old Testament and Greek New Testament. Since a translation can never render the full richness or various nuances and peculiarities of the original language, it is advisable to use several translations in your search for the intended meaning of the biblical text. This is why these volumes provide two of the more reliable versions, the NKJV and the ESV, before each section of commentary. In the course of the commentary, the commentator may refer to one of these versions, another Bible version, or provide his or her personal translation that renders the original text more faithfully. Read your passage in these two versions. It is the opinion of the editors that sometimes the NKJV is better (especially for the Old Testament) and sometimes it is the ESV that is better (especially for the New Testament). Note that the biblical passages introducing the commentary have been determined according to the structure of the biblical text, and not according to the chapter division. This arrangement not only allows for a closer contact with the biblical text, but it also takes in consideration its literary organization.

3. As you consult the commentary, note the frequent biblical references given in parentheses. These help explain and provide the canonical understanding of the text that is commented on.

4. Read carefully the introduction of each book to grasp the general background, the theology, and the outline ("literary structure") of the book.

5. Use the index at the end of the last volume in your study on a certain topic ("tithe," sanctuary," "death," "resurrection," etc.). This consultation will provide you with the biblical texts that deal with your topic and an explanation and discussion of these texts.

6. Get acquainted with the glossary of technical terms (in alphabetic order),

which are used throughout the commentary; this list varies depending on the commentator and is located before each volume (see p. 11).

7. Apply the Word of God to your personal life and existence from the perspective of the great controversy between Christ and Satan, and particularly in light of God's revelation in Jesus Christ. There is a two-way process between the Scriptures and the reader. On one hand, the reading of the inspired text will affect your person and your life. On the other hand, this Spirit-led experience of continuous "conversion" will guide your quest for a right understanding of the biblical text.

Writing a commentary on the Bible is an act of arrogance. This act claims implicitly that the writer who explains, interprets, and comments on the text has a firsthand (or even a better) knowledge of what the biblical author meant to say. Yet the fact is quite the opposite. The experience of writing a commentary on a text that comes from another culture and another time far removed from us all, a text we believe has been inspired by the infinite God of the universe, inevitably brings the potentially "arrogant" commentator to humility.

This has been my personal experience. Commenting on the book of Genesis, the first book of the Bible, which touches everything and is so rich and complex and yet so personal and simple, has been a humbling and exciting journey.

Our first contact with this book is ambivalent. On the one hand, we marvel that the great God of the universe, who created this great masterpiece—our world—and gave life to humankind, planted the lush Garden of Eden, and set the colorful rainbow in the sky, also condescended to come close to humans, speak with them, and tenderly care for their personal needs. These are astonishing stories of divine wonder that convey lessons of ethics, faith, and hope. On the other hand, and in counterpoint, we stumble on sad and sordid stories about men and women of the flesh. They are cowards (Adam and Eve), liars (Abraham), doubters (Abraham and Sarah), gluttons (Isaac), deceivers (Jacob), murderers (Simeon and Levi), they envy (the sons of Jacob), sleep with prostitutes (Judah); and yet, these sinful humans manage to leave a legacy of high moral and spiritual standards. This paradox carries a relevant message for all of us. These men and women are anything but untouchable heroes or disembodied saints; they are flesh and blood sinners, with genuine stories that have been written for our benefit. Their experiences of overcoming teach us crucial lessons "for doctrine, for reproof, for correction, for instruction in righteousness" (2 Tim 3:16).

As the poet John Donne put it, "no man is an island." Likewise, this commentary is not an island. Although I have strived to have a fresh reading of the text of Genesis, I have learned from preceding and contemporary attempts, ranging from the traditional Jewish and Christian commentaries to more scholarly works. In addition, I have not ignored the readings intimated by Ellen White as they often suggested to me an interpretation worth exploring. I am also particularly indebted and most grateful to my friends and co-bearers of this project, the Executive Members of the SDAIBC who, in spite of their heavy and urgent charges, made time to read my manuscript. Their pertinent questions, editorial and theological suggestions, and helpful corrections have considerably contributed to straighten, enrich, and clarify my writing of this commentary.

Jacques B. Doukhan

ECHO. Repetition of sounds, words, or ideas from a passage, suggesting some kind of connection with that passage. The common words *'anokhi* "I" and *hinneh* "behold" used by both Abraham and God in their dialogue (15:1–3) is an echo that suggests a relation of dependence between Abraham's doubts and God's assurances. The use of the specific words *'ot* "sign" and *mo'ed* "season" in the creation account (1:4–19) and in the context of the sanctuary (Exod 12:13; 30:36) suggests a common association of thoughts between creation and the sanctuary. Note that this is a case of **intertextuality**. The common use of the same specific words, grammatical forms, and sentence constructions between the divine reprobation to Eve (3:16) and the divine reprobation to Cain (4:7) suggests that the two texts should shed light on each other. This is another case of intertextuality, which may also be called **inner-textuality**, as the two texts belong to the same book. The use of the same words and motifs *zera'* "seed," "crush," "foot" in Genesis 3:15; 4:25; 2 Samuel 7:13; Psalm 110:1; Romans 16:20; and Revelation 12:1–6 suggests a common messianic interpretation. Note that this last example attests a case of "intertextuality" except for Genesis 4:25 ("innertextuality").

INCLUSIO. This term refers to a word, an expression, or a whole line that appears in the beginning and at the end of a passage. The function of an inclusio is to frame and mark the borders of a text. In the creation story, the phrase "create heavens and earth" is used in the introduction (1:1) and in the conclusion (2:4a) to mark the beginning and the end of the unit, but also to relate the broad creation of the universe (1:1) to the more particular creation of our human world during the creation week (2:4a).

KEYWORD. This is a specific word that is repeated several times in the text, thus indicating an emphasis or a general intention. So, for instance, the word *toledot* "genealogy," the most important keyword of the book of Genesis, suggests the intention of an emphasis on history and serves as a landmark in the organization of the structure of the whole book of Genesis. The repetition of the word *bagad* "garment" (39:12 [2x], 13, 15–16, 18) in the story of Joseph in his confrontation with Potiphar's wife indicates an intention of emphasis and a way to suggest the significance of Joseph's garment in this incident. Joseph's garment points to Joseph's brothers who also used Joseph's garment to support their lie (37:32–33). Also, the Hebrew word *beged* for "garment" hints at another meaning of the root *bagad* "to deceive" or "to lie" (Isa 24:16).

LITERARY STRUCTURE. The biblical text has often been shaped in the mold of a particular structure that is made visible through its rhythm and the regularity of its patterns (refrains, keywords, number of words, etc.). The literary structure is important for it may suggest the general and fundamental intention of the biblical writer, and thus orient our interpretation and help prevent false directions from the very outset. One of the most prevailing structures used in the Ancient Near East and the Bible is the **chiastic** structure (also called **chiasmus**); its form ABCC₁B₁A₁ suggests the Greek letter *chi* (X), hence its name "chiastic." The chiasmus can also be seen as a sequence ABC followed by the same sequence in reverse (CBA), giving the effect of a mirror image.

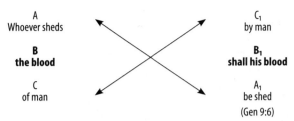

A
Whoever sheds

B
the blood

C
of man

C₁
by man

B₁
shall his blood

A₁
be shed

(Gen 9:6)

Note that this literary device focuses the attention on the central element, called **apex** (in bold in the above example), thus suggesting the central idea of the passage ("blood").

MERISM. This word designates a pair of contrasting (even opposite) words or phrases used to refer to a totality or completeness. So, the phrase "the heaven and the earth" (1:1) is a merism suggesting the totality of the created world. Likewise, the expression "the evening and the morning" (1:5) refers to the two opposite extremities of the day to suggest the entire day. The reference to the river of Egypt in the far south and to the Euphrates in the far north (15:18) is also a merism, meaning the totality of the world.

PARALLELISM. This literary device, certainly the most noteworthy characteristic of Hebrew poetry, consists in balancing one thought, word, phrase, or even whole texts by a corresponding thought, phrase, or text. The parallelism is often made between synonyms, which helps in understanding the meaning of a word or phrase. The fact that the verb *bara'* "create" is used in parallelism with the verb *'asah* "**make**" or *yatsar* "shape" (2:4; 6:7) reinforces the idea that the verb *bara'* "create" refers to a making process. The fact that the two creation stories are written in parallelism to each other suggests a literary unity and complementarity between the first text (1:1–2:4a), which emphasizes the universal perspective, and the second text (2:4b–25), which emphasizes the particular and personal perspective.

WORDPLAY. Some biblical writers like to play with the sound of words, make a pun, suggest a meaning or thought, or connect two words or two concepts. The wordplay on *'arum* "naked" (2:25) and *'arum* "cunning" (3:1) suggests a connection between the innocence and vulnerability of Adam and Eve and the temptation of the serpent. The repetition of the same sound *shup* "bruise," "crush" (3:15) suggests a connection between the two attacks, one on the heel of the Messiah, which depends on the other on the head of the serpent. The wordplay between the word *tsedaqah* "righteousness" and the word *ze'aqah* "outcry" suggests a contrast between the two conditions (18:19–20).

ABBREVIATIONS

BIBLICAL BOOKS

OLD TESTAMENT

Gen	Genesis	**Eccl**	Ecclesiastes
Exod	Exodus	**Song**	Song of Songs
Lev	Leviticus	**Isa**	Isaiah
Num	Numbers	**Jer**	Jeremiah
Deut	Deuteronomy	**Lam**	Lamentations
Josh	Joshua	**Ezek**	Ezekiel
Judg	Judges	**Dan**	Daniel
Ruth	Ruth	**Hos**	Hosea
1 Sam	1 Samuel	**Joel**	Joel
2 Sam	2 Samuel	**Amos**	Amos
1 Kgs	1 Kings	**Obad**	Obadiah
2 Kgs	2 Kings	**Jonah**	Jonah
1 Chr	1 Chronicles	**Mic**	Micah
2 Chr	2 Chronicles	**Nah**	Nahum
Ezra	Ezra	**Hab**	Habakkuk
Neh	Nehemiah	**Zeph**	Zephaniah
Esth	Esther	**Hag**	Haggai
Job	Job	**Zech**	Zechariah
Ps/Pss	Psalm/Psalms	**Mal**	Malachi
Prov	Proverbs		

NEW TESTAMENT

Matt	Matthew	**1 Tim**	1 Timothy
Mark	Mark	**2 Tim**	2 Timothy
Luke	Luke	**Titus**	Titus
John	John	**Phlm**	Philemon
Acts	Acts	**Heb**	Hebrews
Rom	Romans	**Jas**	James
1 Cor	1 Corinthians	**1 Pet**	1 Peter
2 Cor	2 Corinthians	**2 Pet**	2 Peter
Gal	Galatians	**1 John**	1 John
Eph	Ephesians	**2 John**	2 John
Phil	Philippians	**3 John**	3 John
Col	Colossians	**Jude**	Jude
1 Thess	1 Thessalonians	**Rev**	Revelation
2 Thess	2 Thessalonians		

ELLEN G. WHITE

AA	Acts of the Apostles, The
AG	God's Amazing Grace
AH	Adventist Home, The
ApM	Appeal to Mothers, An

AY	Appeal to the Youth
BLJ	To Be Like Jesus
CC	Conflict and Courage
CCh	Counsels for the Church
CD	Counsels on Diet and Foods
CE	Christian Education
CET	Christian Experience and Teaching
CEv	Colporteur Evangelist, The
CG	Child Guidance
CH	Counsels on Health
ChL	Christian Leadership
ChS	Christian Service
CL	Country Living
CM	Colporteur Ministry
COL	Christ's Object Lessons
Con	Confrontation
COS	Christ Our Saviour
CS	Counsels on Stewardship
CSW	Counsels on Sabbath School Work
CT	Counsels to Parents, Teachers, and Students
CTBH	Christian Temperance (Ellen G. White) and Bible Hygiene (James White)
CTr	Christ Triumphant
CW	Counsels to Writers and Editors
DA	Desire of Ages, The
DG	Daughters of God
Ed	Education
Ev	Evangelism
EW	Early Writings
FE	Fundamentals of Christian Education
FH	From the Heart
FLB	Faith I Live By, The
FW	Faith and Works
GC	Great Controversy, The
GC88	Great Controversy, The (1888 edition)
GW	Gospel Workers
GW92	Gospel Workers (1892 edition)
HL	Healthful Living
HP	In Heavenly Places
HS	Historical Sketches of the Foreign Missions of the Seventh-day Adventists
Hvn	Heaven
LDE	Last Day Events
LHU	Lift Him Up
LLM	Loma Linda Messages
LP	Sketches From the Life of Paul
LS	Life Sketches of Ellen G. White
LS88	Life Sketches of James White and Ellen G. White (1888 edition)
Lt	Letter, Ellen G. White
LYL	Letters to Young Lovers
Mar	Maranatha: The Lord Is Coming

MB	Thoughts From the Mount of Blessing
1MCP	Mind, Character, and Personality, Vol. 1 (2MCP for Vol. 2; 2 vols.)
MH	Ministry of Healing, The
ML	My Life Today
MM	Medical Ministry
1MR	Manuscript Releases, Vol. 1 (2MR for Vol. 2, etc.; 21 vols.)
Ms	Manuscript, Ellen G. White
MYP	Messages to Young People
1NL	Notebook Leaflets, Vol. 1 (2NL for Vol. 2; 2 vols.)
OFC	Our Father Cares
OHC	Our High Calling
PaM	Pastoral Ministry
PC	Paulson Collection of Ellen G. White Letters, The
PK	Prophets and Kings
PM	Publishing Ministry, The
PP	Patriarchs and Prophets
Pr	Prayer
RC	Reflecting Christ
RY	Retirement Years, The
SA	Solemn Appeal, A
1SAT	Sermons and Talks, Vol. 1 (2SAT for Vol. 2; 2 vols.)
SC	Steps to Christ
SD	Sons and Daughters of God
1SG	Spiritual Gifts, Vol. 1 (2SG for Vol. 2, 3SG for Vol. 3; 3 vols.)
SJ	Story of Jesus, The (adapted from SC)
SL	Sanctified Life, The
1SM	Selected Messages, Vol. 1 (2SM for Vol. 2, 3SM for Vol. 3; 3 vols.)
1SP	Spirit of Prophecy, The, Vol. 1 (2SP for Vol. 2, etc.; 4 vols.)
SpTA	Special Testimonies, Series A (Nos. 1–12)
SpTB	Special Testimonies, Series B (Nos. 1–19)
SpTBCC	Special Testimonies to the Battle Creek Church
SpTEd	Special Testimonies on Education
SpTMMW	Special Testimonies Relating to Medical Missionary Work
SpTMWI	Special Testimonies to Managers and Workers in Institutions
SpTPH	Special Testimonies to Physicians and Helpers
SR	Story of Redemption, The
SW	Southern Work, The
SW (date)	Southern Watchman (if with date)
1T	Testimonies for the Church, Vol. 1 (2T for Vol. 2, etc.; 9 vols.)
TA	Truth About Angels, The
TDG	This Day With God
Te	Temperance
TM	Testimonies to Ministers and Gospel Workers
TMK	That I May Know Him
TSA	Testimonies to Southern Africa
TSB	Testimonies on Sexual Behavior, Adultery, and Divorce
TSDF	Testimony Studies on Diet and Foods
TSS	Testimonies on Sabbath-School Work (1900)
1TT	Testimony Treasures, Vol. 1 (2TT for Vol. 2, 3TT for Vol. 3; 3 vols.)

UL	Upward Look, The
VSS	Voice in Speech and Song, The
WM	Welfare Ministry
WLF	Word to the "Little Flock," A
YRP	Ye Shall Receive Power
1888	Ellen G. White 1888 Materials, The

OTHER SOURCES

ÄAT	Ägypten und Altes Testament
AB	Anchor Bible
ABD	*Anchor Bible Dictionary.* Edited by D. N. Freedman. 6 vols. New York: Doubleday, 1992
AEL	*Ancient Egyptian Literature.* M. Lichtheim. 3 vols. Berkeley: University of California Press, 1971–1980
AJBI	*Annual of the Japanese Biblical Institute*
AnBib	Analecta Biblica
ANE	Ancient Near East
ANEP	*The Ancient Near East in Pictures Relating to the Old Testament.* 2nd ed. Edited by J. B. Pritchard. Princeton: Princeton University Press, 1994
ANET	*Ancient Near East Texts Relating to the Old Testament.* 3rd ed. Edited by J. B. Pritchard, Princeton: Princeton University Press, 1969
ASAE	*Annales du Service des antiquités de l'Egypte*
ASOR	American School of Oriental Research
AUSS	*Andrews University Seminary Studies*
b.	Babylonian Talmud
BA	*Biblical Archaeologist*
BASOR	*Bulletin of the American Schools of Oriental Research*
BDB	F. Brown, S. R. Driver, and C. A. Briggs, *A Hebrew and English Lexicon of the Old Testament*
BHS	*Biblia Hebraica Stuttgartensia*
Bib	*Biblica*
BMik	*Beit Mikra: Journal for the Study of the Bible and Its World*
BN	*Biblische Notizen*
BTCB	Brazos Theological Commentary of the Bible
CAD	*The Assyrian Dictionary of the Oriental Institute of the University of Chicago.* Chicago: The Oriental Institute of the University of Chicago, 1956–2006
CAH	Cambridge Ancient History
CBQ	*Catholic Biblical Quarterly*
CBRFJ	*Christian Brethren Research Fellowship Journal*
CHANE	Culture and History of the Ancient Near East
CJB	Complete Jewish Bible
COS	*The Context of Scripture.* Edited by W. W. Hallo. 3 vols. Leiden: Brill, 1997–2002
DAA	*Documentation for Ancient Arabia.* K. A. Kitchen. 2 vols. Liverpool: Liverpool University Press, 1994–2000
DJPA	*Dictionary of Jewish Palestinian Aramaic.* M. Sokoloff. Ramat-Gan: Bar Ilan University Press, 1990
EBC	The Expositor's Bible Commentary. Edited by F. E. Gaebelein. 12 vols. Grand Rapids: Zondervan, 1976–1992
ErIsr	*Eretz-Israel*
ESV	English Standard Version
EvQ	*Evangelical Quarterly*

GKC	*Gesenius' Hebrew Grammar.* Edited by E. Kautzsch. Translated by A. E. Cowley. 2nd ed. Oxford: Clarendon, 1910
HALOT	*The Hebrew and Aramaic Lexicon of the Old Testament.* L. Koehler, W. Baumgartner, and J. J. Stamm. 4 vols. Leiden: Brill, 1994–1999
HR	*History of Religions*
HUCA	*Hebrew Union College Annual*
IBHS	*An Introduction to Biblical Hebrew Syntax.* B. K. Waltke and M. O'Connor. Winona Lake, IN: Eisenbrauns, 1990
ICC	International Critical Commentary
IDB	*The Interpreter's Dictionary of the Bible.* Edited by G. A. Buttrick. 4 vols. New York: Abingdon, 1962
IDBSup	*The Interpreter's Dictionary of the Bible: Supplementary Volume.* Edited by K. Crim. Nashville: Abingdon, 1976
IEJ	*Israel Exploration Journal*
ISBE	*International Standard Bible Encyclopedia.* Edited by G. M. Bromiley. 4 vols. Grand Rapids: Eerdmans, 1979–1988
ISV	International Standard Version
JAOS	*Journal of the American Oriental Society*
JATS	*Journal of the Adventist Theological Society*
JBL	*Journal of Biblical Literature*
JE	*The Jewish Encyclopedia.* Edited by I. Singer. 12 vols. New York: Funk & Wagnalls, 1925
JETS	*Journal of the Evangelical Theological Society*
JNES	*Journal of Near Eastern Studies*
JNSL	*Journal of Northwest Semitic Languages*
Joüon	P. Joüon, *A Grammar of Biblical Hebrew.* Translated and revised by T. Muraoka. Rome: Gregorian & Biblical Press, 2011
JPOS	*Journal of the Palestine Oriental Society*
JPS	Jewish Publication Society
JQR	*Jewish Quarterly Review*
JR	*Journal of Religion*
JSOT	*Journal for the Study of the Old Testament*
JSOTSup	Journal for the Study of the Old Testament Supplement Series
JSS	*Journal of Semitic Studies*
JTS	*Journal of Theological Studies*
KBL	L. Koehler and W. Baumgartner. *Lexicon in Veteris Testamenti libros.* 2nd ed. Leiden: Brill, 1958
KJV	King James Version
Klio	*Klio: Beiträge zur Alten Geschichte*
LXX	Septuagint
m.	Mishnah
NAB	New American Bible
NAC	New American Commentary
NASB	New American Standard Bible
NBD	*New Bible Dictionary.* Edited by D. R. W. Wood, H. Marshall, J. D. Douglas, and N. Hillyer. 3rd ed. Downers Grove: InterVarsity, 1996
NEAEHL	*The New Encyclopedia of Archaeological Excavations in the Holy Land.* Edited by E. Stern. 4 vols. New York: Simon & Schuster, 1993
NEASB	*Near East Archaeological Society Bulletin*
NET	New English Translation
NICOT	New International Commentary on the Old Testament

NIDOTTE *New International Dictionary of the Old Testament Theology and Exegesis.* Edited by W. A. VanGemeren. 5 vols. Grand Rapids: Zondervan, 1997

NIV   New International Version

NJB   New Jerusalem Bible

NJPS   New JPS Translation

NKJV   New King James Version

NLT   New Living Translation

NRSV   New Revised Standard Version

NT   New Testament

OBO   Orbis Biblicus et Orientalis

OBT   Overtures to Biblical Theology

OEAE   *The Oxford Encyclopedia of Ancient Egypt.* Edited by D. Redford. 3 vols. Oxford: Oxford University Press, 2001

OMRO   *Oudheidkundige Mededelingen uit het Rijksmuseum van Oudheden te Leiden*

Or   *Orientalia* (NS)

OT   Old Testament

OTL   Old Testament Library

PTMS   Pittsburg Theological Monographs Series

QH   *Qumran Hodayot* (Thanksgiving Hymns)

QM   *Qumran Milkhamah* (*War Scroll*)

RB   *Revue Biblique*

REB   Revised English Bible

RIMA   The Royal Inscriptions of Mesopotamia, Assyrian Periods

RLA   *Reallexicon der Assyriologie.* Edited by E. Ebeling et al. Berlin: de Gruyter, 1928–

SBLMS   Society of Biblical Literature Monograph Series

SDABC   Seventh-day Adventist Bible Commentary

SDAIBC   Seventh-day Adventist International Bible Commentary

Sem   *Semitica*

StPatr   Studia Patristica

TA   *Tel Aviv*

TDOT   *Theological Dictionary of the Old Testament.* Edited by G. J. Botterweck and H. Ringgren. Translated by J. T. Willis et al. 8 vols. Grand Rapids: Eerdmans, 1974–2006

TNIV   Today's New International Version

TNK   Tanakh: The New JPS Translation of the Holy Scriptures, 1985

TWOT   *Theological Wordbook of the Old Testament.* Edited by R. L. Harris, G. L. Archer Jr., and B. K. Waltke. 2 vols. Chicago: Moody Press, 1980

TynBul   *Tyndale Bulletin*

UF   *Ugarit-Forschungen*

VT   *Vetus Testamentum*

WBC   Word Biblical Commentary

y.   Jerusalem Talmud

YLT   Young's Literal Translation

ZA   *Zeitschrift für Assyriologie*

ZÄS   *Zeitschrift für ägyptische Sprache und Altertumskunde*

ZAW   *Zeitschrift für die alttestamentliche Wissenschaft*

[ ]   Corresponding reference in the Hebrew Bible

For other abbreviations used in this commentary, but not listed in this section, consult *The SBL Handbook of Style*, 2nd ed., 2014.

TRANSLITERATION

HEBREW CONSONANTS

א	alef	'
בּ	bet	b
ג	gimel	g
ד	dalet	d
ה	he	h
ו	vav	w
ז	zayin	z
ח	khet	kh
ט	tet	t
י	yod	y
כּ, ך	kaf	k
ל	lamed	l
מ, ם	mem	m
נ, ן	nun	n
ס	samek	s
ע	ayin	'
פּ, ף	pe	p, f
צ, ץ	tsade	ts
ק	qof	q
ר	resh	r
שׂ	sin	s
שׁ	shin	sh
ת	tav	t

HEBREW VOWELS

_	patakh	a
_	furtive patakh	a
ָ	qamets	a
הָ	final qamets he	ah
ֶ	segol	e
ֵ	tsere	e
ֵי	tsere yod	e
ִ	short hireq	i
ִ	long hireq	i
ִי	hireq yod	i
ָ	qamets khatuf	o
ֹ	holem	o
וֹ	full holem	o
ֻ	qibbuts	u
וּ	shureq	u
ֳ	khatef qamets	o
ֲ	khatef patakh	a
ְ	silent sheva No transliteration	
ְ	vocal sheva	e
ּ	dagesh Double letter (xx)	

GREEK		
α	a	
β	b	
γ	g	
γ	n	(before g, k, x, c)
δ	d	
ε	e	
ζ	z	
η	ē	
θ	th	
ι	I	
κ	k	
λ	l	
μ	m	
ν	n	
ξ	x	
ο	o	
π	p	
ϱ	r	
ϱ̇	rh	
σ, ς	s	
τ	t	
υ	y	(when not in diphthong)
υ	u	(in diphthongs: au, eu, ēu, ou, ui)
φ	ph	
χ	ch	
ψ	ps	
ω	ō	
ʽ	h	(with vowel or diphthong)

GENESIS

INTRODUCTION

THE IMPORTANCE OF GENESIS

The book of Genesis has been called "the most important book ever written."[1] As the first book of the Bible, it not only contains or anticipates all the biblical truths, it is also the book that, more than any other biblical book, has impacted the whole of Scripture,[2] and theology at large.[3] Without the book of Genesis, the Bible would be incomprehensible. It is highly significant that the canonical Bible, which begins with Genesis, the creation of heaven and earth (1–2) and the description of the Garden of Eden (3), comes full circle in Revelation with references to Genesis, the re-creation of heaven and earth (Rev 21:1) and eternal life in the Garden of Eden (Rev 22:1–5). It is as though the book of Genesis was meant to provide us with the key to the whole Bible.

The book of Genesis is foundational because of its universal scope. Genesis deals with the origin of the whole of our human universe. This function of the book is reflected in the Hebrew title of the book, *Bere'shit*. This is the first word of the book, meaning "in the beginning." The same idea is attested in the English title "Genesis," which is derived via the Latin transliteration from the Greek Septuagint *genesis*, meaning "origin." Indeed, the book of Genesis informs us about the beginning/origin of the world, of life, of humankind (1–2), of nations, languages, culture (3–11), and Israel (12–50).

Though primarily a book about "beginnings," Genesis also provides a hint of the end—the goal of human history. The account of creation, of life in the Garden of Eden free from death or war, where hu[4]mans lived in perfect harmony with the world and its Creator, inspire and nurture the nostalgia of all humankind. The book of Genesis is not only speaking about our origins, it also gives us a picture of our destination. It is a book of hope. Thus, it is an important book for all humanity.

More than any other book of the Bible, Genesis has shaped the three major monotheistic religions in our world today—Judaism, Christianity, and Islam—which share many of the same Genesis stories and ethical teachings. But even beyond religion, the accounts in Genesis have significantly influenced world culture, art, music, literature, and philosophy. In art, Genesis references span from Michelangelo's *Creation of Adam* on the ceiling of the Sistine Chapel and Rembrandt's painting of *The Sacrifice of Isaac* to Chagall's painting of *The Creation*, his scenes from the life of

---

1   Henry M. Morris, *The Genesis Record* (Grand Rapids: Baker, 1976), 17.

2   See Rolf Rendtorff for whom the book of Genesis provides "an all-embracing framework, as the fundamental, all-underlying premise for any talk about God, the world, and the individual," in *Canon and Theology*, ed. and trans. M. Kohl (Minneapolis: Fortress, 1993), 107–108.

3   Kenneth A. Mathews, *Genesis: 1–11:26*, NAC 1A (Nashville: Broadman & Holman, 1996), 22.

4   Verses without a book cited refer to Genesis.

Abraham, and R. Crumb's comic book of Genesis. In music, we note Joseph Haydn's oratorio on creation, Igor Stravinsky's cantata on Genesis 11, and several anguished Negro spirituals. Literary references appear in works by John Milton and Victor Hugo to modern Egyptian poet Amal Dunqul. And in philosophy, Genesis shows up from the analysis of Edmund Husserl to the questions of Søren Kierkegaard and the discussions of Jacques Derrida. Clearly, the book of Genesis has left profound marks on human culture. In fact, the book of Genesis lends itself to universal interest. It has it all: sex, violence, wars, famine, worldwide disasters, gastronomical interests, ethical dilemmas, suspense, and intrigue—all wrapped up in a true and timeless story with cosmic bearings and eternal repercussions.

For Seventh-day Adventists, the book of Genesis is of special significance. Not only does it explain and justify their keeping of the seventh-day Sabbath as a people united in a covenant with the God of Israel, it also substantiates their "advent" hope, when the world will be restored to its original "Genesis" state. It is noteworthy that nearly all Seventh-day Adventist beliefs are both found in and founded on this book: the seventh-day Sabbath (2:2–3), the unity of human nature (1:26; 2:7), conditional immortality (2:17; 3:19), the Law of God (2:16; 26:4–5),[5] the great controversy (3:15; 7:17–20; 12:1–3; 22:1–3; 22:15–18), salvation (3:15), substitutionary atonement (3:21; 3:15), the practice of tithe (14:20; 28:22), the ideal of a plant-based diet (1:29–30; 9:3), the distinction between clean and unclean meats (7:2–3; 8:20), the meaning of baptism (1:1–3; cf. 1 Pet 3:21), the cosmic significance of the sanctuary doctrine (2:2; cf. Exod 40:38), the creation (1:1), the Trinity (1:2, 26; 3:22; 18:2, 22), the responsibility of mission to the nations (4:26; 12:3), and the gift of prophecy (3:15; 20:6).

The book of Genesis is therefore the ideal place to start our study, not only because it will help us understand our origins and destination, but also because it teaches us how to engage with and reach out to others. In the process, we will be surprised by a God of love and mercy, whose first revelation is reported in the book of Genesis.

THE AUTHOR OF GENESIS

THE COMPOSITION OF GENESIS AND BIBLICAL CRITICISM

For almost eighteen centuries, no one questioned the Mosaic authorship of the book of Genesis. Except for a few,[6] Jewish and Christian scholars all agreed that the book of Genesis was wholly the work of Moses. It was only in the eighteenth century that the first significant disputes about the unity and the authorship of the book of Genesis took place. Biblical scholars began to approach the Scriptures from a *historical-critical* point of view, and thus to question the traditional acceptance of the Mosaic authorship of the book of Genesis. Philosopher Baruch Spinoza (1632–1677) was perhaps the first to challenge the Mosaic authorship of the Pentateuch, the Torah, which he attributed to Ezra. But the critical school of thought started with the 1753 publication of a work by French physician Jean Astruc (1684–1766) who

---

5   For the presence of the Ten Commandments in the book of Genesis, see Jo Ann Davidson, "The Decalogue Predates Mount Sinai: Indicators From the Book of Genesis," *JATS* 19, no. 1 (2008): 61–81.

6   See, for instance, the discussion of Ibn Ezra (1092–1167) who raised critical questions regarding the inclusion of some passages of the Pentateuch (e.g., Deut 34).

noticed variations in the use of divine names. Significantly, Astruc's original observation was based on the first two chapters of Genesis. Noting that Genesis 1:1–2:4a used the name *'Elohim* while Genesis 2:4b–25 used the name *YHWH*, Astruc extended his analysis to the rest of the Pentateuch and came to the conclusion that the book of Genesis was a composite of two parallel sources, one of which referred to Him as "*Yahweh*" and the other as "*'Elohim*." For Astruc, these were only ancient sources, which Moses merely brought together as redactor, but did not author. Although Astruc's view did not receive immediate support, several years later (1780), German historian and biblical scholar J. G. Eichhorn developed Astruc's thesis into a more systematic study, adding other criteria supporting multiple sources in Genesis and the Pentateuch. In the latter part of the nineteenth century and the beginning of the twentieth century, Julius Wellhausen impacted the theory with his evolutionary views, which remain influential even to this day.

It is beyond the scope of this commentary to trace all the steps in the development of the theories regarding the composition of the Pentateuch within the history of biblical criticism. Instead, our discussion will focus on the book of Genesis.[7] The consensus of these biblical critics is that Genesis is the result of the following three (and perhaps even four) distinct literary sources:[8]

1. The Yahwist source (J), dated to the tenth century BC, is thought to originate in Judah. This source covers history from the creation (2:4b) to the death of Moses (Deut 34:5–7). It is mostly biographical, presenting God through anthropomorphic images and, as such, is deemed to be the most primitive source.

2. The Elohist source (E), dated to the ninth century BC, is thought to originate in northern Israel. The source covers roughly the same historical period, but starts with the Abram narrative. It is mostly cultic, dealing with rituals. In this source, God could only be apprehended through dreams and visions. Then, it is proposed that an unknown "redactor" (R) living in the mid-seventh century BC combined these two sources (J and E) into a new composite document called JE.

3. The Priestly source (P), dated to the fifth century BC, is thought to come from priestly circles in Jerusalem after the Babylonian exile. Unlike J and E, P is not concerned with history but with Israel's sacral institutions (genealogies and the details of sacrifices and other rituals), insofar as these relate to and explain that history. Thus, the creation story (1:1–2:4a) is given to provide the reason for the institution of the Sabbath, just as the story of the covenant with Abraham (17:1–27) is produced to justify circumcision. According to critical scholars, the Priestly source develops a theory of religion that grew out of these institutions and is therefore more theological and spiritual. As such, it is considered the most advanced thinking and consequently the most recent source.

4. The Deuteronomic source, whose influence on Genesis had been first suggested by de Wette (1805), is an interpretation widely held among critical scholars today.[9]

---

7   For a thorough discussion of the critical approach to Genesis from a conservative point of view, see Mathews, *Genesis: 1–11:26*, esp. 68–85, and all throughout his commentary; cf. Gleason L. Archer, Jr., *A Survey of the Old Testament Introduction*, rev. and enl. ed. (Chicago: Moody Press, 1994), 89–189; cf. also, Temper Longman III and Raymond B. Dillard, *An Introduction to the Old Testament*, 2nd ed. (Grand Rapids: Zondervan, 2006), 40–62.

8   For the appearance of sources throughout Genesis according to critical scholars, see Victor P. Hamilton, *The Book of Genesis: 1–17*, NICOT (Grand Rapids: Eerdmans, 1999), 16.

9   See, for instance, David Carr's argument of the Deuteronomic language in the book of Genesis (e.g., in Genesis 15) in *Reading the Fractures of Genesis: Historical and Literary Approaches* (Louisville: Westminster John Knox, 1996), 165–166; cf. Gordon Wenham, "The Date of Deuteronomy: Linch-pin of Old Testament Criticism," *Themelios* 10, no.

Later scholars endorsed the classic Wellhausen theory, though using the tools of new scholarly disciplines such as *form criticism* (Hermann Gunkel, 1901) in which J and E were not single authors but schools of thought, and *tradition criticism* (Gerhard von Rad and Martin Noth, 1940–1980) in which J and P were neither single authors nor schools but vague oral traditions. While this theory, which was called the "Documentary Hypothesis" (or "the JEDP theory") has recently been sharply criticized from within the critical school itself, it still remains the basic paradigm from which critical biblical scholars continue to work and propose new solutions.[10] Yet the increasing realization of the speculative and subjective nature of this methodology has caused more people to move away from the diachronic approach to the synchronic approach. So that, instead of being interested in the development of the composition of the biblical document (diachronic approach), one prefers to pay attention to the text as it is, in its final state (synchronic approach).

This new trend has germinated under the influence of recent literary studies, particularly that of rhetorical criticism, which focuses on the style and the rhetorical aspects of the text. It is interesting that although these scholars are not as interested in the historical factors playing a role in the composition of the text, this new approach to the biblical text often leads these scholars to a conclusion regarding the historical composition of the text that is consistent with the prior recognition of the unity of the book of Genesis and even the possibility of its connection to Moses. One representative of this new school is Isaac Kikawada who, with Arthur Quinn,[11] demonstrates the unity of Genesis 1–11 on the basis of literary connections, especially through the chiastic structures.

Additionally, these scholars observe a five-part structure that very closely mirrors the five-part structure in the Akkadian Epic of Atrahasis (eighteenth century BC), a point that should have some implications regarding the antiquity of the book of Genesis. It is interesting that while they acknowledge the values of the Documentary Hypothesis and pay homage to it in their book's first pages,[12] they reach an opposite conclusion at the end: "We offer a persuasive refutation of the documentary analysis of Genesis 1–11 … One thing, if anything, we are certain of: the Documentary Hypothesis at present is woefully overextended."[13] Likewise, Gary Rendsburg, who observes parallels and correspondences between Genesis 12:1–9 (classified as mostly

. . .

3 (April 1985): 15–20; 11, no. 1 (September 1985): 15–18.

10   One of the most controversial critiques of the Documentary Hypothesis has been advocated by John Van Seters who, focusing on what he calls the Abrahamic tradition (12–26), defends his own reconstruction of the literary development in five stages (1. pre-Yahwistic first stage: J1; 2. pre-Yahwistic second stage: E; 3. Yahwistic: J; 4. Priestly: P; and 5. post-Priestly stage). Thus, Van Seters rejects the classic Wellhausen theory and instead erects his own Documentary Hypothesis of J1, J2 (=E), J, P1, and P2. Everything in 12–26 belongs to one or the other of the five segments (see J. Van Seters, *Abraham in History and Tradition* [New Haven, CT: Yale University, 1975]). Another important attack against the Documentary Hypothesis has been carried out by Rolf Rendtorff. However, the ghost of the Documentary Hypothesis is still haunting his theory. Although Rendtorff acknowledges, "the traditional Documentary Hypothesis has come to an end" (R. Rendtorff, "The Paradigm Is Changing: Hopes and Fears," *Biblical Interpretation* I [1992]: 11), he still ends up with a multilayered Genesis (see R. Rendtorff, *The Problem of the Process of Transmission in the Pentateuch*, JSOTSup 89, trans. J. J. Scullion [Sheffield: JSOT Press, 1987]). Instead of speaking of the three sources J, E, and P, Rendtorff simply detects in the book of Genesis two blocks of traditions (first, history made of sagas, myths, genealogies, and theological narratives in 1–11 and patriarchal history made of Abraham, Isaac, and Jacob/Joseph cycles in 12–50).

11   I. M. Kikawada, "The Shape of Genesis 11:1–9," in *Rhetorical Criticism: Essays in Honor of James Muilenburg*, eds. J. J. Jackson and M. Kessler, PTMS 1 (Pittsburg, PA: Pickwick, 1974), 18–32; I. M. Kikawada and A. Quinn, *Before Abraham Was: The Unity of Genesis 1–11* (Nashville: Abingdon, 1985).

12   Kikawada and Quinn, *Before Abraham Was*, 9.

13   Ibid., 125.

from J) and Genesis 22:1–19 (classified as mostly from E), concludes that these two texts have been written by the same person.[14] Thus, in the light of his study, Rendsburg suggests that the Documentary Hypothesis is "untenable" and should be "discarded."[15]

From this brief discussion on the composition of the book of Genesis, we may conclude that the classical Documentary Hypothesis is not a satisfactory option for the following three reasons:

1. The contradictions between the various proponents of the critical school in their delimitations of sources, and the present shift of interest, from a diachronic approach to a synchronic one, calls for a reconsideration of the critical proposals.

2. It is clear that two philosophical presuppositions inspired the idea and determined the shaping of these theories: First, the evolutionist paradigm, which implied a necessary development, from the most primitive and concrete thinking to the most advanced and spiritual thinking. And secondly, the skeptical methodology of rationalism, which implied systematic doubt towards any supernatural process and excluded the option of faith, thus rejecting the idea of miracles such as creation, the flood, and other extraordinary events recorded in the book of Genesis.

3. It is also important to notice that these proposals are, for the most part, indebted to the study of classical (Greek and Latin) literature where myths were a way of expressing and illustrating abstract concepts. Thus, the myth of Plato's Cave is an allegory used by the Greek philosopher Plato in his work *The Republic* to illustrate his thoughts regarding human perception of the world. In other words, Plato proceeds from thought to the story (as a myth), a method that will be later expressed by French philosopher Descartes in his *cogito ergo sum*: "I think, therefore I am." In the biblical worldview, on the other hand, the primary focus is on history, and the thinking process moves from there. It is history that triggers and inspires thinking and not thinking that produces the shaping of history. In the biblical worldview, the Cartesian maxim is reversed: "I am, therefore I think." For example, according to these critics (see the discussion on Genesis 1 below), the biblical story of creation should not be understood as an expression or illustration of the Israelite concept of redemption. Yet this is *exactly* what the biblical worldview proposes. The idea of the myth of creation was not subordinate to the spiritual idea of salvation, as critical scholars have often argued. On the contrary, it is the event of creation that was later used by the prophets of Israel to elaborate their theology of redemption (Exod 15:8, 15; Isa 40–45; Rev 21–22).[16]

MOSAIC AUTHORSHIP

While the critical theories have not been convincing in promoting the idea of multiple authors or sources for the book of Genesis, the testimony of the Scriptures and tradition, as well as the internal evidence from the Pentateuch itself, clearly supports the Mosaic authorship of the book of Genesis.

---

14 Gary A. Rendsburg, *The Redaction of Genesis* (Winona Lake, IN: Eisenbrauns, 1986), 32–34.

15 Ibid., 104–105.

16 For a discussion on the debate on creation and redemption, see Jacques B. Doukhan, *The Genesis Creation Story: Its Literary Structure*, Andrews University Seminary Doctoral Dissertation Series (Berrien Springs, MI: Andrews University, 1978), 227–233.

The Testimony of Scripture

Although the book of Genesis is anonymous and its author is not explicitly designated, many passages claim that Moses is the author of specific records contained in these books (Exod 17:14; 24:4; 34:27; Num 33:1–2; Deut 31:9). In the Old Testament, outside the Pentateuch, several passages relate the name of Moses in one way or another to the Law, the Torah of the Pentateuch (Josh 1:7–8; 8:31, 35; 23:6; 1 Kgs 2:3; 8:53, 56; Ezra 6:18; 7:6; Neh 9:14; 13:1; Dan 9:11–13; Mal 4:4). Following the practice of the Old Testament, the New Testament generally refers to the Pentateuch, as a whole or in part, as "the Law of Moses" (Luke 16:29, 31; John 5:46–47; 7:19, 22; Acts 3:22; Rom 10:5). Jesus Himself uses the expression "the Law of Moses" to designate the first of the three sections of the Hebrew Bible:[17] "These are the words which I spoke to you while I was still with you, that all things must be fulfilled which were written in **the Law of Moses and the Prophets and the Psalms** concerning Me" (Luke 24:27, 44).[18]

The Testimony of Tradition

Ancient rabbinic tradition attributes the whole of the Pentateuch, the Torah proper, to Moses,[19] with the exception of the last eight verses of Deuteronomy, which record the death of Moses. According to one opinion, these verses could have been written by Joshua, or, according to another opinion, by Moses himself at the dictation of God.[20] Similarly, Philo and support the idea that Moses wrote the whole Pentateuch.[21] Early prominent Christians such as Melito (AD 175), Cyril of Jerusalem (AD 348–386), and Hilary (AD 366), as well as later ones (the Reformers Martin Luther [1483–1546] and John Calvin [1509–1564]), likewise believed in the Mosaic authorship of the book of Genesis.

Internal Evidence

The tradition of the Mosaic authorship of the Pentateuch is consistent with the content of the accounts reported in the Pentateuch. There are details related to the life of Moses that only an eyewitness could have known: the details associated with the story of the birth of Moses, the description of the ark of bulrushes with asphalt and pitch, and the specific conversation between Moses' sister and the daughter of Pharaoh (Exod 2:1–10); the historical and geographical allusions; the information about the change of Pharaoh (Exod 1:8; 2:23); the precise count of the twelve springs of water and of the seventy palm trees at Elim (Exod 15:27); the comparison of the land of Canaan "like the land of Egypt as you go toward Zoar" (13:10); the report of the appearance and taste of the manna, which looked like coriander seed and which was colored like the color of bdellium (Num 11:7) and which tasted like "wafers made with honey" (Exod 16:31); the strong Egyptian connection and the precise details specific to the Egyptian civilization.

Also, the language of the Pentateuch, its archaisms, its unique expressions, and

---

17   See the Jewish traditional name *TaNaKh*, which is the acronym for *Torah* (Pentateuch), *Nebiim* (Prophets), and *Ketubim* (Writings).

18   Unless otherwise noted, Bible texts in this book are from the New King James Version (NKJV).

19   m. 'Aboth 1:1.

20   b. Bat. 14b, 15a.

21   Philo, *On the Life of Moses* 3.39, and Flavius Josephus, *Jewish Antiquities* 4.8.48.

the numerous Egyptianisms (indicated along the way in this commentary)[22] likewise testify to the antiquity of this section of biblical literature. Although the names of some places were later adjusted by copyists to help the reader identify them (see, for instance, the name of Dan in 14:14 for the city of Laish, cf. Judg 18:29), this does not affect the fundamental Mosaic attribution for the book of Genesis.

It is suggested in this commentary that Moses was indeed responsible for the book of Genesis, either by recording oral traditions, which were passed down over the centuries and/or by receiving direct revelation from God. In both cases, Moses, under the control and the guidance of the Holy Spirit, would have then written down the records of oral tradition, the words of God and the visions of the great events of the past.

THE SETTING AND THE PURPOSE OF GENESIS

The story of Genesis begins with creation and the Garden of Eden (1–2) and ends with a coffin and the anticipation of the Exodus experience (50:24–26). Thus creation, and by implication the first history of humankind (1–11), is related not just to patriarchal history (12–50), but also to the future Exodus event. While hinting at the unity of the book, this connection also suggests the profound theological purpose underlying the writing of Genesis for the Mosaic community: the God who will save the Israelites from Egypt is not just the God of the patriarchs, He is also the God of the universe, the God of creation. This association of thoughts was reassuring for Moses and even for the weak Israelites who might have doubted their power (Num 13) and questioned the legitimacy of their enterprise (Exod 4:1).[23] In fact, the literary and theological bridge between creation and the Exodus event suggests that the book of Genesis was written by someone with the event of the Exodus in mind. This supports the Mosaic-Exodus setting and origin of the book of Genesis. In that respect, it is no accident that the ten words (commandments) of God in the Decalogue echo the ten words (speeches) of God in the creation story.[24] This numeric parallel suggests that the two documents are responding to each other. The Law of God is put in the perspective of creation to alert the reader of its universality. Prior to the giving of the Law, God expressly presents creation as the reason for Israel to accept the covenant: "for all the earth is Mine" (Exod 19:5). Indeed, God's covenant with Israel and the Law given to them in the desert of Sinai had universal claims: they concerned all humans. For the Torah, the Word of God for all humans, was the very purpose of creation.[25] This is precisely the message registered in the framework of the book of Genesis, which begins with creation and ends with the promise of God's visitation.

---

22   For the Egyptian connection of the Pentateuch, see especially A. S. Yahuda, *The Language of the Pentateuch in Its Relation to Egyptian* (London: Oxford University Press, 1933); and more recently, P. J. Wiseman, *Clues to Creation in Genesis* (London: Marshal, Morgan and Scott, 1977), 47, 103; K. A. Kitchen, *The Bible in Its World* (Downers Grove: InterVarsity, 1978); J. K. Hoffmeier, *Israel in Egypt* (New York: Oxford University Press, 1997); J. D. Currid, *Ancient Egypt and the Old Testament* (Grand Rapids: Baker Books, 1997).

23   See Rashi's comment on Genesis 1:1, in Miqraot Gedolot, ad loc.

24   In the creation story (1:1–2:4a) God speaks ten times, for the phrase *wayyo'mer 'Elohim* "God said" occurs ten times, although the expression applies to the work of creation only nine times (see below).

25   Rashi, the great eleventh-century rabbinic commentator, refers to an ancient rabbinic tradition that the book of Genesis (and the Pentateuch) should have begun with Exodus 12:2, and not with Genesis 1 (see his commentary in Miqraot Gedolot on Genesis 1:1). Cf. R. R. Reno, "God creates for the sake of his commandments, for the sake of the Torah." See R. R. Reno, *Genesis*, BTCB (Grand Rapids: Brazos, 2010), 30.

The book of Genesis also ends with the expectation of the Exodus: "God will surely visit you, and bring you … to the land of which He swore to Abraham, to Isaac, and to Jacob" (50:24). This anticipation is repeated a second time as a solemn oath: "God will surely visit you, and you shall carry up my bones from here" (50:25). These two verses not only mention the future event of the Exodus and give a reference to the transportation of the bones of Joseph from Egypt to the Promised Land, they also name the three patriarchs and their role in the preparation of Israel. The repeated reference to Jacob and Joseph in the first verses of the book of Exodus (Exod 1:1, 5–6), and again the mention of Joseph with regard to the new Pharaoh (Exod 1:8), connect the first verses of Exodus to the last verses of the book of Genesis. It is also noteworthy that the same words of hope and divine promise that wrap up the book of Genesis are heard again when Moses encounters God, *YHWH*, the Lord, for the first time in the desert of Midian: " '*God will surely visit you*, and bring you out of this land to the land of which He swore *to Abraham, to Isaac, and to Jacob.*' Then Joseph took an oath from *the children of Israel*, saying, **'God will surely visit you'** … *in Egypt*" (50:24–26). These same words (italicized in the quotations) that Joseph pronounced to his brothers, "the children of Israel" (50:25), are repeated by Moses to "the children of Israel" (Exod 3:15): "Thus you shall say to *the children of Israel*: 'The Lord God of your fathers, the God of *Abraham*, the God of *Isaac*, and the God of *Jacob*, has sent me to you … The Lord God of your fathers, the God of *Abraham*, of *Isaac*, and of *Jacob*, appeared to me, saying, '*I have surely visited you* and seen what is done to you *in Egypt*' " (Exod 3:15–16).

This echo is not only comprehensive in that it covers words, expressions, and even whole sentences—not to mention the repetition of the last phrase "in Egypt" (Exod 3:16), but it is also a unique echo in the Scriptures suggesting that Moses was recalling Joseph's oath. Because these words cover the last lines of the book of Genesis, we are led to think that the whole book of Genesis was either already completed when Moses alluded to it during his encounter at the burning bush, or that he composed the conclusion of Genesis in light of his last experience, from God's promise at the burning bush. At this point, Moses, eighty years of age (Exod 7:7), had reached the end of his forty-year sojourn in Midian (Acts 7:30). As such, we can appreciate that the last verses of Genesis, like the first verses of Exodus, were indeed shaped from within the hope of and longing for the return from Egypt.

Thus, we conclude that the book of Genesis was written some fifteen hundred years before Christ, during the rule of Thutmose III (1482–1450).[26] This was the pharaoh from whom Moses fled, and who ruled during the years that Moses was a refugee in the desert of Midian and the children of Israel were still under the oppression of their Egyptian taskmasters.[27]

---

26 In this commentary, we have adopted the view of the fifteenth century BC theory of the Exodus.

27 Speaking of Moses' sojourn in Midian, Ellen G. White writes: "As the years rolled on, and he wandered with his flocks in solitary places, pondering upon the oppressed condition of his people, he recounted the dealings of God with his fathers and the promises that were the heritage of the chosen nation, and his prayers for Israel ascended by day and by night. Heavenly angels shed their light around him. Here, under the inspiration of the Holy Spirit, he wrote the book of Genesis. The long years spent amid the desert solitudes were rich in blessing, not alone to Moses and his people, but to the world in all succeeding ages" (PP 251).

THE STRUCTURE OF GENESIS

Through the analysis of the content of Genesis, attention to the literary forms of its texts and observation of recurring keywords, scholars have been able to recognize the organization of the book and thereby identify its structure. Two main proposals have been suggested and, on the basis of these, we are suggesting a third:

1. The Humankind-Patriarchal Structure

Most commentators have divided the book of Genesis into two main sections: The first section deals with the origins of humankind (1–11), which is universal and walks us through the creation of heaven and earth (1:1–2:4a), the first human beings from Adam (1:4b–5) to Noah (5–9) and the origins of nations (10–11). The second section deals with Patriarchal History and is a more limited history in that it focuses on certain elected individuals, beginning with Abraham and his son Isaac (12–27), then Jacob and his brother Esau (27–36), and concluding with Joseph and his brothers (37–50). Although the Humankind-Patriarchal Structure seems convenient after a cursory reading, it could, however, be misleading as it might give the impression that the first chapters of Genesis are merely introductory and designed primarily to prepare the reader for the following chapters on patriarchal stories, yet without otherwise having any real connection to them. Furthermore, this literary division, generally supported by critical scholars, betrays the philosophical bias of the presupposition that identifies Genesis 1–11 as myth,[28] as opposed to Genesis 12–50, which is considered to refer to actual stories recalled from oral traditions. One of the arguments supporting the mythological character of the first section is the identification of parallels between the stories of that section and the Mesopotamian mythological accounts of the second millennium BC.[29] Yet it should be noted that the recognition of these parallels is often questionable and does not necessarily imply a dependence between the two pieces of literature.[30] Furthermore, this two-part structure ignores the literary, linguistic, and theological connections between the two sections. The main lesson that could be drawn from these parallels is that they testify to the antiquity of the Genesis 1–11 narrative.[31]

2. The Genealogical Structure

An attentive reading of the book of Genesis reveals a more complex structure based on the use of the formula *'elleh toledot* "this is the history of," "this is the genealogy of" (2:4; 6:9). This formula appears in the following eleven passages[32] (for the

---

28   For a discussion of these views, see Hamilton, *Genesis: 1–17*, 56.

29   These are especially the Babylonian Epic of Atrahasis (*ANET*, 104–106); see also Bill T. Arnold and Bryan E. Beyer, eds., *Readings From the Ancient Near East: Primary Sources for Old Testament Study* (Grand Rapids: Baker Academic, 2002), 21–31, and the Sumerian flood story, also called "Eridu Genesis" (*ANET*, 42–44; see also Arnold and Beyer, ibid., 13–15). For parallels with the Epic of Atrahasis, see I. M. Kikawada, "Literary Convention of the Primeval History," *AJBI* 1 (1975): 3–21; cf. I. M. Kikawada and A. Quinn, *Before Abraham Was*, 36–53. For parallels with the Sumerian flood story, see T. Jacobsen, "The Eridu Genesis," *JBL* 100 (1981): 513–529.

30   On the discussion about the weaknesses of these reconstructions, see Gordon J. Wenham, *Genesis 1–15*, WBC 1 (Waco: Word Books, 1987), xl.

31   Ibid., xlii–xliv.

32   Verse 5:1a has *zeh sefer toledot* "this is the book of the genealogy," thus differing from all the other formulas, yet implying the same pattern of expression, with the word *toledot* preceded by the demonstrative *zeh* "this," which is the masculine singular equivalent to the plural demonstrative *'elleh* "these." Rashi, following Gen. Rab. 24, suggests that this exception, stressing on the word *sefer* "calculation," "enumeration" is intended to single out these generations

sake of consistency, all the occurrences have been translated with the same word "genealogy"), thus suggesting twelve sections to the book of Genesis:

1. "This is the genealogy of the heavens and the earth" (2:4a), concludes the first section and introduces the second section
2. "This is . . . the genealogy of Adam" (5:1a), introduces the third section
3. "This is the genealogy of Noah" (6:9a), introduces the fourth section
4. "This is the genealogy of the sons of Noah" (10:1a), introduces the fifth section
5. "This is the genealogy of Shem" (11:10a), introduces the sixth section
6. "This is the genealogy of Terah" (11:27a), introduces the seventh section
7. "This is the genealogy of Ishmael" (25:12a), introduces the eighth section
8. "This is the genealogy of Isaac" (25:19a), introduces the ninth section
9. "This is the genealogy of Esau" and his wives (36:1–2), introduces the tenth section
10. "This is the genealogy of Esau" (36:9), introduces the eleventh section
11. This is the genealogy of Jacob (37:2a, our literal translation), introduces the last and twelfth section

The significance of the *toledot* phrase for the structure of Genesis is still debated as it raises a number of problems. First, it is unclear whether the phrase should be understood as the introduction to what follows (superscript) or as the conclusion to what precedes (subscript).[33] Secondly, its placement is not always judicious since it sometimes separates sections that normally belong together (36:1, 9). And thirdly, there is no symmetry or correspondence between the various *toledot* sections, which differ in both length and nature, some being genealogies and others narratives (cf. 2 and 3; 5 and 11).

The function of the *toledot* phrase as a sign marking the various sections of the book of Genesis is therefore to be reconsidered (see below).

3. The "Go!" Genealogical Structure

Our shaping of the Genesis structure will build upon the lessons we have learned from the preceding remarks, namely, the structural function of chapters 1–11 as an introductory section (see "the Humankind-Patriarchal Structure") and the function of the phrase *ʾelleh toledot* "this is the genealogy of" as a key phrase (see "the Genealogical Structure"). Taking into consideration the findings and the weaknesses of the preceding proposals, we suggest the following chiastic structure (ABCB₁A₁), which has been determined on the basis of the following additional observations:

1. The two key phrases *lek leka* "go" and *ʾelleh toledot* "this is the genealogy." The particular phrase *lek leka* "go!" (12:1; 22:2) marks the literary center of the book of Genesis. These two unique occurrences echo each other and frame the middle section (**C: 12:1–22:19**). The key phrase *ʾelleh toledot* "this is the genealogy of" appears

---

. . .
who have succeeded Adam through Seth and have survived, thanks to Noah, unlike the preceding generations who disappeared in the flood.

33   The majority view that the *toledot* phrase functions as the introduction to what follows has been challenged by Wiseman and Harrison, who read this phrase as the colophon-conclusion to what precedes (P. J. Wiseman, *New Discoveries in Babylonia About Genesis* [Nashville: Nelson, 1985], 41–42; cf. Roland K. Harrison, *Introduction to the Old Testament* [Grand Rapids: Eerdmans, 1969], 543–547). These scholars base their argument on the use of that phrase in nonbiblical literature as well as in the biblical examples where the information about the name contained in the *toledot* phrase appears before that name (see, for instance, the cases of Adam in 5:1 and of Jacob in 37:2).

symmetrically, five times before Genesis 12 and five times after Genesis 22,[34] thus confirming the location of the center of the book marked by *lek leka,* "go."

2. The four great geographical movements within the book of Genesis: the first, from Eden to Babel (B: 3–11); the second, from Babel to the Promised Land (**C: 12:1–22:19**); the third, from the Promised Land to Egypt (B₁: 22:20–48:20); and the fourth, from Egypt to the Promised Land (A₁: 48:21–50:26).

3. The heroes of Genesis, the ancestors of humankind and the patriarchs: Adam (A: 1–3); Adam/Seth, Noah, Shem, Terah (B: 3–11); Abraham (**C: 12:1–22:19**); Ishmael, Isaac, Esau, Jacob/Joseph (B₁: 22:20–48:20); and the sons of Israel (A₁: 48:21–50:26).

4. The echo between the two extremities of the book, namely, its introduction and its conclusion (inclusio). The book begins with the story of creation, God's blessing upon humankind, and life in the Garden of Eden (A: 1–2) and ends with Israel's blessing and the prospect of the Promised Land (A₁: 48:21–50:26). As such, the structure of Genesis would resemble the following chiastic structure (ABCB₁A₁):

A Eden: Adam (1–2)

    B From Eden to Babel (3–11), Genealogies 1, 2, 3, 4, 5: Adam/Seth, Noah (2x), Shem, Terah

        C From Babel to Promised Land (12–22:19), no Genealogy: Abraham (Abrahamic Covenant 15–17)

    B₁ From Promised Land to Egypt (22:20–48:20), Genealogies 6, 7, 8, 9, 10: Ishmael, Isaac, Esau (2x), Jacob (Joseph)

A₁ Prospect of Promised Land: Israel (48:21–50:26)

It is interesting to note that there is no genealogy in the Abraham narrative: C (12–22:19). For although Abraham belongs to the genealogy of Terah (11:27), he himself—the core figure in the scheme of *lek leka*—is suspended in the void, having no genealogy (cf. the case of Melchizedek in Heb 7:3). While this exception notes the literary intention to mark the center of Genesis, it may also carry a lesson about the outstanding significance of Abraham who embodies the destiny of *lek leka* (see the comments on 12:1).

THE THEOLOGY OF GENESIS

For critical scholars, the very notion of "a theology of Genesis" does not make sense. Depending on the literary presuppositions of the Documentary Hypothesis, some scholars would rather refer to the theology of the Yahwist (J) or of the Elohist (E) or of the Priestly source (P), or to the theology of a certain narrative cycle. Each source would contain a theology of its own—coming from different times and expressing different theological views—with no real theological connection to the rest of the book. Other scholars might focus on the theology of the "first history" of Genesis 1–11 in contradistinction to the patriarchal legends of Genesis 12–50, again assuming that these two sections of Genesis are different in character and belong to different settings. For these critical interpreters, the book of Genesis is made of composite material and

---

34 The first occurrence in 2:4a stands by itself, since it belongs to the general introduction (1:1–2:4a), which governs the whole book. See Wenham, *Genesis 1–15,* 55.

therefore could not warrant a unified and coherent theological investigation.

On the other hand, the established fact that the book is received and read in the community of faith is an invitation to take the book at face value for the purpose of exploring its theological meaning. This traditional call is in fact supported from within the book by its structure, which testifies to the intention of conveying a unified theological message. We observed that this structure was determined by four clues: (1) the recurring and strategic position of the key phrase 'elleh toledot "this is the genealogy of," (2) the marking of the middle section signaled by the play on the stylistic expression lek leka; (3) the symmetrical geographical movements between the Garden of Eden–Promised Land and the Exile (Babel, Egypt); and (4) the stories about the heroes of salvation history. It is around these four structural indicators that we shall trace and construct the general contours and direction of the theology of Genesis. Then we will analyze to what extent these theological lessons are related to each other, and produce a coherent and unifying theological message that has significance for our present existence and our understanding of redemption.

1. Theology of History

As the most important keyword in the book of Genesis, the noun toledot "history," is "a structural sign that sacral history leading up to the people of Israel is being dealt with."[35] What makes this history a "sacral history" is primarily the fact that God is behind the events of that history. Throughout the book of Genesis, we are confronted with the Living God, "the only character whose presence pervades every narrative."[36] The God who controlled the elements and created the heavens and the earth is also the God who controls the personal lives of the patriarchs. Significantly, toledot also characterizes the great history of the creation of the universe and the small particular histories of Adam, Noah, Abraham, Isaac, and Jacob. But the making of history that is described in Genesis has nothing to do with determinism or fatality (the Moira of the Greeks, Mektub of the Muslims, or the "good fortune" of the horoscopes). Human history is not arbitrarily or independently determined from above. On the contrary, the God who created humans in His image works in association with them.

In the book of Genesis, history is essentially described as the result of a covenant between the Almighty God and humans. The act of the divine covenant is at the heart and center of Genesis, between the two divine calls of lek leka: "go!" (12:1; 22:2). In the middle of this central section (15–17), the divine covenant is dramatized through an extraordinary sacrificial ceremony and paralleled through the institution of circumcision. The process of God's covenant with Abraham, and through him with humankind, is thus unveiled. In this covenant, God chooses to come down and substitute Himself for Abram. And so we note that the fundamentals of righteousness by faith are already laid down at the center of Genesis (15:6; cf. Rom 4:3, 9). Abraham has simply to believe and "go," suspended in the void, without knowing where he was going or how he would sustain himself and his family—in complete dependence upon God.

The covenant's focus on human dependence upon God is already implied from the very outset of Genesis, when the Almighty God of the universe 'Elohim (1:1–2:4a) comes down to also be YHWH, the personal God of human history (2:4b–25). Moreover, God begins the history of His covenant with humans on the Sabbath, the first

---

35   J. Screiner, "yalad," TDOT 6:78–79.

36   James McKeown, Genesis (Grand Rapids: Eerdmans, 2008), 273.

full human day. From that day onwards, God has been a personal God who delights to be in relationship with His children. In other words, Genesis presents not just the God of the universe, but as the God of Adam and Eve, the God of Abraham and Sarah, the God of Jacob and Rachel, and the God of the sons and daughters of Jacob. It is not that God is found exclusively in existential, subjective, and emotional experiences (the encounter of the Existentialists). God is transcendent and beyond human understanding, but He also condescends to be a personal God in the sense that He is comprehensively involved in the minutiae of our personal histories. God walks with humans. In response to God's initiative of covenant, Abraham and through him we all are called to "go" (*lek leka*) by faith.

Another aspect of God's role in the book of Genesis is God's breaking into the human scene to "judge" and evaluate the course of events. For example, God judges Adam and Eve, Cain and the wicked antediluvians before the flood, the builders of Babel, and the men of Sodom. God tests Abraham, wrestles with Jacob, and warns the sons of Jacob. But the overarching purpose of God's judgments is redemptive. Thankfully, the Judge is also the Creator who can bring good out of a negative situation (Rom 8:28). Here we can see that the wonder of creation is suggested at each step of the Genesis history: when God turns the curse against humankind into salvation (3:15), when He puts a seed in Eve's womb to replace the murdered Abel (4:25), when He turns the flood into a re-creation (8–9:17), when He makes the aged Sarah fertile (17:17–19), when He calls Abraham to be a blessing to the nations (12:1–4), when He provides the ram and saves the son of the promise (22:1–19), when He appears at Bethel and connects the earth to heaven (28:10–27), when He changes Jacob into Israel (32:22–32), and when He turns what was meant as evil into good (50:20).

At the end of the road, and against all expectation, we see the systematic unveiling of and surprising evidence for a God who is always in control. This theology of history anticipates the subsequent events of the history of Israel. Along the same lines, Israel will be taken out of Egypt and be saved out of the wilderness and out of the waters. This carries a powerful message of hope not only at the universal level of lost humanity, but also at the more modest scale of our personal daily existence: the God of the universe and the God of Abraham is also the God of the earth and my personal God.

2. Theology of Birth

The main manifestation of the theology of history is "birth," since the word *toledot*, which is derived from the verb *yalad* "to bear children," also means "generations." Thus, we see that, in Hebrew, the two concepts of "history" and "birth" are related. Salvation history will be built through the events of births, which constitute the main hub around which the book of Genesis revolves. This emphasis on giving birth is supplied through the genealogies, which record the births of those who are born from Adam, Noah, Shem, Terah, Ishmael, Isaac, Esau, and Jacob. Another indication of the importance of "birth" as a unifying theme is the keyword *zera'* "seed." This word is not only frequently repeated in the book of Genesis (59x), it also occurs in all the main narratives, with a special concentration in the patriarchal narratives (47x), where concern lies with the genealogical lineage of the elected family.[37]

Beyond the literary indication of these keywords, the narrative plot of Genesis

---

37   See T. Desmond Alexander, "Genealogies, Seed, and the Compositional Unity of Genesis," *TynBul* 44 (1993): 259–260.

expands on the birth stories. We begin with the births of the first humans, the three sons of Adam (4:1–2, 25); followed by the births of Ishmael (16) and Isaac (17; 18; 21:1–7); followed by the births of Jacob and Esau (25:21–26) and the births of the eleven sons of Jacob (30:1–24); then comes the birth of his twelfth son (35:16–18); and finally the births of the two sons of Joseph (41:50–52). These stories of births do not just punctuate the whole book of Genesis, as do the lists of births (the *toledot*); nor are they important just because they occupy much of the territory of the book. These stories are extraordinary primarily because they reveal God's presence and active intervention. For example, the first time the word "seed" appears in the context of human birth, it forms part of the Genesis 3:14–16 prophecy, where birth is identified as the process by which the cosmic redemption of humankind will be implemented. Furthermore, the seed of the woman, which will win the cosmic victory over the serpent in Genesis 3:15, is also related to the act of childbirth by the woman in Genesis 3:16. This first prophecy, also called the *protoevangelium* "first Gospel," hints at the mysterious process of divine incarnation that will, through the channel of human births, prepare and shape the messianic seed of redemption. From Adam to Seth to Noah to Abraham to Jacob, the seed-line and sacred *toledot* mark the articulation of the plot of Genesis. However, these promises of births concern more than the mere shaping of a people. The "seed" lineage was designed for the salvation of "all the families of the earth" (12:3; Acts 3:25).

The author of Genesis insists that God is the One who makes the act of birth possible, for the *toledot* is first of all an act of creation. In fact, Genesis begins with this statement: the event of creation of the heavens and the earth is *toledot* (2:4a). This truth is reaffirmed throughout the stories of extraordinary births in the patriarchal families. This is why the theology of birth based on creation is also a theology of blessing. As the Creator, God provides humans with the capacity to create and reproduce. Moreover, God will interfere in the process and even "create" fruitfulness and success out of barrenness and hopelessness. As such, births are not the mere result of a natural process. Instead, these births are the direct product of God's blessing. Therefore, the theology of birth is interwoven with a theology of blessing. Like the word *toledot*, the Hebrew word for "blessing" (*barak*) is a keyword in the book of Genesis. In fact, more than half of the 160 occurrences in the Pentateuch appear in Genesis. Furthermore, blessing is prominent in the creation story where it is pronounced three times: first, for the birds and the fish (1:22); secondly, for humans (1:28); and thirdly, for the Sabbath (2:3). The blessing is, then, renewed in connection with the ancestors of humankind and the patriarchs of Israel (see above). Genesis concludes with Jacob blessing all his sons (48:1–49:28). Blessing always appears in connection with the promise of or the actual event of birth.[38] Moreover, the two words, *barak* and *zera'*, are often associated.[39] From the first prophecy in Genesis 3:15 to the call of Abraham and then ultimately to the patriarchal stories of extraordinary births, God's blessing is encapsulated in His promise that there *will* be a seed. Significantly, the promise of descendants is by far the most important and most recurring promise in the book of Genesis.[40]

---

38 See 1:28; 9:1; 12:2–3; 17:16, 20; 22:17; 28:3–4; 32:29–32 (for the connection of blessing and fruitfulness in this passage, see our commentary below ad loc.); 48:3–4, 19–20; 49:25.

39 See 12:2–3 (7–8); 17:16, 20 (7–8, 19); 22:17 (17–18); 28:3 (4, 14); 32:29 (12); 47:10 (19, 23); 48:16, 20 (4, 11, 19). References in parenthesis are for *zera'*, while nonparenthetic references are for *brk*.

40 David Clines isolates three major promises in the book of Genesis (and in the Pentateuch): descendants, relationship, and land. The promise of descendants occurs nineteen times, the promise of land occurs thirteen times, and the

In connection with the theme of birth, the theme of "divine promise" has traditionally been recognized by Old Testament theologians as "the connecting bridge,"[41] uniting all the Genesis narratives.[42] Von Rad compares "the promise to the patriarchs" to the "scaffolding supporting and connecting" all the material contained in Genesis: "This whole variegated mosaic of studies is given cohesion of subject-matter … by means of the constantly recurring divine promise."[43] Yet, the connecting function of the divine promises does not limit itself to the patriarchal stories. The theme of the divine promise of a "seed," which is the guarantee for all the other promises, not only connects all the patriarchal cycles with each other but also with the first divine promise of the "seed" in Genesis 3:15. Therefore, the theological scope of the divine promise in Genesis concerns more than the mere physical survival of Abraham's elected descendants. It primarily concerns the spiritual fate of all humanity and brings to light the cosmic sweep of salvation.

3. Theology of the End

The most important implication of this theology of history is that we understand that God rules behind the scenes of human events. In fact, the final accounts of the various stories reveal God as they reveal His works. So, while Genesis is known as a book about beginnings, it is also a book about the end. Yet it seems paradoxical to expect a message about the end to undergird the book of Genesis. This relation between beginning and end was sensed by Hermann Gunkel in his classic *Shöpfung und Chaos in Urzeit und Endzeit* ("Creation and Chaos in Beginning and End"),[44] and revisited later by Claus Westermann,[45] and has been further understood and rediscovered by more recent scholars. Warren A. Gage[46] and John H. Sailhamer[47] in particular have shown how the messianic hope is already contained in the beginning of the book, especially in Genesis 1–7. These authors have noted striking correspondences between themes of the beginning as recorded in Genesis and the biblical discourses of eschatological redemption. Just as the theme of creation foreshadows the postdiluvian re-creation, the Garden of Eden foreshadows the future heavenly city of Zion. Thus, the contours of the future cosmic deliverance are traced and anticipated in the stories of origin, inviting a deeper reading of Genesis, beyond the mere information of events that birthed the human cosmos. So, while the primary design of Genesis is to provide a report of this history of beginnings, it also "paved the way for … the structure of biblical eschatology."[48]

Our study of the structure of the book of Genesis traces this eschatological intention even further. This theology of the end is indeed carried by the whole book of Genesis. It is not only the first history of Genesis 1–7 that allows theological thinking

---

...

promise of relationship occurs thirteen times. David J. A. Clines, *The Theme of the Pentateuch*, JSOTSup 10 (Sheffield: Sheffield Academic Press, 1978), 32–43.

41   Hamilton, *Genesis: 1–17*, 39.

42   For the importance of the theme of promise in the Old Testament and in biblical theology, see Walter C. Kaiser, Jr., *Toward an Old Testament Theology* (Grand Rapids: Zondervan, 1978), 1–69.

43   Gerhard von Rad, *Old Testament Theology*, trans. D. M. G. Stalker (New York: Harper & Row, 1962), 1:167.

44   Hermann Gunkel, *Schöpfung und Chaos in Urzeit und Endzeit* (Göttingen: Vandenhoeck/Ruprecht, 1895).

45   Claus Westermann, *Beginning and End in the Bible*, trans. Keith Crim (Philadelphia: Fortress Press, 1972).

46   Warren. A. Gage, *The Gospel of Genesis: Studies in Protology and Eschatology* (Eugene, OR: Wipf and Stock, 2001).

47   John H. Sailhamer, *The Meaning of the Pentateuch* (Downers Grove: IVP, 2009).

48   John H. Sailhammer, *The Pentateuch as Narrative* (Grand Rapids: Zondervan, 1992), 109.

about a future universal redemption, but also the geographical movements from Eden to Babel, from Babel to the Promised Land, from the Promised Land to Egypt, and then the future prospect of the return to the Promised Land. Beyond the patriarchal blessings, these movements point to the hope of a future eschatological Eden.

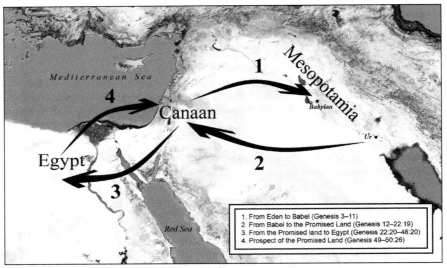

1. From Eden to Babel (Genesis 3–11)
2. From Babel to the Promised Land (Genesis 12–22:19)
3. From the Promised land to Egypt (Genesis 22:20–48:20)
4. Prospect of the Promised Land (Genesis 49–50:26)

Theological Movements in Genesis Source: Felipe A. Masotti

The theological reading of this geographical feature has generally been limited to the theme of the "land" (*'erets*), another important unifying theme in Genesis, as noted by Ottosson: "The promise of the land runs through the patriarchal narratives like a red thread (12:7; 13:15; 17:8; 24:7 [pl. "lands"]; 26:12; 35:12; 48:4; 50:24)."[49] Yet, the connection with the first history (1–11) has been overlooked, since the Hebrew word *'erets* occurs more than eighty times in that section, more than one-tenth of the totality of its occurrences in the book of Genesis. Although the word is often used in that section in a cosmological sense, referring to the "earth," it also applies to the "land" as a circumscribed territory (2:11–13; 11:28), something seen with most usages in Genesis 12–50, where it refers to the Promised Land. Therefore, there is no serious reason why we should exclude this section in the study of "land" in the book of Genesis since the word holds the same ambiguous meaning in both sections, implying that the "land" as unifying thread should also include chapters 1–11. Furthermore, the literary play on the word *'erets* "land" in the two creation stories (1–2) suggests an interesting connection between the two meanings of *'erets*: in the first creation story (1:1–2:4a), *'erets* occurs twenty-one times (7x3), while it occurs seven times in the second creation story (2:4b–25). This parallel between the two usages suggests that the cosmic perspective of the land (1:1–2:4a) is somehow related to the particular perspective associated with the chosen land of the Garden of Eden (2:4b–25). In the light of this observation, it becomes clear that the concept of "the land" in the book of Genesis conveys, by association, also an allusion to the Garden of Eden. The reference to the land *'erets* does not only imply God's creation of the earth

---

49 M. Ottosson, "*'erets*," *TDOT* 1:403.

in a cosmic sense, it also communicates, beyond this cosmic evocation, God's choice of this particular piece of land for human happiness.

This means that in the book of Genesis the theology of the land is more than a mere nationalistic concept. God, the Creator, the owner of the earth, is behind that special land, whether the Garden of Eden or the Promised Land. Interestingly, this is the very lesson that is suggested by the structure of Genesis. The book begins in Eden and ends with the prospect of the Promised Land. The literary device of inclusio is designed to draw the reader's attention to the connection between the two places. Behind the hope of the Promised Land looms the hope of the Garden of Eden. The same lesson is taught by the larger structure of the whole Pentateuch (the first five books of the Bible) in which the Genesis Garden of Eden is echoed at the end of Deuteronomy with Moses' panoramic view of the Promised Land. Here also, beyond the view of the earthly Promised Land (Deut 34:4) looms *another* Promised Land. We may even wonder whether the repetition of the death motif at the end of both Deuteronomy and Genesis—containing the same association with the Promised Land and hinting at the Garden of Eden—might be intentionally suggesting the hope in the eschatological resurrection of the dead. Although the fulfillment of God's blessings to the patriarchs and their descendants through the possession of the Promised Land is not explicitly identified as a return *to* Eden, these blessings bear in themselves significant aspects *of* Eden. This explains why many features of the Garden of Eden are found in the sanctuary and in the Jerusalem temple and, reversely, why many features of the sanctuary are found in the Garden of Eden,[50] a connection noticed as far back as the early stages of rabbinic literature.[51] For just as the Garden of Eden is seen as the first dwelling place of God, the first sanctuary (later the tabernacle and the Jerusalem temple) will be seen as reminiscent of the Garden of Eden. God's blessings to the patriarchs and to the people of Israel, although well received and fully enjoyed, were not their complete fulfillment. Instead, these blessings functioned as markers in the pages of their painful history intended to evoke the blessing of another order.

Thus, the geographical moves in the book of Genesis—from Eden to Babel to the Promised Land to Egypt to the prospect of the return to the Promised Land—suggest a profound theological lesson. For beyond the divine promise of the land of Canaan is heard the divine promise of a return to the Garden of Eden. Through these nomadic journeys of the seed-family, never arriving, never satisfied, always longing for home, the book of Genesis vibrates with the pulsation of hope. Although they tasted of the divine blessings, signs of God's faithful fulfillment of His promise, Adam, Noah, and the patriarchs continued to wait for the ultimate divine victory over evil and death. For only this would bring them, and us, the entire creation, back to the Garden of Eden. Revisiting the theme of birth, Paul in his letter to the Romans resonates with the same hope: "For we know that the whole creation groans and labors with birth pangs together until now. Not only that, but we also who have the first-fruits of the Spirit, even we ourselves groan within ourselves, eagerly waiting for the adoption, the redemption of our body" (Rom 8:22–23).

---

50   See Wenham, "Sanctuary Symbolism in the Garden of Eden Story," in *Proceedings of the Ninth World Congress of Jewish Studies* (Jerusalem: World Union of Jewish Studies, 1986), 19–20; cf. L. E. Stager, "Jerusalem and the Garden of Eden," *ErIsr* 26 (1999): 188–190; cf. Sailhamer, *The Meaning of the Pentateuch*, 577.

51   Gen. Rab. 16:5. For the recognition of this connection in rabbinic literature, see J. D. Levenson, "The Temple and the World," *JR* 64 (1984): 284–285.

1. CREATION: ADAM AND EVE IN EDEN

GENESIS 1–2

THE PLACE OF CREATION

The importance of creation in the Bible can be seen through the extensive and numerous references to creation within the Hebrew Scriptures. In the Pentateuch, creation is explicitly mentioned in the book of Genesis in the creation story (1:1–2:25), in relation to the event of the Exodus (Exod 15:8, 17), and in connection to the Law (Exod 20:11). In the prophetic section, creation reappears in the context of the Israelites' return from Babylonian captivity (Isa 40–45; Jer 4:23–26; 31:35–57). Creation is also an important motif in Wisdom literature. The book of Proverbs describes the creation as a poetic meditation promoting the search for wisdom (Prov 8:22–36); in the book of Job, creation is presented as God's response to human suffering (Job 38); in the book of Ecclesiastes, it shows up as a meditation about the vanity of the world, the human condition (Eccl 1:1–11), and as an ethical encouragement (Eccl 11:10); and in the Psalms, creation hymns respond to God in the context of worship (Pss 29:2; 95:1–6; 139:13–14; 145:15). In the book of Daniel, creation inspires hope via a cosmic and eschatological perspective (see especially Dan 7–8; 12).[52] In the New Testament, creation plays an important role as an expression of faith (Heb 11). Creation is especially prominent to suggest the process of salvation in Christ (Heb 1:2; Col 1:16), the response to God's act of salvation (2 Cor 5:17), and even the eschatological solution (Rev 21–22). Indeed, creation is an important theme in the Bible.

The biblical weight given to creation is also indicated by the fact that the Bible begins its narrative with the creation account. From the medieval Jewish commentator Rashi to modern Christian theologians Claus Westermann and Gerhad von Rad, the readers of the first chapter of Genesis have been intrigued by this observation and have generally suggested various theological explanations for it.[53] The Bible begins with creation for historical, literary, and theological reasons.

The first reason has to do with the historical intention of the text since creation is chronologically situated as the first event that precedes all others. In other words, Genesis grounds the creation as the historical event that introduces and generates every other event in Scripture. It is the first event, the first genealogy without which all other events and genealogies could not have taken place. The fact that creation is the preamble of the history of Israel—and of the world—not only gives it a cosmic perspective, but also affirms and emphasizes its historical quality, which becomes the groundwork and foundation for all subsequent events. As such, to question the historicity of the creation story would be akin to doubting the historicity of all other accounts reported in the book of Genesis.

The second reason Genesis begins with the creation account has to do with the

---

52   See Jacques B. Doukhan, "Allusions à la création dans le livre de Daniel: Dépistage et Signification," in Adam van der Woude, ed., *The Book of Daniel in the Light of New Findings* (Leuven: Leuven University Press), 285–292; see also André Lacocque, "Allusions to Creation in Daniel 7," in J. J. Collins and P. W. Flint, eds., *The Book of Daniel: Composition and Reception*, vol. 1 (Leiden: Brill, 2002), 114–131.

53   See Claus Westermann, *The Genesis Accounts of Creation* (Philadelphia: Fortress Press, 1964), 2; Gerhard von Rad, *Old Testament Theology* (New York: Harper & Row, 1962), 1:450.

literary organization of the book. The text marks the first step of the structure of the book of Genesis: its literary introduction, which anticipates and sets the tone for all ensuing steps. In essence, the creation account already encapsulates the three themes that articulate the structure of the whole book of Genesis: "genealogy" (*toledot*), creation blessing, and land.

Theology is the third reason why the creation story has been put in the beginning of Genesis. The event of creation is the primary foundation for human faith in God. To believe in creation, to believe that I owe my existence and the reality of the world to Someone whom I do not see and who was before I was, is the first act of faith. It is noteworthy that the only biblical definition of faith is related to creation; as the author of the epistle to the Hebrews puts it: "Now faith is the substance of things hoped for, the evidence of things not seen" (Heb 11:1). Creation is the only event in history that took place when humans were not yet present to see it and attest to it. Creation is therefore the event par excellence that requires faith and, by implication, revelation from above. It is also significant that the same author begins his list of faithful acts with creation: "By faith we understand that the worlds were framed by the word of God, so that the things which are seen were not made of things which are visible" (Heb 11:3). Theological thinking begins with the idea that God is not a mere opinion generated by human thinking, but that He precedes all human thought. In short, theological thinking, like faith, must first begin with the acknowledgment of creation.

THE BEAUTY OF CREATION

Although the creation story is a true and meaningful narrative that provides evidence to a historical reality that expresses a profound theology, it is likewise a poetic masterpiece celebrating beauty: "a literary choreography in which every word has been carefully chosen and precisely positioned."[54] In fact, its rhythm, its play on words and sounds, and the symmetric construction of its literary structure are intentional. These textual constructs appeal to the ears, and even the eyes, from the first moment the reader embarks upon the text. This delightful experience is the result of thoughtful choice.

THE RHYTHM OF SEVEN

The rhythm of seven dominates the passage. Indeed, the number seven is seen in the structure of this account not only in that it covers a period of "seven" days, but also through multiple instances of the repetition of sounds, words, or even specific phrases seven times. This play on seven starts from the very beginning of the text in verse 1. The Hebrew verse is not only composed of seven words: *bereshit bara' 'Elohim et hashamayyim we'et ha'arets* "In the beginning God created the heavens and the earth," but the verse itself is also divided into two equal sections of letters: fourteen letters (7x2) in the first section until the word *'Elohim* "God"—marked by the most important accent that separates the verse in two sections (the disjunctive *atnach*)—and fourteen letters (7x2) in the second section. The second verse is likewise composed of fourteen (7x2) words. The keyword *bara'* "create" occurs seven times; both

---

54 McKeown, *Genesis*, 19.

the key phrase *wayyar'eh 'Elohim … ki tov* "God saw … that it was good" and the key phrase *wayehi ken* "and it was so" occur seven times. The word *'Elohim* "God" occurs thirty-five (7x5) times. The word *ha'arets* "the earth" occurs twenty-one (7x3) times.

THE LITERARY STRUCTURE

The first creation story begins in Genesis 1:1 and ends in Genesis 2:4a. This delimitation is suggested through the literary device of the inclusio, in which the introduction and the conclusion echo each other:

Introduction: "In the beginning God created the heavens and the earth" (1:1)
Conclusion: "This is the history of the heavens and the earth when they were created" (2:4a)

In addition, linguistic and thematic correspondences between the first creation story (1:1–2:4a) and the second creation story that follows (2:4b–25) suggest a parallelism between the literary structures of the two texts:

1:1–2:4A	2:4B–25
INTRODUCTION (1:1–2)	**INTRODUCTION** (2:4b–6)
In the beginning,	In the day,
'Elohim created heavens and earth	*YHWH 'Elohim* made earth and heavens
Earth without form and void and darkness	No … not yet
Spirit on the surface of waters	Mist on the surface of the ground
DAY 1. And God said (1:3–5)	**STEP 1.** And Y. God formed (2:7)
Light/darkness	Man/dust
DAY 2. And God said (1:6–8)	**STEP 2.** And Y. God planted (2:8)
Firmament: heaven	Garden: Eden
DAY 3. And God said (1:9–13)	**STEP 3.** And Y. God made grow (2:9–15)
Waters and land, plants	Waters and land, plants; human dominion
DAY 4. And God said (1:14–19)	**STEP 4.** And Y. God commanded (2:16–17)
Luminaries: light/darkness	Tree of knowledge: good/evil (death)
DAY 5. And God said (1:20–23)	**STEP 5.** And Y. God said (2:18)
First animal creation, birds and fish	First need of companion for man
DAY 6. And God said (1:24–31)	**STEP 6.** And Y. God formed (2:19–22)
Animals in relationship to man	Animals in relationship with man
Dominion of man over animals	Dominion of man over animals
Man created as male and female	Man created as male and female
DAY 7. Heaven-earth finished (2:1–3)	**STEP 7.** Man-woman finished (2:23–24)
Divine involvement	Divine involvement
Separation from preceding work	Separation from parents
Blessing and holiness	Unity of couple
CONCLUSION (2:4a)	**CONCLUSION** (2:25)
Presentation of heavens and earth as created	Presentation of man and woman as created

We may also note the same rhythm of seven steps in the second creation story (2:4b–25) as in the first (1:1–2:4a). These are observed through key words in the text: *'erets* "earth" occurs seven times, and *'adam* "man" occurs fourteen times (7x2). The last verse of the second creation story (2:25) also echoes the first verse of the first creation story with the same rhythm of seven words.

THE HISTORICITY OF CREATION

The literary beauty of the text does not imply that the text of the first creation story should be understood merely as a poetic creation of the imagination. In fact, the literary construction of the text warns us against this deduction, for not only is it written as a genealogy, but (as with the second creation story) it also stands in opposition to the other Ancient Near Eastern (ANE) cosmogonies.

THE STYLE OF GENEALOGY

The text of the first creation story is explicitly identified as a genealogy by its author: "this is the genealogy of heavens and earth" (2:4a lit. trans.); and it truly presents all the literary features that characterize a genealogy: (1) the same regular unfolding by successive degrees with the same introductory and concluding formulas; (2) the same dry character and lack of human life with the same report tone; and (3) the same function of marking a turning point in history, a (new) beginning.[55] The first implication of this stylistic observation concerns the historical intention of this text. The primary function of the *toledot*, the "genealogy," is indeed to establish the historical character of a story or to attest to the historical identity of a person. In Near Eastern culture, the historical identity of a person was and still is validated insofar as he or she can situate himself or herself within his or her genealogy, to say whose son or daughter they are.[56] In the Bible, we note this when, in seeking to identify David, Saul asked him: "Whose son are you?" (1 Sam 17:58). Likewise, the writers of the New Testament had to authenticate Jesus' Davidic and divine lineage in order to identify Him as the Messiah (Matt 1:1–17; 22:42; Luke 3:22–38). Thus, we see that the choice to dress the creation story in the literary garment of a genealogy was meant to affirm the authenticity of the reported event, that it truly happened and had a historical identity.

As has been noticed by biblical scholars,[57] the creation story has been written within the genealogical literary genre in order to connect it with the other genealogies within the framework of the book of Genesis. Old Testament scholar Edmond Jacob emphasizes this point when he observes that the same author "uses the term *toledot* for the creation of the heavens and the earth (2:4) as well as for the genealogy of the patriarchs and still today the Jews express the unity of creation and history by

---

55   For more details on the genealogy style of the creation story, see Doukhan, *The Genesis Creation Story*, 175–182.

56   This custom is even reflected in the names of persons, which are composed with the prefix *ben* "son of," Ben Berak, "son of Berak" (Josh 19:45); Ben Hadad, "son of Hadad" (1 Kgs 15:18); Ben-Hur, "son of Hur" (1 Kgs 4:8); and has remained the usage after the biblical times (see names such as Ben Sira, Ben-Asher, Ben-Gurion, etc.). It is noteworthy that this practice is also attested in Western cultures (see Mendelsohn, Nielsen, Davidson, Richardson, etc.).

57   See Gerhard von Rad, *Genesis: A Commentary*, trans. John H. Marks, rev. ed., OTL (Philadelphia: Westminster, 1972), 65; cf. Claus Westermann, *Creation* (London: SPCK, 1974), 24.

dating their calendar from the creation of the world."[58] The reason for this stylistic connection, then, was to suggest creation's historical-human dimension. In other words, creation belongs to human history to the same degree as the lives of the patriarchs.

THE CONNECTION BETWEEN THE TWO CREATION STORIES

The fact that our creation story in Genesis 1:1–2:4a is connected to the historical narrative in Genesis 2:4b–25 provides the reader with a key of interpretation and implies a number of lessons regarding how we should understand the language of the creation story.

1. The parallel between the two creation stories suggests the author's intention to communicate his report on the creation of the universe as an event belonging to the same historical nature as the formation of human beings.

2. Another lesson of this connection is to draw our attention to the "not yet" condition of this creation in comparison to the actual present condition of the human world. Already this observation about the goodness and perfection of creation was mentioned repeatedly in the first creation story through the rhythm of the seven phrases: "It was good." Now the connection with Genesis 2:4b–25 is more specific. Not only was creation good, perfect, and complete, it was also pure and undefiled, not yet touched by the woes of evil, sin, and death. This is the main lesson of the second creation story. Man has not yet sinned and death has not yet come (2:16–17). And this lesson appears not only at the core of the story, but also in the introduction and conclusion of our text as an *inclusio*, a literary device used to notify the reader that this is intended to be the central idea of the passage. In the introduction (2:5), the keywords are "not" (*'ayin* and *lo'*) and "not yet" (*terem;* 2x) and suggest the perspective of the writer. In other words, what characterizes this contemporary world of ours was "not yet" there when God created it. In the conclusion (2:25), the use of the Hebrew word *'arum* (which means "naked" in this verse and will mean "cunning" in the next verse [3:1]) betrays the intention of the author to imply that the tragedy, which will later involve the serpent and human beings, has not yet struck. Indeed, one of the intentions of the function of chapter 2 is to affirm and emphasize the perfect state of creation as it came from the hand of God, one *not yet* sullied by evil, sin, and death.

3. This view also suggests a clear rejection of the theory of evolution, for it implies that just as humans have been created as perfect, finished beings, the heavens and the earth must have also been created as perfect, finished objects—with no need to evolve into higher forms. From our own perspective, this process of creation may appear inconceivable because our present human experience requires a "time" factor for humans to reach the stage of maturity and completeness: humans are not born adults. It is precisely this "abnormality" that is addressed in the second creation story. By connecting the two creation stories, the author is suggesting that the same "time" factor, which operated in the creation of humans, was also at work in the creation of the heavens and the earth. They did not need millions of years to reach a stage of maturity that allowed them to function correctly.

---

58 Edmond Jacob, *Theology of the Old Testament* (New York: Harper & Row, 1958), 139.

THE POLEMIC INTENTION

The biblical creation story is not just embedded in the context of the book of Genesis and the Bible, it is also situated in the context of its Ancient Near Eastern cultural environment. The biblical author is well aware of the cultural world around him and its mythological cosmogonies, to which he responds in a strong polemic manner.[59]

1. The Introduction

This is perhaps the only place where the biblical text seems to deliberately echo the ANE texts of cosmogony (especially the Babylonian introduction).[60] Indeed, both sources display a parallel structure and motif:

A. A clause that refers to time ("when"): general introduction, reference to heaven and earth

B. A parenthetic clause: description of earth at the stage of "not yet," water element

C. The main clause: God's action of "creation …"

The Biblical Text

A. In the beginning God created heavens and earth

B. The earth was without form, and void (*tohu wabohu*); and darkness was on the face of the abyss (*tehom*), and the spirit of God was hovering on the face of waters

C. Then God said, "Let there be light!" … (1:1–3)

The Babylonian Text (*Enuma Elish*)[61]

A. When on high the heaven had not been named, nor firm ground below …

B. Naught but primordial Apsu, their begetter (and) Mummu-Tiamat, she who bore them all, their waters commingling as a single body; no reed hut had been … no marsh had appeared … When no gods whatever had been brought into being uncalled by name, their destinies undetermined …

C. Then it was that the gods were formed within them[62]

This apparent parallel should not mislead us, however. Instead of being an argument on behalf of the Babylonian influence on the biblical text, thus undermining the original inspiration of the biblical text, it is, on the contrary, a significant clue to the author's polemic intention against these accounts. Indeed, this literary connection between these two introductions constitutes a classic polemic means commonly used in ancient literature to refute the opposing view. A good illustration of this polemic literary device can be found in Job 18–19:

---

59   See Gerhard F. Hasel, "The Significance of the Cosmology in Gen 1 in Relation to ANE Parallels," *AUSS* 10 (1972): 1–20; cf. Gerhard F. Hasel, "The Polemic Nature of the Genesis Cosmology," *EvQ* 46 (1974): 81–102.

60   See also the Egyptian cosmogony, which describes the stage of pre-creation in terms of "not yet" (Hermann Grapow, "Die Welt vor der Schöpfung," *ZÄS* 67 [1931]: 34–38), quoted in Claus Westermann, *Genesis 1–11* (Minneapolis: Augsburg, 1984), 75.

61   The Babylonian Epic of Creation was called *Enuma Elish*, "when on high," after the first words of the poem, consisting of seven tablets. For the translation of the whole text of the epic, see E. A. Speiser, "Akkadian Myths and Epics," in *ANET*, 60–72.

62   *ANET*, 60–61.

Bildad the Shuhite answered and said: "**How long** till you put an end to **words**?" (Job 18:1–2)
Then Job answered and said: "**How long** will you torment … with **words**?" (Job 19:1–2)

To be sure, the parallels are not perfect; the introduction of the polemic texts does not exactly duplicate the text it responds to. There are many important differences that should not be overlooked. Yet the parallels between the introductions of the Genesis creation story and those of the ancient Babylonian texts, just as these between the introduction of Job's speech and Bildad's, are significant enough to suggest that they are intended for polemic purposes.

The fact that our text has been written with a polemic objective directed against mythological material suggests the author's intention to affirm the independence of his inspiration. His account is not the mere product of literary influence. It is not a myth, but a truthful historical event, which has been revealed to him.

This strong polemic intention does not mean, however, that the biblical author was determined by his polemic and shaped his whole account under its pressure, thus affecting the content of his report. The very fact that after the introduction the parallels and the polemic hints become only sporadic and accidental constitutes a strong indication to the contrary.

2. The Lamps

The sun and the moon (1:15) are not given their usual names of *shemesh* "sun" and *yareakh* "moon," which would open the possibility of confusing them with *Shamash*, "the sun god" of the Akkadians, Assyrians, Babylonians, and Canaanites, and *Yarih*, "the moon god" of the Canaanites. Instead, they are *me'orot* "luminaries," a word that is always used in the Pentateuch to designate lamps; the only other use of this term refers to the "luminaries" of the sanctuary (Exod 25:6; 27:20; 35:8, 14; 39:37; Lev 24:2; Num 4:9, 16). The sun and the moon are presented as lamps, which are designed to illuminate the world, just as the lamps of the sanctuary are used to illuminate the sanctuary.

3. The Great Fish

It is noteworthy that the technical verb *bara'* "create" is associated only with three creations: the general creation of heaven and earth (1:1), the creation of human beings (1:27), and the creation of the fish and the birds (1:21). Significantly, the reference to *hattanninim hagedolim* **the great sea creatures**, which is the only biblical occurrence, comes first in the list after the verb *bara'* "create." This particular attention on the "great sea creature" is intentional to emphasize the nondivine nature of this animal, which was worshiped as a god in both Babylonian and Egyptian religions. The big fish of the ancient cosmogonies is just an ordinary fish for Genesis.

4. Water Before Creation

In the Genesis creation story, the water of the introduction (1:2) is associated with *khoshek* "darkness," *tohu wabohu* "without form and void," and *tehom* "deep" in order to counteract the ideas promoted in both Babylonian and Egyptian cosmogonies that viewed the waters as the living god who generates the world (*Nun* in Egypt and *Tiamat* in Babylon). These waters are, therefore, qualified in the immediate context of the biblical creation story using the negative terms of darkness and emptiness. This lesson is again confirmed through the parallelism with the second creation story. The description of the state of the earth before God's initial word of creation given in terms of water in 1:1–2 parallels the description of the state of the earth in 2:4b–6 given in terms of "not yet" and "not" (of course, here from the particular perspective of the sixth day). Although the author refers to real water, an element that might have been created before this creation week, the text does not speak about it, nor does it say when or how this element might have been created. The author's concern is not so much water per se, but rather to deny the mythological view that the first element of water was a divine agent of life, a concept that was common in the ANE world. For the biblical author, life was distinct from and outside of water: "The Spirit of God was hovering over the face of the waters" (1:2). What you believe to be the divine producer of life, says Genesis, is just plain water, a "neutral" element associated with darkness, emptiness, and nothingness. Life comes from another source: God.

5. Ex-nihilo Creation

According to Genesis, the act of creation was not performed through any pre-existing divine substance—the blood, sperm, or saliva of a god—as is the case in other ancient cosmogonies (Egyptian and Babylonian).[63] The biblical account was not a creation "out of God," what one would call an *ex-divino* creation. Neither was it the result of a struggle between already existing gods—as was the case in Egyptian cosmogony where the sun god *Re* fights the ocean god *Nun*, or in Babylonian cosmogony where *Marduk*, the god of order, struggles against *Tiamat*, the divine sea serpent. The God of Genesis did not create water, or any element, out of Himself, out of another person, or out of something. God created *ex nihilo*, that is, "out of nothing" through His spoken word and not through magical utterances, as in Egypt.

Also the fact that the creation story is a genealogy betrays the author's concern to provide a polemic against the mythical idea of divine procreation. It is, indeed, significant that our biblical genealogy tells us that creation did not take place as the result of some kind of sexual procreation; it is instead the creative act of a God who precedes and determines the power of giving life.

6. The Creation of Humans

Unlike the other ANE accounts of origins that describe a god who creates for his own benefit,[64] the biblical creation story depicts God as One who creates for the happiness of humankind. The ANE myths were not interested in the creation of humans; and when the creation of man *was* mentioned, it was only incidental and only for the purpose of serving the gods.[65] In Genesis 1, on the other hand, it is God Himself who serves humans (1:29) in anticipation of their creation. Moreover, the

---

63   See the Mesopotamian myths of *Atrahasis* and *Enuma Elish* where the blood of a god is used to create humanity (Kenton L. Sparks, *Ancient Texts for the Study of the Hebrew Bible* [Peabody, MA: Hendrickson, 2005], 313, 315); cf. the Egyptian myths of "Atum Creation Stories" and the "Creations of Re" where creation is achieved though masturbation, sneezing, and spitting (ibid., 323, 326).

64   See the Mesopotamian myth where human beings are created "to carry the toil of the gods" (Sparks, *Ancient Texts*, 313).

65   See, for instance, *Atrahasis* 1:190–197 (W. G. Lambert and A. R. Millard, *Athrahasis: The Babylonian Story of the Flood* [Oxford: Oxford University Press, 1969], 57) and *Enuma Elish* 6:33–36 (*ANET*, 68).

creation of humans is the crowning event in the creation story, for only when humans are created does God say, "it is very good" (1:31).

7. The Sabbath

Unlike the other ANE traditions, which view divine rest as a benefit that the gods enjoyed thanks to human service, the biblical account refers to the Sabbath day as God's good gift to humankind. Thus, while in the other ANE traditions humans worked to allow the gods to rest, in the biblical story God works for humans that they may rest from work they have not performed. It is also noteworthy that while in other Near Eastern cultures the special days of rest (e.g., the Mesopotamian *shapattu*) were often considered unlucky days, the biblical Sabbath is a day of joy and blessing. Moreover, while the Babylonian days of rest were determined by the lunar cycle, implying their gods' involvement in nature, the biblical Sabbath is entirely independent from any celestial movement, testifying "that God is wholly outside of nature."[66] This is why the observance of Sabbath was unique to Israel in the ANE.

THE HISTORICAL INTENTION

Another essential difference between the Genesis creation account and the origin texts of ANE literature concerns their lack of "historical" intention. Unlike the creation stories of Genesis 1 and 2, the ANE stories are not meant to be "creation stories." Instead of speaking about the origin of "the heavens and the earth," the ANE cosmogonies are mainly anthropocentric.[67] They are primarily concerned with the present human condition and aim to explain the existence of evil in the world, with the explicit intent to "silence evil."[68] In ancient Egypt as in ancient Babylon, the knowledge about the origins of the world was not acquired through a special "prophetic" revelation, or even through spiritual or intellectual speculation. Instead, stories of origins were essentially inspired from the observation of natural geographical and physical phenomena: the rise and fall of the Nile for the Egyptians,[69] or the seasonally destructive rains and the rising of the Tigris-Euphrates river system for the Babylonians.[70] The purpose of these observations was to explain present conditions, not to inform about the origins of the world.

The biblical creation story is thus to be considered as the only text that intends to report the actual, historic event of creation. Unlike ANE cosmogonies, which intend to be anthropocentric and functional, responding to philosophical or theological concerns, the biblical creation story intends to testify about an actual event from which its theological lessons are derived and not the other way around. Therefore, the biblical story should be read *respectfully*, with attention to the presented data as it stands: a historical account that accurately describes the content and progression of the creation event as opposed to a mythological story invented for theological or ethical purposes. Written within Hebrew categories, the creation narrative is first of all a history and only secondly a theology that finds its ground within this

---

66   Nahum M. Sarna, *Genesis* (Philadelphia: Jewish Publication Society, 1989), 15.

67   See Susanne Bickel, *La Cosmogonie égyptienne avant le Nouvel Empire*, OBO 134 (Göttingen: Vandenhoek & Ruprecht, 1994), 213.

68   *Coffin Texts*, Spell 1130 (VII462c).

69   See Françoise Dunand and Christiane Zivie-Coche, *Gods and Men in Egypt: 3000 BCE to 395 CE*, trans. Avid Lorton (Ithaca: Cornell University Press, 2002), 47.

70   See Sabatino Moscati, *The Face of the Ancient Orient* (Garden City: Doubleday, 1962), 77.

history.[71] In other words, the spiritual and theological meaning of creation cannot exist apart from its historical reality, and these should be derived from it.

THE CREATION OF HEAVENS AND EARTH (1:1–2:4A)

After a brief prologue (1:1–2) describing the condition of the heavens and earth before the seven-day creation, the account of creation develops in seven days, not only in parallel to its counterpart in the second creation story (2:4b–25; see above), but also with its own proper structure: The first three days (1, 2, 3) parallel the second three days (4, 5, 6). The first three days describe the forming of the unformed universe, while the second three days report its filling, naming the content of this previously empty universe. Thus, we note that on day one the light appeared with God as its agent (1:3–5)[72] || on day four, the light is carried by the luminaries (1:16). On day two, the sky and waters are separated (1:6–8) || on day five, inhabitants of sky (birds) and water (fish) are created (1:20–23). On day three, dry land and vegetation appear (1:9–13) || on day six, inhabitants of land (animals and humans) are created (1:24–31). As for the seventh day, it stands outside of this 3/3 parallel and marks the climax of creation. This last literary observation does not mean, however, that the intention of the biblical author is to emphasize the spiritual message of the creation account at the expense of its historicity. In biblical thinking, the spiritual lesson is rooted in history, a view that applies particularly to the Sabbath (see the comments on 2:3).

1:1–2. THE PROLOGUE

GEN 1:1–2 NKJV	GEN 1:1–2 ESV
1 In the beginning God created the heavens and the earth.	**1** In the beginning, God created the heavens and the earth.
2 The earth was without form, and void; and darkness *was* on the face of the deep. And the Spirit of God was hovering over the face of the waters.	**2** The earth was without form and void, and darkness was over the face of the deep. And the Spirit of God was hovering over the face of the waters.

1:1 In the beginning. The Hebrew word *bere'shit* "in the beginning" is emphasized: "In *the* beginning" (see JPS). Not only is it put in the beginning of the sentence, but it also receives the emphatic accent (*tipkha*), which singles this word out and thus forces the emphasis on it.[73] The phrase *bere'shit* is in fact a technical expression specifically associated with the creation story.[74] It is indeed significant that this expression is very rarely used in the Hebrew Bible. Outside of this verse, it occurs

---

71 See above our discussion on the "Historical-Critical Method."

72 The symbol || stands for parallel.

73 The Hebrew words of the biblical text receive two kinds of accents: the "disjunctive," which marks emphasis on the word that carries it and indicates various degrees of separation between the words, and the "conjunctive," which indicates that the word is to be connected to the next one. These accents also play a role in the chanting of the text in the synagogue. On the function of emphasis of the disjunctive accents, see William Wickes, *Two Treatises on the Accentuation of the Old Testament* (New York: Ktav Publishing House, 1970), part 1: 32–35, part 2: 4.

74 For a thorough discussion of the various possible translations of this word, see Jiři Moskala, "Interpretation of *bereshit* in the Context of Genesis 1:1–3," *AUSS* 49, no. 1 (2011): 33–44.

only four times, and only in Jeremiah where it belongs to a regular stylistic formula alluding to the introductory words of the creation story (Jer 26:1; 27:1; 28:1; 49:34–35), although the messages themselves have no direct reference to the creation account.

The word *bere'shit* refers not only to the creation of planet Earth,[75] but also to the creation of the whole universe,[76] including our planet. The two readings are strongly indicated in the Hebrew grammar of the text and confirmed in tradition. My suggestion, then, is that we accept the two readings together.[77] One way of rendering these two readings would be to first read the verse as a general statement referring to the universal creation and then to read the verse as a more specific statement focusing on the particular creation of our planet. This double reading has the merit of accounting for the existence of elements, such as the waters (1:2, 7); the heavens (1:7); and the sun, the moon, and the stars (1:14–18), which are already present at the moment of that creation. This contrasted reading may seem confusing and trouble our rational Western minds. Yet, the fact is that from the very first word it testifies to the tension and complementarity that governs the process of creation. The same contrast is registered in the parallel between the two creation accounts: the one with the name of God as *'Elohim* (1:1–2:4a) emphasizes the absolute transcendent and universal perspective, and the other with the name of God as *YHWH* (2:4b–25) emphasizes the relative, immanent, and personal perspective. The lesson to be gained from this contrasted understanding is highly significant: The God who created our world and who created me is also the God who created the universe. The beginning of *our* "heavens and earth" has the same absolute quality of beginning as the beginning of the whole universe. Thus, the divine operation of creation is not to be understood in a broad sense, excluding the specifics and allowing subsequent events to evolve by themselves. God involved Himself also in the details of the particular creation until it was thoroughly completed.

God. The emphasis on the absolute character of this "beginning" is reinforced by the exclusive use of the Hebrew name *'Elohim* "God" to designate God in the creation story (1:1–2:4a). This name is derived from the root *'alah*, which conveys the idea of strength and preeminence. The plural form confirms this accent since it is a literary expression of intensity and majesty, rather than an indication of a numerical plural "gods," which would imply a non-Israelite polytheistic belief in several gods.[78] This name refers to the great God who transcends the universe. The rhythm of the verse resonates with the message of the preeminence of *'Elohim*. The word

---

75 The reading of the word *bere'shit* as referring to our human universe is supported by the grammatical form of the word *bere'shit* that normally requires a genitive connection (called "construct") with the following word (see Jer 26:1; 27:1; 28:1; 49:34). The word should, then, be translated: "In the beginning of the creation by God" or "When God began to create." In that case, 1:1–3 is read in one single breath including a parenthesis about the negative state of the earth: "In the beginning of the creation by God … as the earth was without form and void … God said." This reading is attested in Bible translations (e.g., NJPS, NAB, TNK) and in Jewish tradition (see Rashi in Miqraot Gedolot on 1:1).

76 The reading of the word *bere'shit* as referring to the whole universe including ours is supported by the presence of a disjunctive accent on the word *bere'shit*, which separates it from the next word. In that case, 1:1 is read alone, separated from the next verses, referring to the total creation of the cosmos: "In the beginning God created the heavens and the earth" (1:1). This reading is attested in Bible translations (e.g., NKJV, ESV, JPS, NIV) and in old traditions (see *BHS* apparatus ad loc.).

77 This double reading of the word *bere'shit* is supported by the verses of Jeremiah where it always occurs with a disjunctive accent although a genitive connection (construct) is intended. (For the use of the genitive form without genitive sense, see Joüon §96 A *l*, *m*, *q*, §97 B *c*, C *b*, and F *a*.) This double reading would also explain why a strong Jewish tradition reads the word with the flow of a genitive connection (construct) in spite of the disjunctive accent noted by the Massoretes.

78 See *GKC* §124g.

'Elohim signals the center of the verse, not only in terms of the number of words, but also in terms of the number of letters. In addition, the accent (a disjunctive atnach) that separates the verse into two equal parts is attached to the word 'Elohim "God," which, in the traditional chanting in the synagogue, marks the pause and the climax of the verse. "God" is the most important word of the verse, not only because He is the subject of the sentence, but also because of the rhythm of the phrase.

Created. The sounds of the verb bara' "create" are already contained in the first word bere'shit, which begins with the same three letters br'. Although these two words are not derived from the same root, this play of words already suggests the fundamental lesson conveyed in the word bara', namely, that it implies beginning. Indeed, the word br' describes the special and unique act of divine creation and therefore its beginning. The word occurs seven times in the creation story (1:1, 21, 27 [3x]; 2:3; 2:4a), thus indicating its inherent belonging to that particular event of "creation." Moreover, in the Hebrew Bible bara' "create" is always and exclusively used in connection with God as its subject. The verb bara' appears in our immediate context of creation as well as in the Bible at large in synonymous parallelism with the verbs 'asah "make" or yatsar "shape" (2:4; 6:7; Exod 34:10; Isa 41:20; 43:7; 45:12), kun "establish" (Isa 45:18), yasad "found" (Ps 89:12 [11]), and khadash "renew" (Ps 51:12 [11]). The trend of this usage favors the idea of "creating," rather than "separating," as it has sometimes been suggested.[79]

The heavens and the earth. Here we note the use of a merism, a literary device in which opposites are used to refer to a totality ("all"). This phrase does indeed point to the totality of the universe. The intention of this line, however, is not to suggest that the whole of the universe has been created at the same time, in that first week, but simply that all has been created by God. Note that the phrase "heavens and earth" is the direct object of the verb bara', implying that all has been created by God. Both the vast cosmic universe (which includes the heavenly abode of God) and the known human universe (which includes planet Earth) have been created by God. Yet the Genesis account does not inform us about the creation(s) that have preceded the creation of our planet. It simply mentions their existence without explaining the when or how of their genesis. The only affirmation is that God created them.

On the one hand, the biblical creation account of Genesis 1:1–2:4a focuses on the human world—the heavens and earth that were brought into existence at that time, the heavens and earth that would soon become corrupted. This reading is confirmed by biblical eschatology, which uses the same words, "heavens and earth," to describe the redemption of our broken human world: "For behold, I create new heavens and a new earth; and the former shall not be remembered or come to mind" (Isa 65:17). The same human world, the same "heavens and earth," now corrupted, will no longer exist after the eschatological re-creation. It is clear that the word "heavens" refers here to the human "heavens," the heavens surrounding planet Earth where birds fly (Jer 7:33) and the heavens that affect our human life through the function of the luminaries; the heavens of rain and clouds (Deut 11:11) and the heavens of unbearable drought (Lev 26:19).

On the other hand, the biblical account of creation implies that we are not alone

---

79   See Westermann, *Genesis 1–11*, 99; cf. Ellen van Wolde, *Reframing Biblical Studies: When Language and Text Meet Culture, Cognition, and Context* (Winona Lake: Eisenbrauns, 2009), 185–200. For a discussion of this view, see R. van Leeuwen, *"br,'" NIDOTTE* 1:731–732.

in the universe. The creation of our world is a part of an infinitely greater project, which concerns the whole universe. The word "heavens" in the phrase "heavens and earth" also refers to a space and a universe that existed before the creation of our world and is far beyond our world, a universe that does not belong to our corrupted, bound-to-be re-created world. These are the heavens that exist far above (Deut 4:39; cf. Josh 2:11), where God dwells (1 Kgs 8:27; Job 16:19; Matt 5:16) seated upon His throne (Ps 11:4), where He is worshipped by the angelic hosts (Neh 9:6); these are the heavens of heavens, which God also made (Neh 9:6). The notion of the two heavenly orders is also clearly present in the mind of the psalmist who, in the same text, refers to the "heavens" that "dropped rain" and are associated with the shaking of the earth (Ps 68:8 [9]) and to the "heaven of heavens," which is described as existing "of old" (*qadam*), an expression designating a distant, primal past (cf. Deut 33:15). This ambivalence of the heavens is clearly implied in the next word, "the earth."

1:2 The earth. In the Hebrew phrase, the word "earth" is emphasized, being put at the head of the sentence as a way of indicating that the focus is on our human earth. In addition, the word "earth" is preceded by a *waw* "and," which in Hebrew is a conjunction marking a contrast, that is, indicating that the following sentence is to be understood in contrast to the preceding sentence. Thus, the following state of the earth, which will be described as "without form and void," "darkness," and "deep" stands in contrast to the heavens of the preceding sentence. This observation carries a meaningful lesson since it suggests that the "heavens" of verse 1 refer to a place where life and light were already present and created (the first heavens, the abode of God). Amazingly, it is against this heavenly backdrop of life, light, and beauty—where God dwells—that the creation of our earth will be operated. God created planet Earth, having in mind the beauty and goodness of the great heavens in which He dwelt (see Exod 25:9, 40; Ps 78:69), a methodology that will reach its climax with God's rest on the Sabbath (2:2–3).

Without form, and void. The Hebrew words convey the meaning of the phrase through their sounds: *tohu wabohu* "without form and void," which evoke waste and void (onomatopoeia). The word *tohu* means "nothingness" (Isa 29:21) or "desert" (Job 6:18). The word *bohu*, which is always paired with the word *tohu*, reinforces the same concept of emptiness (Jer 4:23; Isa 34:11). The association with "darkness," "the deep," and the explicit word "water," underline the idea of the void, an absence of life. Later on, both "darkness" and "waters" will be associated with the idea of death (Job 10:21; Ps 144:7). The fundamental view of this state, as rendered both phonetically and semantically, is negative. It is also interesting to note that this section of the first creation story (1:2) parallels the section of the second creation story (2:5) that describes the state of the earth in terms of "not yet" and "not." The fundamental idea is that God has created something from nothing—from what is "not" or "not yet."

This accent on the negative character of the earth prior to God's creation does not mean, however, that the earth that is described "without form and void" and the element of the waters do not exist and should therefore be interpreted symbolically. The waters did exist in reality as well as the "void" earth, implying a previous act of creation before this creation week.[80] Yet, all this vastness is still empty and devoid of life.

---

80 For a discussion of the various "gap theories" speculating on this pre-creation, see Richard M. Davidson, "The Genesis Account of Origins," in *The Genesis Creation Account and Its Reverberations in the Old Testament*, ed. Gerald A. Klingbeil (Berrien Springs, MI: Andrews University Press, 2015), 59–129.

Furthermore, this emphasis on the negative state of the earth before creation also suggests a polemic intention to refute the general Near Eastern theories of origins. Indeed, the biblical author, under inspiration, dares to imagine a creation that took place out of something entirely void of life and apart from any divine material, as advocated in the Ancient Middle Eastern views of creation (see above). In other words, God did not create this world and its inhabitants from preexisting materials. Thus, commenting on the phrase "in the beginning" from Genesis 1:1, John could say that all came from the word of God, which he identified with God Himself: "in the beginning was the Word ... and the Word was God ... All things were made through Him, and without Him nothing was made that was made" (John 1:1, 3). Whether one refers to the creation that took place during the first week (1:1–2:4a) or to the creation(s) that took place before (1:1), nothing that was made was made apart from Him. Indeed, there is no room here for the idea that things or beings may have come into existence by themselves as was imagined by the ancient Egyptians through the principle of *kheper*[81] or as was elaborated much later in modern scientific theories of evolution. Creation was triggered from outside by God: "It is He who made us, and not we ourselves" (Ps 100:3).

The Spirit of God. The reference to the "spirit" or "air" of God fits nicely into this context of creation. The *ruakh* "wind," "spirit," or "air" is the principle of life in the Old Testament: "You take away their breath [*ruakh*], they die and return to their dust. You send forth Your Spirit [*ruakh*], they are created" (Ps 104:29–30). It is also significant that the air coming from God's mouth plays the decisive role in the creation of humans (2:7; cf. Job 32:8). The ambiguous meaning of the word *ruakh*, referring to biological as well as spiritual categories, is worth noticing. Spirituality implies life; for "the dead do not praise the Lord, nor any who go down into silence" (Ps 115:17). It is the *ruakh* of God, His breath, that gives humans wisdom and understanding (Job 32:8); without the spirit of God, His *ruakh*, we cannot have a spiritual life. It is also the *ruakh* of God that creates and gives life (Job 33:4). The presence of the *ruakh*, the Spirit/Wind/Air of God hovering upon the lifeless and lightless waters, carries the promise of life beyond this current state of nothingness. Moreover, the promise goes even beyond the mere gift of life; it anticipates God's continuous, faithful support and sustenance of His creation. Even after creation is finished, God's creative acts on behalf of His creation, as well as His power, will continue to be provided amidst the backdrop of darkness and death. In short, hope is present from the very first manifestation of God.

This same imagery of the Spirit of God hovering above the waters is used in Psalm 18 where God the Creator is seen as riding "upon the wings of the wind [*ruakh*]" (Ps 18:10 [11]) blowing at the waters of the abyss in terms that evoke the event of creation: "The foundations of the world were uncovered at your rebuke, O Lord, at the blast of the breath [*ruakh*] of Your nostrils" (Ps 18:15 [16]). And from this evocation of creation, David, the author of this psalm, infers his lesson of hope: "He sent

---

81   The Egyptian notion of *kheper*, which means "evolve" or "become," was conceived by the ancient Egyptians based upon the natural observation of the scarab or "dung beetle" (*kheper*), which was believed to have created itself through an evolutive process. According to Egyptian cosmogony, creation took place when the god *Atum* evolved into the world and became the world through the process of self-evolution; the god was called *khpr-djs.f* "he who evolved by himself." The same notion reappears in the name of the sun god *Khepri* "Evolver," which is represented by a scarab. On the idea of evolution in ancient Egypt, see Siegfried Morenz, *Egyptian Religion* (New York: Cornell University Press, 1992), 159–182.

from above, He took me; He drew me out of many waters. He delivered me from my strong enemy" (Ps 18:16–17 [17–18]).

The Spirit of God is not a natural element, a mere wind blowing upon the water.[82] Although the physical idea of "wind" or "air" may also be implied, the participle "hovering" clearly suggests a distinct person. The expression *ruakh 'Elohim* "Spirit of God" refers to a divine Person who will be later credited as foreknowing and producing historical events (41:38).[83]

1:3–5. DAY ONE

GEN 1:3–5 NKJV	GEN 1:3–5 ESV
3 Then God said, "Let there be light"; and there was light.	**3** And God said, "Let there be light," and there was light.
4 And God saw the light, that *it was* good; and God divided the light from the darkness.	**4** And God saw that the light was good. And God separated the light from the darkness.
5 God called the light Day, and the darkness He called Night. So the evening and the morning were the first day.	**5** God called the light Day, and the darkness he called Night. And there was evening and there was morning, the first day.

1:3 **God said.** This is the first of ten similar formulas that occur in this chapter (1:3, 6, 9, 11, 14, 20, 24, 26, 28,[84] 29) and the third time that God's presence is mentioned as the subject of a verb: first, we saw the God who "creates"; then, the God who "hovers"; and now we hear of the God who "says." The spirit/breath word sequence is an interesting connection as it suggests that the Word shares the same divine nature as the Spirit, just as the spoken word pertains to the breath emanating from the mouth.

Let there be light. It is significant that God's first word of creation affects the darkness that characterizes the state of the earth. The first created thing, then, is light, the first necessary step that will ground the rest of creation. For light is the first prerequisite for life and is often associated with life (see the expression of "light of life" *'or khayyim* in Ps 56:13 [14]). For example, reflecting and commenting on that passage of the Genesis creation story, John associates life to light: "In Him was life, and the life was the light of men" (John 1:4). God's first order is made of two words, *yehi 'or* **let there be light,** immediately followed, as in echo, by the same two words, *wayehi 'or* **and there was light**. The exact repetition of these words suggests the perfect fulfillment of the order. This does not mean, however, that light was created at this time; for light existed before the creation of this earth and outside of the earth (see the above comment on the word "earth" in 1:2 and the comment below on the naming of "light" in 1:5).

1:4 **God saw the light.** The specification of the object "the light" in the refrain phrase **and God saw *the light*, that it was good** is irregular. Normally, the refrain

---

82 As in Tg. Onq. and Tg. Ps.-J.; cf. NRSV: "A wind from God swept over the face of the waters." (See also NJB, NAB.)

83 See Jürgen Moltmann, *Gott in der Schöpfung: Ökologische Schöpfungslehre* (Munich: Kaiser, 1985), 110.

84 In 1:28, the phrase is stylistically different, "God said to them," thus breaking the regular pattern "God said" found in the other nine occurrences. Note that the rhythm of nine is paralleled in the second creation account, which also counts nine divine operations of creation.

phrase is **and God saw that it was (very) good**, without object (1:10, 12, 18, 21, 25, 31). This exceptional formula suggests an essential difference between the evaluation of the light on the first day and the evaluation of what He made on each of the other days. While on the other days the refrain phrase has to do with what God did, or what the elements did at God's command, the variation on the first day speaks only of the result of creation, the object of the light itself, without referring to the act of creation that produced it. This irregularity may be due to the fact that what takes place in the first day is only the appearance of the light, implying that the actual creation of the light belongs to another time that is not mentioned in this account. What is evaluated in the first day is not so much the divine work of creation, which led to the eruption of the light, but rather the finished object of the light itself.

Note that the light is not just "seen by God," it is also appreciated: **It was good** (1:4). The Hebrew word *tov* "good" means more than the simple reference to the efficiency of the function of the light. It also includes aesthetic as well as ethical considerations. The light works well and is beautiful.

The source of light is God Himself. The sun and the moon have not yet been mentioned. As such, the function of separation, which will be held by the luminaries from the fourth day onwards, is now accomplished by God Himself:

God divided the light from the darkness (1:4)
God set them (the luminaries) **to divide the light from the darkness** (1:17)

The parallel between the function of light on the first day and the function of the luminaries on the fourth day, and the fact that the same exact phrase is used to describe the function of separation in both cases ("divide the light from the darkness"), suggests that the function held by the luminaries on the fourth day is the same as the function held by God on the first day; and hence the same solar day of approximately twenty-four hours is intended.

1:5 God called the light Day. This identification of the "light" (*'or*) as "day" (*yom*) again confirms that the "light" that came as a result of God's command ("let there be light") is limited to the human sphere; it is the result of the solar system that will be set in motion on the fourth day (1:14–18). The naming is an important feature of the creation account in that naming gives or confirms existence. God gives names to the day, night, earth, and sea. It is noteworthy that this divine prerogative of the Creator will be extended by God to Adam, as seen in his naming of the animals (2:19–20).

After the creation of light, the "day-night" sequence, which prioritizes the day over the night, might be intended to suggest that the creation of both entities is derived from the same source, the light. In other words, the night is not to be seen as a subproduct of the darkness, which was a part of the state of pre-creation. Instead, both the night as well as the day pertain to the light as two complementary facets of life.

The evening and the morning. Likewise, the "evening-morning" sequence immediately following the reference to the night suggests that the day as a whole has its source in the night, including it within its time.[85] In other words, the day contains both the darkness of the night and the light of the day. The use of the words "evening"

---

85 For a discussion of this formula and an examination of the biblical evidence supporting its legitimacy, see J. Amanda McGuire, "Evening or Morning: When Does the Biblical Day Begin?" *AUSS* 46, no. 2 (2008): 201–214.

and "morning" is a merism that points to the extremities of the day to denote its totality. The concept of the twenty-four-hour solar day, already implied in the separation of the light from the darkness and by extension in the creation of the day and night, is now confirmed in the refrain "evening and morning." Thus, it has been suggested that "each subsequent day is a reenactment of that sequence of events that moves from darkness (chaos) to light."[86] The sequence of evening-morning is in a sense a reminder of and testimony to the miraculous process of creation that transforms the pre-creation state of darkness into the life of light. This expression applies both to the first three days—before the appearance of the sun—as well as to the three days that follow. The seventh day (2:2–3) is the only day that does not contain this refrain for the obvious reason that this is the only day of creation week when humans are present; we do not need the specific mention "evening and morning" because the temporal reality of "evening and morning" has now become the tangible experience of humans.

The expression "evening and morning" is unique to the Genesis creation story; so far it has never been found in other ANE texts as a modifier of or substitute for the concept of "day." In addition, the sixfold emphatic repetition of this very distinctive phrase indicates the deliberate intention of the author to convey a specific message in contradistinction to the other Near Eastern cultures, and perhaps with some polemic intention. Unlike ancient Egypt, for instance, where the day begins at sunrise with the light that wakes humans, the Genesis creation story makes the day begin at sunset with the night, when humans go to bed. In ancient Egypt, sunset marks the end of the day and by implication symbolizes death; the west is the place of the dead. According to Genesis 1, sunset marks the beginning of the day so that the night is an integral part of life. This different concept of what constitutes "day" may reflect both a different understanding of life and a different way of relating to the divine. While the Egyptians associate death (the night) with life (the day), in the biblical economy of creation death is totally absent and God's creation is made of pure life. While the Egyptians believed in a god they could see, the sun god, the god that is present when they wake up, the biblical religion dares to believe in the God who is not seen, yet who is present even during the night hours (Ps 121:4).

In short, this formulation contains a spiritual lesson about the invisible God of grace who creates for us even while we are not around, the God who fights for us while we hold our peace (Exod 14:14), and the God who is present even in our darkest hours. It has also been suggested that the sequence of evening-morning parallels the process of creation and testifies to the sequence of events that move from darkness (chaos) to light (order). The evening-morning sequence as lived in the Sabbath would, then, express faith in the miracle of creation, and rest in God's power to bring light out of darkness.

1:6–8. DAY TWO

GEN 1:6–8 NKJV	GEN 1:6–8 ESV
6 Then God said, "Let there be a firmament in the midst of the waters, and let it divide the waters from the waters."	**6** And God said, "Let there be an expanse in the midst of the waters, and let it separate the waters from the waters."

---

86 McGuire, "Evening or Morning," 214; cf. von Rad, *Genesis*, 52–53.

7 Thus God made the firmament, and divided the waters which *were* under the firmament from the waters which *were* above the firmament; and it was so.	**7** And God made the expanse and separated the waters that were under the expanse from the waters that were above the expanse. And it was so.
8 And God called the firmament Heaven. So the evening and the morning were the second day.	**8** And God called the expanse Heaven. And there was evening and there was morning, the second day.

Firmament. The Hebrew word *raqia'* "firmament" does not refer to a solid sheet of metal,[87] as the etymology of the Latin translation *firmamentum* (from the Vulgate) may suggest. The word occurs mostly in poetic texts (Job 37:18; Ezek 1:25–26; Isa 42:5) and should therefore be understood figuratively to evoke "an expanse" (ESV). The function of this expanse is not so much to cover like a "dome" (NRSV) or a "vault" (REB), but rather to **divide the waters from the waters** (1:6; cf. 1:7). The fact that the punishment for a disobedient Israel would be in finding the heavens like iron (Lev 26:19) or like bronze (Deut 28:23), meaning that they would not produce rain, clearly implies that these heavens are not originally metallic. What is created is not some kind of solid object, but the space or the atmosphere above humans where luminaries are set (1:14–15, 17; Dan 12:3) and birds fly (1:20).

The name **heaven** (1:8) that is given to designate this firmament confirms that the author does not intend to refer to its real substance but rather to the way the firmament is perceived from a human "phenomenological" perspective. The word "heavens" refers here to the human heavens. The fact that it is the same word that is used to refer to the divine heavens suggests some kind of relation between the two entities, although they are essentially different in nature. The word "heavens" refers to an order that is essentially other than the human earth and is seen above it. That God is situated in the heavens means that He belongs to a space that is not ours, a space that is infinitely far from us and infinitely greater than ours, one that Solomon designates with the superlative "heavens of heavens" (1 Kgs 8:27). This is why God is often called "God of heaven" (24:7; 28:17; Dan 2:18; Ezra 1:2). The verbal repetition **under the firmament ... above the firmament** (1:7) emphasizes the efficiency of the command of creation: the firmament fulfills its exact function, as ordered by God, which is to separate the waters. Once again we see that the Genesis creation contains a polemic intention against ANE cosmogonies, where the heavens and waters were gods. Here, however, the heavens and waters are not divine: **God made the firmament** (1:7).

1:9–13. DAY THREE

GEN 1:9–13 NKJV	GEN 1:9–13 ESV
9 Then God said, "Let the waters under the heavens be gathered together into one place, and let the dry *land* appear"; and it was so.	**9** And God said, "Let the waters under the heavens be gathered together into one place, and let the dry land appear." And it was so.
10 And God called the dry *land* Earth, and the gathering together of the waters He called Seas. And God saw that *it was* good.	**10** God called the dry land Earth, and the waters that were gathered together he called Seas. And God saw that it was good.

---

87 For a discussion on the meaning of the word *raqi'a* "firmament," see Randall W. Younker and Richard M. Davidson, "The Myth of the Solid Heavenly Dome: Another Look at the Hebrew *raqia'*," *AUSS* 49, no. 1 (2011): 125–147.

11 Then God said, "Let the earth bring forth grass, the herb *that* yields seed, *and* the fruit tree *that* yields fruit according to its kind, whose seed *is* in itself, on the earth"; and it was so.	**11** And God said, "Let the earth sprout vegetation, plants yielding seed, and fruit trees bearing fruit in which is their seed, each according to its kind, on the earth." And it was so.
12 And the earth brought forth grass, the herb *that* yields seed according to its kind, and the tree *that* yields fruit, whose seed *is* in itself according to its kind. And God saw that *it was* good.	**12** The earth brought forth vegetation, plants yielding seed according to their own kinds, and trees bearing fruit in which is their seed, each according to its kind. And God saw that it was good.
13 So the evening and the morning were the third day.	**13** And there was evening and there was morning, the third day.

1:9 After the creation of the "heavens" and the separation of waters in that space, the author moves down to the creation of the "earth" and the separation of waters in this space. The text does not speak about the creation of the earth but about its appearance: **let the waters … be gathered … and let the dry land appear** (1:9). The divine command is immediately followed by its perfect fulfillment, **and it was so**, indicating that what God creates is the motion of the waters, a separation that results in the existence of the dry earth. It is not clear whether God created the earth matter on the third day or whether He had created it earlier.

1:9–10 The appearance of the earth separates the mass of water (1:9) into what are called **seas**. This is the final stage in the separation of waters begun on the first day, and is why we must wait until now for the second mention of divine appreciation: **it was good**. What is clear, however, is that the capacity of the earth to produce the grass, the seed, and hence the fruit, does not reside within the earth itself. Because the earth is not divine, it cannot hold in itself the power to generate. It is God who creates this process from the outside, according to the same method of the divine command: **let the earth bring forth grass … seed, and the fruit**.

1:11–12 The fulfillment is again signified by the regular formula **and it was so** (1:11) and the verbatim repetition of the divine command in the response of the earth, **and the earth brought forth grass … seed … and fruit** (1:12). While in the ancient world fertility was deified, our text affirms that it is created by God. Yet, it is not just fertility, namely, the mere capacity to reproduce that is created. Creation also concerns the last stage of the event, the fruit. It is interesting to note that the immediacy of the fulfillment excludes the time factor that underlies the hypothesis of creation by evolution.

1:14–19. DAY FOUR

GEN 1:14–19 NKJV	GEN 1:14–19 ESV
14 Then God said, "Let there be lights in the firmament of the heavens to divide the day from the night; and let them be for signs and seasons, and for days and years;	**14** And God said, "Let there be lights in the expanse of the heavens to separate the day from the night. And let them be for signs and for seasons, and for days and years,
15 and let them be for lights in the firmament of the heavens to give light on the earth"; and it was so.	**15** and let them be lights in the expanse of the heavens to give light upon the earth." And it was so.

16 Then God made two great lights: the greater light to rule the day, and the lesser light to rule the night. *He made* the stars also.	**16** And God made the two great lights—the greater light to rule the day and the lesser light to rule the night—and the stars.
17 God set them in the firmament of the heavens to give light on the earth,	**17** And God set them in the expanse of the heavens to give light on the earth,
18 and to rule over the day and over the night, and to divide the light from the darkness. And God saw that *it was* good.	**18** to rule over the day and over the night, and to separate the light from the darkness. And God saw that it was good.
19 So the evening and the morning were the fourth day.	**19** And there was evening and there was morning, the fourth day.

The creation of the fourth day (luminaries) corresponds to the creation of the first day (light). Except for the creation of humans on the sixth day, the creation of the luminaries on the fourth day covers more space than any other day of the creation week. Note also that this creation is located in the middle (fourth day) of the seven-day arrangement. This emphasis is perhaps due to the intention of the biblical author to highlight the sanctuary connection.[88] Significantly, the biblical writer does not use the specific words *shemesh* for the "sun" (15:17; Josh 10:12) and *yareakh* for the "moon" (Josh 10:12–13; Ps 72:5). Instead he uses the word *maʾor* **light** (plural *meʾorot*, **lights**), which is always used to designate the sanctuary lamp in the tabernacle (Exod 35:14; Num 4:9, 16). In addition, both Hebrew terms for **signs** (*ʾot*) and **seasons** (*moʿadim*) belong to the language of rituals. The word *ʾot* "sign" refers to rituals (17:11; Exod 12:13; Ezek 20:12, 20) and the word *moʿadim* "seasons" refer to places and times of meeting with God. The tabernacle is called *ʾohel moʿed* "tabernacle of meeting" (Exod 30:36; Num 17:4). The *moʿadim* refer also to the worship assemblies (Ps 74:4, 8) or to the "feasts of the Lord" (Lev 23:2; Hos 9:5). The function of the luminaries was not just to divide the day and the night or to determine the lunar or solar calendar, it was also designed to determine the appointed moment of the yearly feasts (Ps 104:19; Zech 8:19), which followed the rhythm of the agricultural seasons. These echoes of language, which evoke the life of the sanctuary, suggest that the blueprint of creation is derived from a greater pattern of a supernatural order: "He built His sanctuary like the heights, like the earth He has established forever" (Ps 78:69).

Another reason why the Hebrew names of the sun and the moon are not mentioned is to avoid any potential confusion with the pagan Canaanite gods of the sun and the moon, which were known by the same names. Instead, here the sun and the moon are simply instruments of light. The construction of the phrase, with the *lamed* of purpose, suggests that it was not the sun and the moon that were created by God on the fourth day but rather their function[89] as ruling the day and the night, and dividing light from darkness:

Let there be lights … for the purpose of dividing the day from the night (1:14)
God made the two great lights … for the purpose of ruling the day and the night (1:16)

---

88 On the significance of sanctuary symbolism in the creation account, see Laurence A. Turner, "A Theological Reading of Genesis 1:1," in *In the Beginning*, ed. Bryan W. Ball (Nampa, ID: Pacific Press, 2012): 73–77; cf. Richard M. Davidson, "Cosmic Metanarrative for the Coming Millennium," *JATS* 11 (2000): 109–111.

89 See also, Jiři Moskala, "A Fresh Look at Two Genesis Accounts: Contradictions?" *AUSS* 49, no. 1 (2011): 57–58.

God set them … for the purpose of ruling over the night and the day and dividing the
light from the darkness (1:18)

Note that the function of the luminaries **to divide the light from the darkness**
(1:18) had been previously held by God from day one, as suggested by the parallels
and echoes between the two passages:

God divided the light from the darkness (1:4)
God set them (the luminaries) … to divide the light from the darkness (1:18)

God is then acknowledged as the ultimate source of light, an idea that is clearly
implied in the parallel text of Psalm 104 where God is described as covering Himself
"with light as with a garment" (Ps 104:2).[90]

As for the creation of the stars, the construction of the phrase **the stars also** (1:16)
suggests that "they are only mentioned as extra information, like some kind of appendix."[91] Neither their function nor the time when they were created is indicated.

1:20–23. DAY FIVE

GEN 1:20–23 NKJV	GEN 1:20–23 ESV
20 Then God said, "Let the waters abound with an abundance of living creatures, and let birds fly above the earth across the face of the firmament of the heavens."	**20** And God said, "Let the waters swarm with swarms of living creatures, and let birds fly above the earth across the expanse of the heavens."
21 So God created great sea creatures and every living thing that moves, with which the waters abounded, according to their kind, and every winged bird according to its kind. And God saw that *it was* good.	**21** So God created the great sea creatures and every living creature that moves, with which the waters swarm, according to their kinds, and every winged bird according to its kind. And God saw that it was good.
22 And God blessed them, saying, "Be fruitful and multiply, and fill the waters in the seas, and let birds multiply on the earth."	**22** And God blessed them, saying, "Be fruitful and multiply and fill the waters in the seas, and let birds multiply on the earth."
23 So the evening and the morning were the fifth day.	**23** And there was evening and there was morning, the fifth day.

The creation of the fifth day (fish and birds) corresponds to the creation of the
second day (division of waters and firmament) in that it fills the space previously
made. The text here focuses on the content of the waters and earthly skies, with
special attention given to the creatures in the waters. The distinctive feature of the
fifth day is the unexpected use of one of the seven occurrences of the verb *bara'* "create" here applied to the *tanninim* **sea creatures** (1:20) and the first reference to the
notion of *barak* "blessing." The phrase **God blessed** (1:22) is associated with *parah*
"fruitfulness" and *rabah* "abundance." Besides the poetic play on the phonetic similarity of those terms (prh-rbh-bra-brk), which highlights their connection, the use of
the verb *bara'* in connection to the "sea creatures" may be theologically intended.

---

90 See Davidson, "The Genesis Account of Origins," 119.

91 Doukhan, *The Genesis Creation Story*, 45.

Sea creatures. The specific use of the verb *bara'* "create" for the *tannin* "sea creatures" is surprising, for it is normally associated either with the creation of heavens and earth (1:1; 2:3–4) or the creation of humans (1:27). In fact, this association with the *tannin* belongs to the same cosmic perspective. For the *tannin* is the sea monster, the divine chaos monster in the Ugaritic myths of creation. In Isaiah 27:1, it is symbolically identified as the Leviathan, the serpent, who is God's enemy. The use of *bara'* "create" betrays therefore a deliberate polemic intention directed against the mythological views of the ANE. The ordinary nature of the big serpent is revealed; it is nothing but an animal, a mere fish that was created by God.

Blessed. This is the first occurrence of "blessing" (*barak*). It implies abundant fruitfulness (1:22, 28; 9:1, 7; 17:6, 20; 28:3; 41:52; 48:4) and is therefore quite striking in its immediate context. For against the background of the ANE chaos monster, the divine blessing—and hence its promise of full life—means the victory of life over the power of chaos. On the fifth day, the affirmation of life reaches a particular intensity; this passage (1:21) contains the first explicit reference to "**life**" (*khay*). It appears in the idiomatic expression **every living thing** (*kol nepesh hakhayyah*), which recurs in the context of the Levitical dietary laws of clean and unclean animals (Lev 11:10, 46). This particular echo, among other linguistic and thematic links between this passage and the text in Leviticus, suggests that the legislation of the Levitical dietary laws was somewhat dependent on the creation text. This common emphasis on life may even be read as a clue in regard to the spiritual principle at work behind the dietary differentiation between animals, which concerns the very sacredness of life.

1:24–31. DAY SIX

GEN 1:24–31 NKJV	GEN 1:24–31 ESV
24 Then God said, "Let the earth bring forth the living creature according to its kind: cattle and creeping thing and beast of the earth, *each* according to its kind"; and it was so.	**24** And God said, "Let the earth bring forth living creatures according to their kinds—livestock and creeping things and beasts of the earth according to their kinds." And it was so.
25 And God made the beast of the earth according to its kind, cattle according to its kind, and everything that creeps on the earth according to its kind. And God saw that *it was* good.	**25** And God made the beasts of the earth according to their kinds and the livestock according to their kinds, and everything that creeps on the ground according to its kind. And God saw that it was good.
26 Then God said, "Let Us make man in Our image, according to Our likeness; let them have dominion over the fish of the sea, over the birds of the air, and over the cattle, over all the earth and over every creeping thing that creeps on the earth."	**26** Then God said, "Let us make man in our image, after our likeness. And let them have dominion over the fish of the sea and over the birds of the heavens and over the livestock and over all the earth and over every creeping thing that creeps on the earth."
27 So God created man in His *own* image; in the image of God He created him; male and female He created them.	**27** So God created man in his own image, in the image of God he created him; male and female he created them.
28 Then God blessed them, and God said to them, "Be fruitful and multiply; fill the earth and subdue it; have dominion over the fish of the sea, over the birds of the air, and over every living thing that moves on the earth."	**28** And God blessed them. And God said to them, "Be fruitful and multiply and fill the earth and subdue it and have dominion over the fish of the sea and over the birds of the heavens and over every living thing that moves on the earth."

2 9 And God said, "See, I have given you every herb *that* yields seed which *is* on the face of all the earth, and every tree whose fruit yields seed; to you it shall be for food.

2 9 And God said, "Behold, I have given you every plant yielding seed that is on the face of all the earth, and every tree with seed in its fruit. You shall have them for food.

3 0 Also, to every beast of the earth, to every bird of the air, and to everything that creeps on the earth, in which *there is* life, *I have given* every green herb for food"; and it was so.

3 0 And to every beast of the earth and to every bird of the heavens and to everything that creeps on the earth, everything that has the breath of life, I have given every green plant for food." And it was so.

3 1 Then God saw everything that He had made, and indeed *it was* very good. So the evening and the morning were the sixth day.

3 1 And God saw everything that he had made, and behold, it was very good. And there was evening and there was morning, the sixth day.

The creative acts of the sixth day dealing with the land animals (beasts and humans) and the common vegetation food assigned to them correspond to the creative acts of the third day dealing with the land and its vegetation. The author devotes more space to the sixth day than to any other day and divides it into two sections: (1) the creation of the **beast of the earth,** *each* **according to its kind** (1:24–25), which ends with the regular divine appreciation *it was* **good** (1:25); and then (2) the creation of humans, which is the climax of the sixth day and takes up more space than the creation of animals. Finally, the entire sixth-day account concludes with the highest divine appreciation: **indeed** *it was* **very good** (1:31).

1:24–25 **Living creature according to its kind.** Like the animals of the waters (1:21), the animals of the land are created **each according to its kind** (1:24–25), a language that is found again in the context of the Levitical dietary differentiation of animals (Lev 11:10, 22, 46). Once again the linguistic and thematic link between Genesis 1 and Leviticus 11 suggests a connection of theological significance: the reference to the divine creation underlines the dietary legislation that deals with fundamental common themes, the affirmation of "life" and the divine control over the various "kinds" of animals. This word does not refer here to "species" as understood in modern science, thus implying the idea of fixity of species.[92] Rather, the Hebrew word *min* "kind" refers to general categorizations and is used to emphasize the multiplicity of animals in contrast to the unity of human beings; significantly, this word is consistently absent whenever human beings are referred to.[93]

1:26 **Let Us make man in Our image.** There is an essential difference between the creation of animals and the creation of humans. Animals are created "according to their kind" (1:21, 24–25), a statement made in the third person and indicating a relation to themselves: *leminehem/leminehu/leminah.* Humans, on the other hand, are created *ketsalmenu* "according to Us" (1:26 lit. trans.) referring to Someone outside of themselves—God. Furthermore, animals are defined within the natural domain, according their "kinds" and are described as derived from the earth (1:24), while humans are defined in terms of a special and direct reference to God. One of the fundamental implications from this contradistinction between the creation of the beasts and the creation of humans is that humans do

---

92 For a discussion of this interpretation and its scientific implication, see Rahel Davidson Schafer, "The 'Kinds' of Genesis 1: What Is the Meaning of *Min*?" *JATS* 14, no. 1 (2003): 86–100.

93 P. Beauchamp, "*min*," *TDOT* 8:290.

not derive from the beasts, as taught in the evolutionist hypothesis.

Let Us make. The creation of humans necessitates special deliberation within the Deity. The use of the plural form to refer to God's creation of humans in His image is particularly intriguing, as it suggests that God shared His creative operation with one or more beings. It is certainly not a plural of majesty, since the Genesis account already includes the Spirit of God in the work of creation (see 1:2). Also, the fact that the image of God in humans is in the plural ("let *them* have dominion," 1:26b) suggests that this image reflects God in the plural. In addition, the textual shift from previously mentioning God in the singular to, in this particular instance, the plural suggests the deliberate intention of plurality. Although there is a diversity of opinions regarding the identity of this or these other beings involved in this creation in the "image of God," the majority of interpretations recognize that a real plurality is meant here. Generally speaking, both Jewish and Christian traditions have acknowledged the genuine plural intent of this formula. While the traditional Jewish interpretation held that the plural included God's heavenly court of angels,[94] Christian theologians from the time of the Church Fathers[95] and the Reformers[96] to our time[97] have generally interpreted "Us" as a plural within deity, referring to Christ and/or the Trinity. This act of sharing within the Godhead is thus understood to be an inherent quality of God Himself. The logic of the creation story, which identifies God as the only One who creates—the only One who is the subject of the verb *bara'* (see 1:27)—excludes the involvement of non-divine beings (Jewish tradition) and suggests indeed that only the Divine is involved in this self-deliberation. And since the plural is indeed intended, the application to the Trinity is a reasonable interpretation.[98]

Man in Our image, according to Our likeness. With this phrase, which marks the last work of creation, we reach the boldest affirmation of the remarkably unique relationship between humans and God—humans resemble God. This scriptural definition of the human being is a rich revelation of biblical anthropology, for not only does it affirm the unity of human nature, it also underscores the miracle of human individuality, as we will explore in the following. Incidentally, this concept of the "image of God" in humans provides us with a better picture of God and should therefore have a bearing on biblical theology.

The Unity of Human Nature. Traditionally, and under the influence of Platonic dualism, the boldness of this affirmation has been tempered by emphasizing the spiritual (immaterial) aspects of the human likeness to God at the expense of the physical (material) resemblance. The image of God has thus been relegated to the spiritual/religious or intellectual/rational side of humans. More recently, this biblical statement has been interpreted in functional terms, where the "image of God" refers to the representative function of humans. One example is that humans, as representatives of God, have the responsibility of stewardship over creation.[99] Although this

---

94   See Rashi in Miqraot Gedolot on 1:26; cf. Gen. Rab. 8:8.

95   See R. Wilson, "The Early History of the Exegesis of Genesis 1:28," StPatr 1 (1957): 420–437.

96   See M. Luther, *Lectures on Genesis 1–5*, ed. J. Pelikan, *Luther's Works*, vol. 1 (Saint Louis: Concordia, 1958), 58; J. Calvin, *A Commentary on Genesis*, trans. and ed. J. King (London: Banner of Truth, 1965), 92.

97   See D. J. A. Clines, "The Image of God in Man," *TynBul* 19 (1968): 68–69; Gerhard F. Hasel, "The Meaning of 'Let Us' in Gen 1:26," *AUSS* 13 (1975): 65–66.

98   See Jiři Moskala, "Toward Trinitarian Thinking in the Hebrew Scriptures," *JATS* 21, no. 2 (2010): 255–256.

99   For the "representative" interpretation, the "image of God" applies to the human dominion over the animals and is supported by the biblical text (1:26; cf. 9:6) as well as by the testimony of ANE parallels. See C. John Collins, *Genesis 1–4: A Linguistic, Literary, and Theological Commentary* (Phillipsburg, NJ: P&R Publishing, 2006), 62–63.

interpretation is supported on the basis of the term "rule" (*radah*), which appears in the immediate context (1:26, 28), it is still a limited application of the "image of God." The creation of humans in the "image of God" has also been seen as referring to the human function of relationship,[100] that is, to our God-given capacity to relate to God and one another. This view is also substantiated by the biblical context, particularly concerning the relational bond between the first couple, which is given as a component of the "image of God": So **God created man in His own image … male and female He created them** (1:27). Additionally, humans are the only creatures with whom God specificly relates and speaks: **God said to them** (1:28).

Yet these functional interpretations are incomplete insofar as they are again ignoring the physical and material dimensions of the human individual. Indeed, a careful examination of the biblical formula and its parallels in the ANE has led a significant number of scholars to the conclusion that the "image of God" should be understood in a more comprehensive manner to include both the spiritual/functional as well as the physical/material domains.[101] This interpretation is well supported on a semantic level by the language of the Hebrew text. The term *tselem* "image"—which is etymologically related to the Arabic *tsalama* "to chop off" or "to carve" and is used to designate a statue or even an idol (Num 33:52; 2 Chr 13:17)—refers to the physical image, the visible and shaped form of the human body. On the other hand, the term *demut* "likeness," which is derived from the verb *damah* "to compare," means "comparison" (Isa 40:12–31), "something like" (2 Chr 4:3), and refers to abstract qualities and nonphysical traits. This application to both the physical and the spiritual is also supported in the Ancient Near East, where the statues of the king, which were designed to functionally represent the king in his dominion and spiritual capacities, were also shaped in his physical resemblance. This double application also has the merit of being consistent with the wholistic view of the Bible that never dissociates the spiritual/functional dimension of the human being from his or her physical/material reality. As Gerhard von Rad emphasizes in his commentary on this text: "One will do well to split the physical from the spiritual as little as possible: the whole man is created in God's image."[102]

The Individuality of the Human Person. The "image of God" includes both the physical and spiritual dimensions of the human person and underscores the incarnational nature of the divine act of creation. God has created the human being not only as an abstract spiritual entity but, equally important, as a concrete physical body.

It is highly significant that only humans have been created in God's image. While in the Near Eastern context animals are often chosen to represent an aspect of the deity and be the image of the god, in the Genesis text it is exclusively humans—as male and female—who represent God and are the image of God. It is noteworthy

---

100 The "relational" interpretation has been especially represented by Karl Barth for whom the "image of god" means that God can enter into personal relationship with humans (see Karl Barth, "The Doctrine of Creation," in *Church Dogmatics*, vol. III, part 4 [Edinburg: T&T Clark, 1961, repr., 2000], 117). Karl Barth does not, however, take the Genesis account of creation as a historical event and interprets the story only in existential and ethical terms (see ibid., 28–31).

101 For a review and discussion of the various interpretations of the "image of God," see Richard M. Davidson, "The Nature of the Human Being From the Beginning: Genesis 1–11," in *What Are Human Beings That You Remember Them? Proceedings of the Third International Bible Conference, Nof Ginosar and Jerusalem, June 11–21, 2012*, ed. Clinton Wahlen (Silver Spring, MD: Biblical Research Institute, 2015).

102 Von Rad, *Genesis*, 58; cf. John Goldingay, *Israel's Gospel*, vol. 1 of *Old Testament Theology* (Downers Grove: InterVarsity, 2003), 102–103; cf. Ellen G. White, "When Adam came from the Creator's hand, he bore, in his physical, mental, and spiritual nature, a likeness to his Maker" (Ed 15).

that, although biblical symbolism includes the use of things (e.g., rock: Ps 18:2; ladder: 28:12; John 1:51) or animals (e.g., lamb: Rev 5:6; dove: Matt 3:16) to illustrate an aspect of God's nature or function, in the biblical narrative God always chooses to show Himself as a human being and never as a thing or an animal. The book of Daniel, which situates itself within the same cosmic and creative perspective as Genesis 1, uses the human domain to represent the divine spiritual dimension, but the animal domain to represent human political, nonspiritual powers. Thus, we note that the "Son of Man" (Dan 7:13) initiates and represents the kingdom of God while the four animals represent earthly kingdoms (Dan 7:1–8, 17). It is also particularly telling that the divine incarnation took place in the human sphere; God became an individual, the human Jesus of Nazareth. Within the immediate context of the sixth day, which underlines the special character of the creation of humans in contrast to the other creations, the concept of the "image of God" indicates the uniqueness that characterizes this last creation. In other words, from the idea that humans are the only beings created in the image of God, we may indeed infer that they have been created as distinct and unique individuals. Humans are *'akhad* "one," "unique," just as God is *'akhad* "one" and "unique" (Deut 6:4; cf. 1 Cor 8:4–6). As McKeown comments, "Although it is difficult to ascertain the meaning of the 'image,' it is closely associated with the uniqueness and distinctiveness of humans."[103] This view has an important implication in regard to the individual nature of humans. For while all humans share the same human nature, every human being is unique because he or she is created in the image of God. "Every human being, created in the image of God, is endowed with a power akin to that of the Creator—individuality."[104] Everyone is unique just as God is unique. This principle of "the image of God" is in fact reflected in the divine requirement, "you shall be holy; for I am holy" (Lev 11:44–45).

The idea of individuality is also paradoxically implied in the fact that God created humans of a different nature than Himself. As it has been pointed out, "it is by acknowledging this eternal Creator who is outside of me that I as human reach and maintain any genuine humanity."[105] Unlike the ANE myths of origins that made humans out of the divine (from his spit, or from his sperm), hence of the same nature,[106] the Bible reveals the creation of humans out of what God is *not*, of that which is essentially *different* from Him. Humans are not gods. And yet it is this very difference that, paradoxically, makes humans like God. Succinctly stated, humans are in God's image not only because they resemble God physically and spiritually, but also because they have not been created as another "Himself," a mere mechanical reproduction of God, obliged to say "yes" to God, but as free and different beings capable of saying "no" to God. Yet, as we shall learn from the following accounts, it is only in their saying "yes" to God that humans can preserve their status "in the image of God" and therefore blossom as free and unique individuals.

The Idea of God. The biblical definition of humans in "the image of God" has important implications in regard to our understanding of God. Being physical as

---

103 McKeown, *Genesis*, 27.

104 Ellen G. White, Ed 17.

105 Paul Petersen, "Biblical Theology and the Doctrine of Creation," in *In the Beginning*, ed. Bryan W. Ball (Nampa, ID: Pacific Press, 2012), 119.

106 See the Mesopotamian myths of *Atrahasis* and *Enuma Elish* where the blood of a god is used to create humanity (Sparks, *Ancient Texts*, 313, 315); cf. the Egyptian myths of "Atum Creation Stories" and "The Creations of Re" where creation is achieved through masturbation, sneezing, and spitting (ibid., 323, 326).

well as spiritual beings, individual humans—because they are created in God's image—testify to the unity of God as a physical as well as a spiritual Being and hence to the historical nature and individuality of God's person. God is not an abstract concept or mere spiritual reality. God is not a principle. As a physical and historical being, God exists by Himself as a unique individual and therefore apart from human theological or philosophical imagination and reflection. In that sense, even though God is a physical Being, He remains far beyond our comprehension (Deut 4:15–16). In addition, our experience of existing as a physical and material reality testifies to the similarly real existence of God. God exists as humans exist.

1:27 So God created man. The statement specifying "God created man" parallels the statement on the creation of beasts:

> And God made the beast of the earth according to its kind (1:25)
> And God created man in His image (1:27)

The parallel between the two statements confirms the correspondence (by contrast) between the creation of the beasts and the creation of humans. The creation of humans "in His image" is opposed to the creation of the beasts "according to its kind." The use of the technical verb *bara'* for the creation of humans reminds one of the same polemic intent used for the sea creatures: humans are created, they are not divine. It is interesting and certainly significant that the phrase **male and female He created them** parallels the phrase **in the image of God He created him**. This parallel between "him" and "them" indicates that in the first phrase the pronoun "him" that refers to Adam is inclusive; it means that both the man and the woman have been created in God's image. A better way to render this idea would be to translate it as "humankind" (NRSV, NET, CJB).[107] This will immediately be confirmed in the next statement (1:28) where the divine blessing and commission to dominate is attached again to the plural pronoun "them." This observation not only prevents us from thinking that only the man is to dominate over the world (including the woman), but it also excludes the idea that man had originally been created androgynous, that is, biologically bisexual.[108] Clearly *two* persons, one male and the other female, are meant, just as it was for the animals (7:2–3). Also, the use of the singular "him," which is inclusive and refers to both the man and the woman, clearly implies that the "image of God" concerns the human person: each individual, either male or female, was made in the image of God. The interplay between "him/them" precludes, then, any kind of corporate interpretation suggesting that the image of God is only obtained as a couple, the man having received one part of the image of God and the woman another part.

1:29–30 I have given you every herb … for food. Unlike the ANE mythology where humans were created by the gods only to serve and supply them with food,[109] Genesis 1 presents humans as the ultimate purpose of creation. Instead of humans providing the gods with food, God provided humans with food (plants). Food is

---

107 Other versions have translated with the phrase "human beings" (NLT, TNIV).

108 For a discussion of this interpretation, see Richard, M. Davidson, "The Theology of Sexuality in the Beginning: Genesis 1–2," *AUSS* 26, no. 1 (1988): 7. The legend of the "androgynos" (Gk. *andros* man, *gune* woman), which came originally from Greek and Egyptian mythologies found its way into rabbinic literature (see Gen. Rab. 8:1; cf. '*Erub.* 18a and *Ber.* 61a).

109 See, for instance, the Babylonian *Atrahasis Epic* 1. 190–191 and the *Enuma Elish* 6:35–37.

then the first divine gift to humans. This text contains the first biblical occurrence of the verb "give" (*natan*) associated with God as the giver and humans as receivers. Food is thus declared as the first affirmation of human dependence on God, the first and most fundamental experience of the recognition of God as the Creator. No wonder the blessing of the meal is one of the most common practices throughout the religions of the world.

Remarkably, the original diet here provided by the Creator does not involve killing. Instead, humans and animals share the same plant-based diet, a tradition that is also attested in many other ancient cultures.[110] What was created on the third day, "Herb that yields seed ... and the tree that yields fruit" (1:12) is listed on the sixth day as the menu for Adam and Eve (1:29). Thus, the first statement concerning the human diet refers to both the herb and the tree in language indicative of a merism (the lowest and the highest) to suggest that all the products of the earth were available to humans for food, a universal reference as implied in the following expression "all the earth." The second statement concerning the animal diet (1:30) cites only "every green herb." Yet, this last expression does not imply some kind of restriction in comparison to the food assigned to humans. The mention of the birds (1:30) implies that the fruit of the trees were part of their diet. This is because the Hebrew word *'eseb* "herb" is usually a generic term for food from plants in general (Exod 10:12; Ps 105:35), that is, anything that grows on the earth, meaning every plant. The first statement on human diet is longer than the statement on animal diet, simply because the human sphere receives more attention than the animal one. The plant-based diet is thus a gift "given" to all living creatures as food coming from God who, in this statement, affirms Himself as the Giver of life. Any comment regarding poisonous and potentially deadly plants would be irrelevant here as death was not yet a threat for humans.[111]

1:31 **Then God saw everything that He had made, and indeed it was very good.** This is the seventh and last refrain phrase in the creation story. Yet it differs from the other regular refrain phrases in three ways. First, like the initial phrase, here too the object is specified: "everything that He had made." This irregular specification betrays the intention to focus on the universal scope of God's regard. The difference is that this phrase concerns, for the first and only time, the entire creation. The word "everything" (*kol*) is a key term in the creation story (seventeen occurrences). Secondly, instead of simply saying "saw that it was good," the phrase is introduced with the word *wehinneh* "and indeed" (also translated "and behold," ESV, JPS). This introductory word marks a pause and expresses the desire to highlight the new observation. Thirdly, instead of simply evaluating things as "good," the adjective "very" is now added to the adverb "good." The work is not just "really good" as had previously been emphasized; it is now intensified, simply because, for the first and only time, this "good" marks the seventh (and last) step of creation; it concerns "everything" and expresses completeness.

---

110 See Westermann, *Genesis 1–11*, 163–164.

111 See Jacques B. Doukhan, "When Death Was Not Yet: The Testimony of Biblical Creation," in *The Genesis Creation Account and Its Reverberations in the Old Testament*, ed. Gerald A. Klingbeil (Berrien Springs, MI: Andrews University Press, 2015), 329–342.

2:1–3. DAY SEVEN

GEN 2:1–3 NKJV	GEN 2:1–3 ESV
1 Thus the heavens and the earth, and all the host of them, were finished.	**1** Thus the heavens and the earth were finished, and all the host of them.
2 And on the seventh day God ended His work which He had done, and He rested on the seventh day from all His work which He had done.	**2** And on the seventh day God finished his work that he had done, and he rested on the seventh day from all his work that he had done.
3 Then God blessed the seventh day and sanctified it, because in it He rested from all His work which God had created and made.	**3** So God blessed the seventh day and made it holy, because on it God rested from all his work that he had done in creation.

The seventh day is fundamentally different from the other days. The regular refrains present in the other days ("God said," "the evening and morning") are absent. Also, the seventh day has no corresponding day in the previous sections of creation, as is the case for the other days (1, 2, 3 || 4, 5, 6). The seventh day stands, then, outside the 3 || 3 pattern of the creation week.

It is probably the observation of these striking differences that prompted medieval scholars to place the dividing point between chapters 1 and 2 at precisely this verse. Yet, the section of the seventh day belongs to the same literary process as the creation story. In fact, it is linked with Genesis 1:1 through the same chiastic structure (ABB₁A₁), thus implying that the seventh day embraces the whole of creation:

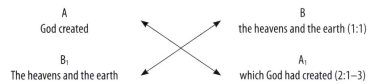

This literary observation suggests that the designation "heavens and earth" not only refers to all that has been created in the course of the week (the human world), but also to the creation of the whole universe, including the heavens of God. The Sabbath contains not only a historical lesson reminding us that God created us and our world, it also carries a cosmic lesson: this God who created us is the same God who created the vast universe. Thus, the Sabbath is not only relevant and meaningful for the human earth, which was created in a week's time, it is also significant for the whole universe, because it is a reminder that *all* has been created by God. In fact, the word **all** (*kol*) is repeated three times in the paragraph on the Sabbath (2:1–3).

Seventh day. The reason for all these differences between the Sabbath and the other days is not that the seventh day belongs to another context but, on the contrary, that the seventh day is the counterpoint to the works of creation. God ceases to create. Yet God is still active (as we shall see, He is the subject of four verbs). While on the previous six days God had created things and beings, on the seventh day God's actions concern only a time, "the seventh day," a phrase repeated three times (or five times, if we count the two pronouns that refer to the seventh day). God's actions on this day are recorded in four verbs, according to a regular pattern (imperfect/subject-imperfect), and display two parallel lines. The first line describes what God did *on* the seventh day (finished and rested). The second line describes what God did *to* the seventh day (blessed and sanctified it). The parallel between the two lines, the meaning and the form of the verbs all suggest that the second verb in each line should be read as an action resulting from the first one:

God finished (*wayekal 'Elohim*) on the seventh day ...
and therefore He rested (*wayishbot*) on the seventh day

God blessed (*wayebarek 'Elohim*) the seventh day ...
and therefore He sanctified (*wayeqaddesh*) it

2:2 God ended. Although God's works of creation "were finished" (2:1) on the sixth day and evaluated as "very good" (1:31), the completion of creation occurs only on the seventh day. The grammar does not support the idea that the verb should be translated "and he had finished,"[112] thus referring to the past creation. Indeed, the form of the verb "God ended" is the same as the form *wayyo'mer 'Elohim*, which means "God said" and not "God had said," as if the action had taken place before. Furthermore, the use of the same form *wayekal* "He ended" as in its parallel line *wayebarek* "He blessed" confirms that the same time is implied.

The fact that creation is really completed only when it reaches the seventh day affects the way we understand "work." In the first place, it means first that without the seventh day, our work is never fulfilled. Without the Sabbath, this moment of grace and faith that reminds us that God did and does work for us, *our* work will *never* be completely achieved.

It means also that the seventh day is an integral part of the week of creation and therefore of the same nature as the other days of the creation week. It is not to be understood as a symbolic-spiritual-eschatological time outside of the historical reality of creation. In fact, the seventh day is intended to be the day more than any other day of the creation week that belongs to human history: it is the first and only full day of the creation week that is lived by humans. It was experienced by our first parents as the definite day. This is why "the seventh day" *yom hashevi'i*, like "the sixth day" *yom hashishi*, is indicated as *the* day with the Hebrew demonstrative article, a characteristic that is absent for the other days, which are merely described as "second day," "third day," "fourth day," and so on (without the article). Adam and Eve were only partially present on the sixth day, but totally present on the seventh day. This may also explain why the specification "evening and morning" is exceptionally and intentionally omitted in the text. Not because it is a day outside of time, "viewed as eternal,"[113] but, on the contrary, because it is the only day of creation week that is

---

112 See Wenham, *Genesis 1–15*, 35.

113 Mathews, *Genesis 1–11:26*, 181.

experienced by humans, the only day of creation week that humans (Adam and Eve) lived from sunset to sunset.

The spiritual lessons of the Sabbath are therefore embedded in its historical reality. The seventh day, which concludes the creation story, is also the first human day, the dawn of human history. The first application of this lesson concerns then our human history: the Sabbath is not a mere spiritual entity; it should be observed in the historical reality of our human time.[114] Also, when we regularly experience the "end" of creation every Sabbath, we receive a message of hope and are reminded that there will be an end. Our miseries and troubles, our human and earthly sojourn, will all come to an end. In other words, the Sabbath day reminds us that the process of our salvation requires the cosmic event of creating a new heaven and new earth, which necessarily implies the end of this one (Isa 65:17; Rev 21:1). It is noteworthy that the phrase "finished the work" is found again at the end of the seven stages of building the sanctuary in the desert (Exod 40:33) and at the end of the seven years of building of Solomon's temple (1 Kgs 7:40, 51). The sanctuary temple is thus identified with God's creation of the world, a significant hint at the cosmic process of salvation (cf. Ps 78:69).[115]

He rested. God's resting on the seventh day is derived from God's finishing on the seventh day. In other words, God's resting is part of the finishing. In fact, the rest *is* the finishing and vice versa. The practical and concrete lesson of this identification is that the rest of the seventh day is possible insofar as we have faith that "all" has been finished. Now, the irony is that the verb "rest" is applied to God—who does not need to rest (Isa 40:28). The author describes God's rest in human terms, as if God had come down and become incarnated into human flesh. Because God meets humans on their own turf, His divine rest becomes their rest; it is shared *with* humans. A second irony is that humans did not need nor deserve to rest, since they did no work during the creation week; God worked for them, while they were still absent. As such, this rest is pure grace, an undeserved gift from God to humans, indeed it is God's rest they are invited to enter (Matt 11:28; Heb 3:18; Heb 4:1–11). Significantly, this day will later be qualified with the technical name as "the Sabbath of the Lord" (Exod 20:10; cf. Exod 16:25), which the Lord had "given" to them (Exod 16:29).

It is noteworthy that the term "Sabbath," used to designate the seventh day of the creation week, is absent. Only the verb is used here with God as its subject. This omission of the noun *Sabbath* and the use instead of the verb *shabbat*, which grammatically relates to God as its originator, may therefore be intended to draw attention to the essential connection existing between the Sabbath and God. It has also been suggested that the author avoided the use of the term *shabbat* in order to not have it confused with the Babylonian *Shapattu*, which was the fifteenth day of the month, the day of the full moon, and was considered an unlucky day.[116] Although this interpretation is attractive, it has remained "unprovable";[117] not only is the technical word *shapattu* not etymologically related to the Hebrew word *shabbat*, but the nature of

---

114 For a discussion of the argument that the Sabbath of Genesis 2:1–3 did not imply observance, see Ross Cole, "The Sabbath and Genesis 2:1–3," *AUSS* 41, no. 1 (2003): 6–7.

115 See also G. K. Beale, *The Temple and the Church's Mission: A Biblical Theology of the Dwelling Place of God* (Downers Grove: IVP, 2004), 31–38.

116 Umberto Cassuto, *A Commentary on the Book of Genesis*, vol. 1, trans. Israel Abrahams (Jerusalem: Magnes Press, 1961), 65–68.

117 Wenham, *Genesis 1–15*, 35.

the respective days is fundamentally different.[118] It seems more probable that the biblical author, within his own system of thought, preferred not to use the word *shabbat* simply to avoid having it confused with other *Shabbat* feast days in the Hebrew calendar (Lev 23:32, 39; Isa 1:13). Unlike the other "Sabbaths," which were linked to the fourth day of creation week's astronomically computed "seasons" and "feasts," the seventh-day Sabbath is given here as an independent time that is separate from all of these feasts and relates only to the event of God's sovereign work of creation. This distinctive character of the Sabbath versus the festivals has been emphasized by Abraham Heschel:

> The date of the month assigned for each festival in the calendar is determined by the life in nature. Passover and the Feast of Booths, for example, coincide with the full moon, and the date of all festivals is a day in the month, and the month is a reflection of what goes on periodically in the realm of nature, since the Jewish month begins with the new moon, with the reappearance of the lunar crescent in the evening sky. In contrast, the Sabbath is entirely independent of the month and unrelated to the moon. Its date is not determined by any event in nature, such as the new moon, but by the act of creation.[119]

2:3 God blessed. Although the preceding statements describe what God did *during* the time of the seventh day ("He rested"), the following statement concerns what He did *to* the time of the seventh day. God's first action in this direction is to bless the seventh day. That God blessed the Sabbath is surprising for God had not blessed any of the other days of creation. So far only living creatures had been blessed, these included fish and humans. It is also surprising because the act of blessing is normally associated with the promise of fruitfulness and a successful future (1:22; 28). It is indeed paradoxical that the seventh day, the only time when people were not to work, not to be involved in producing something, is the only day that is pregnant with the promise of fruitfulness and the anticipation of abundance. The reason for this wonder is that this is the first and only day of creation week when everything and everyone—humans, God, and the world—are finally present in relationship with one another. The future and the prospect of fruitfulness depend on that relationship. The message of the Sabbath is not merely intended to teach humans to cease working in order to become more efficient and hence more productive. God's blessing of the Sabbath contains more than just wisdom aimed at our health, wealth, or ecological balance. The blessing of a nonworking day is the result of our relationship with the Creator; it implies faith in production though we are not working, and only God has worked for us. The blessing encapsulated in the only day designated as the "Sabbath of the Lord," His rest, means the realization that the only work that counts and lasts, the only work that is not vanity, is the work of God's grace and His gift for us (Eccl 2:24; 5:18).

Sanctified. God's blessing of the Sabbath is followed by His sanctification of the Sabbath.[120] Because God blessed this day and filled it with His beneficent presence, He sanctified it (cf. Exod 3:5; 29:43). This is the first time that the word "sanctify"

---

118 For a discussion on this, see Hasel, "Sabbath," *ABD* 5:850; cf. Niels-Erik A. Andreasen, *The Old Testament Sabbath*, Dissertation Series 7 (Missoula, MT: SBL, 1972), 94–102.

119 Abraham Heschel, *The Sabbath: Its Meaning for Modern Man* (New York: Farrar, Strauss and Giroux, 2001), 10.

120 See Cole, "The Sabbath and Genesis 2:1–3," 10–11.

(*qadash*) is used in the Bible. The work of creation had previously been qualified as *tob* "good, beautiful." The use of this new character of "holiness" (*qadash*) suggests that in entering the Sabbath we move from the appreciation of the beautiful and good of the created things to the experience of the "holiness" of time and of the people around us.[121]

This word does not mean that the time of the Sabbath has been made holy in a magical and static manner. In the Old Testament, "time is bound up with its content and even identified with it."[122] Thus, time is tied up with the living person. When we die, there is no longer time. The sanctification of the time of the Sabbath is tied up with the human person as well as with the divine Person. That God has sanctified the Sabbath means that He has separated this time and made it special, and that does not depend on anything other than God Himself.

Yet, the sanctification of the Sabbath cannot be fulfilled in our lives as long as we do not respond to that divine appointment. In other words, if we do not sanctify our time of Sabbath, if we do not sanctify ourselves, we cannot enter God's rest. On the other hand, my personal sanctification of the Sabbath will not occur if I am the one who determines the chronological time of the Sabbath observance and the spiritual activities that fill it. Instead, the sanctification of the Sabbath must be the result of a special relationship between God and humans. In that sense, it can be said that the Sabbath reaffirms the fundamental teaching of Scripture, namely, that "God Himself is personal"[123] and that we are fulfilled only through a personal relationship with Him. Not only does God sanctify the Sabbath (Exod 20:11), but God's people are also told to sanctify the Sabbath (Exod 20:8–9; Deut 5:12–13). So that when Israel is described as a "holy nation" (Exod 19:6) and the priests are called "HOLINESS TO THE LORD" (Exod 28:36; Lev 20:26), it is to affirm this special relationship between God and His people. To apply the word *qadash* "sanctify" to the Sabbath means not only that this time has been separated *from* the other days but also separated *for* a special relationship with God. The time of this day is sanctified insofar as it is lived in relationship with God. The Sabbath is not merely a day of rest, a holiday for the benefit of humans; more importantly, it is a day that God has set apart to enjoy a special relationship with humans. God's act in sanctifying the Sabbath is His last, crowning act of creation, His deliberate invitation to humans to respond to Him and meet with Him in a personal relationship.

2:4A. CONCLUSION

GEN 2:4A NKJV	GEN 2:4A ESV
4a This *is* the history of the heavens and the earth when they were created	**4a** These are the generations of the heavens and the earth when they were created

This is the history of the heavens and the earth when they were created. As we discussed in the introduction, this phrase concludes the creation story: it echoes both its introduction (1:1) and the conclusion of its parallel text (2:25).

History. The technical word *toledot* "history" or "genealogy" ties this account to

---

121 See Heschel, *The Sabbath*, 8–10.

122 See E. Jenni, "Time," *IDB* 4:646.

123 E. Edward Zinke, "A Theology of the Sabbath," *JATS* 2, no. 2 (1991): 148.

the rest of the book of Genesis. The word *toledot* warns the reader from the beginning that our text not only belongs to the literary structure of Genesis as a whole, but also that it is of the same historical quality as the patriarchal stories from Abraham to Joseph.

The heavens and the earth. The verbatim echo between the conclusion and the introduction (1:1) suggests that "heavens" should also include the divine heavens, since that is the case in the introduction. Interestingly, here as there, the expression "heavens and earth" is followed in the next sentence by the shift of focus to the earth: **the *earth* and the heavens** (2:4b, 5; cf. 1:1–2). Thus, the "heavens" of the following account concern only the heavens of the earth, the human heavens. Indeed, the only other occurrence of the word "heavens" in our text applies to the heavens of the birds (2:20). Thus, while the first expression "the heavens and the earth" (2:4a), which puts its emphasis on "heavens," includes the divine heavens, the second expression "the earth and the heavens" (2:4b), which puts its emphasis on "earth," refers strictly to the human heavens.

THE GARDEN OF EDEN (2:4B–25)

This text is to be understood in relation to the preceding text. Its seven-step structure parallels the seven-day structure of Genesis 1:1–2:4a. The two accounts display two complementary perspectives of God's creation in contrast to each other. The first creation story embraces the whole (human) universe; the scope is defined as "the heavens and the earth" (1:1). The second creation story focuses on the earth and the scope is defined as **the earth and the heavens** (2:4b). While in the first creation humans occupy a small place among other creations, in the second creation story humans occupy the whole space of the narrative. Also, while the first creation story presents God as the transcendent God, with the name of *'Elohim*, in the second creation story He is presented as a personal God in close relationship with humans, with the name of *YHWH 'Elohim*. This different perspective explains the apparent chronological contradictions between the two accounts of creation in regards to plants and animals. The second creation account is not concerned with the creation of the plants as such and their chronological appearance, as is the first creation account, but rather with humans in their relationship with plants as their home and their food in the Garden of Eden. In the same manner, the second creation account is not interested in the creation and chronological appearance of the animals, but focuses rather on their relationship with humans as a preparation for the human couple (see the comments on 2:19–22).[124] More importantly, these two texts belong together, for they both cover the same unique quality of time when the divine creation was still in pristine perfection, straight from the hands of the Creator, and not yet defiled by the curse of sin, evil, and death.

---

124 For the presentation of this argument in the literary context of the creation texts, see Doukhan, *The Genesis Creation Story*, 174.

2:4B–6. PROLOGUE

GEN 2:4B–6 NKJV	GEN 2:4B–6 ESV
4b in the day that the L<small>ORD</small> God made the earth and the heavens,	**4b** in the day that the L<small>ORD</small> God made the earth and the heavens.
5 before any plant of the field was in the earth and before any herb of the field had grown. For the L<small>ORD</small> God had not caused it to rain on the earth, and *there was* no man to till the ground;	**5** When no bush of the field was yet in the land and no small plant of the field had yet sprung up—for the L<small>ORD</small> God had not caused it to rain on the land, and there was no man to work the ground,
6 but a mist went up from the earth and watered the whole face of the ground.	**6** and a mist was going up from the land and was watering the whole face of the ground—

2:4b The prologue of the second creation story points back to the prologue of the preceding text and begins, like the first creation story, with a temporal phrase: **in the day** (2:4b) (|| "in the beginning," 1:1).

2:5 This prologue also situates itself in regard to the following chapter. The Hebrew word *terem* "**before any**" (2:5), meaning literally "not yet," is repeated twice in the verse. The negative word *terem* "not yet" is associated with two other negations, *lo'* "not" and *'ayin* "no," and refers to the negative state of the unplanted earth in parallel to the negative state of the empty earth described in the corresponding place in the first creation story (1:2). It also anticipates what is "not yet" here, that is, the future earth, after the fall: **before any plant of the field … and before any herb of the field**. It is important to note that the Hebrew expressions designating the plants *siakh hassadeh* "plant of the field" and *'eseb hassadeh* "herb of the field" are not the same as in Genesis 1.[125] There we have instead *deshe'* "grass" (1:11), *'eseb mazri'a zera'* "herb that yields seed" (1:11), and *'ets peri 'oseh peri* "tree that yields fruit" (1:12). This different language suggests that the biblical author refers to two different botanical realities. The term *siakh* "plant" that is used in Genesis 2 designates some kind of dry shrub or bush that grows in the desert (21:15; Job 30:4, 7).[126] The fact that the expression *'eseb hassadeh* "herb of the field" that is associated with the expression *siakh hassadeh* reappears in Genesis 3 in parallel with "thorns and thistles" (3:18) confirms this interpretation. In that context, the phrase "herb of the field" clearly refers to the food painfully obtained as a result of human sin.[127] There is therefore no chronological contradiction between the two creation accounts in regards to the plants. While in Genesis 1 the biblical author refers to the perfect vegetation that has not yet been affected by sin, in Genesis 2 the biblical author refers, on the contrary, to the kind of plant that has not yet appeared on the earth and will come only after the fall.

The next two sentences emphasize the "not yet" perspective of the account. The phrase **the L<small>ORD</small> God had not caused it to rain** alludes to the future flood when for the first time rain will fall on the earth (7:4). And the information that **there was no man to till the ground** anticipates the "toil" and "sweat" that will characterize humans' work after the fall (3:18–19).

---

125 See Randall W. Younker, "Genesis 2: Second Creation Account?" in *Creation, Catastrophe, and Calvary*, ed. John T. Baldwin (Hagerstown, MD: Review and Herald, 2000), 72–73.

126 See *HALOT* 4:1320–1321.

127 See Umberto Cassuto, *The Documentary Hypothesis*, trans. I. Abrahams (Jerusalem: Magnes, 1961), 90–91.

2:6 **A mist went up from the earth.** Since there was no rain before the flood, the "mist" or "dew" was coming out of the ground to water the ground.[128] In parallel with the *ruakh* "Spirit"—wind that blows on the face of the water before the first divine word of creation out of the water (1:2)—the "mist" rises on the face of the ground, anticipating the first divine work of creation from the earth.

2:7. STEP ONE: THE FORMATION OF HUMANS

GEN 2:7 NKJV	GEN 2:7 ESV
7 And the Lord God formed man *of* the dust of the ground, and breathed into his nostrils the breath of life; and man became a living being.	**7** then the Lord God formed the man of dust from the ground and breathed into his nostrils the breath of life, and the man became a living creature.

2:7 God's first creative work in this account concerns His creation of man out of dust, which parallels the first creation story—the creation of light out of darkness. The creation of man precedes everything else for the focus will be on him. We are situated here in the context of the sixth day. But while in the first creation story the author only describes the creation of man and the principle of his creation in the image of God, in the second creation story he explains the process of this creation.

Formed. The Hebrew verb *wayyitser* "He formed" suggests the image of a potter (Jer 18:2; Ps 139:13–15; cf. Job 10:8). While this verb describes God's artistic activity (Isa 44:9–10), it also emphasizes the dependence of human beings on their Creator (Isa 29:16).

Breath of life. The idea of God's personal and even intimate involvement, which is implied in the touch of His creating hands, is reinforced in God's subsequent act of breathing into man's nostrils. The human creature is thus the result not of two materials, dust and breath—but of two divine actions. Yet nothing in this description could support the idea of a soul distinct from the body. Both divine operations concern the physical domain. On the one hand, the body is compared to a piece of clay; on the other hand, this body receives breath that allows it to breathe. The Hebrew word *neshamah* does not refer to any spiritual entity' but simply denotes breath. The word *neshamah* is derived from the verb *nasham*, which means "to breathe" (Isa 42:14). God gives humans the capacity to breathe. And *nepesh* "being," which has sometimes been translated as "soul" (JPS, KJV), simply means "living being." In fact, the word can even be used to designate animals (1:21). The etymology of the word *nepesh* also conveys the basic meaning of "breathing" as the related words *nashap*, *nashab*, and *nasham* testify. There may even be a play on words between *neshamah* and *nepesh*, suggesting the common meaning of "breathing" is intended. So that is to say "man became a living being" would mean that he became a living, breathing being.

---

128 See Ellen G. White, PP 96–97.

2:8. STEP TWO: PLANTS IN THE GARDEN

GEN 2:8 NKJV	GEN 2:8 ESV
8 The Lᴏʀᴅ God planted a garden eastward in Eden, and there He put the man whom He had formed.	**8** And the Lᴏʀᴅ God planted a garden in Eden, in the east, and there he put the man whom he had formed.

Just as God **had formed** man, He **planted** the Garden. These are two divine works of creation. The Garden is not a symbol. It is presented as a real place, situated in geographic terms. It is precisely located **in** a region called **Eden** and **eastward**. When Cain had to flee, the biblical text specifies that he "dwelt … on the east of Eden" (4:16), implying that Eden was still within view at that time. The meaning of the Hebrew name *'eden* should be sought in relation to the Hebrew root *'adan*, which has the connotation of "pleasure" and "delight" (Ps 36:8; Jer 51:34), a sense that would be supported by the Old Aramaic root *'adan*, meaning "enrich."[129]

2:9–15. STEP THREE: TREES IN THE GARDEN

GEN 2:9–15 NKJV	GEN 2:9–15 ESV
9 And out of the ground the Lᴏʀᴅ God made every tree grow that is pleasant to the sight and good for food. The tree of life *was* also in the midst of the garden, and the tree of the knowledge of good and evil.	**9** And out of the ground the Lᴏʀᴅ God made to spring up every tree that is pleasant to the sight and good for food. The tree of life was in the midst of the garden, and the tree of the knowledge of good and evil.
10 Now a river went out of Eden to water the garden, and from there it parted and became four riverheads.	**10** A river flowed out of Eden to water the garden, and there it divided and became four rivers.
11 The name of the first *is* Pishon; it *is* the one which skirts the whole land of Havilah, where *there is* gold.	**11** The name of the first is the Pishon. It is the one that flowed around the whole land of Havilah, where there is gold.
12 And the gold of that land *is* good. Bdellium and the onyx stone *are* there.	**12** And the gold of that land is good; bdellium and onyx stone are there.
13 The name of the second river *is* Gihon; it *is* the one which goes around the whole land of Cush.	**13** The name of the second river is the Gihon. It is the one that flowed around the whole land of Cush.
14 The name of the third river *is* Hiddekel; it *is* the one which goes toward the east of Assyria. The fourth river *is* the Euphrates.	**14** And the name of the third river is the Tigris, which flows east of Assyria. And the fourth river is the Euphrates.
15 Then the Lᴏʀᴅ God took the man and put him in the garden of Eden to tend and keep it.	**15** The Lᴏʀᴅ God took the man and put him in the garden of Eden to work it and keep it.

The author focuses on two characteristic features of the Garden, the trees and the rivers. The **trees** are for humans, which provide them with food (2:9), and the **rivers**, which water the Garden are for the trees.(2:10). In addition, the trees and the rivers will play a special role in the Garden. The trees provide the setting for the tree of the

---

129 A. R. Millard, "The Etymology of Eden," *VT* 34 (1984): 103–106.

knowledge of good and evil and the tree of life. And the rivers help to situate the Garden of Eden within the geography of the earth.

2:9 **God made every tree grow.** The growing of these trees, already laden with fruit immediately after their planting, suggests a supernatural shortening of time. This is consistent with the creation process by divine command reported in the first creation story: God said *yehi wayehi* "let it be … and it was" (1:3). In other words, the planting and growing of the trees are not submitted to the natural laws of time. They are the immediate result of divine creation, not of laborious gardening. This supernatural aspect of creation, as having instantaneously reached peak maturity, may be explained in that it helps promote the enjoyment of life. This setting of creation is not just implied by its parallelism, but is explicitly brought to mind by mentioning the keyword of the first creation story, **good** (2:9), as qualifying the food of these trees. Furthermore, the fact that man is assigned to **tend and keep** (2:15) the Garden also implies that he has been created not as an infant, but as a fully mature man and is capable of doing the job—thus created within the same categories of time as the rest of creation.

The tree of life … and the tree of the knowledge of good and evil. Significantly, the two trees are both in the midst of the Garden, near to each other. This proximity suggests that, somehow, the two trees are paradoxically related, thus reinforcing the element of choice between the two ways represented by the two trees. The eating from the tree of life will depend on the non-eating from the tree of the knowledge of good and evil: **in the day that you eat of it you shall surely die** (2:17). The verbal form *mot tamut* "you shall surely die" puts the emphasis on the certainty and reality of death. Although Adam did not die immediately, the sentence of death was now pronounced (legal death) and the biological process of dying began. That Adam did not die right away was the result of God's grace through the sacrifice of Christ who volunteered to take his place (cf. 3:15).[130] And indeed, as soon as Adam and Eve took from the tree of the knowledge of good and evil, they were forbidden to have access to the tree of life (3:22). The lesson of that relation between the trees is twofold. First, life is not a natural inherent human quality. Humans have not been created immortal. Even in the Garden of Eden, Adam and Eve were still dependent on an external source for life. And secondly, life is not just a biological condition; it is also a spiritual matter pertaining to the moral issue of good and evil. The reflection of Wisdom literature on the tree of life confirms this understanding. The book of Proverbs in particular describes the tree of life as wisdom (Prov 3:18) and as promoting the capacity to live a righteous and ethical life (Prov 11:30; 15:4).

The tree of life. The meaning of these trees has perplexed Bible students from the earliest stages of its interpretation. The meaning of the "tree of life," however, has not raised too much controversy, primarily because the concept of the tree of life is simple and easy to grasp. As the name indicates, it provides life; yet it does not contain life in itself, apart from God, as though through some innate magical power. This would be totally foreign and diametrically opposed to the biblical worldview. The Bible insists that the Creator God is the only source of life (Ps 36:9). Our text explicitly indicates that God is the One who planted the tree and made it grow (2:8–9). Thus, the tree was represented in the tabernacle through the shape of the menorah (the stylized

---

130 Ellen G. White comments on this passage that "the instant man accepted the temptation … Christ stood between the living and the dead, saying 'Let the punishment fall on me' " (SDABC 1:1085).

golden candlestick) whose light symbolized the gift of life to Israel.[131] Similarly, the tree of life was also a familiar motif within the Ancient Middle Eastern culture.[132]

The tree of knowledge. The tree of the knowledge of good and evil, on the other hand, is more problematic. This tree is mentioned only once in the Bible, in this chapter of Genesis (though it is implied in 3:3–6), and unlike the tree of life, it has no close analogy in ANE texts. Thus, it has received numerous interpretations ranging from moral discernment to omniscience and wisdom.[133] The association between the tree of knowledge and the tree of life suggests a direct correlation. Just as the tree of life (which has been planted by God) indicates its connection to life, so the tree of the knowledge of good and evil (which has likewise been planted by God) indicates its connection to good and evil. This means that eating its fruit—and thus disobeying God—will bring the experience of "evil" into the "good" normally associated with the other trees (2:9) and with creation (1:4, 10, 12, 18, 21, 25, 31). Note that this "evil" experience must have been known by the serpent since the serpent is located near or even on the tree (3:1–6), suggesting that he must have consumed from the tree. Yet, contrary to the serpent's allegation (3:5) and ironically to most commentators, this acquisition of "good" together with "evil" does not indicate progress or "human advancement,"[134] but is, on the contrary, a symptom of human corruption.

2:10–14 Now a river went out … and became four riverheads. The mention by name of these four rivers—two of which, the Tigris and the Euphrates, are well known and well identified—confirms the reality of the Garden and is probably intended to mark the location of the Garden of Eden. The location of the Garden of Eden is thus evaluated concretely from the point of view of a post-flood geography. On the basis of the Tigris and the Euphrates, the majority of interpreters have suggested that the Garden of Eden must have been located somewhere in Mesopotamia. Others have opted for Armenia, Arabia, or even Persia. A number of considerations may suggest a different interpretation, pointing rather to the country of Canaan, the Promised Land of the patriarchs and Israel:

1. The strategic positions of the rivers—on the northeast the **Hiddekel,** also known as the Tigris (ESV), and the **Euphrates**, and on the southwest the Nile (around Cush, which would imply Egypt)—mark the ideal boundaries of the land promised to Abraham (15:18), which inspire the prophetic and eschatological visions of hope (Isa 19:23; 35:8; Zech 9:10).[135] This topographical description suggests that just as the third and the fourth rivers, the Tigris and Euphrates, mentioned in the text delimitate the northeastern boundary (Mesopotamia-Assyria), the first and the second rivers mentioned, the **Pishon** and **Gihon**, delimit the southwestern boundary (Egypt-Ethiopia). The first and the second rivers surround the countries of **Havilah**

---

131 See Jacques B. Doukhan, *Secrets of Revelation* (Hagerstown, MD: Review and Herald, 2002), 197–198; cf. C. L. Meyers, *The Tabernacle Menorah*, ASOR Dissertation Series 2 (Missoula, MT: Continuum International Publishing Group, 1976), 118–120, 174–181.

132 *ANET*, 95–100.

133 For a summary of these interpretations, see Wenham, *Genesis 1–15*, 63–64; cf. Mathews, *Genesis: 1–11:26*, 203–206.

134 Mathews, *Genesis 1–11:26*, 204. See Ellen G. White's comments, "Man lost all because he chose to listen to the deceiver rather than to Him who is Truth, who alone has understanding. By the mingling of evil with good, his mind had become confused, his mental and spiritual powers benumbed. No longer could he appreciate the good that God had so freely bestowed" (Ed 25).

135 The same boundaries are implied in Daniel's eschatological vision of the two heavenly beings whom he sees once in connection with the river of Babylon (Dan 8:2) and once in connection with the river of Egypt (Dan 12:6).

and **Cush**. Although the biblical account refers to two distinct rivers, the Pishon and Gihon, a couple of observations suggest that these two rivers are related to the Nile.[136] The rhyme between Pishon and Gihon and the parallelism between the two lines referring, respectively, to the Pishon and Gihon, even using the same verb "**encompass**" (*sabab*), suggests a connection between the two rivers. In addition, the association between the two names, Havilah and Cush, in the table of nations (10:7) and the traditional identification of Cush as the South of Egypt, that is, Ethiopia (10:6–8) or Egypt (Isa 20:3–5; Nah 3:9) suggests that the names "Havilah" and "Cush" refer to the same region that is roughly Egypt/Ethiopia.

2. The numerous parallels and common motifs between the Garden of Eden and the temple or sanctuary (the cherubim, the menorah tree, the flowing water, the precious stones),[137] while testifying to the memory of God's heavenly temple, at the same time points forward to the Promised Land, the future place of the earthly temple. Obviously, the author of Genesis did not have in mind all the connections between Zion, the temple of Jerusalem, and the Garden of Eden, which belong to a later time (Ps 48:1–2).[138] Yet, the fact that Moses alludes to the Promised Land as he is writing about the Garden of Eden (cf. Joel 2:3) suggests that he places the hope of the Promised Land in the *perspective* of the Garden of Eden. This association also inspired the structure of the book of Genesis, which begins with the Garden of Eden and ends with the prospect of the Promised Land (see our introduction to the book). Does that mean that the Garden of Eden was really located in the country of Canaan, precisely on the site of Jerusalem? A clear answer to that question is not possible. Although the Genesis story speaks about the Garden of Eden and the events that took place there as real and historical, it remains intentionally elusive in regard to its precise location. After all, the biblical story tells us that the Garden of Eden is no longer accessible (3:24); not to mention the effect of the flood, which would have made it difficult, if not impossible, to situate the former location of the Garden. The ultimate lesson that the Bible has retained is the prophetic promise that one day we shall return to the Garden of Eden.

2:15 **To tend and keep it.** Paralleling God's planting and growing noted in the second section (2:8), man is assigned the responsibility of cultivating the Garden and keeping it. It is not enough to cultivate the Garden; they also had to keep it. The ecological lesson is included in the duty of culture. Humans have the duty to plant, grow, and produce fruit; but they are also responsible for the earth. The Hebrew word *shamar* "keep" implies the idea of responsibility. This is the very word Cain uses to refer to his responsibility as a brother (4:9). In the word "keep" is also implied the idea of preserving and of being faithful to a past revelation, to keeping the law (Exod 20:6; Ps 119:57), and to protecting (28:15). Humans have the responsibility to "keep" the earth in the state it has been given to them, to protect it, which already points to the threat of the enemy and the underlying cosmic conflict. It is also noteworthy that the juxtaposition of these two verbs is associated with the priestly role in the

---

136 It is interesting that both rivers have been identified as the Nile: Pishon for Rashi (Miqraot Gedolot), Gihon for the Septuagint followed by Josephus (*Jewish Antiquities* 1.1.3).

137 See Gordon J. Wenham, "Sanctuary Symbolism in the Garden of Eden Story," in *Proceedings of the Ninth World Congress of Jewish Studies*, eds. Moshe H. Goshen-Gottstein and David Assaf (Jerusalem: Magnes, 1986), 400–403; Davidson, "Cosmic Metanarrative for the Coming Millennium," 102–119.

138 See Jon D. Levenson, *Sinai and Zion, an Entry Into the Jewish Bible* (Minneapolis: Winston Press, 1985), 129–131; cf. Gage, *The Gospel of Genesis*, 50–61.

tabernacle (Num 3:7–8; 8:26; 18:5–6; cf. Exod 12:25), another example of the connection between the Garden of Eden and the Israelite sanctuary and an evidence of humankind's function as priests in the pre-fall Edenic sanctuary.[139] This language may suggest the sacredness of the work. In fact, the biblical worldview has no room for a secular place where the divine reference would be absent. Work is a part of religious life. Significantly, the Hebrew word for "work" *'abodah* means also "worship" and designates religious service (Num 4:23).

2:16–17. STEP FOUR: THE FIRST COMMANDMENT

GEN 2:16–17 NKJV	GEN 2:16–17 ESV
16 And the LORD God commanded the man, saying, "Of every tree of the garden you may freely eat;	**16** And the LORD God commanded the man, saying, "You may surely eat of every tree of the garden,
17 but of the tree of the knowledge of good and evil you shall not eat, for in the day that you eat of it you shall surely die."	**17** but of the tree of the knowledge of good and evil you shall not eat, for in the day that you eat of it you shall surely die."

God relates to man through a commandment: **God commanded** (2:16). This is the first time that the verb "command" is used. From the Hebrew word *tsawah* "command" is derived the word *mitswah* "commandment." This word concerns more than just ethical duties or ritual observances. God "commanded" the creation of the world (Ps 33:9; Isa 45:12). God's commandments are not just requests in the form of imperative orders, things we should do, or prohibitions, things we should not do. God's commandments are His gift to humans (Exod 24:12; Neh 9:13), intended for their own happiness and wisdom (Ps 19:8 [9]; Deut 4:5–6). As the psalmist sings, "Give me the grace of Your law" (Ps 119:29 lit. trans.); God's commandments are the expression of His grace. Grace is not incompatible with the Law.

2:16 The first commandment exemplifies this identification of God's commandment as grace. Significantly, it starts with the gift of all the trees: **of every tree … you may freely eat**. Grace is not only in the gift; it is even contained in the prohibition that follows, which ensures life, for the eating of the forbidden fruit will result in death. It is noteworthy that the form of the Hebrew verb expressing God's positive grace to eat from all the trees, *'akhol to'khel* "you may surely eat" (ESV), is the same as the form of the verb expressing the negative prospect of death if man eats from the forbidden tree: **you shall surely die** (*mot tamut*). Both verbs are in the infinitive absolute, expressing the certainty of both actions. This echo between these two forms suggests that God's grace, His generous gift of life, is as certain as the prospect of death, the privation of life. This unexpected parallel means, first of all, a message of hope: the prospect of death should not discourage us, for it is countered by the promise of life. Secondly, the experience of life not only reveals the absurdity of death, but it is also a warning: the full enjoyment of life should not deceive us and be taken as evidence of eternity—for life is not an inherent human quality. Adam received life from God's breath (2:7), and the continuation of life was ensured only through eating from the tree of life (3:22). Only God is immortal (1 Tim 6:16).

---

139 For a discussion of the "priestly status of both Adam and Eve in the Garden of Eden, see especially T. Desmond Alexander, *From Eden to the New Jerusalem: An Introduction to Biblical Theology* (Grand Rapids: Kregel, 2008), 22–27.

2:18. STEP FIVE: THE LONELINESS OF MAN

GEN 2:18 NKJV	GEN 2:18 ESV
18 And the Lᴏʀᴅ God said, "*It is* not good that man should be alone; I will make him a helper comparable to him."	**18** Then the Lᴏʀᴅ God said, "It is not good that the man should be alone; I will make him a helper fit for him."

This is the first time in the second creation story that God speaks within Himself. Just as God deliberated before creating man in His image (1:26), He, once again, deliberates before creating a companion for man. This parallel suggests that the creation of a human companion is also submitted to the same requirement of the image of God. The divine self-deliberation is made of two statements, which justify and describe the formula of this creation.

2:18 **It is not good that man should be alone.** This first statement responds to the sevenfold refrain of Genesis 1, "God saw ... that it was (very) good." This divine judgment implies that the creation of Adam's companion was included in the divine observation "it was good." For without the creation of this companion, God could not have said "it was good." Even worse, the creation would have been "not good." This flashback to the creation of Genesis 1, while confirming the literary complementary unity of these two accounts, also reveals the importance of the particular creation of man's companion. This is the only case retained by the biblical author that could have compromised the "good" quality of God's whole project of creation. Without the creation of the woman, instead of the "very good," which means "*more than good*," sanctioning God's work of creation at that concluding place, the work would have been labeled "not good," meaning it would have been "less than good."[140] This exceptional evaluation by God on His creation suggests that the creation of that companion is of great significance not only for the domestic happiness of humans, but also an indicator of the high ("very good") quality of creation.

A helper comparable to him. This second statement describes in terse language (only two words in Hebrew), the complexity and the rules of the relationship between men and women.

A helper. The Hebrew word '*ezer* "helper" conveys more than the mere idea of "helping" or "being of assistance." The verb '*azar* "help" is frequently used in the Bible with God as the subject and humans as the object (49:25; 1 Sam 7:12). The noun '*ezer* "helper" often refers to God (Pss 10:14; 30:10 [11]); is used as a synonym to the words *magen* "shield," a metaphor which applies to God (Deut 33:29; Pss 33:20; 115:9–11); and is even associated with the word "salvation" (Pss 63:7 [8]; 27:9). Calling the woman "helper" does not mean, then, that the woman's role is only limited to assisting the man where he is the one who does the job. The word, which refers to divine assistance and salvation, should therefore illuminate the theological significance of the role of the woman in the process of salvation.

Comparable to him. The Hebrew phrase is made of two prepositions. First, *ke* "like," which emphasizes the sameness and the parity, implying harmony and mutual understanding. Unlike the animals, which Adam will encounter first, the woman is of the same "human" nature as the man, a person with whom he could relate. Second,

---

140 The expression "not good" does not mean "evil," but refers rather to a deficient ("less than good") and imperfect condition or behavior (Prov 25:27).

negdo "comparable to him," made of the preposition *neged*—"in front of" (1 Kgs 20:27), "against" (Job 10:17)—and the pronoun referring to the third person, which emphasizes the difference and even the opposite, contains therefore the idea of "counterpart," implying "equality" and "partnership." Such a complex definition tying together opposite concepts establishes from the outset the nature of the relationship that should characterize the human couple. On one hand, it affirms the principle that humans should only couple within the same human category (against bestiality); on the other hand, it excludes as inappropriate any human coupling within the same gender (against homosexual relationships). Beyond the strict sexual application, the cohabitation of the same and the different is a guarantee of genuine relationship and dialogue. A relationship made of individuals who are only like each other or only different from each other is bound to die. The two components are necessary to ensure a right and genuine relationship.

2:19–22. STEP SIX: A COMPANION FOR MAN

GEN 2:19–22 NKJV	GEN 2:19–22 ESV
19 Out of the ground the Lᴏʀᴅ God formed every beast of the field and every bird of the air, and brought *them* to Adam to see what he would call them. And whatever Adam called each living creature, that *was* its name.	**19** Now out of the ground the Lᴏʀᴅ God had formed every beast of the field and every bird of the heavens and brought them to the man to see what he would call them. And whatever the man called every living creature, that was its name.
20 So Adam gave names to all cattle, to the birds of the air, and to every beast of the field. But for Adam there was not found a helper comparable to him.	**20** The man gave names to all livestock and to the birds of the heavens and to every beast of the field. But for Adam there was not found a helper fit for him.
21 And the Lᴏʀᴅ God caused a deep sleep to fall on Adam, and he slept; and He took one of his ribs, and closed up the flesh in its place.	**21** So the Lᴏʀᴅ God caused a deep sleep to fall upon the man, and while he slept took one of his ribs and closed up its place with flesh.
22 Then the rib which the Lᴏʀᴅ God had taken from man He made into a woman, and He brought her to the man.	**22** And the rib that the Lᴏʀᴅ God had taken from the man he made into a woman and brought her to the man.

The reference to the creation of the animals **every beast of the field and every bird of the air** (2:19) at this juncture is not chronologically intended, as it was in the first creation story (1:20, 25). The apparent chronological contradiction between the two accounts is due to their different perspective and emphasis. While the first creation story is meant to report the chronicle of their creation per se, the second creation story is meant to put these creations in connection to humans. Thus, plants and animals are related to the humans, plants serve as their environment (2:8) or their food (2:16), and animals serve as their companions (2:18–19) and prefigure the human couple (2:20).[141] The repetition of the phrase "a helper comparable to him" at the end of the animal parade (2:20) not only acknowledges that no animal could qualify, it also anticipates the creation of the woman. In fact, the creation of the woman is the goal of the whole section. The suspense is maintained as Adam

141 For a discussion of the discrepancies between the two accounts of creation and suggested solutions, see Jiří Moskala, "A Fresh Look at Two Genesis Creation Accounts: Contradictions," *AUSS* 49, no. 1 (2011): 59–62.

reviews all the animals and gives them their proper names. The text suggests, not without some humor, that during his encounter with the animals, Adam might have experienced some kind of identity crisis. Reviewing all these animals, Adam must have wondered about who he was, since he could not identify with any one of these creatures. His frustration in not finding someone like him is not only noticed by the author (2:20), it is also implied in Adam's later exclamation when meeting the woman (2:23). It has been suggested that unlike the animals, which were created with a mate, Adam alone was without a female counterpart and this observation must have puzzled and troubled him, and perhaps played a role in his frustration.[142]

2:21 **And the Lord God caused a deep sleep to fall on Adam.** That God needed to cause Adam to sleep in order to create Eve has intrigued the ancient rabbis. There is an old story reported in the Talmud: The emperor one day said to Rabban Gamliel, "Your God is a thief for He caused man to sleep and then stole from him a rib." Then the rabban's daughter asked the emperor, "Please send me a guard." "Why do you need a guard?" asked the emperor. "Thieves visited us last night and robbed us of a clay pitcher, leaving a golden one in its place." "I wish," exclaimed the emperor, "such thief would visit us every day!" "Ah!" she answered, "was it not to Adam's gain that he was deprived of a rib and a wife presented to him instead?"[143] If this humorous story does not indicate the exact reason of God's operation, the lesson it suggests points in the right direction. Adam's sleep was not designed as a means of deception, but on the contrary, for his advantage. It was to allow God to work by Himself, just as He had done for the rest of His creation. It is significant indeed that all of the divine works of creation begin in the evening (1:5). God uses the same deep sleep to keep those around Saul from interfering with divine plans (1 Sam 26:12). Likewise, Abraham's deep sleep is intended to allow for God's unique act: "Yahweh's covenant with Abraham is to be ascribed entirely and exclusively to Yahweh's own initiative."[144]

The woman is then identified as an expression of divine grace like all the other acts of creation that were performed by God alone, without the presence or participation of humans. Additionally, it recalls the "rest" of the Sabbath, which was given to humans as a work God had done for them. On the other hand, that man was asleep and totally passive was also important for the woman. For if man had been awake while God was making the woman, he might have offered his advice and perhaps even tried to become involved as a partner to the Creator, subsequently rendering the woman subservient to him as his co-creation. As such, the equality and wholeness of the nascent couple requires that the creation of the woman stay exclusively in God's hands and entirely beyond man's control or perception.

He took one of his ribs. The reason for the choice of the *tsela'* "rib" has intrigued many Bible readers. Most interpreters have considered its symbolic significance. The rib means "side"[145] and could therefore represent companionship, equality, or direction ("at his side"). Or it could be interpreted as "rib" within the body imagery, meaning humility as opposed to the head. Adam's interpretation in the next verse suggests that he had understood "rib" in the sense of intimacy and identification, **bone of my bones**

---

142 See Rashi in Miqraot Gedolot on 2:21.

143 Sanh. 39a

144 M. Oeming, "*rdm*," *TDOT* 13:339.

145 This interpretation is already attested in the Septuagint, which translates with the word *pleuro/pleura* "side."

and flesh of my flesh (2:23).[146] In his epistle to the Ephesians, Paul alludes to our passage and quotes from it (Eph 5:31). He seems to follow Adam's line of thought and infers from it the same lesson of love and intimacy: "So husbands ought to love their own wives as their own bodies; he who loves his wife loves himself" (Eph 5:28).

2:22 Then the rib ... He made into a woman. The verb *banah* "build," here translated as "made," is a regular term in ANE texts to describe the creation of human beings.[147] One of the divine titles in Ugaritic literature is *bny bnwt* "*Builder of creatures.*"[148] The verb *banah* is also used in Amos 9:6 to describe God's work of creation. It is noteworthy that this verb is the root for the word *bayit* "house" or "family." The idea of family is therefore also implied in this "construction" of the woman. Yet, beyond the existential application to the relationship between the man and the woman, the fact that the word *tsela'* "rib" is also a specialized term in sacral architecture language may also prove an interesting direction to explore. It is indeed noteworthy that this word appears most frequently in the construction of the tabernacle and Solomon's temple.[149] This allusion to the sanctuary is confirmed by its association in our text with the verb *banah* "build," which is also a keyword in the accounts reporting the construction of the sanctuary (Ps 78:69) and the temple (1 Kgs 6:2, 5, 7 [3x], 9–10, 12, 15–16 [2x], 38).[150] The reference to the "rib" as the basis for the "construction" of the woman may then be a part of the numerous hints at the tabernacle, which, as we already observed, is found in the setting of the Garden of Eden. This parallel of the rib-woman with the sanctuary is interesting as it suggests that the creation of the woman means more than the comfort of companionship to man; it may, in fact, have bearings on the salvation of humankind (see below on 3:15).

2:23–24. STEP SEVEN: THE FINISHED COUPLE

GEN 2:23–24 NKJV	GEN 2:23–24 ESV
23 And Adam said: "This *is* now bone of my bones and flesh of my flesh; she shall be called Woman, because she was taken out of Man."	**23** Then the man said, "This at last is bone of my bones and flesh of my flesh; she shall be called Woman, because she was taken out of Man."
24 Therefore a man shall leave his father and mother and be joined to his wife, and they shall become one flesh.	**24** Therefore a man shall leave his father and his mother and hold fast to his wife, and they shall become one flesh.

2:23–24 This is the first and only time that man speaks in the account; this solitary phrase, we might call it his "only word," responds to the "only word" of God (2:18).

2:23 This is now. In God's word, the need for companionship was noted. Only

---

146 This interpretation also fits the general understanding of the Old Testament, which uses the expression "bone and flesh" in the sense of kinship (see, for instance, 29:14; Judg 9:2; 2 Sam 5:1; 19:12–13 [13–14]; 1 Chr 11:1).

147 See Westermann, *Genesis 1–11*, 230–231.

148 See Cyrus H. Gordon, *Ugaritic Textbook*, vol. 3, Analecta Orientalia 38 (Rome: Pontifical Biblical Institute, 1965), 373.

149 Of the thirty-nine occurrences, the word appears nineteen times in connection to the tabernacle (Exod 25:12; 26:20, 26–27; 27:7; 30:4; 36:31–32; 37:3, 5, 27; 38:7). For its connection to Solomon's temple, see 1 Kings 6:5, 8, 15–16, 34; 7:3.

150 This association is also noted by Rashi who points out that the term *tsela'* is also used to refer to the "side" of the tabernacle in Exodus 26:20 (see Miqraot Gedolot on 2:21).

now does the man recognize that this need has been fulfilled. Man's language marks this point of arrival: "now." The literal Hebrew translation would be "this time." The definite article before the word "time" is expressed in the emphatic demonstrative, meaning "this time finally" (see NJB, TNK: "this one at last"; ESV: "this at last"). This is the first time in the account that man speaks. Although he previously gives names to the animals, the narrative does not report any word on his part. He simply does his assignment and perhaps mentally records their names. Only *now* is Adam's voice heard, and this time his pronouncement is not merely a name to register in the columns of natural science. Indeed, Adam exclaims a poem. The keyword is *z'ot* "this," pointing emphatically to the woman. This word is repeated three times in two lines; it appears in the beginning, at the end, and in the middle, more precisely, every five words:

z'ot (five words) *z'ot* (five words) *z'ot*.

In the first line, "bone of my bones, flesh of my flesh," Adam expresses his relationship with the woman, the sameness that he shares with her as opposed to the animals. In the second line, "She shall be called Woman, because she was taken out of Man," Adam refers to God's act of creation. As the first line has no verb, there is no action; Adam is simply admiring the quality of the product: "bone of my bones, flesh of my flesh." The second line, on the other hand, is made up of two verbal clauses reporting an action—God's action. Significantly, the two verbs are in the passive mode, denoting God as the subject ("divine passive").[151] The first phrase in this line refers to the giving of the woman's name; in contrast to the animals, it is God—and not man—who names the woman. The verbal form *qara' le* "called" that is used in connection with the woman is only used to describe God's giving of names in the creation account (1:5 [2x], 10).[152] Even in this name God marks her difference from the animals. The woman is not defined as simply the female counterpart of the male. It is noteworthy that the technical terms *zakhar* "male" and *nekebah* "female" are not used, but rather *'ish* and *'ishah*, to emphasize, through the repetition of sounds,[153] the identity of the nature of man and woman, their equality and the relationship that exists between them on that level.[154] The second verb refers to God's work in the creation of the woman through His taking of man's rib. The preeminence of the woman is also affirmed here in that God makes the woman after He makes man; she is a special creation, unlike the creation of female animals, which were created simultaneously with the male animal.

2:24 All the preceding information grounds the special and unique connection between man and woman, a bond so powerful and exclusive that it will tolerate no other connection—not even that with parents. The introductory word *'al-ken* **therefore** belongs to cognitive language regarding the origin of a name, a custom, or a proverb (16:14; 32:32; Esth 9:26). It indicates that the following comment about the marriage of the man-woman couple conveys a universal duty, transcending all cultures and times.

---

151 On the use of the divine passive, see the comments on the phrase "were finished" (2:1).

152 The formula describing Adam's giving names to the animals (2:20) is different: the phrase is *qr' shemot le* "call names to" (lit. trans.) versus *qara' le*.

153 These two words do not seem to be etymologically related; their association simply denotes a popular etymology.

154 N. P. Bratsiotis, "*'ish*," *TDOT* 1:227.

Shall leave … be joined … become one flesh. The process of the conjugal relationship is described using three verbs, which indicate three aspects of this relationship. The verb forms suggest "a description of divine intention rather than of habitually observed fact."[155] The first verb, "leave," suggests the permanence of this commitment: the man and the woman are now disconnected from their roots (father and mother) and cannot return to their original condition; their commitment is forever. The second verb, "joined," suggests the exclusive character of that relation. And the third verb, "become one flesh," suggests the profound, comprehensive, and intimate nature of that relation.

The first two verbs *'azab* "leave" and *dabaq* "join" belong to covenant language (Deut 28:20; Hos 4:10),[156] which is here applied to the conjugal covenant, as it is in the case of Ruth (Ruth 1:14–16). The fact that it is the man who is described as the one who "shall leave" to "be joined" to the woman and not the other way around has been explained by the rabbis of the Talmud from the point of view of the psychology of men versus women: "because it is in the nature of man to actively pursue the woman and it is not the nature of women to actively pursue the man. If a person loses something, who seeks out whom? It is the one who loses something who seeks it out and not vice versa."[157] Yet, most commentators have been puzzled by the first part of the sentence that requires the man to leave his parents, particularly as it is inconsistent with the patriarchal trend that characterizes biblical culture.[158] The interpretation that this statement echoes a memory of a matriarchal tradition has not been convincing.[159] Yet, precisely because this statement is made against the patriarchal tendency of the biblical society (24:8; 38:11; Deut 25:5–10), it intentionally emphasizes the exceptional force of this covenant. If the formula had been the other way around, the woman being the one having to leave her parents to follow her husband, it would not have carried the same weight, for this was a normal and natural reaction. This unusual and upsetting statement is to be understood as a hyperbolic expression to bring into relief the importance of the new marital covenant. Powerful though they may be, even patriarchal ties should not prevail over the conjugal bond.[160]

One flesh. The ultimate reason for this new condition is that the man and woman have become "one flesh." The Hebrew word for "flesh" (*basar*) refers not only to the physical body but often appears in the sense of "human being" (Lev 13:18, 24). The expression *kol basar* "all flesh" has the meaning of "all humankind," "every human." The expression therefore means more than the unity achieved through a physical, sexual relationship. Becoming "one flesh" means that the man and woman have become one person, implying all aspects of being human—emotional, spiritual, as well as physical and economic. This language suggests that the marital covenant is

---

155 Robert B. Lawton, "Genesis 2:24: Trite or Tragic?" *JBL* 105, no. 1 (1986): 98.

156 See Mathews, *Genesis 1–11:26*, 222; cf. Hamilton, *Genesis: 1–17*, 181.

157 Qidd. 2b.

158 See von Rad, *Genesis*, 85; cf. Davidson, "The Theology of Sexuality in the Beginning," 21.

159 Westermann, *Genesis 1–11*, 233.

160 See Ellen G. White's reflections on the sacred circle of the human couple: "There is a sacred circle around every family which should be preserved. No other one has any right in that sacred circle … I have been shown that there should be a sacred shield around every family. The home circle should be regarded as a sacred place, a symbol of heaven, a mirror in which to reflect ourselves. Friends and acquaintances we may have, but in the home life they are not to meddle. A strong sense of proprietorship should be felt, giving a sense of ease, restfulness, trust" (AH 177–178).

not only pointing to the past to say that this covenant is stronger than even the ties that engage a son to his parents, but it also points to the future to affirm the inviolability of this covenant against any other potential relationship. Malachi uses this passage to defend monogamy and reject divorce (Mal 2:15–16). Being "one flesh," the couple is now inseparable. This is precisely Jesus' conclusion as He quotes and comments on this text: "For this reason a man shall leave his father and mother and be joined to his wife, and the two shall become one flesh … Therefore what God has joined together, let not man separate" (Matt 19:5–6). On the basis of this text, Jesus infers, then, the absolute lesson that according to God (versus tradition) divorce is not an option (Matt 19:7–9). Jesus' main argument (as Malachi's) is that God is personally involved in that relationship, thus making it inviolable. Marriage is not just a human affair concerning only the man and woman; it is essentially a religious affair. The biblical text has hammered this idea in many ways. First, God is actively present in that history; He is the main, if not the only, responsible agent. He is the One who "built" the house-family through the rib-woman and He is the matchmaker, the very One who initiated the marriage, "He brought her to the man." It is a divine institution. Secondly, the linguistic parallels with the sanctuary temple reinforce the intention of the author to emphasize the sacred character of this institution. Thirdly, the message of the parallel literary structure of the second creation story sets this sacred divine institution with another divine institution, the Sabbath (2:1–3). Marriage and the Sabbath are thus presented as the first divine institutions for human society, institutions that predate sin and have been set up in the context of the Garden of Eden. Furthermore, this connection between the Sabbath and marriage informs us about the holiness of marriage (Heb 13:4) and the humanness of the Sabbath (Mark 2:27). Biblical tradition has well retained this association between the Sabbath and family life, with an emphasis on the woman (Lev 19:3)[161] that Jewish tradition has enormously elaborated.[162]

2:25. CONCLUSION

GEN 2:25 NKJV	GEN 2:25 ESV
25 And they were both naked, the man and his wife, and were not ashamed.	**25** And the man and his wife were both naked and were not ashamed.

2:25 **They were both naked … and were not ashamed.** This is the conclusion of the second creation story in parallel to that of the first creation story (2:4a). Just as the conclusion of the first creation story objectively presents the state of heavens and earth as "they were created," the conclusion of the second creation story objectively presents the man and the woman as they were created, that is, "naked." This condition is not a reference to some distant stage of history when humans did not wear clothes or to some psychological embarrassment in regards to sensuality and sexuality. They are in a state that has "not yet been" affected by sin. As we already

---

161 Note that the text prioritizes the mother over the father, "his mother and his father," while the normal order is usually the reverse "father and mother" (Exod 20:12; 21:15; Deut 21:13, etc.).

162 The woman is the one who should mark the beginning of the Sabbath; she is the one who is praised on that evening with the reading of *'ishet hayil* (Prov 31:10–31). The Sabbath is even compared to the beloved woman. See Michael Kaufman, *The Woman in Jewish Law and Tradition* (Northvale, NJ: Jason Aronson, 1995), 215–218; cf. Ellen G. White's recommendations in 6T 356–359.

observed in our introduction to Genesis (cf. 2:5), this account of creation has been written from the "not yet" perspective. Their condition of nakedness is to be understood in connection with the preceding statement describing their condition of oneness. Being one flesh they feel totally confident and do not feel threatened before each other. Nakedness is a state of vulnerability only when one is exposed to all kinds of possible attacks. It is significant that in all the Old Testament passages where nakedness is associated with shame it is in the context of war, when people are threatened by surrounding enemies (Isa 20:4; 47:3; Mic 1:11; Nah 3:5). The last passage is particularly enlightening as it explains the state of nakedness and shame that will characterize Nineveh as being "laid waste" in contrast to Amon "that had the waters around her, whose rampart was the sea" (Nah 3:8). Nakedness is a state of being uncovered, unsheltered, or unprotected. The result is "shame."

But the Hebrew word *bosh*, translated "shame," carries a different nuance than the English. While the English stresses the psychological condition "to feel ashamed," the Hebrew refers to the physical condition of disgrace that is, in most cases, the result of defeat at the hands of the enemy (Mic 1:11; cf. Jer 2:26)[163] or of public disgrace (Ezek 16:52). The use here of the reflexive form (*hitpael*) suggests that they are not ashamed before each other and are without fear or inhibitions. That the man and the woman are "naked" but[164] "not ashamed" means that they have "not yet" been attacked by the enemy—that is, the enemy who is to come. It is precisely this "not yet" situation that the author intends to suggest through the play on words that connects the "nakedness" of the first couple with the "cunningness" of the serpent (2:25; 3:1). Although the two words are derived from two different roots, in Hebrew one hears the same sounds. The word for "naked" (*'arumim*) sounds like the word for "cunning" (*'arum*) and thus leads us to anticipate what is to come. This literary method, termed *prolepsis*,[165] has been interpreted as a "key to what follows."[166]

---

163 See B. K. Waltke, "*bosh*," *TWOT* 97–98.

164 The conjunction "and" in the phrase "*and* were not naked" is a *waw* of contrast and opposition and could be translated "but" (NET) or "yet" (TNK, NAB).

165 Jerome T. Walsh, "Genesis 2:4b–3:24: A Synchronic Approach," *JBL* 96, no. 2 (1977): 163–164.

166 L. Alonso-Schökel, "Sapiential and Covenant Themes in Genesis 2–3," in *Studies in Ancient Israelite Wisdom*, ed. J. Crenshaw (New York: Ktav, 1976), 475.

2. FROM EDEN TO BABEL: SETH-NOAH-SHEM

GENESIS 3–11

Three crucial events form this section. The first event (3:1–24) is the fall of the first parents who listen to the serpent's arguments and eat from the forbidden tree, despite God's warning. This precipitates their leaving Eden. Their expulsion is, however, tempered with the divine promise to save them: the "seed" of the woman will overcome the seed of the serpent (3:15). Evil reaches its climax with the crime of Cain who has then to go farther into exile (4:1–26). The future is then constructed through Adam's other line, Seth (5:1–32). The second event (6:1–7:24) is the flood, which shakes the earth and seems for a moment to compromise the "good" of creation. The whole Cainite tribe vanishes in the flood along with vegetation and animal life; yet God recreates from this watery abyss and gifts the rainbow as a sign of the new covenant with Noah, the descendant of Seth (8:1–10:32). The third event is the tower of Babel (11:1–32), which humans erect to challenge divine sovereignty; God descends and scatters the builders of Babel. From rebellion to rebellion, from exile to exile, Adam, Seth, Noah, and his son Shem experience both the consequences of their iniquities as well as God's faithful and compassionate response.

THE FALL (3:1–24)

From the perfect creation depicted in Genesis 1–2 and the serene life in the Garden of Eden, we now fall into a scene of trouble. Humans disobey God's first commandment and, as a result, evil and death strike. It is in this context of hopelessness that the first word of hope is sounded. Significantly, the first messianic prophecy is located exactly in the center of the literary structure of the chapter, clearly marking the author's intention to highlight its message.

THE LITERARY STRUCTURE

The ideas and the events of the whole passage are organized according to a chiastic structure, a literary device often used in the Bible and ANE literature. The name "chiasmus" is given in reference to the Greek letter *chi* X, which indicates that the sequence ABC is followed by its reverse $C_1B_1A_1$, as indicated below:

$$
\begin{array}{ccc}
A & B & C \\
 & X & \\
C_1 & B_1 & A_1
\end{array}
$$

A Serpent-Eve, God absent: Temptation to eat from the tree (3:1–5)
    B Adam-Eve: Human clothing (3:6–8)
        C God-Adam-Eve: Temptation (3:9–13)
            D God-Serpent: Messianic prophecy (3:14–15)
        C_1 God-Eve-Adam: Suffering (3:16–19)
    B_1 Adam-Eve: Divine clothing (3:20–21)
A_1 God alone: Forbiddance to eat from the tree (3:22–24)

Our commentary will follow the various sections of the chapter as delineated by this structure.

3:1–5. THE SERPENT AND EVE: TEMPTATION

GEN 3:1–5 NKJV	GEN 3:1–5 ESV
1 Now the serpent was more cunning than any beast of the field which the Lᴏʀᴅ God had made. And he said to the woman, "Has God indeed said, 'You shall not eat of every tree of the garden'?"	**1** Now the serpent was more crafty than any other beast of the field that the Lᴏʀᴅ God had made. He said to the woman, "Did God actually say, 'You shall not eat of any tree in the garden'?"
2 And the woman said to the serpent, "We may eat the fruit of the trees of the garden;	**2** And the woman said to the serpent, "We may eat of the fruit of the trees in the garden,
3 but of the fruit of the tree which *is* in the midst of the garden, God has said, 'You shall not eat it, nor shall you touch it, lest you die.'"	**3** but God said, 'You shall not eat of the fruit of the tree that is in the midst of the garden, neither shall you touch it, lest you die.'"
4 Then the serpent said to the woman, "You will not surely die.	**4** But the serpent said to the woman, "You will not surely die.
5 For God knows that in the day you eat of it your eyes will be opened, and you will be like God, knowing good and evil."	**5** For God knows that when you eat of it your eyes will be opened, and you will be like God, knowing good and evil."

The chapter begins explosively with "the serpent" and a dialogue between the serpent and the woman on the issue of the forbidden tree.

3:1 **Now the serpent.** The construction of the phrase indicates that the emphasis is on **the serpent**. The word "serpent" is the first word of the chapter, and it is used with the definite article, meaning "as for the serpent" (3:2, 4, 13–14). The animal is thus individualized. This serpent is unique and familiar to the writer and, supposedly, to the reader as well. From the very beginning, we learn about the superiority of the serpent; it is "more …" than "all" the other animals. The word *kol* "all" or "any" is repeated three times ("*all* the cattle," "*all* beasts of the field," "*all* the days"). In our context, this word is loaded with universalistic overtones (2:1–3, 5–6, 9–11, 19). The serpent is therefore not a ordinary snake, but is presented as a supernatural being of cosmic proportions. The Hebrew Scriptures know this serpent figure well and identify it as the enemy of God (Isa 27:1; Ps 74:13–14). Likewise, ANE mythology represents the serpent as the personification of evil. In Babylonian as well as in Egyptian mythologies, the ancient serpent is a familiar symbol for the evil enemy against which the gods are called to fight.[167]

In the light of these evidences, Cassuto, commenting on this passage of Genesis, identifies the serpent as "the symbol of evil," "the foe of man."[168] In the book of Revelation, the serpent is explicitly called the "serpent of old … the Devil and Satan, who deceives the world" (Rev 12:9).

He said … Has God indeed said? The woman's first surprise is that the serpent speaks. This is the first deception of the Devil, to disguise himself as someone else:

---

167 For the Babylonian, see *ANET*, 61–68, 501–503; for the Egyptian, see Edward Conklin, *Getting Back Into the Garden of Eden* (Lanham: University Press of America, 1998), 49.

168 Cassuto, *Genesis*, 1:142, 160.

"The serpent had not the power of speech, but Satan used him as a medium. It was Satan that spoke, not the serpent. Eve was deceived, and thought it was the serpent."[169] As Mathews notes, "the serpent's trickery is ultimately the voice of Satan."[170] Behind the serpent, God clearly identifies and denounces the real but unseen enemy (3:15), as does the New Testament (John 8:44; 1 John 3:12; Rom 16:20).

The woman's second surprise is that the serpent seems to resonate like God. The serpent does not challenge the word of God nor argues against it. In fact, he presents himself as God's expositor, implying that Eve had not understood Him well. The serpent "said," just as "God said" (ten times in Genesis 1, and one time in Genesis 2). The same verbal form *wayyo'mer* "he said" is used for both. The only difference is that when God is talking, the divine subject is always mentioned: *wayyo'mer* (*YHWH*) '*Elohim* "God [*YHWH*] said." The only other time we encounter the same verbal form is with Adam as the subject (2:23). The construction of the phrase in this case, however, is troubling, for the subject of *wayyo'mer* "said" is not indicated. In fact, this is the only case in this entire passage where the subject is not explicitly indicated. Furthermore, the verb is even preceded by the name '*Elohim* "God," so that the Hebrew sentence has the following sequence of words: "*YHWH* God he said to the woman … he said." In other words, it appears as if God is the One speaking. In this, we note that the serpent cloaks his first appearance and usurps the role of God by posing as YHWH Himself.

You shall not eat of every tree. Significantly, the serpent reports God's prohibition as if it applied to "every tree." While the phrase "every tree" was, in God's original statement, associated with His grace and generosity—"of every tree … you may freely eat" (2:16)—in the serpent's words the phrase is associated with His interdiction. The God of grace has now become the hard God of oppression. It is clear, however, that the serpent is addressing the issue of the forbidden tree, as the woman's response will confirm, in which case this suggests that the woman is near that tree, an indication that she had already been attracted to it. It is also noteworthy that the serpent does not mention the tree of the knowledge by name; instead, it has been neutralized and included in "every tree," thus implying that this particular tree is like the other trees. Evil is not recognized as real evil. The serpent is suggesting that evil is relative (one among others) and therefore God's interdiction has lost its absolute force.

3:2 The woman said to the serpent. The woman responds to the serpent and is now fully engaged in conversation with him. The dialogue form recalls the only previous dialogue, between God and Adam, which was also articulated with the same *wayyo'mer* "he said." The God-man dialogue has now been replaced with the serpent-woman dialogue, suggesting again the usurping interference of the serpent.

3:3 God has said, You shall not eat it. The woman corrects the serpent and intends to report an accurate version of God's words. She even appears to defend God, since her version of God's statement is more precise than the serpent's report. Paradoxically, her care in reporting the *exact* report of the divine words is suspect; it hides her worry and insecurity concerning God's commandment and shows that her relationship with God has already been affected. Without knowing it, she has already adopted the theology of the serpent. Like the serpent, she uses the name of God '*Elohim* rather than *YHWH* '*Elohim*. While the name '*Elohim* connotes the

---

169 Ellen G. White, 3SG 39.

170 Mathews, *Genesis 1–11:26*, 234.

power and transcendence of a God far removed from humans, the name *YHWH* connotes the immanence of a personal God who engages in close relationships with humans (see the comments on 1:1). For Eve, God has become *'Elohim*, a force and abstract idea far from her. He is no longer *YHWH*, the personal God who spoke with her. He is no longer her God. No wonder she also shares the same view of evil as the serpent. For if there is no God or if He is far removed from us, why be concerned about "good and evil"? Like the serpent, she does not identify the tree of knowledge by name; she simply calls it **the tree in the midst of the garden** (3:3).

3:4–5 The serpent said … You will not surely die. For the first time, the subject before the verb "said" is explicitly designated: "the serpent." Also for the first time, the serpent unmasks himself and speaks directly to the woman, no longer using allusions or diplomatic questions. Previously, the serpent had seemed to even respect God's words; he simply commented on them and provided her with the "right inter-pretation." Now, for the first time, the serpent contradicts God and negates His words. Although the serpent is answering the woman and repeats her words, the arrows of his statement go beyond her, being aimed directly at God and couched with the brazen implication that God is a liar. The reason for this new boldness and lack of subtle diplomacy is that the serpent realizes that the woman is now close enough and willing to hear his argument. For this subject is of importance for Eve; it concerns her immortality and, indirectly, her desire of becoming like God. In essence, the serpent has seen that his own ambition of usurpation has resonated well with the woman. This is why he goes beyond mere insinuations, as he did before, to now openly denouncing God as a deceptive and selfish Overlord who wants to keep immortality only to Himself.

For God knows … This phrase is introduced with the conjunction *ki* "for" to explain why God does not want humans to eat from the tree of knowledge. The serpent relates this statement to the preceding sentence about the prospect of death: "You will surely not die *for* God knows that in the day you eat of it you will be like God, knowing good and evil." In other words, the serpent is suggesting to Eve that God's prohibition to eat from the tree of knowledge concerns not only the knowledge of good and evil, but also her immortality. The serpent explains that if only she could eat from the tree of knowledge, she would not die. By eating from the forbidden tree, Eve will acquire the knowledge of good and evil and thus become like God, knowing good and evil, and beyond the threat of death. The serpent is subtly suggesting that the tree of knowledge has the same virtue as the tree of life, that it may, in fact, be the same tree (another argument to convince the woman that she is entitled to it). In short, the serpent's accusation was that God was greedily hoarding the fruit from the tree of knowledge so as to reserve for Himself the gift of immortality.

3:6–8. ADAM AND EVE: HUMAN CLOTHING

GEN 3:6–8 NKJV	GEN 3:6–8 ESV
6 So when the woman saw that the tree *was* good for food, that it *was* pleasant to the eyes, and a tree desirable to make *one* wise, she took of its fruit and ate. She also gave to her husband with her, and he ate.	**6** So when the woman saw that the tree was good for food, and that it was a delight to the eyes, and that the tree was to be desired to make one wise, she took of its fruit and ate, and she also gave some to her husband who was with her, and he ate.

7 Then the eyes of both of them were opened, and they knew that they *were* naked; and they sewed fig leaves together and made themselves coverings.

8 And they heard the sound of the LORD God walking in the garden in the cool of the day, and Adam and his wife hid themselves from the presence of the LORD God among the trees of the garden.

7 Then the eyes of both were opened, and they knew that they were naked. And they sewed fig leaves together and made themselves loincloths.

8 And they heard the sound of the LORD God walking in the garden in the cool of the day, and the man and his wife hid themselves from the presence of the LORD God among the trees of the garden.

When Eve shares the forbidden fruit with her husband, the couple makes a significant move. Discovering their nakedness, they seek to solve the problem by themselves and cover themselves.

3:6 The woman saw that the tree was good. The phrase is reminiscent of God's evaluation of His creation: "God saw that it was good" (1:4, 10, 12, 18, 25, 31). This echo between God's words and her words suggests that Eve has already replaced the divine Creator with her own opinion. And indeed she behaves like God: **She *took* of its fruit and … *gave* to her husband with her, and he *ate*.** These three verbs (italicized in the quotation) have so far only been associated with the Creator. God "gave" to "eat" (1:29); God "took" the man (2:15); and God "took" one of his ribs (2:21). Even the verbal form (consecutive imperfect) *wayyòkhal* "and he ate," describing Adam's response to Eve's offer, is the same as that used to describe the fulfillment of the divine orders of creation, *wayehi* "and there was" (1:3), "and it was so" (1:7). Eve identifies herself with the Creator and one-sidedly imposes her "rule" on Adam, as suggested by Adam's automatic response to Eve, which literally echoes her move: *wattokhal* "and she ate" and *wayyòkhal* "and he ate." Without thinking, Adam mechanically repeats Eve's actions (see the comments on 3:17).

With her. The Hebrew preposition *'immah* "with her" reinforces this impression. In this context, it is preferable to understand the preposition *'im* in its comparative sense, "like" or "as,"[171] indicating that Adam behaved "like" or "as" Eve (Job 9:26), rather than in the sense of accompaniment, suggesting that Adam is standing nearby. The idea of proximity could be rendered, if desired, by the preposition *'etsel* "beside," "with" (13:1; 19:30; cf. Prov 8:30). Note that the preposition *'im* may also refer to the fellowship or companionship between two persons, without them necessarily standing next to each other (3:12; 21:10). The two meanings may well be implied in that preposition. With that in mind, the serpent speaks only "to the woman" (3:1) and Adam's silence in the course of the dialogue between Eve and the serpent suggests that he is not physically present. Thus, the phrase means that Adam ate the fruit just as she had done.

3:7 The verse contains the same association of words as in Genesis 2:25, *sheneyhem* **both of them** and **naked**. Moreover, as we already observed the word for "naked," *'arum* points to the word for the "cunning" *'arum* of the serpent. These echoes convey the message that their passing from nakedness without shame to nakedness with shame is due to the cunningness of the serpent. The human tragedy, then, is not a just a human event. An external power has interfered and played a decisive role in that drama. The wordplay between human nakedness and the serpent's

---

171 See *IBHS*, 219–220.

cunningness implies that the serpent's aim was precisely human nakedness.

They knew that they were naked. For the first time, the man and the woman experience disconnection from God. They are no longer covered and protected by Him. They have severed their relationship with the divine. The use of a slightly different form of "naked" (*'eyrumim* instead of *'arumim*) in this context suggests an intentional nuance between the two experiences of nakedness. While the former word *'arumim,* describing Adam and Eve's nakedness before the fall, often denotes the condition of being "lightly dressed" (Isa 20:2, 4; 58:7; Mic 1:8, etc.), the latter word *'eyrumim* may refer to a different kind of nakedness. Though the text does not explicitly indicate what kind of nakedness characterized the first couple before the fall, we may infer from the parallel passage of Psalm 104 that they were originally clothed with garments of light and glory, thus reflecting the divine appearance (Ps 104:1–2).[172] Commenting on our passage, the Targum of Jerusalem has preserved that very tradition: "His skin was a bright garment, shining like his nails; when he sinned this brightness vanished, and he appeared naked" (Tg. Yer. Gen 3:7).[173] Likewise, speaking of the garment Adam and Eve wore in the Garden of Eden, Ellen White notes "a beautiful soft light, the light of God, enshrouded the holy pair. This robe of light was a symbol of their spiritual garments of heavenly innocence. Had they remained true to God it would ever have continued to enshroud them. But when sin entered, they severed their connection with God, and the light that had encircled them departed. Naked and ashamed, they tried to supply the place of the heavenly garments by sewing together fig leaves for a covering."[174]

They ... made themselves. The verb "make" has so far only been used in relation to God, the Creator. Significantly, Adam and Eve's reaction to address their problem is to put themselves in the place of God and become divine, a move that had already been initiated by the woman. They want to cover themselves and thus solve the problem of their sin—an error that Paul will denounce as righteousness by works (Gal 2:16). By doing this, the human couple is in fact "usurping divine prerogatives as well as explicitly disobeying God's express word. When God makes the couple clothes of skin in 3:21, this is both an act of grace and a reassertion of the creator's rights."[175] It is worth noticing that the human couple has now joined the serpent's project: usurping God's role. Their nakedness now identifies with the serpent's cunning, reinforcing the significance of the play on words with *'arum* "naked."

3:8 **And they heard the sound of the Lord God.** The name of *YHWH 'Elohim* is used again, after a significant hiatus since its last occurrence in Genesis 3:1. Yet, the presence of the Lord is only "heard." It is not even the Lord Himself they hear; it is His *qol* "voice," translated "sound" (NKJV). Adam and Eve shift from the immediate world of seeing and touching, which is associated with the deception of the serpent, to the world of hearing, which implies the distance of the divine presence (Deut 6:4). While the serpent has come closer, God has seemingly become distant. Previously, humankind could see God, now they can only hear Him (Job 42:5). The reference to the "hearing" experience also suggests that Adam is startled. He did not

---

172 Cf. Richard M. Davidson, *The Flame of Yahweh: Sexuality in the Old Testament* (Peabody: Hendrickson, 2007), 55–58.

173 Cf. Gen. Rab. 11:1.

174 Ellen G. White, COL 310.

175 Wenham, *Genesis 1–15,* 75.

see God coming. The violent shock of hearing and the frenzied activity of Adam and Eve (the four verbs are all in the imperfect) contrast with the unique verb describing God's **walking,** associated with the divine voice. The *hitpael* participle form of the verb *mithallek* "walking" suggests relaxation, repetition, and duration.[176] The coming of the Lord (or of His voice) appears to be in the normal course of events. Humans have changed while God remained the same, as if nothing happened. He is walking as usual. Furthermore, this form of the verb (*hitpael*) refers to God's presence in the sanctuary (Lev 26:12; 2 Sam 7:6–7). While this use reaffirms the particular link between the Garden of Eden and the sanctuary, it also reinforces the relational dimension of the Lord *YHWH*, still available and open to relationship. Just as God has taken the initiative to come down and create (1:1), God takes now the initiative to come down and meet with humans and save them.

In the cool of the day. The Hebrew phrase literally means "in the wind of the day" and refers to the evening time (TNK: "at the breezy time of day"), suggesting quietness and freshness, which are also discordant with the stressful behavior of Adam and Eve. The text is full of irony: terrified by rustling leaves they chose to hide behind the leaves of those trees, more precisely the trees that are located **among the trees of the garden** (2:8). The preposition *betokh* "among" is the same as the preposition situating the place of the tree that was forbidden by God (3:3). It appears, then, that Adam and Eve hide behind the very trees that caused their problems, as if they could hide from the Lord God who planted the trees (2:8–9). This reflex also suggests that their relationship with God was not just of a "spiritual" nature, but also involved a tangible physical reality: God could see them just as they could see Him.

3:9–13. GOD, ADAM, AND EVE: HIDING BEFORE GOD

GEN 3:9–13 NKJV	GEN 3:9–13 ESV
9 Then the Lord God called to Adam and said to him, "Where *are* you?"	**9** But the Lord God called to the man and said to him, "Where *are* you?"
10 So he said, "I heard Your voice in the garden, and I was afraid because I was naked; and I hid myself."	**10** And he said, "I heard the sound of you in the garden, and I was afraid, because I was naked, and I hid myself."
11 And He said, "Who told you that you *were* naked? Have you eaten from the tree of which I commanded you that you should not eat?"	**11** He said, "Who told you that you were naked? Have you eaten of the tree of which I commanded you not to eat?"
12 Then the man said, "The woman whom You gave *to be* with me, she gave me of the tree, and I ate."	**12** The man said, "The woman whom you gave to be with me, she gave me fruit of the tree, and I ate."
13 And the Lord God said to the woman, "What *is* this you have done?" The woman said, "The serpent deceived me, and I ate."	**13** Then the Lord God said to the woman, "What is this that you have done?" The woman said, "The serpent deceived me, and I ate."

The irony continues. The Lord plays a game of hide-and-seek, and pretends that He does not know where they are. Significantly, God will address Adam and Eve only with questions: "Where are you?" (3:9) "Who told you that you were naked?

---

176 See Joüon §53i, n. 4.

Have you eaten from the tree?" (3:11) "What is this you have done?" (3:13). The original order of appearance of the actors (serpent, woman, man: 3:1–5) is reversed (man, woman, serpent: 3:9–13) and will be restored in the following scene (serpent, woman, man: 3:14–19).

3:9–10 The first question **where are you?** (3:9) is rhetorical. God knows where Adam is. The same question is used when God asks Cain: "Where is Abel?" which is followed by God's recognition, "the voice of your brother's blood cries out to Me from the ground" (4:9–10), an indication that God knows very well where Abel is. Going down to the human level, God plays the role of the Judge or "the prosecutor in a court of law"[177] who interrogates the culprit in order to make him realize his fault and prepare him for the forthcoming sentence (3:14–19), eventually prompting him to repent, thus leading him (and her) to salvation (3:15). The whole scenario evokes the proceedings of what biblical scholars call the "covenant lawsuit,"[178] whereby God's judgment is established. Old Testament theologian Claus Westermann describes it as "an investigative trial judgment conducted by God."[179] This legal process, which involves God's descent to confront humans and judge them, is in fact one of the most recurring motifs throughout the book of Genesis; it reappears in connection to Cain (4:9–10), the tower of Babel (11:5), the flood (6:5–8), Sodom and Gomorrah (18:21), and is alluded to in many other passages (12:10–20; 15:14; 16:5; 20:1–18; 22:1, 12; 26:6–11; 29:31; 30:6; 31:53; 38:7–10; 50:25).[180] In the wider scope of the book of Genesis, these divine-judgment incursions into the human sphere carry a message of eschatological significance, pointing to the salvation of humankind. It is not accidental that our present context (the judgment of Adam and Eve) contains at heart the first eschatological prophecy that unfolds the process of salvation (3:15).

In the meantime, God's concern for the human sinner is to restore lost communication. God's intention is already expressed in the first verb that introduces His question. God **called** (3:9). The Hebrew verb *qara'* "call" is often used to describe God's call to establish communication (Exod 19:20; Lev 1:1). The reason why God's call is specifically aimed at Adam does not imply that Eve has already been relegated to a secondary and inferior role. The preceding verse gives us a hint at why God chose to address only Adam rather than Eve, or both together. The construction of the Hebrew phrase suggests that Adam is the one who initiated the move to hide: "And Adam hid himself and also his wife" (3:8 lit. trans.). This is clearly indicated both from the sequence Adam-Eve and also from the verb in the masculine singular, referring to Adam. The fact that this use of the masculine singular occurs in a context where, up to this point, only the plural had been used to refer to the pair ("they were not ashamed," "they knew," "they sewed," "they made," "they heard") is striking enough to suggest the intention to refer to only Adam. It is also interesting that Adam speaks only about himself: "I hid myself" (3:10). His first reaction to hide shows that he is the one who was the most conscious of the transgression. Secondly, his lack of courage is consistent with his earlier

---

177 Phyllis Trible, *God and the Rhetoric of Sexuality*, OBT (Philadelphia: Fortress, 1978), 117.

178 For a discussion on the divine covenant lawsuit in the Scriptures, see Richard M. Davidson, "The Divine Covenant Lawsuit Motif in Canonical Perspective," *JATS* 21, no. 1 (2010): 45–84.

179 Westermann, *Creation*, 96.

180 See Davidson, "The Divine Covenant Lawsuit," 72–73.

response to Eve where he did not have the fortitude to stand up against her (3:6).

Instead of directly referring to his act of disobedience, or to his wife (as he will do later), Adam's first excuse is his nakedness: **I was naked** (3:10). Significantly, Adam refers to his nakedness despite the fact that he and Eve are covered with fig leaves. This suggests that by "nakedness" Adam means more than physical nudity and refers instead to his condition of "being unmasked."[181] Adam is now aware of his sin and feels exposed.[182] The reason for his hiding, then, is attributed to his human nature. The description of his natural state as naked is put in the beginning as an emphasis and is followed by the personal pronoun: *'eyrom 'anokhi* "naked, I" (lit. trans.). What Adam is suggesting, then, is that his mistake is a result of the way he was created: "You made me so." In other words, the Creator is the One responsible for Adam's behavior. God is the cause of evil. Hence God's two follow-up questions.

3:11 God's second question **who told you that you were naked?** unveils the true agent responsible for this whole matter. The question points to a person *mi*, "Who?" implying that besides man and God there is a third party involved in the plot. Instead of the word *'amar* "to say," which was used to introduce the words of the serpent, significantly God uses a new word, *higgid* "told," which is often used in prophetic contexts to refer to the proclamation of special revelation (41:25; Hos 4:12; Isa 19:12).[183] God's speech has then an ironic tone: "Who is the one who claims to speak on My behalf, who revealed this truth to you?" God then confronts Adam with the direct question: **Have you eaten from the tree of which I commanded you that you should not eat?** God refers here to the past gift of the law—the same words are used (2:16–17)—and thus appeals to Adam's memory.

3:12 Again, Adam blames God: **the woman whom You gave**. His two answers respond to God's two questions. To the first question, "Who told you?" Adam answers: "the woman." But he specifies that God is behind the woman, "whom You gave." She is the one who "gave me of the tree." To the second question, "Have you eaten?" Adam simply reports, "and I ate," which is related to the woman's offer, and offers no other comment, as if there were no other alternative.

3:13 **What is this you have done?** The demonstrative "this" refers back to what Adam has just reported about Eve who gave him the fruit. This is God's last and most direct question, the only one that concerns an admitted action. Eve's answer echoes Adam's answer:

She gave me . . . and I ate (3:12)
The serpent deceived me, and I ate (3:13)

Deceived. The Hebrew word *nasha'* "deceive" means to make people believe in false hopes and false securities, thinking that God is supporting them while such is not the case (2 Kgs 19:10; Isa 37:10; Jer 49:16; Obad 7). Adam and Eve disobeyed God not necessarily thinking that they were doing evil, but on the contrary, being convinced that they were doing the right thing, even with God's support. The worst evil is not so much doing evil as it is doing evil with the illusion that we are doing right, with the profound conviction that "God is with us."

---

181 Westermann, *Creation*, 95.

182 See Davidson, *The Flame of Yahweh*, 57.

183 F. Garcia-Lopez, "*ngd*," *TDOT* 9:178.

3:14–15. GOD AND THE SERPENT: MESSIANIC PROPHECY

GEN 3:14–15 NKJV	GEN 3:14–16 ESV
14 So the Lᴏʀᴅ God said to the serpent: "Because you have done this, you *are* cursed more than all cattle, and more than every beast of the field; on your belly you shall go, and you shall eat dust all the days of your life.	**14** The Lᴏʀᴅ God said to the serpent, "Because you have done this, cursed are you above all livestock and above all beasts of the field; on your belly you shall go, and dust you shall eat all the days of your life.
15 And I will put enmity between you and the woman, and between your seed and her Seed; He shall bruise your head, and you shall bruise His heel."	**15** I will put enmity between you and the woman, and between your offspring and her offspring; he shall bruise your head, and you shall bruise his heel."

LITERARY STRUCTURE

This section constitutes the apex of the chiastic structure of Genesis 3, a literary way of "focusing attention on the central element."[184] The themes and the rhythm of the words suggest two distinct and contrasted stanzas. The first stanza (3:14) is made of six lines with an irregular word rhythm in Hebrew (2, 2, 3, 3, 2, 3), following an introductory statement of three Hebrew words: *ki 'asitah zo't* "Because you have done this." The second stanza (3:15) is made of four lines with a regular word rhythm in Hebrew (4, 4, 3, 3), following one Hebrew word: *'eybah* "Enmity." The first stanza contains a negative message of judgment against the serpent. The second stanza brings a positive message of hope for humankind:

First stanza (3:14)
Because you have done this
1. You are cursed (2 words)
2. More than all cattle (2 words)
3. And more than every beast of the field (3 words)
4. On your belly you will go (3 words)
5. And you shall eat dust (2 words)
6. All the days of your life (3 words)

Second stanza (3:15)
Enmity
1. I will put between you and the woman (4 words)
2. Between your seed and her Seed (4 words)
3. He shall bruise your head (3 words)
4. And you shall bruise His heel (3 words)

3:14 **Because you have done this.** The phrase "you have done this" refers back to the preceding phrase, which was addressed to Eve, "What is this you have done?" (3:13). This repetition is an indication that the judgment has now moved to the serpent and has reached its last step. It is noteworthy that God does not address any questions to the serpent as He did to Adam and Eve, for the serpent has no excuse.

---

184 Wilfred G. E. Watson, *Traditional Techniques in Classical Hebrew Verse*, eds. David J. A. Clines and Philip R. Davies, JSOTSup 170 (Sheffield: Sheffield Academic Press, 1994), 17.

The judgment against the serpent inaugurates all the judgments, which are given in reverse order from the sins, in a chiastic arrangement:[185]

Sins: man (3:9–11), woman (3:12), serpent (3:13)
Judgments: serpent (3:14–15), woman (3:16), man (3:17–19)

You are cursed. Note that the curse is originally directed to the serpent and only later to the earth (3:17). Significantly, the curse against the serpent echoes the statement about his cunningness. Just as he is **more cunning than any beast of the field**, he is **more cursed than every beast of the field**. In Hebrew, we have exactly the same words: *mikol khayyat hassadeh* "more than every (any) beast of the field." Also the word "cursed" *'arur* sounds like the word "cunning" *'arum*, a play on words suggesting that the serpent's cunningness turned out to be his curse. Furthermore, the curse on the serpent also points back to the creation text referring to the animals (1:24). That only the cattle and the beast of the field are now mentioned, without the "creeping things," emphasizes the fact that the serpent is now identified with that particular category. The curse is the opposite of the blessing (12:3); it implies exclusion from the community of those who are blessed by God (4:11) and therefore banishment from relationship with God and from enjoying future productivity (Josh 9:23; Judg 21:18). The phrase "more cursed than" does not imply that the other animals are also cursed (but less). This is a superlative expression to emphasize that the serpent receives the greatest curse.

It is clear that the curse alludes to the physical condition of the serpent as an animal: **on your belly you shall go**. This description initially implies that crawling on its belly was not the serpent's original way of motion. This reference to the present lowest level (dust) also suggests the highest level of the serpent's former way of motion, which corroborates the various traditions of an ancient flying serpent (see Isa 30:6).[186] Ellen White describes the ancient serpent as "one of the wisest and most beautiful creatures on the earth. It had wings, and while flying through the air presented an appearance of dazzling brightness, having the color and brilliancy of burnished gold."[187] Once the most wonderfully striking animal, the serpent now becomes the most abhorrent of creatures.

It is noteworthy that the language of the curse is echoed in the technical words describing the serpent in the list of unclean animals (Lev 11:42). This commonality of language between the two passages[188] suggests that they hint at each other. It is indeed interesting that the serpent is classified in a unique category of animals, the "creeping things … on the earth" (Lev 11:42), the only category that is "all" impure, in contrast to the other categories of animals, some of which *may* be pure. Additionally, the superlative character of the Genesis curse reappears in Leviticus 11. There the serpent is more impure than "all" the others. Significantly, the word *kol* "all" is repeated six times in the passage (cf. Lev 20:25). The reason for this exception is the particular association of these animals with the earth, which often denotes the underground, the place of death (Exod 15:12; Jonah 2:7; Ps 22:30). Now, in Genesis 3, death

---

185 For further expansion on the reverse order in Genesis 2 and 3, see Zdravko Stefanovic, "The Great Reversal: Thematic Links Between Genesis 2 and 3," *AUSS* 32, no. 1 (1994): 47–56.

186 Note that among other cultures the ancient Mesoamericans and Egyptians who, although they never met and lived centuries and thousands of miles apart, both worshipped the feathered-serpent deity.

187 Ellen G. White, PP 53.

188 These are the only two passages in the Hebrew Bible that have the word *gakhon* "belly."

is even more apparent in the curse as the serpent is specifically associated with dust, which also denotes the grave and the underworld (Isa 26:19; Ps 22:16, 30; Dan 12:2). The curse of the serpent, so embedded with the perspective of death may, therefore, explain the superlative prohibition and abomination associated with the impurity of the "creeping things" in Leviticus 11. It is not the creeping condition of the serpent that has inspired the story of the curse. It is rather the other way around; the event of the fall with its inauguration of death has eventually determined the dietary law. This explanation becomes more forceful in its universality when we realize that all ritual impurity has death "as its common denominator."[189]

You shall eat dust all the days of your life. The language of "eating dust" is obviously symbolic, suggesting victory over the serpent enemy (Ps 72:9; Isa 49:23; Mic 7:17). This image also means that the serpent feeds himself with death. Death is his substance.

All the days of your life. This expression refers to the duration of the tragic condition of the serpent, which will last until the crushing of his head at the end of time, as the rest of verse 15 makes plain. In the immediate context of the Garden of Eden, this association between "eating" and "life" also takes on a paradoxical significance through its allusion to the "tree of life." While "eating" was normally associated with the "tree of life" for the purpose of life, for the serpent "eating" is also associated with life (in the phrase "all the days of your *life*") but for the purpose of death. Once again the deceptive nature of the serpent is revealed.

3:15 **Enmity.** In the Hebrew sentence, the word "enmity" is placed in the beginning of the prophecy to mark an emphasis. From the outset, the basic and most important idea of the passage is pointed out: it is a cosmic and permanent conflict; the word "enmity" points to the categories of the cosmic conflict, the so-called "great controversy."[190] Significantly, the same Hebrew word *'eyba* "enmity" recurs in two other biblical passages (Ezek 25:15; 35:5) with the connotation of a lasting situation for all time. As Westermann comments, "The two Ezekiel passages use the word with the same meaning as here; never-ending or perpetual enmity from long ago. The purpose is to describe the phenomenon that enmity exists not merely in a determined situation but has grown to a continual state, something like an institution."[191]

I will put. The verb *'ashit* "I will put" has God as subject. This enmity is supernatural. It is God who puts enmity. The only other biblical passage that uses the same association of words is Psalm 110. There the same verb in the same form, *'ashit* "I will put," with the same subject, God, appears in connection with "enmity." The words of the psalm *'ashit 'oybeykha* "I make your enemies" are indeed a verbal repetition of the Genesis promise *'eyba 'ashit* "I will put enmity." This echo is particularly significant as it suggests that the author of the psalm believed this first phrase of Genesis 3:15 referred to the Davidic Messiah.

Her Seed. The main issue here concerns whether "her seed," should be

---

189 Jacob Milgrom, *Leviticus 1–16: A New Translation With Introduction and Commentary*, AB (New York: Doubleday, 1991), 686.

190 See Ellen G. White's comments: "The enmity referred to in the prophecy in Eden was not to be confined merely to Satan and the Prince of life. It was to be universal. Satan and his angels were to feel the enmity of all mankind. 'I will put enmity,' said God, 'between thee and the woman, and between thy seed and her seed; it shall bruise thy head, and thou shalt bruise his heel' (Genesis 3:15). The enmity put between the seed of the serpent and the seed of the woman was supernatural" (1SM 254).

191 Westermann, *Genesis 1–11*, 259.

understood in a collective sense, referring to distant "offspring" or "descendants," as most of the modern translations (ESV, NIV, etc.) suggest, or in the narrow sense, referring to an individual. It is noteworthy that the nearest biblical use of this word referring to the "seed" of the woman is found in Genesis 4:25, where it also appears associated with the technical verb *'ashit* "put," from which is derived the name of Seth, the third son of Adam. The verb refers to the fact that God "put" (*shat*) a "seed" in the place of the murdered Abel. The fact that in this parallel and nearby passage the word "seed" refers to a specific individual, "Seth," may support the interpretation that our passage should likewise refer to a particular individual.

He shall bruise. The subject of the verb "bruise" that is implied in the pronoun *hu'* "he" is not precisely identified. It is therefore not immediately clear whether this pronoun refers to the "seed" as a collective or specific individual. It is first important to notice that this pronoun receives special emphasis in the construction of the phrase. It is located precisely in the middle of the stanza, when the poetic rhythm shifts from four beats to three. It functions as the hinge of the passage. In addition, the word order is unusual: the pronoun is the first word in the sentence and occurs before the verb. Normally, in the Hebrew phrase, the subject follows the verb, unless emphasis is intended. This strong emphasis on the "He" suggests the idea that this person, who is not clearly identified, is the One who will bring the final solution to the "enmity" that was just mentioned: "I will put enmity, but He is the One who will bruise." This relation between the "I" of God and the "He" of this unidentified person suggests at least a particular relationship between the two agents, especially in regards to that redemptive mission. The "He" will fulfill the purpose of the divine "I."

It is interesting that we find the same configuration in 2 Samuel 7:11–13, which shares a number of common words with our text, namely, "enemy" (2 Sam 7:9, 11), "seed" (2 Sam 7:12), and "He" (2 Sam 7:13):

I will set up your *seed* after you ...
He shall build a house for My name, and I will establish the throne of his kingdom for ever

As in Genesis 3:15, God is the subject of the prophecy, speaking in the first person. The same pronoun *hu'* "He" is emphasized preceding the verb and stands for the same antecedent "seed." These significant echoes suggest that the writer of 2 Samuel 7 had Genesis 3:15 in mind and applied the pronoun "He" to the "seed," which was to be his son Solomon, ultimately pointing to the Davidic Messiah whose kingship would be established forever (2 Sam 7:13). In light of the reading of 2 Samuel 7, we may interpret the "He" of Genesis 3:15 as implying the antecedent "seed" and referring to a specific individual (in this immediate context, Solomon) and not to a neutral collectivity. It is therefore not surprising that the Septuagint attests to this particular reading of Genesis 3:15, since the Hebrew pronoun *hu'* "He" has been translated there with the pronoun *autos* "He," which implies neither a woman nor a neutral collective but refers specifically to a masculine singular human individual. This conclusion is also confirmed by lexical studies of the word "seed" in the Old Testament that have established that when the word "seed' means a collective, the pronoun that refers to it (referent) is plural, but when the word "seed" means a singular person, then the pronoun that refers to it (referent) is singular (cf. 22:16–18).[192]

He shall bruise your head, and you shall bruise His heel. Although the same Hebrew form *shup* "bruise" is used for the head and for the heel, it is derived from two different roots. The first *shup* derives from a verb meaning "to trample," implying the idea of "crushing," while the second *shup* derives from a verb meaning "to gasp, pant after," implying the idea of biting. The repetition of the same sound, *shup*, is an intentional play on words suggesting the parallel and simultaneous character of the two actions: the *shup* "bruising" ("crushing") of the head, and the *shup* "bruising" ("biting") of the heel are dependent on each other and belong to the same event. The visual image describing the course of the event confirms that impression: The heel is hit while the head is crushed. In fact, the heel is hit *because* it is with the heel that the head of the serpent has been crushed.

Although the heel and the head are mentioned as being "bruised," each antagonist is affected in the totality of his person. Both attacks are mortal. This is clearly suggested through the imagery of the heel versus the head: the serpent because it is hit on its head, and the posterity because the venomous serpent has hit Him on the heel. Note that the two extremities (head and heel) are involved, implying the idea of totality (merism), thus suggesting the completeness of the operation. This idea is also expressed in the grammatical forms, as indicated in the following literal translation: "He will bruise you (*yeshupka*), [through] the head and you will bruise him (*teshupennu*), [through] the heel." Both antagonists will die as a result of the attack (*shup*). The serpent dies because it has been hit (*shup*) on the head; and the posterity (He) dies because He has been hit (*shup*) on the heel. It is noteworthy that in Psalm 139:11 and Job 9:17, the only two other biblical passages where the verb *shup* occurs, it is also the whole person that is concerned. It is also interesting that Psalm 110, which shares unique links with our passage (see above), is once more related to it via the interplay between the foot and the head arranged as an inclusio: The psalm begins with a reference to the foot, "till I make Your enemies Your footstool" (Ps 110:1) and ends with a reference to the head, "He crusheth the head over a wide land" (Ps 110:6 JPS). All these parallels and echoes between the two passages suggest that Psalm 110 was referring to Genesis 3:15 and interpreted it in a messianic sense. The author of Psalm 110 identified the one portrayed in Genesis 3:15 as crushing the serpent as the future Davidic Messiah, even the Lord Himself: "The Lord said to my Lord, 'Sit at My right hand, till I make Your enemies Your footstool'" (Ps 110:1).

EXEGESIS AND INTERPRETATION OF GENESIS 3:15

A number of observations suggest that this text is a "messianic prophecy," the first in the Bible, referring to the redemptive mission of the Messiah:

1. The divine involvement and the universal scope of the prophecy. The divine connection is implied in Psalm 110, which identifies the Lord Himself as the One who crushes the head in Genesis 3:15 (Ps 110:1). The "enmity" is perpetual in length and cosmic in scope.

2. The individual identity of the prophetic figure. The word "seed" refers here to an individual and not to a corporate entity. The pronoun "He" refers to a specific

---

192 See Afolarin Ojewole, "The Seed in Genesis 3:15: An Exegetical and Intertextual Study" (PhD diss., Andrews University, 2002), 192–195.

person, a man and not to the neutral "seed" (see 4:25; cf. 2 Sam 7:13; the testimony of the Septuagint).

3. The messianic application is attested to in the Hebrew Scriptures (Ps 110; 2 Sam 7:11–13).

4. The substitutionary mechanism of redemption. The "He" of Genesis 3:15, identified as the Davidic Messiah and the Lord, will hit the serpent on his head but in the same process will be hit on the heel by the serpent and will die. The death of the serpent, and therefore our deliverance from death and evil, coincides with the death of the "He." This prophetic scenario of salvation is signified in the Levitical sacrifice, where forgiveness and hence the life of the sinner cost the life of the animal (Lev 4:1–26), a process that is also suggested in the substitutionary death of the Suffering Servant (Isa 52:13–53:12).

5. The strong testimony of the New Testament, which alludes and refers to Genesis 3:15, applies this text to Jesus Christ (Rom 16:20; Heb 2:14; Rev 12:1–6, 11).

6. The testimony of some Jewish and Christian traditions (although not unanimous regarding the messianic interpretation of this passage):

Jewish tradition. The Palestinian *Targum* (first century AD), the Aramaic translation of the Old Testament, identifies the serpent of Genesis 3:15 as the Devil who will be overcome at the end of time by the Messiah. *Bereshit Rabbah*, an old commentary of the book of Genesis (AD 425), concludes from the reading of this passage that the struggle against the serpent "will last until the days of the Messiah."[193]

Christian tradition. The messianic application of Genesis 3:15 is attested to in the writings of the Church Fathers as early as the second century with Justin Martyr (ca. AD 160)[194] and Irenaeus of Lyons (ca. AD 180)[195] who first called Genesis 3:15 the *protoevangelium*, "the first Gospel" of the Bible.

3:16–19. GOD, EVE, AND ADAM: SUFFERING

GEN 3:16–19 NKJV	GEN 3:16–19 ESV
16 To the woman He said: "I will greatly multiply your sorrow and your conception; in pain you shall bring forth children; your desire *shall be* for your husband, and he shall rule over you."	**16** To the woman he said, "I will surely multiply your pain in childbearing; in pain you shall bring forth children. Your desire shall be for your husband, and he shall rule over you."
17 Then to Adam He said, "Because you have heeded the voice of your wife, and have eaten from the tree of which I commanded you, saying, 'You shall not eat of it': "Cursed *is* the ground for your sake; in toil you shall eat *of* it all the days of your life.	**17** And to Adam he said, "Because you have listened to the voice of your wife and have eaten of the tree of which I commanded you, 'You shall not eat of it,' cursed is the ground because of you; in pain you shall eat of it all the days of your life;
18 Both thorns and thistles it shall bring forth for you, and you shall eat the herb of the field.	**18** thorns and thistles it shall bring forth for you; and you shall eat the plants of the field.
19 In the sweat of your face you shall eat bread till you return to the ground, for out of it you were taken; for dust you *are*, and to dust you shall return."	**19** By the sweat of your face you shall eat bread, till you return to the ground, for out of it you were taken; for you are dust, and to dust you shall return."

---

193 Gen. Rab. 20:9.

194 See "Dialogue With Trypho," ch. 100, in *Fathers of the Church* (New York: Christian Heritage, 1948).

195 See "Against Heresies," bk. 3, ch. 23, 7, and bk. 5, ch. 21, 1, in *The Apostolic Fathers*, ed. A. C. Coxe (Edinburg: American Edition of the Ante-Nicene Fathers, 1885).

Following this promise of salvation, God turns to Eve and Adam to inform them of the consequences of their disobedience: sorrow (3:16–17), conflict (3:16, 18), and death (3:19) will be bound to their human condition. Yet, humans still remain with the prospect of blessing. Neither Eve nor Adam is cursed. Significantly, the word 'arur "cursed" is used only for the earth (3:17), just as it was for the serpent (3:14). This is why even through the gloom are caught glimpses of hope.

Sorrow. It is also interesting that the same word 'itsabon "sorrow," "toil," that characterizes the painful fate of the woman giving birth to the child is the same word as the one that characterizes the **toil** (3:17) of the man reaping the fruit from the earth. In both cases, it is the future—the fertility of both the land and humankind— that is, the perspective of hope for humans and the earth, that is threatened. Although the biblical text does not refer to the curse of the woman (see below), tragically, their sorrow participates in the curse of the earth.

3:16 This verse is one of the most difficult passages of Genesis and certainly one of the most misused. Unfortunately, it has too often been used as a proof-text to justify "harsh exploitive subjugation, which so often characterizes women's lot in all sorts of societies."[196] This ethical consideration obliges us to make a careful analysis of the text in order to discover its genuine intention, that is, as far as possible, free from our cultural biases or misconceptions. The immediate context of this verse, most notably its close literary connection with the preceding verse (3:15), suggests that 3:16 should be read in the light of 3:15.[197]

THE CONNECTION WITH 3:15

> Enmity I will put between you and the woman and between the seed and her seed, He shall bruise your head and you shall bruise His heel (3:15)[198]
> To the woman He said: Greatly I will multiply your sorrow and your conception; in pain you shall give birth; your desire to your husband but he shall rule over you (3:16)

In addition to the fact that 3:15 immediately precedes 3:16, it shares with it a number of common words, grammatical forms, literary parallels, and particular motifs, as indicated below:

1. The two introductions are arranged in chiastic connection with each other (AB || B₁A₁):

> So the Lord God said (A) to the serpent (B) (3:14)
> To the woman (B₁) He said (A₁) (3:16)

2. Both use the same word ha'ishah **the woman.**
3. Both use a similar introductory divine annunciation in the first person:

> Enmity I will put ('ebah 'ashit) (3:15)
> Greatly I will multiply (harbeh 'arbeh) (3:16)

---

196 Wenham, *Genesis 1–15*, 81.

197 For other biblical parallels to this verse, such as 4:7 and Song 7:10 [11], and their implication for the interpretation of 3:16, see the commentaries on these verses.

198 To facilitate the recognition of the parallels, a literal translation is provided.

4. Both use the same reciprocal relation between the masculine third person *hu'* "he" and the second person "you." Note also the chiastic structure between the two lines: he (A)–you (B) || you (B)–he (A):

> He (*hu'*) (A) shall bruise you, but you (B) shall bruise him (3:15)
> To your (B) husband your desire, but he (*hu'*) (A) will rule over you (3:16)

5. Both use a birth motif: in 3:15 with the mention of "seed," and in 3:16 with the words "give birth."

The unique point that links 3:15 with 3:16 is the reference to "the woman," with a special focus on the motif of giving birth. The connection of 3:15 with 3:16 through the motif of childbearing brings to 3:16 a positive perspective associating it with cosmic salvation (cf. 1 Tim 2:14–15).[199] For it is through the incarnational process of bearing a child, the seed of "the woman," the Messiah, that God will prevail over evil, and the messianic hope will be fulfilled.

THE INTERPRETATION OF THE SO-CALLED CURSE OF THE WOMAN

It is first important to realize that God's address to the woman is not identified as a curse by the biblical text. Significantly, the divine address to the woman is the only one that does not contain the word "curse," while this word appears in the context of the other two divine addresses, to the serpent (3:14) and to the man (3:17). We should also note that the idea of the subordination of women to men was never mentioned or implied prior to this passage, and was therefore not a part of God's original plan of creation.

The connection of 3:16 and 3:15 by the inspired writers suggests that instead of reading the text in the negative sense of a curse we should read it in the positive sense of a blessing.[200] In the light of 3:15, we learn that 3:16 should be placed in the perspective of salvation and the hope of the restoration of the original order. The lessons of this contextual reading of 3:16 are important not only because they provide us with the key of interpretation from within the testimony of Scripture, but also because they have direct ethical implications. Whether in the family circle between husband and wife or in social and professional dynamics, these lessons, which place 3:16 in the perspective of salvation, should definitely inspire and govern man-woman relations. Thus, any administrative measure or lifestyle supporting or promoting the idea of the subordination of the woman by the man, would not only deny the prophetic intention of the biblical text, it would also, sadly, run against the divine project of the kingdom of God.

---

199 See William D. Mounce, *Pastoral Epistles*, WBC 46 (Nashville: Thomas Nelson, 2000), 145–146.

200 Note that the parallel text of Song 7:10 [7:11], the only other biblical text that refers to the notion of *teshuqah* "desire" in the context of the relationship between the man and the woman, brings it in a positive context of joy and love (Song 7:6). Furthermore, the song reverses the roles. Instead of the woman, it is the man who feels *teshuqah* "desire" towards the woman. This perspective is already suggested in the original pre-fall scheme of creation when the principle is enunciated that "a man shall leave his father and mother and be joined to his wife" (2:24) and not the other way around (see SDAIBC on Song 7:10). The song takes us, then, beyond the sinful condition of humankind back to the setting of the Garden of Eden when "rule" was not yet tyranny, when the woman and the man could deal with each other in peace and in perfect harmony. For another biblical confirmation of the positive reading of 3:16, see our commentary on 4:7.

EXCURSUS: THE INTERPRETATION OF GENESIS 3:16 IN ELLEN WHITE:
A THEOLOGY OF MAN-WOMAN RELATIONS
BY RICHARD M. DAVIDSON

Ellen White comments directly on the meaning of Genesis 3:16 in two paragraphs of her published writings. In *Patriarchs and Prophets*, she states:

> And the Lord said, "Thy desire shall be to thy husband, and he shall rule over thee." In the creation God had made her the equal of Adam. Had they remained obedient to God—in harmony with His great law of love—they would ever have been in harmony with each other; but sin had brought discord, and now their union could be maintained and harmony preserved only by submission on the part of the one or the other. Eve had been the first in transgression; and she had fallen into temptation by separating from her companion, contrary to the divine direction. It was by her solicitation that Adam sinned, and she was now placed in subjection to her husband. Had the principles joined in the law of God been cherished by the fallen race, this sentence, though growing out of the results of sin, would have proved a blessing to them; but man's abuse of the supremacy thus given him has too often rendered the lot of woman very bitter and made her life a burden (PP 58–59).

She also speaks of this passage in *Testimonies*:

> When God created Eve, He designed that she should possess neither inferiority nor superiority to the man, but that in all things she should be his equal. The holy pair were to have no interest independent of each other; and yet each had an individuality in thinking and acting. But after Eve's sin, as she was first in the transgression, the Lord told her that Adam should rule over her. She was to be in subjection to her husband, and this was a part of the curse. In many cases the curse has made the lot of woman very grievous and her life a burden. The superiority which God has given man he has abused in many respects by exercising arbitrary power. Infinite wisdom devised the plan of redemption, which places the race on a second probation by giving them another trial (3T 484).

Ellen White emphasizes the same points as those that emerge from the biblical text: (1) Before the fall, Adam and Eve were equal "in all things," without hierarchical role distinctions. (2) The hierarchical relationship with asymmetrical "submission on the part of one" came only *after the fall*. (Note that this is in direct contradiction to the traditional interpretation of 1 Timothy 2:12, which sees Genesis 3:16 as merely reaffirming the hierarchical headship of Genesis 1–2.) (3) The hierarchical relationship was a remedial provision, given by God to Adam and Eve so that "their union could be maintained and their harmony preserved." (4) This remedial arrangement was limited to the marriage relation: Eve "was placed in subjection *to her husband*." (5) The subjection of the wife to her husband "was part of the curse," and the "plan of redemption" gave the race "another trial"—the opportunity to reverse the curse and return to the original plan for marriage whenever possible.

Clear indication is also given as to why it was Eve who was placed in subjection to her husband and not the other way around. Ellen White says nothing about "male headship" before the fall; in fact, she denies this by pointing to Eve as "in all things" the equal of Adam. Rather, she gives three reasons for Eve's submission to Adam and not vice versa: (1) "Eve had been the first in transgression"; (2) "she had fallen into temptation by separating from her companion, contrary to the divine direction"; and (3) "it was by her solicitation that Adam sinned." Based upon these three criteria, it is reasonable to assume that if *Adam* had been first in transgression, if *he* had fallen into temptation by separating from his companion, and if it was by *his* solicitation that Eve sinned, then, Adam would have been placed in subjection to his wife and not the other way around.

In the paragraph that immediately follows the above quote from *Patriarchs and Prophets*, Ellen White applies Eve's experience to that of many women in modern times:

> Eve had been perfectly happy by her husband's side in her Eden home; but, like restless modern Eves, she was flattered with the hope of entering a higher sphere than that which God had assigned her. In attempting to rise above her original position, she fell far below it. A similar result will be reached by all who are unwilling to take up cheerfully their life duties in accordance with God's plan. In their efforts to reach positions for which He has not fitted them, many are leaving vacant the place where they might be a blessing. In their desire for a higher sphere, many have sacrificed true womanly dignity and nobility of character, and have left undone the very work that Heaven appointed them (PP 59).

By reading this paragraph in the context of the immediately preceding paragraph cited above, it is clear that the "higher sphere" that Eve hoped to enter was to be *like* God, not to get out from under her husband's rule. The sphere that God had assigned her from the beginning was to be an equal partner "by her husband's side," not to be in submission to her husband's male headship. The asymmetrical submission of one to the other came only after the fall. Likewise, Ellen White's reference to "restless modern Eves" is not describing their attempts to usurp male headship in the home or church, but rather describes any attempt on their part to "reach positions for which He has not fitted them." This principle applies equally to men as to women, as one aspires to a position that he or she does not have the necessary preparation for filling or abandons other work God has given him or her to do in attempts to advance in career or status.

3:17a Then to Adam He said. This is the shortest introduction to the divine address, a way of marking that it is the last one and that the divine word has now reached its climax. This is also the longest address. For the first time, the name of Adam appears as such without the definite article, this emphasizes that the specific Adam—as a person—is concerned and not simply a human being, a meaning that would have been implied had the word "Adam" been used with the article (6:1, 5; 9:6; etc.). The background of the previous events, which took place in the Garden of Eden, is thus recalled.

Because you have heeded the voice of your wife. The Hebrew phrase *shamaʿ leqol* "hear to the voice of" with the preposition translated "heed to the voice of," is an idiomatic expression meaning "obey," normally used in connection with God (Exod 15:26; 1 Sam 15:1; Judg 2:20; Ps 81:12; Jer 18:19; Ezek 20:39). Adam's mistake was to have listened to his wife as if she were God, confirming once again that she had presented herself to him as God's voice, "God's prophet" (see our commentary on 3:6). God repeats verbatim His original prohibition with the words He had spoken only to him (2:16–17). This reminder establishes Adam's failure to honor the divine covenant and hence justifies the divine sentence.

3:17b-19 The divine address to the man echoes the divine address to the serpent in the three words of **curse**, **eat**, and **dust**, and the expression **all the days of your life** (3:17). Just as with the woman, the sentence upon man's tragic condition is placed within the same perspective of hope, namely, the victory over the serpent and hence over evil and death. The chiastic structure underscores the link that exists between man and his environment, between the human activities of work and eating on the one hand, and the curse on the ground and death on the other:

> **A** The ground: Curse
> > **B** Pain, eating herb (hard work)
> > **B₁** Pain, eating bread (hard work)
> **A₁** The ground: Death

3:17b **Cursed is the ground.** Although man is not cursed, the ground has been cursed because of his sin. Adam's iniquity has an impact even beyond himself. The ecological balance has been upset. The echo between A and A₁ on the word *ha'adamah* "the ground" suggests that death is related to the "curse," which helps us to understand the nature of the ecological disruption and human pain.

For your sake. Although the preposition *ba'aburekha* "for your sake" includes the idea "because of you" (see 12:13), it literally means "for the produce or gain of" and contains the nuance of being "for your benefit, advantage, or good" (27:10, 31). The implicit idea is that the experience of this hardship will remind humans of the consequence of sin and will then nurture in their hearts the longing for ultimate deliverance (Deut 8:16; Rom 8:18–22).[201]

In toil you shall eat of it. The same Hebrew word *'itsabon* "toil" is used to characterize the woman's pain in childbirth (3:16) and the man's struggle to reap the fruit from the earth. Both efforts are related to the gift of life. Before sin, life was graciously provided by God through "eating" from the tree of life. Now, "eating" is a struggle, a matter of life and death. It is significant that the keyword "eat," which appears three times in the divine address, echoes the other two occurrences in its introduction, where it concerns the tree of knowledge, whose fruit they were forbidden to eat. The verb "to eat" also points to the serpent, which "shall eat dust" (3:14). Through this wordplay, sin (eating from the forbidden tree) and the human existential condition (eating with pain) are associated with the cosmic struggle between the Messiah and the serpent (eating the dust). They are a part of the great controversy between good and evil. This curse does not suggest, however, that work and effort per se are a part of that curse; man's vocation for work preceded man's iniquity and was to be a blessing (2:15). The new element here is the introduction

---

201 See Ellen G. White's comments: "Under the curse of sin all nature was to witness to man of the character and results of rebellion against God" (PP 59).

of death and the pervasive presence of evil. Now the positive aspects of work and effort are distorted by injustice, cheating, competition, and the violent surprise of accident, disease, and death. These are the unavoidable ingredients of the human condition, which shall last **all the days of your life**. This expression is the same as the one used for the serpent (3:14), a parallel suggesting that this condition will last only as long as the serpent himself, and that with its demise there is the hope of future redemption.

3:18 Thorns and thistles it shall bring forth. The verb *tsamakh* "bring forth" echoes Genesis 2:9 where the same verb is used in connection with the eating from the trees. There the verb *tsamakh* is also used in connection with eating. But it now applies to the "herb of the field," which grows among the "thorns and thistles." This contrast conveys the idea that humans no longer have access to the trees of the Garden of Eden, among which was the tree of life. The contrast between the two diets (fruit versus herbs) is even reflected through the two human postures they connote. Before sin, humans were tall and erect, standing up to pluck the fruit from the trees. Now they are hunched over, bending down to collect the food from the ground. And worse, the herb of the field is difficult and painful to reach because of the thorns and thistles. The irony is that human life is now, like that of the serpent (3:14), dependent on the ground, the dust, the place of death; while before, in the Garden of Eden, they were dependent on fruit from above, from the tree of life and the God of heaven, an attitude that pertains to the categories of faith. For faith is this capacity to depend on the One whom you do not see, the God of heaven in contrast to idolatry that makes you dependent on what you see, things from below that you may be able to control. The same spiritual lesson will be repeated to the people of Israel as they are on the brink of the Promised Land (Deut 11:10–11).

3:19 In the sweat of your face you shall eat bread. This phrase parallels the phrase "in toil you shall eat of it all the days of your life." Both lines begin with the preposition *be* "in" followed by a synonym, *'itsabon* "toil," "pain," "effort" || *ze'at apeykha* "sweat of your face." Then the parallelism continues with the same word "eat" and with the same motif of dust and death:

In toil you shall eat of it || In the sweat of your face you shall eat
Thorns and thistles . . . the herb of the field || Till you return to the ground . . . to the dust

Thus, the curse of the ground concludes with a statement concerning the mortal nature of humans: "dust you are." Because of their origin (dust) and their destiny (dust), human nature is defined as dust: **dust you are** (3:19). In spite of the "image of God" in them, human nature remains essentially "dust." The idea is that humans are mortal by nature. It is noteworthy that when the origin of humans is concerned, the passive form of the verb suggests God as its subject: "out of it you were taken." Yet when the demise of humans is addressed, the subject is exclusively human: "you return to the ground." Although God is behind the gift of life, only man is responsible for death.

3:20–21. ADAM AND EVE: DIVINE CLOTHING

GEN 3:20–21 NKJV	GEN 3:20–21 ESV
20 And Adam called his wife's name Eve, because she was the mother of all living.	**20** The man called his wife's name Eve, because she was the mother of all living.
21 Also for Adam and his wife the Lord God made tunics of skin, and clothed them.	**21** And the Lord God made for Adam and for his wife garments of skins and clothed them.

Unexpectedly, hope erupts against hopelessness. Despite the premonition of death, a bright future is conceived on both human and divine levels. On the human level, Adam finds a name for his wife, which announces future descendants (3:20). And on the divine level, God Himself makes clothes for both of them, a dramatic gesture signifying the future redemption of humankind (3:21).

And Adam called his wife … Eve, because she was the mother of all living. Eve is the first prophetic name of the Bible. In contrast to the name of Adam, which conveyed the idea of death—through its linguistic connection to the word *'adamah* "ground," his origin and destiny (3:17)—the name of Eve carries a message of "life." In the first name giving of his wife (2:23), Adam deciphered a lesson concerning the past, the creation of his wife, who belongs to the same human flesh. Now, in the second name giving of his wife, Adam reads a lesson about the future, the salvation of humankind. The Hebrew name *khawah* "Eve" is derived from the word *khay* "life"[202] and has been translated *Zoe* "life" by the Septuagint. Yet, Eve owes her name not only to the fact that she is the biological mother of all humans, but more importantly in our context to the fact that she is the one who will transmit the messianic seed of Genesis 3:15. Through Eve's name, human salvation will arise; it heralds the victory of the God of life over the serpent of death.

3:21 **The Lord God made tunics of skin, and clothed them.** The association between the two statements suggests that the two actions, Adam's prophecy and God's clothing, are related. Indeed, the language of this verse implies more than the mere act of providing clothes to the naked couple. The divine clothing recalls the human clothing of Genesis 3:7; the same verb in the same form, *wayya'asu/waya'as* "they made"/"He made," is used in both passages. This echo not only emphasizes God as the unique agent of the act of redemption, it also suggests the mechanism of that process: the substitutionary sacrifice.

What is the meaning of the divine clothing? When the Bible refers to the skin of an animal, it often implies that the animal was killed or that it was sacrificed (Lev 5:13; 7:8). The present context of human sin gives sacrificial significance to the slaughter of that animal. The ritual of sacrifice was instituted, then, with "the awareness of substitutionary atonement."[203] In addition to the implicit presence of the sacrifice, the text employs technical terms that belong to sanctuary language, specifically to the clothing of the priests. The word *ketonot* "tunics" is often used of priestly garments (Exod 28:4, 39–40; 29:5, 8; 39:27; 40:14; Lev 8:7, 13; 10:5; 16:4; Ezra 2:69; Neh 7:70 [69]) and the causative form (*hiphil*) of the verb *wayyalbishem*

---

202 BDB 295, 311.

203 Davidson, "The Theology of Sexuality in the Beginning," 127. It is noteworthy that the connection between clothing made of animal skins and the killing of animals and with the institution of the sacrificial system is well attested in ANE traditions; see Westermann, *Genesis 1–11*, 270, cf. Francis A. Schaeffer, *Genesis in Space and Time* (Downers Grove, IL: IVP, 1972), 105–106.

"clothed" is used particularly to refer to the dressing of the priests (Exod 28:41; 29:8; 40:14; Lev 8:13).

When was the animal killed? God's clothing of Adam and Eve is reported here, not because this event takes place at that moment, but because it constitutes the solution to the death problem just mentioned. The sequence is therefore more logical and theological than chronological. Chronologically, the sacrifice must have taken place soon *after* the expulsion and thus outside the Garden of Eden when and where the effect of the curse on the earth—namely, the upsetting of the ecological system and hence the disturbance of seasons—make God's act of clothing physically necessary.[204]

Who killed the animal? The text does not say who killed the animal. But the fact that the text specifies that God was the one who cut the skins to clothe Adam and Eve, yet does not mention that He also killed the animal (as the cutting of the skins and the killing of the animal are both normally reported in the Levitical prescription [cf. Lev 1:6; 7:8]), suggests that God's action was limited to clothing the couple and that the killing was carried out by someone else. Furthermore, the fact that in the Levitical system the guilty person was the one required to kill the sacrificial animal—as an atonement for his sin (Lev 1:5)—suggests that Adam was the one who performed this first sacrifice.

When Adam called his wife Eve, "mother of the living" (3:20), he must have had in mind the significance of the sacrifice, which carried the promise of life through the woman. Indeed, the memory of the promise of Genesis 3:15 was still vivid in Adam's mind, conveying the same lesson of hope: through the woman, the messianic seed, as the Lamb of God, will bring life to the world by His own vicarious death. Ellen White reflects on these matters:

> To Adam, the offering of the first sacrifice was a most painful ceremony. His hand must be raised to take life, which only God could give. It was the first time he had ever witnessed death, and he knew that had he been obedient to God, there would have been no death of man or beast. As he slew the innocent victim, he trembled at the thought that his sin must shed the blood of the spotless Lamb of God. This scene gave him a deeper and more vivid sense of the greatness of his transgression, which nothing but the death of God's dear Son could expiate. And he marveled at the infinite goodness that would give such a ransom to save the guilty. A star of hope illumined the dark and terrible future and relieved it of its utter desolation.[205]

The fact that the expression describing the divine clothing is an idiom specifically applied to the priests carries an unexpected lesson. This suggests that both Adam and Eve were then instituted as priests. Both Eve and Adam were dressed as the priests of the sanctuary, ready to serve the Lord in His tabernacle. The idea that the woman was excluded from the holy priesthood simply because she was a woman is thus denied from the very time of the institution of priesthood.[206]

---

204 See Ellen G. White: "In humility and unutterable sadness they bade farewell to their beautiful home and went forth to dwell upon the earth, where rested the curse of sin. The atmosphere, once so mild and uniform in temperature, was now subject to marked changes, and the Lord mercifully provided them with a garment of skins as a protection from the extremes of heat and cold" (PP 61).

205 Ellen G. White, PP 68.

206 See Jacques B. Doukhan, "Women Priests in Israel: A Case for Their Absence," in *Women in Ministry: Biblical & Historical Perspectives*, ed. Nancy Vyhmeister (Berrien Springs, MI: Andrews University Press, 1998), 29–43.

3:22–24. GOD ALONE: PROHIBITION TO EAT FROM THE TREE

GEN 3:22–24 NKJV	GEN 3:22–24 ESV
22 Then the LORD God said, "Behold, the man has become like one of Us, to know good and evil. And now, lest he put out his hand and take also of the tree of life, and eat, and live forever"—	**22** Then the LORD God said, "Behold, the man has become like one of us in knowing good and evil. Now, lest he reach out his hand and take also of the tree of life and eat, and live forever—"
23 therefore the LORD God sent him out of the garden of Eden to till the ground from which he was taken.	**23** therefore the LORD God sent him out from the garden of Eden to work the ground from which he was taken.
24 So He drove out the man; and He placed cherubim at the east of the garden of Eden, and a flaming sword which turned every way, to guard the way to the tree of life.	**24** He drove out the man, and at the east of the garden of Eden he placed the cherubim and a flaming sword that turned every way to guard the way to the tree of life.

God speaks again and concludes His judgment. God's prohibition to eat from the tree of life echoes His forbiddance to eat from the tree of knowledge. This parallel is more than a literary construction; it establishes the connection between the two acts of eating and, paradoxically, to the two trees in Eden. Because Adam and Eve ate from the forbidden tree of knowledge, they are now cast out from the Garden of Eden and are thus forbidden to eat from the tree of life.

3:22 **The man has become like one of Us, to know good and evil.** The grammatical construction of the sentence (subject-perfect) suggests an anterior time.[207] The verb *hayah* is a "perfect" form and means "was" rather than "has become" as it has often been translated under the influence of the Septuagint. The exact same form has been used to describe the lasting condition of the serpent, which includes an anterior time: "the serpent **was** [*hayah*] more cunning" (3:1). In fact, the same statement has already been uttered by the serpent: "you will be like God, knowing good and evil" (3:5). In this verse, the verb "to be" is also used in the same perfect form, here also to describe a lasting condition and not a becoming.[208] If the idea of "becoming" was the intended Hebrew meaning, it would normally require the use of the preposition *lamed* "to" following the verb "to be" (*hayah*), as we have it, for instance, in Genesis 2:10: "became [*hayah le*] four riverheads." The variation between the two statements suggests, however, a fundamental difference between the two forms of knowledge. In the serpent's statement, the verb "to know" is used in participle form to describe the act of knowing good and evil by Adam and Eve: *yod'ey tob wara'* "knowing good and evil." This form of knowledge concerns the experience of good as well as the experience of evil. In God's statement, the verb "to know" is used in the infinitive to describe the concept of the knowledge of good and evil: *lada'at tob wara'* "as to the knowledge of good and evil" (YLT). This form of knowledge involves discernment, knowing the difference between right and wrong.[209] This discernment was only possible when "Adam *was* like one of Us as in regard to the distinguishing

---

207 See C. H. J. van der Merve, J. A. Naudé, and J. H. Kroeze, *A Biblical Hebrew Reference Grammar* (Sheffield: Sheffield Academic, 2002), §47.2; cf. Z. Zevit, *The Anterior Construction in Classical Hebrew*, SBLMS 50 (Atlanta: Scholars Press, 1998), 15.

208 The first perfect form refers to a past while the second perfect form (with conversive *waw*) refers to a future.

209 See 2 Samuel 14:17 and 1 Kings 3:9 where the same infinitive form is used to express the same concept of discernment between good and evil.

between good and evil."[210] It is only when Adam was like God, completely sinless, that he was still capable of distinguishing between good and evil. The only way to know good and evil is not, as the serpent said, to know the evil *and* the good, but to know *only* the good. Indeed, as soon as man knew evil, he lost his capacity to discern between good and evil, and hence the sense of the "good." Ellen White's comments on this text are to the point: "Man lost all because he chose to listen to the deceiver rather than to Him who is the Truth, who alone has understanding. By the mingling of evil with good, his mind had become confused, his mental and spiritual powers benumbed. No longer could he appreciate the good God had so freely bestowed."[211]

3:23 The Lord God sent him out of the Garden of Eden. There is a wordplay between the verb describing Adam who **put out** his hand to take the fruit (3:22) and the **sending away** from the Garden of Eden. In Hebrew, the same verb *shalakh* is used. The first occurrence of the verb is in the simple form (*qal*), describing simply the idea of "sending." The second occurrence of the verb is in the intensive form (*piel*), implying a stronger "sending." This pun underlines the causal connection between human sin and divine judgment. Sent away from the Garden of Eden humans are now destined to die. The repetition of man's relation with "the ground from which he was taken" (cf. 3:19) brings back the prospect of death, "till you return to the ground."

3:24 So He drove out the man. The Hebrew verb *wayegaresh* "He drove out" echoes the verb "send away" through the use of the same intensive form (*piel*). This verb describes a stronger "sending" than the preceding verb. In the Pentateuch, it often refers to the violent expulsion of the Canaanites from the Promised Land (Exod 23:28–31). The verse is full of motifs evoking the Israelite sanctuary and the temple.

The **cherubim** here point to the cherubim standing over the ark of the covenant of the tabernacle (Exod 25:18; 26:1, 31) and to the cherubim decorating the curtain of the holy of holies (Exod 26:1; 36:8, 35). Even their eastward orientation recalls the tabernacle and temple orientation (Num 3:38; Ezek 10:9; 47:1). The verb *wayyashken* "He placed" from which is derived the word *mishkan* "tabernacle" (Exod 25:8; 29:45; Josh 18:1) is often used to depict God "tabernacling" among His people (Exod 25:8). All these features suggest that the memory of the Garden of Eden was recorded in the structure of the tabernacle and the temple. The knowledge of their ancestors' idyllic life in the Garden of Eden, enjoyed amidst the full presence of the Lord, nurtured the hopes and dreams of the Israelite religion.

Yet, the evocation of the earthly sanctuary in the Garden of Eden goes beyond mere nostalgia. If the Garden of Eden recalls the Exodus sanctuary, it is not just because the author is writing from an Exodus perspective, but also, and more importantly, because it belongs to a broader, universal scope. The strong allusion to the sanctuary in the Garden of Eden presents a cosmic dimension indicating the *other* sanctuary, the heavenly abode of God, which precedes and transcends the Garden of Eden. This allusion to the heavenly order seems to be preferable to the anachronistic Exodus interpretation for several reasons. First of all, the "cherubim" here are real, angelic, living beings who belong specifically to the heavenly realm and are generally associated with worship in the heavenly temple and with the glory of the

---

210 Literal translation; cf.: "And Jehovah God saith 'Lo, the man was as one of Us, as to the knowledge of good and evil'" (YLT).

211 Ellen G. White, Ed 25.

heavenly throne of God (Ps 18:10 [11]; Ezek 9:3; Rev 4:6–9). Secondly, the fact that Moses built the sanctuary in the wilderness according to the already existing heavenly model (Exod 25:40; Num 8:4; Heb 8:5) also supports this interpretation. Furthermore, Scripture explicitly identifies this heavenly temple as "Eden" (Ezek 28:13–14), thus indicating that the earthly Eden sanctuary functioned as an earthly sign of the preexistent heavenly Eden sanctuary (cf. Heb 8:5).

It is interesting to note that this concept of an earthly place of worship being a sign of the heavenly worship center was also encountered in the patriarchal period (see the comments on 28:10–22). The antiquity of this idea of the temple functioning as heaven on earth is also well documented in the ANE, especially in ancient Egypt, where the temple was considered as "the cosmos in microcosm"[212] and the sign of "heaven on earth … an image of the celestial horizon (*akhet*)" where the gods dwelt.[213] Moses, who had been educated in Egypt, was certainly familiar with these Egyptian concepts. There were, of course, "significant and crucial differences" between the two temples and between the two theologies they respectively channeled.[214] Yet, in light of the biblical and ANE testimonies, one may at least recognize that this idea of a heavenly Eden temple preceding and inspiring its earthly counterpart is not a late elaboration. It is therefore reasonable to conclude that the allusions to the sanctuary temple we find here in Eden, in a historical context prior to the existence of the Israelite sanctuary,[215] could in fact refer to this other heavenly temple, which will later serve as a model for the Israelite sanctuary and temple.

In fact, this view fits the paradigm we already noted, namely, that the creation of the planet Earth is given as a part, a blueprint, of the greater cosmos. In a way, the sanctuary evidences of the Garden of Eden suggest the heavenly DNA of our creation and testify to its supernatural, heavenly genesis. It negates that our world is the natural result of a process from below but celebrates it as the extraordinary creation by the heavenly God. Thus, when the Exodus tabernacle and later the temple harken back to the Garden of Eden, it is in part because, like the Garden of Eden, they all point to the same heavenly order (Exod 25:9, 40; cf. 1 Chr 28:11–19; Ps 78:69).

A TIME TO BE BORN, A TIME TO KILL (4:1–26)

The numerous parallels and echoes between Genesis 3 and 4 underscore the unique connection between the two chapters. Both chapters are made up of narratives and dialogues. Many of the scenes are parallel: The description of sin (3:6–8 || 4:8), God's interrogations (3:9 || 4:9; 3:10 || 4:13), the curse (3:14, 17 || 4:11; 3:17–19 || 4:12), God's covering (3:21 || 4:15), and the expulsion (3:24 || 4:14). Not only does the structure of the texts run parallel, but the passages themselves use the same terminology and grammatical constructions (3:16 || 4:7; 3:10 || 4:10). The

---

212 B. E. Schafer, ed., *Temples of Ancient Egypt* (New York: Cornell University Press, 1997), 8.

213 See Jan Assmann, *The Search of God in Ancient Egypt*, trans. David Lorton (Ithaca, NY: Cornell University Press, 2001), 36–37.

214 On the parallels and differences between the two temples, see Lawrence T. Geraty, "The Jerusalem Temple of the Hebrew Bible in Its ancient Near Eastern Context," in *The Sanctuary and the Atonement*, eds. A. Wallenkampf and W. R. Lesher (Washington, DC: Review and Herald, 1981), 59.

215 On the biblical evidence of the antiquity of the sanctuary in the pre-fall Garden of Eden, see Richard M. Davidson, "Earth's First Sanctuary: Genesis 1–3 and Parallel Creation Accounts," *AUSS* 53, no.1 (2015): 65–89.

reason for the strong literary connection between the two chapters is that Genesis 4 fulfills the prediction of the curse pronounced in Genesis 3 and provides us with the immediate illustration of the nature of human sin and of the curse of death. Yet, death is not the final word in the story. The theme of murder alternates with the theme of birth, thus inserting glimpses of hope, while shaping the chiastic structure of the chapter:

> **A** Birth: Adam and Eve: Cain and Abel (4:1–2)
> > **B** Crime: Cain (4:3–16)
> > > **C Birth: Cain: Enoch-Lamech (4:17–22)**
> > **B₁** Crime: Lamech (4:23–24)
> **A₁** Birth: Adam and Eve: Seth (4:25–26)

4:1–2. BIRTHS OF CAIN AND ABEL

GEN 4:1–2 NKJV	GEN 4:1–2 ESV
1 Now Adam knew Eve his wife, and she conceived and bore Cain, and said, "I have acquired a man from the Lᴏʀᴅ."	**1** Now Adam knew Eve his wife, and she conceived and bore Cain, saying, "I have gotten a man with the help of the Lᴏʀᴅ."
2 Then she bore again, this time his brother Abel. Now Abel was a keeper of sheep, but Cain was a tiller of the ground.	**2** And again, she bore his brother Abel. Now Abel was a keeper of sheep, and Cain a worker of the ground.

4:1 Adam knew Eve his wife. The Hebrew verb *yadaʿ* "knew" is an euphemism for sexual-conjugal relationship (cf. 19:8; 24:16; 38:26). The construction of the sentence (subject-perfect) may also indicate anteriority (cf. our comment on 3:22), suggesting that Adam "had known" his wife before he left the Garden of Eden.[216]

I have acquired a man from the Lord. The woman is the first person who mentions the name of the Lord (*YHWH*). The birth of the first child was certainly experienced by Adam and Eve as an extraordinary event. The first woman was so overwhelmed by this wonder that she believed that God Himself had come down and had become the very One she had given birth to: "I have acquired a man, indeed God Himself" (4:1).[217] This literal translation is justified on the basis of grammar, since the name of God (*YHWH*) is introduced by the same word *ʾet* that introduces the name of Cain. It should be noted that the original Hebrew does not have a preposition as generally supplied in translations (NKJV: "I have acquired a man *from* the Lord"; ESV: "I have gotten a man *with the help of* the Lord"). In fact, all the personal names, Eve, Cain, and *YHWH* in this verse, are introduced by the same word. Only the noun *ʾish* "man" does not receive this introduction since it is indefinite.[218] In addition, the phrase *ʾet qayin* "Cain" parallels the phrase *ʾet YHWH* "the Lord," as they both occur at the same place, concluding the respective proposition, thus echoing each other. This literary parallel confirms that the word *ʾet* before the name of God is the same as the word before Cain and is therefore to be identified as the *ʾet* introducing the direct object and not the preposition "with." Moreover, the use of

---

216 Cf. Rashi in Miqraot Gedolot on 4:1.
217 Cf. ISV: "I have given birth to a male child—the Lord."
218 See *GKC* §117*a*.

the word 'et before "the Lord" may even suggest that an emphasis is intended: "indeed the Lord Himself." This identification is just a hint of how Adam and Eve must have felt. Remembering the promise of Genesis 3:15, Eve may have been thinking that she had given birth to her Redeemer: "indeed the Lord Himself."[219]

4:2 Then she bore again. Abel's birth does not receive particular attention. He is only Cain's brother, as he is called seven times in the chapter. Unlike his brother Cain, who received his name with its explanation by his mother, Abel's name is not commented on. Cain is very present; he occupies the whole space and is the only one of the two who speaks in the course of the story. Abel, on the other hand, almost seems absent; he is passive to Cain's aggression and never speaks. The meaning of the two names reflects this difference between the two characters. *Cain* means "to acquire." It denotes possession, acquisition. *Abel* means "vapor." It denotes elusiveness, a transient condition. This is the very word that is used in the book of Ecclesiastes (*hebel*) to express the idea of "vanity." Thus, Cain and Abel already signify in their respective names the contrast between not only their personalities, but also their present occupation and future destinies. While Cain was "a tiller of the ground," a work requiring toughness, physical strength, and a special connection to the ground of death, Abel was "a keeper of sheep," involving the constant care of living creatures and requiring compassion and sensitivity. While Cain has descendants and founds the first civilization (4:17–22), Abel disappears like a vapor, without leaving any trace (4:8).

4:3–16. THE CRIME OF CAIN

GEN 4:3–16 NKJV	GEN 4:3–16 ESV
3 And in the process of time it came to pass that Cain brought an offering of the fruit of the ground to the Lord.	**3** In the course of time Cain brought to the Lord an offering of the fruit of the ground,
4 Abel also brought of the firstborn of his flock and of their fat. And the Lord respected Abel and his offering,	**4** and Abel also brought of the firstborn of his flock and of their fat portions. And the Lord had regard for Abel and his offering,
5 but He did not respect Cain and his offering. And Cain was very angry, and his countenance fell.	**5** but for Cain and his offering he had no regard. So Cain was very angry, and his face fell.
6 So the Lord said to Cain, "Why are you angry? And why has your countenance fallen?	**6** The Lord said to Cain, "Why are you angry, and why has your face fallen?
7 If you do well, will you not be accepted? And if you do not do well, sin lies at the door. And its desire *is* for you, but you should rule over it."	**7** If you do well, will you not be accepted? And if you do not do well, sin is crouching at the door. Its desire is for you, but you must rule over it."
8 Now Cain talked with Abel his brother; and it came to pass, when they were in the field, that Cain rose up against Abel his brother and killed him.	**8** Cain spoke to Abel his brother. And when they were in the field, Cain rose up against his brother Abel and killed him.
9 Then the Lord said to Cain, "Where *is* Abel your brother?" He said, "I do not know. *Am* I my brother's keeper?"	**9** Then the Lord said to Cain, "Where is Abel your brother?" He said, "I do not know; am I my brother's keeper?"

---

219 Ellen White notes on this passage: "The Saviour's coming was foretold in Eden. When Adam and Eve first heard the promise, they looked for its speedy fulfillment. They joyfully welcomed their first-born son, hoping that he might be the Deliverer" (DA 31).

10 And He said, "What have you done? The voice of your brother's blood cries out to Me from the ground.

11 So now you *are* cursed from the earth, which has opened its mouth to receive your brother's blood from your hand.

12 When you till the ground, it shall no longer yield its strength to you. A fugitive and a vagabond you shall be on the earth."

13 And Cain said to the Lᴏʀᴅ, "My punishment *is* greater than I can bear!

14 Surely You have driven me out this day from the face of the ground; I shall be hidden from Your face; I shall be a fugitive and a vagabond on the earth, and it will happen *that* anyone who finds me will kill me."

15 And the Lᴏʀᴅ said to him, "Therefore, whoever kills Cain, vengeance shall be taken on him sevenfold." And the Lᴏʀᴅ set a mark on Cain, lest anyone finding him should kill him.

16 Then Cain went out from the presence of the Lᴏʀᴅ and dwelt in the land of Nod on the east of Eden.

10 And the Lᴏʀᴅ said, "What have you done? The voice of your brother's blood is crying to me from the ground.

11 And now you are cursed from the ground, which has opened its mouth to receive your brother's blood from your hand.

12 When you work the ground, it shall no longer yield to you its strength. You shall be a fugitive and a wanderer on the earth."

13 Cain said to the Lᴏʀᴅ, "My punishment is greater than I can bear.

14 Behold, you have driven me today away from the ground, and from your face I shall be hidden. I shall be a fugitive and a wanderer on the earth, and whoever finds me will kill me."

15 Then the Lᴏʀᴅ said to him, "Not so! If anyone kills Cain, vengeance shall be taken on him sevenfold." And the Lᴏʀᴅ put a mark on Cain, lest any who found him should attack him.

16 Then Cain went away from the presence of the Lᴏʀᴅ and settled in the land of Nod, east of Eden.

It is noteworthy that the first act of worship or religious expression ever recorded in the Bible—an offering to God—becomes the catalyst for the first criminal act. The weight of this religious crime is rendered through the narratives of the respective offerings and dialogues between the brothers and with God.

4:3 In the process of time. The Hebrew expression *qets yamim* "in the process of time" literally means "in the end of days." The fact that both Cain and Abel brought their offering at the same time suggests that this event must have taken place at an appointed religious time; and the fact that this came more specifically at the end of a time period suggests that it was the Sabbath since this day was, then, the only "end" and only appointed religious time they knew.

4:3–4 Cain brought … Abel also brought. While the same verb *hebi'* "brought" is used to describe the commonality between the two offerings, the Hebrew phrase *gam hu'* "also" indicates a difference among them. While the expression is often used in the sense of "in addition to" or "moreover" (see 20:6; Exod 1:10; 1 Kgs 4:15), the adverb *gam hu'* "also" suggests, rather, a contrast between the two offerings. This is captured by some Bible translations: "Abel, on his part also brought of the firstlings of his flock" (NASB); "While Abel, for his part, brought one of the best firstlings of his flock" (NAB).

While Cain chose to take his offering only from **the fruit of the ground** (4:3), Abel, on the other hand, presented "also" or "in addition" to the nonanimal offering **the firstborn of his flock** (4:4). Thus, in contrast to Cain's offering, Abel's offering conformed to the Law. This required that, "in addition to" a vegetable offering, a sacrificial animal be presented for the burnt offering (Exod 29:39–41). Since the sacrificial system was instituted in Eden (see 3:21), it is reasonable to think that the directives of the ritual were given to Adam and Eve at that moment and then passed on to their children. Yet, while Abel complied with the divine instructions, Cain chose to ignore them. The fact that the two offerings correspond to the brothers' respective occupations—Cain, the tiller of the soil, presenting "the fruit of the ground" and Abel, the keeper of sheep, presenting the "firstling of the flock"—also suggests Cain's dramatic dilemma. For in order to offer a right and acceptable sacrifice, Cain, the older brother, would have to request the help of his younger brother. It is likely that Cain's pride prevented him from the humiliation of that request.

4:4–5 The Lord respected Abel and his offering, but He did not respect Cain and his offering. The Hebrew verb *sha'ah*, translated "respect," denotes "close attention with special interest and acceptance." Thus, in Isaiah 17:7–8, God says that one day "a man will look [*sha'ah*] to his Maker," implying that he will recognize God as his Maker. Interestingly, God's acceptance of Abel's offering precedes His rejection of Cain's offering, although Cain's offering preceded Abel's. God's act of grace and love precedes His act of justice. The reason God accepted Abel's offering and rejected Cain's is not explicitly indicated in the text. Yet clues from the text suggest a number of reasons. First, the text says that God's first attention concerns the person who makes the offering. The *waw*, translated "and" before the phrase "his offering," means more than just an addition. It may be used to "specify the sense of the preceding clause"[220] as the following translation suggests: "God looked with interest at Abel, therefore (*waw*) at his offering; but He did not look with interest at Cain, therefore (*waw*) at his offering." This indicates that the reason for God's rejection or acceptance of the offering lies primarily in the spiritual condition of the person and not in their offering per se (Mic 6:7; Isa 1:11). Secondly, a comparison between the two acts of offering reveals a slight nuance between them. While Cain offers "to God," Abel just offers. The mention "to God" is absent for Abel. This little difference is of significance, as it reflects two fundamentally different views of worship. While Cain thinks of his offering as his gift to God, Abel's attention essentially concerns the meaning of the sacrifice itself, namely, God's gift to him. While Cain views his religion as an upward movement *to* God, Abel experiences it as a downward movement *from* God. This contrasting mentality may also explain another difference regarding how the offerings have been chosen. Abel's offering was not, per se, a better offering than Cain's. In fact, Cain's fruit may have even been a better product than the sheep provided by Abel. The difference, however, was that Abel chose from the *bekhorot*, the **first fruits**, the most precious product of the season, according to the Mosaic legislation (Exod 23:19), whereas Cain took any fruit from the land. Against the background of the preceding chapters, each of the two offerings is reminiscent of something different. The fruit offering from the ground (*'adamah*) points to Genesis 3:19, which is associated with human strength and the perspective of death. The animal offering, on the other hand, points to Genesis 3:21 and is associated with divine protection and the perspective of life. Cain's offering was the expression of human effort towards God, whereas Abel's offering was the expression of humanity's need for God's salvation. Furthermore, Abel's offering was related to the promise of the messianic Lamb of 3:15 who would be sacrificed to save the world, whereas Cain's offering was an empty ritual. Note the same contrast between the human clothing (3:7), which uses the vegetal fig leaf, versus the divine clothing, which uses the animal skin and implies the sacrifice of blood (3:21).

---

220 See *IBHS*, 652.

4:5 **Cain was very angry.** The Hebrew expression *wayyikhar leqayin meʾod*, translated "Cain was very angry," refers, in fact, to the psychological state of being depressed.[221] The phrase has been translated "much distressed" (TNK). Significantly, the same language is used to characterize Jonah, whose depressive condition was such that he asked for death (Jonah 4:9). The following phrase, **his countenance fell**, "his face fell" (ESV), an idiom that occurs only here, recalls Job's words: "the light of my face they did not cast down" (Job 29:24 ESV). "His face fell" means that Cain lost "the light of his face." This expression refers to one's favor (Pss 4:6; 44:3; Prov 16:15) and is reminiscent of the priestly blessing to "make [one's] face shine" (Num 6:25). Only God is associated with this expression (Pss 31:16; 67:1; 80:3; Dan 9:17). This helps shed light on the reason behind Cain's depression; for the loss of the light of Cain's face reflected the loss of his special divine-royal-priestly favor.

4:7 This Hebrew verse has been qualified as the most obscure text of the book of Genesis.[222] The meaning of the words is not clear and the identification of the pronouns is difficult. As with Adam (3:9, 11), the Lord approaches Cain first with a question that is designed to make him aware of his sin: **Why are you angry?** (4:6). Again, God engages the guilty in the process of an investigative judgment (cf. 3:9–13).

If you do well. God's recommendation to "do well" concerns, first of all, the right sacrifice Cain is required to offer; but it also refers to Cain's personal struggle against evil and to his way of life. The Hebrew verb *teytib* "do well" has a strong ethical connotation to the relationship between "a man and his neighbor" (Jer 7:5).

Will you not be accepted? This phrase refers back to Cain's "fallen face." The Hebrew word for "accepted" (*seʾet*), which literally means "lifting up," responds to the "fallen face." Essentially, God instructs Cain that the only way to recover what he has lost, the uplifting light of his face, is to "do well." The word *seʾet* "lifting up" is a technical term that refers to the "firstborn's dignity" (see 49:3), thus clarifying the nature of Cain's loss. What is at stake, then, in this incident, concerns Cain's preeminence as the firstborn.[223] God warns Cain that if he behaves correctly he will not lose the "lifting up of face" that is associated with his status of firstborn. It is also significant that the word *seʾet*, from the verb *nasaʾ*, is the technical verb used to express forgiveness (Exod 34:7; Num 14:18); as Onkelos, the ancient Aramaic translation has rendered, "you will be forgiven." What Cain needs to understand is that his salvation and his preeminence as firstborn hinge entirely on God's forgiveness and can in no way be achieved through his own upward achievement.

Sin. The Hebrew word *khattaʾt*, translated "sin," means rather "sin offering" (Lev 4:25) and refers, then, to the atoning sin offering, the sacrificial animal, which provides forgiveness and salvation for the sinner (Lev 7:37; Ezek 40:39).

Lies at the door. The Hebrew verb *rabats* "lies," which describes here the restful posture of an animal, is most often associated with the pasturing herd or flock (29:2; Ps 23:2), and thus implies a message of hope through the promise of atonement. This interpretation has merit in that it fits the immediate theological context that deals precisely with the issue of the right sacrifice confronting Cain and Abel.[224] The reason

---

221 See Mayer I. Gruber, "The Tragedy of Cain and Abel: A Case of Depression," *JQR* 69, no. 2 (1978): 91–93.

222 See Wenham, *Genesis 1–15*, 104.

223 For an examination of the word *seʾet* in this passage and its application to the "firstborn's dignity," see M. Ben Yashar, "Sin Lies for the Firstborn," (Heb.) *BMik* (1963): 116–119, "Zu Gen 4:7," *ZAW* 94 (1982): 635–637.

224 On this interpretation, see Joaquim Azevedo, "At the Door of Paradise: A Contextual Interpretation of Gen 4:7," *BN* 100 (1999): 49.

the Hebrew verb *robets* "lie" is in the masculine singular (although its subject, *khatta't*, is feminine) is because it points to the male sacrificial animal, which is to be offered as a *khatta't* "sin offering." Note that the same stylistic procedure is used in Leviticus 4:25, where the word *khatta't* "sin offering" is also referred to as a masculine singular to imply the sacrificial animal: "The priest shall take some of the blood of the sin offering [*khatta't*, feminine singular] … and pour its [masculine singular] blood at the base of the altar." This reference to the sacrificial animal as a sin offering is consistent with the reference to *petakh* "door," which is a technical term in the Pentateuch to designate "the door of the tabernacle" where the sacrificial animal was to be brought for the sacrifice (Lev 4:4). In our case, the "door" would refer to the entrance of the sanctuary of that time (see the comments on 2:9–15 and 3:21–24), the door of the Garden of Eden, which marked "the border between the sinful and the sinless worlds … the closest place where fallen creatures were allowed to come near to the tree of life."[225]

Its desire is for you, but you should rule over it. The translation of the pronoun as "its" (NKJV, ESV) implies that it is the sin that is supposed to "desire." Yet, a number of Bible versions have opted for the translation "his"[226] as seen in the phrase "his desire" (KJV, NAB). This translation, with the understanding that Abel is being referred to, is supported by the Septuagint and several ancient Jewish commentators.[227] A number of clues from the biblical text itself validate this interpretation:

1. The back-and-forth movement between the two brothers, Cain and Abel (4:1–9), implies a similar alternation between them in 4:7.

2. Cain is generally referred to in the second person, while Abel is only referred to in the third person. Note that the explicit pronoun *'atah* "you" always refers to Cain (4:7, 11), while the explicit pronoun *hu'* "he" refers only to Abel (4:4).

3. This interpretation is also consistent with the biblical usage of the word *teshuqah* "desire," which always refers to a human person (3:16; Song 7:10 [11]).

The identification of Abel behind the pronoun "his" has important implications for the meaning of the words *teshuqah* "desire" and *mashal* "rule." These two words should be understood in a positive sense. The word *teshuqah* "desire," which describes Abel's relationship towards his older brother, as the firstborn, should be understood in the sense of "trust," "respect," and "love." The word *mashal* "rule," which describes Cain's relationship towards his younger brother Abel, should be understood in the sense of "responsibility," "self control," and "love."

TRANSLATION OF 4:7

Along the lines of the interpretation above, two contextual translations have been proposed:

> If you do well [i.e., offer a burnt offering as well as the thank offering], will [it] not be [for you] preeminence [i.e., will you not retain (or be restored to) the 'firstborn's dignity']? But if you do not well [i.e., you do not offer the proper burnt offering], a purification offering [a male sacrificial animal] lies down at the door [of the Garden], for you [to offer for your sin], and [as a result] to you will be his [Abel's] desire and you will rule [again as the firstborn] over him [your brother].[228]

---

225 Ibid., 54.

226 In Hebrew, it is the same pronoun, and there is no difference between "its" or "his."

227 See Rabbi Meir Zlotowitz, *Bereishis*, vol. 1a (New York: Mesorah Publications, 2009), 146.

228 Richard M. Davidson, "Shame and Honor in the Beginning: A Study of Genesis 4," in *Shame and Honor: Pre-*

If you will better your ways, you will have "preeminence of dignity" (49:3) above him [Abel] for you are the firstborn, and you will be the object of his love and desire, and you will rule over him as a master over a servant.[229]

IMPLICATIONS FOR THE INTERPRETATION OF 3:16

The meaning of 4:7 has important implications for the understanding of 3:16, because the two verses are parallels and share numerous echoes with each other (as indicated in the following translations):

And to you will be his [Abel's] desire, and you will rule [again as the firstborn] over him [your brother] (4:7)
And to your husband your desire, but he shall rule over you (3:16)

1. Both verses use the same technical and rare word *teshuqah* "desire" associated with the same word *mashal* "rule" and following the same sequence (desire-rule).

2. Both use the same prepositions at the same place (beginning and end of the phrase): *we'el* "and to" … *be* "over."

3. Both use the same construction of phrase: "to you … but he shall rule over you" ∥ "to you … but you shall rule over him."

4. Both describe the same reciprocal relation between two partners (man-woman ∥ Cain-Abel).

The connection between Genesis 4:7 and 3:16 is particularly significant in regards to the word *mashal* "rule," since Genesis 4:7 is of the three texts (3:16; 4:7; Song 7:10 [11]) the only one that shares this common word with Genesis 3:16. This particular focus suggests that in Genesis 3:16 the word *mashal* "rule" should be understood in a positive sense, as recommended by God when he addresses Cain's responsibility towards his younger brother Abel by reference to the birthright relationship. In addition, the function of "ruling" is tied to the ethical duty of confronting evil and self-ruling: "if you do well" (see the comments on 4:7). Thus, instead of denoting abuse and subordination, the so-called "rule" of man over the woman implies self-rule as well as the spiritual responsibilities and blessings that are associated with the function of birthright.[230]

In addition, this allusion to the birthright in 4:7 implicitly makes the point that no absolute hierarchy is here intended, since in biblical perspective the second may become first. This principle is regularly affirmed throughout the book of Genesis, as exemplified by the cases of Abel and Seth in place of Cain (4:1–2), Shem in place of Japheth (10:1), Isaac in place of Ishmael (17:18–19), Jacob in place Esau (25:25–26), Rachel in place of Leah (29:16), Joseph in place of his brothers (31:1–11), and Ephraim in place of Manasseh (48:8).

4:8 **Now Cain talked to Abel his brother … and killed him.** The use of the phrase *wayyo'mer qayin* "Cain said," echoing the phrase *wayyo'mer YHWH 'el qayin* "the Lord said to Cain" (4:6), implies that Cain was supposed to respond to God. Yet, instead of responding to God by faith, Cain turns to his brother and kills him. It is significant that his crime immediately follows this shift of dialogue from the failed vertical to the

…
senting Biblical Themes in Shame and Honor Contexts (Berrien Springs, MI: Department of World Mission, Andrews University, 2014), 67; cf. Azevedo, "At the Door of Paradise," 59.

229 *HaRechasim LeBikah* (nineteenth century commentary), quoted in Zlotowitz, *Bereichis*, 148.

230 For the blessings and duties of the function of birthright, see the comments on 25:27–34.

horizontal. The mechanism of the first religious crime is thus suggested. The crimes of the zealous ones are not committed because they are right; the crimes of fanaticism and religious intolerance derive, on the contrary, from the failure to respond to God's word. When faith is replaced by human work and control, all kinds of evil ensue. Cain killed his brother, not because he was right and his brother was wrong, but, on the contrary, because he was evil and his brother was righteous (see 1 John 3:12).

4:9 **Where is Abel your brother?** God's question to Cain again echoes His question to Adam in the Garden, "Where are you?" (3:9); this time, however, the question is more personal than the one addressed to Adam. This echo between the two questions suggests a connection between the two sins, the former leading to the latter. It is also noteworthy that, like Adam, Cain hides before God. Cain's crime against his brother is thus related to Adam's sin against God. Killing one's brother is, in fact, a sin against God—it is like killing God—"for in the image of God He made man" (9:6). Cain replies to God's question with another question, **Am I my brother's keeper?** Cain, like Adam, blames God, who is supposed to be the One "who keeps" (Ps 121:4). Although this rhetorical question is directed at God, the Bible gives a clear affirmative answer to that question for humans, requiring loving actions towards one's brother or sister (Lev 19:10–18).

4:10 **The voice of your brother's blood cries out to Me from the ground.** The reference to "the ground" is reminiscent of the "death" associated with the sin of Adam (3:19). Ironically, the same "ground" from which Cain had taken the fruit offering (4:3) has now become the place of the dead. Since Cain does not respond to God, it is the dead "ground" that responds instead. The same line of reasoning is taken by Jesus: "I tell you that if these should keep silent, the stones would immediately cry" (Luke 19:40). Jesus refers explicitly to Abel as a type of the righteous who were murdered (Matt 23:35; cf. Heb 12:24; 1 John 3:12). The book of Revelation alludes to the case of Abel and turns it into the archetype for all "those who had been slain for the word of God and for the testimony which they held" (Rev 6:9). In that perspective, God's judgment is the only answer. Even if humans keep silent, God will hear and grant justice (Rev 6:10).

4:11–16 **You are cursed from the earth.** The Hebrew phrase literally means that Cain is cursed *from* the earth. The Hebrew preposition *min* "from" could also mean that Cain was *more* cursed than the earth, or it could also mean that Cain was cursed *because* of the earth. It is possible that all these meanings are implied. Cain understands that he has lost the special connection he used to enjoy with the ground. Now he is rejected by the ground. Cain, who used to rely on the stability of the *'adamah* "the ground" (translated "the earth"), now sees the same ground disappearing under him, the ground, **which has opened its mouth** (4:11). Cain has now become a fugitive **driven out from the face of the ground** (4:14). This sentiment is immediately echoed in the phrase **from Your face,** suggesting that Cain's expulsion from the earth corresponds to an expulsion from God Himself. The same verb *garash* "drive out" has been used to describe the expulsion of Adam and Eve from the Garden of Eden (3:24). And, like his parents (3:8), Cain also hides "from the presence [face] of the Lord" (4:16). However, the verb translated "hide" is not the same as that used for Adam and Eve. While the verb *khaba'*, which is used for Adam and Eve, implies the idea of "concealing" and "withdrawing" (31:27; Job 29:8), the verb *satar*, which is used for Cain, conveys the idea of protection and refuge (Pss 91:1; 119:114).

The verb *satar* characterizes the dramatic distance separating the sinner from God and, hence, the loss of divine protection (Isa 59:2). This may explain the function of the **mark** God puts on Cain (4:15). The text does not explain the nature of this sign, but the language and the immediate context suggest that it is designed for protection. The change of language suggests that Cain (as noted above) is being driven even farther than Adam and Eve. The phrase, previously used for the Edenic couple (3:24), reappears to describe Cain's departure. The text specifies that he moves **to the east of Eden** (4:16b), suggesting that Cain settles in a land far beyond the view of the Garden of Eden. The name **Nod,** which designates the new location, means "wandering." Far from the grounding influence of the Garden of Eden, Cain the settler has now become an aimless, homeless vagabond.

4:17–22. THE BIRTHS OF ENOCH AND LAMECH

GEN 4:17–22 NKJV	GEN 4:17–22 ESV
17 And Cain knew his wife, and she conceived and bore Enoch. And he built a city, and called the name of the city after the name of his son—Enoch.	**17** Cain knew his wife, and she conceived and bore Enoch. When he built a city, he called the name of the city after the name of his son, Enoch.
18 To Enoch was born Irad; and Irad begot Mehujael, and Mehujael begot Methushael, and Methushael begot Lamech.	**18** To Enoch was born Irad, and Irad fathered Mehujael, and Mehujael fathered Methushael, and Methushael fathered Lamech.
19 Then Lamech took for himself two wives: the name of one *was* Adah, and the name of the second *was* Zillah.	**19** And Lamech took two wives. The name of the one was Adah, and the name of the other Zillah..
20 And Adah bore Jabal. He was the father of those who dwell in tents and have livestock.	**20** Adah bore Jabal; he was the father of those who dwell in tents and have livestock.
21 His brother's name *was* Jubal. He was the father of all those who play the harp and flute.	**21** His brother's name was Jubal; he was the father of all those who play the lyre and pipe.
22 And as for Zillah, she also bore Tubal-Cain, an instructor of every craftsman in bronze and iron. And the sister of Tubal-Cain *was* Naamah.	**22** Zillah also bore Tubal-cain; he was the forger of all instruments of bronze and iron. The sister of Tubal-cain was Naamah.

The introduction to the genesis of Cain's family echoes the introduction to the genesis of Adam's family in Genesis 4:1, 25, as if Cain intended to replace the first father. The genealogy of Cain presents the first real genealogy (4:17–18) and is composed of seven generations. Sadly, it will be marked with the same feats that characterized the father: achievement (4:17, 20–22) and murder (4:23–24).

4:17 **Cain knew his wife.** Obviously, the text refers to one of Cain's sisters, a daughter of Adam (5:4). While brother-sister marriage was clearly forbidden only later by the Mosaic Laws (Lev 18:9), it was permissible during the first generation of humankind. It is interesting that this practice, which was current in ancient Egyptian royal families, was justified on the basis of extensive mythological precedent (see the god Osiris and his sister Isis, Seth and his sister Nephthys), an indication of the memory of ancient traditions. Significantly, Cain, the murderer and wanderer, is the founder of the first city.[231] The need to build responds to his destroying act and the

---

231 See Niels-Erik Andreasen, "Town and Country in the Old Testament," *Encounter* 42 (1981): 262.

creation of the city responds to his erring fate. The name of **Enoch** (*khanok*) from the verb *khanak* "dedicate" not only suggests that Cain "dedicated" the city to his son, but that it was also a religious act. The verb *khanak* "dedicate" often refers to the dedication of an altar (Num 7:11, 84, 88) or of the temple (1 Kgs 8:63). However, God is not mentioned in the process. Cain's first act of building and dedicating remains in the line of his first offering. Cain's religion is still made of his "doing."

4:19–22 It is significant that in the genealogy of Cain Lamech appears at the seventh position from Adam, while in the genealogy of Adam it is Enoch from the line of Seth (not to be confused with the other Enoch from the line of Cain) who occupies the seventh position (5:19). The most wicked Lamech is thus recorded in contrast to the most righteous Enoch. There is indeed a tendency in biblical genealogies to give particular attention to those names occurring in the seventh position.[232] Lamech is the one who transmits the genetic line initiated by Cain, since it is on his name that the genealogy is expressed. Lamech also carries the same character traits as Cain. Like his ancestor, Lamech takes the initiative, thus denoting the same usurping intention towards God. Lamech's first recorded action is his taking two wives: **Lamech took for himself two wives** (4:19); so, Lamech becomes the founder of polygamy. While God is the One who "took" only one wife for Adam, Lamech "took" his wives for himself. The same verbal form *wayyiqakh* "he took" is used for God (2:15, 21). Furthermore, like Cain, Lamech is also an achiever and the father of industry and civilization. The name of Cain reappears in the name of Tubal-Cain, his descendant associated with metallurgy (4:22). More importantly, like Cain, Lamech will be famous for having killed a man.

4:20 Jabal … **He was the father of those who dwell in tents.** This an idiomatic expression found in Semitic cultures expressing that Jabal was the ancestor of Bedouin life and herding.

4:23–24. THE CRIME OF LAMECH

GEN 4:23–24 NKJV	GEN 4:23–24 ESV
23 Then Lamech said to his wives: "Adah and Zillah, hear my voice; wives of Lamech, listen to my speech! For I have killed a man for wounding me, even a young man for hurting me.	**23** Lamech said to his wives: "Adah and Zillah, hear my voice; you wives of Lamech, listen to what I say: I have killed a man for wounding me, a young man for striking me.
24 If Cain shall be avenged sevenfold, then Lamech seventy-sevenfold."	**24** If Cain's revenge is sevenfold, then Lamech's is seventy-sevenfold."

Unlike Cain's murder, which unfolds through the voice of a narrator, Lamech's murder is known solely through the words of the perpetrator. Yet, unlike Cain, Lamech took murder one step further. He presented his killing as a positive and valuable act and literally boasted about it. With Cain, the crime had progressed to a higher degree of evil as he had chosen to remain silent about it. Lamech, in contrast, writes poetry about his murder, exalting his crime through songs. Whereas Cain had asked God for mercy (4:13–14), Lamech ignores God and instead forces his wives to hear of his prowess and even applaud his feat. His self-exaltation may even sound threatening

---

232 See J. Sasson, "Generation, Seven," *IDBSup*, 354–356; "A Genealogical 'Convention' in Biblical Chronology?" *ZAW* 90 (1978): 171–185.

towards them. Indeed, the same paradigm noticed in Cain's crime can be traced here: the failure in the vertical relation (God-human) yields to a violent turning against the human other. In fact, Lamech moves to the opposite of forgiveness. He speaks of revenge, alluding to additional crimes in the future. Even his revenge is given considerable intensification. While Cain is avenged only seven times, Lamech requires an increase to seventy-seven times (4:24). It is noteworthy that Jesus plays on the same intensification of the number seven to urge forgiveness (Matt 18:21–22).

4:25–26. THE BIRTH OF SETH

GEN 4:25–26 NKJV	GEN 4:25–26 ESV
25 And Adam knew his wife again, and she bore a son and named him Seth, "For God has appointed another seed for me instead of Abel, whom Cain killed."	**25** And Adam knew his wife again, and she bore a son and called his name Seth, for she said, "God has appointed for me another offspring instead of Abel, for Cain killed him."
26 And as for Seth, to him also a son was born; and he named him Enosh. Then *men* began to call on the name of the LORD.	**26** To Seth also a son was born, and he called his name Enosh. At that time people began to call upon the name of the LORD.

After Abel's death, the line of salvation was broken and, for a moment, God seems absent—as if hope had departed. The text covering the story of Cain and his descendants is devoid of any reference to God, except in the beginning when it mentions Cain's separation from Him (4:16). With the birth of Eve's new son, Seth, the failed history is resumed and the name of the Lord reappears.

4:25 And Adam knew his wife again. The repetition of the phrase that introduced the birth of the firstborn Cain (4:1) suggests a return to the beginning, as if history had to be swept clean and restarted. In addition, the repetition of the "again" attached to the birth of Seth, echoing the "again" associated with the birth of Abel (4:2), reconnects the broken line of history at this point: Seth will replace Abel. This idea is also registered in the name of the new son, Seth, which means "to put in the place of," as Eve comments: **For God has appointed another seed for me instead of Abel, whom Cain killed**. Furthermore, the Hebrew verb *shat* "appointed," describing God's "appointing" of the "seed" in Eve, is the same verb as the one that describes God's "appointing," "putting" (*shat*) "enmity" between the serpent and the woman (3:15). This echo between the two verses is not accidental. The lesson of this connection is to affirm that history will be repaired and salvation shaped and ensured through the passing of the "seed." Through this allusion to Genesis 3:15, the biblical author points prophetically to the salvation event as manifested in the divine incarnation of Jesus Christ.

4:26 Then men began to call on the name of the Lord. This is the first time since Eve's statement of wonder at the birth of her firstborn (4:1) that the name of the Lord is again mentioned by humans. The Hebrew verb *qara'* "call," which applies to the name of the Lord, does not refer to the act of "worship" but refers instead to the missionary activity of proclaiming the name of the Lord to other people (cf. Exod 33:19; 34:5), as suggested in the NIV translation: "At that time people began to call on the name of the Lord."[233] The line initiated by the replacing of Seth has

---

233 See Jiří Moskala, "Mission in the Old Testament," in *Message, Mission, and Unity of the Church*, ed. Ángel Manuel Rodríguez (Silver Spring, MD: Biblical Research Institute, 2013), 65–66.

restored the presence of God and thus ensured the transmission of the seed of salvation. This verse sets the stage for the following chapter, which records the revised and promising genealogy of Adam.

THE GENEALOGY OF ADAM (5:1–32)

The genealogy of Adam naturally follows the reference to the birth of Seth (4:25), recapturing the broken line and recovering the promised "seed." This is the second time that the keyword *toledot* "genealogy" is used (5:1; cf. 2:4a), thus implying a direct connection with that text. This identification as "genealogy" is confirmed not only by the structure of the text, but also by its functions.

THE GENEALOGICAL STRUCTURE

The genealogical style is characterized by its monotonous tone and by the regularity of its introductory and concluding formula, which mark the successive degrees of its progression. Thus, the creation story regularly begins with the same phrase, "God said" (1:3, 6, 9, 11, 14, 20, 24), and ends with the same phrase, "so the evening and the morning were the *x* day" (1:5, 8, 13, 19, 23). Likewise, the genealogy of Adam begins with the same phrase, "*x* lived *x* years, and he begot" (5:3, 6, 9, 12, 15, 18, 21, 25, 28), and ends with the same phrase, "all the days of *x* were *x*; and he died" (5:5, 8, 11, 14, 17, 20, 27, 31).[234] It is noteworthy that the formula that is used in this genealogy (as in chapter 11) consistently indicates a precise number of years when "he begot," just as it does when "he died." This specification suggests the intention of the biblical author to emphasize the chronological accuracy of this information. In addition, the use of the causative verbal form (*hiphil*) to refer to the begetting process *wayyoled* "he begot" (5:4, 7, 10, etc.) means "a direct physical offspring" (cf. Judg 11:1; 1 Chr 1:34; 8:9; 2 Chr 11:21). This particular feature is unique in the Bible and the ANE.[235] This chronological intention, which parallels the creation story, confirms the chronological nature of the account of creation: the week days have to be taken literally, just as the number of years in the genealogy of Adam.

In addition, a number of specific features characterize this genealogy:

1. The regularity of the flow is broken in connection to four members who are highlighted because of their particular significance. First, we note the prominent place of Adam, which occurs four times in the chapter and its genealogy (5:3–5), is exceptionally prefaced (5:1–3) with a special reference to his creation in Genesis 1:26–28. Secondly, the section on **Enoch**, the seventh in the list (5:21–24), deviates from the usual language. Instead of the regular formula "he lived," we have "walked with God"; and instead of "he died," we have "and he was not, for God took him" (5:24). Thirdly, the section on Lamech, the ninth in the list, elaborates on the hopes associated with Noah (5:29). And finally, the section on Noah (5:32) refers only to the birth of his three sons and does not mention his death, which will be recorded much later in Genesis 9:29. The reason for this focus on Noah, the tenth and last in

---

234 See Doukhan, *The Genesis Creation Story*, 175–176.

235 For a discussion and a refutation of the argument of the Babylonian influence on the literary patterns of those genealogies, see R. Wilson, "Old Testament Genealogies," *JBL* 94, no. 2 (1975): 186–188; cf. G. F. Hasel, "The Genealogies of Gen 5 and 11 and Their Alleged Babylonian Background," *AUSS* 16 (1978): 361–374.

the list, is obviously in anticipation of the upcoming stories about the flood, in which he is the main hero and the second Adam of humankind.

2. The genealogy is exclusive, only focusing on the descendants of Seth and omitting Cain and his descendants. This special attention is intended to bring out the line of Seth, from which the chosen people and the messianic seed will emerge. As for the descendants of Cain, they are not worth mentioning since they will all disappear in the flood and have no further history.

3. The genealogy displays parallels and contrasts with the genealogy of Cain (4:17–22). While the two genealogies refer to common names, or at least similar sounding names (Qenan/Cain; Enoch/Enoch; Methushelah/Methushael; Lamech/Lamech), the supplementary information associated with the respective names is abundant enough to avoid confusion. In addition, the nearly diametrical contrast between some members of the two genealogies suggests a clear intention to oppose them in order to convey a definite theological lesson. For instance, Lamech—the seventh from Cain—a criminal who ignores God is contrasted with Enoch—the seventh from Seth—who walks with God. The last note of the genealogy of Cain, closing with Lamech boasting about his crimes, contrasts also with the last note of the genealogy of Adam, closing with another Lamech boasting of his son, who will bring comfort and life. While the genealogy of Cain is tainted with blood and satisfied with human achievements that abort on the seventh step, the genealogy of Seth reports of descendants walking with God and blessed with long life. They will reach the tenth generation, which extends into the future through Noah's sons, and, through Shem, to the coming of the long-awaited Messiah.

THE FUNCTIONS OF GENEALOGY

The genealogy of Adam plays three definite functions. First, it speaks about the historical nature of the events that occurred from the time of creation to the time of the flood. These events are not the product of mythic imagination or the symbolic illustrations of theological truths. From Adam to Noah, these historical events are associated with real men who lived and died. They belong to time; their days are precisely numbered, each one with a different span of time. Secondly, it underlines the continuity from Genesis 1 to Genesis 5. God's blessing of fruitfulness given at creation (1:28) has been fulfilled. The transmission of the "image of God" has thus been seamlessly passed on and, with it, the hope of the promised seed. The genealogy of Adam thus serves as a bridge from creation to the flood and God's subsequent re-creation; it spans from Adam to Noah who, in a sense, becomes the new "Adam" who will repopulate the world. Thirdly, it reminds us not only of the blessings and transferral of life, but also of the tragic effect of sin's curse and its deadly results. However long these men lived, they were still mortal. So while the genealogy of Adam is separated from the genealogy of Cain and enjoys God's protection and blessing, it remains affected by the fall (3:17–19). Struggling with evil, they cling to the Lord, their only hope of salvation.

5:1–2. THE CREATION OF HUMANKIND

GEN 5:1–2 NKJV	GEN 5:1–2 ESV
1 This is the book of the genealogy of Adam. In the day that God created man, He made him in the likeness of God.	**1** This is the book of the generations of Adam. When God created man, he made him in the likeness of God.

2 He created them male and female, and blessed them and called them Mankind in the day they were created.	**2** Male and female he created them, and he blessed them and named them Man when they were created.

5:1 **This is the book of the genealogy of Adam**. This is the only genealogy that begins with someone who has not been generated. Adam was not born of a woman but begins his life through the hand of his Maker, at creation. This first step reconnects, therefore, with the account of creation as told in Genesis 1, yet with some variations. The title *toledot* "genealogy" echoes the conclusion of the creation story also identified as *toledot* "genealogy" (2:4a). Unlike the genealogy of creation, which is simply called "genealogy" and appears in the conclusion, this genealogy appears in the introduction and is the only one in the book of Genesis that is qualified by the word *seper* "book." The reason for this variation is unclear. Perhaps this contrast is intended to distinguish this genealogy from the one of Cain that has just been given (4:17–22), to suggest that this is the only genealogy, in opposition to the one of Cain, that should be taken into consideration for the survival of humankind.[236]

In the day that God created. This phrase parallels the introductory phrase of the creation story (1:1; cf. 2:4b). The reference to the creation of humans in God's image is given in the abbreviated form *bidmut 'Elohim* "in the likeness of God," using only the word *demut* "likeness" instead of the more complete *betsalmenu kidmutenu* "in Our image, according to Our likeness" of Genesis 1:26.

5:2 **He created them male and female.** The text repeats the same motifs of blessing in connection to the creation of humans as a couple. The only new idea in regard to Genesis 1 is the specification given here of the meaning of the name "Adam" (KJV, JPS) as referring to both the man and the woman (hence its translation by the term "mankind" in the NKJV). This last emphasis on "blessing" both "male and female" and on the generic sense of "Adam" naturally introduces the first genealogy of humankind, in fulfillment of the divine promise of fruitfulness (1:28).

5:3–5. THE FIRST MAN: ADAM

GEN 5:3–5 NKJV	GEN 5:3–5 ESV
3 And Adam lived one hundred and thirty years, and begot a son in his own likeness, after his image, and named him Seth.	**3** When Adam had lived 130 years, he fathered a son in his own likeness, after his image, and named him Seth.
4 After he begot Seth, the days of Adam were eight hundred years; and he had sons and daughters.	**4** The days of Adam after he fathered Seth were 800 years; and he had other sons and daughters.
5 So all the days that Adam lived were nine hundred and thirty years; and he died.	**5** Thus all the days that Adam lived were 930 years, and he died.

5:3 The image of God is transmitted only through Seth. The expression used in Genesis 1:26 is now used in its complete form, this time with the two words *bidmuto ketsalmo*, **in his own likeness after his image,** to avoid any ambiguity. The echo between the two phrases is reinforced through the literary device of the chiasm. Instead

---

236 This explanation has been suggested by the Midrash (Gen. Rab. 24).

of the sequence *tselem-demut* "image-form" of Genesis 1, we have now the sequence *demut-tselem* "form-image." The intention of this reverse formula (chiasm) is made to suggest the faithful transmission of the image of God. On the other hand, the text does not say that Seth (like Adam) was made in the image of God, but in the image of Adam. This shift of language is significant. Although the original "image of God" will be transmitted, it will now be passed on through the sinful human channel.[237]

5:5 All the days that Adam lived. The extraordinary longevity of the first humans before the flood has baffled ancient and modern interpreters.[238] Yet, it makes sense in the theological context of creation associated with God's blessing and gift of life (1:28; cf. 5:2). It is also confirmed by the decreased lifespan after the flood, an indication of regression rather than progression. In addition, the widespread tradition of ancestors with extensive lifespans testifies that this exceptional quality was a common memory among ancient peoples. A number of arguments have been suggested to explain human longevity in early history. According to the SDABC:

> The longevity of the antediluvian race may be attributed to the following causes: (1) the original vitality with which mankind was endowed at creation, (2) superior piety and intelligence, (3) the residual effect of the fruit of the tree of life, (4) the superior quality of the available food, and (5) divine grace in postponing the execution of the penalty of sin.[239]

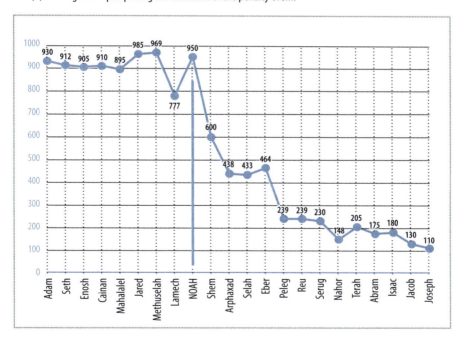

---

237 See Ellen G. White's comments on this text: "Concerning the creation of Adam it is said, 'In the likeness of God made he him;' but man after the Fall, 'begat a son in his *own* likeness, after *his* image.' While Adam was created sinless, in the likeness of God, Seth, like Cain, inherited the fallen nature of his parents" (PP 80).

238 For a discussion on human degeneration and genetic decay, see J. C. Sanford, *Genetic Entropy and the Mystery of the Genome* (Waterloo: FMS Publications, 2008) where the author, a plant geneticist, points to scientific observation and argues against the premises of modern Darwinism that human genomes are not evolving to something better but that they are decaying and degenerating.

239 SDABC 1:245–246.

5:6–20. FROM SETH TO JARED

GEN 5:6–20 NKJV	GEN 5:6–20 ESV
6 Seth lived one hundred and five years, and begot Enosh.	**6** When Seth had lived 105 years, he fathered Enosh.
7 After he begot Enosh, Seth lived eight hundred and seven years, and had sons and daughters.	**7** Seth lived after he fathered Enosh 807 years and had other sons and daughters.
8 So all the days of Seth were nine hundred and twelve years; and he died.	**8** Thus all the days of Seth were 912 years, and he died.
9 Enosh lived ninety years, and begot Cainan.	**9** When Enosh had lived 90 years, he fathered Kenan.
10 After he begot Cainan, Enosh lived eight hundred and fifteen years, and had sons and daughters.	**10** Enosh lived after he fathered Kenan 815 years and had other sons and daughters.
11 So all the days of Enosh were nine hundred and five years; and he died.	**11** Thus all the days of Enosh were 905 years, and he died.
12 Cainan lived seventy years, and begot Mahalalel.	**12** When Kenan had lived 70 years, he fathered Mahalalel.
13 After he begot Mahalalel, Cainan lived eight hundred and forty years, and had sons and daughters.	**13** Kenan lived after he fathered Mahalalel 840 years and had other sons and daughters.
14 So all the days of Cainan were nine hundred and ten years; and he died.	**14** Thus all the days of Kenan were 910 years, and he died.
15 Mahalalel lived sixty-five years, and begot Jared.	**15** When Mahalalel had lived 65 years, he fathered Jared.
16 After he begot Jared, Mahalalel lived eight hundred and thirty years, and had sons and daughters.	**16** Mahalalel lived after he fathered Jared 830 years and had other sons and daughters.
17 So all the days of Mahalalel were eight hundred and ninety-five years; and he died.	**17** Thus all the days of Mahalalel were 895 years, and he died.
18 Jared lived one hundred and sixty-two years, and begot Enoch.	**18** When Jared had lived 162 years, he fathered Enoch.
19 After he begot Enoch, Jared lived eight hundred years, and had sons and daughters.	**19** Jared lived after he fathered Enoch 800 years and had other sons and daughters.
20 So all the days of Jared were nine hundred and sixty-two years; and he died.	**20** Thus all the days of Jared were 962 years, and he died.

Like Adam, every patriarch will ultimately die. The phrase "he died" concludes each paragraph of the genealogy (5:5, 8, 11, 14, 17, 20, 27, 31). However long the patriarch's life was, this advantage did not prevent him from dying. The writer of the book of Ecclesiastes ponders this tragic paradox, which he qualifies as "vanity" (Eccl 6:3–6). Of the five patriarchs following Adam, namely Seth, Enosh, Cainan, Mahalalel, and Jared, nothing is known. Yet they are important insofar as they ensure the passing of the seed—and the image of God—and prepare for the messianic hope (Luke 3:37–38). Each name evokes the presence of God through that process:

Seth (5:6) means "put in the place," alluding to God's replacing the lost Abel (4:25).

Enosh (5:7) is associated with the calling of the Lord (4:26).

Cainan (5:9) is a variation of the name "Cain," reminding us of Eve's exclamation involving God in her first childbirth experience (4:1, see our commentary above). In fact, the reuse of such a name recalling the sad figure of Cain may be intentional to signify the hope of repairing and reshaping the failed history.

Mahalalel (5:16) means "praising God."

Jared (5:18) implies the idea of God's coming down. The name means something like "O (God) come down!" or "May (God) come down" (see 11:5; Exod 34:5; Num 11:25).

5:21–24. THE SEVENTH MAN: ENOCH

GEN 5:21–24 NKJV	GEN 5:21–24 ESV
21 Enoch lived sixty-five years, and begot Methuselah.	**21** When Enoch had lived 65 years, he fathered Methuselah.
22 After he begot Methuselah, Enoch walked with God three hundred years, and had sons and daughters.	**22** Enoch walked with God after he fathered Methuselah 300 years and had other sons and daughters.
23 So all the days of Enoch were three hundred and sixty-five years.	**23** Thus all the days of Enoch were 365 years.
24 And Enoch walked with God; and he *was* not, for God took him.	**24** Enoch walked with God, and he was not, for God took him.

5:21–23 This break from the regular rhythm of the genealogy confirms the historical authenticity of the report. It is with this historical tone that the genealogy places Enoch in the seventh place from Adam. Although the number seven may convey a spiritual message, it is done with the strong assumption that Enoch is a historical individual and not a legendary hero. In fact, his place at the seventh step not only signals some kind of climax in the generations, it also hints at the high effect of his historical presence, the spiritual importance of this individual.

5:24 Enoch walked with God. The change of the text to "walked with God," which is repeated twice (5:22, 24), instead of the usual refrain "he lived," and the change to "he was not, for God took him," instead of the usual "and he died," suggests a significant difference from all the other patriarchs.

The phrase "he walked with God," which is only used for Enoch and Noah (6:9), means intimate and daily companionship with God (1 Sam 25:15). The Hebrew verb *wayyithallek* "he walked" is the same verb describing God's presence in the Garden of Eden (3:8) and in the tabernacle (2 Sam 7:6). The phrase "he was not, for God took him" is also unique to Enoch, focusing on the unexplained fact that he disappeared and no one knew where (Heb 11:5). The same verb *laqakh* "take" is used to describe the assumption of Elijah when the Lord "took" him in a whirlwind into heaven (2 Kgs 2:3, 10–11) and to express the eschatological hope of the psalmist (Ps 73:24).[240] The

---

240 The linguistic echo between the word *'akharit* "end" (Ps 73:17) and the word *'akhar* "after" (Ps 73:24; see YLT: "after honour"; NJB: "in the wake of your glory") suggests that the psalmist has in mind an eschatological event concerning the ultimate destiny of God's children (Ps 73:15) and not an experience that will take place in the course of the present life or even immediately after death.

author of the epistle to the Hebrews explains that Enoch "did not see death" (Heb 11:5). Jewish as well as Christian traditions have retained this interpretation.[241]

5:25–27. THE LONGEST LIFE: METHUSELAH

GEN 5:25–27 NKJV	GEN 5:25–27 ESV
25 Methuselah lived one hundred and eighty-seven years, and begot Lamech.	**25** When Methuselah had lived 187 years, he fathered Lamech.
26 After he begot Lamech, Methuselah lived seven hundred and eighty-two years, and had sons and daughters.	**26** Methuselah lived after he fathered Lamech 782 years and had other sons and daughters.
27 So all the days of Methuselah were nine hundred and sixty-nine years; and he died.	**27** Thus all the days of Methuselah were 969 years, and he died.

Not only did Enoch not die, he also begot the biblical person who would live the longest life—outliving Adam himself. The fact, however, that the Bible does not record anyone living beyond a thousand years, unlike the antediluvian heroic kings of the Sumerians, who were said to reach an age span of six thousand to seventy-two thousand years, illustrates the nonmythological nature of the biblical material.

5:28–31. LAMECH

GEN 5:28–31 NKJV	GEN 5:28–31 ESV
28 Lamech lived one hundred and eighty-two years, and had a son.	**28** When Lamech had lived 182 years, he fathered a son
29 And he called his name Noah, saying, "This *one* will comfort us concerning our work and the toil of our hands, because of the ground which the LORD has cursed."	**29** and called his name Noah, saying, "Out of the ground that the LORD has cursed this one shall bring us relief from our work and from the painful toil of our hands."
30 After he begot Noah, Lamech lived five hundred and ninety-five years, and had sons and daughters.	**30** Lamech lived after he fathered Noah 595 years and had other sons and daughters.
31 So all the days of Lamech were seven hundred and seventy-seven years; and he died.	**31** Thus all the days of Lamech were 777 years, and he died.

The section on Lamech is the longest of all, essentially focusing on his son Noah, whose name is the only one that receives an explanation (5:29). While the name of Noah is etymologically derived from the word *nakh* "rest," it is here related to the word *nakham* "comfort," as explained in the phrase **he called his name Noah, saying this one will comfort us** (5:29). Thus, behind Noah's name we hear the ideas of both "rest" and "comfort," related concepts that Ezekiel 5:13 arranges in a parallel relation: "I will cause my fury to rest [*nakh*] upon them, and I will be comforted [*nakham*]" (KJV). Furthermore, this double meaning anticipates the recurring play on the name of Noah in the flood story through the keywords *nakh* "rest" (8:4), *nakham* "comfort" (6:6 [Heb]), and *nikhoakh* "soothing" (8:21 [Heb]). It is also noteworthy that the Hebrew word *nakham*, translated "comfort," has the connotation of "revenge" (see

---

241 According to Jewish interpretation, Enoch entered alive in the paradise with eight other righteous men (Der. Er. Zut. ch. 1; cf. Sir 49:14; 1 Clem 9:3).

Ezek 5:13 NKJV, NIV). This association of thoughts renders the biblical view of judgment, which relates the dimension of grace in "comfort" and "rest" to the dimension of justice in "avenge."

The reference to the curse of the ground (5:29) recalls the curse after the fall (3:17). In this, we see an expression of Lamech's hope in Noah as the long-awaited "new Adam" through whom the messianic seed will survive and thus ensure the redemption of humankind.

5:32. NOAH'S GENEALOGY

GEN 5:32 NKJV	GEN 5:32 ESV
32 And Noah was five hundred years old, and Noah begot Shem, Ham, and Japheth.	**32** After Noah was 500 years old, Noah fathered Shem, Ham, and Japheth.

Noah's genealogy, the last link mentioned in Adam's bloodline, is the shortest section and incomplete. Yet it will resume after the narrative parenthesis concerning the wickedness and judgment of the antediluvians and conclude much later, following the flood story, with the mention of Noah's death (9:29). Noah's three sons, Shem, Ham, and Japheth, will follow him into the ark and will engender the three branches of humankind (10:1–32). **Shem** is mentioned as the first of Noah's three sons, although he was not the firstborn,[242] because it is through him that Abraham and the chosen people will emerge and, hence, through him that the messianic seed will arise. Their names are not explained, but their meaning may reflect a specific peculiarity associated with the history of the tribes they represent. **Shem** means "name," perhaps alluding to the religious name and reputation of Israel, bearing the name of God. **Ham** may be related to the Egyptian "Keme," meaning the black land, referring to the land of Egypt.[243] The name **Japheth** could be related to the Greek "Iapetos," the name of one of the Greek mythological heroes; in the biblical memory, it also plays on the word *yapt* "extend," referring to the extension of space granted prophetically to Japheth (9:27). Interestingly, the word *shem* "name" of Shem is the only name that does not etymologically refer to an ethnic or space entity but to a spiritual quality.

THE FLOOD (6:1–7:24)

The genealogy of Adam (5:1–32) not only connects with the preceding genealogy, namely, the creation story (2:4a), but it also contains the promise of the survival of humankind through Noah. The mention of Noah who "will comfort" (5:29) anticipates the event of the flood. The Hebrew verb *nakham* recurs in the next chapter, this time to describe God's "regret" (*nakham*) to have "made man on the earth" (6:6). Paradoxically, the divine regret contains the comfort for humankind. The flood, God's response to human wickedness, is given as a second creation. This lesson is conveyed through the structure of the text, constructed on the number seven and the numerous echoes of the creation accounts.

---

242 See SDABC 1:248.
243 For Ham as a synonym of Egypt, see Pss 78:51; 105:23, 27; 106:22.

THE STRUCTURE OF THE FLOOD STORY

Several studies have shown that the flood narrative (6:1–9:17) follows the pattern of a large chiasmus,[244] in which each theme has its corresponding part in a reverse order, like a mirror:

A Divine repentance: Fruitful and multiply, violence (6:1–6)
  B Divine judgment: Resolution to destroy the earth (6:7–22)
    C Command to enter the ark (7:1–10)
      D Beginning of the flood (7:11–16)
        E Rising of waters (7:17–24)
          F Divine remembrance (8:1a)
        E$_1$ Receding of waters (8:1b–6)
      D$_1$ Drying of the earth (8:7–14)
    C$_1$ Command to leave the ark (8:15–19)
  B$_1$ Divine grace: Resolution to preserve the earth (8:20–22)
A$_1$ Divine blessing: Fruitful and multiply, prevention of violence, covenant (9:1–17)

In addition to this larger thematic structure, the event of the flood per se, from its preparation leading to the making of the ark (6:1–22) to its completion with the flooding of the earth (7:1–24), is marked by seven divine actions:

1. "The Lord said" (6:3): human flesh (6:1–4)
2. "The Lord saw" (6:5): great wickedness (6:5)
3. "The Lord was sorry" (6:6): divine repentance (6:6)
4. "So the Lord said" (6:7): divine judgment (6:7–12)
5. "And God said to Noah" (6:13): making the ark (6:13–22)
6. "Then the Lord said to Noah" (7:1): entering the ark (7:1–16a)
7. "And the Lord shut him in" (7:16b): waters on the earth (7:16b–24)

The symmetric character of these structures testifies to "a literary cohesion that can best be explained as the product of one hand."[245]

THE PREPARATION OF THE FLOOD (6:1–22)

6:1–6. DIVINE REPENTANCE

GEN 6:1–6 NKJV	GEN 6:1–6 ESV
1 Now it came to pass, when men began to multiply on the face of the earth, and daughters were born to them,	**1** When man began to multiply on the face of the land and daughters were born to them,
2 that the sons of God saw the daughters of men, that they *were* beautiful; and they took wives for themselves of all whom they chose.	**2** the sons of God saw that the daughters of man were attractive. And they took as their wives any they chose.

---

244 Our structure follows Anderson's proposal with some variations, see Bernard W. Anderson, "From Analysis to Synthesis: The Interpretation of Genesis 1–11, *JBL* 97, no. 1 (1978): 23–39, chart on p. 38.

245 Mathews, *Genesis 1–11:26*, 352–353.

3 And the Lᴏʀᴅ said, "My Spirit shall not strive with man forever, for he *is* indeed flesh; yet his days shall be one hundred and twenty years."	**3** Then the Lᴏʀᴅ said, "My Spirit shall not abide in man forever, for he is flesh: his days shall be 120 years."
4 There were giants on the earth in those days, and also afterward, when the sons of God came in to the daughters of men and they bore *children* to them. Those *were* the mighty men who *were* of old, men of renown.	**4** The Nephilim were on the earth in those days, and also afterward, when the sons of God came in to the daughters of man and they bore children to them. These were the mighty men who were of old, the men of renown.
5 Then the Lᴏʀᴅ saw that the wickedness of man *was* great in the earth, and *that* every intent of the thoughts of his heart *was* only evil continually.	**5** The Lᴏʀᴅ saw that the wickedness of man was great in the earth, and that every intention of the thoughts of his heart was only evil continually.
6 And the Lᴏʀᴅ was sorry that He had made man on the earth, and He was grieved in His heart.	**6** And the Lᴏʀᴅ regretted that he had made man on the earth, and it grieved him to his heart.

Following the genealogy, the text focuses now on the motif of human birth and its multiplying effect. This is the first divine intervention. Yet what was meant to be a divine blessing got disconnected from the divine influence and was thereby reduced to a mere human enterprise: "the sons of God saw the daughters of men" (6:2, 4). As a result, humans began to lose their spiritual vocation (6:3). After an introduction describing the gravity of human evil, God's response is given in four tenses, in a literary fashion that recalls the structure of the creation story:

> When men began to multiply … the sons of God saw the daughters of men … (6:1–2)
> The Lord said (6:3–4)

6:1–2 The sons of God. The identity of the "sons of God" has puzzled interpreters, who have suggested three main options: angels, kings, or the descendants of Seth. The "angel" interpretation has been advocated by some Jewish authors, especially during the Hellenistic period,[246] and adopted by some early Church Fathers.[247] This interpretation was later attested in Rashi's commentary[248] and in modern authors who read this text in relation to Greek and ANE mythologies.[249] The "kings" interpretation has been introduced by Jewish writers of the second century AD, who did not feel comfortable with the "angel" interpretation for the reason that angels could not engage in sexual relations,[250] and by modern interpreters, who relate this text to Akkadian literature.[251] The "Sethite" interpretation was defended by a number of Jewish exegetes, including the traditional Midrash[252] and the great Ibn Ezra,[253] and

---

246 See 1 Enoch 6:22, Jubilees 5:1, the Septuagint ad loc., Philo (*On Giants* 2:17–19), Josephus (*Jewish Antiquities* 1.3.1).

247 See Justin, *Second Apology* 5; Irenaeus, *Against Heresies* 4.36, 4; Clement of Alexandria, *The Instructor* 3.2; Tertullian, *On the Veiling of Virgins* 7; etc.

248 See Miqraot Gedolot, on 6:1–2.

249 See Westerman, *Genesis 1–11*, 378.

250 See Tg. Onq., ad loc.

251 See David J. A. Clines, "The Significance of the 'Sons of God' Episode (Genesis 6:1–4) in the Context of the 'Primeval History' (Genesis 1–110)," *JSOT* 13 (1979): 34–35.

252 Gen. Rab. 26:5.

253 Miqraot Gedolot, ad loc.

on the Christian side by Church Fathers such as Chrysostom[254] and Augustine,[255] and Reformers like Calvin.[256] The "Sethite" interpretation has the advantage of fitting the immediate background of our story, which pits two camps in opposition. The controversy begins with the two brothers, Cain versus Abel, and extends to the family of Cain versus the family of Seth, who replaced Abel.[257] The opposition between the two camps can be established on the basis of the following contrasts:

1. Faith in God versus human works. Cain's offering expressed his will to achieve salvation by his own human works, while Abel's sacrifice expressed his faith in God's act of redemption through the "seed to come" (4:1–15). On the same note, the genealogy of Cain's lineage is characterized by a deliberate omission of any reference to God (4:16–24), while the genealogy of Seth's lineage (5:1–32) is regularly punctuated with the presence of God: in its beginning, with Enosh who initiates the call of the Lord (4:26); in its seventh step, with Enoch who "walked with God" and was taken by Him (5:24); and at its end, with Noah who will reverse the curse of the Lord (5:29) and **found grace in the eyes of the Lord** (6:8).

2. The transmission of God's image versus the transmission of man's image. While the genealogy of Adam begins with a lengthy introduction acknowledging God's creation (5:1–2) and the transmission of God's image to Seth (5:3), Cain's genealogy refers only to himself, ignoring the image of God that is in him. Cain's arrogance is underscored by the different way Adam's and Cain's wives are referred to. While Adam's wife is designated by her name "Eve," Cain's wife is mentioned as such, without any name. With Adam, Eve is recognized and respected as a person; she plays an equal role in the begetting process. Cain's wife, on the other hand, is simply a tool to be used for his own purpose; she is merely a "wife" and therefore only the name of Cain is mentioned.

Implying the begetting process, namely, the giving birth to sons, the phrases "sons of God" and "sons of men" should be understood in the literary context of genealogies. While the line of Adam identifies itself in relation to God, the line of Cain identifies itself only within the human connection, ignoring the divine. This does not mean that the descendants of Cain are ontologically different from the descendants of Adam. Both lines derive from Adam and both carry the same benefit of the image of God. But while the Adam-Seth line is defined in relation to God as "sons of God," an expression that is often used in the Bible to refer to God's people (Deut 14:1; 32:5–6; Isa 1:2; cf. 2 Sam 7:14; etc.), the line of Cain is defined only as "sons of man." The use of this title is also intentional to suggest the contrast with the other group of humans. The phrase "sons of God" should therefore apply to the line of Adam through Seth, while the phrase "sons of man" should apply to the line of Cain.

6:2 They took wives for themselves. The phrase "took wives" is normally used for the act of marriage (11:29; 24:48; Judg 14:3; etc.) and excludes the mythological interpretation involving heavenly beings. Note that Jesus Himself refers to these marrying ones as humans (Matt 24:38). The specification "took for themselves" suggests the intention to counter God's divine operation, when "He took" the wife and

---

254 See *Homilies on Genesis* 22.2.

255 See *City of God* 15.23.

256 See *Commentaries,* 238.

257 See Sven Fockner, "Reopening the Discussion: Another Contextual Look at the Sons of God," *JSOT* 32, no. 4 (2008): 435–456.

brought her to Adam (2:22). The "sons of man" want to usurp God's place, an attitude that is reflected in the phrase **saw … that they were beautiful** (Heb. *tob* "good"), which is reminiscent of God's response to creation: "saw that it was good" (1:4, 10, 12, 18, 21, 25). This replacement of God leads them to actions that are no longer in keeping with God's plan in creation but in line with their own sinful desires. The use of the plural "wives" suggests the introduction of polygamy. The phrase **of all whom they chose** suggests wild and uncontrolled sexual activities outside of the divine Law, including polygamy,[258] bestiality, and adultery.[259]

6:3 The Lord said. The divine word, which originally triggered creation (1:3), is now negating it. The first word of God is *lo'* "not," which affects God's connection with His creation.

My Spirit will not. The first effect of this negation reaches the very source of creation and concerns the first divine initiative of creation, when "the Spirit of God was hovering over the face of waters" (1:2b). The phrase "on the face of waters" resonates in the beginning of the current chapter in the phrase "on the face of the earth," which introduces our story. We are back at the moment of pre-creation, when the earth was still "without form, and void" (1:2a). The word "not" negates, then, the whole process that took place during the creation week. As such, the "not" also negates the biological existence of those living beings who needed the *ruakh* "the breath of life" in order to survive (Ps 104:29–30). And because the "Spirit" (*ruakh*) is also the principle of spirituality (Num 27:18; Isa 63:10–11), the "not" also affects the spiritual domain and their relationship with God.

Strive. The Hebrew verb *yadon* "strive," from the root *dun* "judge," should be interpreted within the context of judgment in the sense of to "plead"—a usage that is attested in Jeremiah (Jer 30:13)—or to "judge" in favor (30:6). The iniquities of the antediluvian patriarchs, just as the Israel of Jeremiah, have reached a stage of incurability (Jer 30:12). God cannot plead for them nor grant forgiveness any longer. The divine pleading grace cannot last forever. It is from that perspective that we may understand the measure of **one hundred years and twenty years** as referring to the time until the advent of the flood, a period of grace to allow for the preparation for that event (1 Pet 3:20).

6:4 They were giants. The qualification of "giants" does not just refer to the Cainites but is a broad statement applying to the general population of that time. The Hebrew word *nepilim* "giants" is unclear;[260] the traditional translation "giant" comes from the Septuagint (*gigantes*). Since the word derives from the root *napal* "fall," it could be argued that the term *nepilim* refers to the "fallen ones," perhaps an allusion to their moral degeneration. On the other hand, the expression *gibborim*, **mighty men,** refers to the violent character of these men (Pss 52:3–5 [1–3]; 120:2–4), a description consistent with the portrayal of the Cainites (4:23–24).

6:5 This is the second divine intervention (cf. 6:1–4). In parallel to the creation

---

258 The construction of the verse, the preposition *mikkol* "of all" suggests that they took many wives and implies the first practice of polygamy. See Davidson, *The Flame of Yahweh*, 184. See D. Clines's translation: "taking for themselves wives of as many women as they chose" ("The Significance of the 'Sons of God' Episode in the Context of the 'Primeval History' [Genesis 1–11]," *JSOT* 13 [1979]: 36).

259 According to Rashi, this phrase refers to adultery, homosexuality, and bestiality; see Miqraot Gedolot, ad loc.

260 The use of the same word *nepilim* in Numbers 13:33 does not necessarily mean that these men are of the same origin, which would mean that they had survived the flood along with Noah and his family; this interpretation would go against the sense of the biblical story. This qualification is a hyperbolic statement used by the fearful spies as an argument to discourage the confrontation.

story, the divine seeing immediately follows the divine word: **The Lord said** (6:3) … **Then the Lord saw … the wickedness of man was great** (6:5). This line also responds to the refrain of creation "and God saw … that it was good" (1:4). But here the original "good" (*tob*) of God's creation has been replaced by its contrary—"wickedness" (*ra'ah*).

Every intent of the thoughts of his heart. The "great wickedness" does not refer to some specific actions or punctual occasions; it describes a thorough and lasting condition. It has reached the root, the profound motivations of the human heart where God finds "only evil" and "continually."

6:6 In this third divine intervention, the language is reminiscent of creation. God regrets that He created man. The divine "regret" is associated with the divine sadness. God **was grieved in his heart**. The Hebrew verb *'atsab* "grieve" is the opposite of joy (Neh 8:10) and refers to mental pain (3:16). God's emotion has to do with His love for humans. Significantly, the Hebrew verb *nakham*, translated "sorry," contains the positive nuance of "grace" and "love." This is why the translation "sorry" for the Hebrew word *nakham* is not satisfactory and does not fully account for God's sentiments. The divine "regret" does not imply that God has changed His mind;[261] instead, it contains elements of grace and "comfort." Thus, the word *nakham* appears sometimes in parallel with the word *shub* "repent" (Jer 4:28; Jonah 3:9), suggesting the "positive sense: 'have mercy.'"[262] The use of the word *nakham* brings hope into the picture—the prospect of salvation through the flood.

6:7–22. DIVINE JUDGMENT: THE DESTRUCTION OF THE EARTH

GEN 6:7–22 NKJV	GEN 6:7–22 ESV
7 So the Lord said, "I will destroy man whom I have created from the face of the earth, both man and beast, creeping thing and birds of the air, for I am sorry that I have made them."	**7** So the Lord said, "I will blot out man whom I have created from the face of the land, man and animals and creeping things and birds of the heavens, for I am sorry that I have made them."
8 But Noah found grace in the eyes of the Lord.	**8** But Noah found favor in the eyes of the Lord.
9 This is the genealogy of Noah. Noah was a just man, perfect in his generations. Noah walked with God.	**9** These are the generations of Noah. Noah was a righteous man, blameless in his generation. Noah walked with God.
10 And Noah begot three sons: Shem, Ham, and Japheth.	**10** And Noah had three sons, Shem, Ham, and Japheth.
11 The earth also was corrupt before God, and the earth was filled with violence.	**11** Now the earth was corrupt in God's sight, and the earth was filled with violence.
12 So God looked upon the earth, and indeed it was corrupt; for all flesh had corrupted their way on the earth.	**12** And God saw the earth, and behold, it was corrupt, for all flesh had corrupted their way on the earth.
13 And God said to Noah, "The end of all flesh has come before Me, for the earth is filled with violence through them; and behold, I will destroy them with the earth.	**13** And God said to Noah, "I have determined to make an end of all flesh, for the earth is filled with violence through them. Behold, I will destroy them with the earth.

---

261 Simian-Yofre, "*nkhm*," *TDOT* 9:344.

262 Ibid., 347.

14 Make yourself an ark of gopherwood; make rooms in the ark, and cover it inside and outside with pitch.	**14** Make yourself an ark of gopher wood. Make rooms in the ark, and cover it inside and out with pitch.
15 And this is how you shall make it: The length of the ark *shall be* three hundred cubits, its width fifty cubits, and its height thirty cubits.	**15** This is how you are to make it: the length of the ark 300 cubits, its breadth 50 cubits, and its height 30 cubits.
16 You shall make a window for the ark, and you shall finish it to a cubit from above; and set the door of the ark in its side. You shall make it *with* lower, second, and third *decks*.	**16** Make a roof for the ark, and finish it to a cubit above, and set the door of the ark in its side. Make it with lower, second, and third decks.
17 And behold, I Myself am bringing floodwaters on the earth, to destroy from under heaven all flesh in which *is* the breath of life; everything that *is* on the earth shall die.	**17** For behold, I will bring a flood of waters upon the earth to destroy all flesh in which is the breath of life under heaven. Everything that is on the earth shall die.
18 But I will establish My covenant with you; and you shall go into the ark—you, your sons, your wife, and your sons' wives with you.	**18** But I will establish my covenant with you, and you shall come into the ark, you, your sons, your wife, and your sons' wives with you.
19 And of every living thing of all flesh you shall bring two of every *sort* into the ark, to keep *them* alive with you; they shall be male and female.	**19** And of every living thing of all flesh, you shall bring two of every sort into the ark to keep them alive with you. They shall be male and female.
20 Of the birds after their kind, of animals after their kind, and of every creeping thing of the earth after its kind, two of every *kind* will come to you to keep *them* alive.	**20** Of the birds according to their kinds, and of the animals according to their kinds, of every creeping thing of the ground, according to its kind, two of every sort shall come in to you to keep them alive.
21 And you shall take for yourself of all food that is eaten, and you shall gather *it* to yourself; and it shall be food for you and for them."	**21** Also take with you every sort of food that is eaten, and store it up. It shall serve as food for you and for them."
22 Thus Noah did; according to all that God commanded him, so he did.	**22** Noah did this; he did all that God commanded him.

God comes down again to conduct a legal trial investigation before sending the destructive flood.[263] This is the fourth divine intervention. It has been suggested that the repeated formulas indicating the divine examination **The Lord saw …** **God looked** (6:5, 12) and the divine determination to act, **I will destroy** (6:7, 13), denote "juridicial overtones, implying both investigation of the facts and readiness for action."[264] Two sides characterize the divine judgment. On the one hand, it is negative, a sentence of death and destruction against the corrupt earth. On the other hand, it is positive, a word of grace and salvation on behalf of Noah and whoever is found to be just. This contrast is rendered in the text through the literary device of the chiasm, which singles out Noah in opposition to his contemporaries:

---

263 See Davidson, "The Divine Covenant Lawsuit," 72.

264 Sarna, *Genesis*, 47; cf. Umberto Cassuto, *A Commentary on the Book of Genesis*, vol. 2, trans. Israel Abrahams (Jerusalem: Magnes Press, 1964), 57.

A Destruction of the earth (6:7)
    B Noah a just man (6:8–10)
A₁ Corruption of the earth (6:11–12)

6:7 **I will destroy.** The Hebrew word *makhah* "destroy" is presented in a word-play with the preceding word *nakham* "sorry," "comfort," which evokes God's sadness and compassion towards humankind through Noah. While *nakham* suggests the positive face of judgment, *makhah* reveals its negative face. Furthermore, the word *makhah* belongs to the language of judgment. It means, more precisely, to "erase." This "erasing" is seen in a physical destruction that operates in reversal to creation, undoing God's creative acts. But beyond the physical destruction, this act of judgment also refers to being spiritually erased from the book of life (Exod 32:32–33; Ps 69:28–29).

It is noteworthy that the language used here is reminiscent of Genesis 1:26–28, dealing with the creation of humans and their lordship over the animals. Now humans are no longer separated from animals, instead both are put on the same level, **both man and beast**. The listing from humans to birds refers backward to the creation account, omitting the fish for the obvious reason that swimming fish will survive the waters of the flood. In addition, the expression **on the face of the earth** (*'al pney ha'adamah*) echoes Cain's complaint when he was driven from *'al pney ha'adamah* "on the face of the earth" (4:14). The iniquity of the antediluvians is of the same vein as Cain's iniquity. Both imply violence, and both have a cosmic impact.

6:8–9 **Noah found grace in the eyes of the Lord.** The expression "found grace in the eyes of" is often used to express love (Ruth 2:2, 10, 13; Esth 2:15). There is also a sound play between the word *khen* "grace" and the name Noah *noakh* in the next verse, which conveys the idea of "rest" (6:8). The point is that, even in His "regret," God has provided for "grace" (*khen*) through "Noah" (*noakh*). The choice of Noah as the father of the new genealogy is justified on the basis of three qualities.

1. The first word *tsaddiq* "just" occurs here for the first time and recurs in Genesis 7:1, where it is given as the reason why Noah and his family have been preserved. This word describes the intrinsic quality of being "righteous" according to God's criteria. To be "just" is a distinct quality and implies a standard that characterizes God Himself or His Law (Deut 32:4). Noah's righteousness was independent and not the result of any external human influence. He was righteous in spite of the corrupt society around him.

2. The second word *tam* "perfect" describes the quality that made Noah so different "in his generations." The word does not suggest that Noah was sinless, but that he was "complete" in his behavior. Noah was not a hypocrite tolerating compromises and half measures. He was entire in his commitment to God. The term *tam* also contains the idea of being "simple," "naïve." Thus, the word is later applied to Jacob "dwelling in tents" (25:27), suggesting that he was "plain" and not sophisticated. Similarly, Abraham was instructed by God to be *tam* before he was promised to become a father at the ripe age of ninety-nine (17:1). Unlike his contemporaries, Noah believed God's warnings and it was his "naïve" quality that saved him.

3. The third expression "Noah walked with God" has already been used for Enoch, suggesting Noah's faithful companionship with God.

6:10 **And Noah begot.** Of all the sons and daughters of Adam, only Noah, the tenth generation, was retained to produce the next *toledot* "genealogy" (6:9) after the genealogy of Adam (5:1). Noah is thus presented as the immediate successor of Adam, the second first ancestor of humankind.

6:11–12 The earth … was corrupt. The word *shakhat* "corrupt" refers to destruction and annihilation (Dan 9:26). This verb often occurs in the context of war (2 Sam 11:1; 1 Chr 20:1) and killing (Judg 20:21, 25, 35, 42; 1 Sam 26:9). The following word *khamas* "violence" clarifies and confirms this particular connotation. What makes the earth "corrupt" is the violence that predominates there. The verb "corrupt" is used three times in this passage and each time in a different form (*niphal* perfect, *hiphil* perfect, and *hiphil* participle) so as to suggest not only the intensity of corruption, but also its totality; all aspects of corruption are implied. The word "earth" also appears three times, thus reflecting the corruption of its inhabitants. The phrase "all flesh" reveals that humans, as well as animals, are included in God's evaluation of "corruption" (7:21).

6:13–22 God's communication with humans is reestablished through Noah. This is the fifth divine intervention. For the first time after the Garden of Eden, God speaks to humans (6:13) and informs them of His plans. Noah is here presented as a prophet, for "the Lord God does nothing, unless He reveals His secrets to His servants the prophets" (Amos 3:7). Like Daniel, Noah is entrusted with an eschatological prophecy, for it concerns the "end" of the world.[265] Significantly, the word describing the destruction of the world is the same word *shakhat*, which refers to the inner corruption of these beings. The "corruption" (*shakhat*) of the earth leads to the "destruction" (*shakhat*) of the earth. Thus, the divine judgment echoes and corresponds to the state of the earth. God's justice is fair. In fact, the self-destruction of the earth anticipates God's destruction. At this point, God's judgment is directed at Noah, but this time His words are intended for salvation. Grace (*khen*) in Noah (*noakh*) is the other side of judgment. Note the play on words (anagram) between the name "Noah" (*noakh*) and the word "grace" (*khen*). This twofold aspect of God's judgment is clearly stated in the middle of the narrative (6:17–18): God's announcement of His destruction of the earth (6:17) is immediately followed by God's promise of His covenant with Noah (6:18a). Before and after the mention of this divine judgment, God commands Noah to "make." Thus, this text is divided into three sections. First, Noah is asked to "make" the ark that will contain the living beings (6:14–16). Second, God enunciates His judgment (6:17–18a). And third, Noah is asked to fill the ark (6:18b–21). Amazingly, the structure of the divine speech recalls the structure of the creation story, which also mentions first the creation of the containers (1:1–13) and then the creation of their respective content (1:14–30). It is noteworthy that the verb *'asah* "make" also appears seven times in the text (6:14–17, 22), thus echoing the rhythm of creation.

6:14 Make yourself an ark. The Hebrew word *tebah* "ark" is a keyword, as it occurs twenty-six times (out of twenty-eight in the whole Bible) in the flood narrative and seven times in this chapter (6:14 [2x], 15, 16 [2x], 18–19). It is, in fact, an Egyptian loan word (*djebaat*), which designates a divine shrine in the form of a "box."[266] The fact that this rare word is also used again for the "ark" in which the

---

265 The word *qets* "end" is a keyword in the book of Daniel where it appears twenty times out of the sixty-seven occurrences in the whole Bible.

266 The Ebla texts have the cognate term *tiba* designating the sacred "ark of the gods" *tibati-illi*, see M. J. Dahood,

infant Moses was hidden (Exod 2:3) suggests a parallel between the two events: in both cases, the "ark" was a means of protection from the water, allowing for the salvation of God's people and, thus, the survival of the "image of God."

Gopherwood. This is the only occurrence of this tree (*goper*) in the Hebrew Bible; it may refer to cypress wood, which is commonly used in shipbuilding. This identification is confirmed by the use of its homonym *koper* "pitch" at the end of the verse, which suggests a resinous wood. The wood of the tree was used to build the frame of the ark and its sap to make the ark watertight inside and out.

6:15–16 How you shall make it. The Hebrew phrase *zeh 'asher ta'aseh* "how you shall make it" introducing and describing the measurements of the ark is also reminiscent of the sanctuary. The same Hebrew phrase is found only once again in the Hebrew Bible—in relation to the sacrifices on the altar of the tabernacle, where it is translated "this is what you shall offer" (Exod 29:38). It is also noteworthy that the dimensions of the ark are given according to the same standard and with the same words used for the construction of the ark in the tabernacle: *x* cubits length, *y* cubits width, *z* cubits height (Exod 25:10). If the cubit equaled 18 inches or 45 centimeters,[267] 300 cubits for the length of the ark would have equaled 450 feet or 135 meters; 50 cubits for its width would have equaled 75 feet or 22 meters; and 30 cubits for its height would have equaled 45 feet or 13 meters. These measurements have no special symbolic significance; they simply suggest the magnitude of the size of the vessel, which was large enough to accommodate the animals and humans on board. Also, these minute architectural details suggest the historical reality of the ark's construction and the divine concern for the success of the operation. In this respect, the ark parallels the sanctuary, for these are the only two structures that are described in such intricate detail in the Bible. From this parallel, Westermann infers a theological lesson: "The parallel between the ark and the tabernacle has a profound meaning. The people of Israel, which alone have in its midst the place where God reveals His glory, are part of the human race which exists now because it has been preserved by the same God."[268]

6:17 I Myself am bringing floodwaters. God unveils His intention to carry out a twofold judgment towards humankind: bring the flood on the earth, and establish His covenant with Noah. The phrase is unequivocal. God assumes full responsibility for His act as indicated in the construction of the phrase, which puts emphasis on the personal pronoun "I." Not only is *'ani* "I" positioned at the beginning of the sentence, it is also repeated in the locution *hinneni* "behold I." It is God alone who will bring the destructive flood and not any other power or a natural cataclysm. The passage shares a number of common words with the introduction of the second creation story introducing God's creation of humans, including, "on the earth," "all in the earth" (2:5) and "breath of life" (2:7).[269] It is the Creator Himself who will now bring about the destructive flood. This strong monotheistic emphasis in the biblical

. . .

"Eblaite and Biblical Hebrew," *CBQ* 44 (1982): 7, 21–22. It is also noteworthy that the tradition of the sacred association of the *tebah* has survived in ancient rabbinic language where it refers to the chest in the synagogue containing the scrolls of the Pentateuch (Sotah 38b).

267 For the equivalence of measures, see Roland de Vaux, *Ancient Israel: Its Life and Institutions* (Grand Rapids: Eerdmans, 1997), 197.

268 Westermann, *Genesis 1–11*, 421.

269 The Hebrew word for "breath" is different though; in Genesis 2:7, it is the word *neshamah*, implying the singularity of God's act of breathing in the creation of Adam, while in Genesis 6:17, it is the word *ruakh*, implying a more universal scope including humans and animals.

flood story contrasts sharply with the polytheistic emphasis of the other ANE flood stories. While, according to the Babylonian, Sumerian, and Egyptian stories, the flood is decided by a multitude of gods in disagreement with other more compassionate gods who oppose that decision, in the biblical story, justice and compassion both derive from the same God. Only one God makes the decision to destroy the earth, and this is the same God who decides to save the righteous.

The flood. The Hebrew word *mabbul* "flood" is an exclusive designation for the Genesis flood; in other words, its only biblical occurrence is in connection to that event (6–11; cf. Ps 29:10). Furthermore, the comprehensive origin of the flood is unique to the Bible. While the Babylonian flood stories refer only to the phenomenon of a heavenly rain without inundation, the Egyptian stories refer only to the phenomenon of an inundation but emerging from below, without rain.[270] Only in the Bible do we find an inundation caused by water coming from above and below.

One important commonality between all these flood stories is the universal scope of the flood, which is always related to other first events of history, such as creation. For all these texts, the flood affects the whole earth and aims at the destruction and, hence, the ultimate restoration of humankind. In the Sumerian version, one of the gods involved in the flood receives the honorific title of "Preserver of the seed of humanity."[271] Another significant evidence of the universality of the flood is the popular recollection of the flood in so many cultures throughout the world. It has been noted that "there is no Old Testament passage that has so many parallels as the flood."[272] Collections of flood stories range from 88 to 302 texts from all over the world.[273] This testimony of flood stories from so many disparate places implies a worldwide phenomenon and is expressed in our biblical text through the use of inclusive language: "under heaven all flesh," "breath of life," "the earth," and "everything." Although these biblical as well as extrabiblical reports are not, per se, an absolute proof of the universal nature of the flood, they testify to a common memory and tradition (from Noah onwards) regarding the cosmic sweep of that event.

Everything that is on earth shall die. The choice of the Hebrew word *yigwa'* "expire," "die" at the end of the verse is fitting, as it refers back to the loss of the **breath of life**, which has just been mentioned.

6:18 This is the first time that the word *berit* "covenant" occurs in the Bible, implying a radically new condition between God and humanity. The rejection of God has, for the first time, reached a worldwide status so that, for the first time in human history, destruction threatens creation. The Hebrew verb *wahaqimoti*, here translated "I will establish," means instead to "confirm"[274] or "fulfill,"[275] implying a preexisting covenant (26:3; Deut 9:5; 2 Sam 7:25). In fact, Noah already enjoyed a covenant relationship with God (6:8–9). In this context, the covenant is not to be understood as a mutual agreement, as has often been argued, but only as God's promise and commitment to the survival of humankind. It is a one-sided decision. The divine promise of covenant is contrasted with the divine threat of destruction

---

270 For a discussion on the difference between the Babylonian and the Egyptian versions of the flood, see Yahuda, *Language of the Pentateuch*, 208–211.

271 Westermann, *Genesis 1–11*, 401.

272 Ibid., 401–402. For a discussion on the ancient parallels to the flood story, see Wenham, *Genesis 1–15*, 159–166.

273 Westermann, *Genesis 1–11*, 402.

274 Wenham, *Genesis 1–15*, 175.

275 Weinfeld, "*berit*," *TDOT* 2:260.

and should, therefore, be understood within these parameters. Previously, God spoke only to Himself, implying His rejection of humans and their impending destruction. Now God speaks to Noah, implying His relationship with humans and their potential salvation. Significantly, the covenant extends beyond Noah and includes his future sons who, though not yet born, are mentioned in this account.[276] This contrast should inform us about the specific meaning of this "new" covenant: relationship versus rejection, life versus death, future prospect versus dead end. The establishment of God's covenant and its mention—even before the coming of the flood—implies the preeminence of grace over justice. Moreover, it means that, against and despite the backdrop of total annihilation, there is still hope for humankind and the earth.

 6:18b–22 You shall go into the ark. The divine discourse resonates as a promise concerning God's establishment of His covenant (6:18). This is the first of the two promises God gives to Noah. The first promise concerns the bringing of humans and animals into the ark (6:18b–20), and the second promise concerns the food to be taken onboard (6:21). Note the numerous echoes with the creation accounts: "male and female" (6:19; cf. 1:27); "after their/its kind" (6:20; cf. 1:11–12, 21, 24–25); and "for food" (*le'okhla*), which is associated with the verb "take" and responds to the verb "give" in the creation account (6:21; cf. 1:30). Note also the same sequence: "birds," "animals," "creeping thing" (6:20; cf. 1:20–24). These echoes hearkening back to creation suggest that Noah has now become a coworker with the Creator. Interestingly, Noah is the subject of the verb "did" (*'asah*), a verb describing God's acts of creation (1:7, 16, 25–26, 31; 2:2 [2x], 3). Also, the word *ken* "so" is reminiscent of creation's first response to the divine word *wayehi ken* "and it was so." However, Noah's creative operation is still dependent on his obedience and dependence on God. The phrase **did according to all that God commanded** appears twice in the text (6:22; 7:5), thus highlighting the grave importance of Noah's obedience. Here, the verb "did" (*'asah*) responds to God's commandment *'aseh* **make!** and is repeated four times: **you shall make** (6:14–16). Noah's obedience concerns, for the moment, only the making of the ark. It is noteworthy that these last two occurrences of the verb *'asah* "make" or "do" in 6:22 complete the number seven, once again hinting at creation. It is also interesting that the phrase "did all according to what God commanded" is a rare technical formula that recurs especially in connection to the erection of the tabernacle (Exod 39:32, 42; 40:16). This parallel confirms the theological association between creation and the tabernacle.

THE COMPLETION OF THE FLOOD (7:1–24)

7:1–10. COMMAND TO ENTER THE ARK

GEN 7:1–10 NKJV	GEN 7:1–10 ESV
1 Then the LORD said to Noah, "Come into the ark, you and all your household, because I have seen *that* you *are* righteous before Me in this generation.	**1** Then the LORD said to Noah, "Go into the ark, you and all your household, for I have seen that you are righteous before me in this generation.

---

276 See SDABC 1:254.

2 You shall take with you seven each of every clean animal, a male and his female; two each of animals that *are* unclean, a male and his female;

2 Take with you seven pairs of all clean animals, the male and his mate, and a pair of the animals that are not clean, the male and his mate,

3 also seven each of birds of the air, male and female, to keep the species alive on the face of all the earth.

3 and seven pairs of the birds of the heavens also, male and female, to keep their offspring alive on the face of all the earth.

4 For after seven more days I will cause it to rain on the earth forty days and forty nights, and I will destroy from the face of the earth all living things that I have made."

4 For in seven days I will send rain on the earth forty days and forty nights, and every living thing that I have made I will blot out from the face of the ground."

5 And Noah did according to all that the LORD commanded him.

5 And Noah did all that the LORD had commanded him.

6 Noah *was* six hundred years old when the floodwaters were on the earth.

6 Noah was six hundred years old when the flood of waters came upon the earth.

7 So Noah, with his sons, his wife, and his sons' wives, went into the ark because of the waters of the flood.

7 And Noah and his sons and his wife and his sons' wives with him went into the ark to escape the waters of the flood.

8 Of clean animals, of animals that *are* unclean, of birds, and of everything that creeps on the earth,

8 Of clean animals, and of animals that are not clean, and of birds, and of everything that creeps on the ground,

9 two by two they went into the ark to Noah, male and female, as God had commanded Noah.

9 two and two, male and female, went into the ark with Noah, as God had commanded Noah.

10 And it came to pass after seven days that the waters of the flood were on the earth.

10 And after seven days the waters of the flood came upon the earth.

his is the sixth divine intervention. After the command (7:1–4), the biblical author recounts Noah's entering into the ark in two complementary versions, using the literary device of Hebrew parallelism, which proceeds from the general picture to the particular (cf. the two creation accounts 1:1–2:4a ‖ 2:4b–25; cf. Daniel 2 ‖ 7).[277] The first narrative A (7:6–9) outlines the broad contours of Noah's move into the ark. The second narrative A_1 (7:10–16a) provides the details of the operation. Each narrative concludes the same way, with the same refrain "as God had commanded" (7:9, 16). We have, thus, the following structure in four steps:

I. Dating:
A 7:6. General date: Noah was six hundred years. General mention of waters: "flood of waters."
A_1 7:10–12. Precise date: Noah was six hundred years, second month, seventeenth day; waters came after seven days. Specific waters: from "fountains of the great deep" and "windows of heaven."

II. Humans entering the ark:
A 7:7. Noah entered the ark with "his sons, his wife, and his sons' wives."
A_1 7:13. Noah and "his sons, Shem, Ham, and Japheth, and Noah's wife and his three sons' wives."

---

277 For this kind of parallelism, see William H. Shea, *Daniel: A Reader's Guide* (Nampa, ID: Pacific Press, 2005), 94. This parallelism is also identified as "parallelism of greater precision" (Watson, *Traditional Techniques*, 16).

III. Animals entering the ark:

A 7:8. Clean beasts, unclean beasts, birds, everything that creeps.

A₁ 7:14–16a. Every beast after its kind, all cattle after their kind, every creeping thing after its kind, every bird of every sort . . . two by two, of all flesh, male and female.

IV. Refrain:

A 7:9. As God had commanded.

A₁ 7:16b. As God had commanded.

7:1–4 Come into the ark. This is the second time that God addresses Noah in the imperative (cf. 6:14), and this time the divine command concerns Noah's entering the ark: *ba'* **come** (7:1). The reason for this command is God's covenant with Noah (6:8–9, 18).

7:1b Righteous before Me. Noah is found righteous in regard to two factors: (1) "before Me," implying that Noah's righteousness is not inherent to himself but is given according to God, and (2) "in this generation," implying that Noah's righteousness is relative, that is, evaluated within the context of his generation. The subsequent verb carries the imperative force *tiqakh* **you shall take** (7:2) and concerns the animals. Earlier it was only stipulated that Noah should bring "two of every sort" of animals, meaning "couples," into the ark. Now, the present command refers to **seven pairs of all clean animals, the male and his mate, and a pair of the animals that are not clean, the male and his mate** (7:2 ESV; cf. NJB, TNK). Here the biblical writer applies the literary method of Hebrew parallelism. First, he gives general and broad instructions; then he narrows down and focuses on more specific and detailed instructions. The number seven is not only reminiscent of creation, it also conveys the idea of inclusiveness to suggest completion. All species of creation (except sea creatures) are included here. Note that seven pairs of each type of clean animal are permitted in the ark, while only one pair of every unclean animal is granted entrance. The greater number of clean animals over the unclean is due to the greater need of clean animals for food and sacrifices after the flood. Furthermore, the reason for this command is that, after seven days, there will be rain for forty days (7:4).

7:5 Noah did according to all that the Lord commanded him. This phrase, which concludes God's command to "come into the ark" (7:1), echoes the phrase that concluded God's command to "make the ark" (6:22).

7:6 Unlike the Mesopotamian flood stories, the biblical account of the flood is precisely situated in time. Its historical timeframe is established in relation to the life of Noah, who will survive the flood: **Noah was six hundred years old** (cf. 7:11). This emphasizes the historical quality of the event, for Noah's life belongs to the same postdiluvian era as that of Abraham and the rest of us. As such, it deserves our attention with all the lessons it carries (Matt 24:37–39; 2 Pet 3:5–7). In addition, the numbers referred to in "seven days" (7:10) and "forty days" (7:12) are considered sacred numbers, traditionally associated with divine providence and the idea that God is in control of time and history. The number seven is essentially connected with the time of creation and is often associated with worship and the times of the feasts (Lev 23). Likewise, forty is also a significant number, pregnant with the idea of judgment and atonement (Exod 24:18; Deut 9:11; Jonah 3:4), and in that perspective marks a transition period preparing for the next step in God's plan (Exod 34:28;

1 Kgs 19:8; Exod 16:35; Matt 4:2). The event of the flood is not only historical, it also contains spiritual lessons to meditate upon. While the event of the coming of the waters is mentioned in general terms in Genesis 7:6, the description of its process is explained in Genesis 7:11. We understand, then, that the eruption of waters obeys the principle of reversing the work of creation in Genesis 1. While in Genesis 1, creation involved the separation of the waters above from the waters below (1:7), the advent of the flood involves the exact opposite, their reunification, since they are no longer maintained within their borders. We are back to the stage of pre-creation.

7:7–10 In contrast to the water's "undoing" of existence, the specific naming of the three sons of Noah reaffirms their historical continuity, pointing back to the preceding genealogy (6:10) and anticipating the next genealogical statement after the flood (9:18). The line of existence is maintained and the survival of humankind is ensured through these three individuals, who are thus identified as the new "progenitors of the nations (chaps. 10–11)."[278] The event of Noah's entering the ark is told twice, each time with a different tense, thus suggesting a different expression of time. The first time (7:7) the verb *wayyabo* "entered" refers to the punctual action of entering. The second time (7:13) the verb *ba'* "had entered" (NAB) refers to an action that has already been completed at that moment.[279] The phrase should be translated "on the very same day Noah … *had already entered* the ark." This grammar suggests that Noah and his sons had entered the ark before the period of the seven days, after which the waters descended upon the earth (7:10).

7:11–16. BEGINNING OF THE FLOOD

GEN 7:11–16 NKJV	GEN 7:11–16 ESV
11 In the six hundredth year of Noah's life, in the second month, the seventeenth day of the month, on that day all the fountains of the great deep were broken up, and the windows of heaven were opened.	**11** In the six hundredth year of Noah's life, in the second month, on the seventeenth day of the month, on that day all the fountains of the great deep burst forth, and the windows of the heavens were opened.
12 And the rain was on the earth forty days and forty nights.	**12** And rain fell upon the earth forty days and forty nights.
13 On the very same day Noah and Noah's sons, Shem, Ham, and Japheth, and Noah's wife and the three wives of his sons with them, entered the ark—	**13** On the very same day Noah and his sons, Shem and Ham and Japheth, and Noah's wife and the three wives of his sons with them entered the ark,
14 they and every beast after its kind, all cattle after their kind, every creeping thing that creeps on the earth after its kind, and every bird after its kind, every bird of every sort.	**14** they and every beast, according to its kind, and all the livestock according to their kinds, and every creeping thing that creeps on the earth, according to its kind, and every bird, according to its kind, every winged creature.
15 And they went into the ark to Noah, two by two, of all flesh in which *is* the breath of life.	**15** They went into the ark with Noah, two and two of all flesh in which there was the breath of life.
16 So those that entered, male and female of all flesh, went in as God had commanded him; and the Lord shut him in.	**16** And those that entered, male and female of all flesh, went in as God had commanded him. And the Lord shut him in.

---

278 Mathews, *Genesis 1–11:26*, 378.

279 See *GKC* §116*f*.

The entering of the animals is connected to the entering of the humans. The two events are governed by the same verb *ba'* **entered** (7:13). Like the three sons of Noah, the entering of the animals is also an affirmation of creation; the animals are qualified with the language of creation: "after its/their kind" (7:14; cf. 1:21, 24–25), "every beast" (7:14; cf. 1:26, 28), "male and female" (7:9; cf. 1:27), and "breath of life" (7:15; cf. 2:7). In contrast to the waters outside, which manifest the *undoing* of creation, those who enter the ark participate in the *doing* of creation. Significantly, the Hebrew word *kol* "all" or "every" is used seven times (7:14–15), marking the listing of the beasts, and the seventh ("all flesh") is repeated twice:

1. every beast
2. all cattle
3. every creeping thing
4. every bird
5. every bird
6. every sort (every winged creature, ESV)
7. all flesh

7:16 **As God had commanded.** This refrain occurs in the beginning (7:9) and at the end of the passage (7:16) in inclusio. Note its slight variation from the longest formula: "Noah did; according to all that God commanded him, so he did" (see the comments on 6:22). Instead of the general phrase "Noah did," we have the description of what he actually did.

And the Lord shut him in. This is God's seventh and last action. This terse phrase (three words in Hebrew) reflects the logistics of the situation, not only suggesting the heavy weight of the door, but also the assurance that water will not infiltrate since the door is sealed from the outside. The phrase is thus loaded with theological meaning. Humans are now completely in God's hands, dependent on His protection. The preposition *ba'ado* "for him" (lit. trans.)[280] suggests that God's action is designed for the benefit of humans (see Ps 3:3); it is an act of grace on His part on behalf of humans.

7:17–24. RISING OF WATERS

GEN 7:17–24 NKJV	GEN 7:17–24 ESV
17 Now the flood was on the earth forty days. The waters increased and lifted up the ark, and it rose high above the earth.	**17** The flood continued forty days on the earth. The waters increased and bore up the ark, and it rose high above the earth.
18 The waters prevailed and greatly increased on the earth, and the ark moved about on the surface of the waters.	**18** The waters prevailed and increased greatly on the earth, and the ark floated on the face of the waters.
19 And the waters prevailed exceedingly on the earth, and all the high hills under the whole heaven were covered.	**19** And the waters prevailed so mightily on the earth that all the high mountains under the whole heaven were covered.

---

280 The preposition *ba'ad* is generally not translated in this verse.

20 The waters prevailed fifteen cubits upward, and the mountains were covered.

20 The waters prevailed above the mountains, covering them fifteen cubits deep.

21 And all flesh died that moved on the earth: birds and cattle and beasts and every creeping thing that creeps on the earth, and every man.

21 And all flesh died that moved on the earth, birds, livestock, beasts, all swarming creatures that swarm on the earth, and all mankind.

22 All in whose nostrils *was* the breath of the spirit of life, all that *was* on the dry *land*, died.

22 Everything on the dry land in whose nostrils was the breath of life died.

23 So He destroyed all living things which were on the face of the ground: both man and cattle, creeping thing and bird of the air. They were destroyed from the earth. Only Noah and those who *were* with him in the ark remained *alive*.

23 He blotted out every living thing that was on the face of the ground, man and animals and creeping things and birds of the heavens. They were blotted out from the earth. Only Noah was left, and those who were with him in the ark.

24 And the waters prevailed on the earth one hundred and fifty days.

24 And the waters prevailed on the earth 150 days.

7:17–20 This section concerns the effect of the flood itself. The first stage of the flood—the falling of the rain (7:17)—lasts forty days. Then the growing intensity of the movement of the waters is described through the use of four key verbs, some of which are repeated: "increased" (2x), "lifted up" (1x), "prevailed" (4x), and "covered" (2x). The crescendo of their intensity is rendered through the repetition of the adverb *me'od* "very," which is used only once the first time (translated "greatly," 7:18) but twice the second time (translated "exceedingly," 7:19). The waters do not just "increase," their power completely overcome the territory. Significantly, the key verb, which recurs most often, *gabar* "prevail," is the one chosen to characterize the waters in the conclusion, leading to the covering of the earth (7:20; cf. 7:24). Interestingly, the verb *gabar* belongs to military language and implies victory, here the victory of the waters over nature (Exod 17:11). This "prevailing" is manifested by the covering of even the highest mountains (7:20) by **fifteen cubits upward** (twenty-two feet or about seven meters).

7:21–22 Death is affirmed twice through the use of two verbs. In the first statement, **all flesh died** (7:21), the verb *wayyigwa'* "died," "expired" (DBY) refers to the act of dying, "perished" (NIV); in the second statement, **all in whose nostrils was the breath ... died** (7:22), the verb *metu* "died" in the perfect tense refers to the resulting condition of death. The two verbs frame the passage in a chiastic fashion, as indicated in our following literal translation, thus emphasizing the completeness of death:

Expired (*wayyigwa'*) ... all flesh
All in whose nostrils ... died (*metu*)

Note that the list of dying creatures parallels the order of creation (from animals to humans) and again enunciates the reversal process of creation.[281]

7:23 God's sovereignty and control are here affirmed through the repetition of the verb *makhah* "destroyed," which is used in the active mood **He destroyed** and

---

281 Turner notes that "apart from this remnant, the reversal of creation is complete." Laurence Turner, *Genesis* (Sheffield: Sheffield Academic, 2000), 48.

in the divine passive **they were destroyed**. It is also significant that the passive form of the verb "destroy," applying to all those outside the ark, is echoed in the other passive form of the verb **remain**, applying to those inside the ark, thus suggesting that both destruction and salvation are God's action. Note that the verb "remain" (*sha'ar*) is often used in the Scriptures to designate God's people, the holy faithful remnant who survive destruction (Jer 23:3; Isa 4:3; Rom 9:27–28).

7:24 One hundred and fifty days. This measure of time (five months of the lunar calendar), which includes the forty days of the falling of the rain, concludes the flood story (see 8:4).

DELIVERANCE FROM THE FLOOD (8–9)

The end of the flood takes us back to creation. What was reversed *from* creation (through the undoing of creation) will now be reversed *to* creation again. This re-creation process is suggested through the literary structure of the text, which not only progresses through seven actions of God, but also parallels the sequence of the seven-day structure of the creation account:

1. God remembered (8:1)
   "Wind" over the "earth," "waters," and "deep" (8:1–2) || First Day (1:2): (no need for the re-creation of light)
   Separation of waters, sky (8:2–5a) || Second Day (1:6–8)
   Appearance of dry ground and plants (8:5b–12) || Third Day (1:9–13)
   Appearance of light (8:13–14) || Fourth Day (1:14–19)
2. God spoke to Noah, saying (8:15)
   Deliverance of animals according to their kind, sacrifice (8:15–20) || Fifth-Sixth Day I (1:20–25)
3. The Lord smelled and said (8:21)
   Redemption of humans, "image of God" (8:21–22) || Sixth Day II (1:26–27)
4. So God blessed (9:1)
   Human dominion over creation, blessing, food (9:1–7) || Sixth Day III (1:28–31)
5. Then God spoke to Noah, saying (9:8)
   Cosmic covenant (9:8–11) || Seventh Day I (2:1–2a)
6. And God said (9:12)
   Rainbow, sign of covenant (9:12–16) || Seventh Day II (2:2b–3)
7. And God said (9:17)
   Rainbow, sign of covenant || Seventh Day III (2:1–3)

The deliverance from the flood encompasses two successive phases. The first phase is presented through a narrative that recounts the story of the end of the flood; it takes place under the first two divine words (8:1–20) and is parallel to days one through five of the creation account. The second phase, on the other hand, looks to the future with God's promise to humans after the flood; it takes place under the last five words (8:21–9:17) and is parallel to days six and seven of the creation account.

THE END OF THE FLOOD (8:1–20)

8:1A. DIVINE REMEMBRANCE

GEN 8:1A NKJV	GEN 8:1A ESV
1a Then God remembered Noah, and every living thing, and all the animals that were with him in the ark.	**1a** But God remembered Noah and all the beasts and all the livestock that were with him in the ark.

The use of the verb *zakar* "remember" does not mean that God had forgotten, implying some kind of deficiency of God's memory. In the Old Testament, "remembering" is often used to express a covenant relationship (Deut 8:2, 18). When the fourth commandment enjoins us to "remember the Sabbath day" (Exod 20:8), it denotes a specific time designed for humans to refresh their relationship with the Creator. When the biblical text speaks about God remembering His creatures, it is to refer to God's act of salvation as He fulfills His promise at the appointed time (19:29). Indeed, the verb *zkr* "remember" means, in this instance, the end of the flood that is precisely marked in time (8:3–6), just as the Sabbath marks an appointed time at the end of the work of creation. It is noteworthy that the Sabbath day also plays a role in the flood's calendar, implying that Noah observed the Sabbath,[282] as the seven-day cycle on both divine and human levels suggests (7:4, 10; 8:10, 12). Note that "these seven-day periods contribute to the structure of the narrative:"[283]

> 7 days of God's waiting (7:4)
> 7 days of God's waiting (7:10)
> 40 days of waters increasing (7:17)
> 150 days of waters prevailing (7:24)
> **God remembered (8:3)**
> 150 days of waters decreasing (8:3)
> 40 days of waters decreasing (8:6)
> 7 days of Noah's waiting (8:10)
> 7 days of Noah's waiting (8:12)[284]

8:1B–6. RECEDING OF WATERS

GEN 8:1B–6 NKJV	GEN 8:1B–6 ESV
1b And God made a wind to pass over the earth, and the waters subsided.	**1b** And God made a wind blow over the earth, and the waters subsided.
2 The fountains of the deep and the windows of heaven were also stopped, and the rain from heaven was restrained.	**2** The fountains of the deep and the windows of the heavens were closed, the rain from the heavens was restrained,
3 And the waters receded continually from the earth. At the end of the hundred and fifty days the waters decreased.	**3** and the waters receded from the earth continually. At the end of 150 days the waters had abated,

---

282 Wenham, *Genesis 1–15*, 177.

283 Ibid., 179.

284 Ibid., 157.

4 Then the ark rested in the seventh month, the seventeenth day of the month, on the mountains of Ararat.	4 and in the seventh month, on the seventeenth day of the month, the ark came to rest on the mountains of Ararat.
5 And the waters decreased continually until the tenth month. In the tenth *month*, on the first *day* of the month, the tops of the mountains were seen.	5 And the waters continued to abate until the tenth month; in the tenth month, on the first day of the month, the tops of the mountains were seen.
6 So it came to pass, at the end of forty days, that Noah opened the window of the ark which he had made.	6 At the end of forty days Noah opened the window of the ark that he had made

8:1-3 The *ruakh* **wind** (8:1) moving over the water-covered earth initiates God's salvation, just as the *ruakh* "wind" over the waters initiated God's work of creation (1:2). The beginning of the deliverance from the flood is thus identified with the beginning of creation. The following event, the separation between the waters from heaven (8:2) and the waters from the earth (8:3), confirms this parallel with creation (1:6).

8:4 The ark **rested** on land exactly one hundred and fifty days (five months) after the beginning of the flood (7:11). The Hebrew verb *tanakh* "rested" (from the root *nuakh*) alludes to the name of Noah (*noakh*) (5:29). It also characterizes the Sabbath, the day of rest (Exod 20:11). It is interesting and certainly significant that the date of the arrival of the ark, on **the seventeenth of the seventh month**, coincides with the time of the Feast of Tabernacles (Lev 23:34), the last festival of the Hebrew calendar, a high feast time of rejoicing (Deut 16:14). It is also noteworthy that this feast has been associated in biblical and Jewish tradition with the blessing of waters (Zech 14:17-18; John 7:37-38; Rev 21:6; 22:1).[285]

On the mountains of Ararat. While the time of the event (the ark's resting) is precise, its location is not. The mention of "mountains" in the plural makes the exact location of the site difficult. According to the biblical record, the precise time of the event—that is, the fact that it historically took place—is more important than the space where it occurred. Ararat is rarely mentioned in the Scriptures and vaguely designates a country situated north of Assyria (2 Kgs 19:37; Isa 37:38; Jer 51:27), now part of eastern Turkey and western Iran.

8:5 Noah's first action took place precisely **in the tenth month, on the first day of the tenth month** (8:5a) when **the top of the mountains were seen**, that is seventy-three days after the ark grounded.

8:6 Now **Noah opened the window of the ark**, which was probably located on its roof. His intention was to verify for himself the situation of the waters.

8:7-14. DRYING OF THE EARTH

GEN 8:7-14 NKJV	GEN 8:7-14 ESV
7 Then he sent out a raven, which kept going to and fro until the waters had dried up from the earth.	7 and sent forth a raven. It went to and fro until the waters were dried up from the earth.
8 He also sent out from himself a dove, to see if the waters had receded from the face of the ground.	8 Then he sent forth a dove from him, to see if the waters had subsided from the face of the ground.

---

285 See the priestly ceremonial of pouring of waters according to the Mishnah (*Sukkah* 5. 1).

9 But the dove found no resting place for the sole of her foot, and she returned into the ark to him, for the waters *were* on the face of the whole earth. So he put out his hand and took her, and drew her into the ark to himself.

10 And he waited yet another seven days, and again he sent the dove out from the ark.

11 Then the dove came to him in the evening, and behold, a freshly plucked olive leaf *was* in her mouth; and Noah knew that the waters had receded from the earth.

12 So he waited yet another seven days and sent out the dove, which did not return again to him anymore.

13 And it came to pass in the six hundred and first year, in the first *month*, the first *day* of the month, that the waters were dried up from the earth; and Noah removed the covering of the ark and looked, and indeed the surface of the ground was dry.

14 And in the second month, on the twenty-seventh day of the month, the earth was dried.

9 But the dove found no place to set her foot, and she returned to him to the ark, for the waters were still on the face of the whole earth. So he put out his hand and took her and brought her into the ark with him.

10 He waited another seven days, and again he sent forth the dove out of the ark.

11 And the dove came back to him in the evening, and behold, in her mouth was a freshly plucked olive leaf. So Noah knew that the waters had subsided from the earth.

12 Then he waited another seven days and sent forth the dove, and she did not return to him anymore.

13 In the six hundred and first year, in the first month, the first day of the month, the waters were dried from off the earth. And Noah removed the covering of the ark and looked, and behold, the face of the ground was dry.

14 In the second month, on the twenty-seventh day of the month, the earth had dried out.

Since he was still unable to see anything other than water, he resorted to using the aid of a raven and a dove. The contrast between these two birds is striking and certainly significant. While the unclean raven keeps going to and fro for indefinite periods of time until the earth **dried up** (8:7; cf. 8:14), the clean dove is sent according to a well-determined rhythm of seven days. It is sent twice, each time for a definite period of seven days (8:10), and then sent again a third time after another period of seven days (8:12). The dove is explicitly assigned a mission, **to see if the waters had abated from the face of the earth** (8:8). The dove then delivers an explicit message: it brings back **a freshly plucked olive leaf** (8:11), a sign that the plants are growing again. The dove has fulfilled its mission, for only then Noah **knew that the waters had abated from the earth** (8:11b), as prescribed verbatim in its mission (8:8). Only the nonreturn of the dove (after its third release) carries significance, since it is the only nonreturn explicitly noticed (8:12). While the raven gives the impression of moving by blind fate through a random process, the dove—determined by the sacred number of "seven" and carrying a meaningful message—suggests, on the contrary, that the natural elements are submitted to the divine order. It is noteworthy that during this course of events, while Noah was locked in the ark, God did not speak to Noah, although He had spoken directly to him before on several occasions (6:13–14; 7:1). God could have informed him about the water's recession and when the earth had dried up. Yet God kept silent, and Noah had to cope with this new experience—God's silence. The story of the dove and the raven presents a rich lesson in this regard. For in it, we observe that God is present even when He may appear absent. God may even speak through what seems to be outside the spiritual domain, the domain of chance and accident, the flow of waters and the moving of the birds. Noah knew that God was there; and, since God was no longer speaking to him directly, Noah used the means at his disposal, expecting that God would find a way to reach him where he was.

8:13–14 This is Noah's second action: **Noah removed the covering of the ark** (8:13). It is also dated with precision, indicating the importance of the event in question. The word "covering" (*mikseh*) is a technical term that specifically designates the covering of the tabernacle (Exod 26:14; 36:19; Num 3:25). This reminiscence of the sanctuary suggests a connection between this event of cosmic deliverance from the flood and the truth of salvation contained in the sanctuary. This is the first time that Noah sees for himself that **the ground was dry** (8:13). Two verbs describe the drying of the earth using different language. The first verb *kharab*, in the sentence **the waters were dried up from the earth,** describes the drying up of the waters. The second verb *yabash*, in the sentence **the earth was dried**, describes the drying up of the earth. This is the same verb as in the creation account, where it is also associated with the word *'erets* "earth" (1:10). This distinctive language suggests that the two sentences refer to two different phases of drying. Thus, the two events receive a different date. The first drying up occurs **in the six hundred and first year, in the first month, the first day of the month** (8:13). The second drying up occurs **in the second month, on the twenty-seventh day of the month** (8:14). This means—considering the fact that the flood began **in the six hundredth year of Noah's life, in the second month, the seventeenth of the month** (7:11)—that it ended exactly twelve lunar months (354 days) and eleven days (365 days) afterwards. In other words, the flood lasted the totality of one solar year.[286]

8:15–19. COMMAND TO LEAVE THE ARK

GEN 8:15–19 NKJV	GEN 8:15–19 ESV
15 Then God spoke to Noah, saying,	**15** Then God said to Noah,
16 "Go out of the ark, you and your wife, and your sons and your sons' wives with you.	**16** "Go out from the ark, you and your wife, and your sons and your sons' wives with you.
17 Bring out with you every living thing of all flesh that *is* with you: birds and cattle and every creeping thing that creeps on the earth, so that they may abound on the earth, and be fruitful and multiply on the earth."	**17** Bring out with you every living thing that is with you of all flesh—birds and animals and every creeping thing that creeps on the earth—that they may swarm on the earth, and be fruitful and multiply on the earth."
18 So Noah went out, and his sons and his wife and his sons' wives with him.	**18** So Noah went out, and his sons and his wife and his sons' wives with him.
19 Every animal, every creeping thing, every bird, *and* whatever creeps on the earth, according to their families, went out of the ark.	**19** Every beast, every creeping thing, and every bird, everything that moves on the earth, went out by families from the ark.

Noah's third and last action inside the ark is, for the first time, triggered by God's command: **Then God spoke to Noah, saying, Go out of the ark** (8:15–16).

---

286 This way of calculating suggests that the author of Genesis, reporter of the event, was acquainted with both the lunar and the solar calendar, an indication of the antiquity of this report since the lunar-solar calendar was already in use in the first Babylonian dynasty (1850–1550 BC); see S. J. De Vries, "calendar," *IDB* 1:484.

Interestingly, Noah had taken the initiative to verify the various stages of the flood-waters and send the birds, but he waited for a sign from the Lord before exiting the ark. The sequence of the divine command is once again followed by Noah's implementation of God's message (6:13–22; 7:1–5), an expression of Noah's faithful obedience. Noah does not go out alone. He and his sons are accompanied by their wives (8:16, 18), just as the animals, who go out of the ark **according to their families** (8:19), paralleling the fifth and the sixth days of the creation week (1:21, 24–25). The same purpose is implied in these specifications: **that they may abound on the earth, and be fruitful and multiply on the earth** (8:17). Thus, both humans and animals are associated under the same blessing, another parallel to the fifth and sixth days of creation week (1:22, 25–26). Likewise, the story of Noah's exiting the ark parallels the creation story (the first couple's exiting of Eden), carrying the same promise of life and a future for humankind. (Note also the structural parallels between the deliverance from the flood and the creation story in "Deliverance From the Flood" above.)

8:20–22. DIVINE GRACE: PRESERVATION

GEN 8:20–22 NKJV	GEN 8:20–22 ESV
20 Then Noah built an altar to the Lᴏʀᴅ, and took of every clean animal and of every clean bird, and offered burnt offerings on the altar.	**20** Then Noah built an altar to the Lᴏʀᴅ and took some of every clean animal and some of every clean bird and offered burnt offerings on the altar.
21 And the Lᴏʀᴅ smelled a soothing aroma. Then the Lᴏʀᴅ said in His heart, "I will never again curse the ground for man's sake, although the imagination of man's heart *is* evil from his youth; nor will I again destroy every living thing as I have done.	**21** And when the Lᴏʀᴅ smelled the pleasing aroma, the Lᴏʀᴅ said in his heart, "I will never again curse the ground because of man, for the intention of man's heart is evil from his youth. Neither will I ever again strike down every living creature as I have done.
22 "While the earth remains, seedtime and harvest, cold and heat, winter and summer, and day and night shall not cease."	**22** While the earth remains, seedtime and harvest, cold and heat, summer and winter, day and night, shall not cease."

8:20 **Then Noah built an altar.** The first thing that Noah does is worship the Lord. This is the first mention of an altar in the Bible.

Clean and unclean. The concept of clean and unclean animals, which was already referred to before entering the ark (7:2, 8), is, for the first time, explicitly applied in a comprehensive manner to "every clean animal and … every clean bird" (cf. 7:2). It is not an accident that this reference to "clean and unclean animals" prolongs the mention of animals created "according to their families" (8:19). This phrase echoes the creation formula "after their kind" (cf. 1:21, 24), which applied to the animals when entering the ark (7:14). This association of the classification "clean and unclean animals" with the creation formula "after their kind," "according to their families" suggests that the classification of "clean and unclean animals" is put in connection to God's act of creation.[287] In addition, the fact that only **some**[288] **of every clean animal** (ESV) were to be sacrificed suggests that this classification of "clean animal"

---

287 See Jiři Moskala, *The Laws of Clean and Unclean Animals in Leviticus 11* (Berrien Springs: Adventist Theological Society, 2000), 210–217.

288 For the partitive sense of the preposition *min*, see *GKC* §119 w2.

is not limited to the sacrifices, but also applies also to the act of eating of these animals, which will be legislated later (9:3–4).

The Hebrew word *'olah* "burnt offering" refers to the oldest and most frequent of all the Old Testament sacrifices. It served two functions. It was both a petition to be forgiven—an expiation for sin (Job 1:5; Lev 1:4; 5:10; 9:7)—and an offering of thanksgiving (Num 15:1–11). Thus, biblical "religion" defines itself more on the basis of what God has done, does, or will do for us than on anything we might do for God. This is the fundamental lesson contained in the biblical sacrifice: It does not describe our way *to* God but instead a way *from* God to us. It concerns, essentially, the event of God who came down to save humankind, the event of God's incarnation and death for us. This lesson, which anticipates the divine sacrifice in Jesus Christ, is the same that was taught through Abel's sacrifice in contrast to Cain's offering. It is that recognition by faith that allows us to draw near to God, welcoming Him into our hearts and into our lives.

8:21 **And the Lord smelled a soothing aroma.** This idiomatic expression conveys the idea of God accepting the sacrifice (Exod 29:18; Lev 1:9; 3:16). The Hebrew adjective *nikhoakh* "soothing," qualifying the smelling, plays on the name "Noah" (*nikhoakh-noakh*), suggesting that the sacrifice has the same "soothing, resting" effect as Noah himself. Again, it is not the sacrifice itself that has an effect on God, which would imply a magical understanding of religion. Noah himself, through his faithfulness and righteousness, is "soothing" and "comforting" God; the implied idea is also that Noah "comforts" God, as is suggested in the word *nakham* "comfort," contained in the name "Noah" (5:29). Here we note that God and Noah share a reciprocal relationship that makes them respond to each other. God receives the one who received Him. God's heart responds to Noah's heart. This resonance between the divine and the human heart is emphasized in the next sentence: **the Lord said in His *heart*, I will never again curse the ground for man's sake, although the imagination of man's *heart* is evil**. The Hebrew conjunction *ki*, translated "although," literally means "for" or "because." It has a causal force. It is a paradoxical statement. God's positive response is given *because* and in spite of man's negative response—it is a response of grace. God forgives and saves humans because and in spite of the iniquity deeply anchored in their hearts. This is the theological meaning of the sacrifice Noah had just performed. On the horizon of this sacrifice looms the divine sacrifice—a bloodstained offering that sinful human nature desperately needs, and which will be given to them through God's unfathomable grace.

8:22 **While the earth remains.** In contrast to human unfaithfulness, the permanence of the earth is the sign of divine faithfulness. The idea of the permanence of the earth is expressed through a merism, using opposing extremities to refer to the totality: **seedtime and harvest and cold and heat and winter and summer and day and night**. The rhythm of time will keep going. Yet, this is not a promise that an eternal time will be granted to the earth. In fact, the duration of the flow of seasons is temporal, since it depends on "all the days of the earth" (lit. trans.). The same expression "all the days of" occurs in Genesis 3:17 among other common words and motifs ("earth," "curse the ground for man's sake"). Note also the echo of the agricultural labor: "seedtime and harvest" || "thorns and thistles it shall bring forth for you, and you shall eat the herb of the field. In the sweat of your face you shall eat bread" (3:18–19). This common language suggests that our text alludes to the curse on the earth in Genesis 3:17–19. Thus, the expression "all the days" designates the time of human life on the cursed earth. Interestingly, this promise of the permanence of the earth, while it applies to a limited time, conveys a message of hope: the curse of the earth will not last forever. In other words, saying that the duration of the seasons will last as long as the curse endures on the earth hints at something else beyond the time of the curse—a time when we shall return to the original blessing of creation.

9:1–17. DIVINE BLESSING

GEN 9:1–17 NKJV	GEN 9:1–17 ESV
1 So God blessed Noah and his sons, and said to them: "Be fruitful and multiply, and fill the earth.	**1** And God blessed Noah and his sons and said to them, "Be fruitful and multiply and fill the earth.
2 And the fear of you and the dread of you shall be on every beast of the earth, on every bird of the air, on all that move *on* the earth, and on all the fish of the sea. They are given into your hand.	**2** The fear of you and the dread of you shall be upon every beast of the earth and upon every bird of the heavens, upon everything that creeps on the ground and all the fish of the sea. Into your hand they are delivered.
3 Every moving thing that lives shall be food for you. I have given you all things, even as the green herbs.	**3** Every moving thing that lives shall be food for you. And as I gave you the green plants, I give you everything.
4 But you shall not eat flesh with its life, *that is*, its blood.	**4** But you shall not eat flesh with its life, that is, its blood.
5 Surely for your lifeblood I will demand *a reckoning*; from the hand of every beast I will require it, and from the hand of man. From the hand of every man's brother I will require the life of man.	**5** And for your lifeblood I will require a reckoning: from every beast I will require it and from man. From his fellow man I will require a reckoning for the life of man.
6 "Whoever sheds man's blood, by man his blood shall be shed; for in the image of God He made man.	**6** "Whoever sheds the blood of man, by man shall his blood be shed, for God made man in his own image.
7 And as for you, be fruitful and multiply; bring forth abundantly in the earth and multiply in it."	**7** And you, be fruitful and multiply, teem on the earth and multiply in it."
8 Then God spoke to Noah and to his sons with him, saying:	**8** Then God said to Noah and to his sons with him,
9 "And as for Me, behold, I establish My covenant with you and with your descendants after you,	**9** "Behold, I establish my covenant with you and your offspring after you,
10 and with every living creature that *is* with you: the birds, the cattle, and every beast of the earth with you, of all that go out of the ark, every beast of the earth.	**10** and with every living creature that is with you, the birds, the livestock, and every beast of the earth with you, as many as came out of the ark; it is for every beast of the earth.
11 Thus I establish My covenant with you: Never again shall all flesh be cut off by the waters of the flood; never again shall there be a flood to destroy the earth."	**11** I establish my covenant with you, that never again shall all flesh be cut off by the waters of the flood, and never again shall there be a flood to destroy the earth."

12 And God said: "This *is* the sign of the covenant which I make between Me and you, and every living creature that *is* with you, for perpetual generations:	**12** And God said, "This is the sign of the covenant that I make between me and you and every living creature that is with you, for all future generations:
13 I set My rainbow in the cloud, and it shall be for the sign of the covenant between Me and the earth.	**13** I have set my bow in the cloud, and it shall be a sign of the covenant between me and the earth.
14 It shall be, when I bring a cloud over the earth, that the rainbow shall be seen in the cloud;	**14** When I bring clouds over the earth and the bow is seen in the clouds,
15 and I will remember My covenant which *is* between Me and you and every living creature of all flesh; the waters shall never again become a flood to destroy all flesh.	**15** I will remember my covenant that is between me and you and every living creature of all flesh. And the waters shall never again become a flood to destroy all flesh.
16 The rainbow shall be in the cloud, and I will look on it to remember the everlasting covenant between God and every living creature of all flesh that *is* on the earth."	**16** When the bow is in the clouds, I will see it and remember the everlasting covenant between God and every living creature of all flesh that is on the earth."
17 And God said to Noah, "This *is* the sign of the covenant which I have established between Me and all flesh that *is* on the earth."	**17** God said to Noah, "This is the sign of the covenant that I have established between me and all flesh that is on the earth."

So God blessed Noah and his sons. The eschatological hope implied in the preceding verse is foreshadowed in the language of the current verse, which indeed takes us back to the time of creation with its initial blessing (1:22, 28; 2:3). In both texts, blessing is associated with the gift of the future through the promise of fruitfulness. Significantly, next to Noah, **his sons** are mentioned for the first time in the flood story, and from now on they will be associated with him (9:8) and with **your descendants** (9:9). This emphasis on the "sons" and the "descendants" opens to the future, thus including all of humankind in history. The divine post-flood message is universal. The text parallels the sixth day of creation, with the same association of motifs:

God blessed Noah and his sons (9:1) || God blessed Adam and Eve (1:28)
Be fruitful and multiply (9:1) || Be fruitful and multiply (1:28)
Fear and dread on every beast (9:2) || Dominion over all the animals (1:28)
Animals for food, as plants (9:3) || Plants given for food (1:29–30)
Life and soul (9:3–4) || Living soul (1:30)
Man in the image of God (9:6) || Man in the image of God (1:26–27)

9:2 And the fear of you and the dread of you shall be on every beast. This is the only motif that marks a significant difference from the creation account. The negative "fear" and "dread" have replaced the positive "dominion" (1:26) due to the change in food options. While in the creation account, humans and animals shared the same plant-based food—thus they were able to eat together without posing a threat to each other—in the new post-flood economy, the eating and, hence, killing of animals implies a new relationship between humans and animals. In addition to the explicit words "fear" and "dread," the phrase "into your hand" implies that pain and abuse will follow (cf. Job 2:6).

9:3 Every moving thing that lives shall be for you. A number of indications suggest that the permission to eat meat was already submitted to the same restrictions we will have under the Levitical laws. First, the specification of "moving thing that lives" excludes the consumption of dead corpses (Exod 22:31; Lev 22:8).

Secondly, Noah was aware of the fact that the classification of "clean and unclean" animals went beyond the sacrificial legislation, since only some of the clean animals were suitable for sacrifice (see the comments on 9:20). Sacrificial animals are all clean animals, but not all clean animals (e.g., deer, fish, locusts) are sacrificial animals (see Lev 11 and Deut 14). As the structure of the flood indicates (see above), Noah was aware of the fact that the classification of clean and unclean animals applied also to the diet:

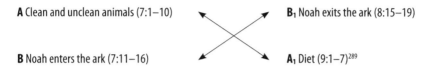

A Clean and unclean animals (7:1–10)   **B₁** Noah exits the ark (8:15–19)

B Noah enters the ark (7:11–16)   **A₁** Diet (9:1–7)[289]

This chiastic parallel (ABB₁A₁) connects the section regarding clean and unclean animals (A) with the section regarding diet (A₁), just as it connects the section about entering the ark (B) with the section about exiting the ark (B₁).

And thirdly, the dietary restriction to "clean animals" is implied in the specification that these animals belong to the classification of creation (8:19–20) and must still be considered to be under divine control, as a gift of God, just as the food in the creation account: **I have given you all things, even as the green herbs**.

9:4 But you shall not eat flesh with its life, that is, its blood. Note that the prohibition of consuming blood applies only to birds or beasts, not to fish or locust's blood (Lev 7:26), which have a different blood system. This commandment confirms once more that Noah is submitted to the same dietary laws that will be later enunciated in the Mosaic legislation (Lev 3:17; 7:26).[290] It is noteworthy that this usage was totally absent in the ANE.

This is the only dietary law for which a reason is given: because "life" is in the blood (cf. Lev 17:11). Thus, the biblical rationale underscores a reverence for life. This consideration takes us, then, back to the context of creation, where death was not yet a reality and only life prevailed.[291] The abstinence from the consumption of blood expresses respect for life and, by implication, a concern for health,[292] which is an essential aspect of the biblical view of holiness (Lev 21:23).[293] Modern science has indeed demonstrated that the consumption of blood can lead to disease and sickness. This association of blood and life is also explained in the book of Leviticus in regard to the atoning function of the blood: "for it is the blood that makes atonement for the soul" (Lev 17:11). Abstaining from blood is therefore related to faith in the God

---

289 Adapted from William H. Shea, "The Structure of the Genesis Flood Narrative and Its Implications," *Origins* 6, no. 1 (1979): 22–23.

290 For a discussion about the prohibition of blood, see Moskala, *The Laws of Clean and Unclean Animals*, 235–237.

291 On the connection between creation and the Levitical diet, see ibid., 210–217.

292 See Moses Maimonides, *The Guide for the Perplexed*, trans. M. Friedländer, 2nd ed., rev. ed. (London: George Routledge, 1910), 362; cf. W. F. Albright, *Yahweh and the Gods of Canaan: A Historical Analysis of Two Contrasting Faiths* (Garden City, NY: Doubleday, 1969), 175–181. Cf. Ellen G. White, "God had given these injunctions to the Jews for the purpose of preserving their health" (AA 192).

293 On the connection between holiness and health, see Jiři Moskala, "The Validity of the Levitical Food Laws of Clean and Unclean Animals: A Case Study of Biblical Hermeneutics," *JATS* 22, no. 2 (2011): 21–22.

of salvation, who forgave through the shedding of blood. These two reasons are related, for both creation and atonement bring life. "The undergirding rationale," for the dietary system, notes Milgrom, is "reverence for life" and pertains to the duty of holiness (Exod 22:30; Lev 11:44–45; Deut 14:4–21).[294]

It is noteworthy that this blood prohibition was still considered to be universal and binding by the early Christians, probably because of the various theological and health reasons. So while the Gentile Christians who joined the church were exempted from circumcision, they were admonished "to abstain … from blood" (Acts 15:20, 29). Addressing the question "Are Christians still forbidden to eat blood?" Old Testament Evangelical scholar G. L. Archer responds on the basis of Acts 15:28–29, "that we are still to respect the sanctity of the blood, since God has appointed it to be a symbol of the atoning blood of Jesus Chris. Therefore it is not to be consumed by any believer who wishes to be obedient to Scripture."[295]

A PRACTICAL QUESTION: EATING MEAT WITHOUT BLOOD?

In practical terms, this prohibition means that the blood of the slain animal must be totally drained at the time of slaughter (Deut 12:24).[296] This is the only biblical practice mentioned to prevent the ingestion of blood along with meat. The Bible does not provide any additional instruction on what to do after the slaughtering in order to eliminate the remaining blood from the animal. Yet, even if current slaughterhouse practices remove most of the blood, a substantial amount of blood remains in the veins of the slaughtered animal. To ensure that all the blood was extracted from the slaughtered animal, a number of preparation techniques became common practice in traditional Judaism. The main technique, known as *melikhah* "salting" involves soaking the drained meat in water and salting (koshering process).[297] Although these rabbinic requirements are not prescribed by the Bible nor required for Christians, they may be helpful for those who wish to avoid blood, as much as possible, when consuming meat. Because of all these complications—and the theology associated with them—and because it is virtually impossible to eliminate all the blood from the animal, the only effective way to avoid the consumption of blood is to discard meat altogether. This view was advocated by Rav Kook, the first Chief Rabbi of pre-state Israel, who endorsed a vegetarian diet and explained that all the elaborate regulations around the slaughtering of animals and preparation were meant by God to discourage us from this dietary practice and, instead, lead us back to God's initial plant-based diet (1:29).[298] The great Jewish Bible commentator Rabbi

---

294 Milgrom, *Leviticus*, 733. Note that the same rationale may also be a part of the rejection of unclean animals, since all the carnivorous animals that consume blood are excluded. (See Moskala, *The Laws of Unclean Animals*, 235; cf. Milgrom, *Leviticus*, 704.)

295 Gleason L. Archer, *Encyclopedia of Bible Difficulties* (Grand Rapids: Zondervan, 1982), 86.

296 Ellen G. White seems to endorse such prohibition: "No creature that was torn, that had died itself, or from which the blood had not been carefully drained could be used as food. By departing from the plan divinely appointed for their diet, the Israelites suffered great loss" (MH 312). "The Gentiles were accustomed to eat the flesh of animals that has been strangled, while the Jews had been divinely instructed that when beasts were killed for food, particular care was to be taken that the blood should flow from the body; otherwise the meat would not be regarded as wholesome. God had given these injunctions to the Jews for the purpose of preserving their health. The Jews regarded it as sinful to use blood as an article of diet. They held that the blood was the life, and that the shedding of blood was in consequence of sin" (AA 191).

297 On postbiblical regulations for koshering meat, see *JE* 6:28, 39.

298 See Abraham I. Kook, "Fragments of Light: A View as to the Reasons for the Commandments," in *Abraham Isaac Kook: The Lights of Penitence, the Moral Principles, Lights of Holiness, Essays, Letters, and Poems*, trans. Ben Zion Bokser (New York: Paulist Press, 1978), 316–321.

Solomon Ephraim Lunchitz of Prague (d. 1619) conveyed the same thinking:

> What was the necessity for the entire procedure of ritual slaughter? For the sake of self-discipline. It is far more appropriate for man not to eat meat; only if he has a strong desire for meat does the Torah permit it, and even this only after the trouble and inconvenience necessary to satisfy his desire. Perhaps because of the bother and annoyance of the whole procedure, he will be restrained from such a strong and uncontrollable desire for meat.[299]

Note that this prohibition does not apply to blood transfusions, since it is strictly limited to oral consumption, that is, eating and drinking. The process of ingesting blood that goes directly to the stomach is also physiologically different from injecting blood directly into the veins. Furthermore, the biblical context of this prohibition concerns appetite and a lack of self-control (1 Sam 14:32) and not medical conditions.

9:5 I will require the life of man. The prohibition of consuming blood is now illustrated through its association with human life in the following verses (9:5–7). It has been pointed out that the consumption of animal blood may stimulate cruelty and incite the killing of humans: "Eating blood may express a secret joy in killing and be an education for murder."[300] Killing animals may indeed affect human sensitivity and prepare for killing humans. Along these lines, the prophet Ezekiel associates the act of eating blood-tinged meat with idolatry and murder (Ezek 33:25–26).

9:6 Whoever sheds man's blood. The reference to "blood" ties the following curse on killing humans, "shedding man's blood," to the preceding commandment not to consume blood. Two arguments are given to show the gravity of the sin of murder and thus justify that curse. The first is focused on the future and looks at the ultimate consequence: **by man his blood shall be shed**. This argument has in view the threat of assassination for revenge that hovers on the murderer (Num 35:27) or refers more specifically to the death penalty for the sin of murder in the ancient Israelite economy (Num 35:30). The gravity of this sin is thus measured by the severity of its fatal outcome. Only life will pay for life. The lesson of this first argument concerns the sacredness of human life that cannot be compensated.[301]

The second argument looks to the past and the special status of man: **in the image of God He made man**. This argument refers back to the creation account to remind us of the divine image in all humans. This implies that killing humans impacts God Himself. Since the human person was made in God's image, God takes murder personally. Although the lives of animals are sacred, as indicated in the blood proscription, it is significant that only human life requires an accounting before God (9:5). Once again, this is because humans are the only beings who have been created in the image of God: **For in the image of God He made man** (9:6). This is why killing humans has been retained as the only killing that is absolutely forbidden. Hebrew language has several verbs for killing. All these verbs apply to both humans and animals except one, the verb *ratsakh*, which applies only to humans. Significantly, it

---

299 Quoted in Abraham Chill, *The Commandments and Their Rationale* (New York: Keter Books, 1974), 400.

300 Benno Jacob, *The First Book of the Bible: Genesis*, trans. Ernest I. Jacob and Walter Jacob (Jersey City, NJ: Ktav, 1974), 63.

301 See Ellen G. White's comment: "The safety and purity of the nation demanded that the sin of murder be severely punished. Human life, which God alone could give, must be sacredly guarded" (PP 516).

is the verb *ratsakh* "kill" (KJV, ASV), "murder" (NIV, ESV), that is used in the Ten Commandments (Exod 20:13). The nuance of this usage does not differentiate between various *circumstances* of killing, between the case of murder and other cases,[302] but between the *object* that is killed—humans and animals. The use of the verb *ratsakh* in the sixth commandment alerts us that the killing implied here concerns only humans (and not animals). The sixth commandment should not be translated "you shall not murder," implying only the specific case of a criminal act,[303] but "you shall not kill humans" in a general sense. The prohibition as "murder" would not make sense for an activity in which most common people would rarely think of engaging.

9:7 **And as for you, be fruitful and multiply.** This conclusion was designed as an inclusio with this section's introduction (9:1); furthermore, the phrase "and as for you" intends to emphasize the duty of men in contrast to the activity of "shedding human blood." Instead of killing and erasing life, humans should produce life: "be fruitful and multiply."[304]

9:8–17 **Then God spoke to Noah … I establish My covenant.** This last section of the flood account covers God's last three words to Noah (9:8, 12, 17), which concern the inauguration of His covenant. The phrase "establish covenant" occurs three times in this section, thus marking its structure: in the beginning (9:9), in the end as an inclusio (9:17), and in the middle after God's first word (9:11). It responds to the first word of God to Noah, promising "I will establish My covenant" (6:18), suggesting that this promise is now being fulfilled. Following the section that corresponds to the sixth day of the creation account, this last section corresponds to the seventh section of the creation account, the Sabbath. Inside the text, the connection with the Sabbath is already suggested through the rhythm marked by the seven occurrences of the word *berit* "covenant" (9:9, 11–13, 15–17). It is also significant that the only other biblical passage that uses the particular expression **sign of the covenant** (9:12–13, 17), involving a cosmic context (9:10, 12–14), concerns the Sabbath (Exod 31:12–17).[305] Thus, the rainbow, the sign of the cosmic covenant between God and humankind, corresponds to the Sabbath, the sign of another cosmic covenant between God and humankind.[306] While the Sabbath is a sign that recalls the event of creation from the primary waters, the rainbow is a sign that reminds us of the event of re-creation from the waters of the flood. Both the Sabbath and the rainbow remind us of God's unilateral action of creation towards humans. Furthermore, the Sabbath and the rainbow convey the same message of peace and reconciliation. The Sabbath brings the message of peace in the context of time as a "break" and "rest,"

---

302 One of the most difficult applications of this observation is the fact that *ratsakh* may also concern the case of killing in Israel's wars for the conquest of Canaan. In fact, a number of biblical evidences suggest that the killing by Israel was not God's intention, for the Lord was supposed to "fight for them" (see Exod 14:13–14, 25; 23:23, 27–28; cf. 2 Chr 20:20–24). For a discussion on the particular case of Israel's wars of conquest and its theological implications, see in the SDAIBC series, R. Davidson's commentary on Exodus and M. Barna's commentary on Joshua.

303 This argument has often been used to justify the killing in war. For the use of that justification and a discussion on recent mistranslations "murder" for *ratsakh*, see Wilma A. Bailey, *"You Shall Not Kill" or "You Shall Not Murder"?: The Assault on a Biblical Text* (Collegeville, MN: Liturgical Press, 2005).

304 Although with a significantly different agenda and ethics, this ideal resonates with the motto launched by the hippies in the sixties, "Make love, not war."

305 The expression "sign of the covenant" appears also for the circumcision (17:11), but, unlike the rainbow and the Sabbath, the circumcision does not involve a cosmic context.

306 Note that it also corresponds to the covenant between the human couple in the seventh section of the second creation story (2:23–24 || 2:1–3).

while the rainbow, which evokes the hunting bow, yet without arrows and inactive—puts it in the context of space as a harmless bow (cf. Rev 4:2). They are both signs of *shalom*.

9:18–19. THE SONS OF NOAH

GEN 9:18–19 NKJV	GEN 9:18–19 ESV
18 Now the sons of Noah who went out of the ark were Shem, Ham, and Japheth. And Ham *was* the father of Canaan.	**18** The sons of Noah who went forth from the ark were Shem, Ham, and Japheth. (Ham was the father of Canaan.)
19 These three *were* the sons of Noah, and from these the whole earth was populated.	**19** These three were the sons of Noah, and from these the people of the whole earth were dispersed.

Note the sequence **Shem, Ham, and Japheth** (9:18), which mentions the youngest brother Shem first, while the eldest brother Japheth (see 10:21; cf. 10:2, 6, 21) is mentioned last. The intention of this sequence is not only to focus on Shem, who will be the ancestor of Abraham and hence of the people of Israel, but also to imply the theological principle underlying the patriarchal births whereby against the general principle the youngest will be selected over the oldest.

The shift of focus from Noah to his sons marks the renewed attention to the future of human history, for **from these the whole earth was populated** (9:19). The verb *naptsah* "populated" is the same verb as the one describing the movements of the peoples who "scattered" "over the face of all the earth" in the story of the tower of Babel (11:4, 8). Within this universalistic perspective, the special mention of **Ham**, as **the father of Canaan** (cf. 10:6, 15) anticipates the perspective of the country of Canaan, the Promised Land (12:5). This association between the future blessing of humankind and the genesis of the chosen people hints at the connection between the blessing of the nations and the election of God's people; indirectly, it anticipates the blessing of Abraham (12:3).

9:20–27. NOAH'S CURSE AND BLESSING

GEN 9:20–27 NKJV	GEN 9:20–27 ESV
20 And Noah began *to be* a farmer, and he planted a vineyard.	**20** Noah began to be a man of the soil, and he planted a vineyard.
21 Then he drank of the wine and was drunk, and became uncovered in his tent.	**21** He drank of the wine and became drunk and lay uncovered in his tent.
22 And Ham, the father of Canaan, saw the nakedness of his father, and told his two brothers outside.	**22** And Ham, the father of Canaan, saw the nakedness of his father and told his two brothers outside.
23 But Shem and Japheth took a garment, laid *it* on both their shoulders, and went backward and covered the nakedness of their father. Their faces *were* turned away, and they did not see their father's nakedness.	**23** Then Shem and Japheth took a garment, laid it on both their shoulders, and walked backward and covered the nakedness of their father. Their faces were turned backward, and they did not see their father's nakedness.

24 So Noah awoke from his wine, and knew what his younger son had done to him.	**24** When Noah awoke from his wine and knew what his youngest son had done to him,
25 Then he said: "Cursed *be* Canaan; a servant of servants he shall be to his brethren."	**25** he said, "Cursed be Canaan; a servant of servants shall he be to his brothers."
26 And he said: "Blessed *be* the Lᴏʀᴅ, the God of Shem, and may Canaan be his servant.	**26** He also said, "Blessed be the Lᴏʀᴅ, the God of Shem; and let Canaan be his servant.
27 May God enlarge Japheth, and may he dwell in the tents of Shem; and may Canaan be his servant."	**27** May God enlarge Japheth, and let him dwell in the tents of Shem, and let Canaan be his servant."

Noah began to be a farmer, and he planted a vineyard. Noah's first act outside of the ark connects him to Adam. For Noah's story of planting a vineyard contains numerous parallels with the story of Adam in the Garden of Eden. Like Adam, Noah eats of the fruit and, as a result of his actions, his nakedness, of which he is not aware (9:21), is revealed (9:22; cf. 3:7) and a covering is provided (9:23; cf. 3:7, 21). Also, both stories end the same way, with a curse and a blessing (9:25–26; cf. 3:14, 17). The parallels between the two stories provide the reader with a key to grasp the ethical and theological lessons of that story.

9:21 Then he drank of the wine. The parallels between wine drinking and the eating of the forbidden fruit subtly suggest a warning against that temptation. A divine indictment may also be implied by the very fact that the first drinking recorded in the Bible is associated with shame and a curse (cf. 19:30–38). The specification of a **beginning** for the culture of wine (9:20) suggests that there is something about that culture, certainly its inebriating effects, that was not known before. Alcoholic wine introduces a new element that is foreign to the divine project of creation. This presumption may explain Daniel's total abstinence from wine drinking. Daniel's abstinence and his plant-based diet are both an expression of his faith in the God of creation, as is implied in his allusion to the text of creation to justify his decision (Dan 1:12; cf. 1:29).[307]

9:22–23 And Ham, the father of Canaan, saw the nakedness of his father. The special note on the act of "seeing" suggests that there was something suspect about it. Ham was not supposed to "see." The biblical text does not elaborate on the nature of the fault. But within the parallels to the story of the Garden of Eden, this verb is reminiscent of the temptation of Eve who "saw" (3:6). Ham's seeing is then more than an accidental or furtive glimpse. Furthermore, Ham goes on and elaborates about it, even trying to get his brothers involved in his iniquity. The reaction of his brothers, who not only cover the nakedness of their father but also manage to avoid seeing it, confirms that the problem was essentially about the seeing of the father's nakedness and not about any implicit sexual misconduct. As Cassuto points out: "If the covering was an adequate remedy, it follows that the misdemeanor was confined to seeing."[308] The issue is more about the respect due to the parent (Exod 20:12; Deut 27:16). In this particular instance, the focus on the father's nakedness, hence on his sex, reinforces the allusion to the father as the progenitor, the one who engenders. Our failure to honor the past that has produced us affects the future that

---

307 Daniel's line (Dan 1:11) is the only other biblical text that contains the same association of Hebrew words (*'khl* "eat," *zr'* "vegetables," *ntn* "give"), which we find in the creation account (1:29).

308 Cassuto, *Genesis*, 2:151.

we shall produce. This is why our obedience or transgression of this commandment directly affects our future accordingly (Exod 20:12), for it is the only commandment associated with a promise (Eph 6:2).

9:24–25 The curse immediately affects Ham's future, one of Noah's sons: **cursed be Canaan** (9:25) This curse is in no way suggesting an ethnic application, thus justifying, for instance, the trade of African slaves in the course of the nineteenth century or the practices of the former apartheid in South Africa. The fact that the curse is restricted to Canaan and is not generalized to all the descendants of Ham, demonstrates the falsity of those through history who have used this passage to support racism against those of African descent. Significantly, the curse focuses on Canaan, Ham's son, probably because the biblical author has in mind some of the unnatural practices of the Canaanites (19:5–7, 31–35).[309] The curse, like the blessing, is essentially concerned with the future and finds its main significance with Canaan's future descendants. The author of Genesis reports this story from the perspective of his present concern, namely, the forthcoming conquest of Canaan. The author of Genesis plays, then, on the name of Canaan to suggest the destiny of the Canaanites, who will be "subdued" by the Israelites and will thus become servants of the Israelites (cf. Josh 9:23; 1 Kgs 9:20–21). Significantly, the name "Canaan" is derived from the root *kana'*, meaning "subdue." The biblical writers have preserved this linguistic connection and often played on the word *kana'* "subdue" to refer to the "subjugation" (*kana'*) of the Canaanites by the Israelites:

On that day God subdued [*kana'*] Jabin king of Canaan [*kana'an*] in the presence of the children of Israel (Judg 4:23)

You subdued [*kana'*] before them the inhabitants of the land, the Canaanites [*kana'anim*], and gave them into their hands (Neh 9:24)[310]

9:26–27 While the curse stays at the human level, the blessing takes us to the divine level: **Blessed be the Lord, the God of Shem** (9:26). It is interesting that while humans are cursed, it is not Shem but only his God who is blessed. The idea is that any blessing derived from Shem originates, in fact, in God (12:3). Also, from the perspective of the blessing in/from God, the prophecy takes us beyond the immediate future of the Pentateuch's history of Israel and opens to the universal horizon of the salvation of humankind. **Japheth** will **dwell in the tents of Shem** (9:27), a wording that also refers to the Israelite tabernacle (Josh 18:1), a prophetic allusion to the Gentiles who will respond to the Israelite message of salvation and join the holy community of Israel (Isa 66:18–20; Rom 11:25).[311] But the fulfillment of that prophecy depends first on the fulfillment of another prophecy that is the subjugation of Canaan. This event is so fundamental in the eyes of the author that he comes back

---

309 See Ellen G. White: "These evil characteristics were perpetuated in Canaan and his posterity, whose continued guilt called upon the judgments of God" (PP 117). It has been suggested on the basis of Leviticus 20:11 that Canaan was the fruit of an incestuous relation between Ham and his mother (see Jon Levenson, "Genesis: Introduction and Annotations," in *The Jewish Study Bible*, eds. Adele Berlin and Mark Zvi [New York: Oxford University Press, 2004], 26).

310 See also Judges 3:30; 11:33; 1 Chronicles 17:10; 20:4.

311 The messianic interpretation of this prophecy can be traced as far as the Targum Pseudo-Jonathan, the Church Fathers, and the Reformers. See John Skinner, *A Critical and Exegetical Commentary on Genesis* (New York: Charles Scribner's Sons, 1910), 185; cf. Mathews, *Genesis 1–11:26*, 424.

165

to it at the end of the blessing note, when for the third time, he refers to Canaan as the servant of Shem: **May Canaan be his servant** (9:27; cf. 9:25–26). The language in the blessing section is given in the style of a prayer: "may … be" (9:26–27). The author, who is contemporary to the time of the Israelite slavery in Egypt, prays for the salvation of Israel, a basic necessary first step towards the salvation of humankind.

9:28–29. NOAH'S DEATH

GEN 9:28–29 NKJV	GEN 9:28–29 ESV
28 And Noah lived after the flood three hundred and fifty years.	**28** After the flood Noah lived 350 years.
29 So all the days of Noah were nine hundred and fifty years; and he died.	**29** All the days of Noah were 950 years, and he died.

These last two verses serve as a hinge, taking us back to the last link of the genealogy of Adam (5:32), again suggesting the role of Noah as a second Adam and anticipating the next genealogy covering all the nations (10:1–32). The lesson of these precise numbers is to inspire trust in the events concerning the flood as well as the events preceding and following the flood. Because Noah's life spans from before to after the flood, he could transmit the great lessons of the creation of the world, the Garden of Eden, the fall, and the first crime—all of which he had heard from his ancestors—as well as give his firsthand personal testimony about the great God who sent the flood and delivered from it.

THE GENEALOGY OF THE SONS OF NOAH (10:1–32)

This list of the nations (10:1–32) has no parallel in the ancient world. As such, it conveys a very unique testimony of the genesis of world nations. According to the results of archaeological research, this table is an ethnographic document of primary importance. Although the table does not aim at completeness (10:5), its authenticity has been confirmed in its essential parts by many inscriptions in the monuments of antiquity (see "The Table of Nations: Geography, History, and Archaeology").

In addition, this genealogical information affirms the reliability of the biblical testimony regarding primary events since the creation of the world, for it gives evidence of a continuous line of witnessing. Abraham was fifty-eight years old at the death of Noah, whose father, Lamech, was fifty-six years old at the death of Adam. The chain of oral tradition from creation to the patriarchs was therefore short enough to maintain a fresh recollection of the events on the basis of direct audible testimony. Furthermore, Isaac and Jacob knew Shem, the son of Noah, as Jacob was fifty years old at the death of Shem.[312] Thus, Jacob was able to teach his children who went to Egypt the lessons he had learned, not only from his father Isaac and his grandfather Abraham, but also directly from Shem, a firsthand witness of the flood.

---

312 For the calculation of these numbers, see Babylonian Talmud, Meg. 16b–17a.

The language and form of the genealogy suggest a theology that is both universal and particular in character, as it relates the history of the diverse nations to the special destiny of Israel. In this "unique list of the nations," according to the *Macmillan Atlas*, "The lands and the world are divided into three main lines: the sons of Shem in Mesopotamia and Arabia, the sons of Ham in Egypt and within its sphere of influence, and the sons of Japheth in the northern and western lands … three spheres of peoples and lands, which meet in the region of the Holy Land."[313] Thus, the genealogy is arranged from the point of view of Israel, a perspective that is reflected in the literary structure of the genealogy, which presents the sons' genealogies in the reverse order of the introduction, thus marking the climax with Shem.

10:1 **This is the genealogy of the sons of Noah: Shem, Ham, and Japheth** … Although the list of the three brothers follows the theological sequence, placing the youngest before the oldest, the genealogy respects the chronological sequence: Japheth, Ham, and Shem.

The sons of Japheth… (10:2)
The sons of Ham… (10:6)
The sons of Shem… (10:21)
These were the families of the sons of Noah (10:32)

In addition to the name of Shem, which marks the climax of the structure, the text draws attention to three other names, names that receive special attention and generate more discussion than the others: Nimrod, the founder of Babel (10:8–11); Canaan, the father of the Canaanites (10:15–19); and Eber, the ancestor of Abraham (10:21) and father of Peleg, who lived during the division of the earth (10:25). Obviously, these pauses and emphases betray the concern of the author and anticipate the forthcoming stories of the tower of Babel (11:1–9) and of the election of Abraham and his descendants (12:1–3). Note that the reference to the actual nations in the table precedes the story of their formation, in classic Hebrew fashion, setting the effect before the cause. In that connection, it is noteworthy that the nation of "Israel" is absent in this table. Most likely this is because Israel is not yet a nation at the time of this composition,[314] which would again support the Mosaic authorship of the book of Genesis. On the other hand, the omission of the "tribes" of Israel may be intended to set them apart. It is indeed significant that the genealogy of Peleg is not given, while his brother's is given (10:26–29). Instead, the genealogy of Peleg will appear in the next chapter under a genealogy exclusively reserved for Shem, leading to Abram (11:17–26). The reason for the omission of the genealogy of Peleg in the table of nations is that it should belong to the line of the elected nation starting with Abram; this branch has been separated from the line of the nations, for it will follow another destiny and deserves special attention. This distinction is also reflected in the language. It is always the general word *goy* that refers to a "nation," a political entity, and never the covenantal term *'am* that refers to a "people" with common racial descent that is normally reserved for Israel (Exod 15:16; Isa 1:3; Hos 1:9). Note here that the classification of the table does not intend to explain the origin of ethnic groups and languages. Thus, the identification as "Japhetite," "Semitic," or "Hamitic"

---

313 Yohanan Aharoni and Michael Avi-Yonah, *The Macmillan Bible Atlas*, rev. ed. (New York: Macmillan, 1977), 15.
314 Mathews, *Genesis 1–11:26*, 431.

does not follow clear criteria. Although Canaanite languages are Semitic, Canaan is counted among the Hamites. Although Cush is a descendant of Ham, he is the father of Nimrod, the founder of Babel. Elam, who belongs to a non-Semitic people, is a son of Shem. As such, the concern of the table is more about ethnogeography (geographic distribution of human groups) than about ethnicity (origin of human races).

Another stylistic peculiarity of the genealogy is its predilection for the number seven. As a whole, there are seventy (seven by ten) nations, and the key terms *beney* "sons of" and *'erets* "earth" or "land" occur fourteen times (2x7). The seven-time repetition is reminiscent of the style of creation and, thus, connects the genealogy to the creation story. As for the number seventy, it foreshadows the seventy members of the family of Jacob (46:27) and the seventy elders of Israel in the wilderness (Exod 24:9). This correspondence between the two "seventies" seems to underlie Deuteronomy 32:8, which speaks of God dividing humankind "according to the number of the children of Israel." Just as there were seventy nations, so there were seventy languages, according to Jewish tradition.[315] In the New Testament, Jesus sends seventy disciples to evangelize the world (Luke 10:1–16).

The genealogy of Noah, the father of the nations of the earth (9:19; 10:32), embodies the fulfillment of God's blessing and promise to Noah, "be fruitful and multiply" (8:17; 9:1, 7), which is also tied with the initial promise and blessing given to Adam at creation (1:28–29). The God of the nations, the Creator of the world, and the Lord of Israel are the same God. This observation has two important theological implications. First, it means that God affects history even beyond the realms of religion. God is also present among the nations. Second, it means that the salvation of the nations also depends on the testimony of Israel. The blessing of the nations will be realized only through Israel (12:3), for only the God of Israel is the true God—"salvation is of the Jews" (John 4:22). The lessons of the Hebrew Bible, the history of Israel, and the events that happened to the Jews and were recorded in the New Testament are of redemptive significance for the nations.

THE TABLE OF NATIONS: GEOGRAPHY, HISTORY, AND ARCHAEOLOGY (10:1–32)
BY MICHAEL G. HASEL

10:1–5. THE SONS OF JAPHETH

GEN 10:1–5 NKJV	GEN 10:1–5 ESV
1 Now this *is* the genealogy of the sons of Noah: Shem, Ham, and Japheth. And sons were born to them after the flood.	**1** These are the generations of the sons of Noah, Shem, Ham, and Japheth. Sons were born to them after the flood.
2 The sons of Japheth *were* Gomer, Magog, Madai, Javan, Tubal, Meshech, and Tiras.	**2** The sons of Japheth: Gomer, Magog, Madai, Javan, Tubal, Meshech, and Tiras.
3 The sons of Gomer *were* Ashkenaz, Riphath, and Togarmah.	**3** The sons of Gomer: Ashkenaz, Riphath, and Togarmah.

---

315 See Tg. Ps.-J on 11:7. The same tradition is behind the belief that the Decalogue was written in seventy languages so that all the nations might understand it (Sotah 7:5); for the same reason, the divine voice at the Mount Sinai was heard in seventy tongues (Shabbat 88b).

4 The sons of Javan *were* Elishah, Tarshish, Kittim, and Dodanim.

5 From these the coastland *peoples* of the Gentiles were separated into their lands, everyone according to his language, according to their families, into their nations.

4 The sons of Javan: Elishah, Tarshish, Kittim, and Dodanim.

5 From these the coastland peoples spread in their lands, each with his own language, by their clans, in their nations.

10:1 **Japheth** is not associated with a nation but is considered to be a person. The descendants of Japheth form those entities north of Israel, in the territories of Anatolia, the Russian steppes, and Europe surrounding the Mediterranean basin. The Table of Nations begins with Japheth because he represents the most distant entities from the territory of Canaan or Israel.

10:2 The sons of Japheth are seven: **Gomer, Magog, Madai, Javan, Tubal, Meshech, and Tiras**.

Gomer appears three times in the Old Testament (1 Chr 1:5–6; Ezek 38:6) and is identified as the Cimmerians.[316] Homer locates this Indo-European people in Europe. They appear for the first time as *gimirrāia* or *gimarraja* in the texts of Sargon II, when they defeat the city of Urartu in 714 BC.[317] Majority opinion, with Herodotus, holds that the Cimmerians came down from the Caucasus steppes, invading Urartu from the north, perhaps pushed down by the Scythians.[318] Another theory is that Gamir, "the land of the Cimmerians," was in the steppes of the Pontis Mountains in Asia Minor.[319] The geographical area of the Crimea retains the name in modern times.

Magog is difficult to identify (cf. Ezek 38:2; 39:2; Rev 20:8). Proposals tend to be confined to the area of Asia Minor or the northern area of the Scythians. The most frequent identification is in relationship to Gyges, king of Lydia (ca. 650 BC),[320] even though this is made difficult by the chronological gap between his reign and the earliest date for the book of Ezekiel and other historical considerations.

Madai are the Medes of the Old Testament (Isa 13:17) or the country of Media (2 Kgs 17:6; 18:11; Isa 21:2). This Indo-European group was located east of the valleys of the Zagros Mountains in the high Iranian plateau. Archaeological excavations have not been extensive in this region. The Medes coalesced by the ninth century[321] and are mentioned frequently in Assyrian sources. Eventually, they join the Babylonians in defeating Nineveh in 612 BC and then merge to become the Medo-Persian Empire.[322]

---

316 A. I. Ivantchik, *Les Cimmériens au Proche-Orient*, OBO 127 (Fribourg: Vandenhoeck & Ruprecht, 1993); Edwin Yamauchi, *Foes From the Northern Frontier: Invading Hordes From the Russian Steppes* (Grand Rapids: Baker, 1982), 49–62.

317 *CAD* 5:75; A. Kammenhuber, "Kimmerier," *RLA* 5, 7/8 (1980): 594–596.

318 C. Burney and D. M. Lang, *The Peoples of the Hills: Ancient Ararat and Caucasus* (London: Weidenfeld and Nicolson, 1971), 318.

319 V. Parker, "Bemerkungen zu den Zügen der Kimmerier und der Skythen durch Vorderasien," *Klio* 77 (1995): 7–34.

320 Sverre Bøe, *Gog and Magog: Ezekiel 38–39 as Pre-text for Revelation 19,17–21 and 20,7–10* (Tübingen: Mohr Siebeck, 2001), 91–99.

321 Stuart C. Brown, "Media in the Achaemenid Period," in *Centre and Periphery Proceedings of the Groningen Achaemenid Workshop*, Achaemenid History III, eds. H. Sancesi-Weerdenburg and A. Kuhrt (Leiden: Nederlands Instituut voor het Nabije Oosten, 1990), 63–76.

322 RIMA 3:68; Brown, "Median (Media)," *RLA* 7, 7/8 (1982): 620.

Javan refers, in the Old Testament, to the Hellenic peoples in general and, specifically, to the Ionians (1 Chr 1:5–7; Isa 66:19; Ezek 27:13; 19), who settled along the eastern coastland of Asia Minor (modern Turkey) between the two geographical spheres of mainland Greece and Anatolia. The archaeology of this region is known from the cities of Priene, Miletos, Ephesos, and others.[323]

Tubal is consistently linked with Gog, Magog, and Meshech (Ezek 27:13; 32:26; 38:2–3; 39:1) and as traders from "the coastlands afar off" (Isa 66:19). The term may refer to the Tibar of Naram-Sin in the third millennium and Tapala of the fifteenth and fourteenth centuries BC in the Hittite sources.[324] Later, the Assyrians refer to them as the Tabal, located in the eastern and southeastern plateau of Anatolia from the reigns of Shalmaneser III (836 BC) to Assurbanipal (668 BC).[325]

Meshech is consistently linked to Gog, Magog, and Tubal (Ezek 27:13; 32:26; 38:2–3; 39:1), where they are described as traders. They are the Mushki or Mushku in Assyrian texts,[326] known as early as Tiglath Pileser I (1100 BC), who defeats five chiefs of the Mushku on the western shore of the Tigris River. Located in southeastern or central Anatolia, they may be the Phrygians or a separate group.[327]

Tiras may be identified with the Tursha, mentioned by Merenptah of Egypt in 1209 BC[328] and later by Ramses III in his Sea Peoples campaign. It is possible that they occur in a Hittite text of the thirteenth century as Taruisha (connected with ancient Troy) and later with the Tyrsenoi/Tyrrhenoi.[329] They have frequently been associated with the later Etruscans that settled in Italy after 800 BC.[330]

10:3 Gomer has three sons: **Ashkenaz, Riphath,** and **Togarmah.**

Ashkenaz (1 Chr 1:6; Jer 51:27) are the classical Scythians (Col 3:11) of Herodotus and the Ashkuza or Iškuzāi of the Assyrian texts of Esarhaddon.[331] This nomadic group lived in the steppes of Russia north of the Black Sea, stretching from Ukraine in the west to Siberia in the east. Archaeological evidence for the Scythians includes Nemirov Gorodische in the Ukraine and burial sites that have produced sophisticated, artistic workmanship in gold.[332]

Riphat does not occur elsewhere in the Old Testament or in ancient sources.

Togarmah is mentioned in Ezekiel 27:14 and 38:6 in association with Tubal, Javan, and Meshech and refers to ancient Tegarama and Takarma, which contained an Old Assyrian trading colony during the early second millennium BC.[333] It is known in the sixteenth century during the campaign of Hantili[334] and later the Hittite king Suppiluliuma captured Carchemish in his campaign against Mitanni. The

---

323 Alan M. Greaves, *The Land of Ionia: Society and Economy in the Archaic Period* (London: Wiley-Blackwell, 2010).

324 Trevor Bryce, *The World of the Neo-Hittite Kingdoms: A Political and Military History* (New York: Oxford University Press, 2012), 140–153.

325 S. Aro, "Tabal," *RLA* 8, 5/6 (1983): 388–391.

326 W. Röllig, "Muški, Muski," *RLA* 8, 7/8:493–495.

327 M. J. Mellink, "The Native Kingdoms of Anatolia," *CAH* III, 2:622–23.

328 On Merenptah's campaign, see Hasel, *Domination and Resistance: Egyptian Military Activity in the Southern Levant, ca. 1300–1185 BC*, Probleme der Ägyptologie 11 (Leiden: Brill, 1998), 178–193.

329 G. Neumann, "Tyrrhener," in *Die Kleine Pauly*, vol. 5 (Munich: Deutscher Taschenbuch Verlag, 1979), 1029.

330 Vedia Izzet, *The Archaeology of Etruscan Society* (Cambridge: Cambridge University Press, 2008).

331 Luckenbill, *Ancient Records of Assyria and Babylonia* (Chicago: University of Chicago Press, 1927), 207 §517, 213 §533.

332 M. I. Artamonov, *The Splendor of Scythian Art: Treasures From Scythian Tombs* (New York: Praeger, 1969); M. I. Artamonov, *Treasures From Scythian Tombs in the Hermitage Museum* (London: Thames and Hudson, 1969).

333 P. Garelli, *Les Assyriens en Cappadoce* (Paris: Maisonneuve, 1965), 117–118.

334 Trevor Bryce, *The Kingdom of the Hittites* (New York: Oxford University Press, 1998), 106.

location is not certain, although it probably was located in central or southeast Anatolia.[335]

10:4 The sons of Javan are **Elishah**, **Tarshish**, **Kittim**, and **Dodanim**.

Elishah is to be identified with the island of Cyprus in the eastern Mediterranean, where habitation, based on excavation, dates back into the third millennium BC.[336] It is attested in second millennium cuneiform sources as Alashia[337] and Egyptian sources as *Isy* or Alasia.[338] The earliest Egyptian text comes from the reign of Amenemhat II (ca. 1900 BC) when an army force is sent to *I3sy* by ship.

Tarshish occurs in the Old Testament as a location of trade and shipping (2 Chr 9:21; 20:36; Ezek 27:12–25; Jonah 1:3; 4:2). It is identified either as Tartessos on the mouth of the Guadalquivir in southern Spain or with Tarsus in Cilicia. Its location in Spain is to be preferred, based on (1) the geographical sequences in Genesis 10:4, (2) the traded metals (silver, Ezek 27:12; Jer 10:9; and gold, Isa 60:9) that are congruent with Tartessos, and (3) the repeated references to ships and shipping (1 Kgs 10:22; 22:49; Isa 2:16; 23:1, 14; 60:9), which seem to indicate a distant place.[339]

Kittim is the people of Kition on the island of Cyprus dating back to the mid-second millennium BC. Areas within Kition, modern Larnaca, have been extensively excavated by several expeditions.[340] The name later was applied to Greeks in general.

Dodanim or **Rodanim** (variant spelling in 1 Chr 1:7 and the Septuagint) is perhaps the Greek island of Rhodes, off of the western coast of Asia Minor. If the reading of Dodanim in Genesis 10:4 is to be preferred, some have suggested that they may be connected to the Dardanayu mentioned in a list of Aegean place names under Amenophis III (1381 BC),[341] and "the land of Dardanya," listed with the Hittite allies in the Battle of Kadesh texts of Ramses II (1275 BC),[342] which some have equated with the classical Dardanoi of Troy.[343]

10:5 The phrase **the coastland peoples** refers to the descendants of Javan, the fourth son of Japheth, and their dispersal into languages, families, and nations. This accords well with the settled and inhabited territory of the islands and coastal areas of the Mediterranean world from Spain (Tartessos) to Cyprus (Elishah, Kittim), and possibly Rhodes (Rodanim).

---

335 O. R. Gurney, *The Hittites*, 2nd ed. (Baltimore: Penguin, 1954), map; Bryce locates it near modern Gürün (*Kingdom of the Hittites*, 106).

336 Sophocles Hadjisavvas, *Cyprus: Crossroads of Civilizations* (Nicosia: Republic of Cyprus, 2010).

337 J. D. Muhly, "The Land of *Alashiya*: References to *Alashiya* in the Texts of the Second Millennium BC and the History of Cyprus in the Bronze Age," in *Proceedings of the First International Cypriote Congress* (Nicosia: Society for Cypriote Studies, 1972), 201–208.

338 K. A. Kitchen, "Alas(h)i(y)a (Irs) and Asiya (Isy) in Ancient Egyptian Sources," in *Egypt and Cyprus in Antiquity*, eds. D. Michaelides, V. Kissianidou, and R. S. Merrillees (London: Oxbow, 2009), 2–8.

339 John Day, "Where Was Tarshish?" in *Let Us Go Up to Zion: Essays in Honour of H. G. M. Williamson on the Occasion of His Sixty-Fifth Birthday*, eds. Iain Provan and Mark Boda, VTSup 153 (Leiden: Brill, 2012), 359–369.

340 E. Gjerstad, *The Swedish-Cyprus Expedition*, vols. 1–3 (Stockholm: Swedish Cyprus Expedition, 1934); Vassos Karageorghis, *Kition* (London: Thames and Hudson, 1976).

341 Elmar Edel and Manfred Görg, *Die Ortsnamenlisten aus dem Totentempel Amenophis III*, ÄAT 50 (Wiesbaden: Harrassowitz, 2005), 22, 25, 33–35.

342 Michael G. Hasel, "The Battle of Kadesh: Identifying New Kingdom Polities, Places, and Peoples in Canaan and Syria," in *Egypt, Canaan, and Israel: History, Imperialism, and Ideology*, eds. S. Bar, D. Kahn, and J. J. Shirley (Leiden: Brill, 2011), 65–86.

343 P. W. Haider, "Troia zwischen Hethitern, Mykenern und Mysern. Besitz der Toianische Krieg einen historischen Hintergrund?" in *Fontes atque Pontes: Eine Festgäbe für Hellmut Brunner* (Wiesbaden: Harrassowitz, 1983), 95–99.

The Sons of Japheth

Gomer	Magog	Madai	Javan	Tubal	Meshech	Tiras
Ashkenaz			*Elishah*			
Riphat			*Tarshish*			
Togarmah			*Kittim*			
			Dodanim			

10:6–20. THE SONS OF HAM

GEN 10:6–20 NKJV	GEN 10:6–20 ESV
6 The sons of Ham *were* Cush, Mizraim, Put, and Canaan.	**6** The sons of Ham: Cush, Egypt, Put, and Canaan.
7 The sons of Cush *were* Seba, Havilah, Sabtah, Raamah, and Sabtechah; and the sons of Raamah *were* Sheba and Dedan.	**7** The sons of Cush: Seba, Havilah, Sabtah, Raamah, and Sabteca. The sons of Raamah: Sheba and Dedan.
8 Cush begot Nimrod; he began to be a mighty one on the earth.	**8** Cush fathered Nimrod; he was the first on earth to be a mighty man.
9 He was a mighty hunter before the Lᴏʀᴅ; therefore it is said, "Like Nimrod the mighty hunter before the Lᴏʀᴅ."	**9** He was a mighty hunter before the Lᴏʀᴅ. Therefore it is said, "Like Nimrod a mighty hunter before the Lᴏʀᴅ."
10 And the beginning of his kingdom was Babel, Erech, Accad, and Calneh, in the land of Shinar.	**10** The beginning of his kingdom was Babel, Erech, Accad, and Calneh, in the land of Shinar.
11 From that land he went to Assyria and built Nineveh, Rehoboth Ir, Calah,	**11** From that land he went into Assyria and built Nineveh, Rehoboth-Ir, Calah, and
12 and Resen between Nineveh and Calah (that is the principal city).	**12** Resen between Nineveh and Calah; that is the great city.
13 Mizraim begot Ludim, Anamim, Lehabim, Naphtuhim,	**13** Egypt fathered Ludim, Anamim, Lehabim, Naphtuhim,
14 Pathrusim, and Casluhim (from whom came the Philistines and Caphtorim).	**14** Pathrusim, Casluhim (from whom the Philistines came), and Caphtorim.
15 Canaan begot Sidon his firstborn, and Heth;	**15** Canaan fathered Sidon his firstborn and Heth,
16 the Jebusite, the Amorite, and the Girgashite;	**16** and the Jebusites, the Amorites, the Girgashites,
17 the Hivite, the Arkite, and the Sinite;	**17** the Hivites, the Arkites, the Sinites,
18 the Arvadite, the Zemarite, and the Hamathite. Afterward the families of the Canaanites were dispersed.	**18** the Arvadites, the Zemarites, and the Hamathites. Afterward the clans of the Canaanites dispersed.
19 And the border of the Canaanites was from Sidon as you go toward Gerar, as far as Gaza; then as you go toward Sodom, Gomorrah, Admah, and Zeboiim, as far as Lasha.	**19** And the territory of the Canaanites extended from Sidon in the direction of Gerar as far as Gaza, and in the direction of Sodom, Gomorrah, Admah, and Zeboiim, as far as Lasha.
20 These *were* the sons of Ham, according to their families, according to their languages, in their lands *and* in their nations.	**20** These are the sons of Ham, by their clans, their languages, their lands, and their nations.

10:6 **Ham** is a person, the son of Noah, and is not associated with a nation, country, territory, or people group. The four sons of Ham—Cush, Mizraim, Put, and Canaan—are discussed below with their descendants who develop into entities within the territories of Africa, Arabia, and Canaan. The sons of Ham are **Cush**, **Mizraim**, **Put**, and **Canaan**.

Cush is referred to in the Old Testament as the territory of Kush, the deserts south of the First Cataract along the Nile extending into Upper Nubia.[344] The territory is first mentioned by Mentuhotep II, founder of the Middle Kingdom, during his military campaigns (ca. 2017–2015 BC).[345] Later, Nubian pharaohs ruled over Egypt.[346]

Mizraim refers to Egypt. The Hebrew word *mitsrayim* is used ninety times for Egypt in the Old Testament. The dual ending (*-ayim*) may reflect the division of Egypt as Upper and Lower Egypt. The term *matsor* is used in poetic passages (2 Kgs 19:24; Isa 19:6; 37:25; Mic 7:12). It is found in cuneiform sources as *misir, misru, musri*.[347] Mizraim (Egypt) "begot" the Ludim, the Anamim, the Lehabim, the Naphtuhim, the Pathrusim, and the Casluhim (10:13–14).

Put is found in conjunction with Cush (Jer 46:9 ESV) and again alongside Persia and Cush (Ezek 38:5). In Nahum 3:9, they are equated with Lubim. It is most frequently identified with Libya in the desert west of Egypt.[348] The Libyan rulers of Dynasty XX included Shoshenq I (Shishak) who attacked Judah and Israel in 925 BC.[349] Put is the only son of Ham for whom no descendants are given.

Canaan is the third people, which refers to the territory of Syria-Palestine in the Old Testament (Deut 1:7; Josh 3:10; Judg 1:3). The boundaries of the land of Canaan are further described in Numbers 34–35. In New Kingdom Egypt, the terms "Canaan" or "Canaanite" are employed for the same territory, often with synonyms such as Djahy, Retenu, and Kharu, beginning with the reign of Amenophis III (1380 BC).[350] In the cuneiform sources, it appears in texts from Mari, Amarna, Ugarit, Assur, and Hattusha.[351] The cities, nations, and peoples that are related belong to this general area of Syro-Palestine.

10:7 The descendants of Cush later extended into East Africa and the Arabian Peninsula. The sons of Cush were **Seba, Havilah, Sabtah, Raamah,** and **Sabtechah;** and the sons of Raamah were Sheba and Dedan (10:7).

Seba, not to be confused with Sheba, is mentioned several times in the Old Testament (Ps 72; Isa 43:3; 45:14). It is somewhat related to Cush and Sheba but located in East Africa (possibly Eritrea/Ethiopia),[352] where Sabeanlike archaeological remains have been found in modern Teha.[353]

---

344 K. A. Kitchen, *On the Reliability of the Old Testament* (Grand Rapids: Eerdmans, 2003), 593n26.

345 E. Brovowski and William J. Murnane, "Inscriptions From the Time of Nebhepetre-Mentuhotep II at Abisko," *Serapis* 1 (1969): 11–33.

346 Lázló Török, *Between Two Worlds: The Frontier Region Between Ancient Nubia and Egypt, 3700–640 BC*, Probleme der Ägyptologie 29 (Leiden: Brill, 2008).

347 W. Röllig, "Misir, Misru, Musur, Musri III, Muzir," *RLA* 8, 3/4 (1994): 264–69.

348 G. Posener, *La première domination perse en Égypte* (Cairo: Institut Français d'Archéologie Orientale du Caire, 1936), 186–187.

349 K. A. Kitchen, *The Third Intermediate Period in Egypt (1100–650 BC)*, 2nd ed. (Warminster, UK: Aris & Phillips, 1996); K. A. Kitchen, "The Shoshenqs of Egypt and Palestine," *JSOT* 93 (2001): 3–12.

350 For complete references, see Michael G. Hasel, "Pa-Canaan in the Egyptian New Kingdom: Canaan or Gaza?" *Journal of Ancient Egyptian Interconnections* 1, no. 1 (2009): 8–17.

351 Anson F. Rainey, "Who Is a Canaanite? A Review of the Textual Evidence," *BASOR* 304 (1996): 1–15.

352 H. von Wissmann, *Über die frühe Geschichte Arabiens und die Entstehen des Sabäerreiches, Die Geschichte von Saba' 1* (Vienna: Academie, 1975), 87–95, 102–105.

353 Kitchen, *On the Reliability of the Old Testament*, 594n34.

Havilah is mentioned in the Old Testament in connection with Ophir, which is east of Egypt (25:18; 1 Sam 15:7) and is a land that contains gold (2:11). It has been identified with northern Arabia, but the more likely identification is with western Arabia. Its name may derive from the Sabaean Hawlan.[354]

Sabtah may derive from Shabwa(t), the capital of the kingdom of Hadramaut. The excavations of the site indicate that the strata date all the way back to the eighteenth or fourteenth centuries BC.[355]

Raamah is listed in the Old Testament with products such as spices, precious stones, and gold (Ezek 27:22–24), suggesting a location in southern Arabia near incense routes. Some have identified it with ancient *rgmtm* (Ragmatum), the ancient capital in north Yemen or the oasis Nagrān[356] in modern southwest Saudi Arabia. The earliest mention of this capital is from an old Sabean inscription dated to 500 BC.[357] Raamah had two sons, **Sheba** and **Dedan**. *Sheba* is named with Raamah as a commercial partner (Ezek 27:22) and is to be located in Yemen in southwestern Arabia. Settlements in this area date to the eleventh century BC. A sequence of rulers extends to at least the tenth century BC.[358] *Dedan* was a commercial settlement (Ezek 27:15–20) whose merchants caused consternation for the Hebrew prophets (Isa 21:13; Ezek 38:13). The site of Khuraybah has been identified as a possible location for the kingdom located on the narrow oasis of modern Al-Ula in northwest Arabia.[359] An inscription naming two kings dates back to the sixth century BC.[360]

Sabtechah only occurs in this context, which suggests that it should also be located in Arabia, possibly the site of Shabaka in Hadramaut, two days' journey west of the ancient kingdom's capital, Shabwat.[361]

The last section dealing with Ham (10:8–20) focuses on the three neighboring peoples who impacted the history of Israel: Babylon-Assyria (10:8–12), Egypt (10:13–14), and Canaan (10:15–19). The association of the three peoples is rendered stylistically by the use of the same introductory phrase: *x* begot (*yalad*) *y* (10:8, 13, 15).

10:8–9 **Nimrod** is Cush's sixth son, who appears unexpectedly after the mention of his other five sons and two grandsons (10:8). The identification of Nimrod continues to be debated. Nimrod is recorded as the founder of a number of city-states: Babel, Erech, Accad, Calneh, in the land of Shinar, or Babylonia in southern Mesopotamia (11:2; Zech 5:11; Dan 1:2). From there, his descendants colonized Nineveh, Rehoboth Ir, Calah, and Resen in northern Mesopotamia, later Assyria. Most of these sites are well known from the cuneiform sources and from archaeological excavation.

10:10 The city of **Babel** is to be identified with ancient Babylon, dating back to the third millennium. It was the capital of Babylonia under Hammurabi in the eighteenth century BC;[362] and in the Neo-Babylonian period, it became the conquering

---

354 K. A. Kitchen, "Sheba and Arabia," in *The Age of Solomon: Scholarship at the Turn of the Millennium,* ed. Lowell K. Handy (Leiden: Brill, 1997), 145; Kitchen, *Reliability of the Old Testament*, 594n30.

355 Abdallah Hassan Al-Shaiba, "Die Ortsnamen in den altsüdarabischen Inschriften," *Archäologische Berichte aus dem Yemen* 4 (1987): 36; *DAA* 2:126–127.

356 W. W. Müller, "Raamah," *ABD* 5:597.

357 J.-B. Chabot, *Répertoire d'Epigraphie Sémitique* 4:393–395; cf. *DAA* 2:509.

358 *DAA* 1:242–245; *DAA* 2:737–747.

359 David F. Graf, "Dedan," *ABD* 2:121–123.

360 *DAA* 1:50–51, 118, 168.

361 H. von Wissmann and M. Höffner, *Beiträge zur historischen Geographie des vorderasiatischen Südarabien* (Wiesbaden: Harrassowitz, 1953), 109; W. W. Müller, "Sabteca," *ABD* 5:862–863.

362 Marc van der Mieroop, *King Hammurabi of Babylon: A Biography* (Marden: Blackwell, 2005).

power to defeat Jerusalem under Nebuchadnezzar (Dan 1:1–3; 2 Kgs 24–25).[363]

The city of **Erech**, mentioned only again in Ezra 4:9, is ancient Uruk, or Warka, one of the first cities of ancient Sumer and home to Gilgamesh and other fabled kings. In the Sumerian King List, it is one of the first cities to be built after the flood.[364] Its extensive ruins were excavated over a period of thirty-nine seasons and revealed a city more than 5.5 square kilometers in area, including temples and domestic buildings.[365]

The city of **Accad** is to be identified with the Sumerian Agade of Sargon I,[366] established as the capital of his dynasty north of Babylon on the Euphrates. Historical sources indicate that this city existed since the third millennium BC and declined sharply in importance after 2000 BC. It has never been identified or excavated.[367]

The city of **Calneh** is not known as a city at the present time, and a number of scholars suggest it should be translated "and all of them" in the land of Shinar, connecting the preceding cities with the land of Shinar.[368]

The area of **Shinar** was equated by some early Assyriologists with ancient Sumer and the Sumerians,[369] but there remain some linguistic difficulties with the identification.[370] It is likely to be a regional designation for all of Babylonia or southern Mesopotamia, an area where writing and cities first developed in the Fertile Crescent.

The name of **Assyria** refers to the northern territory of Mesopotamia colonized by the descendants of Nimrod. Its history goes back to the third millennium BC, when the city-states of Asshur and Nineveh were established.[371] The Assyrian Empire later dominated through a ruthless military expansion, defeating Israel in 722 BC and threatening the kingdom of Judah in 701 BC during the reign of Sennacherib.[372]

10:11 The city of **Nineveh** was Assyria's most prominent city and capital during the eighth century BC.[373] Excavations revealed the massive palaces of Sennacherib and Assurbanipal, temples, gates, and an enormous city that stretched over 750 hectares (1900 acres) surrounded by 12-kilometer brick ramparts.

The name of **Rehoboth Ir** could either designate Nineveh, or it may be identified as Rebit Ninâ. It has been translated as a suburb of Nineveh,[374] as a city of broad streets,[375] or roughly "the broadest city" (cf. Jonah 3:3; 4:11).[376]

The city of **Calah** is the ancient city of Kalhu, modern Nimrud,[377] one of the four

---

363 D. J. Wiseman, *Nebuchadrezzar and Babylon,* Schweich Lectures on Biblical Archaeology (London: Oxford University Press, 1991); Joan Oates, *Babylon* (London: Thames and Hudson, 1986).

364 Westermann, *Genesis 1–11,* 517.

365 Mitchell S. Rothman, ed., *Uruk Mesopotamia and Its Neighbors* (Santa Fe: School of American Research, 2001); M. Liverani, Z. Bahrani, and M. van der Mieroop, *Uruk: The First City* (London: Equinox, 2006).

366 Jerome S. Cooper, *The Curse of Agade* (Baltimore: Johns Hopkins University, 1983).

367 For possible locations, see Harvey Weiss, "Kish, Akkad and Agade," *JAOS* 95 (1975): 434–453; Christophe Wall-Romana, "An Areal Location of Agade," *JNES* 49 (1990): 205–245.

368 J. A. Thompson, "Samaritan Evidence for 'All of Them in the Land of Shinar' (Gen 10:10)," *JBL* 90 (1971): 99–102.

369 Anton Deimel, "Šumer = Šin'ar," *Bib* 2 (1921): 71–74; Anton Deimel, "Nimrod (Gen. 10:8–12)," *Or* 26 (1927): 76–80.

370 Ran Zadok, "The Origin of the Name Shinar," *ZA* 74 (1984): 240–244.

371 A. Leo Oppenheim, *Ancient Mesopotamia,* 2nd ed. (Chicago: University of Chicago Press, 1977).

372 On Assyrian military tactics, see Michael G. Hasel, *Military Practice and Polemic: Israel's Laws of Warfare in Near Eastern Context* (Berrien Springs, MI: Andrews University Press, 2005), 51–94.

373 Mark Van de Mieroop, *The Ancient Mesopotamian City* (Oxford: Oxford University Press, 1997), 95; A. Kirk Grayson, "Nineveh," *ABD* 4:1118–1119.

374 Cassuto, *Genesis,* 2:203.

375 E. A. Speiser, *Genesis,* AB (New York: Doubleday, 1969), 68.

376 Jack M. Sasson, "Rehovot 'Ir," *RB* 90 (1983): 94–96.

377 A. Kirk Grayson, "Calah," *ABD* 1:807–808.

great cities of ancient Assyria in the third and second millennia BC. After an extensive rebuilding program by Assurnasirpal II, it became the capital of Assyria until 700 BC. Excavations revealed a massive temple and ziggurat built during his reign.[378]

10:12 The city of **Resen** has not been identified with a known ancient city or location. It may refer to some type of waterworks within the city of Nineveh or Calah.[379]

10:13 **Ludim** are people that are often associated with Egypt and Cush (Jer 46:9; Ezek 30:5; 27:10), which implies a location in North Africa. Babylonian texts mention *Ludu* in alliance and fighting with Egypt.[380] They are a different group from Lud (Lydia), mentioned as one of the descendants of Shem.

Anamim is an unknown group that has not been clearly identified, although suggestions include the *a-na-mi* of Assyrian texts (Cyrene)[381] or an emendation of the text to *knmtym*, which might correspond to *knmt* in the Libyan desert west of Egypt.[382] The latter suggestion has not been widely accepted.

Lehabim is an alternate spelling for the Lubim, a Libyan group living to the west of Egypt. They are mentioned frequently in the Old Testament (Dan 11:43; 2 Chr 12:3; 16:8) and are placed together with Put, another Libyan group. The Egyptians refer to them as the *rbw*, pronounced *Lebu* in texts of the New Kingdom.[383]

Naphtuhim are people located in Upper Egypt or the delta near the capital Memphis. This conclusion is based on the Egyptian designation Na-Ptah, for the people of Ptah, living in the vicinity of the Great Temple dedicated to Ptah at Memphis.[384]

10:14 **Pathrusim** are the inhabitants of *pa-to-resi* or "the southland" of Upper Egypt, south of the delta region, the Paturesi of Assyrian texts. Old Testament texts (Jer 44:1, 15; Ezek 29:14; 30:14) link Pathros with the origin of the Egyptians. This corresponds to the Egyptian tradition of Menes uniting Upper and Lower Egypt from this territory.[385]

Casluhim are the progenitors of the Philistines and the **Caphtorim**. Because this group originates as the sixth son of Egypt, it is identified as a group originating from Lower Egypt and eventually settling in the Aegean, perhaps Crete, before migrating to the southern coastal plain of Canaan.[386]

Philistines are originated from Caphtor (Jer 47:4; Amos 9:7). If Caphtor is Crete, then Genesis 10:14 may indicate that, in early times, the biblical writers understood Cretans to be "Philistines," or the name was later updated. The name "Philistines" has been found under Ramses III. The Philistine cities (Ashkelon, Ashdod, Gath, Gaza, and Ekron) have been excavated and produced large amounts of Aegean-type pottery, suggesting an origin from the Aegean, including Crete.[387]

---

378 Julian E. Reade, "Nimrud," in *Fifty Years of Mesopotamian Discovery*, ed. John E. Curtis (London: British School of Archaeology in Iraq, 1982), 99–112.

379 James R. Davila, "Resen," *ABD* 5:678; Lipiński, "Nimrod et Aššur," *RB* 73 (1966): 77–93.

380 Simo Parpola, *Neo-Assyrian Toponyms* (Kevelaer: Butzon & Bercker, 1970), 227.

381 William F. Albright, "A Colony of Cretan Mercenaries on the Coast of the Negev," *JPOS* 1 (1920–1921): 187–194.

382 John Skinner, *Genesis*, ICC 12 (New York: Scribner, 1910), 212.

383 Anthony Leahy, ed., *Libya and Egypt, ca. 1300–750 BC* (London: Society for Libyan Studies, 1990).

384 On the great temple, see H. Papazian, "The Temple of Ptah and Economic Contacts Between Memphite Cult Centers in the Fifth Dynasty," in *8. Ägyptologische Tempeltagung*, eds. Monika Dolínska and Horst Beinlich (Wiesbaden: Harrassowitz, 2010), 137–154.

385 Herodotus, *Histories* 2.4.1; 2.99.1.

386 Gary A. Rendsburg, "Gen. 10:13–14: An Authentic Hebrew Tradition Concerning the Origin of the Philistines," *JNSL* 13 (1987): 89–96; cf. Richard S. Hess, "Casluhim," *ABD* 1:877–878.

387 For summaries, see Trude Dothan and Moshe Dothan, *People of the Sea: The Search for the Philistines* (New York: Macmillan, 1992); Trude Dothan, *The Philistines and Their Material Culture* (New Haven: Yale University Press,

Caphtorim destroyed the cities of the coast as far as Gaza and lived in them (Deut 2:23). They are later connected to the Philistines (Jer 47:4; Amos 9:7). Caphtor is the cuneiform *kaptara* mentioned as early as the eighteenth century BC at Mari and known in Egyptian texts as Keftiu,[388] mentioned as early as the reign of Amenophis III.[389] They have been identified as the inhabitants of Cyprus, Cappadocia, Cilicia, or, more commonly, with Crete.[390]

10:15 Canaan, like Cush and Mizraim, "begot" (10:15) his descendants: Sidon, Heth, the Jebusite, the Amorite, the Girgashite, the Hivite, the Arkite, the Sinite, the Arvadite, the Zemarite, and the Hamathite (10:15–18).

Sidon is located along the coast in modern Lebanon. Sidon occurs in Egyptian texts in the mid-second millennium BC (Papyrus Anastasi I and Wenamun)[391] and in the Amarna letters, where the ruler is named Zimreddi.[392] It was the mother city of Tyre (Judg 1:31).[393] The intermittent archaeological excavations of the site reveal a city dating back into the third millennium.

Hittites (from the name "Heth") appear in the Old Testament when Abraham purchases a cave from the "sons of Heth" to bury Sarah, David kills Uriah the Hittite (2 Sam 11; 12:9–10), and Solomon takes a Hittite wife (1 Kgs 11:1). Since these names are all Semitic, they are to be distinguished from the Indo-European Hittites of Anatolia in the mid-second millennium BC. These Hittites later mixed with the population of Canaan.[394] Others suggest that Heth, in fact, refers to the same Hittites of Anatolia, mentioned frequently in Egyptian texts of the New Kingdom and by the Assyrians as *hattú*.[395] In this case, later descendants would have moved into Canaan. The archaeological remains of the Anatolian Hittites, with their capital of Hattusha, are extensively documented.[396]

10:16 **Jebusites** are one of the Canaanite peoples in the Old Testament (Exod 3:8–17; 13:5; 23:23; 33:2; Josh 9:1; 12:8), the inhabitants of Jebus, ancient Jerusalem (Judg 19:11), which was captured by David in the seventh year of his reign (2 Sam 5:6–8). Its first mention is found in the Amarna tablets.[397] Excavations south of the Temple Mount revealed massive fortifications dating to the Middle Bronze Age.[398]

Amorites (Exod 3:8–17; 13:5; 23:23; 33:2; Josh 9:1; 12:8) were known from the Sumerian texts as MAR.TU and from the third millennium and Akkadian texts as

. . .
1982); Sy Gitin, "The Philistines," in *The Book of Kings: Sources, Composition, Historiography and Reception,* eds. Andre Lemaire and Baruch Halpern (Leiden: Brill, 2010), 301–364; Ann E. Killebrew and Gunnar Lehmann, eds., *The Philistines and Other "Sea Peoples" in Text and Archaeology* (Atlanta: Society of Biblical Literature, 2013).

388 M. Weippert, "Kreta," *RLA* 6, 3/4 (1981): 226–227; James Strange, *Caphtor/Keftiu: A New Investigation* (Leiden: Brill, 1980).

389 Edel and Görg, *Ortsnamenlisten,* 27–28.

390 Jean Vercouter, *L' Egypte et le monde égéen préhellénique* (Cairo: Institut Français d'Archéologie Orientale du Caire, 1956).

391 *COS* 1:91; Glenn Markoe, *The Phoenicians* (London: British Museum Press, 2000), 199–201.

392 Moran, *The Amarna Letters* (Baltimore: Johns Hopkins University Press, 1992), 230–242.

393 D. J. Wiseman suggests that the absence of Tyre in the Table of Nations indicates the lists antiquity. "Genesis 10 Some Archaeological Considerations," *925th Ordinary General Meeting of the Victoria Institute* (December 6, 1954), 17. On excavations, see Issam Ali Khalifah, "Sidon," *OEANE* 5:38–40.

394 David W. Baker, "Heth," *ABD* 3:188.

395 J. D. Hawkins, "Hatti," *RLA* 4, 1/4 (1979): 152–159.

396 Kurt Bittel, "Hattuša," *RLA* 4, 1/4 (1979): 162–172.

397 Moran, *Amarna Letters,* 328–329; see Nadav Na'aman, "The Contribution of the Amarna Letters to the Debate on Jerusalem's Political Position in the Tenth Century B.C.E.," *BASOR* 304 (1996): 17–27.

398 R. Reich and E. Shukron, "The Date of the Siloam Tunnel Reconsidered," *TA* 38 (2011): 147–157.

Amurru. They appear both as a geographical and ethnic designation.[399] The Babylonian king Hammurabi had the title "King of Amurru."[400] Amorites widely influenced the development of Semitic languages, such as Canaanite and Hebrew.[401]

Girgashites are unknown outside the Old Testament (15:21; Deut 7:1; Josh 3:10; 24:11; Neh 9:8), where they are listed among the Canaanite peoples in the land.

10:17 **The Hivites** are unknown outside the Old Testament (occurring twenty-five times; cf. 15:21; Deut 7:1; Josh 3:10; 24:11), where they appear among the Canaanite peoples in the land.

Arkites inhabited the Phoenician city of Irqata. The town occurs in Egyptian texts as '3qty; in the Hittite as *ir-qà-ta*; and in Akkadian sources as *ir-qat, ir-qa-ta, ir-qà-ta*; including the Amarna letters, as early as the second millennium.[402] Excavations at the site of Tell Arqa, twelve miles northwest of Tripoli, exposed Bronze through Iron Ages.[403]

Sinites are from Siyannu, known as *syn*, from the archives of its northern neighbor at Ugarit in the fifteenth century BC[404] and mentioned later in the campaign records of Tiglath Pileser III.[405] The site's exact location remains unknown.

Arvadites are from the city of Arvad, modern Ruad, dating to the third millennium BC. It is mentioned in an Egyptian text as *'a-r-du*,[406] in the Amarna tablets allied with Amurru (the Amorites),[407] as well as Assyrian and Babylonian texts, where it is located "in the midst of the sea."[408] This location rightly corresponds to the information found in Ezekiel 27:8, which refers to the Arvadites as seamen.

Zemarites, only occurring here and a parallel text (1 Chr 1:16), were the people of Sumer, classical Simirra (Tell Kazel), located near the mouth of the Eleutheros Valley near the coast. Sumer is mentioned frequently in the campaign accounts of New Kingdom Egypt, beginning with the reign of Thutmose III[409] and in the Amarna letters.[410]

Hamathites were people of Hamath, a city located on the Orontes in west-central Syria. The site is mentioned as the northern border to the later territory of Israel (Num 34:8; 1 Kgs 8:65; 1 Chr 13:5). The Ebla texts refer to the city as *Ematu*, while the Syro-Hittite (Luwian) texts refer to it as *Amatu*.[411] Excavations have revealed a long history of the city stretching back to the third millennium BC.

---

399 Alfred Haider, *Who Were the Amorites?* (Leiden: Brill, 1971), 20, 65–66; Giorgio Buccellati, *The Amorites of the Ur III Period* (Naples: Institutio Orientale di Napoli, 1966); Mario Liverani, "The Amorites," in *Peoples of Old Testament Times*, ed. D. J. Wiseman (Oxford: Clarendon, 1973), 102.

400 J.-R. Kupper, *Les Nomades en Mésopotamie au temps des rois de Mari* (Paris: Belles lettres, 1957), 174–177.

401 George E. Mendenhall, "Amorites," *ABD* 1:200–202.

402 Parpola, *Neo-Assyrian Toponyms*, 31, 176.

403 J.-P. Thalman, "Tell-Arqa (Liban Nord) Campagnes I-III (1972–1974) Chantier I. Repport préliminaire," *Syria* 55 (1978): 1–151; R. Dussaud, *Topographie historique de la Syrie antique at medieval* (Paris: Geuthner, 1927), 80–91.

404 J. Nougayrol, *Le Palais Royal d'Ugarit*, vol. 4 (Paris: Imprimiere Nationale/Klincksieck, 1956), 15–17.

405 Parpola, *Neo-Assyrian Toponyms*, 308.

406 Wolfgang Helck, *Untersuchungen Ägyptens zur vorderasien im 3. Und 2. Jahrtausend v. Chr.*, ÄAT5 (Wiesbaden: Harrassowitz, 1962), 310.

407 H. J. Katzenstein, *The History of Tyre* (Jerusalem: Magnes, 1973), 42; cf. Richard S. Hess, "Arvad," *ABD* 1:468.

408 Wiseman, "Two Historical Inscriptions From Nimrud," *Iraq* 13 (1951): 21–26; Eckhard Unger, "Arwad," *RLA* 1 (1976): 160–161.

409 H. Klengel, "Sumar/Simyra und die Eleutheros-Ebene in der Geschichte Syriens," *Klio* 66 (1984): 5–18; Donald B. Redford, *The Wars in Syria and Palestine of Thutmose III*, CHANE 16 (Leiden: Brill, 2003), 70.

410 Moran, *Amarna*, 132–133, 140.

411 Marie-Louise Buhl, "Hamath," *ABD* 3:33–36.

10:19–20 The borders of Canaan extend up to the city of Sidon on the eastern coast of modern Lebanon, south to Gaza, and westward to the Dead Sea. This corresponds to the cities and territories described in this periscope and the territory promised to Israel.

The Sons of Ham

Cush	Mizraim	Put	Canaan
Seba	Ludim		Sidon
Havilah	Anamim		Hittites
Sabtah	Lehabites		Jebusites
Raamah	Naphtuhites		Amorites
Sheba	Pathrusites		Girgashites
Dedan	Casluhites		Hivites
Sabtechah	Philistines		Arkites
Nimrod	Caphtorites		Sinites
			Arvadites
			Zemarites
			Hamathites

10:21–31. THE SONS OF SHEM

GEN 10:20–31 NKJV	GEN 10:21–31 ESV
21 And *children* were born also to Shem, the father of all the children of Eber, the brother of Japheth the elder.	**21** To Shem also, the father of all the children of Eber, the elder brother of Japheth, children were born.
22 The sons of Shem *were* Elam, Asshur, Arphaxad, Lud, and Aram.	**22** The sons of Shem: Elam, Asshur, Arpachshad, Lud, and Aram.
23 The sons of Aram *were* Uz, Hul, Gether, and Mash.	**23** The sons of Aram: Uz, Hul, Gether, and Mash.
24 Arphaxad begot Salah, and Salah begot Eber.	**24** Arpachshad fathered Shelah; and Shelah fathered Eber.
25 To Eber were born two sons: the name of one *was* Peleg, for in his days the earth was divided; and his brother's name *was* Joktan.	**25** To Eber were born two sons: the name of the one was Peleg, for in his days the earth was divided, and his brother's name was Joktan.
26 Joktan begot Almodad, Sheleph, Hazarmaveth, Jerah,	**26** Joktan fathered Almodad, Sheleph, Hazarmaveth, Jerah,
27 Hadoram, Uzal, Diklah,	**27** Hadoram, Uzal, Diklah,
28 Obal, Abimael, Sheba,	**28** Obal, Abimael, Sheba,
29 Ophir, Havilah, and Jobab. All these *were* the sons of Joktan.	**29** Ophir, Havilah, and Jobab; all these were the sons of Joktan.
30 And their dwelling place was from Mesha as you go toward Sephar, the mountain of the east.	**30** The territory in which they lived extended from Mesha in the direction of Sephar to the hill country of the east.
31 These *were* the sons of Shem, according to their families, according to their languages, in their lands, according to their nations.	**31** These are the sons of Shem, by their clans, their languages, their lands, and their nations.

10:21 **Shem** is not associated with a nation and is considered a person. The descendants of Shem are more complex than the previous lists. They extend beyond the sons and grandsons—tracing the lineage down to the fifth generation after Noah. Shem has five sons that form the nations of Mesopotamia and Iran, but many of the later descendants seem to be names of individuals and not as yet identifiable as nations, countries, territories, cities, or people groups. At this juncture, following the listing of the nonelect families, the author of Genesis focuses on the chosen lineage of the Semites, from whom will come Abraham, the ancestor of the Hebrews, who are alluded to in the phrase **all the children of Eber**. The Hebrew word *'ibri* "Hebrew" is the gentilic form of the name "Eber." This special note anticipates the future nation of Israel from the line of Shem. The verb *yalad* "beget" is used again (cf. 10:8, 13, 15); but here the form is passive, **were born**, suggesting the implicit divine subject.

10:22 Shem has five sons: **Elam, Asshur, Arphaxad, Lud**, and **Aram**.

Elam is the easternmost country named and is mentioned twenty-five times in the Old Testament (14:1–9; Ezra 2:7–31; 4:9; 10:2; Jer 25:25). It is to be identified with the kingdom of Elam located in southwest Iran, near Sumer, which lies near the Persian Gulf. The Elamites are known from the third millennium onwards in texts and through the archaeology of major cities, including Anshan and Susa.[412]

Asshur is the capital Ashur, which gave the Assyrian kingdom its name. The city dates back to the third millennium BC.[413]

Lud is not to be confused with the Ludim mentioned under the descendants of Ham (cf. 10:13). Lud is most frequently identified with Lydia in Anatolia, first attested in the seventh century in Assyrian sources as Gyges of Lydia.[414]

Aram is the ancient nation of the Arameans (22:21; Num. 23:7) and is located in southern Syria with its capital in Damascus.[415] The nation existed from the late second millennium BC until the campaign of Tiglath Pileser III in 732 BC, when Aram was defeated.[416] There are no written documents from the kingdom itself other than the fragments of the Dan stele written in Aramaic and proclaiming a victory over the king of Israel and the house of David.[417]

10:23 Of the five sons of Shem, only the sons of Aram and Arphaxad are given, reflecting their particular connection with the history of the Hebrews. For Aram, however, the genealogy does not go beyond the first generation. Aram's sons are: **Uz, Hul, Gether**, and **Mash**. These names refer to a people who have not yet been identified with certainty and were located in the Aramean territory.

10:24 **Arphaxad** is Shem's son, who receives the most attention. He is the only son whose descendants are given beyond the first generation, reaching to the fourth generation. Significantly, the passage dealing with Arphaxad (10:24–25) contains the greatest concentration of the verb *yalad* "beget" (five occurrences). Arphaxad

---

412 D. T. Potts, *The Archaeology of Elam: Formation and Transformation of the Ancient Iranian State* (Cambridge: Cambridge University Press, 1999).

413 W. Andrae, *Das wiederstandene Assur*, ed. B. Hrouda (Munich: Beck, 1977).

414 Mordecai Cogan and Hayim Tadmor, "Gyges and Ashurbanipal: A Study in Literary Transmission," *Orientalia* 46 (1977): 65–85.

415 Wayne T. Pitard, *Ancient Damascus: A Historical Study of the Syrian City-State From Earliest Times Until Its Fall to the Assyrians in 732 BCE* (Winona Lake, IN: Eisenbrauns, 1987).

416 André Dupont-Sommer, *Les Araméens* (Paris: Depot A. Maisonneuve, 1949); A. R. Millard, "Arameans," *ABD* 1:345–350.

417 Avraham Biran and Joseph Naveh, "An Aramaic Fragment From Tel Dan," *IEJ* 43 (1993): 81–98; William M. Schniedewind, "Tel Dan Stela: New Light on Aramaic and Jehu's Revolt," *BASOR* 302 (1996): 75–90.

has been difficult to identify on the basis of the name alone, although a possible etymological connection of the name *kshdarpakshad* "Arphaxad" with the word *kasdim* "Chaldean" (11:28), on the basis of the common last letters *kshd*, suggests the southern region of Babylonia. Arphaxad's son **Salah** is not easily identified; he is not associated with a city, a nation, a region, or a people group (cf. 11:10–26). He is Eber's father, and, as such, deserves to be mentioned (cf. 10:21; 11:16). Eber begets two sons, Peleg and Joktan (10:25).

10:25 The name **Peleg** means division and may hint at the division of nations, following the incident of the tower of Babel (11:8–9).

10:26 **Joktan** and his descendants settled as various people groups in the territory of Arabia. The names are retained in the geographical and city designations long after they settled in the region. **Sheleph** is to be identified with ancient *Slfn* in the Sabaean texts and the name may be retained in the various *as-Salfs* located in Yemen.[418] **Hazarmaveth** is to be identified with Hadramaut, the territory of Yemen. **Jerah** may be identified with the ruins of the city Yarih mentioned in the Mari letters of the early second millennium BC, later the Yariheans.[419]

Other entities (**Almodad, Hadoram, Uzal, Diklah, Abimael**, and **Obal**) have not been identified with certainty.

10:29 **Jobab** could be the Old South Arabian clan name.

10:30 **Ophir, Havilah**, and **Jobab** are locations in Arabia also listed under Ham with references there. Likewise, the places of these peoples, **Mesha** and **Sephar**, although situated in **the mountain of the east** (10:30), suggesting the Arabian geography, have not been identified with precision and certainty.

10:31 The section on the sons of Shem is concluded the same way as the sections of the two other sons of Noah (cf. 10:5, 20).

The Sons of Shem

Elam	Asshur	Arphaxad	Lud	Aram
		Salah		*Uz*
		Eber		*Hul*
		Peleg		*Gether*
		Joktan		*Mash*
		Almodad		
		Sheleph		
		Hazarmaveth		
		Jerah		
		Hadoram		
		Uzal		
		Diklah		
		Obal		
		Abimael		
		Sheba		
		Ophir		
		Havilah		
		Jobab		

---

418 Wissmann, *Geschichte Arabiens*, 78n1; cf. Kitchen, *On the Reliability of the Old Testament*, 597n41.

419 J.-M. Durand, *Documents épistolaires du palais de Mari*, vol. 2 (Paris: Éditions du Cerf, 1998), 29–30.

10:32. CONCLUSION

GEN 10:32 NKJV	GEN 10:32 ESV
32 These were the families of the sons of Noah, according to their generations, in their nations; and from these the nations were divided on the earth after the flood.	**32** These are the clans of the sons of Noah, according to their genealogies, in their nations, and from these the nations spread abroad on the earth after the flood.

This line closes the whole Table of Nations, referring to all the sons of Noah. The conclusion echoes the language of its introduction in inclusio (cf. 10:1) and anticipates the forthcoming event of the tower of Babel, which will report on the origin and the circumstances of the spreading of these nations (10:9).

THE TOWER OF BABEL (11:1–9)

GEN 11:1–9 NKJV	GEN 11:1–9 ESV
1 Now the whole earth had one language and one speech.	**1** Now the whole earth had one language and the same words.
2 And it came to pass, as they journeyed from the east, that they found a plain in the land of Shinar, and they dwelt there.	**2** And as people migrated from the east, they found a plain in the land of Shinar and settled there.
3 Then they said to one another, "Come, let us make bricks and bake *them* thoroughly." They had brick for stone, and they had asphalt for mortar.	**3** And they said to one another, "Come, let us make bricks, and burn them thoroughly." And they had brick for stone, and bitumen for mortar.
4 And they said, "Come, let us build ourselves a city, and a tower whose top *is* in the heavens; let us make a name for ourselves, lest we be scattered abroad over the face of the whole earth."	**4** Then they said, "Come, let us build ourselves a city and a tower with its top in the heavens, and let us make a name for ourselves, lest we be dispersed over the face of the whole earth."
5 But the Lᴏʀᴅ came down to see the city and the tower which the sons of men had built.	**5** And the Lᴏʀᴅ came down to see the city and the tower, which the children of man had built.
6 And the Lᴏʀᴅ said, "Indeed the people *are* one and they all have one language, and this is what they begin to do; now nothing that they propose to do will be withheld from them.	**6** And the Lᴏʀᴅ said, "Behold, they are one people, and they have all one language, and this is only the beginning of what they will do. And nothing that they propose to do will now be impossible for them.
7 Come, let Us go down and there confuse their language, that they may not understand one another's speech."	**7** Come, let us go down and there confuse their language, so that they may not understand one another's speech."
8 So the Lᴏʀᴅ scattered them abroad from there over the face of all the earth, and they ceased building the city.	**8** So the Lᴏʀᴅ dispersed them from there over the face of all the earth, and they left off building the city.
9 Therefore its name is called Babel, because there the Lᴏʀᴅ confused the language of all the earth; and from there the Lᴏʀᴅ scattered them abroad over the face of all the earth.	**9** Therefore its name was called Babel, because there the Lᴏʀᴅ confused the language of all the earth. And from there the Lᴏʀᴅ dispersed them over the face of all the earth.

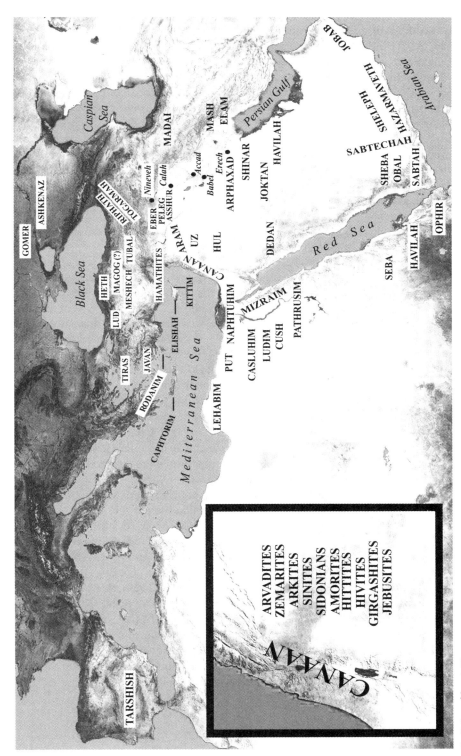

The Nations of Genesis 10 *Source: Felipe A. Masotti*

Like the Table of Nations, the story of the tower of Babel is unique in ANE literature.[420] However, scholars have recognized a number of parallels with the Mesopotamian *ziggurat* and especially with the Babylonian story of Babylon in *Enuma Elish*.[421] Also, archaeological remains of the sacred ziggurats, especially the best preserved one of Ur in Iraq that is made of baked bricks placed in bitumen for mortar, may confirm the authenticity of the biblical story. These towers were made of raised platforms (hence the name "ziggurat"/"ziqqurat" from the Akkadian *zaqaru* "to raise up," "elevate"). These superposed platforms rose up from a large base up to two or even seven floors in progressively narrower levels. The Mesopotamians believed that these towers functioned as a connection between the heavens and the earth. The ziggurat at Babylon was known as *Etemenankia* or "House of the Platform Between Heaven and Earth." One other practical function of the tower was to provide a high place to which one could escape during the annual inundations. Although the buildings had religious significance, they were not temples for public worship. They were believed to be the dwelling place of the gods.

Although the similarities between the two accounts are striking, the differences of architecture and function between the Genesis tower (*migdal*) and the stepladder ziggurat temples are too important to justify the idea that "the narrative in Genesis 11 had its 'starting-point' in the ruins of one of those … ziggurats."[422] At minimum, those parallels may testify to a common memory. It is possible that the ancient Babylonians had simply remembered the story of the tower of Babel but interpreted it differently, applying it to their own history of the founding of the city of Babylon. At any rate, the essential biblical components of the universal language and the dispersion of nations are totally absent from the Babylonian tradition of ziggurats. Also, the story of the tower of Babel fits too well within the biblical context to be suspected of being a foreign addition. To begin with, it was anticipated in the previous chapter, which alludes to that story more than once (10:25, 32) and even refers explicitly to Babel (10:10). Furthermore, in the conclusion (10:32), we look forward to the event of Babel, with its reference to the division of the earth and the sound of the word *mabbul* "flood," which anticipates the name "Babel" (*babel*). In addition, the genealogy of the sons of Noah shares a number of keywords and motifs with our text: the verbs *puts* "scatter" (11:4, 8; cf. 10:18), *banah* "build" (10:11; cf. 11:4–5, 8), the words *'erets* "land," "earth" (10:5, 8, 10–11, 20, 25, 31–32; cf. 11:1–2 [2x], 4, 8–9 [2x]), and *qedem* "east" (10:30; cf. 11:2), the expression **land of Shinar** (10:10; cf. 11:2). The way the story of Babel is situated between the two genealogies of Shem (10:21–32; 11:10–26) is particularly significant. The second genealogy takes over the first one at the stage of Shem and focuses on the branch of Peleg that was missing in the first genealogy, precisely in connection to the incident of Babel, when **the earth was divided** (10:25; 11:16–19). This design is not only of a literary order, intended to witness to the unity of the parts and their interconnection, but it also suggests that the separation of that branch from the nations is somehow related to the incident of Babel. This explains why the story of Babel, although following the Table of Nations, chronologically precedes their formation and dispersal.

---

420 See Frank A. Spina, "Babel," *ABD* 1:561–563.

421 *ANET*, 68–69.

422 Andre Parrot, *The Tower of Babel*, trans. E. Hudson (London: SCM Press, 1955), 17.

LITERARY STRUCTURE AND THEOLOGICAL MESSAGE

The story of the tower of Babel develops in two parts. The first part (11:2–4) describes the actions of the builders of the tower, and the second part (11:5–8) describes God's response to these actions. This organization and the parallels between the sections are indicated in the following chiastic structure:[423]

> **A** Narrative: The whole earth had one language and settling (11:1–2)
>> **B** Human speech (11:3–4)
>>> **C Narrative: Divine judgment (11:5)**
>> **B₁** Divine speech (11:6–7)
> **A₁** Narrative: The whole earth has many languages and scattering (11:8–9)

In addition, the symmetric distribution of the motifs in the chiastic structure suggests a mirror effect with elements of the second part (11:5–9), $A_1B_1C_1D_1E_1F_1$, reflecting elements of the first part (11:1–4), ABCDEF.[424]

> **A** "The whole earth had one language" (11:1)
>> **B** "there" (11:2)
>>> **C** "one another" (11:3)
>>>> **D** "Come, let us make bricks" (11:3)
>>>>> **E** "Come, let us build ourselves" (11:4)
>>>>>> **F** "a city, and a tower" (11:4)
>>>>>>> **G "The Lord came down …" (11:5)**
>>>>>> **F₁** "the city and the tower" (11:5)
>>>>> **E₁** "which the sons of men had built" (11:5)
>>>> **D₁** "Come, let Us … confuse" (11:7)
>>> **C₁** "one another" (11:7)
>> **B₁** "from there" (11:8)
> **A₁** "the language of all the earth" (11:9)

The design of this literary structure suggests two main theological ideas. First, it presents a theology of reversal. The language that is used in the first part to describe the work of the builders of Babel echoes the creation account, with the deliberate intention to reverse the work of creation and replace the God of creation. Already this intention is suggested in the Table of Nations, when Nimrod's foundation of the kingdom of Babel is introduced with the technical word *re'shit* "beginning," which echoes the divine creation account (1:1). Nimrod, whose name means "we shall rebel,"[425] presents himself as the creator of Babel, as God is the Creator of heaven and earth. Likewise, in the story of the tower of Babel, we observe the same usurpation. The phrase *'al peney* "on the face of," which referred to the state of the earth before the divine creation (1:2), reappears here (11:4). While the creation story moved from the one element (waters) to multiplicity and diversity, Babel intends to reverse the state of multiplicity into the one element. The word of God, *wayyo'mer 'Elohim* "God said," has been replaced by their word, *wayyo'meru* **they said** (11:3–4). The divine

---

423 See Moskala, "Toward Trinitarian Thinking in the Hebrew Scriptures," 257.

424 See J. P. Fokkelman, *Narrative Art in Genesis* (Assen: Van Gorcum, 1975), 19–32.

425 Turner, *Genesis*, 58.

fulfillment of creation *wayehi* "and there was" (1:3) has been replaced by the human achievement *wattehi* "and it was" (11:3).[426] The divine self-deliberation or consultation *na'aseh* "let Us make" of the divine Creator (1:26) has been replaced by the human self-deliberation *na'aseh* **let us make** (11:4). The builders of Babel have the same ambition as Eve. They want to be like God (3:5).

On the other hand, in the second part, which describes God's reaction to the Babel builders, the language also suggests a second reversal, designed to reverse the previous reversal (see the structure). This theology of reversal not only denounces the iniquity of Babel and their intention to usurp God's role, it also reveals the result of this human attempt and God's response to it. The theme of Babel will appear across the Scriptures as a warning against any human attempt to embark on the same path that seeks to replace God (Isa 14:12–15; Ezek 28:14–17; Dan 4:31–37; 8:11, 25; Rev 13:4; 14:8–9).

The story of the tower of Babel also conveys a message of hope. There is an "after" Babel: God will come down. This is the central message of the story, which is significantly located in the center of the narrative (11:5). The very fact that God's intervention means the reversal of Babel's reversal of creation suggests that the divine descent will take us back to the situation at the time of creation. The dream of Babel to unite as a world power fails, and the nations are scattered **over the face of all the earth** (11:9), thus bringing us back to God's original plan for the diversity of the peoples, whose reunion will only occur through the blessing of Abraham (12:3). This hope resonates throughout the Scriptures. It is seen in the prophets' vision of the gathering of all nations under the rule of God, when the covenant with Israel will be broadened into a new covenant, one including all the nations (Dan 9:27; Rom 11:24–25). This promise was already experienced by the church at Pentecost (Acts 2:5–13) but will reach its complete fulfillment at the coming of the Day of the Lord (Zeph 3:9; Isa 49:6; Rev 7:9).

11:1 **The whole earth.** The "whole earth" may have been a small number of people for today's standards. It has been suggested that about a thousand people gathered together.[427] The last verse of the preceding chapter had just referred to "the earth" on which the nations were divided (10:32), obviously alluding to the incident of Babel. Since this verse refers only to the nations that were on the Table of Nations, it follows that the branch of Peleg, which is there omitted, should not be counted in that mention. It is then possible that the members of the family of Peleg had already separated themselves from the others and were therefore not involved in the iniquity of Babel. The expression "the whole earth" concerns, then, all the rest of the population. They are united not only in their language, but also in their views.

One language. The phrase "one language" (lit. trans.: "one lip") refers to the common tongue that was shared by the human population before the division of languages. It is not clear, however, whether the branch of Peleg preserved that language, while the others acquired new linguistic instruments. Jewish tradition surmises that, since the name "Hebrew" is derived from the name "Eber," the father of

---

426 The verb "to be" does not appear in the translation "they had bricks for stone" (NKJV); see the literal translation of YLT: "and the brick *is* to them for stone."

427 This conclusion is based on three considerations: (1) the assumption of an average family of ten to twelve children, (2) the calculation of 3.5 generations (forty years for each generation) from the flood to Babel, and (3) there were seventy nations or families in Genesis 10. See Henry M. Morris, *The Biblical Basis for Modern Science* (Grand Rapids: Baker Books, 1984), 414–436.

Peleg and the ancestor of the Hebrews, one may infer that this "one language" was the Hebrew language, which may, then, contain elements of that original prediluvian language.[428]

One speech. The phrase "one speech" (lit. trans.: "words one") refers to the fact that these people used the same words and held the same discourse. They all shared the same mentality and were all cast in the same mold, suggesting a totalitarian society (cf. Dan 3:1–7), which left no room for difference or disagreement, for they all spoke the same language and said the same things with the same words.

11:2 They journeyed from the east. They all agree to move together to another place. The word *miqqedem* "from the east" does not just have a spatial reference indicating a geographical direction. The word may also apply to time, meaning "before," "ancient" (Deut 33:15; Isa 19:11), or "days of old" (Ps 44:1 [2]). The word may even refer to the very beginning of time, the origin, at the time of creation (Prov 8:22–23). The Garden of Eden is situated *miqqedem* (2:8), not only pointing to the eastward location of the Garden, but also implying that it belonged to the most ancient times. The word often has, therefore, the negative connotation of abandoning the original place. It is significant that the same word is used to describe the movement of Adam leaving the Garden of Eden (3:24), Cain leaving the family of God (4:16), and Lot separating from Abraham (13:10–12). The spiritual intention of this movement is immediately confirmed in the next step. They chose **a valley**, which is in blatant contradiction to the preceding locations that contained mountains. The ark of Noah had stranded on mountains (8:4), and the sons of Shem, who apparently did not follow the other groups, were dwelling in a place identified as "the mountain of the east" (10:30). Furthermore, they decided to settle, "they dwelt there" (11:2), at the same spot, which was also in opposition to the divine commission addressed to Noah and his sons to "fill the earth" (9:1). The last time that the verb "dwell" (*yashab*) was used was in connection to Cain, who "dwelt in the land of Nod" (4:16). This echo between the *yashab* "dwelling" of Cain and the *yashab* "dwelling" of the builders of Babel[429] suggests the negative connotation implied in this desire to "dwell." There is something of the mentality of Cain in the builders of Babel.

11:3 Let us make bricks. The language of the builders of Babel anticipates their failure and the forthcoming judgment of God. The first word, an interjection, *habah* "come," which introduces their discourse twice (11:3–4), reappears in God's reaction (11:7). The expression of community collaboration, which is repeated four times in the passage (**let us make bricks**, **let us bake them**, **let us build**, **let us make**), recalls the divine plural of creation "let Us make" (1:26) and betrays, then, their intention to usurp God. This language will be ironically simulated by God in the second part of the story (**let Us go down**, **let Us confuse**). The sounds of the words *nilbena lebenim* "let us make bricks" will also resonate in God's sentence *nabelah* "let us confuse" (11:7) and will sound again in the name of the city *Babel* and the verb *balal* "confuse" (11:9), which explains it.

Brick for stone … asphalt for mortar. The material that is used is their creation.

---

428 See Rashi in Miqraot Gedolot on 11:1; cf. SDABC: "The question as to whether any known language resembles that original speech cannot be answered. It is possible, even probable, that one of the Semitic tongues, such as Hebrew or Aramaic, is similar to the language men spoke before the confusion of tongues. Personal names of the period preceding the confusion of the tongues, as far as they can be interpreted, make sense only if considered to be originally Semitic" (1:283).

429 For other parallels between the two stories, see Mathews, *Genesis 1–11:26*, 478.

The builders of Babel, like the family of Cain, are creative (4:22). Yet, the text does not intend to bring out the industrious virtue of those builders. The language suggests, rather, "the mechanism of the passing from the natural city to the artificial city."[430] The men of Babel are only concerned with the achievement of their industrious project. When they speak to each other, they all say the same thing and it is only about this work. They behave like artificial and mechanical puppets and seem to have lost their humanness.

11:4 **Let us build ourselves a city.** So far, only the family of Cain had engaged in that activity (4:17). The builders of Babel are thus associated with the tradition of Cain. The emphasis on the pronoun "ourselves" suggests that they insist that they are on their own, a way of marking their independence from God. Like the builders of the family of Cain, the builders of Babel intend to create a secular civilization.

A tower whose top is in the heavens. The Hebrew word for "tower" (*migdal*), which qualifies the city of Babel, betrays the aspiration of the builders. The word is related to the word *gadal* "great," implying the idea of ambition and glory, often associated with God Himself (Exod 18:11; Deut 7:21; 2 Sam 7:22). Interestingly, the passage of Daniel 8, which shares a number of linguistic and theological motifs with our text, uses the word *gadal* as a keyword to describe the attempt of the little horn to exalt itself unto God Himself (Dan 8:9–11, 25). In fact, the tower is supposed to reach heaven, a specification that suggests more than just the monumental proportion of the tower. The builders of Babel have the spiritual ambition to replace God.

A name for ourselves. The play on words relating to the words *shamayim* "heaven" and *shem* "name" reveals their intention to replace God. For not only does God dwell in heaven (19:24; 21:17), but He is also the only One who makes a "name great" (12:2) and the only One who can "make" a "name" for Himself (Isa 63:12, 14; Jer 32:20). Since, in biblical culture, a name is bound up with existence (27:36), the giving of names corresponds, indeed, to an act of creation and is therefore the prerogative of the Creator (1:5, 8, 10; cf. Isa 40:26).[431] It is also noteworthy that this intention to "rival the heavens" has been retained in Babylonian tradition in connection with the construction of Babylon.[432] The memory of the event of the flood may also have a played a role in the men's decision to build a tower. Ironically, they had chosen the plain in order to forget the mountains, which were associated in their memory with the event of the flood and the presence of God. On the one hand, they may have built the high tower with the intention of preserving themselves from another flood, a superstition that survived in the tradition of the builders of the ziggurats. On the other hand, they sought to replace the natural mountain with an artificial one, the one they fabricated. The upward movement of the work also betrays their mentality. They push themselves upward because they want to control their destiny and ensure their salvation. They refuse to rely on the invisible God and on His promises. They refuse to believe in the God who comes down. Therefore He will come down (11:5, 7).

11:5 **But the Lord came down to see the city.** The irony of that statement

---

430 André Neher, *De l'hébreu en français* (Paris: Klincksieck, 1969), 54.

431 Even when Adam gave names to the animals it was initiated and monitored by God. In this way, Adam was appointed by God as His coworker, having received from Him the power to rule over the animals (1:26, 28).

432 See E. A. Speiser, "Word Plays on the Creation Epic's Version of the Founding of Babylon," *Or* 25, no. 4 (1956): 319.

should not be missed. In spite of all the efforts of the builders to reach the heavens, God had to come down to meet them anyway. This irony is perceived by the poet of Psalm 2, who probably has the builders of Babel in mind when he hears the Lord laughing at the foolishness of the nations that gathered against Him:

> Why do the nations rage, and the people plot a vain thing? The kings of the earth set themselves, and the rulers take counsel together, against the Lord and His Anointed, saying, "Let us break . . . and cast away . . ." He who sits in the heavens shall laugh; the Lord shall hold them in derision (Ps 2:1–4).

This prospect of the coming down of God is also the irony of God, who has the last word and who will descend against the proud and arrogant end-time Babel. Thus, the prophet Isaiah gives an eschatological application to the story of the tower of Babel, referring to the coming Day of the Lord:

> For the day of the Lord of hosts shall come upon everything proud and lofty . . . upon every high tower [*migdal*] . . . In that day a man will cast away his idols . . . to go into the clefts of the rocks, and into the crags of the rugged rocks, from the terror of the Lord and the glory of His majesty, when He arises to shake the earth mightily (Isa 2:12, 15, 20–21).

Likewise, the prophet Daniel uses the lesson of the tower of Babel to describe the eschatological scenario of the gathering of the nations as the last symptom of human history that will generate the descent of God (Dan 2:43–44; cf. Gen 11:4–5).[433]

The city and the tower which the sons of men had built. Strangely, the process of building has not been registered in the biblical narrative. Since the previous conversation, no word was heard from the builders. They had built in silence, with no human emotions or communication. For the value of the "great" work had prevailed over the value of human beings. This ethical lesson of the story has been noted by the ancient rabbis. An old Jewish tradition comments that, while building the tower, the following occurred: If a worker fell off the tower and was killed, he was ignored and the work continued unabated. However, if a brick fell and broke, there was tremendous upheaval and the workers sat down and wept.[434]

11:7–8 Come, let Us … confuse their language. God's reuse of the same plural form as the builders is not only ironic through mimicry, it also restores the divine prerogative, since it reaffirms the divine agent of creation: "Let Us make" (1:26; see the comments there). Only God can say "Let Us …" and produce one product. The God in plural who is "One" responds to the builders, who are many and fail to be one. The builders' failure to value each other's humanity led to the impossibility of communicating with each other. God came down and interfered with the intimacy of their words and discourse. Suddenly, their speech does not make sense anymore. They sound like fools to each other. The Hebrew writer plays on these words, where the phrase *nablah* "let's confuse," which sounds like *nilbenah* "make bricks," also sounds like *nebalah* "foolishness." Thus, the text reveals that the foolishness they experience now was already contained in their initial work. They speak and yet do

---

433 See Jacques B. Doukhan, *Secrets of Daniel: Wisdom and Dreams of a Jewish Prince in Exile* (Hagerstown, MD: Review and Herald, 2000), 36.
434 Pirqe R. El. 24.

not understand each other. The text does not say whether they were speaking new languages or whether the divine judgment had simply sanctioned a condition they had created themselves. The fact is, their communication does not function anymore. The same old words they used to say now have different meanings, and new words are now used that have no meaning at all. The good old days when they were "one in language" have been reversed. With some humor, Jewish tradition surmises on that confusion of languages: "Instead of possessing one language, one speech and one dialect, they began to speak to one another in different languages and dialects. And great confusion took place; nobody knew what the other spoke. If one would ask for an ax, the other would hand him a shovel; and getting angry he would throw the shovel at him and kill him. So they left off building the tower, and God scattered them from the face of the earth."[435]

11:9 **Babel.** The name given to the city is an apt summary of the entire Babel story and its lessons. The Babylonians understood the meaning of the name "Babel" as *Bab-ili*, "gate of God." This explanation, which has been retained in the annals of Babylonian history, testifies to the ambition hidden in the project of Babel, namely, to reach the "gate of God." This designation does not merely refer to an object or a place, it points to something more. First, considering the fact that Babel is understood as a city, the word "gate" carries the traditional idea of an essential fortification of the city against a siege (Deut 3:5; 1 Sam 23:5). To reach and control the "gate" means, then, to control the city (Isa 62:10; Judg 16:3). As such, the desire to reach the "gate of God" betrays the ambition of Babel's builders to control God and occupy His territory—to take His place. Playing on the name and word sounds, the author also relates *babel* "gate of God" to the word *balal* "confuse" and alerts his readers to the foolishness of this enterprise. Babel leads to confusion.

11:10–26. THE GENEALOGY OF SHEM

GEN 11:10–26 NKJV	GEN 11:10–26 ESV
10 This *is* the genealogy of Shem: Shem *was* one hundred years old, and begot Arphaxad two years after the flood.	**10** These are the generations of Shem. When Shem was 100 years old, he fathered Arpachshad two years after the flood.
11 After he begot Arphaxad, Shem lived five hundred years, and begot sons and daughters.	**11** And Shem lived after he fathered Arpachshad 500 years and had other sons and daughters.
12 Arphaxad lived thirty-five years, and begot Salah.	**12** When Arpachshad had lived 35 years, he fathered Shelah.
13 After he begot Salah, Arphaxad lived four hundred and three years, and begot sons and daughters.	**13** And Arpachshad lived after he fathered Shelah 403 years and had other sons and daughters.
14 Salah lived thirty years, and begot Eber.	**14** When Shelah had lived 30 years, he fathered Eber.
15 After he begot Eber, Salah lived four hundred and three years, and begot sons and daughters.	**15** And Shelah lived after he fathered Eber 403 years and had other sons and daughters.
16 Eber lived thirty-four years, and begot Peleg.	**16** When Eber had lived 34 years, he fathered Peleg.

---

435 Mendel G. Glenn, *Jewish Tales and Legends* (New York: Hebrew Publishing, 1929), 31.

17 After he begot Peleg, Eber lived four hundred and thirty years, and begot sons and daughters.	**17** And Eber lived after he fathered Peleg 430 years and had other sons and daughters.
18 Peleg lived thirty years, and begot Reu.	**18** When Peleg had lived 30 years, he fathered Reu.
19 After he begot Reu, Peleg lived two hundred and nine years, and begot sons and daughters.	**19** And Peleg lived after he fathered Reu 209 years and had other sons and daughters.
20 Reu lived thirty-two years, and begot Serug.	**20** When Reu had lived 32 years, he fathered Serug.
21 After he begot Serug, Reu lived two hundred and seven years, and begot sons and daughters.	**21** And Reu lived after he fathered Serug 207 years and had other sons and daughters.
22 Serug lived thirty years, and begot Nahor.	**22** When Serug had lived 30 years, he fathered Nahor.
23 After he begot Nahor, Serug lived two hundred years, and begot sons and daughters.	**23** And Serug lived after he fathered Nahor 200 years and had other sons and daughters.
24 Nahor lived twenty-nine years, and begot Terah.	**24** When Nahor had lived 29 years, he fathered Terah.
25 After he begot Terah, Nahor lived one hundred and nineteen years, and begot sons and daughters.	**25** And Nahor lived after he fathered Terah 119 years and had other sons and daughters.
26 Now Terah lived seventy years, and begot Abram, Nahor, and Haran.	**26** When Terah had lived 70 years, he fathered Abram, Nahor, and Haran.

The first genealogical record of Shem (10:21–32) is now continued in this second, more expanded and focused version. Although the main concern of this second genealogy centers on firstborn sons, it covers more generations, ten instead of five, and regularly refers to the birth of sons and daughters. Furthermore, this new genealogy of Shem is also connected to the story of the tower of Babel. The name of Shem echoes the last verse of the story (11:9) with the play on the sounds *shem* "name" and *sham* "there" (2x), which was already heard inside the text (11:4, 7–8). The connection between the two texts is also alluded to in the structure of the genealogy, which brings in the name of Peleg, the one who was contemporary to the incident of Babel (10:25) at its center, four before (Shem, Arphaxad, Salah, and Eber) and four after (Reu, Serug, Nahor, and Terah). The genealogy of Shem also continues the genealogy of Adam, using the same vocabulary and literary patterns, with the same refrain, **sons and daughters**, and concluding the same way with the naming of three sons (5:32; 11:26). The genealogy of Shem and the genealogy of Adam are thus connected. The lesson of this literary connection is clear: the history of the patriarchs, which is introduced here, continues the cosmic history from Adam in the Garden of Eden to Noah and the flood and the story of the tower of Babel. The comparison between the two lists reveals one significant difference: the ages when the men of this list become fathers and die are considerably lower than in the precedent genealogy. This is probably due to climactic and especially dietary changes after the flood, which went from a strictly plant-based diet to one including the flesh of animals (9:3). Another contributing factor to a shortened lifespan was the lessened effect of the fruit from the tree of life, which had only been available to the first family.[436] This specific information suggests that the men of the preceding list, namely Noah and his descendants, could have lived long enough to have witnessed the division of the earth, and even for Shem, the father of the new genealogy, to be a contemporary of Abraham. Indeed, the chronological precision provided by the genealogy starting **two years after the flood** (11:10) allows us to calculate that Noah, who lived 350 years after the flood (9:28), was 701 years old when Peleg was born (11:16); and if we add together the ages of the fathers (from the flood to Abram) including the two years for Shem, when their sons were born after the flood we obtain 292 years; which means that Abram was born 292 years after the flood. Noah lived, then, 58 years (350 minus 292) after Abram was born. Likewise, Shem, who was 100 years old at the beginning of the genealogy (11:10) and lived 600 years (11:11), must have been 392 years (100 plus 292) old when Abraham was born (11:26) and 550 years old at the birth of Jacob. "This would mean that Noah and Abraham were contemporaries as were Shem and Eber with Jacob."[437] All these chronological indications may have been intended to suggest that, from Adam to the patriarchs, there was, as Ellen White put it, an "unbroken line" of God's witnesses.[438] The death of these men did not interrupt the continuity of the testimony. This lesson was, in fact, reflected in the very style of the genealogy. It is noteworthy indeed that this genealogy, which is so similar to the genealogy of Adam in many respects, differs, however, from it in one particular feature: the refrain of death that regularly marks the rhythm of the previous genealogy—the expression "and he died" (5:5, 8, 11, 14, etc.)—is absent here.

11:26 **Terah lived seventy years, and begot Abram, Nahor, and Haran**. This phrase does not mean that the three sons were born at the same time (perhaps as triplets) exactly when Terah was seventy years old. Instead, this is a condensed version of the events intended to place special focus on Abram. This phrase means that Terah had lived seventy years when he began to father his three sons. Abram is listed first, not because he is the firstborn (he is never identified as such), but because of his significance for the following events and particularly in the history of salvation. The fact that Nahor married Haran's daughter (11:29) suggests that Haran was older than Nahor. The list was then given in the reverse order, from the youngest to the oldest, a sequence with a theological lesson that will denote the patriarchal births, namely, that the youngest will prevail over the oldest (see also the sequence "Shem, Ham, and Japheth" in 9:18). Considering the fact that Terah is 205 years old when he dies (11:32), and that Abram leaves to go to Canaan at the death of his father (11:32–12:4; Acts 7:4) when he is 75 years old (12:4), we have the following chronology: Terah is 70 years old when he begets his firstborn Haran and is 130 years old (205 minus 75) when he begets his third son, Abram.[439]

---

436 See Ellen G. White's comment: "The tree of life is a representation of the preserving care of Christ for his children. As Adam and Eve ate of this tree, they acknowledged their dependence upon God. The tree of life possessed the power to perpetuate life, and as long as they ate of it, they could not die. The lives of the antediluvians were protracted because of the life-giving power of this tree, which was transmitted to them from Adam and Eve" (*Review and Herald*, January 26, 1897; cf. 3SG 64).

437 Mathews, *Genesis 1–11:26*, 493.

438 Ellen G. White, PP 125.

439 For an alternative chronology that makes Abraham leave Haran sixty years before Terah's death, see Mathews, *Genesis 1–11:26*, 499; cf. Wenham, *Genesis 1–15*, 274, n.34.

11:27–32. THE GENEALOGY OF TERAH

GEN 11:27–32 NKJV	GEN 11:27–32 ESV
27 This *is* the genealogy of Terah: Terah begot Abram, Nahor, and Haran. Haran begot Lot.	**27** Now these are the generations of Terah. Terah fathered Abram, Nahor, and Haran; and Haran fathered Lot.
28 And Haran died before his father Terah in his native land, in Ur of the Chaldeans.	**28** Haran died in the presence of his father Terah in the land of his kindred, in Ur of the Chaldeans.
29 Then Abram and Nahor took wives: the name of Abram's wife *was* Sarai, and the name of Nahor's wife, Milcah, the daughter of Haran the father of Milcah and the father of Iscah.	**29** And Abram and Nahor took wives. The name of Abram's wife was Sarai, and the name of Nahor's wife, Milcah, the daughter of Haran the father of Milcah and Iscah.
30 But Sarai was barren; she had no child.	**30** Now Sarai was barren; she had no child.
31 And Terah took his son Abram and his grandson Lot, the son of Haran, and his daughter-in-law Sarai, his son Abram's wife, and they went out with them from Ur of the Chaldeans to go to the land of Canaan; and they came to Haran and dwelt there.	**31** Terah took Abram his son and Lot the son of Haran, his grandson, and Sarai his daughter-in-law, his son Abram's wife, and they went forth together from Ur of the Chaldeans to go into the land of Canaan, but when they came to Haran, they settled there.
32 So the days of Terah were two hundred and five years, and Terah died in Haran.	**32** The days of Terah were 205 years, and Terah died in Haran.

The genealogical record of Terah continues the genealogy of Shem. The first link of the genealogy (11:27) is repeated, thus coinciding with the last link of the previous genealogy: "Terah begot Abram, Nahor, and Haran" (11:26). The connection is, then, carried over to these three sons and, more particularly, to Abram. In fact, any reference to the two other sons is given insofar as it is related to Abram and his destiny, as evidenced in the following information.

11:27–28 Haran begot Lot. And Haran died. The mention of the birth of Lot (11:27) and the report of the death of his father Haran (11:28) explain why Lot will later be associated with Abram (11:31; 12:4ff.).

11:29 Abram's wife was Sarai. The endogamous system, which allows marriage within the same family, not only confirms the antiquity of the story, predating the Mosaic interdiction (Lev 18:9; 20:17), it also anticipates the incident of Abraham in Egypt where he referred to his wife as his sister (12:13). Abram is indeed married to Terah's daughter (his half-sister) and Nahor is married to Haran's daughter, who will become the grandmother of the future wife of Abram's son (Rebekah) (24:15). The reference to Nahor's wife Milcah, who has a record of giving birth to children (22:20) and the specification that she is the daughter of Haran, who is also the father of Iscah, are given to contrast with Abram's wife Sarai, whose sterility is underlined through the repetition: **Sarai was barren; she had no child** (11:30). Both brothers, Nahor and Haran, were fruitful and gave birth to children. Abram remained the only one in the family without children. This exception anticipates the miracle of the future birth of Isaac (18:14).

11:31 Although the text reports that **Terah took his son Abram … to go to the land of Canaan,** it is clear that the decision to leave the country came from Abram, since Terah did not go further than Haran (11:32), and only Abram went to Canaan.

Ur of the Chaldeans. The decision to go to Canaan was made when Abram was still in Ur, as the text clearly suggests: **they went out from Ur of the Chaldeans to go to the land of Canaan**. Most scholars have identified Ur of the Chaldeans as the ancient Sumerian city Ur (modern Tell el-Muqayyar), located on the Euphrates in southern Iraq.[440] The specification "of the Chaldeans" accords with historical facts. The Tablets of Mari attest to the presence of Semitic peoples related to the Aramaeans,[441] who had migrated from the north to the region by the end of the third millennium BC. There were also intense commercial and cultural connections between Ur and the northern city of Haran. The business of wool, which was probably a specialty of the Terah clan (13:5–8), was very developed there and the road between Ur and Haran served as the main means of communication between the north and the south. In addition, Ur and Haran shared the same moon god, who was probably one of the many gods worshiped by Abraham's ancestors (Josh 24:2, 14). The name of the moon god may even be recognized in the name of Terah (related to the Hebrew word *yareakh* "moon") and may be traced in the name of Sarah "princess," which was the name of the wife of the Babylonian moon god Sin, and Milcah, which was the name of this moon god's daughter. These strong ties between the two cities also explain why the Terah clan chooses to move to the north, to the city of **Haran**, as it may be the clan's original homeland.[442] Even the report of Haran, who **dwelt there**, is related to Abram, for it anticipates the story of Isaac and Rebekah and explains why Abraham will later refer to that place as still being "my country … my kindred" (24:4 ESV).

11:32 **Terah died in Haran.**[443] In the same manner, death, which strikes in the beginning and in the end of the genealogy as an inclusio, is set in opposition to Abram's destiny. Haran dies **in his native land, in the Ur of the Chaldeans** (11:28), and Terah dies in the place that bears the name of Haran (11:32), perhaps an allusion to the place associated with the memory of Haran. On the other hand, Abram **went out … from Ur of the Chaldeans** and was the only one **to go to the land of Canaan** (11:31). Just as in the previous genealogy, the evocation of life affects the literary composition of the text. In the genealogy of Shem, life was related to the preservation of the divine testimony. In the genealogy of Terah, life is set in the perspective of the land of Canaan, where God's promise will finally materialize.

---

440 For arguments in favor of a northern localization of Ur, see Hamilton, *Genesis 1–17*, 363–365.

441 Their Aramaic identity has been recognized in biblical tradition (Deut 26:5) and is also reflected in their names; a grandson of Nahor was called "Aram" (22:21) and one of his sons was "Chesed" (22:22), which is the Hebrew word *kesed* for Chaldeans (*kasdim*).

442 See Kitchen, *On the Reliability of the Old Testament*, 318. Political reasons may have also played a role in the departure of the Terah clan. Indeed, these events are contemporary to the wars between the Babylonian Hammurabi (a Semite) and the kings of Sumer. In this context, Semitic people like the Terah clan may have been regarded as suspect by the Sumerians of the region.

443 On the chronological issue concerning the age of the patriarch's death, see our comment on 11:26.

3. FROM BABEL TO THE PROMISED LAND: ABRAHAM

GENESIS 12–22:19

We have now reached the literary center of the book (see "The Structure of Genesis" in the Introduction). This central section will cover the stories of Abraham after he leaves Ur of the Chaldeans (11:31; cf. 12:1) to go to the land of Canaan until he finally settles in Beersheba (22:19). Abraham is called *ger* "a stranger" (17:8), a technical term that designates the "alien" who does not enjoy the rights of the resident (cf. Exod 18:3; 23:9). As a result, Abraham is often on the move. It is significant that this "moving" destiny is reflected in the language that covers the stories of his life. The verb "go" (*halak*) is a keyword that pervades the narratives (12:1, 4 [2x], 5, 9, 19; 13:3, 5, 17; 14:11, 24; 15:2 [Heb]; 16:8; 17:1; 18:16, 22, 33; 19:2; 21:14–16, 19, 32; 22:2–3, 5–6, 8, 13, 18). Note that the most important concentrations of *halak* occur in the two poles of the section (five times in 12:1–9, and seven times in 22:1–19). It is also significant that the phrase *lek leka* "go," which emphasizes the sound *lek* "go," frames the spiritual journey of Abraham. This expression appears twice, the first time when Abraham is called to leave his past (12:1), and the second time when he is called to abandon his future (22:2). Suspended in the void, disconnected from his roots, and without any horizon, Abraham depends only on God. Abraham exemplifies "faith." He is, in fact, portrayed by the author of Genesis as the one who "put his faith [*he'emin*] in Yahweh" (15:6 NJB) and will be remembered in the Hebrew Scriptures as the man of faith: "You found his heart faithful [*ne'eman*] before You" (Neh 9:8).[444] In the New Testament, Abraham is one of the most mentioned figures of the Old Testament. His name appears seventy-three times, second only to Moses, whose name appears eighty times. Abraham's life of faith is precisely the lesson that is retained by the author of the letter to the Hebrews: "By faith Abraham obeyed when he was called to go out … By faith he dwelt in the land of promise as in a foreign country" (Heb 11:8–9). "By faith Abraham, when he was tested, offered up Isaac" (Heb 11:17).

THE LITERARY STRUCTURE

Between the two *lek leka* (12:1; 22:2), the stories of Abraham, which are punctuated by seven revelations of God[445] are distributed in a chiastic fashion, echoing each other to suggest literary unity but also to bring out the central idea of the section: the faith of Abraham and the nature of God's covenant with him.

> **A** *Lek leka* "Go!" Call to Abraham to leave his past (12:1–9)
> > **B** Sojourn in Egypt (12:10–13:1a)
> > > **C** Abram and Lot (13:1b–14)
> > > > **D The Abrahamic covenant (15–17)**
> > > **C₁** Abraham and Lot (18–19)
> > **B₁** Sojourn in Gerar (20–21)
> **A₁** *Lek leka* "Go!" Call to Abraham to leave his future (22:1–19)[446]

---

444 The Hebrew word *ne'eman* "faithful," derived from the root *'aman*, is related to the word *'emunah* "faith."

445 See Martin Buber, "Abraham the Seer," in *On the Bible* (New York: Schocken, 1968), 25.

446 Cf. Cairus's suggestion of the following chiastic structure ABCDD₁C₁B₁A₁: *A* Divine commands and Abraham's obedience (11:27–12:9); *B* Threat to wife and family strife (13:1–3); *C* Divine Revelation and care for Lot (13:14–18; 14:1–24); *D* Covenant and secondary offspring (16); *D'* Covenant and secondary offspring (17); *C'* Divine revelation and care for Lot (18–19); *B'* Threat to wife and family strife (20–21); *A'* Divine commands and Abraham's obedience

LEK LEKA "GO!" CALL TO ABRAHAM TO LEAVE HIS PAST (12:1–9)

GEN 12:1–9 NKJV	GEN 12:1–9 ESV
1 Now the Lord had said to Abram: "Get out of your country, from your family And from your father's house, to a land that I will show you.	**1** Now the Lord said to Abram, "Go from your country and your kindred and your father's house to the land that I will show you.
2 I will make you a great nation; I will bless you and make your name great; and you shall be a blessing.	**2** And I will make of you a great nation, and I will bless you and make your name great, so that you will be a blessing.
3 I will bless those who bless you, and I will curse him who curses you; and in you all the families of the earth shall be blessed."	**3** I will bless those who bless you, and him who dishonors you I will curse, and in you all the families of the earth shall be blessed."
4 So Abram departed as the Lord had spoken to him, and Lot went with him. And Abram *was* seventy-five years old when he departed from Haran.	**4** So Abram went, as the Lord had told him, and Lot went with him. Abram was seventy-five years old when he departed from Haran.
5 Then Abram took Sarai his wife and Lot his brother's son, and all their possessions that they had gathered, and the people whom they had acquired in Haran, and they departed to go to the land of Canaan. So they came to the land of Canaan.	**5** And Abram took Sarai his wife, and Lot his brother's son, and all their possessions that they had gathered, and the people that they had acquired in Haran, and they set out to go to the land of Canaan. When they came to the land of Canaan,
6 Abram passed through the land to the place of Shechem, as far as the terebinth tree of Moreh. And the Canaanites *were* then in the land.	**6** Abram passed through the land to the place at Shechem, to the oak of Moreh. At that time the Canaanites were in the land.
7 Then the Lord appeared to Abram and said, "To your descendants I will give this land." And there he built an altar to the Lord, who had appeared to him.	**7** Then the Lord appeared to Abram and said, "To your offspring I will give this land." So he built there an altar to the Lord, who had appeared to him.
8 And he moved from there to the mountain east of Bethel, and he pitched his tent *with* Bethel on the west and Ai on the east; there he built an altar to the Lord and called on the name of the Lord.	**8** From there he moved to the hill country on the east of Bethel and pitched his tent, with Bethel on the west and Ai on the east. And there he built an altar to the Lord and called upon the name of the Lord.
9 So Abram journeyed, going on still toward the South.	**9** And Abram journeyed on, still going toward the Negeb.

The last time God spoke, it was to pronounce judgment at the tower of Babel, resulting in the creation of nations (11:9). The last time God spoke to a person, it was to Noah to assure him of His covenant with all flesh on the earth (9:17). God's new word to Abram reconnects with His other words and carries the promise of their fulfillment: the nations of the earth will be blessed though the blessing of Abram. This first section, introduced by the phrase *lek leka* (12:1), is made up of two paragraphs. The first paragraph (12:1–3) reports the call of God to Abram to **go** (ESV). The second paragraph (12:4–9) reports the actual fulfillment of the divine order: *wayyelek* **went** (ESV), responding to the call to go (*lek*), **as the Lord had spoken to him** (12:4). The keyword *halak* "go" gives the tone to the whole passage, after which the word is used

. . .

(22). See Aecio E. Cairus, "Protection and Reward: The Significance of Ancient Midrashic Expositions on Genesis 15:1–6" (PhD diss., Andrews University, 1988), 242.

no more and will only reappear when Abram returns from Egypt and heads for Bethel (12:19; 13:3). The word is heard seven times (11:31; 12:1 [2x], 4 [2x], 5, 9), if we include its occurrence in the conclusion of the genealogy of Terah, where it is echoed (11:31), and its phonetic allusion in the preposition *leka*, in the phrase *lek leka*.

12:1–3 Go from your country (ESV). Abram's departure from his country (around 1760 BC) was already reported in the conclusion of the genealogy of Terah: **They went out with them from Ur of the Chaldeans to go to the land of Canaan** (11:31). The allusion to this verse is confirmed by the strong linguistic echoes between the two passages.[447] Our text suggests, then, a flashback to the preceding text (11:31–32): Abram had heard this call when he was still in Ur of the Chaldeans—a timeframe that is also supported by other biblical accounts (15:7; Neh 9:7; Acts 7:2–4). This explains the translation: "the Lord had said" (12:1), indicating a previous time. It is no accident that God's call to Abram to leave is heard in the land of Ur of the Chaldeans. It is indeed striking that the ancient Sumerian city of Ur (see the comments on "Ur of the Chaldeans" in 11:31) is located in the region of Babylonia that has the closest association with the incident of Babel, for it provides us—from the fourth millennium (conventional dating)—with the best archaeological testimony to the tower of Babel. That Abram heard the call to leave a place loaded with the memory of Babel makes sense and should not surprise us, not only because of historical and geographical considerations, but also because of its theological implications. From the cry of the prophets to the apocalyptic supplication, the divine call to "get out of Babylon"[448] has a long theological history in biblical tradition (Isa 48:20; Rev 18:4). It means not only deliverance from the oppressive exilic conditions and national restoration to the Promised Land, but also implies a return to the covenant.

---

447 In addition to the echo on the verb *halak*, which relates the two passages (11:31; 12:1), see in particular the echoes between the report of the genealogy of Terah (11:31) and the report of the actual fulfillment of God's command (12:5), which use exactly the same words: *wayyetsu* "they went out," "departed"; *laleket* "to go"; *'artsah* "to the land"; and *kena'an* "Canaan."

448 "Babylon" is the English name (from the Greek *Babulon*) of the Hebrew word *Babel* "Babel."

12:1 From your family and from your father's house. It is noteworthy that the same phrase is used again by Abraham when he refers to the place where he sends his servant to find a bride for his son Isaac (24:4; cf. 24:38–41). It is identified as the city of Nahor, which is located near Haran in northwest Mesopotamia (24:10). God's call to Abram aims, then, beyond the present. Abram must not only leave his present environment, he must also abandon his heritage. The call does not just affect space, it also concerns time and the person of Abram. This meaning, which involves Abram himself, is even rendered in the particular form of the Hebrew phrase *lek leka* "get out," which adds to the imperative *lek* "get out," the dative preposition *lek ah* "to you." This construction may suggest emphasis[449] or simply express an "idea of relation,"[450] that is, "go in order to find yourself, and thus fulfill yourself." In other words, the call to Abram to "get out" of his country and away from his roots should take him to himself—to establish his identity.[451] It is not enough for Abram to get out of Babel; in order to find his real self, Abraham has to get rid of the Babel that is still in him, the idolatry of his fathers and the arrogant mentality of Babel.

LITERARY STRUCTURE

The call to go, *lek leka*, does not stand alone but serves as a basis for the structure of the passage. This feature may be already noted on the phonetic level: the sound *ka* in *lek le**ka*** resounds eleven times in the passage. Furthermore, the verbs of the passage that refer to God's acts are subordinate to the imperative "go." This construction means that Abram must first go so that God may act. The six verbs describing God's actions conclude with a passive on the seventh step, with the observation of the ultimate result. Note the parallel between the structure of the call of Abram and the structure of the creation story: both accounts begin with a negative note (leaving Babel confusion || leaving cosmic chaos), after which they both share the same rhythm of God's six creative actions. Both accounts conclude with the seventh step describing a passive state resulting from the divine action: "all the families of the earth shall be blessed" (12:3) || "the heavens and the earth, and all the host of them, were finished" (2:1):

"Go! . . .
1. that I may show you . . .
2. that I may make you a great nation . . .
3. that I may bless you . . .
4. that I may make your name great . . .
5. that I may bless . . .
6. that I may curse . . .
7. that be blessed in you all the families of the earth"

This structural parallel suggests an underlying theology of creation. The call to Abram to get out of Babel is a word of creation: it brings back the promise of life and

---

449 *GKC* §119s.

450 Joüon §133d.

451 See T. Muraoka's discussion of the so-called "ethical dative": "Basically it serves to convey the impression on the part of the speaker or author that the subject establishes his own identity, recovering or finding his own place by determinedly dissociating himself from his familiar surrounding" ("On the So-Called DATIVUS ETHICUS in Hebrew," *JTS* 29 [1978]: 497).

opens, after the flood and the confusion of Babel, new perspectives of hope regarding the Promised Land. Note also that the phrase "all the families of the earth" (12:3) is reminiscent of the language of the Table of Nations, "the families of the sons of Noah … on the earth after the flood" (10:32; cf. 10:5, 20, 31), thus emphasizing the universal scope of the Abrahamic blessing.

To a land that I will show you. The same language will be used again in Genesis 22:2, where God refers to the mount of Moriah as "the land" He will reveal to Abraham. In contrast to the land of Babel situated in a flat plain, the Promised Land has mountains, which are reminiscent of the landscape surrounding Ararat and thus a reminder of God's presence before the men left for Babel (see the comments on 11:4). God's promise, then, involves more than the mere assurance of a physical home, although this is a vital and necessary component. Beyond the physical fulfillment of the land, the promise aims at the spiritual redemption of the world contained in the Moriah event. Abram does not know where that land is, but he leaves behind what he knows and ventures to a place he does not know, relying entirely on God: this demonstrates total faith on Abram's part. On the other hand, the Promised Land is given by God. Abram does nothing to deserve it: this demonstrates total grace on God's part.

12:2 **I will make you a great nation … and make your name great.** The call of Abram once again stands against the designs of Babel. The builders of Babel wanted to make for themselves a great name and make themselves into a unique universal nation (11:4). In the new perspective, it is God who makes a name great and only God who makes one particular nation great and unique in contradistinction to the other nations. Interestingly, the verb "make" is a keyword of the creation account, where it occurs seven times with God as the subject (1:7, 16, 25–26; 2:2 [2x], 3). The verb was used three times by the builders of Babel to describe their activity (11:4, 6 [2x]) and one instance in particular was in relation to "name" (11:4). Babel stood, then, in place of the Creator. The call to Abram restores God's prerogatives. Only God, as the Creator, can "make"; and only God can "make a name" (see the comments on 11:4). Moreover, only the name of God is described as "great" (Josh 7:9; 1 Sam 12:22; Ps 76:2 [1]; Mal 1:11). This means that to qualify the name of Abram's people as "great" is to suggest a special connection between God and this people; it is as if God is identifying Himself with this people (Hos 1:9), an idea that will be implied again later in the call (12:3). Significantly, the same phrase occurs only in the Davidic covenant (2 Sam 7:9), which suggests, then, the implementation of this promise.

12:2–3 **I will bless.** The word *barak* "bless" is a keyword in our passage, where it appears five times. The use of this word is particularly prominent in the book of Genesis, where it occurs eighty-eight times (against 356 times in the rest of the Hebrew Bible). The Hebrew concept of "blessing" is often associated with the prospect of fruitfulness (1:21–23). Thus, the call to Abram overturns the ideology of Babel. Against the builders of Babel, who refused to go along with the divine plan of creation to multiply, the blessing of Abram restores the forces of creation and the promise of the future. While the builders of Babel founded their security only on themselves and their own homogeneity, in the new perspective the blessing of the nations is solely dependent on the blessing of Abram.

The essential reason for this blessing lies in a future historical event: **in you all the families of the earth shall be blessed** (12:3). The language of the text suggests that the physical person of Abram is implied. The preposition "in you" means "in your seed" or "through your seed"[452] (see NIV). The same language is used by Paul to describe the universal effect of the new covenant: "*in* Christ Jesus neither circumcision nor uncircumcision avails anything, but a new creation" (Gal 6:15; cf. 6:5). In fact, this is the interpretation offered by other biblical passages that quote this text and explicitly refer to the "seed": "In your seed all the nations of the earth shall be blessed" (22:18; 26:4; 28:14). It is not "in Abram" that the blessing is obtained but "in the seed" of Abram. The text refers here to the same messianic seed as in Genesis 3:15, with which our text shares many common grammatical forms and associations of words and thoughts. Both passages are divine prophecies using the same verbal form (imperfect) in the first person; both contain the same association of "blessing" and "curse"[453] and the same Hebrew word *zera'* for "seed." It is noteworthy that the promise is also echoed in the divine prophecy given to David (2 Sam 7:9-13), which shares the same language as that of the call to Abram, and also alludes to Genesis 3:15. The blessing of the nations will happen "through" the messianic "seed" of Abram, which will be identified as the messianic "seed" of David, and then, ultimately, as the Messiah Himself, Jesus Christ (Acts 3:25).

This blessing also contains an implicit commandment. Abram is not just the passive object of God's blessing; the form of the verb suggests that he is also the subject of blessing. The Hebrew form of the verb **you shall be a blessing** (12:2) is an imperative that expresses command and purpose: "so that you will be a blessing" (ESV). From God's blessing, Abram (and his spiritual children) should infer the duty to be a blessing to the nations.[454] The result of being blessed is a missionary lesson: "bringing salvation to all planet earth."[455] That this prophecy and this commandment have been fulfilled can be observed as an objective historical fact. From the beginning of the Christian testimony in the first centuries, the God of Abraham has been worshipped by all nations and the seed of Abraham has become a blessing to all humanity. Even the illustrious rabbi Maimonides, commenting on Genesis 12:3, wondered at the effect of this blessing: "The result of the course which Abraham took, is the fact that most people, as we see at present, agree in praising him [Abraham], and being proud of him; so that even those who are not his descendants call themselves by his name."[456]

12:4-9 Abram departed. The second paragraph of the narrative describes the *halak* "going" of Abram. As already noted, the verb *halak* "go" is the keyword of the passage and marks the progression of that going in four steps. The first *halak* "going" (12:4a) is a general statement qualifying Abram's response; it marks the departure of Abram from Ur of the Chaldeans and introduces and triggers all the following *halak* experiences of Abram. The second *halak* is related to Lot and marks the departure from Haran (12:4b). The third *halak* marks the move to the land of Canaan (12:5-8). The fourth *halak* (12:9) marks the traveling southward, preparing for the next move toward Egypt.

12:4 **So Abram departed as the Lord had spoken.** The verse is constructed in

---

452 The Hebrew preposition *be* "in" means either "in" or "through," "by the means of."

453 Although the word for "curse" in Genesis 3 is different (*'arar* instead of *qalal*) and the blessing is only implied in the victory of the seed over the serpent.

454 See Moskala, "Mission in the Old Testament," 66–67.

455 Walter Kaiser Jr., *Mission in the Old Testament: Israel as a Light to the Nations* (Grand Rapids: Baker, 2000), 13.

456 Maimonides, *The Guide for the Perplexed*, 315.

chiastic connection (ABCC₁B₁A₁) to the divine commandment "the Lord said to Abram: go" (12:1), as the following literal translation indicates:

A The Lord said
    B to Abram
        C Go (*lek leka*)
        C₁ he went (*wayyelek*)
    B₁ Abram
A₁ as the Lord said

This chiastic structure, which makes the move of Abram resonate with the divine command, suggests that Abram's move responded to the call of the Lord at Ur of the Chaldeans. In addition to this historical information, this literary echo conveys the spiritual idea that Abram responded in perfect conformity to the divine command. From the very beginning, Abram is described not only as a man of faith, but also as a faithful servant obedient to the Lord. This quality of Abram's response is even explicitly specified **as the Lord had spoken to him**, the same idiomatic expression that was used to characterize Noah's faithful obedience (6:22; 7:5).

And Lot went with him. The last time that Lot was mentioned was in connection to his grandfather, Terah, when they left Ur of the Chaldeans (11:31). This suggests that Lot's decision to separate from Terah to go with Abram must have taken place after the trip to Haran and, therefore, in Haran. There must have been some discussion and even disagreement about leaving. Then Lot decided to separate from Terah and went instead with Abram. The form of the verb *wayyelek* "went," which duplicates Abram's response, confirms that Lot joined Abram's response. The text does not say how long the clan stayed in Haran before making the decision to leave. Yet it is clear from the language of the report that Terah was determined not to leave with them. The passage, which places the course of events under Terah's control, ends with the use of verb *yashab* "dwell" (11:31). Also, it is not insignificant that the author concludes with the note that Terah died in Haran. This news, which echoes in inclusio (beginning and end of the passage) the news of Haran's death "in his native land, in Ur of the Chaldeans" (11:28), alludes to Haran's attachment to the homeland.

Abram was seventy-five years old when he departed from Haran. The age of Abram is now given, for it is only now that Abram actually leaves for the Promised Land. This is a way of marking the significance of that turning point. Abram's readiness to obey God prevailed over his loyalty to his family (cf. Matt 10:37). This timeline also measures his waiting twenty-five years before he begat his son Isaac (cf. 21:5).

12:5 Then Abram took … the people whom they had acquired in Haran. Abram not only takes care of his family (Sarai and Lot), but he is also attentive to the people around him. The text highlights Abram's missionary activity. The Hebrew word *nepesh* (KJV, JPS: "souls"; NKJV, ESV: "people") cannot refer to children, since Sarah was still barren at that time, or to slaves, since the Hebrew uses another word for "slave" (*'ebed*). This word should therefore refer to the proselytes Abram has been able to win through his testimony.[457] This interpretation fits the meaning of the

---

457 See Cassuto, *Genesis*, 2:320; cf. *Sifrei on Deut* 6:5; cf. Ellen G. White, PP 127.

Hebrew word *nepesh* "breath," which often refers to the "center of religious expression"[458] (Pss 42:2–3; 119:20, 81).

12:5–8 **They departed to go to the land of Canaan.** The repetition of the words "land of Canaan" (12:5) emphasizes the idea of arriving at the final destination, the Promised Land, with all the significance this place implied for the future of salvation history. Yet the report insists on the idea that Abram does not settle. Abram is only passing through (12:6) and moving from one place to another (12:8).

12:6 **The Canaanites were then in the land.** This remark from the author does not imply that, at the time of the writer, the Canaanites were no longer in the land, thus suggesting that this report was given in a post-Mosaic time. This observation is simply designed to emphasize the alien status of Abram: the land is already occupied. Significantly, Abram never goes into the cities he passes by; he always prefers to stay outside, at a tree near Shechem and in the mountain east of Bethel. The paradox of the Promised Land is suggested here: even though Abram should finally feel at home there, he should also understand that he is just passing by. It is interesting, on the other hand, that whenever Abram's settling is recorded it is always in a religious context. Certainly, Abram must have pitched his tent many times as he was traveling from Haran. But those pauses were never mentioned. The reason for this exception is that stops (like the present one mentioned) are significant as they are associated with the building of an altar. It is interesting to note that the last time Genesis reported the building of an altar was when Noah went out of the ark (8:20). The two occasions are similar, marking the turning point between two eras and the redemptive prospect of new horizons. The first site where Abram stops is **Shechem** (12:6), located between Mounts Ebal and Gerizim, east of modern Nablus. It is more precisely near **the terebinth tree of Moreh**, meaning "tree of the teacher," which suggests that this location was associated with some pedagogical activity. It is interesting that the missionary activity (12:5) is followed by a teaching session in connection to worship. There is a play on words relating Moreh to the verb *wayyera'* "appeared," describing God's revelation through a theophany: **the Lord appeared to Abram** (12:7). Also, the verb *wayyera'* "appeared" (lit. trans.: "made Himself seen") resonates with the verb *'ar'eh* "show" (lit. trans.: "cause to see"), promising that the Lord will "show the land" (12:1). The intention of this echo is to suggest that Abram has now reached the goal; he is now in the Promised Land, which the Lord has showed him. At the same time, the appearance of the Lord is identified with the point of destination. The Promised Land is associated with the Lord Himself. From Shechem, Abram moves to a second site, near Bethel (12:8), identified with modern Beitin (ten miles [seventeen kilometers] north of Jerusalem, and three miles [five kilometers] northeast of Ramallah). Bethel anticipates the episode of God's revelation to Jacob (28:19; 31:13). Abram pitches his tent there and builds a second altar. Settling is only allowed insofar as it is placed within the divine perspective, for the land belongs to God (Josh 22:19; cf. 18:1).

---

458 H. Seebass, "*nepesh*," *TDOT* 9:503.

SOJOURN IN EGYPT (12:10–13:1A)

GEN 12:10–13:1 NKJV	GEN 12:10–13:1 ESV
10 Now there was a famine in the land, and Abram went down to Egypt to dwell there, for the famine *was* severe in the land.	**10** Now there was a famine in the land. So Abram went down to Egypt to sojourn there, for the famine was severe in the land.
11 And it came to pass, when he was close to entering Egypt, that he said to Sarai his wife, "Indeed I know that you *are* a woman of beautiful countenance.	**11** When he was about to enter Egypt, he said to Sarai his wife, "I know that you are a woman beautiful in appearance,
12 Therefore it will happen, when the Egyptians see you, that they will say, 'This *is* his wife'; and they will kill me, but they will let you live.	**12** and when the Egyptians see you, they will say, 'This is his wife.' Then they will kill me, but they will let you live.
13 Please say you *are* my sister, that it may be well with me for your sake, and that I may live because of you."	**13** Say you are my sister, that it may go well with me because of you, and that my life may be spared for your sake."
14 So it was, when Abram came into Egypt, that the Egyptians saw the woman, that she *was* very beautiful.	**14** When Abram entered Egypt, the Egyptians saw that the woman was very beautiful.
15 The princes of Pharaoh also saw her and commended her to Pharaoh. And the woman was taken to Pharaoh's house.	**15** And when the princes of Pharaoh saw her, they praised her to Pharaoh. And the woman was taken into Pharaoh's house.
16 He treated Abram well for her sake. He had sheep, oxen, male donkeys, male and female servants, female donkeys, and camels.	**16** And for her sake he dealt well with Abram; and he had sheep, oxen, male donkeys, male servants, female servants, female donkeys, and camels.
17 But the Lᴏʀᴅ plagued Pharaoh and his house with great plagues because of Sarai, Abram's wife.	**17** But the Lᴏʀᴅ afflicted Pharaoh and his house with great plagues because of Sarai, Abram's wife.
18 And Pharaoh called Abram and said, "What *is* this you have done to me? Why did you not tell me that she *was* your wife?	**18** So Pharaoh called Abram and said, "What is this you have done to me? Why did you not tell me that she was your wife?
19 Why did you say, 'She *is* my sister'? I might have taken her as my wife. Now therefore, here is your wife; take *her* and go your way."	**19** Why did you say, 'She is my sister,' so that I took her for my wife? Now then, here is your wife; take her, and go."
20 So Pharaoh commanded *his* men concerning him; and they sent him away, with his wife and all that he had.	**20** And Pharaoh gave men orders concerning him, and they sent him away with his wife and all that he had.
13:1a Then Abram went up from Egypt, he and his wife and all that he had.	**13:1a** So Abram went up from Egypt, he and his wife and all that he had.

The irony is that Abram, who had just arrived in the Promised Land and was grateful for that gift, now decides to leave the country because he is hungry. Although Abram had courage and faith to bear the threat of the Canaanites and remain in the land, he cannot endure the famine. A number of reasons may explain this paradox. While Abram felt close ethnically and culturally to the Canaanites, who were generally hospitable toward him, he must have been disturbed by the hard physical conditions of the land. This new risky environment, whose agriculture depended on rains from above, was in sharp contrast to the secure and stable Tigris-Euphrates valley. In that respect, the land of Egypt and the Nile reminded Abram of his homeland; the fertility of both lands lay in stark contrast with the land of Canaan. Moses himself would later warn the people of the Exodus that "the land which you go to possess is not like the land of Egypt from which you have come, where you sowed your seed and watered it by foot, as a vegetable garden; but the land which you cross over to possess is a land of hills and valleys, which drinks water from the rain of heaven" (Deut 11:10–11). No wonder Egypt was a temptation for Abram, as it would continue to be for the ancient Israelites (Num 11:18; 14:3; Jer 2:18; 42:15). Egypt also represents human reliability (2 Kgs 18:21; cf. Isa 36:6, 9). In Egypt, faith is unnecessary, for the promise is visible there. This new section differs, then, from the preceding one in a significant way. Before, Abram was portrayed as a man of faith who lived according to God's call: Abram left Ur and settled in Canaan in response to God. Now, Abram is depicted as an empirical, realistic politician who relies exclusively on his own wisdom. In fact, when he leaves Canaan and settles in Egypt, God is never mentioned. And yet, God is with him and will bless him anyway, even against and in spite of himself. In fact, God will turn Abram's mistake and lack of faith into a blessing for himself and for all the surrounding nations. Abram will leave Egypt a wealthier man, and Pharaoh will be saved. God will transform evil into good. This promise of blessing will be seen again in the lives of Isaac (22:17–18), Jacob (26:3), and Joseph (50:20). God is present even within the darkness of human iniquity, even when He seems to be absent.

LITERARY STRUCTURE

The structure of the passage reflects this wonder of God's presence. Unlike the preceding trip to the Promised Land, which, from the departure (12:1–3) to the arrival (12:7–8), was full of the presence of God, the trip to Egypt has no mention of God. Abram decides by himself to go to Egypt (12:9), settle there (12:10), and return to Canaan (13:1). While in the trip to Canaan God spoke and appeared and humans never spoke, in the trip to Egypt God never speaks or appears and only humans (Abram, Pharaoh, and Pharaoh's princes) speak to each other. Yet God is present, and His action is recorded in the middle of the chiasm (12:17):

> **A** Descent of Abram to Egypt (12:10)
>   **B** Abram speaks to Sarai about Pharaoh (12:11–13)
>   **C** The princes of Pharaoh speak to Pharaoh about Sarai (12:14–16)
>   **D The Lord plagued (12:17)**
>   **C₁** Pharaoh speaks to Abram about Sarai (12:18–19)
>   **B₁** Pharaoh speaks to his men about Abram (12:20)
> **A₁** Ascent of Abram to Canaan (13:1a)

12:10 **There was a famine in the land.** This is the first contact with Egypt recorded in the Bible. That Abram decides to go to Egypt is not surprising. Already, the fact that Abram had moved to the south of Canaan (12:9) was suspect. We don't understand why Abram moved to the south right after God had appeared to him at Bethel—as a sign that he had arrived at his destination (12:7). It is as if Abram was not totally satisfied and was still looking for something else, as if he was attracted by the land of Egypt and secretly aspired to settle there.

Abram went down … to dwell there. The Hebrew verb *gar* "dwell," "sojourn" is the technical word to describe the state of residence and long-term settlement. Egypt was then considered as the ideal place to live and often attracted many people from the region, especially in times of crisis (26:1; 42:5; 47:11–13). The evidence of infiltrations from Canaan into Egypt because of famine is well attested in Egyptian texts of that time. Thus, in the teaching of Merikare, a text composed during the period of the Middle Kingdom (2060–1700), people coming from Canaan are identified as "miserable Asiatic" (*aamu*) and described as "wretched … short of water … he does not dwell in one place, food propels his foot."[459] A painting in the tomb of Khnumhotep III at Beni Hassan (about 150 miles north of Cairo; from the time of Sesostris II, 1897–1878 BC) represents Bedouin chief Ibsha with his tribe of thirty-seven companions, who traveled to Egypt to purchase grains.[460]

12:11 A woman of beautiful countenance. Sarai is then at least sixty-five years old, which is about midlife, considering her long life expectancy (23:1), and therefore still in good shape. The miracle of her capacity to give birth at the age of ninety is also consistent with the likelihood of her beauty at the age of sixty-five. Sadly, Sarai's beauty becomes a hazard for Abram, who fears that the Egyptians, who do not share his ethical standards, may attempt to harm or even kill him in order to gain his wife (cf. 20:10–13). Abram also knows that Egyptians are fond of the pretty women from the east, as attested in ancient Egyptian literature.[461] Therefore, Abram resorts to lies, and he does this with Sarai's tacit agreement (12:13). Abram's deceitful scheme is consistent with the manner in which he left Canaan and settled in Egypt. Once again, divine providence is not taken into consideration.

12:14–15 The woman was taken to Pharaoh's house. Indeed, Abram was right. The beauty of Sarai is noticed, and the course of events develops according to Abram's fears. The verb "see" is repeated twice. The common Egyptians, as well as the princes, **saw the woman**.

12:15–16 Yet Abram's deception turns against him. It is precisely because Abram lied—claiming that Sarai was his sister—that Pharaoh took her into his harem (12:15; cf. 12:19). Ironically, it is also because Pharaoh believed she was Abram's sister that he treated Abram well (12:16), according to Abram's plans (12:13). The gifts Abram receives from Pharaoh surpass his expectations. To the list of common gratifications, **sheep, oxen, male donkeys, male and female servants**, is added a rare product for that time, **and camels**. This is not an anachronism, for evidence of camels has been substantiated from bones and artistic representations from the fourth or third millennium BC.[462] The story is full of ambiguities. Even when Abram lies, he is telling the truth, for Sarai is both his sister and not his sister; she is his half-sister. Even when Abram is blessed with all the gifts of Pharaoh, he is cursed, for his wife is now in the harem of Pharaoh.

---

459 *AEL* 1:103–104.

460 See *ANET*, 229; cf. *ANEP*, no. 3.

461 See the Egyptian Sinuhe, who marries the daughter of a prince of Canaan (*AEL* 1:226); see also *The Doomed Prince*, who falls in love with an eastern (*Aamu*) princess (*AEL* 2:200–203).

462 See Oded Borowski, *Every Living Thing: Daily Use of Animals in Ancient Israel* (Walnut Creek, CA: Altamira, 1998), 114; cf. Randall W. Younker, "Late Bronze Age Camel Petroglyphs in the Wadi Nasib, Sinai," *NEASB* 42 (1999): 47–54.

12:17 **But the Lord plagued Pharaoh.** God's eruption in the house of Pharaoh is unexpected. The Lord intervenes on behalf of Abram and Sarai (both names are mentioned) despite their iniquity and their obliviousness of God. The plagues here point to the future ten plagues, which will hit Egypt just prior to the exodus of Abram's descendants. In this way, these plagues also anticipate the present deliverance of Abram from Egypt. For the God of Abram is also the God of Moses.

12:18–19 **Pharaoh called Abram and said.** Yet God does not rebuke Abram. Instead, it is Pharaoh who speaks, and his words sound like God's words. The expression is reminiscent of the technical formula describing God's call to man: "the Lord called to Adam and said" (3:9; cf. 21:17; 22:11; 15–16). It is also interesting that the question Pharaoh asks is followed by a series of questions, just as in the call of God to Adam (3:9, 11). This parallel between these two rebukes suggests that Abram's iniquity is of the same vein as Adam's iniquity. In both cases, the unity of the human couple was compromised. Adam refused to take responsibility and, as a result, could have lost his wife, from whom he had dissociated himself (3:12). Similarly, Abram also refused to take responsibility in regards to his wife and almost lost her. The grammar of the phrase implies that Abram lied **so that** (consequently) Pharaoh could have "taken" Sarai for his wife: **Why did you say, "She is my sister," so that I took her for my wife?** (ESV). Note also that Pharaoh's words denote impatience and exasperation: **take her and go your way** (12:19).

12:20 **They sent him away.** The verb "send" is the same that is used to describe God sending Adam away from the Garden of Eden (both passages use *shalakh* in the intensive *piel* form). The irony is that Abram is sent away from Egypt just as Adam was sent away from the Garden of Eden. The difference between the two expulsions, however, is huge. First, Egypt is not the Garden of Eden, although Abram might have for a moment thought so. Secondly, it is not God who sends him away, not even the pharaoh, but his servants. It is, therefore, a humbled Abram who leaves Egypt. It is also significant that the same language will be used again to describe the reaction of the Egyptians and Pharaoh, who will "send" (*shalakh*) the people of Israel out of Egypt—also enriched from the Egyptians and also immediately after the plagues (Exod 12:33; 13:17). These parallels between the two events suggest that Abram leaving Egypt anticipates the future exodus and also carries in itself a message of hope.

13:1a **Then Abram went up from Egypt.** This verse, which concludes the session in Egypt, echoes the introduction (12:10) as an inclusio. Abram's return to Canaan is noted without any comment. Abram is confused. Ironically, he does not return to the land because the famine ended, but because he is expelled from Egypt. Apparently, famine is no longer an issue, so that it seems he went there for no reason. Abram did not lose anything though. He goes back the same way he came, **he and his wife and all that he had**. Yet Lot is mentioned for the second time (cf. 12:4), after the mention of material wealth, like an appendix, hinting at his future separation. Thus, this verse functions as a hinge between the two stories. It serves both as the conclusion of the preceding section covering Abram's journey in Egypt (12:10–20) and as the introduction to the following story covering Abram's return to Canaan (13:1–18).

ABRAM AND LOT (13:1B–14:24)

A bram returns to where he was before. The way the author tells the story suggests that, in his view, Abram should not have left. For he had gone out from the *Negeb* "south" (12:9), and now he is heading for that same place, the *Negeb* **the South** (13:1). It is also noteworthy that Lot is mentioned again. Lot was not mentioned when Abram left Canaan, while he had been mentioned when he had moved to Canaan (12:4). The second trip to Canaan reminds us of the first trip to Canaan, when they were responding to the call of God. All this indicates Abram's intention to repent and repair his relationship with God. In fact, he goes back to Bethel, the very place where he had built the altar and where God had appeared to him (13:3–6). At last, Abram decides to "dwell." The verb "dwell" (*yashab*) is a keyword in this chapter, where it appears six times and serves as a landmark to delimitate the structure of the story. In the first section (13:2–9), it is used with a negation because of their wealth: **they could not dwell together** (13:6). In the same section, it is used a second time in the context of tensions that erupted between the herdsmen of Abram and the herdsmen of Lot, to give one more reason why they cannot dwell together. The land is not enough, for it is already occupied by the Canaanites (13:7). The word is only used positively in the second section (13:12, 18). Abram and Lot are able to "dwell" only when they separate from each other and when Lot decides to "dwell" outside of the Promised Land (13:10–13). More precisely for Abram, this happens when—for the first time since God's call *lek leka* (12:1ff.)—he hears God's voice again (13:14) and finally decides to "dwell" and pitch his tent in the Promised Land (13:18).

13:1B–9. TENSIONS BETWEEN HERDSMEN

GEN 13:1B–9 NKJV	GEN 13:1B–9 ESV
1b and Lot with him, to the South.	**1b** and Lot with him, into the Negeb.
2 Abram *was* very rich in livestock, in silver, and in gold.	**2** Now Abram was very rich in livestock, in silver, and in gold.
3 And he went on his journey from the South as far as Bethel, to the place where his tent had been at the beginning, between Bethel and Ai,	**3** And he journeyed on from the Negeb as far as Bethel to the place where his tent had been at the beginning, between Bethel and Ai,
4 to the place of the altar which he had made there at first. And there Abram called on the name of the LORD.	**4** to the place where he had made an altar at the first. And there Abram called upon the name of the LORD.
5 Lot also, who went with Abram, had flocks and herds and tents.	**5** And Lot, who went with Abram, also had flocks and herds and tents,
6 Now the land was not able to support them, that they might dwell together, for their possessions were so great that they could not dwell together.	**6** so that the land could not support both of them dwelling together; for their possessions were so great that they could not dwell together,
7 And there was strife between the herdsmen of Abram's livestock and the herdsmen of Lot's livestock. The Canaanites and the Perizzites then dwelt in the land.	**7** and there was strife between the herdsmen of Abram's livestock and the herdsmen of Lot's livestock. At that time the Canaanites and the Perizzites were dwelling in the land.

8 So Abram said to Lot, "Please let there be no strife between you and me, and between my herdsmen and your herdsmen; for we *are* brethren.	**8** Then Abram said to Lot, "Let there be no strife between you and me, and between your herdsmen and my herdsmen, for we are kinsmen.
9 *Is* not the whole land before you? Please separate from me. If *you take* the left, then I will go to the right; or, if *you go* to the right, then I will go to the left."	**9** Is not the whole land before you? Separate yourself from me. If you take the left hand, then I will go to the right, or if you take the right hand, then I will go to the left."

13:2–5 And he went … as far as Bethel. For the first time since Canaan, the verb *halak* "go"—responding to the call *lek leka*—reappears. It is used twice (13:1, 5). The first time it refers to the move of Abram to Bethel, more exactly to the place where Abram had built an altar and worshipped God (13:4). Obviously, Abram wants to reconnect and restore what his trip to Egypt had interrupted. Abram has come back to "the old paths" (Jer 6:16; cf. 18:15). He has repented. The second time the verb *halak* "go" is used it refers to the going of Lot. Yet, unlike Abram's, the "going" of Lot has no spiritual connotation; instead, it is associated with his wealth (13:5). Moreover, not only is the way they "go" different, but also the way they "dwell." While Abram relates his "dwelling" to his relationship with God and to the invisible kingdom, Lot views his "dwelling" only in connection to himself and his material possessions. Therefore, they **could not dwell together** (13:6). The difficulty of their cohabitation is not merely due to outside factors—the land, their wealth, or the Canaanites—but it essentially pertains to profound spiritual divergences.

13:7–9 And there was strife. Considering the backdrop of irreconcilable worldviews, tensions were unavoidable. According to the biblical record, only the herdsmen are involved in the strife. Yet the dispute goes beyond the herdsmen, as it involves spiritual matters. Abram's immediate reaction and initiative suggests that the conflict hides the essential divergence between him and Lot: **Abram said to Lot, Please let there be no strife between you and me** (13:8). It is therefore Abram who proposes the separation as the only way to restore peace. The Hebrew word *parad* for **separate** (13:9) is to relate socially (Prov 18:1). The same word is used to describe the dispersal of peoples after the flood and Babel (10:5, 32; cf. 11:8). The separation between Abram and Lot is, then, tragic and irreversible.

13:10–18. THE PROMISED LAND

GEN 13:10–18 NKJV	GEN 13:10–18 ESV
10 And Lot lifted his eyes and saw all the plain of Jordan, that it *was* well watered everywhere (before the Lord destroyed Sodom and Gomorrah) like the garden of the Lord, like the land of Egypt as you go toward Zoar.	**10** And Lot lifted up his eyes and saw that the Jordan Valley was well watered everywhere like the garden of the Lord, like the land of Egypt, in the direction of Zoar. (This was before the Lord destroyed Sodom and Gomorrah.)
11 Then Lot chose for himself all the plain of Jordan, and Lot journeyed east. And they separated from each other.	**11** So Lot chose for himself all the Jordan Valley, and Lot journeyed east. Thus they separated from each other.

12 Abram dwelt in the land of Canaan, and Lot dwelt in the cities of the plain and pitched *his* tent even as far as Sodom.	**12** Abram settled in the land of Canaan, while Lot settled among the cities of the valley and moved his tent as far as Sodom.
13 But the men of Sodom *were* exceedingly wicked and sinful against the Lord.	**13** Now the men of Sodom were wicked, great sinners against the Lord.
14 And the Lord said to Abram, after Lot had separated from him: "Lift your eyes now and look from the place where you are— northward, southward, eastward, and westward;	**14** The Lord said to Abram, after Lot had separated from him, "Lift up your eyes and look from the place where you are, northward and southward and eastward and westward,
15 for all the land which you see I give to you and your descendants forever.	**15** for all the land that you see I will give to you and to your offspring forever.
16 And I will make your descendants as the dust of the earth; so that if a man could number the dust of the earth, *then* your descendants also could be numbered.	**16** I will make your offspring as the dust of the earth, so that if one can count the dust of the earth, your offspring also can be counted.
17 Arise, walk in the land through its length and its width, for I give it to you."	**17** Arise, walk through the length and the breadth of the land, for I will give it to you."
18 Then Abram moved *his* tent, and went and dwelt by the terebinth trees of Mamre, which *are* in Hebron, and built an altar there to the Lord.	**18** So Abram moved his tent and came and settled by the oaks of Mamre, which are at Hebron, and there he built an altar to the Lord.

13:10–13 The land that Lot sees, **all the plain of Jordan** is located outside the confines of the Promised Land. In contrast to Abram who **dwelt in the land of Canaan … Lot dwelt in the cities of the plain** (10:12), the future possession of Lot's descendants, the Moabites and the Ammonites. We should still consider these lands to be God's gift to them (Deut 2:9, 19). Ironically, this region is identified with the Garden of Eden and Egypt (13:10), which hints at Abram's recent trip to Egypt and his possible attraction to that land (see the comments in the introduction on 12:10–20). The irony continues with the mention of the future destruction of Sodom and Gomorrah, and the reference to the wickedness of their inhabitants. What Lot sees is as deceptive as a mirage and will not last long. Our passage begins with the phrase **before the Lord destroyed …** , in connection to the lush beauty of the plain (13:10), and ends with the phrase **against the Lord**, associated with the exceeding wickedness and sinfulness of its inhabitants (13:13). Significantly, Lot moves eastwards (*miqqedem*) (13:11), like Adam when he left the Garden of Eden (3:24), Cain when he left his family (4:16), and the builders of Babel when they left their original settlement (see the comments on 11:2). It is also significant that this move comes from a human initiative: **Lot chose for himself** (13:11). The same language was used by the antediluvians: "they took wives *for themselves* of all whom they *chose*" (6:2). On the other hand, Abram did not choose. This was not only an act of civility and love towards his nephew, this was also an act of faith. Abram allowed God to choose the land for him. This is not the land he would have chosen for himself. Yet this land was to be a gift, received by Abram only through the grace of God.

13:14–18 **And the Lord said to Abram … Lift your eyes now and look.** Unlike Lot who decides by himself to "lift his eyes and see" (13:10), Abram does this (the

209

same Hebrew words are used) only at God's injunction (13:14). This is the first time God speaks to Abram since His initial call to leave Ur (12:1ff.). It is striking that God's involvement in the life of Abram is set in direct connection to Lot's departure. God speaks to Abram only **after Lot separated from him** (13:14). Then God confirms the gift of the land (13:15, 17). The space of the whole land is emphasized. From Bethel, the place where he stands, Abram's eyes should embrace the four directions, **northward**, **southward**, **eastward, and westward** (13:14), just as Jacob will do later, again from the same place (28:14). Then Abram is pressed by God to physically apprehend the reality of the land. He should **walk in the land through its length and its width** (13:17). This walk "represents a symbolic appropriation of the land."[463] Abram's vision is also transported in time, into the future. **All the land** (13:15) will also be given to his descendants (13:15–16). There is a play on words linking the descendants to that land. They will be as numerous as the **dust of the earth** (13:16). The same Hebrew word *ʾarets* "land" that refers to "all the land" given by God is used in the phrase "the dust of the earth" (*ʾarets*, also translated "land" in 13:15, 17). The passage ends with worship. Abram builds an altar (13:18), just as he did in the beginning, when he had first arrived at the Promised Land (12:7–8); and again, it is around trees, like last time. Even Mamre, the name of the place, is reminiscent of Moreh (cf. 12:6). Thus, Abram has recovered his connection with the Lord and his destiny. Having temporarily gone astray, he is now determined to stay in the land. Hebron-Mamre will be the primary settlement of Abram and Isaac (18:1; 35:27) and the burial site of all the patriarchal family (23:2; 50:13).

14:1–24. THE THREAT OF BABEL

After having survived the temptation of Egypt, Abram is now subjected to a military threat from Shinar (14:1), that is, Babel (10:10).[464] This identification is confirmed by Shinar's association with the neighboring king of Elam, which is ancient Persia (modern Iran). Shinar, the place of the tower of Babel (11:2), is mentioned first on the list of the enemies, although Chedorlaomer is the leader (14:5, 9). This accent on Shinar suggests that beyond the military east-west confrontation a theological significance is intended. This spiritual perspective is suggested in the contrast between Abram and Lot underlying these stories. While Lot departed from where he dwelt, Abram still dwells by the terebinth trees of Mamre. While Lot was caught in the midst of troubles and military tensions, Abram lives in peace with his allies (14:13). While Lot was taken captive without being able to do anything (14:12), Abram arms his servants and attacks the enemies (14:14–15). While Lot has lost everything (14:12), Abram is able to recover everything (14:16). While God is ignored in Lot's misfortunes, Abram lives near the altar (14:13; cf. 13:18), gives his tithe (14:20), and invokes "the Lord, God Most High" (14:22).

---

463 Wenham, *Genesis 1–15*, 298.

464 Cf. the Samaritan Pentateuch (14:9), the Targum Onkelos (14:1), and the Genesis Apocryphon (14:1), which specifically state "Babel."

14:1–11. THE COALITION OF BABEL

GEN 14:1–11 NKJV	GEN 14:1–11 ESV
1 And it came to pass in the days of Amraphel king of Shinar, Arioch king of Ellasar, Chedorlaomer king of Elam, and Tidal king of nations,	**1** In the days of Amraphel king of Shinar, Arioch king of Ellasar, Chedorlaomer king of Elam, and Tidal king of Goiim,
2 *that* they made war with Bera king of Sodom, Birsha king of Gomorrah, Shinab king of Admah, Shemeber king of Zeboiim, and the king of Bela (that is, Zoar).	**2** these kings made war with Bera king of Sodom, Birsha king of Gomorrah, Shinab king of Admah, Shemeber king of Zeboiim, and the king of Bela (that is, Zoar).
3 All these joined together in the Valley of Siddim (that is, the Salt Sea).	**3** And all these joined forces in the Valley of Siddim (that is, the Salt Sea).
4 Twelve years they served Chedorlaomer, and in the thirteenth year they rebelled.	**4** Twelve years they had served Chedorlaomer, but in the thirteenth year they rebelled.
5 In the fourteenth year Chedorlaomer and the kings that were with him came and attacked the Rephaim in Ashteroth Karnaim, the Zuzim in Ham, the Emim in Shaveh Kiriathaim,	**5** In the fourteenth year Chedorlaomer and the kings who were with him came and defeated the Rephaim in Ashteroth-karnaim, the Zuzim in Ham, the Emim in Shaveh-kiriathaim,
6 and the Horites in their mountain of Seir, as far as El Paran, which *is* by the wilderness.	**6** and the Horites in their hill country of Seir as far as El-paran on the border of the wilderness.
7 Then they turned back and came to En Mishpat (that *is*, Kadesh), and attacked all the country of the Amalekites, and also the Amorites who dwelt in Hazezon Tamar.	**7** Then they turned back and came to En-mishpat (that is, Kadesh) and defeated all the country of the Amalekites, and also the Amorites who were dwelling in Hazazon-tamar.
8 And the king of Sodom, the king of Gomorrah, the king of Admah, the king of Zeboiim, and the king of Bela (that *is*, Zoar) went out and joined together in battle in the Valley of Siddim	**8** Then the king of Sodom, the king of Gomorrah, the king of Admah, the king of Zeboiim, and the king of Bela (that is, Zoar) went out, and they joined battle in the Valley of Siddim
9 against Chedorlaomer king of Elam, Tidal king of nations, Amraphel king of Shinar, and Arioch king of Ellasar— four kings against five.	**9** with Chedorlaomer king of Elam, Tidal king of Goiim, Amraphel king of Shinar, and Arioch king of Ellasar, four kings against five.
10 Now the Valley of Siddim *was full of* asphalt pits; and the kings of Sodom and Gomorrah fled; *some* fell there, and the remainder fled to the mountains.	**10** Now the Valley of Siddim was full of bitumen pits, and as the kings of Sodom and Gomorrah fled, some fell into them, and the rest fled to the hill country.
11 Then they took all the goods of Sodom and Gomorrah, and all their provisions, and went their way.	**11** So the enemy took all the possessions of Sodom and Gomorrah, and all their provisions, and went their way.

14:1–2 And it came to pass in the days of Amraphel king of Shinar. The Hebrew word *wayehi* "and it came to pass" introduces a new section while providing background information and could better be translated, "At the time when Amraphel … went to war."[465] This is the first **war** (*milkhamah*) recorded in the Bible (14:2).

---

465 Bruce K. Waltke and Cathi J. Fredericks, *Genesis: A Commentary* (Grand Rapids: Zondervan, 2001), 228.

First, the two camps are presented. Three other kings fight alongside Amraphel, king of Babel (14:1). Although these kings have not been identified, the linguistic structure of their names allows at least some recognition. The name "Amraphel" has not been clearly identified, but its "l" ending (from the Akkadian *illu* "god") denotes a Semitic (Babylonian) origin.[466] The name "Arioch" is well attested in Hurrian sources before the second millennium, which "presupposes an ancient and authentic tradition."[467] The name "Chedorlaomer" is also well attested in Elamite sources. Tidal is Hittite, as indicated by a number of Hittite kings with this name. Facing these four kings are five kings of the Dead Sea area. The list of these kings begins with the mention of Sodom and Gomorrah, a rhetorical way to mark their importance for the author. Significantly, both kings of Sodom and Gomorrah receive Hebrew names with the same form and pejorative meaning (**Bera** means "in evil," and **Birsha** means "in wickedness"), suggesting that the names are pseudonyms or at least deliberately mispronounced to emphasize their sinfulness. The two other names **Shinab** and **Shemeber** sound more authentic since they both resemble West Semitic names occurring at that time. The name of the fifth king is not given.

14:3–11 All these joined together. The five Canaanites armies went to war in response to successive attacks conducted by the four Babel armies progressing along the north-south King's Highway (Num 20:17), against the seven peoples in Transjordan who had just rebelled the preceding year against their Mesopotamian suzerains after twelve years of submission (14:4–5). The success of the Babel coalition urged them to also join forces together. The idea of coalition is here emphasized; the same notion appears twice in the narrative, in the beginning and in the end (14:3, 8), and in the same environment, **the Valley of Siddim** (14:10). This method of waging war was typical in Middle Eastern politics especially during that period (2000–1750 BC).[468] The Canaanite coalition faces another coalition: **four kings against five** (14:9) and these coalitions contrast with the camp of Abram who fights alone (14:14–15).[469] It is also noteworthy that this association of the two numbers "five" versus "four," which is designed to suggest the illusion of superiority of the Canaanite camp over the Babel camp, brings out the number nine (five plus four) that is the characteristic number representing the totality of the enemies in Egyptian tradition.[470] From the perspective of Abram and certainly from the perspective of the author, both the five and the four were the enemies.

---

466 The identification with Hammurabi is no longer supported for strong linguistic reasons.

467 Speiser, *Genesis*, 107. Arioch is also the name of a captain of the guard in Babylon in the days of Nebuchadnezzar and Daniel (Dan 2:14), which shows that the tradition of this name was well preserved.

468 See K. A. Kitchen, *Ancient Orient and Old Testament* (Chicago: IVP, 1966), 45.

469 This passage refers only to Abram and his servants as fighters, although Abram asks compensation also for Aner, Eshcol, and Mamre (14:24). Rashi explains this apparent contradiction by suggesting that only Abram's servants went to the battle, while his allies did not join them to guard the camp (Miqraot Gedolot, ad loc.). Note that David will do the same (1 Sam 30:24).

470 See Robert B. Partridge, *Fighting Pharaohs: Weapons and Warfare in Ancient Egypt* (Manchester, UK: Peartree Publishing, 2002), 7–8.

14:12–17. THE RESCUE OF LOT.

GEN 14:12–17 NKJV	GEN 14:12–17 ESV
12 They also took Lot, Abram's brother's son who dwelt in Sodom, and his goods, and departed.	**12** They also took Lot, the son of Abram's brother, who was dwelling in Sodom, and his possessions, and went their way.
13 Then one who had escaped came and told Abram the Hebrew, for he dwelt by the terebinth trees of Mamre the Amorite, brother of Eshcol and brother of Aner; and they *were* allies with Abram.	**13** Then one who had escaped came and told Abram the Hebrew, who was living by the oaks of Mamre the Amorite, brother of Eshcol and of Aner. These were allies of Abram.
14 Now when Abram heard that his brother was taken captive, he armed his three hundred and eighteen trained *servants* who were born in his own house, and went in pursuit as far as Dan.	**14** When Abram heard that his kinsman had been taken captive, he led forth his trained men, born in his house, 318 of them, and went in pursuit as far as Dan.
15 He divided his forces against them by night, and he and his servants attacked them and pursued them as far as Hobah, which *is* north of Damascus.	**15** And he divided his forces against them by night, he and his servants, and defeated them and pursued them to Hobah, north of Damascus.
16 So he brought back all the goods, and also brought back his brother Lot and his goods, as well as the women and the people.	**16** Then he brought back all the possessions, and also brought back his kinsman Lot with his possessions, and the women and the people.
17 And the king of Sodom went out to meet him at the Valley of Shaveh (that *is*, the King's Valley), after his return from the defeat of Chedorlaomer and the kings who *were* with him.	**17** After his return from the defeat of Chedorlaomer and the kings who were with him, the king of Sodom went out to meet him at the Valley of Shaveh (that is, the King's Valley).

After the previous reports of war and especially after we learned that Sodom and Gomorrah had fallen, we are expecting to hear about Lot, for Lot **dwelt in Sodom** (14:12). Lot was the very reason for these reports, yet he is only mentioned incidentally. Lot is **taken captive** (14:14) as an accidental part of the war, among other booty. Obviously, Lot was not among all the others who had fled the city (14:10). Lot's passivity to the events is striking and in stark contrast to Abram, who immediately reacts as soon as he hears of his nephew's predicament. Lot is not just identified as his brother's son (14:12). Abram thinks of Lot as his brother (14:14). Abram is the one who loves, who reaches out, and who will save. Lot, on the other hand, never speaks and never relates to Abram. Abram does not limit himself to his duty to fight and win the battle, but he goes on to pursue the enemies up **as far as Dan** (14:14b). The reference to "Dan" to mark the northern border is a late modernization for the ancient name of Laish, intended to help the contemporary reader follow the story (see also Josh 19:47 where the name "Laish" corresponds to "Leshem"; see also Judg 18:7, 14, 27, 29). The name of Dan also appears in the expression "from Dan even to Beersheba" to designate the limits of Canaan (2 Sam 17:11).

At the end of the campaign, when Lot and his people are finally rescued and return home, it is only the king of Sodom who meets Abram to thank him (14:17). Lot contents himself in being the one who is loved and saved, and he lets others act on his behalf. Ironically, Lot, the one who had taken the initiative and had been the most concerned to be in control of his destiny when he chose his part of the land, is now the one who is the most passive. Abram, on the other hand, who had behaved the most passively, trusting God and giving Lot the right to choose first, is now the one who takes the initiative and controls the course of events. Abram had understood that trust in God and the readiness to lose his benefits was the best way to control his destiny and ensure the best outcome. The same paradoxical lesson is reinforced by Jesus in His Sermon on the Mount: "whoever desires to save his life will lose it, but whoever loses his life for My sake and the gospel's will save it" (Mark 8:35).

14:18. MELCHIZEDEK KING OF SALEM

GEN 14:18 NKJV	GEN 14:18 ESV
18 Then Melchizedek king of Salem brought out bread and wine; he *was* the priest of God Most High.	**18** And Melchizedek king of Salem brought out bread and wine. (He was priest of God Most High.)

14:18 This mysterious king seems completely out of place in our context. First of all, **Melchizedek** comes from the city of **Salem**, the ancient name of Jerusalem,[471] which was not involved in the war. Additionally, the name of *shalem* "Salem," which means "peace," contradicts the activities of war that have been central to the story so far. "Justice" (*tsedeq*), which is included in the name of the king, stands in opposition to the evocations of "evil" and "wickedness" in the names of Bera ("in evil'), king of Sodom, and Birsha ("in wickedness"), king of Gomorrah. Also the place of Salem, which Abraham will later call "the Lord-Will-Provide" (22:14), stands in opposition to Babel, which promotes human control and the usurpation of God. Furthermore, the text is saturated with religious references. Melchizedek is called a **priest of God Most High**. This is the first occurrence in the Bible of the word "priest" (*kohen*), so that Melchizedek's priesthood predates the Levitical priesthood. The fact that Abram uses the same title *'el 'elyon* "God Most High" for his God (14:22) suggests that Abram considered Melchizedek a legitimate priest of the Creator God. And yet, Abram's specific addition of YHWH to the name "God Most High," which was absent in Melchizedek's discourse, suggests also Melchizedek's universal perspective. It is clear, however, that Melchizedek was not Christ. God had chosen him to be His representative among the people of that time, although he belonged to the Canaanite community.[472] Kings bearing the qualifying title of *tsedek* in their royal names are well attested in the history of ancient Canaanite Jerusalem (Josh 10:1). In spite of his foreign origin, Abram still gives him a tithe and is blessed by him. In addition, the strong religious atmosphere of the scene—the numerous references to God, the sacred meal of the bread and the wine, and the poetic blessing addressed to God— reinforces the enigmatic character of the meeting between this king and Abram. All these features suggest that the author is intentionally placing the Canaanite figure of Melchizedek in a spiritual perspective, pointing beyond a simple meeting of kings. Significantly, the subsequent Scriptures maintain the Genesis tradition: Psalm 110

---

471 The first mention of the name "Jerusalem" in the form of Urushalim (or Rushalimum) appears in Egyptian Execration Texts of the nineteenth and eighteenth centuries BC (see J. M. Weinstein, "Jerusalem," *OEAE* 2:199). For the biblical identification of Jerusalem with Salem, see the use of the name "Salem" in parallel to the name "Zion," referring to the temple of Jerusalem (Ps 76:2 [3]); the first century AD Genesis Apocryphon (1 Qap Gen 22:13) clearly identifies Salem with Jerusalem: "he came to Salem, that is Jerusalem"; cf. the Targumim; Josephus, *Jewish Antiquities* 1.10.2 [180–181]; Gen. Rab. 43:6.

472 See Ellen G. White, SDABC 1:1092–1093.

associates Melchizedek with the future Davidic Messiah (Ps 110:4), followed by the authors of the New Testament who relate the unique priesthood of Melchizedek to that of Jesus (Heb 5:5–6:10; 7:1–28), and later by Jewish and Christian interpreters who recognized the religious significance of this particular portrayal of Melchizedek, while still maintaining—the majority of them—that he was a human being.[473]

Bread and wine. The significance of this meal is not clear. In our context, this could be a meal celebrating the recent victory and soldiers' homecoming, along with the recovery of the lost goods. Melchizedek would, then, just be the generous leader who honors his neighbor Abram. Yet, the limitation of the meal to only "bread and wine" suggests that it is a symbolic gesture rather than a real festive banquet. The specific religious accent of the story favors a religious interpretation, especially as it introduces the blessing and giving of the tithe. In that case, this could be a covenant meal between God and Abram signifying the blessing of God the Creator, the One who gives bread and wine.

The same association of words occurs in the blessing of Jacob by Isaac (27:27–29) where the motifs "wine and grain" also occur in connection to the motifs of "blessing," "heaven and earth," and the promise of preeminence over the nations.

The first implication of the connection between the two passages concerns the nature of the wine that was used by Melchizedek. While the Hebrew word *yayin* "wine" used by Melchizedek is ambiguous, referring in 50 percent of the cases to alcoholic wine, in the blessing of Jacob it is the Hebrew word *tirosh* that is used, which unambiguously refers to "grape juice." The frequent association of *tirosh* "grape juice" with "grain" (Deut 7:13; 11:14; 2 Chr 31:50) indicates that these words refer to the fresh product that has been threshed or pressed (Num 18:27). Thus, even when the Hebrew word *yayin* is used (Exod 29:40; Lev 23:13; Num 15:5), it is clear that it refers to unfermented grape juice in the context of a sacrificial offering—a "libation"—precisely because it was associated with unleavened bread (Lev 2:11).[474]my It is also noteworthy that the same association occurs in connection to the giving of tithes (Deut 14:23). There are therefore good reasons to think that the so-called "wine" that was used on Melchizedek's table was nonalcoholic wine, and the bread was unleavened bread; as is the case in other similar occasions in the Bible where "wine" is associated with grain and tithe giving in a ceremony designed to express gratefulness for the divine blessing.

The second implication of these biblical parallels is that the "bread and wine" of Melchizedek have strong religious connotations. It is enlightening that Melchizedek's offering of bread and wine was connected in Jewish tradition with the bread and wine of the Presence in the Sanctuary. In one ancient commentary on 14:18, it is said: "On the verse 'And Melchizedek king of Salem brought out bread and wine' (14:18) …

---

473 A Qumran tradition (11QMelch) identifies Melchizedek as a superior heavenly being, even Michael Himself who atones for the sin of the wicked (see G. Brooke, "Melchizedek (11QMelch)," *ABD* 4:686). But for Philo, Melchizedek was a special, anointed priest, even a high priest before God (Philo, *On the Life of Abraham* 235; cf. Josephus *Jewish Antiquities* 10.2 [180–181]). Rabbinic tradition identifies Melchizedek with Noah's son, Shem (Gen. Rab. 44:7). For Melchizedek in the Christian tradition, see especially Justin Martyr (*Dialogue With Trypho* 19:3–4, 33) and Tertullian (*Against the Jews* 2) who saw in Melchizedek a type of the priesthood of Jesus, which was, like Melchizedek's priesthood, not dependent on circumcision or on the Jewish Law and was carried on by the church.

474 According to the Talmud, wine was formally prohibited as an offering: "One may bring any kind of fruit to the holy Temple, as a token of thanksgiving, but one is not permitted to bring intoxicating alcohol" (b. Hul. 120; cf. 'Arak 11). For the longstanding Jewish tradition that the wine of the offering had to be unfermented grape juice fresh from the press, see also Maimonides, *Code of Maimonides*, Treatise III: Heave Offering (New Haven: Yale University Press, 1949), 5, 25.

Rabbi Samuel ben Nahman said: 'He [Melchizedek] instructed him [Abram] in the laws of the priesthood, *bread* alludes to the bread of the Presence, and *wine* alludes to libations.' "[475] This identification with the bread of the Presence suggests that the wine brought by Melchizedek was unfermented, just as the bread was unleavened bread.[476] Interestingly, we find again the same association of "bread and wine" in the Passover prayer (the *Kiddush*), celebrating the miracle of the Exodus event, a ritual that was subsequently carried over into the Lord's Supper (Luke 22:19–20). All these historical testimonies again support the idea that Melchizedek's "bread and wine" had a definite religious significance.

14:19–20. THE BLESSING OF MELCHIZEDEK

GEN 14:19–20 NKJV	GEN 14:19–20 ESV
19 And he blessed him and said: "Blessed be Abram of God Most High, Possessor of heaven and earth;	**19** And he blessed him and said, "Blessed be Abram by God Most High, Possessor of heaven and earth;
20 and blessed be God Most High, who has delivered your enemies into your hand." And he gave him a tithe of all.	**20** and blessed be God Most High, who has delivered your enemies into your hand!" And Abram gave him a tenth of everything.

That the blessing is directly associated with the "bread and wine" confirms the religious setting of this meal. This is the second blessing after Noah (9:26–27). Melchizedek blesses the God of Abram, just as Noah blessed the God of Shem. The word *barak* "bless" is a keyword in the passage; it occurs three times, an emphasis that points back to the promise of the blessing of Abram (12:1–3), which is now fulfilled for the first time. Abram is blessed by the nations while he is also a blessing to them. The text of the blessing is presented poetically through two parallel verses. The first line takes on a universal scope and refers to the God of creation: **God Most High, Possessor of heaven and earth** (14:19). The Hebrew word *qoneh* "possessor" implies the idea of ownership, acquisition (4:1; Eccl 2:7–8), and creation (Deut 32:6; Ps 139:13). In biblical thinking, the two ideas are related. God possesses the heavens and the earth because He created them (Pss 24:1; 89:11–12). Clearly, the blessing refers to the first verse of Genesis: "In the beginning God created the heavens and the earth" (1:1). The expression "heavens and earth" is a merism associating two extremes to suggest totality. God is the owner of "all" because He created "all." The form of the verb (participle in apposition to "God Most High"), however, suggests also that the heavens and earth are God's possession. This theological proposition is reasserted by Abram (14:22). In Abram's words, however, the universality of God is associated with the name *YHWH*, which adds to the idea of universality, the idea of relationship, and the personal presence of the Lord, as revealed in the second creation story (2:4b–25). This is precisely the perspective that is elaborated in the second line, which affirms the God of salvation who just delivered Abram: the God **who has delivered your enemies into your hand** (14:20). The word *miggen* "delivered" is derived from the root *magan* "give" or "grant,"[477] common to several Semitic

---

475 Gen. Rab. 43:6.

476 According to the testimony of Josephus, the "bread of the presence" (or "showbread") was unleavened bread (*Jewish Antiquities* 3.10.7).

477 See D. N. Freedman and M. P. O'Connor, "*magen*," *TDOT* 8: 85–86.

languages, implying the idea of grace.[478] The idea is that God has graciously "given" Abram's enemies into his hands, as seen in the more common expression "to give into the hand" (Josh 6:2; cf. Hos 11:8). Note that the blessing moved from the universal event of creation to the particular experience of salvation and not the other way around.

14:20 He gave him a tithe of all. Abram "gave" a tithe to Melchizedek in virtue of his priesthood and the priestly blessing he just bestowed upon Abram, but also in direct response to God's gift of creation and salvation. The affirmation of God as "Possessor of heaven and earth" and hence as Creator of "all" is indeed related to the giving of the tithe, which is not only a recognition that "all" belongs to God, but also the expression of gratefulness for God's free gift of salvation. It is noteworthy that the practice of the tithe is set in the context of prayer and worship. This concrete accounting task is unexpectedly placed in the midst of Abram's poetic and spiritual worship experience. As such, the tithe is to be understood as an essentially religious act, directed at the God of creation who owns everything (Heb 7:2–6) and the God of grace who gives us everything we have. Thus, Jacob swears to give *to* God a tithe of "all" that God would give him (28:22). Giving our tithe to God is simply our recognition that God is the Giver of "all." Paradoxically, then, the tithe given by the worshipper to God is identified as a gift from God to the worshipper, not only because it is God who gives the tithe (Num 18:21–28), but also because the practice of the tithe brings God's blessing (Deut 14:28–29).

14:21–24. WAR BOUNTIES

GEN 14:21–24 NKJV	GEN 14:21–24 ESV
21 Now the king of Sodom said to Abram, "Give me the persons, and take the goods for yourself."	**21** And the king of Sodom said to Abram, "Give me the persons, but take the goods for yourself."
22 But Abram said to the king of Sodom, "I have raised my hand to the Lord, God Most High, the Possessor of heaven and earth,	**22** But Abram said to the king of Sodom, "I have lifted my hand to the Lord, God Most High, Possessor of heaven and earth,
23 that I *will take* nothing, from a thread to a sandal strap, and that I will not take anything that *is* yours, lest you should say, 'I have made Abram rich'—	**23** that I would not take a thread or a sandal strap or anything that is yours, lest you should say, 'I have made Abram rich.'
24 except only what the young men have eaten, and the portion of the men who went with me: Aner, Eshcol, and Mamre; let them take their portion."	**24** I will take nothing but what the young men have eaten, and the share of the men who went with me. Let Aner, Eshcol, and Mamre take their share."

Now the king of Sodom said to Abram, Give me … The "give" of the king of Sodom (14:21) echoes the "give" of Abram (14:20). The same verb *natan* "give" is used. The king of Sodom misunderstands the special sense of this giving and interprets it on his level. He asks Abram to "give" to him because he sees him in the action of giving. Indecently and arrogantly, he claims from Abram what he thinks are his rights. Unlike Melchizedek, who gives generously although he did not receive anything, the king of Sodom makes demands although he had just been rescued by

---

478 See the Akkadian *magannu* "gift," "gratis" and the Jewish Palestinian Aramaic *magan* "for nothing," "in vain" (see M. Sokoloff, "*mgn,*" *DJPA* 291).

Abram: **Give me the persons, and take the goods for yourself** (14:21). As their rescuer Abram was entitled to both the people and the property.[479] The king of Sodom is primarily seeking his own interests, as reflected in the sequence of the verbs he uses: "give-take." Contrary to the king of Sodom, Abram does not want to take anything, not even **a sandal strap** (14:23), which represents the smallest and least valuable item (Judg 9:13; Isa 5:27; Matt 3:11). Pointedly, Abram responds to him by referring to Melchizedek's text of blessing, reminding him that "all" belongs to God, and that he therefore owes "all" to God (14:22). Then he conveys the same lesson, subtly and somewhat ironically, through his wordplay between the "tithe" (*ma'aser*) he just gave and his "wealth" (*'ashar*). If Abram is rich, it is because of what he has received from God and implicitly because he gives his tithe to God (Mal 3:10), thus returning to Him what belongs to Him (Lev 27:30). Abram will, then, not accept anything for himself, although as leader and victor of the war he had the right to claim all the booty. Yet, his generosity does not overstep the rights of his allies Aner, Eshcol, and Mamre, who did receive their rightful share because they were guarding the camp, while he was fighting (see the comments on 14:3–11).

THE ABRAHAMIC COVENANT (15–17)

We have reached the center of the section framed by the expression *lek leka* (12–22),[480] which is also the literary center of the whole book of Genesis (see "The Structure of Genesis" in the introduction). This passage should therefore be considered the middle of the central section of the whole book of Genesis. This literary construction suggests the importance of these chapters, which are considered "the very heart of the Abraham story."[481]

This is the crucial moment when God formalizes the covenant He initiated with Abram when He called him from Ur, an event that is specifically referred to (12:7). This is, in fact, God's second covenant, the first being the covenant with Noah (6:18–9:20). The Abrahamic covenant contains the same components as the Noahic covenant. It is initiated by a sacrificial ceremony (15:9; 17:10–14; cf. 8:20–21), brings a promise of birth (15:1–6; 17:8; cf. 9:1) and of the land (15:18–21; 17:8; cf. 8:21; 9:11), and is signified by a sign (17:11; cf. 9:13, 17).

The two ceremonies of the Abrahamic covenant—the sacrificial ceremony that establishes the covenant and the institution of circumcision that signifies it—correspond with each other in a consistent parallelism. Both passages begin with the same divine self-declaratory formula "**I**." The two *'ani* "I" (17:1–4) echo the two *'anokhi* "I" of God's previous speech to Abram (15:1–2). Both passages end with a digression concerning Ishmael, his birth (16:1–16), and his circumcision (17:23–27). They also echo each other with the recurring use of the verb *natan* "give" or "make" (17:2, 5–6, 8, 16, 20; cf. 15:2–3, 7, 10, 18).

In addition, chapter 15 shares with chapter 17 the same structure of two parallel panels (17:1–14, 15–27; cf. 15:1–6, 7–21) involving five successive speeches by God

---

479 See Wenham, *Genesis 1–15*, 318.

480 This section has been identified as the center-apex of the chiastic structure covering the chapters 12–22, see Cairus, "Protection and Reward," 241–245.

481 Westermann, *Genesis 12–36*, 230.

(17:1–2, 9, 15, 19; cf. 15:1, 4, 7–8, 13).[482] In both chapters, Abram falls prostrate (17:3, 17; cf. 15:12). In the second revelation, Abram is less talkative, speaking only once (17:18), whereas he spoke three times in his previous encounter (15:2–3, 8). And when he speaks, it is to suggest Ishmael as a surrogate for a son (17:18), just as he did with Eliezer (15:2–3).

Both revelations of the Abrahamic covenant convey the same promise of birth and land, although the promises are more precise in chapter 17. The promise of birth will not just relate to the physical person of Abram (15:4), it will be with Sarai, and it will be a son whose name will be Isaac (17:19, 21). Likewise, the promise of the land will not just concern a vague territory stretching between the two rivers (15:18), it will be "the land of Canaan" (17:8).

The motif of covenant is also strongly intensified. While there is only one reference to "*a covenant*" (*berit*) in the first revelation (15:18), in the second revelation the word "covenant" appears eleven times, and each time is specifically qualified—nine times as "My covenant" (17:2, 4, 7, 9, 10, 13–14, 19, 21) and two times as "everlasting covenant" (17:7, 19).

Interestingly, the parallels between the two sets of promises suggest some relation between the ritual ceremonies with which they are associated. While in the first revelation the covenant is signified by the slaughter of sacrificial animals cut in two (15:9–10), in the second revelation the covenant is signified by the ritual of circumcision (17:10–14; 17:23–27).

15:1–21. PROMISE OF BIRTH FOR ABRAM: SACRIFICES

The last time God had spoken to Abram it was to confirm His promise about the land and a multitude of descendants (13:14–17). God addresses Abram again on these two themes. This time, however, the word of God is articulated through a pair of dialogues between God and Abram, which parallel each other and carry two promises. The first dialogue brings the promise of descendants: God promises (15:1), Abram doubts (15:2–3), God confirms (15:4–5), Abram believes (15:6). The second dialogue concerns the promise of the land: God promises (15:7), Abram doubts (15:8), God confirms (15:9–21). The sequence of events reinforces the connection between the sacrificial ceremony and the circumcision:

Divine self-declaration (15:1)	Divine self-declaration (17:1)
Promise of birth (15:2–6)	Promise of birth (17:2–7)
Promise of land (15:7–8)	Promise of land (17:8)
Sacrifices (15:9–11)	**Circumcision (17:9–14)**
Precise prophecy (15:12–16)	Precise prophecy (17:15–19a)
God comes down, covenant (15:17–21)	Covenant, God goes up (17:19b–22)

---

482 Kenneth A. Mathews, *Genesis 11:27–50:26*, NAC 1B (Nashville: Broadman & Holman, 2005), 159; cf. S. E. McEvenue, *The Narrative Style of the Priestly Writer*, AnBib 50 (Rome: Biblical Institute, 1971), 149–155.

15:1. DIVINE SELF-DECLARATION

GEN 15:1 NKJV	GEN 15:1 ESV
1 After these things the word of the LORD came to Abram in a vision, saying, "Do not be afraid, Abram. I *am* your shield, your exceedingly great reward."	**1** After these things the word of the LORD came to Abram in a vision: "Fear not, Abram, I am your shield; your reward shall be very great."

15:1 **Do not be afraid.** Abram is afraid, first, because **the Lord appeared in a vision**. This kind of divine manifestation or "theophany" always involves a fearful reaction (21:17; 28:17; Exod 3:6). The vision of the appearance of God does not belong to the common domain and familiar reality. Abram was probably surprised by this new experience. God had spoken to him and to others before. But this is the first time that the phenomenon of **vision** (*makhazeh*) is recorded in the Bible.

Abram's fear, however, is due to more than just the natural and immediate reaction to the supernatural. It is not due to his enemies. He has vanquished them; his present is now ensured. Abram's fears occur **after these things**, that is, after his previous wars. What Abram fears more than anything is his future. When God says "Do not be afraid," it is to reassure him about his future. Significantly, the phrase *'al tira'* "do not be afraid," "fear not," "do not fear" is often associated with the promise of descendants (21:17; 26:24; 35:17; 46:3).

The same promise for the future is contained in the word *magen* **shield**, which echoes the verb *magan* "deliver" (14:20). The lesson of the play on words is that God has made Abram's past experience of salvation (*magan*) into "his shield" (*magen*) against the fears of the future. The word *magen* "shield" is typically used in the Psalms to imply the future salvation of God (Pss 3:3 [4]; 18:30 [31]).

The expression *harbeh me'od* **exceedingly great** alludes to the blessing of fruitfulness. The same phrase is used again later in a slightly different form *'arbeh 'otkha bime'od me'od* "I will multiply you exceedingly" (17:2) to refer to the numerous descendants promised to Abram. To Abram, who is afraid for his future, God responds that He will be his future: "I am your shield, that is, your exceedingly abundant fruitfulness." God is the future of Abram.

15:2–6. PROMISE OF BIRTH

GEN 15:2–6 NKJV	GEN 15:2–6 ESV
2 But Abram said, "Lord GOD, what will You give me, seeing I go childless, and the heir of my house *is* Eliezer of Damascus?"	**2** But Abram said, "O Lord GOD, what will you give me, for I continue childless, and the heir of my house is Eliezer of Damascus?"
3 Then Abram said, "Look, You have given me no offspring; indeed one born in my house is my heir!"	**3** And Abram said, "Behold, you have given me no offspring, and a member of my household will be my heir."
4 And behold, the word of the LORD *came* to him, saying, "This one shall not be your heir, but one who will come from your own body shall be your heir."	**4** And behold, the word of the LORD came to him: "This man shall not be your heir; your very own son shall be your heir."

5 Then He brought him outside and said, "Look now toward heaven, and count the stars if you are able to number them." And He said to him, "So shall your descendants be."

6 And he believed in the LORD, and He accounted it to him for righteousness.

5 And he brought him outside and said, "Look toward heaven, and number the stars, if you are able to number them." Then he said to him, "So shall your offspring be."

6 And he believed the LORD, and he counted it to him as righteousness.

15:2 Abram catches God's allusion to his fruitfulness, since he immediately refers to his lack of descendants: **I go childless**. The adjective *ʿariri* "childless" that Abram uses to describe himself means "stripped" or "destitute" and accounts for his feelings of hopelessness.

15:3 You have given me no offspring. Abram's complaint that God did not "give" him "offspring," which in Hebrew is the word "seed" (*zeraʿ*), suggests a veiled blame on God who did not fulfill His promise (cf. 12:7).

The dialogue between God and Abram displays an interesting dynamic, not without some irony. We note the echo between the *ʾanokhi* (emphatic "I") of God, which introduces God's emphatic assurance that He is his shield (15:1), and the responding *ʾanokhi* of Abram, which introduces his condition of childlessness (15:2). Then Abram keeps speaking, although the use of the form *wayyoʾmer* marks the turning point in the dialogue, expecting God to respond.

15:4 God responds to Abram's challenge with the assurance that his heir shall come "from his own body." The presentative adverb *hinneh* **behold**, "look," which Abram used to point to Eliezer (15:3), is echoed in God's words, which are introduced with the same adverb *hinneh* "behold," "look," insisting that the birth should instead come from his own flesh (15:4).

These echoes in the dialogue suggest that Abram's doubts correspond to God's assurances and vice versa. Abram's skeptical question "What will You give?" and his last resort to the traditional custom[483] to use his servant Eliezer as his heir, clearly betray his doubts.

The same words *zerʿ yetseʾ mimʿeykha* **seed … will come from your body** will be used by the prophet Nathan to David to refer to the future messianic king (2 Sam 7:12).

The Hebrew word *meʿeyka* "from your body" refers more precisely to the inward parts of the body, the sources of procreation (25:23; Isa 48:19; 49:1). The intertextual connection suggests that the text is essentially concerned with the messianic seed, which should come from Abram's own body. Thus, the great number of descendants illustrated by the infinite number of stars in the skies has to be understood in connection to the messianic seed. Abram had already heard the same promise at Ur: "in you" (*bekha*), referring concretely to Abram's body, "all the families of the earth will be blessed" (12:3).

15:6 And he believed in the Lord. The messianic vision of God as his future inspires in Abram faith in his future. Having seen the stars in the sky as an illustration of the divine promise, Abram believed. The Hebrew verb *heʿemin* "believed" describes more than a sentimental or intellectual process as expressed in our English verb "to

---

483 This custom is attested in the Bible (Prov 17:2) and in Nuzi texts (see *ANET*, 219–220).

believe." It means more than the mere reference to the creed, the religious "belief," or the naïve aptitude to swallow anything. In Hebrew, "to believe" is historical and relational, as implied in the root 'aman "firm," "reliable," and especially with the use of the preposition be "in," "on" with the object. Relying on God, Abram "believed" that he will have descendants.

This kind of belief, this faith, God "accounted" as "righteousness."[484] God is the subject of the verb "accounted," as its most immediate antecedent. This reading is confirmed by the use of the divine passive (niphal) of the same verb yekhasheb "accounted," "imputed" in the same idiom elsewhere (Lev 7:18; cf. Ps 106:31), which also have God as the subject.[485] In other words, God "counted" (ESV) this faith as having the same value as righteousness. It is not the human effort and works that produce righteousness; instead, righteousness is a gift from God.

This passage makes sense against the background of ancient Egyptian beliefs. In both systems, counting and righteousness belong to judicial language, and counting is used for the evaluation of righteousness. Yet, the two perspectives are fundamentally different. In ancient Egypt, the weight of human righteousness was evaluated on the basis of the counting of human works against the weight of the Maat, the divine righteousness.[486] In this system, divine righteousness was counted and demanded from humans. Abram's righteousness, on the contrary, is evaluated on the basis of the divine works for him.

In the biblical perspective, "righteousness" (tsedaqah) is a specific divine quality (Isa 45:24; Dan 9:7) and as such righteousness can only be God's gift to man (Deut 6:25; 24:13; Isa 45:24; Ps 24:5). What makes Abram righteous is not the sum of his deeds, but his willingness to rely on God's deeds for him (Rom 4:2–4).

15:7–8. THE PROMISE OF THE LAND

GEN 15:7–8 NKJV	GEN 15:7–8 ESV
7 Then He said to him, "I *am* the LORD, who brought you out of Ur of the Chaldeans, to give you this land to inherit it."	**7** And he said to him, "I am the LORD who brought you out from Ur of the Chaldeans to give you this land to possess."
8 And he said, "Lord GOD, how shall I know that I will inherit it?"	**8** But he said, "O Lord GOD, how am I to know that I shall possess it?"

The second encounter between God and Abram (15:7–21) shifts from the theme of birth to the theme of the land.

As in the first revelation, the vision begins with God who identifies Himself in connection with Abram. The first revelation referred to the historical person of Abram, his past protection, and his descendants (15:1). The second revelation concerns his space, the land, where he comes from and where he will go. The verb yarash "inherit," which was used in relation to Abram's offspring (15:2–4), is now applied to the land (15:7–8), thus suggesting a connection between the two: Abram's

---

484 The complement of the verb "account" (here translated "it") is feminine and refers, then, by anticipation to the feminine word tsedaqah "righteousness."

485 Note that the same verb tsadaq appears in the rare passive form (niphal) nitsdaq "cleansed" in Daniel 8:14, suggesting its dependence on the judicial declaratory formulae of Leviticus.

486 See Jan Assmann, *The Mind of Egypt: History and Meaning in the Time of the Pharaohs* (New York: Metropolitan Books, 1996), 136–137.

descendants will inherit the land. Likewise, the verb *natan* **give** of the land echoes the *natan* **give** of the *zera'* "offspring," "seed" (15:4), here also suggesting that the land and the seed are God's gifts (15:7).

Abram's response to God parallels his first response to God in the first revelation: **Lord God, how shall I know that I will inherit it?** (15:8). We find the same opening formula "Lord God" and the same skeptical reaction. The Hebrew phrase *bammah* "how?" (lit. trans.: "in what?") is used when more supporting evidence is requested (Exod 33:16; Mal 1:6–7).

15:9–11. SACRIFICES

GEN 15:9–11 NKJV	GEN 15:9–11 ESV
9 So He said to him, "Bring Me a three-year-old heifer, a three-year-old female goat, a three-year-old ram, a turtledove, and a young pigeon."	**9** He said to him, "Bring me a heifer three years old, a female goat three years old, a ram three years old, a turtledove, and a young pigeon."
10 Then he brought all these to Him and cut them in two, down the middle, and placed each piece opposite the other; but he did not cut the birds in two.	**10** And he brought him all these, cut them in half, and laid each half over against the other. But he did not cut the birds in half.
11 And when the vultures came down on the carcasses, Abram drove them away.	**11** And when birds of prey came down on the carcasses, Abram drove them away.

15:9 Bring Me … The choice of specific sacrificial animals (the ram, the goat, and the heifer) and the use of the verb *laqakh* "bring," which normally introduces the sacrifice (Lev 9:2–3), anticipates a sacrificial ceremony,[487] such as the Day of Atonement (Lev 16:3, 5). Furthermore, the universalistic character of the sacrifice, involving four species of sacrificial animals, three species of quadrupeds (ram, goat, and heifer) and one species of bird, evokes Noah's offering who "took [*laqakh*] of every clean animal and of every clean bird" (8:20).

The parallels between the two narratives are striking: establishment of a covenant (9:9; cf. 15:18); cosmic sign (9:13; cf. 15:12, 17); promise for the future (8:21; 9:15; cf. 15:13–16); and list of nations (10; cf. 15:18–21).

15:10 Then he brought all these to Him. Abram is involved in the ceremony by three actions. The first action signifies his immediate and faithful response to God's instructions. The verb "brought" (15:10) echoes God's call to "bring" (15:9). Then Abram cuts the animals in two, which implies that he slaughters them, and arranges the sections across from each other in parallel rows. Only the birds are left entire due to their size (Lev 1:17).

This covenant ritual with some variations is well attested in the ANE.[488] Within the Bible, only the text of Jeremiah 34 refers to another covenant ceremony in which an animal is cut in half (Jer 34:18–19). Many ANE texts explain the reason why the covenanter walked between the two parts. The action signifies the identification of

---

487 According to an old Jewish tradition, through that ceremony, God revealed to Abram the atoning function of the sacrifices and showed him the service of the temple and of the sacrifices (see Gen. Rab. 44:17; cf. Rashi in Miqraot Gedolot on 15:8–9).

488 These texts are from the Mari letters (eighteenth century BC) and the Abba-An (also called "Alalakh") treaty text (seventeenth century BC). For a discussion of the connection between these two texts and Genesis 15, see Gerhard F. Hasel, "The Meaning of the Animal Rite in Genesis 15," *JSOT* 19 (1981): 61–78.

the one walking between the pieces with the cut animals themselves.

One testimony of this rationale is found in the covenant of the Assyrian king Ashur-nirari V with his vassal Mati-ilu. After Mati-ilu cuts the head of the ram, the king says: "This head is not the head of the ram, but the head of Mati-ilu ... If Mati-ilu violates the oath, as the head of this ram is struck off, ... so will the head of Mati-ilu be struck off."[489]

15:11 **Abram drove them away.** A comparison between these ceremonies and the one reported in Genesis 15 reveals one important difference. While in the ANE ceremonies only one covenanting party, the inferior one, used to pass between the cut parts, in the ceremony of Genesis 15 both covenanting parties pass between the parts. On one hand, Abram is described as walking "reverently ... between the parts of the sacrifice, making a solemn vow to God of perpetual obedience."[490] However, while Abram's walking between the cut parts is only indirectly implied in his act of driving away the vultures, only God is specifically mentioned as walking between the parts.

The covenant ceremonial of Genesis 15 suggests two lessons about God. First, the fact that the emphasis is put on God rather than on the vassal suggests that God (and not the vassal as in the ANE) has identified Himself with the slaughtered animal, thus alluding to the substitutionary process implied in that covenant (Isa 53:5, 8; 2 Cor 5:21). "It is as if God swears by the divine self to be cut in two in failing to uphold the divine end of the bargain."[491]

Second, God, the Invisible, is the One who takes the initiative and controls the course of that covenant. Abram executes the instructions and prepares the animals; he walks between the parts to indicate his good disposition and signify his commitment. But the covenant remains in God's hands and depends entirely on Him. Only God initiates and "makes the covenant" (15:18). The covenant becomes effective only when God comes down and consumes the offering (cf. 1 Kgs 18:38–39).

Unlike the ANE covenant treaty, which makes the covenant depend on the submission of the vassal, on his good works, the covenant implied in Genesis 15 is unilateral and depends only on God's move. In that connection, the parallels with Noah's covenant, noted above, which is also unilateral (see the comments on 9:8–17), illuminate our understanding of the nature of the ceremony described in Genesis 15. This parallel not only confirms the covenant character of that ceremony, it also identifies the sacrificial nature of the animals slaughtered for that purpose. Yet, in spite of this parallel, the ceremony of Genesis 15 remains different. There is no altar and the sacrificial ceremony is not typical of the Sinaitic legislation. It has been noticed even within the ANE testimony that "the functions and meanings of animal rites differ from each other."[492] This ceremony is as unique in the Scriptures as it is in the ANE context at large. It seems, therefore, that this covenant ceremony is distinctively shaped to serve an extraordinary purpose and is loaded with particular meanings.

---

489 *ANET*, 353–354.

490 See Ellen G. White, PP 137.

491 Paul Borgman, *Genesis: The Story We Haven't Heard* (Downers Grove: IVP, 2001), 68.

492 Hasel, "The Meaning of the Animal Rite in Genesis 15," 68.

15:12–16. PRECISE PROPHECY

GEN 15:12–16 NKJV	GEN 15:12–16 ESV
12 Now when the sun was going down, a deep sleep fell upon Abram; and behold, horror *and* great darkness fell upon him.	**12** As the sun was going down, a deep sleep fell on Abram. And behold, dreadful and great darkness fell upon him.
13 Then He said to Abram: "Know certainly that your descendants will be strangers in a land *that is* not theirs, and will serve them, and they will afflict them four hundred years.	**13** Then the Lord said to Abram, "Know for certain that your offspring will be sojourners in a land that is not theirs and will be servants there, and they will be afflicted for four hundred years.
14 And also the nation whom they serve I will judge; afterward they shall come out with great possessions.	**14** But I will bring judgment on the nation that they serve, and afterward they shall come out with great possessions.
15 Now as for you, you shall go to your fathers in peace; you shall be buried at a good old age.	**15** As for yourself, you shall go to your fathers in peace; you shall be buried in a good old age.
16 But in the fourth generation they shall return here, for the iniquity of the Amorites *is* not yet complete."	**16** And they shall come back here in the fourth generation, for the iniquity of the Amorites is not yet complete."

15:13 Following the ceremony, the prophecy provides its own commentary, decoding step by step its mysterious signs. The first step refers to the struggle of Israel as strangers, slaves, and oppressed victims: **Know certainly that your descendants will be strangers**. This condition of affliction is rendered through the technical term *'anah* **afflict**, which is also used to describe the humbling attitude required at the Day of Atonement (Lev 16:29).

The dramatic moment when the national and spiritual identity of Israel was threatened was signified in the scene of Abram struggling against the threat of the birds of prey, the **vultures** attacking the sacrificial animals, which represented the cult of Israel (15:11).

This phase of threat would last for a period of "**four hundred years,**" which is a round number covering the equivalent of **four generations** (15:16). According to this counting, one generation equals 100 years,[493] probably because it is situated in the specific context of Abram who was 100 years old when the next generation appeared (21:5). According to Paul, the law was given in Sinai 430 years after the covenant with Abram in Haran (Gal 3:16–17; cf. Gen 12:1–3), that is when Abram was 75 years old (12:4). The 400 years should then begin 30 years later, that is, about the time of the first tension between Abraham's two sons (21:9–11; cf. Gal 4:29) and end at the time of the Exodus. The number four was hinted at in the four sacrificial pieces of animals—namely, (1) the heifer, (2) the goat, (3) the ram, and (4) the turtledove and the pigeon, which were not cut (15:9; cf. 15:10).

15:14 The second step refers to the event of the Exodus, when God **will judge** the oppressors of Israel and will save Israel who **shall come out with great possessions** (15:14; cf. Exod 12:36). This divine judgment is alluded to in the **horror and great darkness** (15:12; cf. Exod 10:21–23) that fell upon Abram while he was in a

---

493 For the flexible meaning of the period covered by the word *dor* "generation," see D. N. Freedman and J. Lundbom, "*dor*," *TDOT* 3:174.

deep sleep. Abram's sleeping suggests passivity and safety: God will fight for him (Exod 14:14, 25).

15:15 The vision associates this moment of salvation with the information about the death of Abram, who **shall go … in peace** (15:15). The word *shalom* "peace" is used here for the first time in the Scriptures.

15:16 The deliverance will take place **in the fourth generation**, which coincides with the time of Moses, who belongs to the fourth generation from Levi (Exod 6:16–20).

A theological reason is given to justify the delay in the occupation by Abram's descendants until the fourth generation and, by implication, the expulsion of its inhabitants: **for the iniquity of the Amorites is not yet complete**. The "Amorites" stand for the whole Canaanite population (Amos 2:10), who are known for their depravity (2 Kgs 21:11). The paradox, however, is that God waits until sin reaches its limits to exert His judgment. God's character—His patience and forbearance towards the Canaanites—is evident and brings an unexpected spark of light in the darkness of judgment. In that perspective, justice is balanced and controlled by the power of love.

15:17–21. GOD COMES DOWN: COVENANT

GEN 15:17–21 NKJV	GEN 15:17–21 ESV
17 And it came to pass, when the sun went down and it was dark, that behold, there appeared a smoking oven and a burning torch that passed between those pieces.	**17** When the sun had gone down and it was dark, behold, a smoking fire pot and a flaming torch passed between these pieces.
18 On the same day the LORD made a covenant with Abram, saying: "To your descendants I have given this land, from the river of Egypt to the great river, the River Euphrates—	**18** On that day the LORD made a covenant with Abram, saying, "To your offspring I give this land, from the river of Egypt to the great river, the river Euphrates,
19 the Kenites, the Kenezzites, the Kadmonites,	**19** the land of the Kenites, the Kenizzites, the Kadmonites,
20 the Hittites, the Perizzites, the Rephaim,	**20** the Hittites, the Perizzites, the Rephaim,
21 the Amorites, the Canaanites, the Girgashites, and the Jebusites."	**21** the Amorites, the Canaanites, the Girgashites and the Jebusites."

15:17 **A smoking oven and a burning torch.** The vision returns to Abram's sphere to continue the scene of sunset and darkness (15:12). Now, **the sun went down and it was dark**.[494] The brightness of the fire is all the more vivid. The fire represents the divine presence (Exod 3:3–6). This symbolism is particularly prominent in the context of the Exodus where the fire is identified with God's presence (Exod 13:21; 19:18) and fire and smoke are associated with the theophany (Exod 19:18). The fire passing (*'abar*) between the pieces prefigures the God of Exodus who "will pass through [*abar*] to strike the Egyptians" (Exod 12:23; cf. 12:12), or

---

494 The Hebrew word *'altah* "darkness" in 15:17 is different from the word *khoshek* "darkness" in 15:12; *khoshek* refers to the condition of darkness, while *'altah* describes its surrounding effect.

Israel passing (*'abar*) through the sea (Exod 14:29; cf. Pss 66:6; 78:52–53).[495]

15:18 After the fire has consumed the sacrificial animals, a sign that God has come down into the human sphere, God extends His grace to Abram and promises him the future occupation of the land. This is called "covenant": **The Lord made a covenant**.

The notion of "covenant" that is implied here has nothing to do with an agreement involving two parties. God is alone in the action. As it is for Noah, God's covenant with Abram is unilateral. It is simply a commitment on God's part that His promise will be fulfilled. The covenant is based only on Himself, with no demands in return, although the side note about the Amorites (15:16) contains a veiled warning towards the beneficiaries of the covenant, lest they fall into the same iniquity as the previous inhabitants of the land they have expelled (Lev 18:24–30). The description of the covenant confirms its graceful character: **to your descendants I have given this land**.

The word *natan* "give" is used with the words *'erets* "land" and *zera'* "seed," "descendants." God's gift of the "land" for the "seed" is more than a mediocre reference to earthly properties, although it does not exclude them. The divine covenant extends grace to the far horizons stretching from the river of Egypt to the Euphrates—from Egypt to Babylon, from the south to the north. This is a merism, the covenant refers to the two extremities of the land to suggest the idea of totality. The land encompasses the whole world, from Babylon to Egypt.

It is clear that the prophecy has more in view than the Israelite conquest (Deut 1:7–8) or even the golden age of Solomon (1 Kgs 4:29–31 [5:9–11]). Although some elements may fit these historical fulfillments, the vision of the ideal land mass demarcated in Genesis 15:18 has never been accomplished.

The delimitation is reminiscent of the description of the Garden of Eden, which is also delimited in the south by the *nahar* **river** flowing in Egypt[496] (2:13) and in the north by the "river" (*nahar*) flowing in Assyria, the **Euphrates** (2:14).[497] Note that the same word *nahar* "river" is used to designate the two rivers, not only to suggest that they are equivalent, but also, with deliberate intention, to echo the text describing the Garden of Eden.

God's promise to Abram is more than a nationalistic statement about the historical occupation of the land by Israel. It is a vision about the messianic return to the lost Garden of Eden. The messianic interpretation of this passage is supported by the strong apocalyptic tone of the text: the scene of Abram's intense defense against the vultures, the dramatic atmosphere of darkness and horror falling on Abram sleeping deeply (see Dan 8:18; 10:9), the eruption of the fire, which consumes everything, and the prophecy that announces the far future and takes us beyond the contingent reality into the eschatological event of cosmic salvation.[498] Isaiah uses the

---

495 While the passage in Exodus uses another verb (*halak*), it is the same verb *'abar* "pass" that is used in the Psalms to describe the passing through the sea by the Israelites.

496 Many commentators have identified the "river" of chapter 15 as Wadi el Arish in northeastern Sinai on the basis of the boundaries indicated in Numbers 34:2–12. But in that text the boundaries of Canaan are more restricted and the "river" marking the border of Egypt is called *nakhal* "brook" (34:5), a stream that flows only after the rain, in contrast to the *nahar* "river" (15:18), which never dries up (see L. A. Snijders, "*nakhal*," *TDOT* 9:335). Cf. the Targum of Jonathan, which identifies the "river of Egypt" as the Nile.

497 See John H. Sailhamer, *Genesis*, EBC (Grand Rapids: Zondervan, 1990), 42–44.

498 Note Ellen G. White's eschatological and messianic application of this passage: "The voice of God was heard, bidding him not to expect immediate possession of the Promised Land, and pointing forward to the sufferings of his posterity before their establishment in Canaan. The plan of redemption was here opened to him, in the death of Christ, the great sacrifice, and His coming in glory. *Abraham saw the earth restored to its Eden beauty, to be given him*

same language to evoke the comprehensiveness of the future messianic salvation of Israel (Isa 27:12–13).

15:19–21 The messianic perspective is reinforced by the unusual list of ten nations,[499] which also resonates with messianic overtones.[500] The number ten often has the symbolic meaning of completeness. The only other biblical text that refers to ten nations is Psalm 83, which carries a definite messianic intention. There also the mention of the ten nations, the prototypical enemies of God's people, leads to the messianic vision of their total destruction (Ps 83:13) and the ultimate recognition of God's universal lordship (Ps 83:18). Likewise, the mention of "ten kings" in the book of Daniel describes the last step in human history with the same message of messianic hope: "in the days of these kings the God of heaven will set up a kingdom which shall never be destroyed … it shall break in pieces and consume all these kingdoms, and it shall stand forever" (Dan 2:44; cf. 7:24; 11:45; Rev 16:19).

16:1–16. THE BIRTH OF ISHMAEL

To God's promise of a son, Abram, whose wife was barren, had already responded by referring to his servant Eliezer as a way to help God fulfill His promise. In spite of Abram's skepticism, God had insisted that the birth should come from Abram himself. Now, even after God's last reassuring, prophetic revelation, Abram responds again with the same skepticism. Abram's doubts come from ten years of waiting (16:3; cf. Ruth 1:4).[501] He resorts again to a custom that was in force in his time: the practice of surrogate motherhood, which is attested in the ANE from the third millennium BC.

Considering the environment Abram lived in, his conduct was proper and respectable. He had good reasons to behave that way. But the forthcoming story will show that Abram and Sarai were wrong. Yet, within the mistake, God will insert an unexpected blessing outside the original plan. Hagar will give birth.

The text is made of two parts (16:1–6, 7–16), both consisting of two narratives and two dialogues. The first part involves Abram and Sarai; the second part, the Angel of the Lord and Hagar. The introduction (16:1) and the conclusion (16:15–16) echo each other as an inclusio on the motif of bearing a child: in the introduction, Sarai has not borne Abram children (16:1); in the conclusion, Hagar bore Abram a son (16:16).

Introduction: Narrative: Sarai has not borne children (16:1)

A. Sarai and Abram (16:1–6)
Dialogue: Sarai speaks, Abram responds (16:2)
Narrative (16:3–4)
Dialogue: Sarai speaks, Abram responds (16:5–6a)
Narrative (16:6b)

...

for an everlasting possession, as the final and complete fulfillment of the promise" (PP 137; emphasis supplied).

499 This is the only list of ten nations representing the inhabitants of Canaan; the Bible normally reports six or seven nations. Note the omission of the Philistines, the Ammonites, and the Moabites who confronted the Israelites during the conquest, an indication of the antiquity of that list (see Wenham, *Genesis 1–15*, 333–334).

500 The messianic interpretation of the ten nations has been retained in the Midrash (see Gen. Rab. 45:27; cf. Rashi in Miqraot Gedolot on 15:18).

501 According to a rabbinic tradition, the reason that prompted Sarai to resort to that custom is that after a ten-year period of barrenness the couple was allowed to divorce (Gen. Rab. 45:3; cf. Yebam. 6.6).

B. The Angel of the Lord and Hagar (16:7–16)
   Narrative (16:7)
   Dialogue: The Angel speaks, Hagar responds (16:8)
   Dialogue: The Angel speaks, Hagar responds (16:9–13)
   Narrative: Hagar and Abram (16:14)

Conclusion: Narrative: Hagar bore a son (16:15–16)

16:1–6. SARAI AND ABRAM

GEN 16:1–6 NKJV	GEN 16:1–6 ESV
1 Now Sarai, Abram's wife, had borne him no *children*. And she had an Egyptian maidservant whose name was Hagar.	**1** Now Sarai, Abram's wife, had borne him no children. She had a female Egyptian servant whose name was Hagar.
2 So Sarai said to Abram, "See now, the LORD has restrained me from bearing *children*. Please, go in to my maid; perhaps I shall obtain children by her." And Abram heeded the voice of Sarai.	**2** And Sarai said to Abram, "Behold now, the LORD has prevented me from bearing children. Go in to my servant; it may be that I shall obtain children by her." And Abram listened to the voice of Sarai.
3 Then Sarai, Abram's wife, took Hagar her maid, the Egyptian, and gave her to her husband Abram to be his wife, after Abram had dwelt ten years in the land of Canaan.	**3** So, after Abram had lived ten years in the land of Canaan, Sarai, Abram's wife, took Hagar the Egyptian, her servant, and gave her to Abram her husband as a wife.
4 So he went in to Hagar, and she conceived. And when she saw that she had conceived, her mistress became despised in her eyes.	**4** And he went in to Hagar, and she conceived. And when she saw that she had conceived, she looked with contempt on her mistress.
5 Then Sarai said to Abram, "My wrong *be* upon you! I gave my maid into your embrace; and when she saw that she had conceived, I became despised in her eyes. The LORD judge between you and me."	**5** And Sarai said to Abram, "May the wrong done to me be on you! I gave my servant to your embrace, and when she saw that she had conceived, she looked on me with contempt. May the LORD judge between you and me!"
6 So Abram said to Sarai, "Indeed your maid *is* in your hand; do to her as you please." And when Sarai dealt harshly with her, she fled from her presence.	**6** But Abram said to Sarai, "Behold, your servant is in your power; do to her as you please." Then Sarai dealt harshly with her, and she fled from her.

16:1 The introduction establishes the plot by presenting Sarai's situation: she is barren, but she has a maidservant. The identification of **Sarai** as **Abram's wife** and **Hagar** as **Sarai's maidservant** immediately marks the difference between the two women. The detail that Hagar was Egyptian widens the chasm between them. Hagar is alien, and she bears her status even in her name—the name "Hagar" sounds like *hagger* "the alien." Moreover, this slave comes from Egypt, perhaps a gift souvenir from the pharaoh of Egypt (12:16),[502] the place where Sarai had been humiliated and had almost become a slave and the same place where Israel will later be enslaved. Hagar is therefore associated with the somber perspective of the Exodus.

---

502 The irony of that situation is pointed out in the Midrash, which reports the tradition that Hagar was the daughter of Pharaoh who gave her to Sarai, saying, "Better let my daughter be handmaid in this house than a mistress in another's" (Gen. Rab. 45:1).

16:2-4 So Sarai said to Abram. In the first dialogue, Sarai takes the initiative. She blames God as she explains her condition and justifies her dubious proposal to her husband. Faith is absent. She is not even sure of the outcome of her maneuver; she uses the word "perhaps" (16:2). She has shifted from the divine sphere of wonder and faith to the human domain of strategies and works, from the perspective of the promise from God to the perspective of the achievement from man.

The apostle Paul has in mind these different perspectives of birth when he thinks of the two covenants (Gal 4:21-31) and juxtaposes the two births. The birth from the bondwoman Hagar, "according to the flesh" (Gal 4:23), represents human achievement, the bondage under the works of the law (Gal 4:24); but the birth from the freewoman Sarai, "through promise" (Gal 4:23) and "according to the Spirit" (Gal 4:29), represents freedom under God's grace (Gal 4:26).

Out of consideration for her husband and probably in order to avoid the suspicion of sin, Sarai elevates Hagar's status to that of a "wife" (16:3). Sarai's intention, however, is not to change Hagar's status of servant into that of wife or even of concubine for the rest of her life. Her "gift" to Abram is strictly limited to the function of surrogate mother and is therefore designed to be temporary. In doing so, Sarai is simply applying a well-adopted custom in the ANE society.

Although Sarai is legally right in regards to the laws of her society, she is wrong regarding her own standards. As the course of the story clearly suggests, her choice is in conflict with God's instructions and promises.

The passage describing Sarai in relation to Abram is reminiscent of the story of Eve and Adam in the Garden of Eden, with which it shares common language: the common use of the verbs "take" (*laqakh*) and "give" (*natan*) (16:3; 3:6) and the phrase "heeded the voice" (*shama' leqol*), which occurs only in these two passages (16:2; cf. 3:17). The intentional parallel suggests that "both narratives describe comparable events ... they are both accounts of a fall."[503] At least, they are clear indications of the divine disapproval towards Abram and Sarai and portend future troubles.

On an ethical level, the parallel between the fruit, an object, and Hagar shows Sarai's manipulation and dehumanization of Hagar. It is noteworthy that neither Abram nor Sarai speak to Hagar. She is simply used as an instrument for their own purposes. Apparently doing so is immediately effective, which suggests a unique encounter: **he went in to Hagar, and she conceived** (16:4). The system works like a good mechanism. The construction of the sentence suggests cold and efficient automatism. No emotion is recorded on the part of either Abram or Hagar. Yet, Hagar develops feeling of contempt towards Sarai. Parallel cases in cognate and contemporary literature[504] suggest that Hagar may have even claimed equality with her mistress and therefore had become a threat to her.

16:5-6 Then Sarai said to Abram. This is the second dialogue between Sarai and Abram, and it is Sarai who addresses Abram. Strangely, instead of responding to Hagar's despising, she turns to Abram and blames him for her pain: **"my wrong be upon you"** (16:5). The construction of the phrase is not clear enough to indicate whether this is an invocation (NKJV) or a mere observation of the facts (NIV). Sarai may have had good reasons to be angry at her husband.

The term *khamas* "wrong" suggests lies and betrayal (Ps 27:12; 1 Chr 12:17).

---

503 Werner Berg, "Der Sündenfall Abrahams und Saras nach Gen 16:1-6," *BN* (1982): 10.
504 *ANET*, 172.

Abram's response to his wife's proposal seems too quick not to be suspicious. In addition, Sarai's explicit reference to Abram's intimacy with Hagar ("embrace") suggests more than an innocent affair. This is why she appeals to God's judgment.

This is the second time that Sarai mentions God in her speech to Abram (cf. 16:2). But God remains absent from her life. God never speaks to her, nor does she speak to Him; she only speaks about Him. Abram's zealous response of immediately delivering Hagar into Sarai's hands may in fact be a cover-up for his feelings of guilt. Likewise Sarah's deficiency in her relationship with her husband and her lack of relationship with God may explain her humiliating treatment (*'anah*) against Hagar. Violence and oppression against others often derive from our failure in our relationship with God or a parent.

Hagar does not respond; she cannot defend herself. She chooses to avoid confrontation: **she fled** (16:6), a probable hint of the other meaning of her name "Hagar," which may be related to the Arabic *hadjara* ("flight," "emigration"; cf. the Arabic word "*Hegira*").

16:7–16. THE ANGEL OF THE LORD AND HAGAR

GEN 16:7–16 NKJV	GEN 16:7–16 ESV
7 Now the Angel of the LORD found her by a spring of water in the wilderness, by the spring on the way to Shur.	**7** The angel of the LORD found her by a spring of water in the wilderness, the spring on the way to Shur.
8 And He said, "Hagar, Sarai's maid, where have you come from, and where are you going?" She said, "I am fleeing from the presence of my mistress Sarai."	**8** And he said, "Hagar, servant of Sarai, where have you come from and where are you going?" She said, "I am fleeing from my mistress Sarai."
9 The Angel of the LORD said to her, "Return to your mistress, and submit yourself under her hand."	**9** The angel of the LORD said to her, "Return to your mistress and submit to her."
10 Then the Angel of the LORD said to her, "I will multiply your descendants exceedingly, so that they shall not be counted for multitude."	**10** The angel of the LORD also said to her, "I will surely multiply your offspring so that they cannot be numbered for multitude."
11 And the Angel of the LORD said to her: "Behold, you *are* with child, and you shall bear a son. You shall call his name Ishmael, because the LORD has heard your affliction.	**11** And the angel of the LORD said to her, "Behold, you are pregnant and shall bear a son. You shall call his name Ishmael, because the LORD has listened to your affliction.
12 He shall be a wild man; his hand *shall be* against every man, and every man's hand against him. And he shall dwell in the presence of all his brethren."	**12** He shall be a wild donkey of a man, his hand against everyone and everyone's hand against him, and he shall dwell over against all his kinsmen."
13 Then she called the name of the LORD who spoke to her, You-Are-the-God-Who-Sees; for she said, "Have I also here seen Him who sees me?"	**13** So she called the name of the LORD who spoke to her, "You are a God of seeing," for she said, "Truly here I have seen him who looks after me."
14 Therefore the well was called Beer Lahai Roi; observe, *it is* between Kadesh and Bered.	**14** Therefore the well was called Beer-lahai-roi; it lies between Kadesh and Bered.
15 So Hagar bore Abram a son; and Abram named his son, whom Hagar bore, Ishmael.	**15** And Hagar bore Abram a son, and Abram called the name of his son, whom Hagar bore, Ishmael.
16 Abram *was* eighty-six years old when Hagar bore Ishmael to Abram.	**16** Abram was eighty-six years old when Hagar bore Ishmael to Abram.

16:7 The phrase *mal'akh YHWH* **the Angel of the Lord** is used here for the first time in the Old Testament, where it appears fifty-eight times. In the book of Genesis, this title occurs six times: four in Genesis 16 (7, 9–11), and two in the story of the sacrifice of Isaac (22:11, 15).

The construction of the phrase (construct before proper name) implies a determinate "*the* Angel of the Lord," thus suggesting a unique individual.[505] Jacob refers to him as "the Angel" (48:16; cf. Hos 12:4). The "Angel of the Lord" is often identified with the Lord, *YHWH*, God Himself (18:1, 13, 22; Judg 6:11–22; 13:3–22; Exod 3:2, 4, 6–7; Acts 7:30–34, 38). The Angel of the Lord reveals the face of God (32:30). His name is "wonderful" (*pele'*), which is the name given to the Messiah (Isa 9:6 [5]).

In this passage, the "Angel of the Lord" speaks like God, using the first person like He does (16:10; cf. 22:17), and is identified as the Lord by both Hagar and the author (16:13). This divine identification is further supported by His functions as Redeemer (48:16), Savior (22:11; Ps 34:7 [8]), and Intercessor (Zech 1:11–12; 3:1–5). On these grounds, the "Angel of the Lord" was often identified by the Church Fathers and the Reformers with the Logos, the preincarnate Christ.

The appearing of the Lord marks a turning point in the story. Up to now God has been absent, never interfering in the course of events; He was only evoked twice by Sarai.

The Angel of the Lord found her. This time God takes the initiative, a role that was held before by Sarai. This unexpected parallel is a veiled indication of Sarai's usurpation of God. That God "finds" Hagar suggests God's interest in her while also suggesting that Hagar is passive in the process.

Hagar is found near a spring in the wilderness, where she pauses in need of water. The text specifies **on the way to Shur**, which shows Hagar making her way to Egypt, her native land, since Shur was located near the border of Egypt (Exod 15:22). The "way to Shur" refers probably to the ancient caravan route ("Darb el Shur") that went from Beersheba to Egypt. Hagar must have been found at a walking distance from the tents of Abram, since Abram used to camp between Kadesh and Shur (20:1). Apparently, she was planning to return to her Egyptian family.

16:8 And He said, Hagar … The Angel of the Lord takes the initiative in the first dialogue with Hagar. He calls her by her name just as He does for Abraham when he is about to kill his son (22:11), denoting the same sense of urgency. Both sons of Abraham—Isaac and Ishmael—are imperiled. The Angel's question **Where are you?** reminds us of God's question to Adam (3:9) and to Cain (4:9). In these cases, the person addressed is not supposed to be where he or she is. The question contains, then, a disguised reproach and calls for responsibility.

Hagar responds like Adam and Cain. Like them, she evades the question. On one hand, Hagar responds to the Angel's first question asking where she was coming from. She indicated that she was fleeing from her mistress, thus focusing on her misery and implying that she had the right to flee from her mistress who had abused her. On the other hand, she ignores the Angel's second question asking where she was going. Acknowledging that she was heading for Egypt would have perhaps revealed her secret intention to return to Egyptian idolatry, which would have met the Angel's reprobation. Hagar's dismissal of the Angel's question suggests that she

---

505 See the same construction in "the city of the Lord" (Ps 48:9) or "the city of David" (2 Sam 5:7) to refer to the unique city of Jerusalem.

has something to hide in regards to the choice of her destination: it was not so much because of her condition of oppression that she was fleeing but rather because of a more subtle and spiritual reason.

16:9 In the second dialogue, the Angel seems to ignore Hagar's charge and insists on her duty. The verb *shub* **return** (16:9) does not just refer to the physical return to Sarai, it implies the spiritual idea of repentance. We find the same association of these two words *shub* **return** and *'anah* **submit** (16:9b) in Solomon's prayer about the repentance of Israel (1 Kgs 8:35).

Here in Genesis this use of the Hebrew verb *'anah* "submit" receives an additional intention since it echoes the verb *'anah* "deal harshly" (16:6), which was the cause for Hagar's flight. The Lord presses Hagar to return to her past condition of oppression, a move that He describes in terms of repentance. The Angel alludes here to Hagar's sin of pride and calls her to repent ("return") and to humble herself ("submit") before Sarai, whom she had begun to despise (16:4).

In addition to the need for Hagar to repair the past mistake, the Angel insists on her return for reasons that concern the future. Indeed, Hagar's journey back to Egypt may have compromised the fulfillment of the promise. She has to go back to the house of Abraham in order to enjoy the blessing of Abraham.

This message is emphasized and repeated in the next two communications from the Angel.

16:10 The words of that blessing **I will multiply your descendants exceedingly** are the same as those that make up the blessing to Abraham (15:1; cf. 17:20). The phrase *harbeh 'arbeh* "I will multiply exceedingly" resonates with the name "'Abraham." The next communication is the first birth annunciation that we find in the Scriptures (see 17:19; Isa 8:3–4; Matt 1:21). It is a poem of two stanzas (16:11–12) with four lines each.

16:11 The first stanza refers to God's gracious presence. It announces the birth of a son **Ishmael**, whose name is specifically given and explained by God: "God has heard." The name of this son is explained to Hagar as an expression of God's care for her, **because the Lord has heard your affliction**. Although God has just encouraged Hagar to return to her "affliction" and "submit" herself (see 16:6, 9, where the same word *'anah* is used), He is not indifferent to her pain. God describes Himself as sensitive and loving, a God who is in touch with humans and communicates with them (Mic 7:7).

16:12 The second stanza refers to the human domain. It describes the fate of Ishmael in connection with the present situation of Hagar and Ishmael. Prenatal influences will play a role. The difficult circumstances of Hagar and Ishmael in the wilderness, disconnected from the world and free from any civil restraints, will impact the life of Ishmael who will grow and hunt like **a wild man** (lit. trans.: "wild donkey of man"). The image of a "wild donkey" refers to a kind of untamed donkey, roaming in the desert (21:20–21).

Ishmael was involved in the reciprocal conflicts of Sarai against Abram (16:5) and Abram against Sarai (subtly implied in 16:6), Hagar against Sarai (16:4) and Sarai against Hagar (16:6). Ishmael's future will reflect the same dynamic of reciprocal confrontations with his brothers (25:18).[506]

---

506 The same phrase "in the presence of all his brethren" is used in both passages. The Hebrew expression *we 'al peney* "in the presence" should be translated "against," "in confrontation" (Deut 21:16; Isa 65:3).

It would be inappropriate to see here a prophetic reference to the Arabic people or even to the Muslims, who identify themselves as the descendants of Ishmael. First, such an interpretation goes against the biblical view: the prophecy applies essentially to the historical person of Ishmael (21:20; 25:18). Second, not all Arabs are descendants of Ishmael, just as not all Muslims are Arabs. Third, this picture contradicts the facts: while a few Muslims are still nomads, many, like some groups among the Inuit, the Romani, and the New Age travelers, are well settled in cities and involved in modern civilization.

16:13 Hagar's second response to the Angel of the Lord is still a part of the dialogue. The verb *'amar* "say," which frames the dialogue, qualifies her response. She directly addresses the Angel who spoke to her and identifies Him as God: **You are the God who sees**. Her words are extraordinary: the unsophisticated and nontheologically educated "Hagar is the only woman in the OT, indeed the only person in all Scripture to give deity a name."[507] Hagar owes her boldness, and hence her closeness to God, to her humble condition. She may not be able to understand and "see" God, but she knows that she is seen by God. It is interesting that God had defined Himself as the God who hears, an assertion that shaped the name of Ishmael "God heard" (16:11).

The same shift from "hearing" to "seeing" is suggested in Job's experience: "I have heard of You by the hearing of the ear, but now my eye sees You" (Job 42:5–6). Job, just as Hagar, did not actually see God physically, an experience that no one can survive (Exod 33:20; cf. John 1:18). Job describes here the progression of his spiritual experience: before, he had only an abstract and indirect idea about God; now he met Him personally and directly.

There is also a fundamental difference between Hagar's seeing God and God's seeing her. While God sees her directly and completely, *ro'y* "sees me," she only sees *'akharey* "after," "behind" the One who sees. That is, she only sees His back. The same word is used for Moses, who also can only see God's back (Exod 33:23). The use of the same language unexpectedly relates Hagar to Moses. Both of them, indeed, were visited and called by God by name in the wilderness (Exod 3:4ff.). Yet, only Moses could speak with God "face to face" (Exod 33:11; cf. Deut 34:10). Despite obvious important differences between the two figures, what remains fundamentally common between them is their limitation in their perception of the divine.

The primary lesson of this parallel is one of "theological" humility. As far as human perception of God is concerned, we will always be limited. Even the great prophet Moses cannot see more of God than the Egyptian slave Hagar.

16:14 To commemorate the event, Hagar gives the name of the place **Beer Lahai Roi**, which means "the well of the Living who sees me." Interestingly, she does not refer to her experience in her address to the Angel, namely, that she saw God. Instead, she retains the other side of it, namely, that God took the initiative and saw her. The lesson she learned from her encounter with God has to do with God's preeminence. God's move downward to us precedes and is more important than our move upward to God. That God sees us is more important than what we see of God.

Hagar's perspective and emphasis on God's grace and initiative contrasts with Sarai's perspective and tendency to take the initiative (16:2–6). Beer Lahai Roi is

---

507 Davidson, *The Flame of Yahweh*, 229.

mentioned again as the place where Isaac dwelt (24:62; 25:11), not far south of Beer-sheba, Abram's previous station (22:19).

16:15–16 So Hagar bore Abram a son. The section concludes with an echo of the introduction. Beginning with the observation that a birth from Sarai was not possible for Abram, it closes with a birth from Hagar for Abram. It is noteworthy that Hagar is always qualified as "maid" by the author, Sarai, Abram, and the Angel of the Lord, except in this instance when the event of her giving birth and the moment when she conceived are recorded (16:4). Then she is called by her name, as are Sarai and Abram, as if she has achieved equality with them.

While the name of Sarai is mentioned in the introduction, it is conspicuously absent in the conclusion. The name of Abram, however, appears four times and the name of Hagar three times. Abram gives the name of Ishmael to his son, although the Angel had explicitly designated Hagar for this assignment (16:11). The child is thus reaffirmed as Abram's son, although Abram acknowledges Hagar's encounter with the Angel of the Lord and submits himself to the Angel's instruction regarding the choice of the name of Ishmael. While Hagar was in the wilderness, separated from Abram, the son was just hers; Abram was not mentioned. His mention here suggests that Hagar has returned to his house, which allows Abram to recognize Ishmael as his son.

16:16 Abram was eighty-six years old. The noting of Abram's age at this point places the birth of Ishmael as an integral part of Abram's life. It serves also as a landmark in the course of his journey. Abram was seventy-five years old when he arrived in Canaan (12:4); now he is eighty-six years old—eleven years later. Abram will have to wait until age ninety-nine, that is, thirteen more years to receive the next promise of another son, this time with Sarai (17:1, 16).

17:1–27. PROMISE OF BIRTH FOR ABRAHAM WITH SARAI; CIRCUMCISION

After a moment of silence (16:1–16), God speaks again to Abram. For the first time since the initiation of the covenant in Genesis 15, God reconnects with Abram. God's revelation related to the circumcision (17:1–22) parallels God's revelation related to the sacrifices (15:1–16), unfolding here as there in five sections, after the introductory divine self-declaration, with the circumcision in the center of the structure section (17:9–14), like the sacrifices (cf. 15:9–11).

Divine self-declaration (17:1; cf. 15:1)
Promise of birth (17:2–7; cf. 15:2–6)
Promise of land (17:8; cf. 15:7–8)
Circumcision (17:9–14; cf. 15:9–14)
Precise prophecy (17:15–19a; cf. 15:12–16)
God goes up, covenant (17:19b–22; cf. 15:17–21)

17:1. DIVINE SELF-DECLARATION

GEN 17:1 NKJV	GEN 17:1 ESV
1 When Abram was ninety-nine years old, the LORD appeared to Abram and said to him, "I *am* Almighty God; walk before Me and be blameless.	**1** When Abram was ninety-nine years old the LORD appeared to Abram and said to him, "I am God Almighty; walk before me, and be blameless,

Thirteen years after the birth of Ishmael (16:16) and twenty-four years after he arrived in Canaan (12:4) Abram is still waiting for the birth of a son with Sarai. Just as God had revealed Himself as the "shield" (*magen*), God reveals Himself again to Abram, this time as *'El Shaddai* **Almighty God**.

The parallel between the two self-declaratory formulas suggests that we should understand the name *'El Shaddai* as God's promise for the future (see the comments on 15:1). The connection between the name *Shaddai* and the word *shad* "breast" (Song 4:5; 7:3) points indeed to the future, the promise of descendants (see also 49:25).[508] It is significant that all the places in Genesis where the name *Shaddai* appears (17:1; 28:3; 35:11; 43:14; 48:3; 49:25) comes in a context of birth, blessing, and fertility. This interpretation is in the line of Moses' reading of the passage in Exodus 6:3. God "has appeared" (*ra'ah*) to the patriarchs as *'El Shaddai*, the God of promise while now in the time of the fulfillment of the promise He "has made Himself known," "experienced" (*yada'*) as *YHWH*, the God of history.

The name *'El Shaddai* is particularly prominent in the book of Job (thirty-one times against seventeen times in the rest of the Old Testament), although without the denominative *'El*. While this common usage testifies to a common literary origin, it may also reflect the same theology of hope in a state of hopelessness, a longing for God to fulfill His promise.

Walk before Me and be blameless. The key verb associated with Abram, *halak* "go" (see our comment on 2:1), reappears here in the same form as with Enoch (5:24) and Noah (6:9). The parallel is closer to Noah as it shares the common association with the word *tamim* "blameless."

The construction of the phrase indicates, however, a different process in reaching blamelessness. While Noah's blamelessness is derived from "his generation," Abram's blamelessness is achieved from walking before God, as the following literal translation suggests: "walk before God and then be blameless."

Noah (like Enoch) walks "with God" while Abram walks "before" (*lipney*) God. The preposition used for Noah suggests that God is by his side—we see God and Noah together. The preposition used for Abram, however, suggests that the invisible God is behind him, like the shepherd who walks behind his sheep guiding them (48:15).[509]

17:2–7. PROMISE OF BIRTH

GEN 17:2–7 NKJV	GEN 17:2–7 ESV
2 "And I will make My covenant between Me and you, and will multiply you exceedingly."	**2** "That I may make my covenant between me and you, and may multiply you greatly."
3 Then Abram fell on his face, and God talked with him, saying:	**3** Then Abram fell on his face. And God said to him,
4 "As for Me, behold, My covenant is with you, and you shall be a father of many nations.	**4** "Behold, my covenant is with you, and you shall be the father of a multitude of nations.

---

508 For the connection between the idea of "breast" and the name *'El Shaddai*, see D. Biale, "The God With Breasts: El Shaddai in the Bible," *HR* 21 (1982): 180–193.

509 See Jacob, *Genesis*, 109.

5 No longer shall your name be called Abram, but your name shall be Abraham; for I have made you a father of many nations.	**5** No longer shall your name be called Abram, but your name shall be Abraham, for I have made you the father of a multitude of nations.
6 I will make you exceedingly fruitful; and I will make nations of you, and kings shall come from you.	**6** I will make you exceedingly fruitful, and I will make you into nations, and kings shall come from you.
7 And I will establish My covenant between Me and you and your descendants after you in their generations, for an everlasting covenant, to be God to you and your descendants after you."	**7** And I will establish my covenant between me and you and your offspring after you throughout their generations for an everlasting covenant, to be God to you and to your offspring after you."

17:2 The language of the promise echoes that of Genesis 15:1. We find the same verb *rabah* "multiply" with the same qualification *me'od* **exceedingly**, which is now intensified by being repeated twice (cf. 17:6).

17:3 Abram responds to God by worshipping in prayer: **Abram fell in his face**. This is an act signifying respect towards a superior (cf. 37:10; 48:12). But it is often a physical expression of profound reverence before a supernatural apparition of God (17:1; cf. Exod 34:8). Note that this behavior is unique to Abram among the patriarchs (cf. 18:2; 19:1).

17:4–6 The promise refers to the future: The phrase *'ab hamon goyim* **father of many nations** (17:4) is used to justify the new name of Abram. He will no longer be called *'Ab-ram* (17:5), which means "high father," an attribute that was limited to the present situation. Abram was only "high" for his contemporaries. He will be called *'Abraham,* which integrates the word *hamon* "many," "multitude" into the name, which becomes then *'Ab-ra-ham.*

The new name looks now to the future: **I will make you exceedingly fruitful** (17:6). This promise of fruitfulness relates to the old promise of the engendering (and blessing) of many peoples as announced in the call at Ur (12:1–3). Abraham will not only physically engender many peoples and thus become *goy gadol* "a great nation," in him, "all the families of the earth will be blessed" (12:3).

17:7 This promise expands into a covenant that is stylistically reminiscent of the first messianic prophecy (3:15). In both cases, God is the divine subject of the operation:

'ashit … beynekha ubeyn … ubeyn zar'eykha "I will put … between you and your seed" (3:15)
wahaqimoti … beyni ubeynekha ubeyn zar'eykha "I will establish between Me and you and your descendants" (17:7)

The parallel between the two texts suggests that the covenant with Abram concerns more than the promise that he will give birth to many peoples: it contains also the spiritual promise of salvation for all the peoples of the world, as predicted in the first messianic prophecy (3:15).

Everlasting covenant. The qualification "everlasting" refers to the One who makes the covenant and implies His "everlasting" assurance, meaning that God will not change His mind. It also signifies the effect of that covenant, which is eternal life. God's covenant with Abraham contains, then, the promise of the messianic seed and of the sacrifice of Christ that ensures eternal life (Rom 6:23; Titus 1:2).

17:8. PROMISE OF LAND

GEN 17:8 NKJV	GEN 17:8 ESV
8 "Also I give to you and your descendants after you the land in which you are a stranger, all the land of Canaan, as an everlasting possession; and I will be their God."	**8** "And I will give to you and to your offspring after you the land of your sojournings, all the land of Canaan, for an everlasting possession, and I will be their God."

I give to you … the land. The same eternal perspective is attached to the gift of the land. The sense of the text is not that the physical land of Canaan is given eternally to the descendants of Abraham, although that promise applies to a certain extent to the historical possession of the land of Canaan. Its eternal dimension suggests that it transcends this event and aims at another event of an eternal quality.

Furthermore, the connection with the first messianic prophecy (3:15) indicates that this gift of the land belongs to the perspective of salvation as achieved through the sacrifice of Christ. Beyond the local and temporal event of the possession of Canaan, the gift of the Promised Land points to the recovery of eternity in the Garden of Eden. Significantly, God's gift of "an everlasting possession" implies that He "will be their God," a phrase that is normally associated with His favorable presence and proximity (Lev 26:12; 2 Cor 6:16).

17:9–14. CIRCUMCISION

GEN 17:9–14 NKJV	GEN 17:9–14 ESV
9 And God said to Abraham: "As for you, you shall keep My covenant, you and your descendants after you throughout their generations.	**9** And God said to Abraham, "As for you, you shall keep my covenant, you and your offspring after you throughout their generations.
10 This *is* My covenant which you shall keep, between Me and you and your descendants after you: Every male child among you shall be circumcised;	**10** This is my covenant, which you shall keep, between me and you and your offspring after you: Every male among you shall be circumcised.
11 and you shall be circumcised in the flesh of your foreskins, and it shall be a sign of the covenant between Me and you.	**11** You shall be circumcised in the flesh of your foreskins, and it shall be a sign of the covenant between me and you.
12 He who is eight days old among you shall be circumcised, every male child in your generations, he who is born in your house or bought with money from any foreigner who is not your descendant.	**12** He who is eight days old among you shall be circumcised. Every male throughout your generations, whether born in your house or bought with your money from any foreigner who is not of your offspring,
13 He who is born in your house and he who is bought with your money must be circumcised, and My covenant shall be in your flesh for an everlasting covenant.	**13** both he who is born in your house and he who is bought with your money, shall surely be circumcised. So shall my covenant be in your flesh an everlasting covenant.
14 And the uncircumcised male child, who is not circumcised in the flesh of his foreskin, that person shall be cut off from his people; he has broken My covenant."	**14** Any uncircumcised male who is not circumcised in the flesh of his foreskin shall be cut off from his people; he has broken my covenant."

17:10 **Every male child among you shall be circumcised.** The verb "circumcise" (*mul*, from which comes the technical word *milah* "circumcision") refers to the rite that consists of removing the foreskin and thus permanently exposing the glans of the penis. This practice was current in the ANE (Egypt, Canaanites, and Arabs).

The significance of this rite has been discussed and attributed to various reasons (health, fertility, puberty, control of sexuality, initiation to marriage, etc.). While these explanations may have been supported in the context of the ANE cultures, in the Bible, the rite of circumcision has been invested with new meanings illuminated by biblical revelation. It is significant that the passage dealing with God's command concerning the rite of circumcision (17:1–27) has parallels in the chiastic structure of the Abrahamic covenant (15–17). This parallel suggests that the rite of circumcision is connected in some way with the sacrificial system.

17:10–11 The rite of circumcision is explicitly identified as **covenant** (17:10) and then more specifically as a **sign of the covenant** (17:11). The association with the sacrificial system is also reflected in the language that describes the rite of circumcision, which is "a sign" just like "the sign" of the blood of the Passover lamb (Exod 12:13). Indeed, both rites are signs of blood (Exod 4:25). The linkage between circumcision and the Paschal lamb is further established by Exodus, which requires the circumcision of all males who would eat the sacrifice (Exod 12:43–49).

17:12 The moment of the circumcision, on the eighth day, also holds special meaning in connection with the sacrificial system. The sacrificial animals that are used in the ceremony of the covenant with Abram (15:9) appear often in the ceremony of atonement that should take place on the eighth day (Lev 9:1–24; 14:20–23; 15:14–15, 29–30; 29:27–28; Num 6:10–11). These numerous parallels and associations with the sacrifices suggest that the rite of circumcision, because it involves the shedding of blood, was understood in sacrificial categories.[510] This aspect of the theological significance of circumcision does not suggest that circumcision has in itself a salvific effect. The apostle Paul explains that Abraham "received the sign of circumcision, a seal of the righteousness of the faith which he had while still uncircumcised, … that righteousness might be imputed to them also" (Rom 4:11).[511] Along these lines, Old Testament theologian Bruce Waltke comments: "Circumcision reflects God's intent to set apart the procreative elect as the means for salvation of the world. For the Israelites, to circumcise a child reflects the parents' faith in God's promise and commitment to partner with God in effecting his plan of salvation for the world."[512]

This understanding fits perfectly the immediate context, which evokes the messianic prophecy of Genesis 3:15, anticipating the future atoning death of the Messiah. This is why the rite of circumcision is given as the sign of the everlasting covenant (17:13), which, like the gift of the land, points to the messianic event of salvation.

---

510 Interestingly, this association of the blood of circumcision and the blood of the Passover lamb has been noted in rabbinic tradition, which identified circumcision as a sacrifice and ranked circumcision blood as sacrificial blood (Exod. Rab. 12:3–5; 19:5).

511 See Ellen G. White, PP 138.

512 Bruce K. Waltke, *An Old Testament Theology* (Grand Rapids: Zondervan, 2007), 358.

17:15–19A. PRECISE PROPHECY

GEN 17:15–19A NKJV	GEN 17:15–19A ESV
15 Then God said to Abraham, "As for Sarai your wife, you shall not call her name Sarai, but Sarah *shall be* her name.	**15** And God said to Abraham, "As for Sarai your wife, you shall not call her name Sarai, but Sarah shall be her name.
16 And I will bless her and also give you a son by her; then I will bless her, and she shall be *a mother of* nations; kings of peoples shall be from her."	**16** I will bless her, and moreover, I will give you a son by her. I will bless her, and she shall become nations; kings of peoples shall come from her."
17 Then Abraham fell on his face and laughed, and said in his heart, "Shall a *child* be born to a man who is one hundred years old? And shall Sarah, who is ninety years old, bear *a child*?"	**17** Then Abraham fell on his face and laughed and said to himself, "Shall a child be born to a man who is a hundred years old? Shall Sarah, who is ninety years old, bear a child?"
18 And Abraham said to God, "Oh, that Ishmael might live before You!"	**18** And Abraham said to God, "Oh that Ishmael might live before you!"
19a Then God said: "No, Sarah your wife shall bear you a son, and you shall call his name Isaac."	**19a** God said, "No, but Sarah your wife shall bear you a son, and you shall call his name Isaac."

17:15–16 In parallel with the text of Genesis 15, the next item is made a prophecy. For the first time, the attention is directed to Sarah: **as for Sarai your wife** (17:15). God specifies that the son of the covenant shall not only come from Abraham but also from Sarah (17:16). It is interesting that she receives the same treatment as Abraham. Like Abraham, she has her name changed; like him, she receives a *hey* into her name. Abram, who was "high father" only for his contemporaries, becomes Abraham "the father of many nations" expanding to the future. Likewise, Sarai, who was "my princess" only for Abraham, becomes "the princess" for everyone, Sarah. The relative and temporal have shifted to the absolute and universal. She has now become the mother of nations (17:16), just as Abraham had become the father of nations.

This consistent parallel between the patriarch Abraham and the matriarch Sarah emphasizes the equal significance of Sarah, "thus showing that the covenant blessings and promises apply to her—and to women—just as surely as to Abraham and his male descendants."[513] For Abraham, God's promise involving Sarah is unbelievable.

17:17 Abraham's immediate reaction to the divine announcement is silent prostration and awe: **Abraham fell on his face** (17:17). This is the second time Abraham prostrates in silence (cf. 17:3). This time, however, his prostration is followed or accompanied by laughter, the first laughter recorded in the Bible. The meaning of Abraham's laughter is not indicated. We have only Abraham's question, which seems to explain it: **Shall a child be born to a man who is one hundred years old? And shall Sarah, who is ninety years old, bear a child?** It is not clear whether this double question associated with his laughter connotes skepticism or expresses his wonder. There may be a mixture of both. The fact that laughter and questions take place in the context of Abraham's act of worship suggests that wonder predominates.

17:18–19a As soon as Abraham speaks, skepticism prevails. He proposes a reasonable solution that will make this unbelievable promise believable. Abraham refers

---

513 Davidson, *The Flame of Yahweh*, 227; cf. M. Evans, "The Invisibility of Women: An Investigation of a Possible Blind Spot for Biblical Commentators," *CBRFJ* 122 (1990): 37–38.

to Ishmael just as he had done in the past with Eliezer (15:2). Abraham's skeptical recommendation obliges God to become more precise and specific. God squarely negates Abraham's suggestion; the prophecy does not concern Ishmael (17:19). In echo to Abraham's questions concerning both Sarah and himself, God responds with the same words involving both of them. The promise becomes more real. The verbal form in the participle *yoledet* **she is about to bear you a son** (17:19a) marks the imminence of the event. God even gives the name of the son (17:19a). Ironically, *Isaac* means "He laughs," resonating with Abram's laughter. But this time it is God who laughs, for the name "Isaac" implies the name of God, as Semitic and biblical studies of names suggest. In parallel to the name "Ishmael" ("God has heard"), Isaac's name must have also carried at least implicitly the name of God "[God] has laughed."

17:19B–22. COVENANT: GOD GOES UP

GEN 17:19B–22 NKJV	GEN 17:19B–22 ESV
19b "I will establish My covenant with him for an everlasting covenant, *and* with his descendants after him.	**19b** "I will establish my covenant with him as an everlasting covenant for his offspring after him.
20 And as for Ishmael, I have heard you. Behold, I have blessed him, and will make him fruitful, and will multiply him exceedingly. He shall beget twelve princes, and I will make him a great nation.	**20** As for Ishmael, I have heard you; behold, I have blessed him and will make him fruitful and multiply him greatly. He shall father twelve princes, and I will make him into a great nation.
21 But My covenant I will establish with Isaac, whom Sarah shall bear to you at this set time next year."	**21** But I will establish my covenant with Isaac, whom Sarah shall bear to you at this time next year."
22 Then He finished talking with him, and God went up from Abraham.	**22** When he had finished talking with him, God went up from Abraham.

17:19b The word *berit* **covenant** is repeated twice; the first time to specify that this covenant is specifically related to Isaac, and the second time to affirm the everlasting character of this covenant, which involves Isaac's descendants.

17:20–21 In response to Abraham's reference to Ishmael, God specifies that He heard him, playing again on the name "Ishmael." Ishmael will benefit from the same blessing in parallel to Isaac. He will be fruitful and engender twelve princes (17:20), an anticipation of the twelve sons of Jacob. Yet, as the word "but" suggests,[514] the contrast will still remain between the two sons: ***but* My covenant** (17:21). God's covenant will be established only with Isaac, the son of Sarah.

17:22 Then He finished talking with him. The Hebrew verb *wayekal* "He finished" marks the end of God's intervention. It is the same as the verb that concludes the divine work of creation (2:1). There is nothing to add to God's words, a way of asserting that Abraham's case is final and that nothing can keep the birth from taking place.

God went up. This information suggests a visible ascension of God corresponding to "the Lord appeared" at the beginning of the story (17:1). God's move into the space of Abraham gives a historical reality to the divine promise of the birth of Isaac.

---

514 The word "but" translates the *waw* of contrast before the phrase "My covenant."

17:23–27. THE CIRCUMCISION OF ISHMAEL

GEN 17:23–27 NKJV	GEN 17:23–27 ESV
23 So Abraham took Ishmael his son, all who were born in his house and all who were bought with his money, every male among the men of Abraham's house, and circumcised the flesh of their foreskins that very same day, as God had said to him.	**23** Then Abraham took Ishmael his son and all those born in his house or bought with his money, every male among the men of Abraham's house, and he circumcised the flesh of their foreskins that very day, as God had said to him.
24 Abraham *was* ninety-nine years old when he was circumcised in the flesh of his foreskin.	**24** Abraham was ninety-nine years old when he was circumcised in the flesh of his foreskin.
25 And Ishmael his son *was* thirteen years old when he was circumcised in the flesh of his foreskin.	**25** And Ishmael his son was thirteen years old when he was circumcised in the flesh of his foreskin.
26 That very same day Abraham was circumcised, and his son Ishmael;	**26** That very day Abraham and his son Ishmael were circumcised.
27 and all the men of his house, born in the house or bought with money from a foreigner, were circumcised with him.	**27** And all the men of his house, those born in the house and those bought with money from a foreigner, were circumcised with him.

Abraham's first response to God's revelation of the birth is to circumcise himself and Ishmael and, by implication, all foreign males who were born in his house. The inclusiveness of the rite is repeatedly noted through the use of the word *kol* "all" (17:23 [3x], 27). The significance of this act is marked twice chronologically, by the specification of the age of Abraham who was **ninety-nine years old** (17:24) and the repetition of the phrase "that very same day" (17:23, 26), suggesting a turning point in history—the beginning of the Abrahamic covenant including all the nations (17:27).

ABRAHAM AND LOT (18–19)

Following the inclusive covenant involving Ishmael and the foreign males of the house of Abraham, new events bring Lot, Abraham's nephew, and his family to reconnect with the line of Abraham. The two lines remain distinct from each other, however. The hospitable visit of angels to Abraham (18:1–8) contrasts with the inhospitable visit of angels to Lot (19:30–38) and the supernatural birth from Abraham with Sarah (18:9–15) contrasts with the incestuous births from Lot with his daughters (19:30–38).

Abraham's encounter with the Lord (18:16–33) is inserted between the two parallel panels, thus forming the following structure:

A Visit of angels to Abraham (18:1–8)
  B Birth from Sarah with Abraham (18:9–15)
    C Abraham's encounter with the Lord (18:16–33)
A₁ Visit of angels to Lot (19:1–29)
  B₁ Birth from Lot's daughters with Lot (19:30–38)

18:1–8. VISIT OF ANGELS TO ABRAHAM

GEN 18:1–8 NKJV	GEN 18:1–8 ESV
1 Then the LORD appeared to him by the terebinth trees of Mamre, as he was sitting in the tent door in the heat of the day.	**1** And the LORD appeared to him by the oaks of Mamre, as he sat at the door of his tent in the heat of the day.
2 So he lifted his eyes and looked, and behold, three men were standing by him; and when he saw *them*, he ran from the tent door to meet them, and bowed himself to the ground,	**2** He lifted up his eyes and looked, and behold, three men were standing in front of him. When he saw them, he ran from the tent door to meet them and bowed himself to the earth
3 and said, "My Lord, if I have now found favor in Your sight, do not pass on by Your servant.	**3** and said, "O Lord, if I have found favor in your sight, do not pass by your servant.
4 Please let a little water be brought, and wash your feet, and rest yourselves under the tree.	**4** Let a little water be brought, and wash your feet, and rest yourselves under the tree,
5 And I will bring a morsel of bread, that you may refresh your hearts. After that you may pass by, inasmuch as you have come to your servant." They said, "Do as you have said."	**5** while I bring a morsel of bread, that you may refresh yourselves, and after that you may pass on—since you have come to your servant." So they said, "Do as you have said."
6 So Abraham hurried into the tent to Sarah and said, "Quickly, make ready three measures of fine meal; knead *it* and make cakes."	**6** And Abraham went quickly into the tent to Sarah and said, "Quick! Three seahs of fine flour! Knead it, and make cakes."
7 And Abraham ran to the herd, took a tender and good calf, gave *it* to a young man, and he hastened to prepare it.	**7** And Abraham ran to the herd and took a calf, tender and good, and gave it to a young man, who prepared it quickly.
8 So he took butter and milk and the calf which he had prepared, and set *it* before them; and he stood by them under the tree as they ate.	**8** Then he took curds and milk and the calf that he had prepared, and set it before them. And he stood by them under the tree while they ate.

For the first time Abraham receives heavenly guests without knowing it. His actions will be remembered as a model of hospitality (Heb 13:2).

18:1 **The Lord appeared to him.** Instead of engaging right away with the promise, as it is the case in the parallel stories (cf. 12:7; 15:1; 17:1), we have a moment of hospitality. God enters the human sphere. He will be seen, met, and fed by Abraham.

In the heat of the day. This is a time of siesta, when everyone withdraws into the shade. But, instead of having a regular nap inside the tent like others, Abraham is sitting **in the tent door**, as if waiting for someone. This abnormal behavior added to the fact that the event takes place in the familiar worship environment **by the terebinth trees of Mamre** (cf. 13:18) suggests that Abraham may well have secretly been hoping for God to appear.

18:2 **He lifted his eyes and looked, and behold**. This particular expression, often associated with the appearing of God (22:13; Dan 10:5; 24:63–64; 31:10), confirms the special nature of Abraham's expectation.

He ran. The repetition of the verb *rats* **ran** (18:2, 7), reinforced by the repetition of the verb *mahar* **hurried** (18:6) and **quickly make** (18:6), is extraordinary considering Abraham's great age—he is ninety-nine years old and has just been circumcised (17:24).

18:3 **My Lord.** The word *'adonay* "my Lord," like the first person plural "my lords," normally refers to the divinity (20:4; Exod 15:17; Isa 37:24; Ps 35:23) and is the traditional reading (*qere*)[515] of *YHWH*. It is therefore possible that Abraham uses the word *'adonay* to imply God *YHWH* Himself.[516] It seems that Abraham had a vague inkling of the divine nature of One of them, while seeing them at the same time as mere human visitors.

In Your sight. Abraham refers to the second person masculine singular *be'eyneykha* "in thy eyes" (DBY), as Abraham is speaking to the One he calls *'adonay*, "my Lords" (lit. trans.). If Abraham had in mind several people, while saying *'adonay*, he should have used the plural form *be'eyneykem* "in your eyes."

18:4–6 Interestingly, immediately after this particular address Abraham shifts to the second person plural (18:4–5), as he busily attends to his guests and prepares the meal for them. After providing water to wash his guests' feet (18:4), Abraham selects the best for the meal: **fine flour** (18:6 ESV), the kind that later will be used to bake the bread of the Presence (Lev 24:5), and a **tender and good calf** (18:7). Abraham involves all his family in this work. Sarah prepares the bread (18:6) and **the young man**, presumably Ishmael,[517] prepares the calf (18:7). Yet, Abraham humbly qualifies the feast as **a morsel of bread** (18:5). The Hebrew word *pat lekhem* suggests a pita bread. Obviously, Abraham's passion and zeal towards the three visitors derives from his intuition that they hold a special status. The way he addresses one of the visitors suggests that perception.

The fact that Abraham offers food and water to the visitor does not necessarily exclude his recognition of the divine identity. Visitors in the desert are rare and are therefore revered as God Himself (cf. Heb 13:2). The "human" expression of the visitors who physically stand (18:2), eat (18:8), and have articulate conversations (18:9) is a part of the divine strategy of incarnation. This ambivalent perception is immediately confirmed in the following verses.

18:8 He then stands **by them under the tree as they ate**, attentive to their needs and ready to serve them.

18:9–15. BIRTH FROM SARAH WITH ABRAHAM

GEN 18:9–15 NKJV	GEN 18:9–15 ESV
9 Then they said to him, "Where *is* Sarah your wife?" So he said, "Here, in the tent."	**9** They said to him, "Where is Sarah your wife?" And he said, "She is in the tent."
10 And He said, "I will certainly return to you according to the time of life, and behold, Sarah your wife shall have a son." (Sarah was listening in the tent door which *was* behind him.)	**10** The LORD said, "I will surely return to you about this time next year, and Sarah your wife shall have a son." And Sarah was listening at the tent door behind him.

---

515 The *qere* is the traditional reading indicated by the Massoretes for words that should be read differently than what their writing suggests. For instance, in order to avoid pronouncing the name of God *YHWH* the vowels *a o a* from the word *'aDoNaY* are given to the word *YHWH* thus forming the artificial word "Jehovah" to indicate that the word *YHWH* should be read *'adonay*. Note that the vowel *a* (*patach furtive*) under the guttural ' (*'alef*) of *'adonay* becomes *e* (*shewa*) under the solid consonant *Y* (*yod*).

516 See the Targum Onkelos, which translates with *YHWH*. See however, Hamilton's argument that suggests that Abraham did not actually use the word *'adonay* (the Massoretic rendering) and said instead *'adoni* "my lord" (in singular), implying that he did not recognize right away the visitor as divine but came to this recognition only gradually (Victor P. Hamilton, *Genesis 18–50*, NICOT [Grand Rapids: Eerdmans, 1995], 3). Although this interpretation seems to make better sense considering Abraham's offering of food and water to the visitor, we prefer the Massoretic testimony that has preserved the use of *'adonay* in spite of the logical problem, thus suggesting the force of that reading (*lectio difficilior*).

517 The phrase *hanna'ar* "the young man" designates Ishmael (21:17, 20).

11 Now Abraham and Sarah were old, well advanced in age; *and* Sarah had passed the age of childbearing.	**11** Now Abraham and Sarah were old, advanced in years. The way of women had ceased to be with Sarah.
12 Therefore Sarah laughed within herself, saying, "After I have grown old, shall I have pleasure, my lord being old also?"	**12** So Sarah laughed to herself, saying, "After I am worn out, and my lord is old, shall I have pleasure?"
13 And the Lᴏʀᴅ said to Abraham, "Why did Sarah laugh, saying, 'Shall I surely bear *a child*, since I am old?'	**13** The Lᴏʀᴅ said to Abraham, "Why did Sarah laugh and say, 'Shall I indeed bear a child, now that I am old?'
14 Is anything too hard for the Lᴏʀᴅ? At the appointed time I will return to you, according to the time of life, and Sarah shall have a son."	**14** Is anything too hard for the Lᴏʀᴅ? At the appointed time I will return to you, about this time next year, and Sarah shall have a son."
15 But Sarah denied *it*, saying, "I did not laugh," for she was afraid. And He said, "No, but you did laugh!"	**15** But Sarah denied it, saying, "I did not laugh," for she was afraid. He said, "No, but you did laugh."

Only after the angels' question (18:9) is the third person masculine singular used again, **and He said** (18:10). This shift of pronouns from the plural to the singular suggests that the person who is now speaking is the Lord Himself, just as in the beginning of the encounter (18:1). This is clearly indicated by the fact that the promise of the birth is given in the same terms as in God's previous annunciation (17:19). In addition, His promise of a second visit at the time of the birth coincides with the Lord's visit at its fulfillment (21:2).

In the tent, Sarah listens to the conversation and her response echoes Abraham's. Like him, she is skeptical and laughs at this unbelievable promise (18:10–12). Something strange then happens. Although Sarah had laughed **within herself** (18:12), her most intimate thoughts are known, even though the visitor could not see her since his back is to the tent (18:10) and though she denies having laughed (18:14–15). This exceptional capacity indicates to Abraham and Sarah that they are in the presence of the Lord and guarantees the miraculous fulfillment of God's promise. Indeed, the text explicitly states that it is the Lord who is speaking (18:13).

The event will happen *lammo'ed* **at the appointed time** (18:14), language that echoes the Lord's language in the previous annunciation (17:21). Remarkably, the Lord's first comment refers to the domain of wonder: **is anything too hard?** The Hebrew word *pl'* "wondrous" (TNK), "wonderful" (DBY), "too hard" (NKJV) often describes the prodigious miracle of salvation (Exod 3:20; Jer 32:17, 27; Zech 8:6).

The promised son Isaac, **he laughed**, the concrete manifestation of the miracle, turns Sarah's skeptical laughter into an irony of wonder. The Lord's last words, **No, but you did laugh!** (18:15), which insist on Sarah's laughter in spite of her denial, imply the same observation of wonder: just as you have laughed in spite of your denial you will give birth in spite of your skepticism.

This is the first and totally affirmative statement after a series of rhetorical questions: **Where is Sarah your wife?** (18:9), **Why did Sarah laugh?** (18:13), **Is anything too hard for the Lord?** (18:14). The conversation ends with this short statement, implying that there is nothing to add and that the divine word on the fulfillment of the event is final.

18:16–31. ABRAHAM'S ENCOUNTER WITH THE LORD

Abraham continues his hospitality and accompanies his visitors as they depart (18:16). Two of the three men are heading for Sodom (18:16, 22) and will arrive there (19:1). The third man, who will stay with Abraham, is clearly identified as the Lord (18:17, 22).

The passage is made up of two sections. The first (18:16–21) consists of a divine deliberation implicitly addressed to the other men concerning Abraham's righteousness and Sodom's wickedness. The second (18:22–33) consists of a dialogue between the Lord and Abraham concerning the righteous and the wicked in Sodom.

18:16–21. DIVINE DELIBERATION

GEN 18:16–21 NKJV	GEN 18:16–21 ESV
16 Then the men rose from there and looked toward Sodom, and Abraham went with them to send them on the way.	**16** Then the men set out from there, and they looked down toward Sodom. And Abraham went with them to set them on their way.
17 And the Lord said, "Shall I hide from Abraham what I am doing,	**17** The Lord said, "Shall I hide from Abraham what I am about to do,
18 since Abraham shall surely become a great and mighty nation, and all the nations of the earth shall be blessed in him?	**18** seeing that Abraham shall surely become a great and mighty nation, and all the nations of the earth shall be blessed in him?
19 For I have known him, in order that he may command his children and his household after him, that they keep the way of the Lord, to do righteousness and justice, that the Lord may bring to Abraham what He has spoken to him."	**19** For I have chosen him, that he may command his children and his household after him to keep the way of the Lord by doing righteousness and justice, so that the Lord may bring to Abraham what he has promised him."
20 And the Lord said, "Because the outcry against Sodom and Gomorrah is great, and because their sin is very grave,	**20** Then the Lord said, "Because the outcry against Sodom and Gomorrah is great and their sin is very grave,
21 I will go down now and see whether they have done altogether according to the outcry against it that has come to Me; and if not, I will know."	**21** I will go down to see whether they have done altogether according to the outcry that has come to me. And if not, I will know."

18:17 **And the Lord said.** The Lord's speech is directed at the two men. The Lord seems to ask them permission to include Abraham in the process of judgment. This request suggests that the two men are a part of the divine council (Jer 23:18).

18:17–18 **Shall I hide from Abraham what I am doing?** Two reasons are given to justify Abraham's participation. First, Abraham is a prophet and a righteous man. The Lord's rhetorical question implies the special relation entertained between God and His prophets (Amos 3:7). The future will not be hidden from Abraham because he is a man of the future. Abraham will have an impact on the future of the nations of the earth, since **all the nations of the earth shall be blessed in him** (18:18; cf. 12:2–3) as well as the future of his own family (18:19). Although there seems to be a difference between these two destinies, they are blessed by the righteousness offered by God's people.

18:19 This is the purpose of the election of Abraham: **for I have known him.**

The verb *yada'* "know" conveys the idea of election and intimate relations (Jer 1:5; Hos 13:5). This unique knowledge of the Lord implies that Abraham should **command** (*tsawah*) his family that they **keep the way of the Lord**, which is described in ethical terms, as doing **righteousness and justice**.

18:20–21 While the two words "know," and "do" are associated with *tsedaqah* "righteousness" for Abraham, they are associated with *ze'aqah/tse'aqah* "outcry" for the iniquity for Sodom (18:20–21). The symmetric contrast is thus suggested between the line of Abraham and that of Sodom. In the line of Abraham, the "know" expresses God's love and election, whereas in the line of Sodom, it expresses God's inquisitive search and judgment. In the line of Abraham the "do" refers to righteousness, while in the line of Sodom it refers to sin.

The contrast is also heard through the play on words ("paronomasia") on the words "righteousness" (*tsedaqah*) and "outcry" (*ze'aqah/tse'aqah*). The same contrasting play on words will be used by Isaiah when he denounces the lack of social justice among the people of his day: "He looked for justice [*mishpat*], but behold, oppression [*mispakh*]; for righteousness [*tsedaqah*], but behold, weeping [*tse'aqah*]" (Isa 5:7). Sodom and Gomorrah accumulate all evil. The crime of Cain, the iniquity of the generation of Noah, and the pride of Babel are evoked.

The **outcry** (18:20) that has reached God echoes the voice of Abel's blood (4:10). The outcry against Sodom and Gomorrah is described as **great** (*rabbah*), like the sin in Noah's day (6:5), and God will respond to them as He did to the men of Babel. Again God confronts humans with judgment.

The legal process begins with God's investigation: **I will go down now and see** (18:21; cf. 11:5). Although the same prospect of God's descent anticipates the same fate of judgment, the phrase **if not, I will know** (18:21) suggests that there is still some kind of hope for Sodom. God is willing to let Himself be challenged. This is the second reason why God allows Abraham to be involved in His judgment. The Lord will stay with Abraham while the two other men are heading for Sodom to inquire about the situation and thus enlighten the case (18:22). This will give Abraham an opportunity to challenge God's judgment.

18:22–33. ABRAHAM CHALLENGES GOD

GEN 18:22–33 NKJV	GEN 18:22–33 ESV
22 Then the men turned away from there and went toward Sodom, but Abraham still stood before the Lord.	**22** So the men turned from there and went toward Sodom, but Abraham still stood before the Lord.
23 And Abraham came near and said, "Would You also destroy the righteous with the wicked?	**23** Then Abraham drew near and said, "Will you indeed sweep away the righteous with the wicked?
24 Suppose there were fifty righteous within the city; would You also destroy the place and not spare *it* for the fifty righteous that were in it?	**24** Suppose there are fifty righteous within the city. Will you then sweep away the place and not spare it for the fifty righteous who are in it?
25 Far be it from You to do such a thing as this, to slay the righteous with the wicked, so that the righteous should be as the wicked; far be it from You! Shall not the Judge of all the earth do right?"	**25** Far be it from you to do such a thing, to put the righteous to death with the wicked, so that the righteous fare as the wicked! Far be that from you! Shall not the Judge of all the earth do what is just?"

247

26 So the L_ORD_ said, "If I find in Sodom fifty righteous within the city, then I will spare all the place for their sakes."	**26** And the L_ORD_ said, "If I find at Sodom fifty righteous in the city, I will spare the whole place for their sake."
27 Then Abraham answered and said, "Indeed now, I who *am but* dust and ashes have taken it upon myself to speak to the Lord:	**27** Abraham answered and said, "Behold, I have undertaken to speak to the Lord, I who am but dust and ashes.
28 Suppose there were five less than the fifty righteous; would You destroy all of the city for *lack of* five?" So He said, "If I find there forty-five, I will not destroy *it.*"	**28** Suppose five of the fifty righteous are lacking. Will you destroy the whole city for lack of five?" And he said, "I will not destroy it if I find forty-five there."
29 And he spoke to Him yet again and said, "Suppose there should be forty found there?" So He said, "I will not do *it* for the sake of forty."	**29** Again he spoke to him and said, "Suppose forty are found there." He answered, "For the sake of forty I will not do it."
30 Then he said, "Let not the Lord be angry, and I will speak: Suppose thirty should be found there?" So He said, "I will not do *it* if I find thirty there."	**30** Then he said, "Oh let not the Lord be angry, and I will speak. Suppose thirty are found there." He answered, "I will not do it, if I find thirty there."
31 And he said, "Indeed now, I have taken it upon myself to speak to the Lord: Suppose twenty should be found there?" So He said, "I will not destroy *it* for the sake of twenty."	**31** He said, "Behold, I have undertaken to speak to the Lord. Suppose twenty are found there." He answered, "For the sake of twenty I will not destroy it."
32 Then he said, "Let not the Lord be angry, and I will speak but once more: Suppose ten should be found there?" And He said, "I will not destroy *it* for the sake of ten."	**32** Then he said, "Oh let not the Lord be angry, and I will speak again but this once. Suppose ten are found there." He answered, "For the sake of ten I will not destroy it."
33 So the L_ORD_ went His way as soon as He had finished speaking with Abraham; and Abraham returned to his place.	**33** And the L_ORD_ went his way, when he had finished speaking to Abraham, and Abraham returned to his place.

18:22 It has been suggested that the phrase **Abraham still stood before the Lord** (18:22b) is a *tiqun soferim* "scribal correction" to avoid irreverence, which would have been implied in the reverse sequence "God stood before Abraham."[518] The Hebrew expression *'amad lipney* "stand before" characterizes the attitude of humbling and serving ("served," Jer 52:12). It is normally used to describe reverence before God (Deut 10:8; 1 Kgs 17:1; Zech 3:1). Yet, this sequence may well be original, indicating that Abraham was indeed standing before the Lord, praying on behalf of the Sodomites, as translated by the Aramaic Targum of Onkelos: "And Abraham was still ministering in prayer before the Lord." Abraham was praying although the angels had already reached their destination and were about to destroy Sodom (18:22a). This is the first time in the Bible that man prays on behalf of another person. Even Noah had kept quiet in similar circumstances (6:13–22).

18:23 And Abraham came near and said. The Hebrew verb *wayyigash* "came near" suggests Abraham's hesitation and slow approach to God (18:23). Abraham is bold yet remains respectfully conscious of God's distance. Tactfully, he addresses God with a total of seven questions. Abraham's first question to God is a rhetorical

---

518 See the apparatus of *BHS*; cf. Rashi in Miqraot Gedolot on 18:22.

question: **would You also destroy the righteous with the wicked?** (18:23). Abraham engages God in a bargaining session, moving from the assumption of fifty down to ten. If there were *x* righteous within the city, would God spare it for their sake? Each time God's answer is affirmative: God would spare the place for their sake.

This encounter between Abraham and God presents two stylistic features. The decreasing progression of Abraham's argument to God, from his longest speech in the beginning to his shortest address at the end, using fewer and fewer words denotes his growing hesitancy and increasing consciousness of God's rightness. Abraham's back and forth reference to God (18:25, 30, 32) and to him (18:27, 31) brings out the majesty of God in contrast to the smallness of Abraham (cf. Dan 9:7).

18:24 **Suppose there were fifty righteous within the city**. The choice of the number fifty is not clear. It has been suggested on the basis of Amos 5:3 that fifty stands for half a small city, which contains a minimum of one hundred men (cf. Judg 20:10). Abraham starts his challenge with the assumption of equal numbers of righteous and wicked in the city.

18:25 The event even takes a cosmic turn. Abraham calls God **Judge of all the earth** (18:25).

18:32 **Suppose ten should be found there**. Abraham feels that he has now reached the limit and therefore promises that he will not go beyond that number: **I will speak but once more**. The number ten will be used in Jewish tradition as a symbol of the idea of minimum. The number ten will later be represented by the *yod*, the smallest letter of the Hebrew alphabet (see Matt 5:18). Later the number ten will become in Judaism the minimum required for the worshipping community (*minyan*).[519]

That ten righteous would be enough to save the collective community is a "revolutionary" concept, as pointed out by Gerhard Hasel:

> In an extremely revolutionary manner the old collective thinking, which brought the guiltless member of the guilty association under punishment, has been transposed into something new: the presence of a remnant of righteous people could have a preserving function for the whole … For the sake of the righteous remnant Yahweh would in his *tsedaqah* forgive the wicked city. This notion is widely expanded in the prophetic utterance of the Servant of Yahweh who works salvation for many (Isa 53:5, 10).[520]

18:33 After six responses (18:26, 28–29, 30–32) God abruptly ends His conversation with Abraham. Although God consented to consult with humans, He remains sovereign of His judgment.

19:1–29. VISIT OF ANGELS TO LOT

The new course of events involving Lot parallels in many respects the stories involving Abraham, bringing out the contrast between the two destinies (see the comment on 18:17). The events are situated in time, thus marking the steps of their progression. It is "the evening" (19:1) when the two angels come to Sodom. "Before they lay down" (19:4), the threatening Sodomites surround the house. "When the

---

519 Ber. 6a.

520 Gerhard F. Hasel, *The Remnant: The History and Theology of the Remnant Idea From Genesis to Isaiah,* 2nd ed. (Berrien Springs, MI: Andrews University Press, 1974), 150–151.

morning dawned" (19:15), Lot is pressed to leave the city. "The sun had risen upon the earth" (19:23) when the destruction begins. It is "early in the morning" (19:27) when Abraham returns to the place where he had stood before the Lord.

19:1–3. IN THE EVENING

GEN 19:1–3 NKJV	GEN 19:1–3 ESV
1 Now the two angels came to Sodom in the evening, and Lot was sitting in the gate of Sodom. When Lot saw *them*, he rose to meet them, and he bowed himself with his face toward the ground.	**1** The two angels came to Sodom in the evening, and Lot was sitting in the gate of Sodom. When Lot saw them, he rose to meet them and bowed himself with his face to the earth
2 And he said, "Here now, my lords, please turn in to your servant's house and spend the night, and wash your feet; then you may rise early and go on your way." And they said, "No, but we will spend the night in the open square."	**2** and said, "My lords, please turn aside to your servant's house and spend the night and wash your feet. Then you may rise up early and go on your way." They said, "No; we will spend the night in the town square."
3 But he insisted strongly; so they turned in to him and entered his house. Then he made them a feast, and baked unleavened bread, and they ate.	**3** But he pressed them strongly; so they turned aside to him and entered his house. And he made them a feast and baked unleavened bread, and they ate.

19:1–3 The two angels move speedily. They had just left Abraham in the afternoon after the meal (18:1, 16) and arrived in the evening of the same day at Sodom, which is probably located at the south of the Dead Sea, about forty miles from Mamre, just north of Hebron, a journey that would normally take two days. The encounter between the messengers and Lot reminds us of their encounter with Abraham. This parallel highlights the contrast between the two encounters.

19:1 **Lot was sitting in the gate.** While Abraham is sitting "in the tent door," Lot is sitting "in the gate of Sodom." Abraham is described as a nomad (18:1), while Lot is a sedentary associated with a city. The mention of the gate suggests that Lot may have held an administrative office in Sodom (Deut 21:19; 22:15; Ruth 4:1; Job 5:4), perhaps even as a judge (19:9). While Abraham runs towards the messengers, Lot simply "rose to meet them." Abraham appears to be more eager to meet with the men and more apt to run than his nephew, who does not move easily and may be heavier (19:16, 20). The haste that characterized Abraham is absent here.

19:2 **My lords.** The same plural form is used by Abraham *'adonay* "my lords" in 18:3. While Abraham applies this plural form to only one person, Lot applies the plural form to several persons. This grammatical difference confirms the identity of the Lord in Abraham's address to Him (see the comment on 18:2–3).

19:3 **He insisted strongly.** While the angels immediately accepted Abraham's hospitality (18:5), they turn down Lot's offer, opting to camp outside (19:2), and he has to insist. The Hebrew verb *patsar* will be repeated to describe the Sodomites who "pressed hard" (*patsar*) against the man Lot (19:9). Ironically, Lot's insistence anticipates the Sodomites' insistence. Even Lot's zeal is potentially harmful. Even Lot's meal does not stand in comparison to Abraham's: it is described vaguely as **a feast** and only the unleavened bread is noted, in contrast to the more elaborated description of the meal prepared by Abraham (18:6–8).

19:4–14. IN THE NIGHT

GEN 19:4–14 NKJV	GEN 19:4–14 ESV
4 Now before they lay down, the men of the city, the men of Sodom, both old and young, all the people from every quarter, surrounded the house.	**4** But before they lay down, the men of the city, the men of Sodom, both young and old, all the people to the last man, surrounded the house.
5 And they called to Lot and said to him, "Where are the men who came to you tonight? Bring them out to us that we may know them *carnally*."	**5** And they called to Lot, "Where are the men who came to you tonight? Bring them out to us, that we may know them."
6 So Lot went out to them through the doorway, shut the door behind him,	**6** Lot went out to the men at the entrance, shut the door after him,
7 and said, "Please, my brethren, do not do so wickedly!	**7** and said, "I beg you, my brothers, do not act so wickedly.
8 See now, I have two daughters who have not known a man; please, let me bring them out to you, and you may do to them as you wish; only do nothing to these men, since this is the reason they have come under the shadow of my roof."	**8** Behold, I have two daughters who have not known any man. Let me bring them out to you, and do to them as you please. Only do nothing to these men, for they have come under the shelter of my roof."
9 And they said, "Stand back!" Then they said, "This one came in to stay *here*, and he keeps acting as a judge; now we will deal worse with you than with them." So they pressed hard against the man Lot, and came near to break down the door.	**9** But they said, "Stand back!" And they said, "This fellow came to sojourn, and he has become the judge! Now we will deal worse with you than with them." Then they pressed hard against the man Lot, and drew near to break the door down.
10 But the men reached out their hands and pulled Lot into the house with them, and shut the door.	**10** But the men reached out their hands and brought Lot into the house with them and shut the door.
11 And they struck the men who *were* at the doorway of the house with blindness, both small and great, so that they became weary *trying* to find the door.	**11** And they struck with blindness the men who were at the entrance of the house, both small and great, so that they wore themselves out groping for the door.
12 Then the men said to Lot, "Have you anyone else here? Son-in-law, your sons, your daughters, and whomever you have in the city—take *them* out of this place!	**12** Then the men said to Lot, "Have you anyone else here? Sons-in-law, sons, daughters, or anyone you have in the city, bring them out of the place.
13 For we will destroy this place, because the outcry against them has grown great before the face of the LORD, and the LORD has sent us to destroy it."	**13** For we are about to destroy this place, because the outcry against its people has become great before the LORD, and the LORD has sent us to destroy it."
14 So Lot went out and spoke to his sons-in-law, who had married his daughters, and said, "Get up, get out of this place; for the LORD will destroy this city!" But to his sons-in-law he seemed to be joking.	**14** So Lot went out and said to his sons-in-law, who were to marry his daughters, "Up! Get out of this place, for the LORD is about to destroy the city." But he seemed to his sons-in-law to be jesting.

19:4 **Now before they lay down, the men of the city … surrounded the house.** The men of Sodom waited until the guests were preparing for the night, when they supposedly were the most vulnerable (1 Sam 26:5; Isa 51:20). The idea that the totality of the population became involved in this threatening action is mentioned five times: **the men of the city**, **the men of Sodom**, **both old and young**, **all the people**, **from every quarter**. The word *kol* "all," "every" is repeated. The merism "old and young" is used to imply the idea of totality. This emphasis is intentional to anticipate the total judgment that will fall later. Contrary to what Abraham was hoping in his bargaining with God (18:23–32), there is no exception. Even Lot's sons-in-law may have been involved in this assault (see the comments on 19:14).

19:5 And they called to Lot. The fact that the men of Sodom "called" suggests that they are still at a distance outside, but it may also suggest their passion. They are shouting.

That we may know them. The sexual intention of their request is clearly implied in the verb *yada'* "know," a technical term that often describes sexual intercourse (4:1). The same verb will be used later by Lot with the same meaning, when he refers to his "two daughters who have not known [*yada'*] a man" (19:8). The language clearly refers to the Sodomites' intention to engage in homosexual relations with the men (Jude 7), a practice condemned by Old Testament law as "an abomination" (Lev 18:22). It is because Lot had understood this threat that he offered his daughters in exchange, thinking in his confused set of values that his option was less reprehensible. The wickedness of Sodom became proverbial (Isa 3:9; Lam 4:6; 2 Pet 2:7–10; Jude 7). For Ezekiel, the sexual iniquity of Sodom was associated with wealth, idleness, and a lack of compassion for the poor and needy (Ezek 16:49).

19:6–11 So Lot went out. The description of Lot's reactions is full of irony. First, he shuts the door behind him, which excites the men of Sodom against him. This is precisely the door they are about to break (19:9). Lot behaves like someone who is close to them and feels that as one of them he would be qualified to protect the strangers from them. He is reminded, however, that in spite of his function as a judge (19:9) and all his efforts to fit in and settle in the city, he remains himself a stranger like the other strangers. Lot was never adopted by the clan of Sodom.

Ironically, while Lot meant to protect his guests, it turns out that it is these guests who will **shut the door** behind him (19:10) and thus protect him. The irony is pushed further with the next miracle, which will strike "all" the Sodomites with blindness and make them unable to find the door (19:11). This other merism, this time applied to the size of the Sodomites **small and great,** echoes the one before that was applied to their age **old and young**.

Second, Lot offers his two daughters in place of his two guests, which irritates the Sodomites, who now plan to deal worse with him (19:9). Although Lot shows his hospitality towards his guests, his proposal denotes insensitivity towards his daughters. The deal Lot is negotiating with the Sodomites is highly questionable. Lot is sacrificing his daughters' virginity for the welfare of two strangers. Thus, Lot places himself on the same level as the Sodomites, whom he calls "my brethren" (19:7). Ironically, at the end of the story, Lot will find himself playing the role of sex object he intended to impose on his daughters (19:30–38), although the two conditions are highly incomparable. While Lot will not be aware of his daughters' acts on him, and will be remembered as the ancestor of two nations, his daughters were in full conscience of what would have happened to them and would not have survived rape by an entire city of hostile men.

19:12–13 Have you anyone else here? After this painful experience demonstrating the wickedness of the Sodomites, it is the perfect time for the messengers to announce their forthcoming destruction. Yet, grace precedes justice. Before the destruction, God gives Lot's family members the opportunity to prepare themselves.

It is interesting that the first persons who are mentioned are the **sons-in-law** (19:12). God warns them of the forthcoming destruction and justifies it (19:13).

19:14 So Lot went out. Significantly, Lot has to go out in order to find his sons-in-law. The same verb in the same form *wayyetse'* is used for Lot "went out" to meet with the Sodomites (19:6). This echo suggests that the sons-in-law were sharing the same mentality as "all" the Sodomites. They are located in the same place as the wicked Sodomites. No wonder, then, that they do not take Lot seriously. They find him "funny" (*metsakheq*).

The word *khatan* translated "sons-in-law" does not necessarily refer to a married person; it may simply designate a man who is promised to a woman before their marriage.[521] That seems to be the case since the verb in the participle *loqkhey* "taking" suggests an imminent future. The phrase *loqkhey benotaw* **who had married his daughters** (NKJV) means instead "who were to marry his daughters" (ESV) or "who were pledged to marry his daughters" (NIV). This semantic clarification is consistent with Lot's declaration about his daughters **who have not known a man** (19:8).

19:15–22. AT DAWN

GEN 19:15–22 NKJV	GEN 19:15–22 ESV
15 When the morning dawned, the angels urged Lot to hurry, saying, "Arise, take your wife and your two daughters who are here, lest you be consumed in the punishment of the city."	**15** As morning dawned, the angels urged Lot, saying, "Up! Take your wife and your two daughters who are here, lest you be swept away in the punishment of the city."
16 And while he lingered, the men took hold of his hand, his wife's hand, and the hands of his two daughters, the Lᴏʀᴅ being merciful to him, and they brought him out and set him outside the city.	**16** But he lingered. So the men seized him and his wife and his two daughters by the hand, the Lᴏʀᴅ being merciful to him, and they brought him out and set him outside the city.
17 So it came to pass, when they had brought them outside, that he said, "Escape for your life! Do not look behind you nor stay anywhere in the plain. Escape to the mountains, lest you be destroyed."	**17** And as they brought them out, one said, "Escape for your life. Do not look back or stop anywhere in the valley. Escape to the hills, lest you be swept away."
18 Then Lot said to them, "Please, no, my lords!	**18** And Lot said to them, "Oh, no, my lords.
19 Indeed now, your servant has found favor in your sight, and you have increased your mercy which you have shown me by saving my life; but I cannot escape to the mountains, lest some evil overtake me and I die.	**19** Behold, your servant has found favor in your sight, and you have shown me great kindness in saving my life. But I cannot escape to the hills, lest the disaster overtake me and I die.
20 See now, this city *is* near *enough* to flee to, and it *is* a little one; please let me escape there (*is* it not a little one?) and my soul shall live."	**20** Behold, this city is near enough to flee to, and it is a little one. Let me escape there—is it not a little one?—and my life will be saved!"
21 And he said to him, "See, I have favored you concerning this thing also, in that I will not overthrow this city for which you have spoken.	**21** He said to him, "Behold, I grant you this favor also, that I will not overthrow the city of which you have spoken.
22 Hurry, escape there. For I cannot do anything until you arrive there." Therefore the name of the city was called Zoar.	**22** Escape there quickly, for I can do nothing till you arrive there." Therefore the name of the city was called Zoar.

---

521 See E. Kutsch, "*khtn*," *TDOT* 5:273.

The lightness of the sons-in-law who do not take Lot's information seriously contrasts with the seriousness of the next scene. The messengers urge Lot to leave the place quickly. Paradoxically, even Lot does not seem to realize the gravity and emergency of the situation. While the messengers insist on hurrying, Lot, on the contrary, lingers and negotiates for more time.

19:15 **The morning dawn.** The urgency is already sensed with the first words, which place the action in the earliest moments of the day. The sun has not yet risen. The *shakhar* is the time when the darkness of the night just begins to lighten. The first verb underscores the messengers' call to hurry. The Hebrew verb *'uts* **urge to hurry** implies intense pressure; it is used, for instance, to describe the Egyptian taskmasters who forced the Israelites to hurry to finish their daily quota of work (Exod 5:13).

The first word we hear is the command **arise**, implying that Lot is still in bed and not moving.

Take your wife and your two daughters. The absence of the so-called "sons-in-law" from Lot's house confirms their status of not-yet married (see the comments on 19:14) and indicates that they are not joining the journey. The reminder of the threat, **lest you be consumed**, again suggests that Lot is still hesitating and not fully aware of the danger.

19:16 **While he lingered, the men took**. Lot had just been asked to "take" his wife and his daughters. Lot does not seem to react, since it is the men who **took hold of his hand, his wife's hand, and the hands of his two daughters**. Even Lot himself needs to be taken by hand. The narrative comments that this move pertains to the Lord's mercy. The Hebrew word *khamal* **merciful** referring to God is used to express the idea of pity for the poor man who lost his property (2 Sam 12:4) or for the child exposed on the river (Exod 2:6).

19:17 **Escape … Do not look behind.** Although Lot is brought outside by the men, he is still slow to move. He may be pausing. The word "escape" is given twice: the first time with a positive argument, for the sake of his life; the second time with a negative argument, to avoid destruction. We note the sound play between the Hebrew verb *malat* "escape" and the name of Lot (*lot*). This insistence on the part of the men and their need to repeat their command suggests that Lot is still lingering and taking his time. Even his body language seems to indicate that he is about to look behind, hence the men's warning.

19:18–19 At last, Lot speaks. He has finally recovered his senses. His first word is "no." He uses exactly the same words *'al na'* **Please no!** (19:18) he already used towards the men of Sodom to dissuade them from acting wickedly (cf. 19:7).

Although the narrative reports that Lot is addressing a plural—"Lot said to them"—the following sentence clarifies that he is actually speaking to the Lord. He now shifts to the singular and uses language that reminds us of Abraham's first response to the Lord, with the same shift from the plural to the singular:

18:2–3: "to meet them … My Lord [*'adonay*], if I have now found favor in Your sight [masc. sing.] … Your servant [masc. sing.]"
19:18–19: "said to them … my lords [*'adonay*] your servant [*'abdkha*, masc. sing.) has found favor in your sight [*be'eyneyka*, masc. sing.]"

Lot is subtly blaming God for the evil he is enduring. He identifies God with the wicked Sodomites. Then, it seems that Lot realizes his arrogance, and his tone becomes more humble. For the first time, he calls himself "your servant" (19:19) and acknowledges his debt to the One who saved his life.

The language Lot uses indicates that he has God in mind. This association of words, *gadal* "great" and *khesed* "grace," is always related to God (Pss 57:11; 86:13; 145:8; 1 Kgs 3:6). The verb *khay* in the causative form (*hiphil*, "to make alive"), here translated "saving my life," normally applies to God (45:7; 2 Kgs 5:7; Isa 57:15; Ezek 13:18).

But Lot's words of gratefulness are only diplomatic. They precede his request for God to spare him from going to the mountains. This, however, was God's plan for him, since the mountains were the only place that had not yet been contaminated by the iniquities of the plains. Lot is not really worried about the iniquity of the place. He prefers to remain in the plains, either because the mountains are too far away, or simply because the plains demand less effort, less faith, and are immediately reward-ing (13:10–12). Lot claims that he is afraid that an "evil" (*ra'ah*) would catch him. But he used the same word *ra'ah* "evil," wickedness" to refer to the "evil" of the people of the plains (19:7).

19:20–22 Lot's argument is pathetic. The city where he wants to flee is just *mits'ar* **a little one**. Obviously, Lot is bargaining with God, just like his uncle Abra-ham. There is one important difference, however. Whereas Abraham is concerned with the salvation of the city for the sake of the righteous living there, Lot is con-cerned only with himself, with his own little happiness. Righteousness is not an issue for him. Lot is fully aware of the iniquity pervading that "little" city. But it is not because there are some righteous people there that the city deserves God's pity but simply because it is just "a little one." The degree of sin is not as large as in the other cities, not because there is less sin, but because of the population; it is a little city.

19:21 **I have favored you.** The Hebrew phrase *nasa' panim* "have favor" is an idiomatic expression referring to God's acceptance and forgiveness. The same phrase is used by God to promise gracious forgiveness to Cain (4:7) and is a part of the priestly benediction, "The Lord lift up His countenance [*nasa' panim*] upon you" (Num 6:26). God may bless and forgive even the one who does not deserve to be blessed and accepted. To the other graces, God adds that one **also**. God's grace is always a supplement, a surplus, something that is beyond and above what is normally expected.

19:22 The story ends as it began (19:15) with an imperative: **hurry, escape**. The first imperative marked the beginning of Lot's move "arise." The last imperative marks the end of Lot's journey, his arrival to safety: "escape." The Hebrew verb *malat* "escape" has already occurred several times, for a total of five times in the passage (19:17 [2x], 19–20, 22). Amazingly, God makes His action dependent on Lot's move, **I cannot do anything until you arrive there** (19:22). Just before Lot arrives in the "little" city, the name of the city **Zoar** (*tso'ar*) is given. The name resonates with the words "little" (*mits'ar*) that punctuated Lot's bargain with God. Humans are part of God's decision, even in their littleness. And God comes down and makes Himself little to accommodate them and to save them. The "I cannot" (*lo' 'ukhal*) of grace of the Lord corresponds ironically to the "I cannot" (*lo' 'ukhal*) of the limitation of Lot (19:19).

19:23–26. AFTER SUNRISE

GEN 19:23–26 NKJV	GEN 19:23–26 ESV
23 The sun had risen upon the earth when Lot entered Zoar.	**23** The sun had risen on the earth when Lot came to Zoar.
24 Then the LORD rained brimstone and fire on Sodom and Gomorrah, from the LORD out of the heavens.	**24** Then the LORD rained on Sodom and Gomorrah sulfur and fire from the LORD out of heaven.
25 So He overthrew those cities, all the plain, all the inhabitants of the cities, and what grew on the ground.	**25** And he overthrew those cities, and all the valley, and all the inhabitants of the cities, and what grew on the ground.
26 But his wife looked back behind him, and she became a pillar of salt.	**26** But Lot's wife, behind him, looked back, and she became a pillar of salt.

19:23 Lot enters Zoar when the sun rises, barely half an hour after dawn (19:15). Often sunrise marks new beginnings and the promise of a glorious future (32:31). Here the sunrise is deceptive. The arrival of Lot the refugee inaugurates the terrible destruction.

19:24–26 The account of the destruction is relatively short, only three verses sandwiched between eight verses reporting the preparation of Lot's escape (19:15–22) and three verses commenting on his actual deliverance (19:27–29). The intention of this structural organization is to emphasize that salvation is more important than destruction. Instead of describing the course of events, the narrative focuses on three ideas: first, the Lord is the author of the destruction (19:24); second, the destruction is complete (19:25); and third, there is an unfortunate collateral result—Lot's wife is lost in the process (19:26).

19:24 The Lord rained … from the Lord. The report insists that it is the Lord who "rained." So far there has been no reference to the Lord; this is the first time that He is explicitly mentioned. The grammar and the style of the text reflect this emphasis. The subject, "the Lord," is put at the beginning of the sentence and is repeated toward the end of the line in a chiastic fashion. Although the destruction involves natural agents, God takes total responsibility for the manifestation of judgment. He is the One who operates the destruction.

The same verb *himtir* "cause to rain" is used to describe the flood, "I will cause it to rain [*himtir*] on the earth" (7:4; cf. 2:5). The judgment against Sodom and Gomorrah is thus related to the judgment of the flood. Interestingly, the first occurrence of the verb is found in the context of the second creation story to inform us that the Lord had not yet "caused it to rain" (2:5). While this specification is an indication of the way the ground was watered (not by rain but by the rising mist), it is also an allusion to the first rain of the flood. The One who "caused to rain" the water of the flood and the fire on Sodom is the Creator Himself.

The allusion to creation suggests a difficult theological lesson: Paradoxically, this destruction, an expression of the divine judgment, is associated with the idea of creation. The same paradigm was present in the event of the flood (see the comments on 6:17 and 8:1). The same lesson will be heard again in the eschatological promise of the creation of the new earth and the new heavens, which will necessarily entail that "the former shall not be remembered or come to mind" (Isa 65:17), "for the first heaven and the first earth had passed away" (Rev 21:1).

19:25 So He overthrew those cities. The verb *hapak* "overthrow" occurs several times in the passage (19:21, 25, 29). It becomes the key term associated with the destruction of Sodom in biblical memory, reappearing in the classic expression *kemahpekat-sedom* "like the overthrow of Sodom" (Deut 29:23; Amos 4:11; Isa 13:19; cf. 1:7; Jer 49:19). The specific phrase *wayyahapok* "He overthrew" with the Lord as subject is used to refer to God reversing the wind of the locusts back to the Red Sea (Exod 10:19) and reversing the curse of Balaam into a blessing (Deut 23:5).

What characterizes the event of Sodom is the phenomenon of reversal. Just as the flood is a reversal of creation (see the comments on 6:7), the destruction of Sodom is a reversal of the Garden of Eden (13:10). This overthrow is total and concerns all aspects (the word "all" is used twice): cities, plains, inhabitants, and plants. At the same time, this overthrow anticipates creation. The destruction is necessary for the new creation to take place, just as it was necessary for the flood and will be necessary for the future eschatological salvation.

19:26 But his wife. The grammar of the phrase suggests a contrast that implies that Lot's wife's actions run contrary to the normal course of events, which are designed for her deliverance. She looks back behind her husband's back, doing exactly what the messenger had warned Lot not to do, and as he intended to (19:17). His wife, "on the other hand," looked back, because she already missed the place and the culture she was leaving. It was a part of herself she was losing. She would have liked the past to last longer; therefore, she became frozen in that past. Because she identified with Sodom she became like Sodom: **a pillar of salt**. The prophet Isaiah will warn his contemporaries of the same danger: if they identify with the evil city, they will ultimately become "like Sodom" (Isa 1:9).

19:27–29. EARLY IN THE MORNING

GEN 19:27–29 NKJV	GEN 19:27–29 ESV
27 And Abraham went early in the morning to the place where he had stood before the Lᴏʀᴅ.	**27** And Abraham went early in the morning to the place where he had stood before the Lᴏʀᴅ.
28 Then he looked toward Sodom and Gomorrah, and toward all the land of the plain; and he saw, and behold, the smoke of the land which went up like the smoke of a furnace.	**28** And he looked down toward Sodom and Gomorrah and toward all the land of the valley, and he looked and, behold, the smoke of the land went up like the smoke of a furnace.
29 And it came to pass, when God destroyed the cities of the plain, that God remembered Abraham, and sent Lot out of the midst of the overthrow, when He overthrew the cities in which Lot had dwelt.	**29** So it was that, when God destroyed the cities of the valley, God remembered Abraham and sent Lot out of the midst of the overthrow when he overthrew the cities in which Lot had lived.

19:27–29 And Abraham went early in the morning. This is the next "early morning," after another night has passed. The overthrow of Sodom is finished. What Abraham sees as he looks toward Sodom and Gomorrah is just **the smoke of the land** (19:28).

Abraham and not Lot notes the denouement of the whole event. This is surprising and theologically meaningful. First, it shows once again the passivity of

Lot who simply endures the tragedy and seems to ignore the turn of events. Only Abraham is here, as if he is the only one awake and following events. The main reason, however, for his presence has to do with his personal involvement in that judgment.

Significantly, the scene takes place **where he had stood before the Lord** (19:27) and pleaded for God to save the city for the sake of the righteous in it (18:23–32). The passage concludes with this important information, which resonates with that former discussion. Lot was saved, not because of his merits, but for the sake of the righteous—because **God remembered Abraham** (19:29). The contrast between the Abraham now and the Abraham then is striking. Then Abraham was loquacious. Now he is silent.

19:30–38. BIRTH FROM LOT'S DAUGHTERS WITH LOT

GEN 19:30–38 NKJV	GEN 19:30–38 ESV
30 Then Lot went up out of Zoar and dwelt in the mountains, and his two daughters were with him; for he was afraid to dwell in Zoar. And he and his two daughters dwelt in a cave.	**30** Now Lot went up out of Zoar and lived in the hills with his two daughters, for he was afraid to live in Zoar. So he lived in a cave with his two daughters.
31 Now the firstborn said to the younger, "Our father *is* old, and *there is* no man on the earth to come in to us as is the custom of all the earth.	**31** And the firstborn said to the younger, "Our father is old, and there is not a man on earth to come in to us after the manner of all the earth.
32 Come, let us make our father drink wine, and we will lie with him, that we may preserve the lineage of our father."	**32** Come, let us make our father drink wine, and we will lie with him, that we may preserve offspring from our father."
33 So they made their father drink wine that night. And the firstborn went in and lay with her father, and he did not know when she lay down or when she arose.	**33** So they made their father drink wine that night. And the firstborn went in and lay with her father. He did not know when she lay down or when she arose.
34 It happened on the next day that the firstborn said to the younger, "Indeed I lay with my father last night; let us make him drink wine tonight also, and you go in *and* lie with him, that we may preserve the lineage of our father."	**34** The next day, the firstborn said to the younger, "Behold, I lay last night with my father. Let us make him drink wine tonight also. Then you go in and lie with him, that we may preserve offspring from our father."
35 Then they made their father drink wine that night also. And the younger arose and lay with him, and he did not know when she lay down or when she arose.	**35** So they made their father drink wine that night also. And the younger arose and lay with him, and he did not know when she lay down or when she arose.
36 Thus both the daughters of Lot were with child by their father.	**36** Thus both the daughters of Lot became pregnant by their father.
37 The firstborn bore a son and called his name Moab; he *is* the father of the Moabites to this day.	**37** The firstborn bore a son and called his name Moab. He is the father of the Moabites to this day.
38 And the younger, she also bore a son and called his name Ben-Ammi; he *is* the father of the people of Ammon to this day.	**38** The younger also bore a son and called his name Ben-ammi. He is the father of the Ammonites to this day.

Lot's story began like Abraham's story with the visit of the messengers of the Lord. The final episode of Lot's story parallels the final episode of Abraham's story. Both men wind up with the same prospect of births.

Yet, the difference between the two accounts is important. While in Abraham's case the Lord is present and is the One who initiates the promise of birth, in Lot's case the Lord is absent and the promise of birth is initiated by his daughters. While Abraham's case is concerned with only one birth and is for a later time, in Lot's case the births are plural and immediate. While Abraham is active and even challenges the Lord's views, Lot again is passive, drunk, and unaware of what is happening to him. As soon as Lot is settled in the mountains (19:30), his two daughters conceive schemes to obtain children by him (19:31–32). The story of the births progresses rapidly and evolves smoothly, involving successively the first and the second daughters (19:33–35). Eventually, both daughters bear a son (19:36–38).

19:30 Ironically, the story reports that Lot **was afraid to dwell in Zoar** and is now forced to leave the place he had begged the angel to save (19:20). He settles **in the mountains**, the place where he had asked not to go (19:19). The events confirm the rightness of God's judgment about Zoar and oblige Lot to finally fulfill God's original plan (19:17).

19:31–32 The firstborn said to the younger, Our father is old. As the firstborn, the daughter feels her responsibility to preserve the lineage of her father (19:32). She repeats the argument, the first time as a general principle (19:32), the second time to encourage her sister when her turn comes (19:34). She is concerned because her father is old and because there is no man available (19:31).

The first reason was given by Sarah to justify her skepticism regarding the promise of birth (18:12). While for Sarah Abraham's old age becomes the occasion for God's wonder to take place, for Lot's daughter it is the excuse to commit incest with her father. Faith in God has no place in the whole scenario. Lot's daughters are only relying on themselves. The form of the verbs in their discourse reminds us of the conversation between the men of Babel: **Come, let us make** (19:32; cf. 11:3).

The second reason—that **there is no man on the earth**—is even more questionable. The destruction only affected a limited part of the earth and there were other inhabitants present on the planet as well as the rest of Abraham's family. But the daughters do not even consider that option. Although they had been engaged to Sodomite men, they prefer incest over having to allow "other" men from outside the clan to mingle in their lineage. This attitude not only implies that the Sodomites were well accepted into their Lot clan, it also suggests that the daughters were not open to other relationships outside their Lot-Sodomite clan.

The same way of thinking, the refusal of the difference, is a mark of the homosexual choice. The new sin of incest is congruent with the Sodomite lifestyle and shows how well adjusted and experienced in that culture Lot's daughters had become. Both practices were clearly regarded as wrong in the ANE and in the Hebrew Bible (Lev 20:12–13).

The fact that Lot's daughters had to resort to the use of wine in order to achieve their schemes shows that they knew very well that they were breaking the law and that their father would not have approved. While the context of Sodom may explain the behavior and the perverted choice of Lot's two daughters, it also brings out the irony of the situation. The angels had rescued the two virgin daughters from the

259

hands of the Sodomites, that they may save their virginity and the father's honor. Now when there is no more danger, they are ready to sacrifice their virginity and their father's honor.

19:33–35 So they made. They do as they had planned, without any hesitation, immediately, "that night" (19:33). The flow of the narrative suggests that the events are fulfilled without any obstacle or any thinking; the daughters act mechanically. The younger daughter replicates what the older daughter did, as suggested by the exact repetition of the same phrases (19:33; cf. 19:35).

19:36–38 Thus both the daughters of Lot were with child. The whole enterprise is successful. Both daughters give birth to sons. Lot is completely passive in the whole process. Even the names of the sons are given by the two daughters against the normal practice (16:15; 21:3). The first name "Moab" ("from the father") reminds us of the incestuous origin of this birth. The second name "Ben-Ammi" ("son of my people") reveals the secret intention of the two daughters to stay within their clan (see above).

SOJOURN IN GERAR (20–21)

The journey to Gerar echoes the one to Egypt (12:10–20) with the same association of verbs "journey" (*nasa*') and "sojourn" (*gar*) as in Genesis 12:9–10. The parallel between the two introductions anticipates similar experiences. Indeed, the two narratives, in spite of some significant differences, parallel each other with the same motifs and follow more or less the same sequence of events: Abraham's lie regarding his relationship, presenting his wife as his sister (20:2; cf. 12:13); the abduction of Sarah (20:1–2; cf. 12:14–15); divine punishment (20:3, 17–18; cf. 12:17); gifts offered to Abraham (20:14; cf. 12:16); Abraham's sojourn in Canaan (21:34; cf. 13:1); the birth of Isaac (21:1–7; cf. 15:1–6); the departure of Hagar and Ishmael (21:8–21); a covenant between Abraham and a Canaanite king (21:22–34; cf. 14:18–24).

20:1–18. ABRAHAM AND ABIMELECH

Abraham relapses into the same faithless and deceitful behavior. He has forgotten the lessons of the past and is not acting consistently with the high spiritual image he has just projected. While this failure is surprising, it creates, on the brink of the birth of Isaac, great suspense in regard to the fulfillment of God's promise.

The story is shaped according to the following chiastic structure:

A Abduction of Sarah by Abimelech (20:1–2)
    B God's threat against Abimelech (20:3–7)
        C Fear of God (20:8)
    B₁ Abimelech's threat against Abraham (20:9–13)
A₁ Restoration of Sarah and Abimelech (20:14–18)

20:1–2. ABDUCTION OF SARAH

GEN 20:1–2 NKJV	GEN 20:1–2 ESV
1 And Abraham journeyed from there to the South, and dwelt between Kadesh and Shur, and stayed in Gerar.	1 From there Abraham journeyed toward the territory of the Negeb and lived between Kadesh and Shur; and he sojourned in Gerar.
2 Now Abraham said of Sarah his wife, "She *is* my sister." And Abimelech king of Gerar sent and took Sarah.	2 And Abraham said of Sarah his wife, "She is my sister." And Abimelech king of Gerar sent and took Sarah.

20:1 Abraham … sojourned in Gerar (ESV). In contrast to Lot who moves with the intention to "dwell" (*yashab*) (19:30), Abraham intends to "sojourn" (*gar*) in the place where he dwells (*yashab*) (20:1). The sound play between the words *gar* "sojourn" and the name of the place *gerar* "Gerar," located on the southeastern border of Canaan (10:19), emphasizes again the moving destiny of Abraham.

While Abraham's journey to Egypt is justified—"there was a famine in the land"— (12:10), no reason is given for Abraham's journey to Gerar. The fact, however, that Abraham chose to sojourn "in the land of the Philistines many days" (21:34) suggests that he felt comfortable there and related well with the people of the land.

20:2 She is my sister. Abraham once again lies in order to gain protection against Abimelech, as he did against the pharaoh of Egypt. The repetition of his mistake does not mean that the biblical text is made of two different sources, as it is argued by some critical scholars. Not only does this echo belong to the literary intention to parallel with the previous story (see above), it also simply witnesses to the human frailty of Abraham. Apparently, Abraham did not learn his lesson from his previous experience, namely, that lying will not help but will instead worsen his condition. Either after twenty-five years (12:4; cf. 21:5) he had forgotten, or his evaluation of the situation was more convincing to him than his faith in God. Abraham was not naïve; he tended to be skeptical (15:2; 17:17–18) and even ready to challenge God (18:22–32).

Abimelech sent and took Sarah. *Abimelech*, meaning "Melech is my father" or "the king is my father," recurs in Genesis 26. It is a title name, referring to his function as ruler, the equivalent of Pharaoh in Egypt or even Melchizedek for the city of Salem (see the comments on 14:18–24). That Sarah was abducted for the harem of a king is strange. She was sixty-five years old when she was taken by Pharaoh and could, at that time, still be beautiful. Now she is ninety years old.

Two explanations have been proposed to solve this incongruity. The ancient rabbis of the Talmud assumed the difficulty of the story and attributed Sarah's attractiveness to the miracle of her imminent pregnancy.[522] Other more natural explanations have been suggested, referring to socioeconomic considerations and to Abimelech's motive to strengthen his relationship with the powerful clan of Abraham. While the political consideration may have played a role in Sarah's abduction (21:22–34), it does not eliminate the possibility of Sarah's real beauty, which was the main reason for Abraham's first lie (12:11). Abimelech, like Pharaoh, did not know how old Sarah was, and the fact that God had to intervene in order to keep Abimelech from touching her (20:6) suggests that Abimelech's intentions were more than mere

---

522 b. Bava Metsi'a, 87a.

cold economical calculations. Sarah still had forty years to live, which implies that she could be considered young by our standards.

20:3–7. GOD'S THREAT AGAINST ABIMELECH

GEN 20:3–7 NKJV	GEN 20:3–7 ESV
3 But God came to Abimelech in a dream by night, and said to him, "Indeed you *are* a dead man because of the woman whom you have taken, for she *is* a man's wife."	**3** But God came to Abimelech in a dream by night and said to him, "Behold, you are a dead man because of the woman whom you have taken, for she is a man's wife."
4 But Abimelech had not come near her; and he said, "Lord, will You slay a righteous nation also?	**4** Now Abimelech had not approached her. So he said, "Lord, will you kill an innocent people?
5 Did he not say to me, 'She *is* my sister'? And she, even she herself said, 'He *is* my brother.' In the integrity of my heart and innocence of my hands I have done this."	**5** Did he not himself say to me, 'She *is* my sister'? And she herself said, 'He *is* my brother.' In the integrity of my heart and the innocence of my hands I have done this."
6 And God said to him in a dream, "Yes, I know that you did this in the integrity of your heart. For I also withheld you from sinning against Me; therefore I did not let you touch her.	**6** Then God said to him in the dream, "Yes, I know that you have done this in the integrity of your heart, and it was I who kept you from sinning against me. Therefore I did not let you touch her.
7 Now therefore, restore the man's wife; for he *is* a prophet, and he will pray for you and you shall live. But if you do not restore *her,* know that you shall surely die, you and all who *are* yours."	**7** Now then, return the man's wife, for he is a prophet, so that he will pray for you, and you shall live. But if you do not return her, know that you shall surely die, you and all who are yours."

20:3 **God came to Abimelech in a dream by night.** The same language is used in relation to Laban (31:24) and Balaam (Num 22:20). In both cases, just as for Abimelech, God reveals Himself through a dream by night to an outsider to save His people. In this instance, it is God's very promise of a son to Abraham through Sarah that is in jeopardy, hence, God's dramatic threat, **you are a dead man**.

The Hebrew phrase means literally "you are about to die." Abimelech needs to understand the urgency of the situation. He does not need a lesson about the iniquity of adultery. He recognizes it as iniquity, as it is generally the case in the ANE and in the Mosaic legislation (Deut 22:22). What matters most at this stage for Abimelech is not so much understanding that he has acted wrongly but that he has to be stopped.

20:4–5 **But Abimelech had not come near her.** This observation by the author clears Abimelech of the charge of adultery. The expression "come near" (*qarab*) is used to describe illicit sexual relations (Lev 18:6, 14). Furthermore, this declaration of innocence observed by the author is confirmed by Abimelech who speaks to God like Abraham (18:31) and has the same concern for the righteous as Abraham (18:23–32), except that he has the kind of righteousness Abraham was pleading for (20:4; cf. 18:23). Abimelech affirms his innocence. The reason for Abimelech's move towards Sarah is that not only Abraham but also Sarah herself had lied to him (20:5). In this instance, Abimelech is the one who is righteous, and not Abraham nor Sarah. As far as he is concerned, he is completely pure in his heart and intentions as well as in his hands and actions (20:5).

20:6–7 Through the repetition of the supernatural communication, Abimelech's innocence is reaffirmed by the God who knows the heart: **I know that you did this in the integrity of your heart** (20:6). Yet even then, Abimelech has no merit from his innocence, for it is God Himself who prevented him from committing sin. Even when we resist sin and are tempted to boast about our righteousness, we should remember that it is God who enabled us to overcome and thus helped us to remain in the right.

Yet it is not enough for Abimelech to be righteous, even if it was God Himself who had so declared him righteous. Abimelech has to return Sarah to Abraham. It is also important that we repair the mistake we made, even if we did it innocently, even if we were not aware of the problem, and even if we were deceived into it. Sin remains a sin even if we did not intend to do it. The reason given to Abimelech sounds like an irony. Although Abimelech was treated like a prophet, he now learns that it is Abraham who is the prophet and that he will in fact owe his salvation to him, since Abraham will pray for him.

The Hebrew word *nabi'* for **prophet** (20:7) is used here for the first time in the Scriptures. This does not mean that there was no prophecy before that time. Rather, this first occurrence suggests that an emphasis on the special prophetic calling of Abraham is intended. The word *nabi'* "prophet" is a passive derived from the Akkadian root *nabu* "to call." *Nabi'* means "the one who is called (by God) to speak on God's behalf (Exod 4:16; 7:1) and thus function as His mediator (Num 12:1–2)."

The rabbis who translated the Septuagint rendered the Hebrew word *nabi'* by the Greek word *prophetes*. This refers to the person who stood as the mediator between the god and the people to communicate the will and revelation of the god. Abraham in that sense is the prophet par excellence, since he will become the mediator between God and the nations. Through him, God will reveal Himself, and thus all the nations will be blessed. This includes the nation (*goy*) of Abimelech, which is here mentioned (20:4; cf. 12:1–3).

Abimelech and his nation owe their salvation to the future birth of the son promised to Abraham and Sarah. Had Abimelech engaged in sexual relationships with Sarah, God's project would have been compromised; Isaac would not have been born. This is why God's warning is so strong. The formula is the same as God's threat to Adam, *mut tamut* "you shall surely die" (2:17), and is also used to signify capital punishment (Exod 21:16).

20:8. FEAR OF GOD

GEN 20:8 NKJV	GEN 20:8 ESV
8 So Abimelech rose early in the morning, called all his servants, and told all these things in their hearing; and the men were very much afraid.	8 So Abimelech rose early in the morning and called all his servants and told them all these things. And the men were very much afraid.

Abimelech as well as his people take God's warning seriously: **Abimelech rose early in the morning**, a move that indicates zeal to respond to God (22:3). As for the people who heard Abimelech, it is reported that they **were very much afraid**, a phrase that describes great anxiety for what is about to happen (Exod 14:10; cf. 1 Sam 17:24).

This reference to the "fear of God" marks the apex, the center of the chiastic structure, an indication of the emphasis of the passage. The "fear of God" was found in the very place where Abraham had suspected it would not be (20:11). This lesson of humility and tolerance should be meditated on by all religious people. Sometimes the Gentile and the nonbeliever may have more fear of God than the man or the woman of God in religious communities may anticipate.

20:9–13. ABIMELECH'S THREAT AGAINST ABRAHAM

GEN 20:9–13 NKJV	GEN 20:9–13 ESV
9 And Abimelech called Abraham and said to him, "What have you done to us? How have I offended you, that you have brought on me and on my kingdom a great sin? You have done deeds to me that ought not to be done."	**9** Then Abimelech called Abraham and said to him, "What have you done to us? And how have I sinned against you, that you have brought on me and my kingdom a great sin? You have done to me things that ought not to be done."
10 Then Abimelech said to Abraham, "What did you have in view, that you have done this thing?"	**10** And Abimelech said to Abraham, "What did you see, that you did this thing?"
11 And Abraham said, "Because I thought, surely the fear of God *is* not in this place; and they will kill me on account of my wife.	**11** Abraham said, "I did it because I thought, 'There is no fear of God at all in this place, and they will kill me because of my wife.'
12 But indeed *she is* truly my sister. She *is* the daughter of my father, but not the daughter of my mother; and she became my wife.	**12** Besides, she is indeed my sister, the daughter of my father though not the daughter of my mother, and she became my wife.
13 And it came to pass, when God caused me to wander from my father's house, that I said to her, 'This *is* your kindness that you should do for me: in every place, wherever we go, say of me, "He *is* my brother."'"	**13** And when God caused me to wander from my father's house, I said to her, 'This is the kindness you must do me: at every place to which we come, say of me, "He is my brother."'"

20:9–13 The vertical dialogue between God and Abimelech shifts to the horizontal dialogue between Abimelech and Abraham: **And Abimelech called Abraham** (20:9). Biblical religion is not made up only of our relationship with God, it should also affect our relationships with other humans. God cannot forgive Abimelech as long as he has not settled his problem with Abraham and Sarah. The same principle is implied in the Lord's Prayer: "Forgive us our debts, as we forgive our debtors" (Matt 6:12). Abimelech's behavior conforms to the moral laws of the Bible, which enjoin us to meet with our neighbors so that we may forgive them and not bear a grudge against them (Lev 19:17; cf. Matt 18:15).

The pagan Abimelech shows more righteousness than the man of God. While Abimelech confronts Abraham openly, with direct questions to know Abraham's true intentions (20:9–10), Abraham remains elusive, justifying himself by referring to his unfounded suspicions (20:11) and his half lie about his sister-wife (20:12–13). While Abimelech displays integrity, courage, and generosity, Abraham appears to be cowardly, deceptive, and calculating.

Outside of the church and our religious community, in the world, there may be people with more noble characters than inside. This observation warns us against spiritual pride and a spirit of superiority that some Christians may be tempted to entertain toward the outsider who does not share the same faith. At the same time, we are reminded that God had chosen Abraham, not because of his qualities, but in spite of his human imperfections. The honest description of Abraham, which does not ignore his flaws and his mistakes, is a mark of the authenticity of the text.

20:14–18. RESTORATION OF SARAH AND ABIMELECH

GEN 20:14–18 NKJV	GEN 20:14–18 ESV
14 Then Abimelech took sheep, oxen, and male and female servants, and gave *them* to Abraham; and he restored Sarah his wife to him.	**14** Then Abimelech took sheep and oxen, and male servants and female servants, and gave them to Abraham, and returned Sarah his wife to him.
15 And Abimelech said, "See, my land *is* before you; dwell where it pleases you."	**15** And Abimelech said, "Behold, my land is before you; dwell where it pleases you."
16 Then to Sarah he said, "Behold, I have given your brother a thousand *pieces* of silver; indeed this vindicates you before all who *are* with you and before everybody." Thus she was rebuked.	**16** To Sarah he said, "Behold, I have given your brother a thousand pieces of silver. It is a sign of your innocence in the eyes of all who are with you, and before everyone you are vindicated."
17 So Abraham prayed to God; and God healed Abimelech, his wife, and his female servants. Then they bore *children*;	**17** Then Abraham prayed to God, and God healed Abimelech, and also healed his wife and female slaves so that they bore children.
18 for the Lord had closed up all the wombs of the house of Abimelech because of Sarah, Abraham's wife.	**18** For the Lord had closed all the wombs of the house of Abimelech because of Sarah, Abraham's wife.

Abimelech does not content himself with talking to Abraham and rebuking him. Having heard Abraham's explanations he now wants to reassure him concretely of his good disposition.

20:14 Abimelech took sheep. The list of Abimelech's gifts to Abraham recalls Pharaoh's gifts (12:16), except that donkeys and camels are missing here. Not that Abimelech is less generous than Pharaoh. The additional gifts, the land and the money (see below), suggest the contrary. The reason for this omission may be simply that Abraham is no longer the nomad he was when he came to Egypt. He, therefore, does not need so many donkeys and camels now, for these animals are used rather for bearing burdens and transportation. Abraham is progressively passing to the sedentary stage, as indicated in Abimelech's gift of land.

He restored Sarah his wife. The specification "his wife" suggests Abimelech's recognition of Sarah's status, which was not affected by her sojourn in his house. Sarah had remained "Abraham's wife," a guarantee that she will still give birth to Abraham's promised son.

20:15 See, my land is before you; dwell where it pleases you. Abimelech's language is an invitation to Abraham to settle and "dwell" (*sheb*). This gift marks a fundamental difference from the gifts offered by Pharaoh. While Pharaoh was anxious to see Abraham move away, outside of his land, Abimelech offers his land. The association of the restoration of Sarah, who will give birth to a son, with the gift of the land, anticipates the twofold fulfillment of God's promise. It also contains legal legitimation for Abraham to settle in Canaan. While the land is God's gift to Abraham, it is also spontaneously offered by the native Abimelech and not violently taken from him.

20:16 I have given your brother a thousand pieces of silver. "Your brother," rather than "your husband," reminds Sarah of her duplicity. A thousand pieces of silver is a considerable sum of money, considering that one hundred is the price for a piece of land (33:19). The purpose of that money is to serve as some kind of compensation, **a covering of the eyes** for the embarrassing situation. The author comments that Sarah is then completely restored in her righteousness. The very fact that the money is given to Abraham and not to Sarah indicates Abimelech's recognition of Abraham as her husband.

20:17-18 So Abraham prayed to God. The restoration of Sarah's righteousness is followed by Abraham's prayer on behalf of Abimelech and God's healing of Abimelech and his wife, to allow them to bear children. The connection is explicitly stated: it is because of Sarah, who is explicitly qualified as **Abraham's wife,** that the house of Abimelech had been affected with sterility (20:17). Note that this qualification points to God's promise when Sarah was for the first time called Abraham's wife (15:4). This last observation anticipates the next story of Sarah giving birth.

The two miracles are interdependent, suggesting an interesting theological lesson: although these miracles are the manifestation of God's grace, they nevertheless work within the parameters of human righteousness. God's forgiveness of Abimelech depends on Abimelech's forgiveness of Abraham, and God's forgiveness of Abraham depends on Abraham's forgiveness of Abimelech (Matt 6:12).

21:1-7. THE BIRTH OF ISAAC

GEN 21:1-7 NKJV	GEN 21:1-7 ESV
1 And the LORD visited Sarah as He had said, and the LORD did for Sarah as He had spoken.	**1** The LORD visited Sarah as he had said, and the LORD did to Sarah as he had promised.
2 For Sarah conceived and bore Abraham a son in his old age, at the set time of which God had spoken to him.	**2** And Sarah conceived and bore Abraham a son in his old age at the time of which God had spoken to him.
3 And Abraham called the name of his son who was born to him—whom Sarah bore to him—Isaac.	**3** Abraham called the name of his son who was born to him, whom Sarah bore him, Isaac.
4 Then Abraham circumcised his son Isaac when he was eight days old, as God had commanded him.	**4** And Abraham circumcised his son Isaac when he was eight days old, as God had commanded him.
5 Now Abraham was one hundred years old when his son Isaac was born to him.	**5** Abraham was a hundred years old when his son Isaac was born to him.
6 And Sarah said, "God has made me laugh, *and* all who hear will laugh with me."	**6** And Sarah said, "God has made laughter for me; everyone who hears will laugh over me."
7 She also said, "Who would have said to Abraham that Sarah would nurse children? For I have borne *him* a son in his old age."	**7** And she said, "Who would have said to Abraham that Sarah would nurse children? Yet I have borne him a son in his old age."

The announcement of the birth of Isaac is given as a fulfillment. This idea of fulfillment is emphasized several times and in diverse manners.

21:1 The event is described in reference to a past promise: **the Lord visited.** The Hebrew verb *paqad* "visit" (21:1a) has the connotation of "remembering" (see

Jer 3:16). That God remembers implies a divine word from the past, which is explicitly referred to and repeated, **as He had said**, **as He had spoken**. The announcement of the birth of Isaac was first given some twenty-five years earlier (12:4) and after that was regularly recalled (13:16; 15:4–5; 17:15–16; cf. 18:10).

21:2 At the set time. Even the time had been mentioned previously to Abraham, since it is a **time of which God had spoken to him**.

21:3 The name "Isaac" given by Abraham (21:3) responds to God's former injunction, "you shall call his name Isaac" (17:19).

21:4–5 The time element is again underlined in regard to the circumcision, when Isaac **was eight days old** (21:4). Here also the practice refers to a past divine word, **as God had commanded him** (21:4). The mention of Abraham's age at that particular moment **one hundred years** (21:5) reinforces this focus on time.

21:6–7 Likewise Sarah evokes her past reaction (and Abraham's) when she comments on the verb **laugh** (*tsakhaq*) contained in the name "Isaac" (21:6–7; cf. 17:17; 18:12). This latest reference to "laughter," however, takes on a new meaning. While Sarah's past laughter expressed doubt and incredulity, this time laughter is a gift from God (21:6). It expresses God's grace and is therefore a laughter of gratefulness and joy (Pss 113:9; 126:2). Thus, Sarah's exclamation *mi millel* **who would have said?** (21:7) is to be understood as an expression of wonder, as is the case in the similar expression, "who can utter [*mi yemallel*] the mighty acts of the Lord" (Ps 106:2).

21:8–21. DEPARTURE OF HAGAR AND ISHMAEL

The story of the birth of Isaac is followed by the story of the expulsion of Ishmael, as if the presence of Isaac would exclude the need for the other son. Indeed, Sarah has good reasons to be concerned about Ishmael—that he might compete with Isaac and ultimately attempt to supplant him. The feast celebrating the weaning of Isaac is associated with Ishmael's laughter (21:8–13) and thus becomes the occasion for his departure (21:14–21).

21:8–13. THE LAUGHTER OF ISHMAEL

GEN 21:8–13 NKJV	GEN 21:8–13 ESV
8 So the child grew and was weaned. And Abraham made a great feast on the same day that Isaac was weaned.	**8** And the child grew and was weaned. And Abraham made a great feast on the day that Isaac was weaned.
9 And Sarah saw the son of Hagar the Egyptian, whom she had borne to Abraham, scoffing.	**9** But Sarah saw the son of Hagar the Egyptian, whom she had borne to Abraham, laughing.
10 Therefore she said to Abraham, "Cast out this bondwoman and her son; for the son of this bondwoman shall not be heir with my son, *namely* with Isaac."	**10** So she said to Abraham, "Cast out this slave woman with her son, for the son of this slave woman shall not be heir with my son Isaac."
11 And the matter was very displeasing in Abraham's sight because of his son.	**11** And the thing was very displeasing to Abraham on account of his son.

12 But God said to Abraham, "Do not let it be displeasing in your sight because of the lad or because of your bondwoman. Whatever Sarah has said to you, listen to her voice; for in Isaac your seed shall be called.	**12** But God said to Abraham, "Be not displeased because of the boy and because of your slave woman. Whatever Sarah says to you, do as she tells you, for through Isaac shall your offspring be named.
13 Yet I will also make a nation of the son of the bondwoman, because he *is* your seed."	**13** And I will make a nation of the son of the slave woman also, because he is your offspring."

21:8 **So the child grew and was weaned.** This detail about Isaac reaching his physiological independence relates to the preceding verse with Sarah nursing Isaac (21:7). The weaning of the child, which used to take place only after three to five years in the ANE, had some spiritual significance and was associated with the consecration of the child to the Lord (1 Sam 1:22; cf. 1 Sam 1:11). Abraham organizes a **great feast** for this occasion, something he did not do for Ishmael. This will make Ishmael jealous.

21:9 **And Sarah saw the son of Hagar … scoffing.** Sarah's laughter (21:6), rich with hope and joy, is ironically echoed and thus distorted in the laughter of Ishmael. The same Hebrew root *tsakhaq* "laugh" resonates again here, but this time the laughter takes on a new nuance. The verb is now used in the intensive form (*piel*) and in the participle (*metsakheq*), implying a causative sense, meaning "cause to laugh" or "mock."

Who or what is the object of the laughter—the weaning, Sarah, or Isaac—is not indicated. The vagueness of the language leaves open the intention of the laughter, which makes it all the more suspect to Sarah, who takes it personally. Because she had predicted that people would laugh (21:6), she could identify the potential of evil contained in that laughter.

Another meaning of the verbal form *tsakhaq* in the intensive form (*piel*) is "to play" (Exod 32:6). The Septuagint (like the Latin Vulgate) explicitly identifies Isaac as the missing object of the verb in the Hebrew version: "sporting with Isaac her son." This reading suggests that Ishmael was playing with Isaac in a way that looked suspect to Sarah. The large age difference between Isaac (about five years old) and Ishmael (about seventeen years old) makes Ishmael's play with Isaac seem unnatural and therefore suspect.

21:9–13 **The son of this bondwoman shall not be heir with my son.** Sarah observes Ishmael's behavior (21:9) and concludes that, in the games shared between the two sons, there is a danger for Isaac to lose his rights as the legitimate heir. In the way Ishmael mocks or plays with Isaac, Ishmael presents himself as the rightful heir to be taken seriously versus the joke represented by Isaac (as also implied in his name). This is the reason Sarah gives to justify her apprehension and her decision to expel Hagar and her son (21:10). This interpretation agrees with Paul's perception that Ishmael intended to harm Isaac and that he "persecuted him" (Gal 4:29). God confirms Sarah's fears and therefore supports her decision.

Abraham is intensely "displeased" and even angry (21:11)[523] with Sarah's decision. He hesitates, perhaps playing with the idea that Ishmael may be the rightful heir. But God not only supports Sarah's request, He also insists: **In Isaac your seed shall be**

---

523 The Hebrew verb *ra'a'* "be displeasing" implies the idea of anger and resentment (Num 11:10; Jonah 4:1).

called. The Hebrew verb in the passive form (*niphal*) *yiqqare'* "be called" is used to characterize the divine calling of Abram who became Abraham (17:5) and Jacob who became Israel (35:10).

This language should remind Abraham that the seed of Isaac is the one that was set apart by God for messianic purposes. Although the special election does not exclude God's care for the other son, the divine promise limits itself here to the physical blessing: from Ishmael, God will only **make a nation** (21:13; cf. 17:20). It is indeed interesting and intriguing that the same word *zera'* "seed" is used to refer to Isaac as well as to Ishmael; they are both identified as "seed." Yet only the "seed" of Isaac is "called" (*yiqqare'*), thus implying the divine initiative. Only Isaac is called to transmit the seed that will lead to the Davidic line and then to the Messiah.

21:14–21. THE DEPARTURE OF ISHMAEL

GEN 21:14–21 NKJV	GEN 21:14–21 ESV
14 So Abraham rose early in the morning, and took bread and a skin of water; and putting *it* on her shoulder, he gave *it* and the boy to Hagar, and sent her away. Then she departed and wandered in the Wilderness of Beersheba.	**14** So Abraham rose early in the morning and took bread and a skin of water and gave it to Hagar, putting it on her shoulder, along with the child, and sent her away. And she departed and wandered in the wilderness of Beersheba.
15 And the water in the skin was used up, and she placed the boy under one of the shrubs.	**15** When the water in the skin was gone, she put the child under one of the bushes.
16 Then she went and sat down across from *him* at a distance of about a bowshot; for she said to herself, "Let me not see the death of the boy." So she sat opposite *him*, and lifted her voice and wept.	**16** Then she went and sat down opposite him a good way off, about the distance of a bowshot, for she said, "Let me not look on the death of the child." And as she sat opposite him, she lifted up her voice and wept.
17 And God heard the voice of the lad. Then the angel of God called to Hagar out of heaven, and said to her, "What ails you, Hagar? Fear not, for God has heard the voice of the lad where he *is*.	**17** And God heard the voice of the boy, and the angel of God called to Hagar from heaven and said to her, "What troubles you, Hagar? Fear not, for God has heard the voice of the boy where he is.
18 Arise, lift up the lad and hold him with your hand, for I will make him a great nation."	**18** Up! Lift up the boy, and hold him fast with your hand, for I will make him into a great nation."
19 Then God opened her eyes, and she saw a well of water. And she went and filled the skin with water, and gave the lad a drink.	**19** Then God opened her eyes, and she saw a well of water. And she went and filled the skin with water and gave the boy a drink.
20 So God was with the lad; and he grew and dwelt in the wilderness, and became an archer.	**20** And God was with the boy, and he grew up. He lived in the wilderness and became an expert with the bow.
21 He dwelt in the Wilderness of Paran; and his mother took a wife for him from the land of Egypt.	**21** He lived in the wilderness of Paran, and his mother took a wife for him from the land of Egypt.

21:14–21 The language describing Abraham's actions suggests that he is particularly concerned about Hagar and the child. The fact that **Abraham rose early in the morning** (21:14) and that he himself supplies Hagar with the provisions, which are basic (perhaps hoping that Hagar will not go very far), indicates that he cares for her and the child. Abraham himself puts the **skin of water** (21:14), a kind of bottle made of skin, on her shoulder, allowing her to have a free hand for Ishmael (cf. 21:18). The child who was around seventeen years old (cf. 16:16; 21:5, 8) was old enough to walk by himself. Note that the term *na'ar* "lad" (21:12; 17:25) refers to a teenager. This age is not in contradiction with Hagar's move when **she placed the boy under one of the shrubs** (21:15). The Hebrew verb *wattashlek* "she placed" is also "a technical term for exposure"[524] (see 21:15; Jer 38:6; Ezek 16:5) and is especially used in the case of casting dead bodies (Josh 8:29). "The term suggests Hagar was in despair anticipating her son's imminent death."[525] This tragic story of Ishmael exposed to death is echoed in the story of Isaac when he will, in his turn, be exposed to death. The same phrase "So Abraham rose in the morning" marks Abraham's departure to the "sacrifice of Isaac" (22:3). This echo between the two texts suggests an intention to connect the story of Ishmael's expulsion and the story of the sacrifice of Isaac. Abraham is personally involved and intensely active in both accounts. The same verb *wayyiqakh* **he took** initiates his action in both narratives (21:14; cf. 22:3, 6). Both sons come to the point of death, and both are saved through the intervention of **the angel of God … out of heaven** (21:17; cf. 22:11, 15). We find the same element of surprise—the well that was not visible (21:19), and the ram hidden in the bush (22:13). Finally, both stories take place near Beersheba (21:14; cf. 22:19).

These parallels, which attest to God's presence near the other son of Abraham (see 21:20), also bring out the fundamental difference between the two destinies. The sacrifice of Isaac has a spiritual horizon. It leads to Mount Moriah and the prospect of God's salvation through the atoning substituted animal. The expulsion of Ishmael, however, has only a physical denouement. It leads to Ishmael's survival and his military preparation against any threat. Ishmael **became an archer** (21:20) and married an Egyptian woman (21:21). Beyond the spiritual lessons this last information implies is an interesting irony: Sarah's aggressive censure against Ishmael's laughter led to an armed Ishmael in the camp of Egypt. The account concludes with a veiled note of threat, which anticipates the next episode.

21:22–34. COVENANT WITH ABIMELECH

As implied in the preceding account, Abraham is still not completely safe. Although he has a son—the fulfillment of God's promise—and although he is now wealthy, he remains a vulnerable refugee. Yet it is Abimelech, the native of the land, who worries and therefore is the one who initiates a covenant with Abraham (21:22–26). Abraham responds positively by offering seven ewe lambs (21:27–30). The ceremonial takes place at Beersheba, whose name will memorize the covenant (21:31–34). This account of a covenant made with the Philistines is an indication of its antiquity, since later the Israelites were forbidden to engage in treaty-making with the inhabitants of Canaan (Exod 23:31–33; cf. Lev 20:26).

---

524 See Morton Cogan, "A Technical Term for Exposure," *JNES* 27, no. 2 (1968): 133–135.
525 Gordon Wenham, *Genesis 16–50* (Dallas: Word, 1994), 85.

21:22–26. THE CALL FOR COVENANT: ABIMELECH

GEN 21:22–26 NKJV	GEN 21:22–26 ESV
22 And it came to pass at that time that Abimelech and Phichol, the commander of his army, spoke to Abraham, saying, "God *is* with you in all that you do.	**22** At that time Abimelech and Phicol the commander of his army said to Abraham, "God is with you in all that you do.
23 Now therefore, swear to me by God that you will not deal falsely with me, with my offspring, or with my posterity; but that according to the kindness that I have done to you, you will do to me and to the land in which you have dwelt."	**23** Now therefore swear to me here by God that you will not deal falsely with me or with my descendants or with my posterity, but as I have dealt kindly with you, so you will deal with me and with the land where you have sojourned."
24 And Abraham said, "I will swear."	**24** And Abraham said, "I will swear."
25 Then Abraham rebuked Abimelech because of a well of water which Abimelech's servants had seized.	**25** When Abraham reproved Abimelech about a well of water that Abimelech's servants had seized,
26 And Abimelech said, "I do not know who has done this thing; you did not tell me, nor had I heard *of it* until today."	**26** Abimelech said, "I do not know who has done this thing; you did not tell me, and I have not heard of it until today."

21:22 Abimelech and Phichol, the commander of his army. Abimelech sends an ambivalent message to Abraham. On one hand, he recognizes that Abraham is under God's protection; on the other, he has the commander of his army standing next to him. The name "Phichol," probably of Anatolian origin, confirms the Philistine identity of Abimelech (21:32, 34; cf. 26:1), since the Philistines originally came from the Aegian region or Anatolia, via Caphtor (10:14), the Hebrew name for Crete (Jer 47:4).[526] The Philistine coast was also called "Negeb of the Cherethites (1 Sam 30:14, ESV), and the word "Philistines" is in parallelism with the name "Cherethites" (Eze 25:16; Zeph 2:5, ESV).

21:23 Now therefore, swear to me. The root of the word "swearing" (*shaba'*) reappears in the number seven *sheba'*, referring to the "seven" ewes Abraham will give to Abimelech (21:28), and the name Abraham will give to the place "Beersheba" (21:31), meaning the "well" (*be'er*) of the "seven" (*sheba'*) or of the "swearing" (*shaba'*). Abimelech's request to Abraham not to **deal falsely** with him and his words **according to the kindness that I have done to you** allude to his previous encounter with Abraham. Then Abraham did indeed deal "falsely" with him (20:9), yet Abimelech had been kind to him (20:14–16).

21:24 I will swear. Abimelech asks Abraham to take the initiative to **swear by God**, although he himself did not swear right away (cf. 21:31). The construction of the sentence—placing the subject before the verb, although the subject normally follows the verb—suggests emphasis on the pronoun, thus implying that the "swearing by God" belongs especially to Abraham. The ancient rabbis of the Talmud interpreted this grammatical form to imply Abraham's reluctance to allow Abimelech to swear by his idol.[527] The narrative focuses on Abraham's oath although they both swore (21:31). This is a subtle way to suggest that only the oath to the God of Abraham would guarantee its validity.

---

526 See J. D. Ray, "Two Etymologies: Ziklag and Phicol," *VT* 36 (1986): 358–361.

527 Sanh. 3a.

21:25 **Then Abraham rebuked Abimelech.** Abraham's complaint to Abimelech concerning a well taken by Abimelech's servants may also be a reason why Abraham insists on being the only one to swear. He is the only one capable of honoring his oath, since Abimelech is apparently unable to honor his word (20:15).

21:26 **I do not know.** Abimelech's reference to his ignorance not only justifies himself, but implies at the same time his incapacity to control his servants. Abimelech's only excuse is that Abraham did not communicate with him about the matter, a way to blame Abraham, while reminding him of his previous fault when he failed to report to Abimelech the status of his sister-wife Sarah (20:9).

21:27–30. THE CEREMONIAL OF COVENANT: ABRAHAM

GEN 21:27–30 NKJV	GEN 21:27–30 ESV
27 So Abraham took sheep and oxen and gave them to Abimelech, and the two of them made a covenant.	**27** So Abraham took sheep and oxen and gave them to Abimelech, and the two men made a covenant.
28 And Abraham set seven ewe lambs of the flock by themselves.	**28** Abraham set seven ewe lambs of the flock apart.
29 Then Abimelech asked Abraham, "What *is the meaning of* these seven ewe lambs which you have set by themselves?"	**29** And Abimelech said to Abraham, "What is the meaning of these seven ewe lambs that you have set apart?"
30 And he said, "You will take *these* seven ewe lambs from my hand, that they may be my witness that I have dug this well."	**30** He said, "These seven ewe lambs you will take from my hand, that this may be a witness for me that I dug this well."

21:27 **Abraham took sheep and oxen.** Note that it is Abraham who, once again, takes the initiative in making the covenant. This specification is in line with Abimelech's initial request that Abraham should swear by God (21:23), and it suggests that Abraham is perceived as the superior. Significantly, it is Abraham who, this time, gives "sheep and oxen" to Abimelech and not the other way around, as it was in their preceding meeting, when Abimelech was depicted as the wealthy and generous host versus Abraham the needy refugee (20:14). Abraham's gift of the sheep is designed for the sacrifice that is required in the covenant ceremony, which involves the "cutting" of the animals (15:9–17; cf. Jer 34:18–19). The Hebrew phrase *karat berit* (usually translated "make covenant") means literally to "cut a covenant."

21:28–30 **Seven ewe lambs of the flock.** The additional gift of the "seven ewe lambs" to surprise Abimelech, who asks for an explanation (21:29). Abraham does not content himself with a formal covenant, which should guarantee a future peaceful relationship with his neighbor. Abraham founds the promise for the future on the present reality—namely, the well in question—to establish from the very beginning the seriousness of that covenant. The issue of the well becomes, then, the test for the validity of the covenant. The "seven ewe lambs" should witness that he "dug this well" (21:30).

21:31–34. THE MEMORY OF COVENANT: BEERSHEBA

GEN 21:31–34 NKJV	GEN 21:31–34 ESV
31 Therefore he called that place Beersheba, because the two of them swore an oath there.	**31** Therefore that place was called Beersheba, because there both of them swore an oath.
32 Thus they made a covenant at Beersheba. So Abimelech rose with Phichol, the commander of his army, and they returned to the land of the Philistines.	**32** So they made a covenant at Beersheba. Then Abimelech and Phicol the commander of his army rose up and returned to the land of the Philistines.
33 Then *Abraham* planted a tamarisk tree in Beersheba, and there called on the name of the Lord, the Everlasting God.	**33** Abraham planted a tamarisk tree in Beersheba and called there on the name of the Lord, the Everlasting God.
34 And Abraham stayed in the land of the Philistines many days.	**34** And Abraham sojourned many days in the land of the Philistines.

21:31 Beersheba. The name of the place "Beersheba" is a play on the word *sheba'*, which is heard in the word *shaba'* "swear" as well as in the word "seven" (*sheba'*). The name "Beersheba" will function as a reminder of the two basic components of the covenant between Abraham and Abimelech—their oath and the seven ewe lambs.

21:32 They returned to the land of the Philistines. This information indicates that Abimelech and his army commander were foreigners and that Beersheba was not under Philistine control. Because the Philistines appear for the first time in Egyptian sources only in the thirteenth century BC, the mention of the Philistines in this passage has been interpreted as anachronistic. It has been suggested, however, that the name "Philistines" is "a blanket term for non-Canaanite Aegean people."[528] This is consistent with the identification of Phichol as an Anatolian name (see the comments on 21:22). The name "Philistines" designates, then, the non-Canaanite peoples, including the Aegean peoples and the Sea Peoples mentioned in Ugaritic documents (northern Syria), before the fifteenth century BC.

The fact that at that time those Philistines did not feel at home in the land of Canaan suggests a much earlier stage, when the Philistines were not yet settled in the country, as will be the case later in the time of the Judges (1 Sam 4:1–10; Judg 13–15). This observation on the alien status of the Philistines is important because it legitimizes Abraham's claim for the land and the well. Abimelech, like Abraham, has no historical rights to the land.

21:33–34 Abraham planted a tamarisk tree. The tamarisk tree is an evergreen that can reach thirty feet (ten meters), and is ideal for providing shade. Saul is described as sitting under one (1 Sam 22:6), and his bones were buried beneath another one (1 Sam 31:13). Abraham's act of "planting a tree" is accompanied by his prayer to the One he calls "the Everlasting God," thus, expressing his hope to settle permanently in that land. His prayer is heard since the next verse informs us that Abraham **sojourned in the land many days** (21:34).

---

528 Kitchen, *On the Reliability of the Old Testament*, 341.

LEK LEKA "GO!" CALL TO ABRAHAM TO LEAVE HIS FUTURE
(22:1–19)

This section covers the end of the central part of the book of Genesis, which started with the call of God to Abraham to "go" (*lek leka*) (12:1–9).[529] This text marks also the fourth section of the book of Genesis and covers the stories of Abraham and Isaac (22–28:9). The story of the "sacrifice of Isaac" has been called in Jewish tradition the *'aqedah*, reference to the tying up (*'aqad*) of Isaac (22:9). The text has become a classic in world literature, as noted by German philosopher Erich Auerbach in his book *Mimesis*.[530] It has inspired philosophers like Kant and Kierkegaard and artists like Rembrandt. In addition, it has remained a fundamental text in Jewish, Christian, and Muslim traditions. It is remembered in the Jewish liturgy of Rosh Hashanah and Kippur, in the Christian celebration of the Lord's Supper, and in the Muslim feast of Id-al Kabir.

The meaning of this story has baffled ancient and modern commentators. They have been troubled by the shocking picture of God commanding a father to sacrifice his son. The passage not only raises difficult ethical issues, it is at odds with the divine repulsion and prohibition toward human sacrifices (Lev 18:21) and contradicts God's promise of an eternal covenant with the posterity of Isaac (15:5).

THE LITERARY STRUCTURE

The beauty and the intricacies of the literary form of the narrative engage our attention as they are used to express the author's intention to convey a specific message. The passage displays the following chiastic structure $ABCB_1A_1$.

> **A** Dialogue: God (*'Elohim*) and Abraham ("here I am") (22:1–2)
> > **B** Abraham's walk (22:3–6)
> > **Refrain** "The two of them went together" (*wayyelku sheneyhem yakhdaw*) (22:6b)
> > > **C Dialogue: Abraham and Isaac ("here I am") (22:7–8)**
> > **Refrain** "The two of them went together" (*wayyelku sheneyhem yakhdaw*) (22:8b)
> > **B₁** Abraham's walk (22:9–10)
> **A₁** Dialogue: God (Angel of *YHWH*) and Abraham ("here I am") (22:11–19a)
> **Refrain** "And they went together" (*wayyelku yakhdaw*) (22:19b)

The chiastic structure is supported by the following observations:

1. The symmetric and strategic distribution of keywords: The verb *'amar* "say" occurs six times in the first section (22:1 [2x], 2 [2x], 3, 5), five times in the middle second section (22:7 [4x], 8), and six times again in the third section (22:9, 11 [2x], 12, 14, 16). In a parallel manner, the verb *ra'ah* "see" occurs once in the first section (22:4), once in the second middle section (22:8 [Heb]), and reaches its climax in the third section with three occurrences (22:13–14). The phrase *hinneni* "Here I am" occurs once in the first section (22:1), once in the second middle section (22:7), and again in the third section (22:11).

---

529 A study of the structure of Genesis from the perspective of "work" has led Elisabeth Ostring to identify Genesis 22 as the center of the overall chiastic structure of the book; see Elisabeth Ostring, "The Theology of Human Work as Found in the Genesis Narrative Compared With the Co-creationist Theology of Human Work" (PhD diss., Avondale College of Higher Education, 2015), 227.

530 Erich Auerbach, *Mimesis: The Representation of Reality in Western Literature*, trans. Willard Trask (Princeton, NJ: Princeton University Press, 1953; repr. 2003), 11.

2. The common motifs in Abraham's walk, in B (22:3–6) and in B₁ (22:9–10): "wood," "burnt offering," "the place of which God had told him," "laid on Isaac" (cf. "laid him on," 22:9), and "took the knife."

3. The regularity of the refrain "they went together" (22:6, 8, 19), which marks the borders of the center, just as the expression *lek leka* does for the whole book of Genesis.

22:1–2. GOD AND ABRAHAM

GEN 22:1–2 NKJV	GEN 22:1–2 ESV
1 Now it came to pass after these things that God tested Abraham, and said to him, "Abraham!" And he said, "Here I am."	**1** After these things God tested Abraham and said to him, "Abraham!" And he said, "Here am I."
2 Then He said, "Take now your son, your only *son* Isaac, whom you love, and go to the land of Moriah, and offer him there as a burnt offering on one of the mountains of which I shall tell you."	**2** He said, "Take your son, your only son Isaac, whom you love, and go to the land of Moriah, and offer him there as a burnt offering on one of the mountains of which I shall tell you."

22:1 The first verse introduces us to the story that will follow, informing us about the chronology—it comes "after these things"; and the nature of the event—it is a "test."

After these things. This phrase locates the story with regard to the preceding ones (the covenant with Abimelech and the expulsion of Ishmael) and marks a clear distance between them, thus confirming the chronological indication of the last verse of the last chapter: "Abraham sojourned many days in the land" (21:34 ESV). Isaac is now old enough to confront the next experience. Before, Isaac was called a *yeled*, a "child" of about three to five years old who had reached his weaning time (21:8). Now, he is a *na'ar*, a "lad" in his twenties.[531]

God tested Abraham. The meaning of the Hebrew verb *nissah* "tested" is difficult because it embraces opposite ideas. On one hand, it is a part of judgment—God "tests" in order "to know what was in your heart" (Deut 8:2; cf. Ps 139:1, 23–24; Eccl 12:14). This aspect is clearly enunciated by the Angel of the Lord: "now I know that you fear God" (22:12).

On the other hand, the biblical idea of "testing" goes beyond the mere threatening quiz that God needed to give Abraham in order to evaluate the quality of his faith.

Moses uses the same verb *nissah* "test" in order to reassure his people trembling before the thundering on Sinai (Exod 20:18): "Moses said to the people, 'Do not fear; for God has come to test [*nissah*] you, and that His fear may be before you, so that you may not sin'" (Exod 20:20). The common words ("test," "fear of God") and the same threat of death shared by the two passages suggest that the same theology of "test" is implied. Instead of being an arbitrary and cruel act directed *against* the one tested, the divine testing brings the positive and promising perspective of divine judgment and atonement *on behalf of* the tested and is therefore to be understood in connection with the covenant of grace.[532]

---

531 The Hebrew word *na'ar* may refer to a seventeen-year-old man (37:2) or a man of marriageable age (34:19) or even a warrior (2 Sam 18:5).

532 See C. Dohmen, "*nissah*," *TDOT* 9:450.

Here I am. Abraham's response *hinneni* "Here I am" occurs three times in the narrative—in the beginning (22:1), in the middle (22:7), and at the end (22:11)—thus following the flow of its literary structure. In Hebrew, the English phrase "Here I am" is rendered by one single word *hinneni*, expressing the prophet's total availability and immediate readiness to respond to God and serve Him (31:11; 46:2; Exod 3:4; 1 Sam 3:4; Isa 6:8). Abraham's word responds to only one word from God: "Abraham." The quick back-and-forth between God and Abraham suggests Abraham's familiar relationship with God (see 18:23–33), which underscores his submission.

22:2 **Take now your son ... and go ... and offer him.** God's command consists of three orders, derived from three verbs in the imperative form. Between the "taking" of the son and the "offering" of him, we find inserted the stylistic phrase *lek leka* "go yourself." We previously encountered the phrase in God's call to Abraham (see the comments on 12:1–3).

There is a fundamental difference, however, between the two calls. The first *lek leka* pointed to the past, his father and his Babel country, with all that it implied of memory and idolatrous habits. The second *lek leka* points to the future, his son Isaac and the land of Moriah, the future place of Jerusalem, with all that it implies of hope and promise; it has a prophetic perspective.

Take now your son, your only son Isaac, whom you love. In the Hebrew text, the story rises to a crescendo as it moves from the more general and distant connection "your son" to the more specific ("Isaac"). We note also the parallel of rhythm with God's previous call (12:1). The three designations of the sacrifice Abraham is asked to offer (your son, the only one whom you love, Isaac)[533] parallel the three designations of the place he was asked to leave. There we find the same progression, from the more general and distant ("your country") to the more particular ("your kindred," referring to birthplace or to relatives[534]), and to the most intimate relationship ("your father's house").

The parallel between the texts suggests a similar type of experience. In both cases, Abraham has to make a sacrifice. In the first call (12:1–3), he has to abandon his past, his father, and his roots. Now, he has to risk his future, his son, and his hope. The abnormal repetition "your son, your only son Isaac, whom you love," is necessary because of Abraham's tendency to transfer the promise. When God promised him a son, he responded by either referring to Eliezer (15:2) or to Ishmael (17:18). To avoid that kind of misunderstanding it was necessary for God to become more and more specific, as if He were following Abraham's surmises.

This intensification also emphasizes the pain this request brings Abraham and hence the difficulty of his sacrifice. The choice of words underscores the intention. The Hebrew word *na'* (translated "now"), following the verb "take!" expresses supplication and urgency (as in the phrase "Hosana" from the Hebrew "*Hosha'-na'*," meaning "Save, please!"). The specification "your only," which qualifies the word "your son," signifies the exclusive character of Abraham's relationship with Isaac. Then, the verb "love" (which occurs for the first time in the Hebrew Scriptures) reveals that there is even more between Abraham and Isaac than a mere father-son

---

533 Each of these designations is introduced by the same word *'et*, which occurs, then, three times.

534 The Hebrew word *moledet* derives from the word *yalad* "give birth" (see 48:6, where the two words are related) and may refer either to the birthplace (Lev 18:9; Ruth 2:11) or to relatives (Esth 2:10; Ezek 16:3–4).

relationship. Abraham's deep emotion excludes any interpretation that would suggest callousness and insensitivity.

The land of Moriah. We may hear in the word "Moriah" a play on words (anagram) that resonates with *haharim* **the mountains** as well as with the forthcoming keyword *raʾah* "see." The name is loaded with special significance. It is not an accident that the only places where this name occurs are here and in the story reporting the building of the temple by Solomon (2 Chr 3:1). The linguistic links between the two passages confirm this connection. In addition to the common word "Moriah," we have the words "provided" || "appeared" (*nirʾeh*), "mount" (*har*), "place" (*maqom*).

The story of the choice of that place by David (1 Chr 21:22–30) contains notable parallels with the narrative of the sacrifice of Isaac. In both passages, the appearance of the angel of the Lord is associated with the restraining of the killing hand (22:12; cf. 1 Chr 21:15); and in both stories, the prophet "lifted his eyes and saw" (22:13; cf. 1 Chr 21:16). These numerous parallels between the two passages suggest a significant intention to relate the two events. On the basis of this association with the name "Moriah," Jewish tradition has placed the sacrifice of Isaac on the Temple Mount.[535] On the horizon of the sacrifice of Isaac loom the sacrifices that will be offered in the Jerusalem temple, invested with the same spiritual lesson.

Offer him there as a burnt offering. Strangely and perhaps ironically, God's language in describing this human sacrifice, a Canaanite practice that was prohibited by Him (Lev 18:21; 20:2–5) and even called an "abomination" (Deut 12:31), is the same as in the description of the tabernacle sacrifice (Exod 29:38–45; Lev 1:3–17; Num 15:1–10). The contradiction is all the more disturbing as the two sacrifices express opposite theologies of salvation. While the pagan sacrifice implies the human ascent and work towards God, the Israelite sacrifice signifies, on the contrary, the divine descent and grace on behalf of humans.

Against all expectations, Abraham does not respond to God, nor does he engage in discussion with Him as he liked to do (15:2; 17:18; 18:22–33). Abraham's silence is unusual. Either he is too confused to answer, or God's request fits some lost (dusty) corner of his theology. The silence may also suggest that Abraham has at last reached the stage when he can finally receive God's strange order and trust God in spite of his questions, doubts, and confusion. It is significant that "this time, the last time, the only time, and the most difficult time, there is no promise accompanying the test."[536]

22:3–6. ABRAHAM'S WALK

GEN 22:3–6 NKJV	GEN 22:3–6 ESV
3 So Abraham rose early in the morning and saddled his donkey, and took two of his young men with him, and Isaac his son; and he split the wood for the burnt offering, and arose and went to the place of which God had told him.	**3** So Abraham rose early in the morning, saddled his donkey, and took two of his young men with him, and his son Isaac. And he cut the wood for the burnt offering and arose and went to the place of which God had told him.
4 Then on the third day Abraham lifted his eyes and saw the place afar off.	**4** On the third day Abraham lifted up his eyes and saw the place from afar.

---

535 Gen. Rab. 55:7.

536 Borgman, *Genesis*, 89.

| 5 And Abraham said to his young men, "Stay here with the donkey; the lad and I will go yonder and worship, and we will come back to you." | 5 Then Abraham said to his young men, "Stay here with the donkey; I and the boy will go over there and worship and come again to you." |
| 6 So Abraham took the wood of the burnt offering and laid *it* on Isaac his son; and he took the fire in his hand, and a knife, and the two of them went together. | 6 And Abraham took the wood of the burnt offering and laid it on Isaac his son. And he took in his hand the fire and the knife. So they went both of them together. |

22:3 **So Abraham rose early in the morning … and went to the place.** This localization in time, "early in the morning," suggests that Abraham had his vision during the preceding night. Abraham's response is therefore immediate. The same phrase had previously been used in connection with the expulsion of Ishmael (21:14). The two stories show numerous parallels and echoes: "Abraham rose early in the morning" "and took" (22:3; cf. 21:14); Abraham "put on" (22:6; cf. 21:14); "and he went" (22:3) ‖ "and she went" (21:16); "the boy" (22:5; 21:15); "Abraham *lifted* his eyes" (22:13) ‖ Hagar "*lifted* her voice" (21:16); "the Angel of the Lord called to him from heaven" (22:11) ‖ "the angel of God called to Hagar out of heaven" (21:17); the common theme of fear (22:12; cf. 21:17); the common theme of *ra'ah* "seeing," "providing" (22:4, 13; 22:8, 14; cf. 21:16, 19; cf. 16:13–14); the common theme of hearing: Abraham hears the voice of God (22:18) ‖ God hears the voice of the lad (21:17); the common promise of great posterity (22:17–18; 21:18); "Abraham dwelt at Beersheba" (22:19) ‖ Ishmael "dwelt in the Wilderness" (21:21).

Ishmael and Isaac are thus associated in a parallel yet contrasted destiny. While Ishmael, Abraham's natural son, will possess the land and survive in the wilderness by the force of his weapons (21:20), Isaac will inherit the Promised Land and survive by faith through the sacrifice offered at Moriah.

22:4 **On the third day.** Abraham took two full days and part of the third to reach Moriah (the place of Jerusalem). This is the right time for the old man and his loaded donkey to cover the distance from Beersheba, which is fifty to sixty miles (about eighty kilometers). This precision confirms the identification of Moriah, the place of Jerusalem, as his destination. The three days also have a symbolic meaning. They signify a period of preparation for an important event (31:22; 34:25; 40:20; 42:18) and also imply the hope of salvation and resurrection (Jonah 3:3; cf. Josh 1:11; Mark 9:31).

Abraham lifted his eyes and saw. From the moment when Abraham **rose early in the morning** (*wayyashkem*) until the moment when he **saw** (*wayyar'eh*) **the place** (22:4), the narrative counts seven verbs. The verb "saw" marks the seventh step of Abraham's walk toward "the place," an indication that Abraham has reached his destination (see 22:13).

22:5 **Abraham said to his young men … The lad …** The same word *na'ar* that designates "the young men" is also used for Isaac ("the lad") and even for Ishmael (21:12, 17, 20). It is not clear whether the writer refers to "servants" or to other individuals. The Aramaic Targum, referring to the common wording of the two designations (*na'ar*), suggests that the "two young men" who accompanied them may have been Eliezer and Ishmael, since these are the two other "young men" of Abraham's household and both were former candidates for the divine election.[537] If this interpretation is correct, their presence and particularly the presence of Ishmael, who must have traveled from far away for the occasion, underscores the gravity and the significance of this journey in which they all play a part.

I will go yonder and worship. Abraham identifies the goal of his journey as an act of worship. The Hebrew verb for "worship" (*hishtakhaweh*) refers to a religious act; implying prayers, sacrifices, and prostration on the ground expressing adoration and service to God (Ps 5:7 [8]; 95:6; Neh 8:6). The verb is often associated with the reference to creation (Pss 29:2; 100:3; see the comments on "The Place of Creation"). Abraham knows that he will meet with the great God of life. Thus, he engages in this difficult journey with the faith that he will return with his son. On one hand, Abraham accepts God's command to sacrifice his son; and, on the other, he trusts God and His promise that Isaac will be the father of the chosen people and the ancestor of the Messiah. This is why, in spite of the prospect of death, Abraham is sure that he will return with his son. He does not dismiss God's order, just as he does not dismiss God's promise. Taking God's word seriously, whether as His unbearable command or as His glorious promise, Abraham therefore must have thought of resurrection (Heb 11:17–18; cf. Rom 4:17).[538]

22:6 The two of them went together. The phrase occurs three times—here, at the end of Genesis 22:8, and in Genesis 22:19 (where the incomplete phrase appears, which will be discussed below). It marks the three sections of the story, as a refrain, and highlights its center (22:7–8). The key verb *wayyeleku* "and they went" echoes and responds to God's initial command "go!" (22:2): Isaac is a part of Abraham's obedient response to the divine word. The phrase sounds tragic, as it underlines the silent walk of father and son. Abraham thinks of Isaac's impending death, and Isaac wonders about Abraham's act of murder.

22:7–8. DIALOGUE: ABRAHAM AND ISAAC

GEN 22:7–8 NKJV	GEN 22:7–8 ESV
7 But Isaac spoke to Abraham his father and said, "My father!" And he said, "Here I am, my son." Then he said, "Look, the fire and the wood, but where *is* the lamb for a burnt offering?"	**7** And Isaac said to his father Abraham, "My father!" And he said, "Here am I, my son." He said, "Behold, the fire and the wood, but where is the lamb for a burnt offering?"
8 And Abraham said, "My son, God will provide for Himself the lamb for a burnt offering." So the two of them went together.	**8** Abraham said, "God will provide for himself the lamb for a burnt offering, my son." So they went both of them together.

22:7–8 But Isaac spoke. The silence is broken by Isaac's voice. It is the first and only time that Isaac speaks in this story. The father-son dialogue appears at the center of the chiastic structure of the text, a way of highlighting its significance. The poignant nature of the dialogue, made up of silences and unanswered questions, emerges in the following literal translation (shown in italics), along with our comments:

And Isaac said to Abraham his father: In the Hebrew text, the first "say" of Isaac

---

537 See Tg. Ps.-J.

538 The tradition of Isaac's resurrection has been preserved in both Jewish and Christian writings; see Pirke R. El. 31; Origen, *Homily on Genesis 8:1*; and Augustine, *Exposition on Psalms 51:5*; see also Ellen G. White, 3SG 106.

is not immediately followed by the words of Isaac. It is as if Isaac intended to say something but stopped and could not proceed. This detail, overlooked in translations, suggests Isaac's distress. He is full of contradictory thoughts and overwhelming emotions.

And he said: "my father": When Isaac finally is able to speak, he can only say one Hebrew word *'abi* "my father!" which reminds us of his relationship with the one who is preparing for the slaughter.

And he said: "Here I am, my son": the stylistic location of Abraham's response to his son "here I am" (*hinneni*) in the exact middle of the section underlines its importance. Abraham's response to Isaac's call is the same as his response to the divine call (22:1). The lesson of this parallel is clear. Abraham's disposition towards Isaac is equivalent to Abraham's disposition towards God. In Abraham's religion, the vertical (his relationship with God) is balanced by the horizontal (his relationship with the human other).

The word "my son" (*beni*) corresponds to the word "my father" (*'abi*). Thus, it answers Isaac's concern about Abraham's relationship with him. Isaac should be reassured. Abraham has remained his father. The father loves the son, and the intensity of that love for his only son makes the sacrifice all the more painful (cf. John 5:20).

He said: here is the fire and the wood, but where is the lamb for the burnt offering? Isaac's response begins with the same word used by Abraham to reassure Isaac: "here" (*hinneh*). In this instance, the word is used to introduce Isaac's trembling question: "Where is the lamb?" This is another way of defining the terrible reality, without having to explicitly state: "Am I the lamb?"

And Abraham said: "God will see in connection to Himself, the lamb, my son": The construction of the phrase and of the expressions is particularly telling. First, the word "God" is put in the beginning of the sentence before the verbal form. This goes counter to the Hebrew regulation, which normally places the verb before its subject. The intention of this irregularity is to emphasize "God," to indicate that the solution is only in God. It is God who will see.

The expression "see in connection to Himself" is awkward. It is unique in the Hebrew Scriptures. It has the same form as the phrase *lek leka* "go in connection to yourself," "go to yourself," or, in a reflexive sense, "go yourself." As with *lek leka*, the subject of the verb and the object of the preposition are the same. The verbal form *yr'eh lo* (generally translated "He will provide") should therefore instead be translated: "He will see in connection to Himself," "He will see Himself," or "He will provide for Himself" (ESV, NASB).[539]

The parallel with *lek leka* suggests that *yr'eh lo* should be understood in a similar manner. In that case, this phrase could mean that Abraham was called to go to the land in order to fulfill himself; he foresees that God will see the lamb in order to fulfill Himself. The phrase could be translated as follows: "God will see (for) Himself as the lamb," which means that God will provide Himself as the lamb.

"The lamb" is not preceded by the term *'et*, the Hebrew word that normally introduces the definite object (not translated in English). The word "lamb" is not to be

---

539 See 1 Samuel 16:1, which uses the similar expression *ra'iti ... li* "I have provided for myself" (ESV), "I have provided Myself" (NKJV), "I have selected ... for Myself" (NASB). In this expression, however, the language is slightly different. While in 22:8 the preposition follows immediately the verb: "He will see Himself, the lamb," in 1 Samuel 16 the preposition follows the object: "I have selected a king for Myself" (NASB).

understood as the object of the verb "see." The word "lamb" is in apposition to the phrase "He will see Himself," meaning He will see Himself, (as) the lamb. The lamb is here identified as God. Thus, the lamb that is referred to here is not merely the physical animal that Isaac had in mind, it is God Himself.

The animal that will be slaughtered is not a lamb but, for some reason, a ram (see the comments below). What is in view in this phrase is therefore more than the ram that Abraham will offer. Beyond this sacrifice is "seen" the sacrifice offered by God of Himself through Jesus Christ. Jesus may allude to that prophetic intuition of Abraham when He says, echoing Abraham's emphasis on "seeing," "providing" (22:8; cf. 22:14): "Your father Abraham rejoiced to *see* My day, and he *saw* it and was glad" (John 8:56).[540]

With this hope concerning the future messianic event, Abraham and Isaac resume their silent walk (22:8). It is important to note that this line is situated at the very center of the chiasm of the *'aqedah*; it constitutes its apex, around which all the ideas of the text have been organized.[541] More precisely, it is the end of the central section, thus, marking its climax. This means that the prophetic event, which Abraham describes as "God will see Himself as the lamb," is to be understood as the essence, the very heart of the story.

22:9–10. ABRAHAM'S WALK

GEN 22:9–10 NKJV	GEN 22:9–10 ESV
9 Then they came to the place of which God had told him. And Abraham built an altar there and placed the wood in order; and he bound Isaac his son and laid him on the altar, upon the wood.	**9** When they came to the place of which God had told him, Abraham built the altar there and laid the wood in order and bound Isaac his son and laid him on the altar, on top of the wood.
10 And Abraham stretched out his hand and took the knife to slay his son.	**10** Then Abraham reached out his hand and took the knife to slaughter his son.

Abraham built an altar … to slay his son. As soon as they arrive at the place designated by God, Abraham gets busy. Six verbs describe his activities, ending with a seventh verb in the infinitive that marks the conclusion and the goal of all this activity: **built … placed … bound … laid …** (22:9) **stretched … took … to slay** (22:10).

The language belongs to the sacrificial domain. This is attested by the expression "built an altar" (8:20; 12:7–8; 13:18; 26:25; 35:7; Exod 17:15; 24:4; Josh 22:11; etc.), the phrase "placed the wood in order" (Lev 1:7) and the verb "slay" (Lev 1:11). The verb "bind" (*'aqad*), which occurs only here in the Hebrew Scriptures, was used in the Mishnah to refer technically to the tying of the *tamid* lamb on the altar.[542] The

---

540 See Ellen G. White's comments on this passage, which she associates with the story of the *'aqedah*: "Abraham had greatly desired to see the promised Saviour. He offered up the most earnest prayer that before his death he might behold the Messiah. And he saw Christ. A supernatural light was given him, and he acknowledged Christ's divine character. He saw His day, and was glad. He was given a view of the divine sacrifice for sin. Of this sacrifice he had an illustration in his own experience. The command came to him, 'Take now thy son, thine only son Isaac, whom thou lovest … and offer him … for a burnt offering.' Genesis 22:2 … This terrible ordeal was imposed upon Abraham that he might see the day of Christ, and realize the great love of God for the world" (DA 468, 469).

541 See R. L. Alden, "Is the High Point of the Psalm's Chiasmus the Point of the Psalm?" (paper presented at the Annual Meeting of the SBL, Chicago, IL, November 1988).

542 *Tamid* 4, 1. The word *'aqedah* "binding" will become later, in rabbinic literature, the technical term for the sacri-

tying of Isaac means more than a mere evocation of the sacrificial lamb. This technical detail suggests that Isaac lets himself be tied, showing profound trust and a high level of self-control, thus silently allowing his old father to take him to the slaughter,[543] just as the Suffering Servant (cf. Isa 53:7). The phrase "stretched out the hand" (*shalakh yad*) is frequently used to express the determined intent of hostility and violence (37:22; Ps 125:3), hence the sudden intervention by the Angel of the Lord.

22:11–19. THE ANGEL AND ABRAHAM

GEN 22:11–19 NKJV	GEN 22:11–19 ESV
11 But the Angel of the Lord called to him from heaven and said, "Abraham, Abraham!" So he said, "Here I am."	**11** But the angel of the Lord called to him from heaven and said, "Abraham, Abraham!" And he said, "Here am I."
12 And He said, "Do not lay your hand on the lad, or do anything to him; for now I know that you fear God, since you have not withheld your son, your only *son*, from Me."	**12** He said, "Do not lay your hand on the boy or do anything to him, for now I know that you fear God, seeing you have not withheld your son, your only son, from me."
13 Then Abraham lifted his eyes and looked, and there behind *him was* a ram caught in a thicket by its horns. So Abraham went and took the ram, and offered it up for a burnt offering instead of his son.	**13** And Abraham lifted up his eyes and looked, and behold, behind him was a ram, caught in a thicket by his horns. And Abraham went and took the ram and offered it up as a burnt offering instead of his son.
14 And Abraham called the name of the place, The-Lord-Will-Provide; as it is said *to* this day, "In the Mount of the Lord it shall be provided."	**14** So Abraham called the name of that place, "The Lord will provide"; as it is said to this day, "On the mount of the Lord it shall be provided."
15 Then the Angel of the Lord called to Abraham a second time out of heaven,	**15** And the angel of the Lord called to Abraham a second time from heaven
16 and said: "By Myself I have sworn, says the Lord, because you have done this thing, and have not withheld your son, your only *son*—	**16** and said, "By myself I have sworn, declares the Lord, because you have done this and have not withheld your son, your only son,
17 blessing I will bless you, and multiplying I will multiply your descendants as the stars of the heaven and as the sand which *is* on the seashore; and your descendants shall possess the gate of their enemies.	**17** I will surely bless you, and I will surely multiply your offspring as the stars of heaven and as the sand that is on the seashore. And your offspring shall possess the gate of his enemies,
18 In your seed all the nations of the earth shall be blessed, because you have obeyed My voice."	**18** and in your offspring shall all the nations of the earth be blessed, because you have obeyed my voice."
19 So Abraham returned to his young men, and they rose and went together to Beersheba; and Abraham dwelt at Beersheba.	**19** So Abraham returned to his young men, and they arose and went together to Beersheba. And Abraham lived at Beersheba.

. . .

fice of Isaac. It was used in the Middle Ages to refer to the martyrdom of the Jews during the pogroms associated with the Crusades. Along the same lines, Elie Wiesel, Nobel Peace Prize winner and survivor of the Holocaust, alluded to the story of the sacrifice of Isaac when for the first time he used the word "holocaust" to refer to the Jewish genocide of the Second World War.

543 It is this observation that prompted Holocaust scholars and thinkers (including Elie Wiesel) to prefer the Hebrew term *Shoah*, instead of the current term "Holocaust," which they felt was inappropriate since the Jews were not voluntary victims.

22:11 But the Angel of the Lord called … and said, Abraham, Abraham! So far the text is referring to God as *'Elohim*, a name that evokes the transcendence of God (see the comments on Genesis 1). Suddenly, it is the Angel of the Lord who intervenes, the Person who has been identified with *YHWH* Himself. This change of the divine name does not presuppose another source, as critics have often suggested. The use of the name *YHWH* may have theological reasons to point to the immanent God who draws near to humans, walks with them, and saves them (2:4b–25; 16:7).

The repetition "Abraham, Abraham!" shows the urgency of the situation (see Exod 3:4; 1 Sam 3:10; Acts 9:4); the divine messenger wants to make sure that Abraham will hear him. That repetition is needed also suggests Abraham's concentration in his zeal to perform the fatal operation. Abraham responds immediately with the same formula *hinneni* "Here I am" that he had already used to respond to God the first time and to his son.

22:12 Do not lay your hand on the lad, or do anything to him. The divine command is also given in a repetitive manner, echoing Abraham's two actions. "Do not lay your hand on the lad" refers to Abraham's first action, the stretching of his hand. This time, however, Abraham's stretching the hand is directed toward the lad, while the first stretching was only to the knife (22:10).[544] "Or do anything to him" refers back to Abraham's second action, the slaying. God, by His insistence, is making sure that Abraham understands the message, since earlier he had heard another, opposite command. The divine repetition suggests that Abraham needed to know and understand the meaning of God's inconsistency and the strange scenario.

All the works of Abraham—his multiple zealous activities, his painful journey, and even his willingness to obey and sacrifice to the Lord even the best of himself— were for nothing. Abraham was like the "unprofitable servant" of Jesus' parable who learned that he had worked for nothing (Luke 17:7–10). But he must have understood the principle of grace, that it is not our works for God that count and save, but it is instead God's works for us.

This truth may have struck him when he ended his journey and arrived at "the place" (*hammaqom*) (22:9), the common designation for the tabernacle (Exod 15:17; 23:20; Lev 4:24) and the temple (1 Chr 15:3; 2 Chr 3:1; Ps 26:8; Jer 19:3–4), the place where the Lord supplied with a sacrifice. The truth of grace was thus affirmed at the very place where the sacrificial lamb, prefiguring the divine sacrifice of Jesus Christ, was regularly slaughtered on the altar.

Abraham may have puzzled over the mysterious mechanism of grace, the free gift of salvation, impossible to be understood or known, which Paul would call "the unsearchable riches of Christ" (Eph 3:8; cf. Rom 11:33). The idea advocated by critics since Hermann Gunkel,[545] that behind the story lies an old etiological version testifying to an ancient Hebrew practice of child sacrifice, goes against the point of the story. The story instead emphasizes the need of God's grace for humans versus the vanity of human work for God.

Now I know. Abraham may not know, but God now knows. According to the Angel of the Lord, the Lord Himself, the purpose for this "test" was that God may know; this does not mean that God did not know. He certainly did know. But this

---

544 It is the same expression *shalakh yad* "stretch hand" (22:10) that is repeated here.

545 This view, which is still shared by a number of critics (see, for instance, G. W. Coats), has been deemed as "speculative" and unfounded for the lack of serious evidence (Wenham, *Genesis 16–50*, 105).

recognition by the Angel is a way to confirm God's covenant with Abraham. The "test" was not designed to frighten Abraham but to reassure him of His grace. Moses refers to the same notion of "test" to encourage Israel who was frightened: "Moses said to the people, 'Do not fear; for God has come to test you, and that His fear may be before you, so that you may not sin'" (Exod 20:20).

You have not withheld your son, your only son, from Me. The relationship between God and Abraham is thus reaffirmed, as implied in the personal pronouns "your ... Me." Abraham was willing to lose his son and risk his future for God. The language of this verse does not suggest, however, that Abraham was willing to slaughter his son for God's sake, as implied in the theology of Moloch. The Hebrew verb *khasakh mimenni* (usually translated "withhold from me") conveys the idea of trust. The same expression is used by Joseph when he refers to the trust of Potiphar: "everything he owns he has entrusted to my care ... My master has withheld nothing from me [*khasakh mimenni*] except you" (39:8–9 NIV).

The virtue that is recognized by the Angel regarding Abraham is not so much his capacity to sacrifice for God, but rather his capacity to trust God, to put his faith in Him. Abraham so trusted God that he even entrusted to Him his son, "his only son" (echoing God's terrible request, 22:2), knowing that "He will see." From a New Testament perspective, the father Abraham who gives his only son evokes God the Father who "so loved the world that He gave His only begotten Son, that whoever believes in Him should not perish but have everlasting life" (John 3:16).

22:13 **Then Abraham lifted his eyes and looked.** This phrase once again marks the last step of Abraham's activities, this time in regard to the sacrifice of Isaac. It contains the seventh verb, *wayyar'eh* "looked," a formula that "usually intimates that what is to be seen is of great significance (cf. 18:2; 24:63; 33:1, 5; 43:29)."[546]

And behold, ... a ram (ESV). What Abraham sees takes him by surprise, as indicated by the word "and behold" (*wehinneh*). The *'ayil* "ram" stands as the fulfilled reality of his expectation of faith. Even when we pray to God with faith and ask Him for something, the fulfillment of our request always surprises us, for our faith never measures up to God's response.

In this instance (22:7), Abraham was expecting a *seh*, that is, some kind of sacrificial animal. The Hebrew word *seh* translated "lamb" (NKJV) is the generic term for small cattle, referring in a general sense to "sheep" (NAB, TNK; cf. Exod 34:19; Josh 6:21), and could apply to a ram (Ezek 34:17).[547] Now Abraham is confronted with the specific "ram." His prayer turns from a vague, future, and abstract hope to the present, particular, and tangible reality.

Abraham understands that this animal has been provided by God in the place of Isaac. Thus, it signifies substitutionary atonement. The ram was God's gift, because Abraham was unable to provide for it. The intention of this story was not to answer the question of the origins of animal sacrifices or to prescribe what humans have to do and give to God in order to obtain salvation. The ram that took Isaac's place was God's gift to Abraham.

The process of salvation originates in God, as Paul emphasized: "God was in Christ reconciling the world to Himself" (2 Cor 5:19). Yet, beyond this substitutionary function of the animal, the ram as a burnt offering contains profound theological

---

546 Wenham, *Genesis 16–50*, 107.

547 See KBL, 916.

lessons. The nature of the sacrifice expressed its spiritual meaning. The burnt offering was the only sacrifice that required the burning of the totality of the animal: "The priest shall burn all on the altar as a burnt sacrifice" (Lev 1:9). The burnt offering pointed, then, to the wholeness of God's sacrifice through Jesus Christ for the salvation of humankind (Heb 9:12; 10:10). It is highly significant that the burnt offering— whether offered continuously, night and day, on the altar (Lev 6:9–13), as a voluntary sacrifice (Lev 1:2–3), or for the consecration of priests (Lev 9:2–3)—did not deal with specific sins, but rather with "the ingrained sinfulness of human nature."[548]

The burnt offering implied the people's "constant dependence upon the atoning blood of Christ"[549] and contained the great message of hope of the gospel—that our salvation depends entirely on God. John the Baptist thought of the same process when he identified Jesus Christ as "the Lamb of God who takes away the sin of the world" (John 1:29; cf. 1 John 3:2–3). Note that he did not refer to some specific sins but to "*the* sin of the world." John referred to the intrinsically sinful nature of the world and, hence, in essence its fundamental need for the atoning blood of Christ. The burnt offering does not just take care of the occasional sin. What is at stake is the salvation of the one who is a sinner by nature. Thus, this continual sacrifice before God "came to be seen as the most essential sacrifice."[550]

The sacrifice offered by Adam and Eve under God's instruction and supervision, the first sacrifice ever recorded in the Bible, was a burnt offering (3:21). We conclude this because only this sacrifice involved the use of the animal skin by the priests (Lev 7:8).[551] Abel also offered a burnt offering,[552] as did Noah as soon as he went out of the ark (8:20). Likewise a burnt offering was offered on the Day of Atonement (Lev 16:3, 5). More than any other biblical passage, this one shares the language with the text of the *'aqedah*. We find the same association of the words *'olah* "burnt offering" (22:13; cf. Lev 16:3, 5), *ra'ah* "appear," in the same passive form (*niphal*) (22:14; cf. Lev 16:2), *yiqqakh* "he took" (22:13; cf. Lev 16:5), and "one ram" (22:13; cf. Lev 16:6).[553] The presence of the "ram as a burnt offering" on the Day of Atonement, therefore, may have served not only as a way to convey the symbolic lessons implied

---

548 John E. Hartley, *Leviticus*, WBC 4 (Dallas: Word Books, 1992), 122.

549 Ellen G. White, PP 352.

550 Andrew E. Steinmann, *Daniel* (Saint Louis: Concordia, 2008), 396; cf. Ellen G. White, 1SM 343–344.

551 See Davidson, *The Flame of Yahweh*, 57–58.

552 Ibid., 49–52; cf. Ellen G. White, 3SG 47.

553 The majority of commentators suggest emending the word *'akhar* "behind" into *'ekhad* "one." Indeed, a number of observations would support the reading *'ekhad* "one" instead of *'akhar* "behind," implying a copyist mistake; the *daleth* (ד) and the *resh* (ר) look alike and could have easily been confused by a copyist (note that the mistake from the square shape of *daleth* to the round shape of *resh* is more likely to happen than the reverse; on the confusion of *daleth* and *resh* as one of the most frequent scribal misreadings, see Ernst Würthwein, *The Text of the Old Testament: An Introduction to the Biblia Hebraica* [Grand Rapids: Eerdmans, 1979], 107). 1. Textual argument: The testimony of many manuscripts and the support of the Septuagint, the Syriac, the Vulgate, and the Targum (see *BHS* Critical Apparatus). 2. Grammatical argument: The analysis of the Hebrew word *'akhar* "behind" as an adverb or as a preposition in a locational sense, meaning "at the back" or "behind" (see Joüon §103a) without the mention of a noun complement object (cf. 19:6) makes the syntax awkward, obliging the translator to supply the missing complement ("behind him," see NKJV, ESV; contra NIV, TNK, which translate "a ram"). 3. Stylistic argument: The analysis of this word in a temporal sense, meaning "after" ("and behold a ram *after* it was caught in the thicket") will nullify the force of the effect of abrupt surprise and temporal immediacy implied in the just mentioned *wehinneh* "and behold." Furthermore, this stylistic practice is not attested in biblical Hebrew, especially after the idiomatic phrase "lifted the eyes, saw, and behold" (see, for instance, 18:2; 24:63; 31:10; 33:1; 37:25; Josh 5:13; Dan 8:3; 10:5; etc.). Intertextual argument: The examination of the use of the phrase *'ayil 'akhad* "one ram" in the Hebrew Scriptures reveals that it is a technical expression generally referring to the sacrificial animal (see, for instance, Num 7:15; 28:27; 29:36), as it is here the case in the *'aqedah* (22:13). More importantly, the Levitical text, which is related to our passage on the basis of common words, has also the same expression *'ayil 'akhad* "one ram" (Lev 16:5).

in the burnt offering (see above), but also to remind the reader of the incident of the 'aqedah.

This unique intertextual connection suggests that the writer of the legislation of the Day of Atonement had the text of the 'aqedah in mind and that he deliberately set the story of the 'aqedah in the perspective of the Day of Atonement. Through such biblical allusions, it has thus been suggested that the story of Abraham's offering and binding of Isaac goes beyond the private religious experience of an individual and is "identified with the communal worship of God's people in which divine reality appears."[554] That the ram was provided by God points typologically to the eschatological Day of Atonement wherein God accepts that sacrifice for the historical fulfillment of the atonement of His people (Dan 8:14), in view of the kingdom of God (Dan 7:9–14).

So Abraham went. The Hebrew verb *wayyelek* "he went" echoes the divine call *lek leka* "go!" which started the story (22:2), just as the other words of the sentence echo God's initial command ("took," "offered for burnt offering," "his son").

Instead of his son. This is the second time that the process of substitution takes place. First, God Himself had been "provided" as ("instead of") the lamb for the sacrifice (22:8), and thus implicitly "instead" of the son. It is the ram, which is now substituted by God as the sacrifice, "instead of" the son. God, the lamb, and the ram are involved in the same drama, as if they were identified with each other. This redemptive substitution, which costs the death of God behind the lamb and the ram, reminds us of the scenario of the prophecy of Genesis 3:15 where the messianic seed will die for the salvation of humankind (3:15). It evokes the substitutionary atonement, which characterized the sacrificial system of Israel (Lev 6:6–7; 16:5–6; 1 Pet 2:24; Heb 9:28).

22:14 **And Abraham called the name of the place, The Lord-Will-Provide.** The prophecy that Abraham pronounced to his son, "God will see Himself as the lamb" (22:8), is now repeated in an abbreviated version. After Abraham offers the ram, the name he gives the place is *YHWH Yir'eh* "the Lord will see" (lit. trans.), "God will see." To justify this naming, Abraham changes the form of the verb *ra'ah* "see." Instead of the simple form (*qal*) *yir'eh* "He will see," he uses the passive form (*niphal*) *yera'eh* "He will be seen" (lit. trans.). This is the same passive form that is used in Leviticus 16 to describe the appearance of the Lord on the Day of Atonement: *'era'eh* "I will appear" (lit. trans.: "I will be seen") "in the cloud above the mercy seat" (Lev 16:2).

The grammatical correspondence suggests that Abraham has in view, through the offering of the ram he just performed, the service of the Day of Atonement, when the Lord (already identified as the lamb) will appear on the mercy seat. Jewish tradition has not only related the 'aqedah (22:7) to Passover,[555] it also associated the 'aqedah and the Day of Atonement.[556] In addition, the 'aqedah is a prominent motif in the liturgies of Rosh Hashanah and the Day of Atonement.[557]

The connection between the 'aqedah and the Day of Atonement can also be found

---

554 S. D. Walters, "Wood, Sand and Stars: Structure and Theology in Gen 22:1–19," *Toronto Journal of Theology* 3 (1987): 305–306, 309–310.

555 *Mekhilta de-Rabbi Ishmael* 2. 3. 2.

556 *Ta'an.* 2:4, 16a; b. Rosh Hashanah 16a; Gen. Rab. 56:9.

557 See, for instance, the *Musaf* of the New Year liturgy in Joseph H. Herz, *The Authorized Daily Prayer Book* (New York: Bloch Publishing, 1948), 880–883.

in Romans 8:32, which parallels God's offering of His Son to the ʿaqedah in terms evoking the Day of Atonement (Rom 8:32).[558]

In the Mount of the Lord. This expression always refers to the place of the temple in Jerusalem (Isa 2:3; Mic 4:1; Zech 8:3; Isa 30:29), thus confirming Moriah as the place of the temple.

22:15 **Then the Angel of the Lord called … a second time out of heaven.** The Angel of the Lord calls again to Abraham "out of heaven." The repetition of the same introductory phrase "the Angel of the Lord called … out of heaven" (22:15; cf. 22:11), the specification "a second time," and the repetition of the same reference to Abraham's action, "you have … not withheld your son, your only son" (22:16; cf. 22:12), places this call in the line of the first call. This time, however, it is no longer a dialogue. Only the Angel speaks.

22:16 **And said: By Myself I have sworn, says the Lord.** The Angel of the Lord is now identified with the Lord Himself (see the comments on 16:7). Of the seventy-five occurrences of the verb "swear" (*shabaʿ*) in the passive form (*niphal*) with God as the subject, in only five instances God swears by Himself (22:16; Exod 32:13; Isa 45:23; Jer 22:5; 49:13). That God swears by Himself is to affirm the certainty of the promise (it is God who swears) and to emphasize that its fulfillment depends only on God (by Himself). The rhythm of the seven Hebrew verbs[559] that make up the divine discourse reinforce the sacredness of the divine oath.

22:17–18 **Blessing I will bless you.** The blessing is certain, as expressed in the verbal form (infinitive absolute). It will have an impact on the future: It concerns not only the future of Abraham himself, who will have many descendants, but also concerns the future of the nations. The promise that Abraham's descendants will **possess the gate of their enemies** means symbolically the promise of victory of the "seed" (*zeraʿ*) over the enemy. This is reminiscent of the prophecy of Genesis 3:15, which also promises the victory of the messianic seed (*zeraʿ*) over the enemy. The Hebrew has ʾoybaw "*his* enemies" (masculine singular), an indication that the "seed" refers to one single individual and not in a corporate way to a people. The reference again to the "seed" (*zeraʿ*) in verse 18 confirms the allusion from a positive perspective: the blessing of Abraham, which implies victory of the "seed" over the enemies, leads to the blessing of the nations by the "seed" (Gal 3:14–16).

The experience of the ʿaqedah thus opens up a cosmic perspective, namely, the salvation of the world. This lesson seems to have been retained in the epistle to the Hebrews, which applies the blessing concluding the ʿaqedah (22:17; cf. Heb 6:14) to the extraordinary moment of the Day of Atonement when the High Priest could penetrate "behind the veil" (Heb 6:19; cf. Lev 16:2, 15).

22:19 **Abraham returned.** Only Abraham returns. Strangely, Isaac is not mentioned. This omission has intrigued many interpreters who speculated about Isaac's fate. But this omission may be intentional to include this time not only Abraham and Isaac, but also the two other servants (or sons) in the return journey.

---

558 See Paba Nidrani De Andrado, *The Aqedah Servant Complex: The Soteriological Linkage of Genesis 22 and Isaiah 53 in Ancient Jewish and Early Christian Writings* (Peeters: Leuven, 2013), 162. On early traces of Christian tradition connecting the ʿaqedah and the Day of Atonement, see Daniel Stökl Ben Ezra, *The Impact of Yom Kippur on Early Christianity* (Tübingen: Mohr Siebeck, 2003), 150–151. For a discussion on the allusion to the ʿaqedah in this passage, see James D. G. Dunn, *Romans 1–8*, WBC 38A (Dallas: Word Books, 1988), 501–502.

559 We count the following verbs: *nishbaʿti* "I have sworn," *barek* "blessing," *ʾabarekkha* "I will bless you," *harbeh* "multiplying," *ʾarbeh* "I will multiply," *weyirash* "shall possess," and *wehitbareku* "shall be blessed."

The story starts with Abraham, who is described as alone in the journey to "the place" *wayyelek* "went" (22:3). Then he continues with Isaac, *wayyelku shneyhem yakhdaw* "the two of them went together" (22:6, 8), and ends with everyone together. Significantly, the verb *wayyelku* "they went" (22:19) that corresponds to God's call to "go" has no subject explicitly indicated. Now, after the sacrifice, everyone is part of the journey. The final lesson of the *'aqedah* is universal.

4. FROM THE PROMISED LAND TO EGYPT:
ISAAC-JACOB-JOSEPH

GENESIS 22:20–48:22

After the double call of *lek leka*, which marked the life of Abraham (12:1–22:19), section 4 of the book of Genesis (B₁: 22:20–47:26) moves in parallel to section 2 (B: 3:1–11:32). Both sections are oriented with the same perspective, toward Babel in section 2 and toward Egypt in this section (4). Similar to the focus in section 2 on the three great generators of the history of humankind after Adam (Seth, Noah, and Shem), section 4 focuses on the three great generators of the people of Israel after Abraham, namely, Isaac, Jacob, and Joseph (22:20–48:22). As in section 2, the three patriarchal cycles are not clearly delineated; when the new cycle begins, the preceding patriarch is still alive and the preceding cycle is therefore still in effect to a certain extent while the attention has shifted to the new patriarch.

22:20–25:18. ISAAC

Now that Isaac has survived the test of the *'aqedah*, his future, which was for a moment at risk, is ensured. The focus thus far has been on Abraham; Isaac has been relegated to the shadows. The emphasis now shifts to Isaac who emerges as the hero, the new patriarch of the chosen people. However, the message conveyed through the following stories remains ambivalent. Hope is associated with death and the insecurity of exile. The genealogical news regarding Abraham's brother Nahor (22:20–24) carries both the reminder of Abraham's exilic condition and the promise of a bride for Isaac (22:23). Similarly, the report of Sarah's death and burial (23:1–20) not only reinforces Abraham's consciousness of his alien status (23:4), but also the prospect of Isaac receiving comfort from Rebekah (24:67). The listing of Abraham's sons with his new wife Keturah (25:1–4) is associated with his special commitment to his son Isaac (25:5–6), and the report of Abraham's death and burial (25:7–11) is coupled with the genealogy of Ishmael (25:12–18).

GENEALOGY OF REBEKAH (22:20–24)

GEN 22:20–24 NKJV	GEN 22:20–24 ESV
20 Now it came to pass after these things that it was told Abraham, saying, "Indeed Milcah also has borne children to your brother Nahor:	**20** Now after these things it was told to Abraham, "Behold, Milcah also has borne children to your brother Nahor:
21 Huz his firstborn, Buz his brother, Kemuel the father of Aram,	**21** Uz his firstborn, Buz his brother, Kemuel the father of Aram,
22 Chesed, Hazo, Pildash, Jidlaph, and Bethuel."	**22** Chesed, Hazo, Pildash, Jidlaph, and Bethuel."
23 And Bethuel begot Rebekah. These eight Milcah bore to Nahor, Abraham's brother.	**23** (Bethuel fathered Rebekah.) These eight Milcah bore to Nahor, Abraham's brother.
24 His concubine, whose name was Reumah, also bore Tebah, Gaham, Thahash, and Maachah.	**24** Moreover, his concubine, whose name was Reumah, bore Tebah, Gaham, Tahash, and Maacah.

22:20 This genealogy seems out of place right after the story of the *'aqedah*. However, the use of the same introductory phrase **Now it came ... after these things** (22:20; cf. 22:1) suggests some type of connection between the two accounts. In both cases, Abraham is surprised by an unexpected announcement. In the first account, Abraham hears the sentence of death against Isaac, thus crushing all hopes for the future. In the second instance, Abraham hears news of birth and thus of promise for the future. This second report is directly related to the preceding story and is a direct response to the experience of the *'aqedah*. The message of hope implied in the sacrifice is beginning to be fulfilled.

Milcah also has borne children. The small Hebrew word *gam* "also" is a subtle allusion to the preceding story concerning Abraham's "only" son Isaac, who recently escaped death, and thus indirectly relates Rebekah to Isaac. In the report of births, Rebekah is the only girl and the only child that belongs to the next generation.

22:21 **Kemuel the father of Aram.** This pause on the name of Aram, which also refers to Mesopotamia, anticipates the future residence of Jacob (24:10; 35:9), where he will father his twelve sons. This Aramean origin of the one who will become Israel will be an identification mark for the Israelite descendants (Deut 26:5).

22:22–23 **Bethuel begot Rebekah.** The sequence of the names, beginning with Huz the firstborn (22:21) and ending with Bethuel (22:22), suggests that Bethuel is the youngest of eight sons, a hint at the divine process of election, working beyond the natural rights of the firstborn (25:23). Rebekah, the only daughter in the genealogy, appears as the climax and the last link of these genealogies (22:23), an indication that she was the reason for the genealogy.

The parallel between the twelve sons of Nahor (22:20–24), the twelve sons of Jacob (35:22–26), and the twelve sons of Ishmael (17:20; 25:12–16) suggests that God is in control of all of these genealogical histories. God's blessing on Abraham has an effect on the destiny of his relatives.

SARAH'S DEATH AND BURIAL (23:1–20)

The story of the death of Sarah prepares the reader for the first steps of Isaac as an independent patriarch who will marry and father the elected descendants. The attention given to the story of the purchase of the burial place (which covers most of the chapter), rather than to the story of Sarah's death, emphasizes the physical connection to the Promised Land. The structure of this report is marked by the keyword *wayyaqom* "stood up," "deeded" that indicates, after the introduction about Sarah's long life and death (23:1–2), the three steps of the legal procedure (22:3–6, 7–16, 17–20). The Hebrew verb *wayyaqom* "stood up," "deeded" appears four times, twice referring to Abraham who "stood up" (23:3, 7) and twice referring to the fulfillment of the legal operation (23:17, 20; translated "were deeded"), thus suggesting the following structure:

23:1–2 Introduction: Sarah's long life
23:3 *wayyaqom*, Abraham's request (23:3–6)
23:7 *wayyaqom*, Abraham's transaction (23:7–16)
23:17 *wayyaqom*, fulfillment of deed/Sarah (23:17–19)

23:20 *wayyaqom,* fulfillment of deed/Abraham's descendants

The first two occurrences describe Abraham's position "stood up" (23:3, 7), and the third and fourth occurrences signals the fulfillment of the legal procedure: "deeded" (23:17).

23:1–2. SARAH'S LONG LIFE

GEN 23:1–2 NKJV	GEN 23:1–2 ESV
1 Sarah lived one hundred and twenty-seven years; *these were* the years of the life of Sarah.	**1** Sarah lived 127 years; these were the years of the life of Sarah.
2 So Sarah died in Kirjath Arba (that *is*, Hebron) in the land of Canaan, and Abraham came to mourn for Sarah and to weep for her.	**2** And Sarah died at Kiriath-arba (that is, Hebron) in the land of Canaan, and Abraham went in to mourn for Sarah and to weep for her.

23:1 Sarah lived one hundred and twenty-seven years … the life of Sarah. Note the inclusion of the words *khayyey sarah* "life of Sarah," which begins and ends the Hebrew verse. This theme of a long life is echoed in the beginning of the next chapter in relation to Abraham, who is also qualified as **old, well advanced in age** (24:1). This echo between the two texts marks the delimitations of the passage, while relating Abraham's and Sarah's old ages with the forthcoming marriage of Isaac. Sarah is the only woman in the Old Testament whose number of years is recorded, an indication of her importance; she thus receives the same status as the patriarchs (25:7; 35:28; 47:28). Because Sarah is ninety years old when Isaac is born (17:17; cf. 21:5), he is thirty-seven years old when she dies.

23:2 So Sarah died in … the land of Canaan. The mention of the phrase "in the land of Canaan," which is repeated twice in relation to Sarah's death (23:19), underlines the rooting of Sarah's death and burial (23:19) in God's promise of the land.

Kirjath Arba. The name of the city means "city of four," probably referring to a group of cities (cf. Josh 21:39), a notion already implied in the name of **Hebron**, which is derived from the Hebrew verb *khabar,* meaning "group." This term appears in the Mari documents to designate "an association of wandering families which have been drawn into closer union as a result of their nomadic status."[560] The name has also been explained as "the city of Arba" after the name of Arba, a giant Canaanite (Josh 14:15; 15:13).

23:3–6. ABRAHAM'S REQUEST TO THE SONS OF HETH

GEN 23:3–6 NKJV	GEN 23:3–6 ESV
3 Then Abraham stood up from before his dead, and spoke to the sons of Heth, saying,	**3** And Abraham rose up from before his dead and said to the Hittites,
4 "I *am* a foreigner and a visitor among you. Give me property for a burial place among you, that I may bury my dead out of my sight."	**4** "I am a sojourner and foreigner among you; give me property among you for a burying place, that I may bury my dead out of my sight."

---

560 A. Malamat, "Man and the Bible: Some Patterns of Tribal Organization and Institutions," *JAOS* 82 (1962): 145.

5 And the sons of Heth answered Abraham, saying to him,	**5** The Hittites answered Abraham,
6 "Hear us, my lord: You *are* a mighty prince among us; bury your dead in the choicest of our burial places. None of us will withhold from you his burial place, that you may bury your dead."	**6** "Hear us, my lord; you are a prince of God among us. Bury your dead in the choicest of our tombs. None of us will withhold from you his tomb to hinder you from burying your dead."

23:3 **Then Abraham stood up.** The fact that Abraham "stood up" suggests that he must have been sitting, which is the position of mourning (Isa 3:26; 47:1; Job 2:13), thus indicating that Abraham has moved **from before his dead** wife, ready for action.

23:4 Abraham initiates the conversation with **the sons of Heth**. The Hittites were one of the ten nations from whom Abraham was supposed to inherit the land (15:20; cf. Josh 1:4). They should not be identified with the Hittites of the Hittite Empire, who occupied the territories expanding from Anatolia (modern Turkey) to the kingdom of Kadesh (on the Orontes), or with the Hittites of Syria, who were connected to the Judean kingdoms (1 Kgs 10:29).[561] Their names were notably Semitic (e.g., Ephron) instead of properly Hittite (an Indo-European language), and they seemed to speak a common language with Abraham, although probably with some foreign accent.[562]

Give me property. Abraham presents himself as **a foreigner and a sojourner** (ESV), which means a "resident alien." Abraham is not simply interested in acquiring a piece of land for the special occasion of Sarah's death.

23:5–6 **Our burial places.** The change of terms from "a property" to "our burial places" betrays the Hittites' intentions. Note their emphasis on the phrase "our burial places," which appears in the beginning of the sentence and on the personal pronoun, which twice refers to their possession of burials ("our," "his"). Obviously, they are not willing to abandon their land. Their exaggerated politeness (**my lord**, **mighty prince**)[563] is suspect. Yet, as reflected in the following lengthy discussion between Abraham and the sons of Heth, Abraham is primarily concerned in establishing himself permanently in the Promised Land.

23:7–16. ABRAHAM'S TRANSACTION WITH EPHRON

GEN 23:7–16 NKJV	GEN 23:7–16 ESV
7 Then Abraham stood up and bowed himself to the people of the land, the sons of Heth.	**7** Abraham rose and bowed to the Hittites, the people of the land.
8 And he spoke with them, saying, "If it is your wish that I bury my dead out of my sight, hear me, and meet with Ephron the son of Zohar for me,	**8** And he said to them, "If you are willing that I should bury my dead out of my sight, hear me and entreat for me Ephron the son of Zohar,

561 See Waltke and Fredericks, *Genesis*, 317; cf. H. A. Hoffner, "The Hittites and Hurrians," in *Peoples of Old Testament Times*, ed. D. J. Wiseman (Oxford: Clarendon, 1973), 213–214.

562 See Rabin's suggestion on his observation of the awkward spelling of the concluding *lo* (23:5) in C. Rabin, "L-With Imperative (Gen 23)," *JSS* 13 (1968): 113–124.

563 The Hebrew phrase *nasi' 'elohim* means literally "prince of God," but the use of the name *'Elohim* "God" is probably to be understood as a superlative (see *IBHS*, 14, 5b).

9 that he may give me the cave of Machpelah which he has, which *is* at the end of his field. Let him give it to me at the full price, as property for a burial place among you."

9 that he may give me the cave of Machpelah, which he owns; it is at the end of his field. For the full price let him give it to me in your presence as property for a burying place."

10 Now Ephron dwelt among the sons of Heth; and Ephron the Hittite answered Abraham in the presence of the sons of Heth, all who entered at the gate of his city, saying,

10 Now Ephron was sitting among the Hittites, and Ephron the Hittite answered Abraham in the hearing of the Hittites, of all who went in at the gate of his city,

11 "No, my lord, hear me: I give you the field and the cave that *is* in it; I give it to you in the presence of the sons of my people. I give it to you. Bury your dead!"

11 "No, my lord, hear me: I give you the field, and I give you the cave that is in it. In the sight of the sons of my people I give it to you. Bury your dead."

12 Then Abraham bowed himself down before the people of the land;

12 Then Abraham bowed down before the people of the land.

13 and he spoke to Ephron in the hearing of the people of the land, saying, "If you *will give it*, please hear me. I will give you money for the field; take *it* from me and I will bury my dead there."

13 And he said to Ephron in the hearing of the people of the land, "But if you will, hear me: I give the price of the field. Accept it from me, that I may bury my dead there."

14 And Ephron answered Abraham, saying to him,

14 Ephron answered Abraham,

15 "My lord, listen to me; the land *is worth* four hundred shekels of silver. What *is* that between you and me? So bury your dead."

15 "My lord, listen to me: a piece of land worth four hundred shekels of silver, what is that between you and me? Bury your dead."

16 And Abraham listened to Ephron; and Abraham weighed out the silver for Ephron which he had named in the hearing of the sons of Heth, four hundred shekels of silver, currency of the merchants.

16 Abraham listened to Ephron, and Abraham weighed out for Ephron the silver that he had named in the hearing of the Hittites, four hundred shekels of silver, according to the weights current among the merchants.

23:7 Abraham's first address is directed generally to the sons of Heth before whom he stands (*wayyaqom*). Abraham does not respond to their compliments; although they call him "prince" he bows himself and humbly pleads his case with all parties.

23:8 **Meet with Ephron the son of Zohar.** The Hebrew verb *paga'* (translated "meet") means "to intercede" (Jer 7:16) and may denote violence (1 Kgs 2:25). Abraham requests that the sons of Heth put strong pressure on Ephron, the owner of the plot. The fact that Ephron is identified by his father's name, which is rare for a non-Israelite, suggests that Ephron was well known by the family of Abraham or that he was a prominent leader (cf. 34:2).

23:9 **Machpelah.** This name derives from the root *kapal*, meaning "double" (the Septuagint translates "double cave"), perhaps referring to the multiple occupancy of the cave. Abraham must have also thought of using that place for himself and his descendants (25:9; 49:30). This location is identified today with the tomb located in the Arab mosque called *Haram el-Khalil* "holy place of the friend," situated in the town of Hebron. Abraham's qualification of the place of the tomb **at the end of his field** is his argument that the selling of the cave will in no way affect the value of the field.

Full price. This may be a legal expression referring to paying cash for the totality of the price, thus suggesting the irrevocability of the sale. By offering "full price," Abraham shows not only his wealth, but also his generosity, to ensure Ephron's positive response.

23:10 **The gate of his city.** The typical setting at the city gate in the presence of witnesses (**the sons of Heth, all who entered**) gives formal legality to the transaction. The phrase "enter the gate of the city" is technical language designating the involvement of the elders of the city in a legal affair.[564]

23:11–16 **I give you the field and the cave.** This abnormal generosity on the part of the one who sells the cave is suspect. Ephron will later demand **four hundred shekels** (23:15). Because silver coinage was a later development, the transaction was therefore made on the basis of weight. A shekel is estimated to be approximately 0.403 ounces (11.424 grams);[565] therefore, four hundred shekels would be equivalent to approximately 10 pounds (4.57 kilograms), which was high compared to the fifty shekels David paid for the temple site (2 Sam 24:24). Ephron pretends to offer the cave and even adds the field in the deal in order to gain Abraham's confidence and eventually obtain more than the actual value of the property. Another reason for Ephron's generosity is that he wants to maintain his rights over the land. Regardless of Ephron's motivations, Abraham understands Ephron's strategy. The narrative plays on the verb "give," which occurs seven times in the passage, thus reflecting the interchange between Ephron and Abraham. The bargaining discussion is typically Middle Eastern, each one emphasizing that he is "giving" to the other. Whereas Ephron uses the verb "give" three times (23:11 [3x]), Abraham uses it four times (23:4, 9 [2x], 13 [Heb]), showing that he is willing to go the extra mile and give even more than requested. Abraham does not even discuss the price but accepts Ephron's proposal as it is: **Abraham weighed out the silver for Ephron which he had named** (23:16). The exact repetition of Ephron's terms and the precise report of the paid sum (**four hundred shekels of silver, currency of the merchants**) give to the transaction its legal character and value. The Hebrew word *kesep* refers to the metal silver, which was then the common item of exchange. A system of coinage was not used in Egypt before the sixth century BC under Greek influence.

23:17–20. THE FULFILLMENT OF THE DEED

GEN 23:17–20 NKJV	GEN 23:17–20 ESV
17 So the field of Ephron which *was* in Machpelah, which *was* before Mamre, the field and the cave which *was* in it, and all the trees that *were* in the field, which *were* within all the surrounding borders, were deeded	**17** So the field of Ephron in Machpelah, which was to the east of Mamre, the field with the cave that was in it and all the trees that were in the field, throughout its whole area, was made over
18 to Abraham as a possession in the presence of the sons of Heth, before all who went in at the gate of his city.	**18** to Abraham as a possession in the presence of the Hittites, before all who went in at the gate of his city.

---

564 H. Reviv, "Early Elements and Late Terminology in the Descriptions of Non-Israelite Cities in the Bible," *IEJ* 27 (1977): 83–88.

565 See *IDB* 4:832. SDABC estimates that it is the equivalent of $116, which is not certain because the value depended on the time and place.

19 And after this, Abraham buried Sarah his wife in the cave of the field of Machpelah, before Mamre (that *is*, Hebron) in the land of Canaan.	**19** After this, Abraham buried Sarah his wife in the cave of the field of Machpelah east of Mamre (that is, Hebron) in the land of Canaan.
20 So the field and the cave that *is* in it were deeded to Abraham by the sons of Heth as property for a burial place.	**20** The field and the cave that is in it were made over to Abraham as property for a burying place by the Hittites.

Deeded. The Hebrew verb *wayyaqom* "deeded" is placed at the beginning of the sentence. It is a commercial term meaning that the contract was solid, literally "standing." Note that the term is used twice, referring to the two aspects of possession. The first time ownership is connected to the legal operation (23:17), and the second time it relates to the burial of Sarah (23:19–20). Abraham owns the place legally because of the legal procedure and physically because of the physical presence of Sarah.

A WIFE FOR ISAAC (24:1–67)

This is the longest chapter of the book of Genesis. That the story of the betrothal of Isaac and Rebekah is given immediately after the story of Sarah's death, more precisely three years later (25:20), suggests that the two events are related, a notion that is reinforced by two pieces of information framing the whole plot. In the beginning of the story, Abraham's insistence that Isaac not settle outside of Canaan because of God's promise to give this land to his descendants (24:7) points to the previous chapter where Abraham has just purchased the land in view of that same perspective. Similarly, at the end of the story, Isaac's move to bring Rebekah to Sarah's tent and the notation that Isaac's love for Rebekah comforted him **after his mother's death** (24:67) points back to the preceding chapter that tells of Sarah's death. Given that his father is old and his mother is dead, it is time for Isaac to sever the umbilical cord. However, it is still the father who seeks a wife for his son, a unique case in the book of Genesis. This particular initiative from Abraham indicates something about the personality of Isaac, who is not so eager to leave home, and makes a statement about the importance of marriage. This marriage is extremely crucial to Abraham because of the future of salvation history, and the transmission of the messianic seed depends on it. Abraham is therefore highly concerned and wants to ensure that the Abrahamic line gains a proper foothold. The story is also a lesson about God's providence. In this chapter, the Lord (*YHWH*) who never speaks is, however, mentioned seventeen times. This emphasis is notable after the preceding chapter where He is not mentioned at all. The prayers and the miracles that punctuate this story convey the message that it is ultimately God who controls events, in spite of human maneuvers. Another keyword of the chapter is the verb "go" (*halak*), which also occurs seventeen times, seven of which are related to Rebekah, who becomes the "female Abraham."[566] Isaac's passivity could also be interpreted as an attitude of faith. Isaac, who is the hero of the plot, significantly appears last, after the interventions of Abraham, the servant, and Laban.

---

566 Wenham, *Genesis 16–50*, 138.

295

LITERARY STRUCTURE

The story takes place in Canaan, in Mesopotamia, and then in Canaan again, in five different settings, following the journey of the servant. The parallels and echoes between the diverse sections in connection to the respective geographical locations suggest an ABCB₁A₁ chiastic structure:

A Canaan, in Abraham's house: Abraham and the servant (24:1–9)
 B Mesopotamia, by the well: The servant and Rebekah (24:10–27)
  C Mesopotamia, in Rebekah's house: The servant and Laban (24:28–61)
 B₁ Canaan, by the well: Isaac (the servant) and Rebekah (24:62–65)
A₁ Canaan, in Sarah's tent: Isaac (the servant) and Rebekah (24:66–67)

24:1–9. IN CANAAN, IN ABRAHAM'S HOUSE

GEN 24:1–9 NKJV	GEN 24:1–9 ESV
1 Now Abraham was old, well advanced in age; and the Lᴏʀᴅ had blessed Abraham in all things.	**1** Now Abraham was old, well advanced in years. And the Lᴏʀᴅ had blessed Abraham in all things.
2 So Abraham said to the oldest servant of his house, who ruled over all that he had, "Please, put your hand under my thigh,	**2** And Abraham said to his servant, the oldest of his household, who had charge of all that he had, "Put your hand under my thigh,
3 and I will make you swear by the Lᴏʀᴅ, the God of heaven and the God of the earth, that you will not take a wife for my son from the daughters of the Canaanites, among whom I dwell;	**3** that I may make you swear by the Lᴏʀᴅ, the God of heaven and God of the earth, that you will not take a wife for my son from the daughters of the Canaanites, among whom I dwell,
4 but you shall go to my country and to my family, and take a wife for my son Isaac."	**4** but will go to my country and to my kindred, and take a wife for my son Isaac."
5 And the servant said to him, "Perhaps the woman will not be willing to follow me to this land. Must I take your son back to the land from which you came?"	**5** The servant said to him, "Perhaps the woman may not be willing to follow me to this land. Must I then take your son back to the land from which you came?"
6 But Abraham said to him, "Beware that you do not take my son back there.	**6** Abraham said to him, "See to it that you do not take my son back there.
7 The Lᴏʀᴅ God of heaven, who took me from my father's house and from the land of my family, and who spoke to me and swore to me, saying, 'To your descendants I give this land,' He will send His angel before you, and you shall take a wife for my son from there.	**7** The Lᴏʀᴅ, the God of heaven, who took me from my father's house and from the land of my kindred, and who spoke to me and swore to me, 'To your offspring I will give this land,' he will send his angel before you, and you shall take a wife for my son from there.
8 And if the woman is not willing to follow you, then you will be released from this oath; only do not take my son back there."	**8** But if the woman is not willing to follow you, then you will be free from this oath of mine; only you must not take my son back there."
9 So the servant put his hand under the thigh of Abraham his master, and swore to him concerning this matter.	**9** So the servant put his hand under the thigh of Abraham his master and swore to him concerning this matter.

The first scene takes place in Canaan and involves Abraham, who initiates the conversation, and his servant.

24:1–2 The qualification **oldest** (*zakan*) **servant** (24:2), which echoes the reference to the old (*zaken*) Abraham (24:1), suggests the intimate relation between the two persons; Abraham and his servant share the same faith and worldview. The use of the word "old" does not necessarily mean that this servant is old in age. Whereas the adjective "old" is explicit for Abraham as "advanced in age," the adjective for the servant is connected to the house, suggesting that he is the elder of the house, the senior administrator of the house. This servant is perhaps Eliezer, the very one who was born in Abraham's house (15:3) and whom Abraham previously considered as his heir (15:2–3), and likely the one who attended the Moriah experience (22:3).

24:3 I will make you swear. The ceremony of swearing consists of two components, a gestural one and a verbal one. The gestural component is commanded by Abraham upon his servant: **put your hand under my thigh** (24:2). The "thigh" (*yerek*), being a euphemism for genitalia, was perceived as the seat of procreation (46:26; Exod 1:5). This evocation of the future births of the Abrahamic line resonates with the text of the verbal component, which refers to the God of creation **the Lord, the God of heaven and the God of the earth**. The association of "the God of heaven" with "the God of the earth" points to Genesis 1:1, which speaks of God as the Creator of the heavenly universe and the planet Earth. The two names of God, which signify the two perspectives in Genesis 1 and 2, are here mentioned together: "the Lord" *YHWH* and "God" *'Elohim*. The name *'Elohim* is associated with the creation of the heavens and the earth (1:1–2:4a), and the name *YHWH* is associated with the close Presence of the Lord who works for the salvation of humankind (2:4b–25). Swearing by this God is, first of all, a prayer for God's powers of creation and salvation with direct bearing on the births of Abraham's descendants; more specifically, this swearing contains the promise of Abraham's descendants, those who will come from the "thigh" of Abraham, including the Messiah Himself. Implied in this hope is also the promise for the servant that this God will be with him and will control the operation. The old Abraham is also particularly concerned that in the event of his death his servant will not take a wife for his son **from the daughters of the Canaanites, among whom I dwell** (24:3). The word "dwell" (*yashab*) is reminiscent of Abraham's previous self-identification with the sons of Heth when he refers to himself as a "sojourner" (*toshab*) (23:4). Abraham may be alluding to his most recent experience with the Canaanites, which gave him some insight into their mentality.

24:4 But you shall go to my country and to my family. This recommendation is not simply dictated by the custom obliging marriage within the family (endogamy). Despite certain polytheistic trends (31:34), Abraham's family was acquainted with his religion if one considers Abraham's personal testimony (see the comments on 12:5), Laban's response to the miraculous story told by the servant, and his familiar reference to the Lord (24:50). Abraham wants to remain faithful to the requirements of his covenant with God and not choose women among the idolatrous Canaanites; he is thus the first to enunciate and implement this principle, which will be clearly stated in the Mosaic legislation, in order to avoid apostasy and idolatry (Exod 34:15–16; Deut 7:3–4; cf. Num 25; Ezra 9:2, 12).

24:5 Perhaps the woman will not be willing to follow me to this land. The servant's concern is legitimate. Not only does Rebekah not know her future husband, she would also have to leave her family and follow a complete stranger. The scenario obliging Isaac to move to Mesopotamia would then be a possible alternative. The use of the verb *halak* to characterize Rebekah's going from her place echoes the verb *halak* that Abraham used to characterize his own going from that place (24:4). Abraham subsequently relates Rebekah's going to his own going. Rebekah's going pertains to the same quality of faith.

24:6–8 Abraham's response to his servant is immediate and without ambiguity. That Isaac would go there is absolutely not an option. The Hebrew verb *hishamer leka*, translated **beware** (24:6), denotes an extremely strong reaction to an unacceptable idea (31:24, 29; Exod 34:12; Deut 4:9). Abraham's reasoning is coherent with God's requirement to leave the place of his kindred (12:1) and His promise that He would give Canaan to his descendants (12:7). Abraham therefore possesses the faith that God will remain consistent and facilitate the operation. The reference to the **Angel of the Lord** is an allusion to the experience of the *ʿaqedah,* where the Angel of the Lord was sent to rescue Isaac from being slaughtered by his father (22:11). The same angel who saved Isaac with regard to his death will save him with regard to his marriage. Abraham's reference to **the God of heaven** (24:7) is also congruent with the coming of this Angel who calls from heaven (22:11). The qualification "God of heaven" points also to the previous title (24:3), where it is associated with "the God of the earth." This association of "heaven and earth" is an allusion to the God of creation (cf. 1:1; 14:19). By mentioning only the first part of the title, Abraham underlines the majestic and cosmic dimension of this God, in order to reassure his servant. The God who controls the universe is able to control forthcoming events. However, Abraham leaves open the possibility that the woman will not respond to God's call. As powerful as this God may be, humans remain free before Him. Although Rebekah's departure is intended to be part of God's plan, she retains her freedom of choice. The only issue upon which Abraham will not compromise is that Isaac should not go back **there** (24:8). That the country is not even referred to by name is significant; it is only designated by the word *sham* "there," which is repeated four times (24:5–8), implying a derogatory intention.

24:9 The mention of the oath, which seals the ritual, echoes the mention of the oath, which mentions its promise, thus forming an inclusio (cf. 24:3). (On the significance of the gesture of putting one's hand under the thigh, see the comments in 24:2.)

24:10–27. MESOPOTAMIA, BY THE WELL: THE SERVANT AND REBEKAH

GEN 24:10–27 NKJV	GEN 24:10–27 ESV
10 Then the servant took ten of his master's camels and departed, for all his master's goods *were in* his hand. And he arose and went to Mesopotamia, to the city of Nahor.	**10** Then the servant took ten of his master's camels and departed, taking all sorts of choice gifts from his master; and he arose and went to Mesopotamia to the city of Nahor.
11 And he made his camels kneel down outside the city by a well of water at evening time, the time when women go out to draw *water*.	**11** And he made the camels kneel down outside the city by the well of water at the time of evening, the time when women go out to draw water.
12 Then he said, "O Lᴏʀᴅ God of my master Abraham, please give me success this day, and show kindness to my master Abraham.	**12** And he said, "O Lᴏʀᴅ, God of my master Abraham, please grant me success today and show steadfast love to my master Abraham.

13 Behold, *here* I stand by the well of water, and the daughters of the men of the city are coming out to draw water.

14 Now let it be that the young woman to whom I say, 'Please let down your pitcher that I may drink,' and she says, 'Drink, and I will also give your camels a drink'—*let* her *be the one* You have appointed for Your servant Isaac. And by this I will know that You have shown kindness to my master."

15 And it happened, before he had finished speaking, that behold, Rebekah, who was born to Bethuel, son of Milcah, the wife of Nahor, Abraham's brother, came out with her pitcher on her shoulder.

16 Now the young woman *was* very beautiful to behold, a virgin; no man had known her. And she went down to the well, filled her pitcher, and came up.

17 And the servant ran to meet her and said, "Please let me drink a little water from your pitcher."

18 So she said, "Drink, my lord." Then she quickly let her pitcher down to her hand, and gave him a drink.

19 And when she had finished giving him a drink, she said, "I will draw *water* for your camels also, until they have finished drinking."

20 Then she quickly emptied her pitcher into the trough, ran back to the well to draw *water*, and drew for all his camels.

21 And the man, wondering at her, remained silent so as to know whether the Lord had made his journey prosperous or not.

22 So it was, when the camels had finished drinking, that the man took a golden nose ring weighing half a shekel, and two bracelets for her wrists weighing ten *shekels* of gold,

23 and said, "Whose daughter *are* you? Tell me, please, is there room in your father's house for us to lodge?"

24 So she said to him, "I *am* the daughter of Bethuel, Milcah's son, whom she bore to Nahor."

25 Moreover she said to him, "We have both straw and feed enough, and room to lodge."

26 Then the man bowed down his head and worshiped the Lord.

13 Behold, I am standing by the spring of water, and the daughters of the men of the city are coming out to draw water.

14 Let the young woman to whom I shall say, 'Please let down your jar that I may drink,' and who shall say, 'Drink, and I will water your camels'—let her be the one whom you have appointed for your servant Isaac. By this I shall know that you have shown steadfast love to my master."

15 Before he had finished speaking, behold, Rebekah, who was born to Bethuel the son of Milcah, the wife of Nahor, Abraham's brother, came out with her water jar on her shoulder.

16 The young woman was very attractive in appearance, a maiden whom no man had known. She went down to the spring and filled her jar and came up.

17 Then the servant ran to meet her and said, "Please give me a little water to drink from your jar."

18 She said, "Drink, my lord." And she quickly let down her jar upon her hand and gave him a drink.

19 When she had finished giving him a drink, she said, "I will draw water for your camels also, until they have finished drinking."

20 So she quickly emptied her jar into the trough and ran again to the well to draw water, and she drew for all his camels.

21 The man gazed at her in silence to learn whether the Lord had prospered his journey or not.

22 When the camels had finished drinking, the man took a gold ring weighing a half shekel, and two bracelets for her arms weighing ten gold shekels,

23 and said, "Please tell me whose daughter you are. Is there room in your father's house for us to spend the night?"

24 She said to him, "I am the daughter of Bethuel the son of Milcah, whom she bore to Nahor."

25 She added, "We have plenty of both straw and fodder, and room to spend the night."

26 The man bowed his head and worshiped the Lord

27 And he said, "Blessed *be* the Lᴏʀᴅ God of my master Abraham, who has not forsaken His mercy and His truth toward my master. As for me, being on the way, the Lᴏʀᴅ led me to the house of my master's brethren."	**27** and said, "Blessed be the Lᴏʀᴅ, the God of my master Abraham, who has not forsaken his steadfast love and his faithfulness toward my master. As for me, the Lᴏʀᴅ has led me in the way to the house of my master's kinsmen."

The next action takes place in Mesopotamia around a well where the servant will become acquainted with Rebekah, whom he will immediately recognize as the ideal candidate following a series of tests. This episode is framed by prayers, his request for God's guidance in the beginning (24:12–14) and his thankfulness for God's response at the end (24:27).

24:10–11 The servant responds immediately and with full commitment to his master's commission. The verb **took** (*laqakh*) and **departed** (*halak*) echo the same two verbs **go** (*halak*) and **take** (*laqakh*) used by Abraham in his command (24:4). The reference to the ten camels, which were relatively rare (see the commentary on 12:16), suggests the wealth of merchandise the servant is taking with him (**all his master's goods**). This is also an allusion to his faith as well as to Abraham's confidence in the success of the operation, since all these luxuries were destined to serve as the bride-price.

Mesopotamia. The Hebrew expression *'Aram naharayim*, meaning literally "Aram of the two rivers" (Deut 23:4; Judg 3:8 NIV), refers to the area situated between the Euphrates on the west and the Habur on the east (the Septuagint applies the dual plural to the Tigris and the Euphrates, hence the word "Mesopotamia," which means "between the rivers"). The same word *Nhrn* is used in Egyptian to designate this country. The city of **Nahor**, which bears the name of Abraham's brother, is an actual city attested to in the Mari tablets under the name of Nahuru, east of the Balikh River.

The journey must have taken one month, which the author ignores, for the focus is on the real action to come. It is evening **time**, the propitious moment for prayer to be heard (Dan 9:21; Ps 141:2; 1 Kgs 18:36), which is also the time when women come to the well to draw water for the clan (Exod 2:16; 1 Sam 9:11). Knowing of this custom, the servant stops here hoping that the women will come, among whom one may fulfill his plans. His evening prayer and the coming of the women are thus associated.

24:12–14 The servant's prayer includes three components: First, the identification of the God he is praying to: this God is not merely a vague natural deity but a specific, personal, and historical **God of my master Abraham** (24:12), similar to a later designation of God as the "God of Abraham, Isaac, and Jacob" (50:24; Exod 3:6). Second, a general request: he asks for the success of the operation. The Hebrew verb *haqr'eh* derives from the verb *qarah*, which means "to happen" and conveys the idea of "chance" (Ruth 2:3). The servant asks God to produce the chance of this encounter. The notion of accidental chance has no room here. The fact that God is in control of chance means that He will operate within the parameters of what appears to be chance from a human viewpoint. He is the God of providence, who can cause the event to occur. This view is reinforced by the fact that the servant goes so far as to determine not only the moment of this event (it should be right away, **this day** [24:12]), but also the place where the event should occur (it should be right here, where the servant has **made his camels kneel down** [24:11] and where he stands, **by the well of water** [24:13]). To ensure the fulfillment of his prayer, the servant refers to God's **kindness**. The word is repeated three times in his prayers (24:12, 14, 27). The Hebrew word *khesed* refers to more than mere "kindness." The quality of *khesed* refers to one of the most important attributes of God's character (Exod 20:6; Deut 5:10; Ps 136) and designates God's powerful and miraculous acts of grace (Neh 13:14; Isa 55:3). The word is also often associated with covenant, implying a relation of faithfulness and loyalty (Deut 7:9; Ps 25:10; 1 Sam 20:8, 14, 16). Third, the conditions of the realization of his request: to determine the selection of the woman, the servant proposes a test to God. The candidate woman must not only **let down** her **pitcher** to him, a stranger (24:14), but must also volunteer to give a drink to his ten camels, a test that is nearly impossible to pass. The difficulty of the test will establish whether God is behind it—**by this I will know that You have shown** (24:14; cf. Judg 6:36–40). This test is obviously not merely a supernatural sign showing God's approval, it is also "a shrewd character test"[567] that will reveal the personality of that woman—her generosity and kindness, her willingness to serve beyond what is required, her hospitality, but also her physical strength and endurance for hard work.

24:15 The fulfillment of the servant's prayer had already begun even before that very prayer: **it happened, before he had finished speaking** (cf. Dan 9:21). Jesus witnesses to the same truth: "your Father knows the things you have need of before you ask Him" (Matt 6:8).

The entire section reports the details of that fulfillment. It begins with a surprise, which is rendered by the word **behold** (*hinneh*) introducing **Rebekah**, who is identified as **born to Bethuel, son of Milcah, the wife of Nahor, Abraham's brother**. In addition, the description of **her pitcher on her shoulder** echoes the terms of the servant's request to God (cf. 24:14) and suggests that she is the candidate for the test.

24:16 The report then proceeds to specify the physical qualities of that woman: her beauty and her virginity. Her family background and her gender qualify her to marry Isaac. The spatial information that **she went down to the well** suggests the difficulty of the test and adds to the suspense.

24:17 The servant is anxious to know; he is also very thirsty after his long trip in the wilderness. **The servant ran to meet her and said, "Please let me drink a little water from your pitcher."**

The scenario of a woman who meets a stranger at a well who asks her for a drink parallels the New Testament story of the Samaritan woman who meets Jesus at a well who asks her for a drink (John 4:7). Interestingly, in both cases, the story has a messianic perspective. The Samaritan woman finds the Messiah (John 4:25–26; cf. 29:1, 10; Exod 2:16, 21). For the servant, the test also has a messianic significance. This woman will give birth to the ancestor of the Messiah; hence, the importance of the test.

24:18–21 To the servant's amazement, all the requirements of the test are accurately met by Rebekah. She **let her pitcher down** (22:18), just as the servant had described in his prayer (24:14). She also volunteers to draw water and give a drink to the camels (24:19), just as the servant had stipulated (24:14).

Rebekah goes even beyond the servant's expectations. She does not merely fulfill

---

567 Meir Sternberg, *The Poetics of Biblical Narrative* (Bloomington, IN: Indiana University Press, 1987), 137.

her duties by giving a drink to the servant but adds an express invitation: **drink, my lord**. She also exudes zeal, enthusiasm, and efficiency in her work. The spirit of Abraham, which inspires the servant, inhabits her. Similar to Abraham, the servant "ran to meet … and said" (24:17; cf. 18:2–3). Similar to Abraham, Rebekah provided **a little water** (24:17; cf. 18:4), **quickly** (24:18, 20; cf. 18:6 [2x]), and **ran** (24:20; cf. 18:7). Note that the parallel not only uses the same words, but also their same frequency in both passages ("little water" [1x]; "quickly" [2x]; "run" [1x]).

The servant's reaction is silent awe (24:21). Although he prayed for it, he wonders at the unbelievable miracle. His faith remains mixed with doubts; he does not **know whether** he has been successful or not (24:21). Only after the entire drinking operation is finished does he understand that she is the right woman, whereupon he **took** (24:22) the gifts he had prepared for this occasion. The servant did not actually "put" the ring in Rebekah's nose (see the comments on 24:47). The procedure of piercing the nose and of hanging the ring would have been complex, and a servant touching a woman would be inappropriate. It is also noteworthy that only Rebekah's hands (*yadeyha* translated "wrists") are mentioned, whereas Rebekah's nose is not. The Hebrew phrase indicates that the servant put the jewels "on" her hands.[568] This interpretation is consistent with the later observation that Laban saw the **ring, and the bracelets upon his sister's hands** (24:30 JPS). The servant's gifts amount to a handsome sum of money (**half a shekel**, or 5.5 grams of gold for the ring, and **ten shekels**, or 110 grams of gold for the bracelets). The nature of the gifts, their expensive value, and the fact that they are given only when Rebekah fulfills the servant's prayer (24:14) suggest that these luxuries are more than a mere reward for her kindness but are meant as bridal gifts (34:12). The servant's bold gift-giving gesture seems to suggest his anticipation (by faith) that Rebekah will respond favorably to his proposal. Rebekah must have had some inkling of the significance of that gesture; thus, her further excitement and her rush toward her mother (24:28). That she might have given some thought to that prospect may explain her spontaneous positive answer and readiness to leave immediately with the servant (24:58). Note that Rebekah offers hospitality, food, and lodging without even asking permission from her parents. The short word *gam* **moreover** (24:25) indicates her enthusiastic welcome. Beyond Rebekah's generosity, the servant discerns the hand of God. Paradoxically, instead of thanking Rebekah directly, he thinks of God and reveres Him (24:26), which is a typical Near Eastern expression of gratitude.

24:27 **Blessed be the Lord God … the Lord led me to the house of my master's brethren.** The blessing marks the sentiment of arrival at the destination and the fulfillment of prophecy (Ezra 7:27–28; Dan 12:13). The servant refers to the two goals of his journey: first, the finding of the bride, implied in the recognition of God's **mercy and truth** toward his master (24:27); second, the leading to "the house," which also responds to Rebekah's assurance that he can stay there. Although in his first prayer he had simply mentioned "kindness" (*khesed*) (24:12), he now adds the word "truth" (*'emet*). The notion of *khesed* is now complemented by the notion of "truth" and "reliability," which is implied in the Hebrew word *'emet*. This is a keyword in this chapter, occurring in three (24:27, 48–49) of the six occurrences in the book of Genesis. The actual event of Rebekah's fulfilling the exact words of his prayer makes

---

568 The Hebrew preposition is *'al*, which means "on" (NAB).

the servant understand that God is not merely a God of love and grace, but a God of truth and action who causes events to occur.

24:28–61. IN MESOPOTAMIA, IN REBEKAH'S HOUSE

GEN 24:28–61 NKJV	GEN 24:28–61 ESV
28 So the young woman ran and told her mother's household these things.	**28** Then the young woman ran and told her mother's household about these things.
29 Now Rebekah had a brother whose name *was* Laban, and Laban ran out to the man by the well.	**29** Rebekah had a brother whose name was Laban. Laban ran out toward the man, to the spring.
30 So it came to pass, when he saw the nose ring, and the bracelets on his sister's wrists, and when he heard the words of his sister Rebekah, saying, "Thus the man spoke to me," that he went to the man. And there he stood by the camels at the well.	**30** As soon as he saw the ring and the bracelets on his sister's arms, and heard the words of Rebekah his sister, "Thus the man spoke to me," he went to the man. And behold, he was standing by the camels at the spring.
31 And he said, "Come in, O blessed of the Lᴏʀᴅ! Why do you stand outside? For I have prepared the house, and a place for the camels."	**31** He said, "Come in, O blessed of the Lᴏʀᴅ. Why do you stand outside? For I have prepared the house and a place for the camels."
32 Then the man came to the house. And he unloaded the camels, and provided straw and feed for the camels, and water to wash his feet and the feet of the men who *were* with him.	**32** So the man came to the house and unharnessed the camels, and gave straw and fodder to the camels, and there was water to wash his feet and the feet of the men who were with him.
33 *Food* was set before him to eat, but he said, "I will not eat until I have told about my errand." And he said, "Speak on."	**33** Then food was set before him to eat. But he said, "I will not eat until I have said what I have to say." He said, "Speak on."
34 So he said, "I *am* Abraham's servant.	**34** So he said, "I am Abraham's servant.
35 The Lᴏʀᴅ has blessed my master greatly, and he has become great; and He has given him flocks and herds, silver and gold, male and female servants, and camels and donkeys.	**35** The Lᴏʀᴅ has greatly blessed my master, and he has become great. He has given him flocks and herds, silver and gold, male servants and female servants, camels and donkeys.
36 And Sarah my master's wife bore a son to my master when she was old; and to him he has given all that he has.	**36** And Sarah my master's wife bore a son to my master when she was old, and to him he has given all that he has.
37 Now my master made me swear, saying, 'You shall not take a wife for my son from the daughters of the Canaanites, in whose land I dwell;	**37** My master made me swear, saying, 'You shall not take a wife for my son from the daughters of the Canaanites, in whose land I dwell,
38 but you shall go to my father's house and to my family, and take a wife for my son.'	**38** but you shall go to my father's house and to my clan and take a wife for my son.'
39 And I said to my master, 'Perhaps the woman will not follow me.'	**39** I said to my master, 'Perhaps the woman will not follow me.'
40 But he said to me, 'The Lᴏʀᴅ, before whom I walk, will send His angel with you and prosper your way; and you shall take a wife for my son from my family and from my father's house.	**40** But he said to me, 'The Lᴏʀᴅ, before whom I have walked, will send his angel with you and prosper your way. You shall take a wife for my son from my clan and from my father's house.

41 You will be clear from this oath when you arrive among my family; for if they will not give *her* to you, then you will be released from my oath.'

42 "And this day I came to the well and said, 'O Lᴏʀᴅ God of my master Abraham, if You will now prosper the way in which I go,

43 behold, I stand by the well of water; and it shall come to pass that when the virgin comes out to draw *water*, and I say to her, "Please give me a little water from your pitcher to drink,"

44 and she says to me, "Drink, and I will draw for your camels also,"—*let* her *be* the woman whom the Lᴏʀᴅ has appointed for my master's son.'

45 "But before I had finished speaking in my heart, there was Rebekah, coming out with her pitcher on her shoulder; and she went down to the well and drew *water*. And I said to her, 'Please let me drink.'

46 And she made haste and let her pitcher down from her shoulder, and said, 'Drink, and I will give your camels a drink also.' So I drank, and she gave the camels a drink also.

47 Then I asked her, and said, 'Whose daughter *are* you?' And she said, 'The daughter of Bethuel, Nahor's son, whom Milcah bore to him.' So I put the nose ring on her nose and the bracelets on her wrists.

48 And I bowed my head and worshiped the Lᴏʀᴅ, and blessed the Lᴏʀᴅ God of my master Abraham, who had led me in the way of truth to take the daughter of my master's brother for his son.

49 Now if you will deal kindly and truly with my master, tell me. And if not, tell me, that I may turn to the right hand or to the left."

50 Then Laban and Bethuel answered and said, "The thing comes from the Lᴏʀᴅ; we cannot speak to you either bad or good.

51 Here *is* Rebekah before you; take *her* and go, and let her be your master's son's wife, as the Lᴏʀᴅ has spoken."

52 And it came to pass, when Abraham's servant heard their words, that he worshiped the Lᴏʀᴅ, *bowing himself* to the earth.

53 Then the servant brought out jewelry of silver, jewelry of gold, and clothing, and gave *them* to Rebekah. He also gave precious things to her brother and to her mother.

41 Then you will be free from my oath, when you come to my clan. And if they will not give her to you, you will be free from my oath.'

42 "I came today to the spring and said, 'O Lᴏʀᴅ, the God of my master Abraham, if now you are prospering the way that I go,

43 behold, I am standing by the spring of water. Let the virgin who comes out to draw water, to whom I shall say, "Please give me a little water from your jar to drink,"

44 and who will say to me, "Drink, and I will draw for your camels also," let her be the woman whom the Lᴏʀᴅ has appointed for my master's son.'

45 "Before I had finished speaking in my heart, behold, Rebekah came out with her water jar on her shoulder, and she went down to the spring and drew water. I said to her, 'Please let me drink.'

46 She quickly let down her jar from her shoulder and said, 'Drink, and I will give your camels drink also.' So I drank, and she gave the camels drink also.

47 Then I asked her, 'Whose daughter are you?' She said, 'The daughter of Bethuel, Nahor's son, whom Milcah bore to him.' So I put the ring on her nose and the bracelets on her arms.

48 Then I bowed my head and worshiped the Lᴏʀᴅ and blessed the Lᴏʀᴅ, the God of my master Abraham, who had led me by the right way to take the daughter of my master's kinsman for his son.

49 Now then, if you are going to show steadfast love and faithfulness to my master, tell me; and if not, tell me, that I may turn to the right hand or to the left."

50 Then Laban and Bethuel answered and said, "The thing has come from the Lᴏʀᴅ; we cannot speak to you bad or good.

51 Behold, Rebekah is before you; take her and go, and let her be the wife of your master's son, as the Lᴏʀᴅ has spoken."

52 When Abraham's servant heard their words, he bowed himself to the earth before the Lᴏʀᴅ.

53 And the servant brought out jewelry of silver and of gold, and garments, and gave them to Rebekah. He also gave to her brother and to her mother costly ornaments.

54 And he and the men who *were* with him ate and drank and stayed all night. Then they arose in the morning, and he said, "Send me away to my master."

54 And he and the men who were with him ate and drank, and they spent the night there. When they arose in the morning, he said, "Send me away to my master."

55 But her brother and her mother said, "Let the young woman stay with us *a few* days, at least ten; after that she may go."

55 Her brother and her mother said, "Let the young woman remain with us a while, at least ten days; after that she may go."

56 And he said to them, "Do not hinder me, since the LORD has prospered my way; send me away so that I may go to my master."

56 But he said to them, "Do not delay me, since the LORD has prospered my way. Send me away that I may go to my master."

57 So they said, "We will call the young woman and ask her personally."

57 They said, "Let us call the young woman and ask her."

58 Then they called Rebekah and said to her, "Will you go with this man?" And she said, "I will go."

58 And they called Rebekah and said to her, "Will you go with this man?" She said, "I will go."

59 So they sent away Rebekah their sister and her nurse, and Abraham's servant and his men.

59 So they sent away Rebekah their sister and her nurse, and Abraham's servant and his men.

60 And they blessed Rebekah and said to her: "Our sister, *may* you *become the mother* of thousands of ten thousands; and may your descendants possess the gates of those who hate them."

60 And they blessed Rebekah and said to her, "Our sister, may you become thousands of ten thousands, and may your offspring possess the gate of those who hate him!"

61 Then Rebekah and her maids arose, and they rode on the camels and followed the man. So the servant took Rebekah and departed.

61 Then Rebekah and her young women arose and rode on the camels and followed the man. Thus the servant took Rebekah and went his way.

The next setting occurs at the "House of Abraham's brethren." In order to obtain Rebekah as a bride for Abraham's son, the servant engages in a long and detailed report of his commission and journey for the purpose of providing evidence of God's providence in this matter.

24:28 Her mother's household. Rebekah's next move is consistent with her previous behavior. She **ran**, thus showing again her zeal and enthusiasm in regard to her encounter. That she first goes to her mother's house to tell her story suggests that she feels that this encounter means something important for her as a woman. This reference to her mother (cf. 24:53, 55) is also in line with the special attention given to the women in this context (Milcah in 22:20; 24:15, 24, 47, and Sarah in 23:1–2, 19, 24; 24:36, 67). Although this emphasis pertains to the concern of birth that permeates these stories, it also witnesses to the matriarchal side that often characterized patriarchal societies (see also Rebekah's leading role in 27:5–16).

24:29–33 Laban. The brother's active participation in the hospitality ceremonials (24:32–33) and in the discussion that follows (24:33, 50, 55) may be explained by the protective role brothers played on behalf of their sisters (34:7, 31). However, Laban's motivation seemingly exceeds his brotherly concern for his sister. Unlike his sister, who runs to graciously serve and receive her guest, Laban's running **to the man by the well** (24:29) and his invitation to "come in" are not unrelated to the fact that he saw the jewels on his sister's hands—**when he saw the nose ring, and the bracelets on his sister's wrists … he went to the man … and he said, "Come in …"**

(24:30–31). His gesture of hospitality is therefore not devoid of self-interest. Note also his concern for the ten camels, which he mentions in his words of welcome, and which are the first thing he noticed by the well. At that time, camels were a rare and luxurious type of transport. All of these reactions betray Laban's greed, which will later motivate his abuses of Jacob (29:25–27; 30:27–36; 31:2–8, 28–29, 38–42).

The servant is therefore prudent. He refuses to enjoy Laban's hospitality and eat with him before he has exposed the object of his journey (24:33). Consistent with the practice in other covenant ceremonials, only after he settles the matter will he be able to relax with confidence and share meals with the other party (24:54; cf. 31:43–54; Luke 22:30).

24:34–36 The servant begins his report by demonstrating Abraham's wealth, which is already implied in the way he introduces himself. He is merely **Abraham's servant** (24:34); the wealth he is displaying suggests the tremendous wealth of his master. The servant insists that this fortune originates from God's blessing (24:35). The Hebrew word qualifying the degree of blessing is *me'od* (translated "greatly"), meaning "very," suggesting that this blessing is beyond ordinary measure. To that emphatic qualification he adds that God has made him **great**; he subsequently produces as evidence a detailed list of all his master's possessions (24:35). Against this backdrop, the servant introduces Abraham's son, specifying that this son was born when Sarah was old (24:36), which not only suggests the miraculous characteristic of his birth (21:2, 5), but also implies that this son is still young enough to marry Rebekah. This son is also the only heir of Abraham. This additional information is designed to convince Rebekah's family that this young man could be an excellent partner for her.

24:47 **I put the nose ring.** The use of the Hebrew verb *sim* "put" suggests that Rebekah is already wearing the jewels. Although the servant did not actually "put" the jewels on Rebekah (see the commentary on 24:22), he endorses the operation, because as the giver of the jewel, he is the one who initiated the whole process. Note that the word *sim* may also mean "give" (Num 6:26; Isa 61:3).

24:48 **The way of truth.** The expression "way of truth" in the phrase "the Lord … led me in the way of truth" recaptures the association he had made in his prayer, where the phrase "being on the way, the Lord led me" immediately follows the reference to "His truth" (24:27). The dimension of "truth" (*'emet*), which refers to the concrete efficiency of God leading the operation, means that this way is reliable.

24:49 **You will deal kindly and truly.** The servant now refers to both notions together, "kindness" (*khesed*) and "truth" (*'emet*), as he delivers his final address and presents his final argument to convince the family. The two main attributes of God are now applied to them. The servant wisely suggests that by responding positively to his request, they will align themselves with God Himself.

24:50–54 The awkward sequence that puts the father after the son, **Laban and Bethuel**, is consistent with the father's absence elsewhere in the story. This downplay of the father suggests that he was either too old to be involved in the discussions and the hospitality negotiations or that his wife was the one who governed the household, as implied in other passages (24:28, 53, 55). The family connection, Abraham's blessing, the miraculous manner in which the events occurred, the response of Rebekah, and the fulfillment of the servant's prayer are all evidence for Laban and Bethuel that "the thing comes from the Lord" (for their reference to the Lord, see the commentary on 24:4). Consequently, they cannot further argue one way or another (24:50). Their consent triggers a series of actions. The servant again worships the Lord, an expression of gratefulness to God for the success of the enterprise. The servant then distributes gifts not only to Rebekah, in addition to his other gifts, but this time he adds gifts **to her brother and to her mother** (24:53). These gifts are now an explicit recognition of the forthcoming wedding, to be considered as the formal dowry (34:12). Only then could they relax; they ate, drank, and went to bed (24:54).

24:55–61 Although Laban and Bethuel had clearly indicated that Rebekah could follow him immediately (24:51), the brother, this time in the company of his mother, seemingly has second thoughts about the affair and begins to try to gain some time, as Laban will subsequently do to Jacob (29:27). The Hebrew idiom *yamim ʾo ʿasor* **a few days** means, literally, "days or ten." The word *yamim* "days" could be understood as referring to years (Lev 25:29; Num 9:22). The Targum and the Midrash Rabbah (60.12) read "one year and ten months." As the servant turns down their request, referring to the Lord, they then turn to Rebekah, hoping that she will support their view and stay at home longer. Without any hesitation, Rebekah responds with one word *ʾelek* **I will go** (24:58), which is echoed in the feminine plural *watelakhna* **followed**, referring to the maids, and finally in the word *wayyelek* **departed** related to the servant, which marks the last occurrence of the key verb *halak* "go." Rebekah's determination is striking in this patriarchal context, where the woman was not supposed to have a say in her marriage. In spite of the appearance and all the preparations of Abraham and the servant, Rebekah remains sovereign. This is not the normal procedure of an arranged marriage. All depends on her "yes" or "no" as she has the last word on this matter. Moreover, Rebekah's response is identified with the response of the patriarch Abraham. The verbs echo the departure verb of Abraham when he left Mesopotamia, *wayyelek* **departed** (12:4).

The twofold blessing offered by Rebekah's family to her resonates with that echo to Abraham. These blessings evoke the two texts framing Abraham's journey, when he was called to leave Ur and when he was called to sacrifice Isaac. Similar to Abraham, Rebekah will become many nations (24:60a; cf. 12:1–4) and will **possess the gates of** the enemy (24:60b; cf. 22:17).

24:62–65. IN CANAAN, BY THE WELL

GEN 24:62–65 NKJV	GEN 24:62–65 ESV
62 Now Isaac came from the way of Beer Lahai Roi, for he dwelt in the South.	**62** Now Isaac had returned from Beer-lahai-roi and was dwelling in the Negeb.
63 And Isaac went out to meditate in the field in the evening; and he lifted his eyes and looked, and there, the camels *were* coming.	**63** And Isaac went out to meditate in the field toward evening. And he lifted up his eyes and saw, and behold, there were camels coming.
64 Then Rebekah lifted her eyes, and when she saw Isaac she dismounted from her camel;	**64** And Rebekah lifted up her eyes, and when she saw Isaac, she dismounted from the camel
65 for she had said to the servant, "Who *is* this man walking in the field to meet us?" The servant said, "It *is* my master." So she took a veil and covered herself.	**65** and said to the servant, "Who is that man, walking in the field to meet us?" The servant said, "It is my master." So she took her veil and covered herself.

From this point onward, Isaac and Rebekah are at the forefront of the scene. The servant plays a secondary role. He is no longer in charge of the operation but only responds to either Rebekah (24:65) or Isaac (24:66). This section parallels section B (24:10–27). Similar to the servant, Isaac is located by a well, **from the way of Beer Lahai Roi** (24:62). This is the well where Hagar had been saved by the Angel of the Lord (16:14). Similar to the servant, Isaac is praying in the evening (24:63; cf. 24:11). The Hebrew verb *suakh* **meditate** has been understood in rabbinic tradition in the sense of "prayer."[569] The verb may also connote an attitude of depression or distress, as implied in the related verb *siakh*, which is associated with the verb "comfort" (Ps 77:3–4; cf. 24:67). Isaac may be praying, in his sadness associated with the loss of his deceased mother, asking God for comfort. At that very moment, similar to the servant, he is surprised by the coming of Rebekah (24:63; cf. 24:15). The same word *wehinneh* **there** is used in both places to express that surprise.

24:64–65 The sighting of Isaac by Rebekah also parallels the sighting of Rebekah by the servant (24:16), which suggests that Rebekah must have been impressed by the figure of Isaac, just as the servant had been impressed when he first saw Rebekah (24:16). The fact that **when she saw Isaac she dismounted from her camel** (24:64) suggests her particular interest in the stranger she wants to identify (24:65), just as the servant had been interested when he saw Rebekah and had asked for her identity (24:23). Just as the servant had put a golden nose ring on her when he identified her as Isaac's future bride, Rebekah covered her face with a veil when the servant identified him as her prospective bridegroom (24:65). The servant's sober response, **it is my master** consist of only two words in Hebrew. The first word *hu'* "he" puts the accent on the pronoun, suggesting emphasis on "him." Isaac is now called "my master" in the place of Abraham.

24:66–67. IN CANAAN, IN SARAH'S TENT

GEN 24:66–67 NKJV	GEN 24:66–67 ESV
66 And the servant told Isaac all the things that he had done.	**66** And the servant told Isaac all the things that he had done.
67 Then Isaac brought her into his mother Sarah's tent; and he took Rebekah and she became his wife, and he loved her. So Isaac was comforted after his mother's *death.*	**67** Then Isaac brought her into the tent of Sarah his mother and took Rebekah, and she became his wife, and he loved her. So Isaac was comforted after his mother's death.

The journey now reaches its final destination. This last action develops in two steps. First, **the servant told Isaac all the things that he had done** (24:66). This was likely the same detailed report he had given to Laban. Although he had been commissioned by Abraham, the servant chooses to give this report to Isaac, who is present with him. After all, this matrimonial matter concerns him directly. Isaac's new status as prospective bridegroom also makes him the next patriarch, the new master of the house (24:65). Note that Abraham had already assigned him as his formal heir (24:36; cf. 25:5). Second, Isaac responds to the servant's report, which must have essentially addressed Rebekah, since the next line refers to Rebekah as

---

569 Gen. Rab. 60:14; cf. Tg. Onq, ad loc.

"her"; **Isaac brought her into his mother Sarah's tent** (24:67). The evocation of Sarah is consistent with the identification of Isaac as the master. Rebekah succeeds Sarah just as Isaac succeeds Abraham. The repeated mention of Sarah at the end of the section also echoes the mention of Abraham in its beginning (24:1–2). Isaac's bringing Rebekah into his mother's tent also has profound psychological significance. This act implies an important lesson regarding how the new husband will treat his wife. The memory of his mother will affect his behavior and will inspire his respect toward this other woman in his life. The biblical author then skips all the side information regarding the course of events that must have occurred before the wedding; this would have included the presentation of the bride to the community, the preparation for the wedding, and the wedding feast, not to mention the period of settling in by the newcomers (29:22–23). The following observation that Isaac loved Rebekah only after his marriage may be surprising and does not appear romantic. This particular remark is, however, consistent with the biblical view of love as a conjugal experience (29:32). Although love may not be absent before marriage (29:18), it reaches its mature stage and blossoms only after marriage, as a result of life together, with its ups and downs, its struggles and joys, and the long and difficult process of learning to understand, to respect, and to appreciate each other. In Western civilization, we marry because we love, or we feel that we love; it is this feeling that triggers our commitment and justifies it. When we feel that we do not love anymore, we choose to end the marriage. According to the Bible, love is constructed in the breath of conjugal life. We love because we live together; we do not live together because we love. This is why love implies faithfulness, the duty to "enjoy life with the wife whom you love" (Eccl 9:9 ESV). This Hebrew concept of love has significantly inspired the Hebrew theology of religion. The experience of conjugal love has been used as a model for the covenant between God and His people (Hos 2:2; 3:1). "Love" in the Old Testament is an integral part of "covenant"; the two words are often associated (Deut 7:9). Thus, when God calls humans to love Him, He is not referring to a momentary sentimental experience; to love God implies the commitment to live with Him for life (Deut 6:5–9; Exod 20:6). Conversely, it is our relationship with God that should inspire our conjugal relationship (Eph 5:25).

The note about the comfort that Isaac received from Rebekah **after his mother's death** (24:67) suggests closure and marks the conclusion of the entire passage since Sarah's death and burial (23:20). This conclusion also anticipates the following story about Abraham's new marriage.

ABRAHAM'S NEW WIFE (25:1–6)

GEN 25:1–6 NKJV	GEN 25:1–6 ESV
1 Abraham again took a wife, and her name *was* Keturah.	**1** Abraham took another wife, whose name was Keturah.
2 And she bore him Zimran, Jokshan, Medan, Midian, Ishbak, and Shuah.	**2** She bore him Zimran, Jokshan, Medan, Midian, Ishbak, and Shuah.
3 Jokshan begot Sheba and Dedan. And the sons of Dedan were Asshurim, Letushim, and Leummim.	**3** Jokshan fathered Sheba and Dedan. The sons of Dedan were Asshurim, Letushim, and Leummim.

4 And the sons of Midian *were* Ephah, Epher, Hanoch, Abidah, and Eldaah. All these *were* the children of Keturah.	**4** The sons of Midian were Ephah, Epher, Hanoch, Abida, and Eldaah. All these were the children of Keturah.
5 And Abraham gave all that he had to Isaac.	**5** Abraham gave all he had to Isaac.
6 But Abraham gave gifts to the sons of the concubines which Abraham had; and while he was still living he sent them eastward, away from Isaac his son, to the country of the east.	**6** But to the sons of his concubines Abraham gave gifts, and while he was still living he sent them away from his son Isaac, eastward to the east country.

The mention of Abraham's new marriage immediately after the mention of Isaac's marriage, using the same language **took … wife** (25:1), suggests the same effect of comfort.

25:1 Keturah. The identity of this new wife is unclear. Whereas the biblical text may imply that she is another concubine in addition to Hagar (25:6; cf. 1 Chr 1:32), other evidence suggests that she could be identified with Hagar, a view that has been adopted in ancient rabbinic texts.[570] The chronicler associates Keturah's sons with Ishmael's, and Hagar's name is not mentioned, whereas Keturah's name is (1 Chr 1:32–33; cf. 1 Chr 1:29). This identification could also be supported by the fact that Abraham treats her sons in the same manner as he treated Hagar's son; he sends them away lest they should supplant Isaac (25:6; cf. 21:14). They are notably sent eastward, an expression implying that they are separated from God's people (13:11). Whatever the interpretation, the biblical text clearly implies that the children of this new marriage, in addition to Hagar's children (Gal 4:24–25),[571] should not pose a problem for Isaac's heritage since **Abraham gave all that he had to Isaac** (25:6; 24:36).

DEATH OF ABRAHAM (25:7–11)

GEN 25:7–11 NKJV	GEN 25:7–11 ESV
7 This *is* the sum of the years of Abraham's life which he lived: one hundred and seventy-five years.	**7** These are the days of the years of Abraham's life, 175 years.
8 Then Abraham breathed his last and died in a good old age, an old man and full *of years*, and was gathered to his people.	**8** Abraham breathed his last and died in a good old age, an old man and full of years, and was gathered to his people.
9 And his sons Isaac and Ishmael buried him in the cave of Machpelah, which *is* before Mamre, in the field of Ephron the son of Zohar the Hittite,	**9** Isaac and Ishmael his sons buried him in the cave of Machpelah, in the field of Ephron the son of Zohar the Hittite, east of Mamre,
10 the field which Abraham purchased from the sons of Heth. There Abraham was buried, and Sarah his wife.	**10** the field that Abraham purchased from the Hittites. There Abraham was buried, with Sarah his wife.

---

570 Gen. Rab. 61:4.

571 Since the Old Testament never refers to Hagar as having other children than Ishmael, the text of Galatians probably refers to the sons of Ishmael, Hagar's descendants.

11 And it came to pass, after the death of Abraham, that God blessed his son Isaac. And Isaac dwelt at Beer Lahai Roi.	**11** After the death of Abraham, God blessed Isaac his son. And Isaac settled at Beer-lahai-roi.

The paradoxical principle of the second taking the place of the first (cf. Eccl 4:15) was already hinted at in the last verses of the preceding chapter, which presented Isaac as "master" in the place of Abraham (24:65) and Rebekah as the new Abraham (24:58, 60). The death of Abraham (25:7–11) and the death of Ishmael (25:12–18) give way to Isaac, who will now, without any question, take the place of both his father Abraham and his older brother Ishmael (25:19–21).

Abraham is one hundred and seventy-five years old when he dies (25:7), that is, about forty years after Sarah's death (23:1). Abraham is still alive when Isaac marries at the age of forty (25:20) and when the twins are born from this marriage twenty years later (25:26). The inspired author comments on Abraham's death in the exact terms as the old prophecy God had given to Abraham when He made His covenant with him, predicting that he would die in a good old age (25:8; cf. 15:15). Yet, Abraham does not simply die at a very old age; the biblical testimony adds that he was "contented" (TNK). The verb *saba'* has generally been translated "full" (NKJV, ESV) based on the Septuagint, which relates this satisfaction to the "days." However, the word implies an inner attitude. Abraham had reached the stage of satisfaction, a rare, if not exceptional, case. The book of Ecclesiastes uses the same verb to state that, even though a man may live many years, his soul will never be "satisfied" (Eccl 6:3). The expression **was gathered to his people** (25:8), which is also used for Ishmael (25:17), is not an allusion to the survival of an immortal soul. This idiom refers to the practice of family burial, as expressed in the kindred phrase "buried with his fathers" (15:15; 47:30). The association of his burial in the cave of Machpelah (25:9) with Sarah his wife (25:10) marks the end of this generation. God's blessing passes, then, to his son Isaac (25:11). The following information about Isaac dwelling at Beer Lahai Roi (25:11) indicates Hagar's spiritual experience and suggests that Isaac also acknowledges the blessing of Ishmael.

GENEALOGY OF ISHMAEL (25:12–18)

GEN 25:12–18 NKJV	GEN 25:12–18 ESV
12 Now this *is* the genealogy of Ishmael, Abraham's son, whom Hagar the Egyptian, Sarah's maidservant, bore to Abraham.	**12** These are the generations of Ishmael, Abraham's son, whom Hagar the Egyptian, Sarah's servant, bore to Abraham.
13 And these *were* the names of the sons of Ishmael, by their names, according to their generations: The firstborn of Ishmael, Nebajoth; then Kedar, Adbeel, Mibsam,	**13** These are the names of the sons of Ishmael, named in the order of their birth: Nebaioth, the firstborn of Ishmael; and Kedar, Adbeel, Mibsam,
14 Mishma, Dumah, Massa,	**14** Mishma, Dumah, Massa,
15 Hadar, Tema, Jetur, Naphish, and Kedemah.	**15** Hadad, Tema, Jetur, Naphish, and Kedemah.

16 These *were* the sons of Ishmael and these *were* their names, by their towns and their settlements, twelve princes according to their nations.	**16** These are the sons of Ishmael and these are their names, by their villages and by their encampments, twelve princes according to their tribes.
17 These *were* the years of the life of Ishmael: one hundred and thirty-seven years; and he breathed his last and died, and was gathered to his people.	**17** (These are the years of the life of Ishmael: 137 years. He breathed his last and died, and was gathered to his people.)
18 (They dwelt from Havilah as far as Shur, which *is* east of Egypt as you go toward Assyria.) He died in the presence of all his brethren.	**18** They settled from Havilah to Shur, which is opposite Egypt in the direction of Assyria. He settled over against all his kinsmen.

From the allusion to Hagar and Ishmael by means of the reference to Beer Lahai Roi, the focus moves to the genealogy of Ishmael, whose identity as the son of Sarah's maidservant is recalled (25:12). Although the verb "bless" does not appear here in reference to Ishmael, whereas it was used in connection with Isaac (25:11), it contains all the ingredients of blessings. Ishmael will die after a long life at the age of 137 years (25:17), although not as old as Isaac, who will die at the age of 180 years (35:28). The language that describes the course of Ishmael's destiny echoes the ancient prophecies, thus suggesting the fulfillment of the divine promises. He will, like Jacob, beget twelve princes (25:16; 17:20)[572] and will settle "over against all his kinsmen" (25:18b ESV; 16:12), an allusion to the future antagonism opposing the sedentary lifestyle represented by the Israelites who will settle in Canaan and the nomadic one represented by the Bedouin Ishmaelites.[573] Ishmael's descendants will dwell outside the Promised Land, "from Havilah to Shur" (25:18a ESV), which is roughly from Arabia to Egypt. As for the name "Assyria," it should not be confused with the country of Assyria in northern Mesopotamia. This "Assyria" refers to a place near Egypt, most likely in Sinai (This "Assyria" refers to a place near Egypt, most likely in Sinai (see "Asshurim," 25:3; "Asshur," Num 24:22, 24). The history of these Ishmaelite tribes will notably remain part of the biblical prophetic interest (Isa 21:13; Jer 25:24) and is even included in the eschatological hope of the kingdom of God (Amos 9:11–12; cf. Acts 15:16–17; Isa 42:11–12; 60:7–12).

THE CYCLE OF JACOB (25:19–35:26)

The cycle of Jacob (25:19–35:26) is symmetrically preceded by the death of Abraham (25:7–11) and the genealogy of Ishmael (25:12–18) and is followed by the death of Isaac (35:27–29) and the genealogy of Esau (36:1–43). The stories of Jacob are organized in a mirror-image or chiastic structure, whose apex brings out the birth of Jacob's children:[574]

---

572 See also the twelve sons of Nahor, Abraham's brother and Rebekah's grandfather (22:20–24).
573 See Wenham, *Genesis 16–50*, 165.
574 Ibid., 169.

Prelude Death of Abraham and Genealogy of Ishmael (25:7–18)
  A Birth of Isaac's sons, struggle at birth (25:19–34)
    B Isaac and Abimelech (26:1–33)
      C Jacob steals the blessing from Esau (26:34–28:9)
        D Encountering God at Bethel (28:10–22)
          E Jacob arrives at Laban's house (29:1–14)
            F Laban deceives Jacob (29:15–30)
              G Birth of Jacob's children (29:31–30:24)
            F$_1$ Jacob deceives Laban (30:25–31:2)
          E$_1$ Jacob leaves Laban (31:3–55 [32:1])
        D$_1$ Encountering God at Peniel (32:1–32 [2–33])
      C$_1$ Jacob returns the blessing to Esau (33:1–17)
    B$_1$ Dinah and Shechem (33:18–34:31)
  A$_1$ Jacob's sons, struggle at birth (35:1–26)
Postlude Death of Isaac and genealogy of Esau (35:27–36:43)

BIRTH OF ISAAC'S SONS (25:19–34)

After an introduction affirming Isaac as Abraham's true heir (25:19–21), this status is established based on Rebekah's pregnancy, which reproduces the miracle of Sarah; both are barren (25:21; cf. 11:30; cf. 30:22). The birth of Jacob and Esau anticipates, then, the wonders of salvation history. The ominous nature of the relationship between the twin brothers is manifested in the womb (25:22–23), at birth (25:24–26), and later around a meal (25:27–34).

25:19–21. ISAAC, ABRAHAM'S TRUE HEIR

GEN 25:19–21 NKJV	GEN 25:19–21 ESV
19 This *is* the genealogy of Isaac, Abraham's son. Abraham begot Isaac.	**19** These are the generations of Isaac, Abraham's son: Abraham fathered Isaac,
20 Isaac was forty years old when he took Rebekah as wife, the daughter of Bethuel the Syrian of Padan Aram, the sister of Laban the Syrian.	**20** and Isaac was forty years old when he took Rebekah, the daughter of Bethuel the Aramean of Paddan-aram, the sister of Laban the Aramean, to be his wife.
21 Now Isaac pleaded with the L ORD for his wife, because she *was* barren; and the L ORD granted his plea, and Rebekah his wife conceived.	**21** And Isaac prayed to the L ORD for his wife, because she was barren. And the L ORD granted his prayer, and Rebekah his wife conceived.

25:19 Unlike Ishmael, who is identified as Abraham's son by means of the Egyptian servant of Sarah (25:12), Isaac is simply identified as **Abraham's son** (25:19). Isaac is the true heir of Abraham.

25:20–21 The fact that **Isaac was forty years old** (25:20) suggests that he had been waiting for twenty years before he became a father (cf. 25:26). This explains the specific mention of his prayer: **Isaac pleaded with the Lord for his wife** (25:21). Note that while Isaac follows his father's example of praying to obtain the healing of Abimelech's barren wife and servants (20:17) he does not resort to concubinage.

Interestingly, Isaac is the only patriarch who remained monogamous.

25:22–23. IN THE WOMB

GEN 25:22–23 NKJV	GEN 25:22–23 ESV
22 But the children struggled together within her; and she said, "If *all is* well, why *am I like* this?" So she went to inquire of the LORD.	**22** The children struggled together within her, and she said, "If it is thus, why is this happening to me?" So she went to inquire of the LORD.
23 And the LORD said to her: "Two nations *are* in your womb, two peoples shall be separated from your body; *one* people shall be stronger than the other, and the older shall serve the younger."	**23** And the LORD said to her, "Two nations are in your womb, and two peoples from within you shall be divided; the one shall be stronger than the other, the older shall serve the younger."

25:22 **The children struggled.** The Hebrew verb *ratsats* "struggled" suggests violence (Judg 9:53; Isa 36:6) and its reflexive form (*hithpael*) indicates that reciprocal blows are being exchanged between the children. Rebekah, who became pregnant as a result of prayer (25:21), prays to God about the troubling nature of her pregnancy (25:22). The two prayers are, however, different. Whereas Isaac's prayer (*'atar*) is an intercessory prayer (cf. Exod 8:30 [26]), Rebekah's prayer (*darash*) is a question that demands or seeks an answer (9:5; 2 Sam 11:3; Judg 6:29). Rebekah asks God the reason for this violent struggle in her womb: **why?** No mention is made of any magical technique Rebekah could have used to ascertain the divine response, as was generally the case in ANE religions. Rebekah's inquiry is direct. In response, the divine answer is also given directly in the form of a poem; it is a double parallelism composed of two lines each; the second line explains or emphasizes the information of the first one:

1. The two children represent two nations. These two peoples will be separated from the very moment they leave the womb.
2. One people shall be stronger than the other. The older shall serve the younger.

25:23 **Two nations.** The descendants of Esau, the Edomites (for the name of "Edom," see 25:30), will oppose the Israelites during the wilderness sojourn (Num 20:14–21). Biblical prophecy will refer to Edom as the traditional enemy of Israel (Num 24:18; Obad 10). Jewish tradition will identify Edom with Rome and later with traditional Christianity, as Jews suffered under the oppression of Rome and the persecution of the Christian church.

From your body. The separation of the peoples begins as soon as the children are born. This prophecy applies to Esau and Jacob, who will be separated by their physical appearance (25:25), their temperament (25:27), and the love of their parents (25:28); and will always live separated from each other (27:43; 28:5; 31:38; 33:16–17; 36:6).

One people shall be stronger. The text does not identify which of the two is the stronger one. This omission seems to be intentional, because of the ambiguity regarding the understanding of who is "strong." Esau will always present himself as the stronger one (32:6–7; 33:1; 36:31), and yet it is Jacob, the one who seems weaker, who will ultimately triumph.

The older will serve the younger. Jacob, the younger child, is viewed by prophecy as becoming greater than his brother because he will be served by Esau, the older one. This prophecy may seem unjust for the stronger, but the reverse would also be unjust for the weaker; yet this alternative seems more logical and natural. The point of this reversal is to challenge our natural scale of values. This paradoxical principle, which opposes natural custom (29:26; 37:10–11; Job 32:6), is an expression of the grace of God. It is Jacob's weakness that will ultimately become his strength (32:28; Joel 3:10; 1 Cor 1:27; 12:10).

25:24–26. AT BIRTH

GEN 25:24–26 NKJV	GEN 25:24–26 ESV
24 So when her days were fulfilled *for her* to give birth, indeed *there were* twins in her womb.	**24** When her days to give birth were completed, behold, there were twins in her womb.
25 And the first came out red. *He was* like a hairy garment all over; so they called his name Esau.	**25** The first came out red, all his body like a hairy cloak, so they called his name Esau.
26 Afterward his brother came out, and his hand took hold of Esau's heel; so his name was called Jacob. Isaac *was* sixty years old when she bore them.	**26** Afterward his brother came out with his hand holding Esau's heel, so his name was called Jacob. Isaac was sixty years old when she bore them.

As previously indicated, the contrast between the twin brothers (25:24) appears from the beginning, inspiring their respective names and signifying their respective destinies. **The first** (25:25) is described by his appearance; he was red and hairy. His hairy aspect (*se'ar*) is related to the name of *'Esaw* "Esau" through the first two consonants in reverse (*s-'/'-s*); it also points to the name of *Se'ir* "Seir," Esau's future home (32:3). **Afterward his brother** (25:26) is described by his action; **his hand took hold of Esau's heel** (*'aqeb*), pointing to his name *Ya'aqob* "Jacob," which anticipates Jacob's future act of supplanting his brother (27:36). Thus, the two names of the brothers are like prophecies, which signify their respective destinies. This "prophetic" explanation of the name does not exclude the existence of this name elsewhere outside of the Bible. The name of Jacob is well attested to in the ANE. This name was, for instance, borne by some of the Hyksos rulers in ancient Egypt.[575]

25:27–34. AROUND A MEAL

GEN 25:27–34 NKJV	GEN 25:27–34 ESV
27 So the boys grew. And Esau was a skillful hunter, a man of the field; but Jacob was a mild man, dwelling in tents.	**27** When the boys grew up, Esau was a skillful hunter, a man of the field, while Jacob was a quiet man, dwelling in tents.
28 And Isaac loved Esau because he ate *of his* game, but Rebekah loved Jacob.	**28** Isaac loved Esau because he ate of his game, but Rebekah loved Jacob.
29 Now Jacob cooked a stew; and Esau came in from the field, and he *was* weary.	**29** Once when Jacob was cooking stew, Esau came in from the field, and he was exhausted.

---

575 For instance, Yaqub-Har (or Yaqub-Baal), whose seals bearing his name have been found from Gaza to Kerma, see Nicolas Grimal, *A History of Ancient Egypt* (Malden, MA: Blackwell, 1992), 187.

30 And Esau said to Jacob, "Please feed me with that same red *stew*, for I *am* weary." Therefore his name was called Edom.	**30** And Esau said to Jacob, "Let me eat some of that red stew, for I am exhausted!" (Therefore his name was called Edom.)
31 But Jacob said, "Sell me your birthright as of this day."	**31** Jacob said, "Sell me your birthright now."
32 And Esau said, "Look, I *am* about to die; so what *is* this birthright to me?"	**32** Esau said, "I am about to die; of what use is a birthright to me?"
33 Then Jacob said, "Swear to me as of this day." So he swore to him, and sold his birthright to Jacob.	**33** Jacob said, "Swear to me now." So he swore to him and sold his birthright to Jacob.
34 And Jacob gave Esau bread and stew of lentils; then he ate and drank, arose, and went his way. Thus Esau despised *his* birthright.	**34** Then Jacob gave Esau bread and lentil stew, and he ate and drank and rose and went his way. Thus Esau despised his birthright.

25:27 The contrast between the two brothers becomes more striking as they grow up. The age of the twins is not explicitly indicated. The term *na'ar* **boys** refers broadly to a young man; it is used for Joseph when he is seventeen years old (37:2). Like Ishmael (21:20), Esau is a **skillful hunter, a man of the field**, whereas Jacob is **a mild man** who prefers **dwelling in tents**.

25:28 Esau is loved by his father, while Jacob is loved by his mother. The spiritual and sensitive nature of Jacob contrasts with the tough, physical nature of Esau. The Hebrew word *tam* (translated "mild"), which qualifies Jacob, is the same word that characterizes Job (Job 8:20) and Noah (6:9). Likewise, the verb *yashab* (translated "dwelling"), meaning "sitting," suggests the quiet and meditative temperament of Jacob (cf. Pss 84:4; 91:1).

25:29–31 This information regarding their characters anticipates the incident of the meal, which will determine their respective destinies.[576]

The red color of the stew, *'adom*, is related to the name of *'Edom* "Edom," another name for Esau (25:30), thus making a connection between this incident around the meal and Esau's destiny. The Hebrew word *na'* "please" in the phrase **please feed me** (25:30) suggests that Esau was begging. The Hebrew verb *la'at* "feed" suggests avid swallowing: "let me gulp down" (NAB). Famished with hunger from his hunting party in the field, Esau was concerned only with the present and his immediate needs, **for I am weary** (25:30; cf. 25:32). Jacob understands the situation and responds, **sell me … as of this day** (25:31). Jacob's quick reaction, without any hesitation, suggests that his action was premeditated.

25:34 Jacob has considered the spiritual significance of the **birthright** he wants so passionately to obtain, whereas Esau does not consider beyond the present life and is not interested in what could take place after his death. Jacob is aware of the divine promise that would concern the descendants of Abraham, namely the Promised Land and the messianic hope. Before the institution of the priesthood, "the birthright included not only an inheritance of worldly wealth, but also spiritual preeminence. He who received it was to be priest of his family."[577] As implied in Esau's reflections, which dissociated birthright from blessing (27:36), birthright did not at that time necessarily imply immediate material blessing. What Esau despised was of

---

576 On the significant role of meals in the Genesis plot, see Turner, *Genesis*, 119.

577 Ellen G. White, PP 177; cf. Rashi in Miqraot Gedolot on 25:31.

a spiritual nature (25:34; cf. Heb 12:16–17) and was not associated with any immediate and visible **profit** (25:32). Unlike Esau who is present-oriented, Jacob is
future-oriented and particularly sensitive to spiritual values; yet Jacob is so eager to
secure this birthright at this moment that he uses material means for that purpose.
Ironically, Jacob has enough faith to "see" spiritual values and the future profit of a
birthright but not enough faith to trust God for it (cf. 27:41–45).

ISAAC AND ABIMELECH (26:1–33)

Just as the two former episodes of Abraham and Abimelech (20:1–18; 21:22–34),
the following two episodes about Isaac and Abimelech are associated with the
stories of the conception and birth of Jacob (25:21–26; cf. 21:1–7), implying the
dismissal of Esau (26:26–34; cf. 21:8–21). This parallel confirms that our text is not
misplaced here, whereas it suggests the same theological intention to relate the secur-
ing of the Promised Land, through the digging of wells, to the birth of the promised
son. Furthermore, the episodes of Isaac and Abimelech parallel the episodes of Abraham and Abimelech. They both are presented in pairs and both occur successively
at Gerar (20:1; 26:1–22) and Beersheba (21:32; 26:23–33). The structure of the chapter follows the geographical distribution in a parallel manner:

26:1–6 Divine promises in Gerar   **26:23–25** Divine promises in Beersheba
26:7–16 Isaac-Abimelech in conflict in Gerar   **26:26–31** Isaac-Abimelech at peace in Beersheba
26:17–22 Isaac digs wells in conflict in Gerar   **26:32–33** Isaac digs a well in peace in Beersheba

26:1–6. DIVINE PROMISES IN GERAR

GEN 26:1–6 NKJV	GEN 26:1–6 ESV
1 There was a famine in the land, besides the first famine that was in the days of Abraham. And Isaac went to Abimelech king of the Philistines, in Gerar.	**1** Now there was a famine in the land, besides the former famine that was in the days of Abraham. And Isaac went to Gerar to Abimelech king of the Philistines.
2 Then the LORD appeared to him and said: "Do not go down to Egypt; live in the land of which I shall tell you.	**2** And the LORD appeared to him and said, "Do not go down to Egypt; dwell in the land of which I shall tell you.
3 Dwell in this land, and I will be with you and bless you; for to you and your descendants I give all these lands, and I will perform the oath which I swore to Abraham your father.	**3** Sojourn in this land, and I will be with you and will bless you, for to you and to your offspring I will give all these lands, and I will establish the oath that I swore to Abraham your father.
4 And I will make your descendants multiply as the stars of heaven; I will give to your descendants all these lands; and in your seed all the nations of the earth shall be blessed;	**4** I will multiply your offspring as the stars of heaven and will give to your offspring all these lands. And in your offspring all the nations of the earth shall be blessed,
5 because Abraham obeyed My voice and kept My charge, My commandments, My statutes, and My laws."	**5** because Abraham obeyed my voice and kept my charge, my commandments, my statutes, and my laws."
6 So Isaac dwelt in Gerar.	**6** So Isaac settled in Gerar.

A famine obliges Isaac to move to Gerar, the land under the rule of the Philistine Abimelech. It is in Gerar that Isaac will for the first time receive God's blessing.

26:1 A famine. This motif ties in, not without some irony, with the preceding episode referring to the hungry Esau around a meal (25:29–34).

Besides the first famine that was in the days of Abraham. The explicit evocation of the preceding case of famine indicates clearly that this is a second occurrence; our present story is therefore not to be interpreted as a redundant doublet implying the same event. As for **Abimelech**, this story clearly cannot be the same Abimelech of Genesis 20, but rather two individuals with the same name, as is the case with his army commander, Phichol (26:26; 21:22). Another Abimelech appears in the time of David (Ps 34:1), identified as Achish (1 Sam 21:10–15). "Abimelech" is therefore a name for an honorary function or a throne name. (Regarding the presence of the Philistines in Canaan, see the commentary on 21:32.)

26:2 Do not go down to Egypt. God's recommendation to Isaac echoes Abraham's concern that Isaac should not leave Canaan (24:6). This insistence on not leaving the land is coherent with the Genesis theology of the Promised Land. It is a land that is given by God, **the land of which I shall tell you.** Any time a patriarch must leave Canaan is related to extenuating circumstances, such as famine (Abraham, Isaac, Jacob, and Joseph) or troubles at home (Jacob).

26:3–6 I will be with you and bless you. The divine blessing on Isaac is reminiscent of the divine blessing on Abraham. The same language is used, reminding the reader of the two poles of the cycle of Abraham. The phrase **all the nations of the earth shall be blessed** (26:4) points to the first call of Abraham: "all the families of the earth shall be blessed" (12:3). The phrase **the oath which I swore to Abraham your father** (26:3) and the promise to **multiply descendants as the stars of heaven** clearly refer to the second call of Abraham, which concludes with the oath God swore to Abraham at Moriah: "By Myself I have sworn, says the Lord" (22:16) and the promise to "multiply your descendants as the stars of the heaven" (22:17). The blessing on Isaac is notably justified based on Abraham's faith: **because Abraham obeyed My voice** (26:5), which echoes the *aqedah*: "because you have obeyed My voice" (22:18). The threefold repetition of words referring to the Law, **My commandments, My statutes, and My laws,** suggests the comprehensiveness of Abraham's obedience. The fact that the same covenant language will be used again by Moses to exhort his people to keep the laws of the Sinaitic covenant (Deut 4:40; 30:16) suggests that those laws were already known in the time of Abraham.[578] The introductory words of that reference, **kept My charge,** are a play on the word *shamar* "keep" (*wayyishmor mishmarti*), making the verb *wayyishmor* "kept" resonate with the word *mishmarti* "My charge." This echo between God's charge and Abraham's response suggests the quality of Abraham's faithfulness. His obedience corresponds perfectly to God's intention. Similar to the blessing on Abraham, the blessing on Isaac concerns both the inheritance of the land and the multiplication of descendants, implying a profound connection between the land and the descendants. The hope of the Promised Land has something to do with the hope of the messianic seed. The parallel between the two blessings as a consequence of Abraham's faith implies a parallel between Abraham's faith and Isaac's faith. The

---

578 For pre-Sinai evidence in the book of Genesis for the Decalogue Commandments, see Jo Ann Davidson, "The Decalogue Predates Mount Sinai."

paragraph ends with the remark that **Isaac dwelt in Gerar** (26:6), which responds to God's injunction to Abraham to **dwell in the land** (26:2 ESV), **sojourn in this land** (26:3 ESV).

26:7–16. ISAAC AND ABIMELECH IN CONFLICT

GEN 26:7–16 NKJV	GEN 26:7–16 ESV
7 And the men of the place asked about his wife. And he said, "She *is* my sister"; for he was afraid to say, "*She is* my wife," *because he thought*, "lest the men of the place kill me for Rebekah, because she *is* beautiful to behold."	**7** When the men of the place asked him about his wife, he said, "She is my sister," for he feared to say, "My wife," thinking, "lest the men of the place should kill me because of Rebekah," because she was attractive in appearance.
8 Now it came to pass, when he had been there a long time, that Abimelech king of the Philistines looked through a window, and saw, and there was Isaac, showing endearment to Rebekah his wife.	**8** When he had been there a long time, Abimelech king of the Philistines looked out of a window and saw Isaac laughing with Rebekah his wife.
9 Then Abimelech called Isaac and said, "Quite obviously she *is* your wife; so how could you say, 'She *is* my sister'?" And Isaac said to him, "Because I said, 'Lest I die on account of her.'"	**9** So Abimelech called Isaac and said, "Behold, she is your wife. How then could you say, 'She is my sister'?" Isaac said to him, "Because I thought, 'Lest I die because of her.'"
10 And Abimelech said, "What *is* this you have done to us? One of the people might soon have lain with your wife, and you would have brought guilt on us."	**10** Abimelech said, "What is this you have done to us? One of the people might easily have lain with your wife, and you would have brought guilt upon us."
11 So Abimelech charged all *his* people, saying, "He who touches this man or his wife shall surely be put to death."	**11** So Abimelech warned all the people, saying, "Whoever touches this man or his wife shall surely be put to death."
12 Then Isaac sowed in that land, and reaped in the same year a hundredfold; and the LORD blessed him.	**12** And Isaac sowed in that land and reaped in the same year a hundredfold. The LORD blessed him,
13 The man began to prosper, and continued prospering until he became very prosperous;	**13** and the man became rich, and gained more and more until he became very wealthy.
14 for he had possessions of flocks and possessions of herds and a great number of servants. So the Philistines envied him.	**14** He had possessions of flocks and herds and many servants, so that the Philistines envied him.
15 Now the Philistines had stopped up all the wells which his father's servants had dug in the days of Abraham his father, and they had filled them with earth.	**15** (Now the Philistines had stopped and filled with earth all the wells that his father's servants had dug in the days of Abraham his father.)
16 And Abimelech said to Isaac, "Go away from us, for you are much mightier than we."	**16** And Abimelech said to Isaac, "Go away from us, for you are much mightier than we."

In order to ensure prosperity in the foreign land, Isaac does not hesitate to expose his wife.

26:7 In the following scene, Isaac is not immediately present. We first hear about **the men of the place** who are asking about **his wife** (26:7). The construction of the Hebrew phrase is unclear as to whom their question is addressed (see the KJV where the pronoun "*him*" is italicized, indicating its absence in the original Hebrew). Isaac is keeping a low profile and responds as if this woman does not concern him.

She is my sister. Isaac uses exactly the same phrase as his father Abraham (20:2), stressing the word "sister," which also appears at the beginning of the sentence. However, Isaac's situation differs from Abraham's. Whereas Abraham could argue that Sarah was his sister, that is, "she is the daughter of my father" (20:12), Isaac cannot do so because Rebekah is his cousin. Although Sarah supported Abraham in his claim (20:5), Rebekah does not.

She is beautiful to behold. The same expression *tobat mar'eh* was used to qualify Rebekah when she was found by Abraham's servant (24:16). This echo suggests that at the time, that is, at least seventeen years after the birth of the twins (25:27), Rebekah is still as beautiful as Sarah.

26:8–9 **Abimelech ... saw Isaac laughing with Rebekah** (ESV). The Hebrew word *metsakheq* is a wordplay on the name *yitskhaq* "Isaac" (21:6, 9). The verb is here used in the intensive form (*piel*), which may have sexual connotations (39:14, 17) to the degree that Abimelech understands that Isaac's relationship with Rebekah is not just of a brotherly nature (26:9). The chronological note that this episode takes place after **a long time** suggests that Isaac's fear is not justified, since nothing has happened so far.

26:10–11 Instead of bringing blessings to peoples, as designed by God's promise (26:4), Isaac brings troubles. Abimelech's question is the same as God's to Eve when she ate the forbidden fruit: **what is this you have done?** (26:10; cf. 3:13). Abimelech is the one who speaks for God and behaves righteously. Whereas Isaac has selfish concerns at the expense of others, the pagan king Abimelech has ethical concerns and issues a decree to protect Isaac and his family (26:11).

26:12–16 Although Isaac prospers, his success becomes a threat to others; **the Philistines envied him** (26:14). Ultimately, Isaac will have to leave this place, precisely because of his success. The same Abimelech who had protected Isaac now asks him to **go away** for he has become **much mightier** than them (26:16). This story contains an important lesson in matters of geopolitics. Becoming rich with no concern for others, although this wealth may have been acquired honestly and been blessed by God, will sooner or later end in conflict. Ironically, Isaac, who was so concerned with settling himself in the foreign land, and who had even **sowed in that land** (26:12), an activity that is unique among the patriarchs, is now obliged to move elsewhere. Isaac's success in settling became the cause for unsettling.

26:17–22. ISAAC DIGS WELLS IN GERAR

GEN 26:17–22 NKJV	GEN 26:17–22 ESV
17 Then Isaac departed from there and pitched his tent in the Valley of Gerar, and dwelt there.	**17** So Isaac departed from there and encamped in the Valley of Gerar and settled there.
18 And Isaac dug again the wells of water which they had dug in the days of Abraham his father, for the Philistines had stopped them up after the death of Abraham. He called them by the names which his father had called them.	**18** And Isaac dug again the wells of water that had been dug in the days of Abraham his father, which the Philistines had stopped after the death of Abraham. And he gave them the names that his father had given them.

19 Also Isaac's servants dug in the valley, and found a well of running water there.

20 But the herdsmen of Gerar quarreled with Isaac's herdsmen, saying, "The water *is* ours." So he called the name of the well Esek, because they quarreled with him.

21 Then they dug another well, and they quarreled over that *one* also. So he called its name Sitnah.

22 And he moved from there and dug another well, and they did not quarrel over it. So he called its name Rehoboth, because he said, "For now the Lᴏʀᴅ has made room for us, and we shall be fruitful in the land."

19 But when Isaac's servants dug in the valley and found there a well of spring water,

20 the herdsmen of Gerar quarreled with Isaac's herdsmen, saying, "The water is ours." So he called the name of the well Esek, because they contended with him.

21 Then they dug another well, and they quarreled over that also, so he called its name Sitnah.

22 And he moved from there and dug another well, and they did not quarrel over it. So he called its name Rehoboth, saying, "For now the Lᴏʀᴅ has made room for us, and we shall be fruitful in the land."

Once again Isaac attempts to settle. The verb *yashab* "dwell" is used a second time (26:17). Isaac previously attempted to settle through sowing. This time, Isaac's settling revolves around digging wells. Three times Isaac engages in digging a well and each time it ends with a strike.

26:17 Pitched his tent. The Hebrew verb *khanah* "pitch" (ESV: "encamp") typically appears in the context of the Exodus when the Israelites "camped in the wilderness" (Exod 19:2; 14:2; Num 33:5–49). The use of that same verb suggests that, despite his eagerness to settle, Isaac, similar to the Israelites, is not yet settled and is still on the move toward the Promised Land.

26:18–21 Isaac's choice to dig the old wells that had already been dug and possessed by his father (21:30–31) denotes his intense intention to settle; he also **called them by the names which his father had called them**; a way of reaffirming his ownership. No reaction is reported on the part of the men of Gerar. They likely do not dare to confront Isaac, because of their respect for the patriarch, and considering the history of those wells (21:23–33). However, as soon as Isaac's servants venture to dig new wells (26:19), they vehemently object, claiming that these wells belong to them (26:20). This mishap occurs on two occasions. Each time the digging ends with a conflict, and each time Isaac gives a name to the well commemorating the nature of the confrontation. The first well was called *'eseq*, a word that occurs only here, which means "quarrel." The second well was called *sitnah*, which means "accusation" (Ezra 4:6). The names suggest a crescendo in the confrontation, which begins with a dispute that challenges Isaac's claim to the well and ends with an accusation that settles the matter against him. Only on the third incident does Isaac experience relief and calls the name of the well accordingly; "Rehoboth" is derived from the word *rakhab*, meaning "spacious." Isaac at last feels at ease in the land and infers from this new comfort that he has finally reached the point to **be fruitful in the land** (26:22). Yet, the fact that he leaves that place to go to Beersheba (26:23) suggests that, despite his good feelings, he was not ready to settle.

26:23–25. DIVINE PROMISES IN BEERSHEBA

GEN 26:23–25 NKJV	GEN 26:23–25 ESV
23 Then he went up from there to Beersheba.	23 From there he went up to Beersheba.
24 And the Lᴏʀᴅ appeared to him the same night and said, "I *am* the God of your father Abraham; do not fear, for I *am* with you. I will bless you and multiply your descendants for My servant Abraham's sake."	24 And the Lᴏʀᴅ appeared to him the same night and said, "I am the God of Abraham your father. Fear not, for I am with you and will bless you and multiply your offspring for my servant Abraham's sake."
25 So he built an altar there and called on the name of the Lᴏʀᴅ, and he pitched his tent there; and there Isaac's servants dug a well.	25 So he built an altar there and called upon the name of the Lᴏʀᴅ and pitched his tent there. And there Isaac's servants dug a well.

As soon as Isaac arrives at Beersheba, the **same night** the Lord reveals Himself as the God of Abraham, and with the same words of encouragement He used when He revealed Himself to Abraham: **do not fear** (26:24; cf. 15:1). Similar to Abraham, Isaac has recently survived a conflict against the kings of Canaan when he hears from God (26:14–22; cf. 14:1–17). Isaac has the same fear as Abraham of not having a future in this land. God's words to Isaac are thus the same as His words to Abraham. They are words about the future, conveying the same promise of a multitude of descendants (26:24; cf. 15:5). Similar to Abraham, Isaac responds in worship (26:25; cf. 15:9–11). Isaac subsequently feels reassured and adopts the same attitude he had taken when he moved to the valley of Gerar; he pitches his tent (26:25, cf. 26:17) and thus places himself in the perspective of the Promised Land (see the commentary on 26:17). Isaac reaffirms his ownership of the land and his hope in the future of that land by digging a well (26:25; cf. 26:18).

26:26–31. ISAAC AND ABIMELECH IN PEACE IN BEERSHEBA

GEN 26:26–31 NKJV	GEN 26:26–31 ESV
26 Then Abimelech came to him from Gerar with Ahuzzath, one of his friends, and Phichol the commander of his army.	26 When Abimelech went to him from Gerar with Ahuzzath his adviser and Phicol the commander of his army,
27 And Isaac said to them, "Why have you come to me, since you hate me and have sent me away from you?"	27 Isaac said to them, "Why have you come to me, seeing that you hate me and have sent me away from you?"
28 But they said, "We have certainly seen that the Lᴏʀᴅ is with you. So we said, 'Let there now be an oath between us, between you and us; and let us make a covenant with you,	28 They said, "We see plainly that the Lᴏʀᴅ has been with you. So we said, let there be a sworn pact between us, between you and us, and let us make a covenant with you,
29 that you will do us no harm, since we have not touched you, and since we have done nothing to you but good and have sent you away in peace. You *are* now the blessed of the Lᴏʀᴅ.'"	29 that you will do us no harm, just as we have not touched you and have done to you nothing but good and have sent you away in peace. You are now the blessed of the Lᴏʀᴅ."
30 So he made them a feast, and they ate and drank.	30 So he made them a feast, and they ate and drank.

31 Then they arose early in the morning and swore an oath with one another; and Isaac sent them away, and they departed from him in peace.	**31** In the morning they rose early and exchanged oaths. And Isaac sent them on their way, and they departed from him in peace.

Abimelech initiates visiting Isaac with two of his high officers: Ahuzzath, his civil officer, and Phichol, his military officer. The qualification of Ahuzzath as **friend** designates a royal official (2 Sam 15:37; 16:16; 1 Kgs 4:5) and is the equivalent of the Egyptian title "friend," which designates the counselor of the king. This Phichol cannot be the Phichol who visited Abraham with Abimelech of that time, since this event occurred some sixty years earlier (21:22, 32). That Abimelech is accompanied by his two main officers indicates the formal nature of his approach to Isaac (26:26). However, Isaac is suspicious of Abimelech's intentions, considering his previous trouble with him (26:27; cf. 26:16). Abimelech's response reveals his desire to reassure Isaac. He not only acknowledges that Isaac has been blessed (26:28–29), but places himself in a subordinate position. He is the one who asks Isaac for a covenant between them (26:28) because he is afraid that Isaac might harm him, implicitly recognizing Isaac's preeminence over him (26:29). Isaac's response in providing the covenant meal is not simply a gesture of hospitality but confirms his superior position as a suzerain (26:30; cf. 2 Sam 3:20; cf. Ps 23:5). Abimelech departs the next day **in peace** (*beshalom*) (26:31) and thus concludes the meeting. Abimelech had used the same word to describe Isaac's departure from Gerar (26:29); just as Isaac had left Abimelech unharmed, that is, in peace, Abimelech was to leave Isaac unharmed and in peace.

26:32–33. ISAAC DIGS A WELL IN PEACE IN BEERSHEBA

GEN 26:32–33 NKJV	GEN 26:32–33 ESV
32 It came to pass the same day that Isaac's servants came and told him about the well which they had dug, and said to him, "We have found water."	**32** That same day Isaac's servants came and told him about the well that they had dug and said to him, "We have found water."
33 So he called it Shebah. Therefore the name of the city *is* Beersheba to this day.	**33** He called it Shibah; therefore the name of the city is Beersheba to this day.

Unlike the wells he had dug in Gerar, this is the first time that Isaac digs a well and can enjoy its water. Until now, either the men of Gerar (26:20–21) opposed him or he had to leave for some other reason (26:23). Now, a well had been dug (26:25), although water had not yet been found. Significantly, both the good news of the dug well and of the finding of water are delivered to Isaac on the **same day** (26:32) when peace is concluded with Abimelech. Once again, Isaac names the well. The previous names of Esek, Sitnah, and Rehoboth reflected the circumstances of acquiring the wells. This time, Isaac gives the well its old name, Beersheba, which had been given to it by Abraham. However, in the case of Abraham, the name referred to the *seven* ewe lambs offered by Abraham to Abimelech on the occasion of their covenant (21:29–30) and to the *oath* they swore to each other (21:31). The words "seven" and "oath" have the same root (*sheba'* and *shaba'*) in Hebrew. In our passage, the word *shaba'* only refers to the oath Abimelech and Isaac swore to each other. No mention is made of "seven ewe lambs," although they may be implied in the covenant ceremony. Isaac had already used the old names Abraham had given to the wells (26:18), although those names are unknown. This is the first time the name "Beersheba" is explicitly indicated. The reason for this difference is that, in the time of the writing of the account, the place was then referred to as Beersheba (26:33), thus anticipating the inheritance of the Promised Land.

JACOB STEALS THE BLESSING FROM ESAU (26:34–28:9)

The use of the introductory word *wayehi* (lit. trans.: "and it was so, when") linguistically marks the shift to a new section.[579] The reappearance of Esau also thematically signals a turning point, returning to the moment when "Esau despised the birthright" (25:34) and thus anticipating that the blessing of Jacob will proceed at the expense of the frustrated blessing of Esau. The structure of the section reflects the dependent relation between the two blessings, which is introduced and concluded by the same reference to Esau's poor choices of women (26:34–35; 28:6–9). This inclusio provides the negative background of Esau, which, along the lines of his despising of the birthright, prepares for the selective blessing. The report of the blessing of Jacob alternates with the report of the frustrated blessing of Esau, suggesting the following chiastic structure ($ABCB_1A_1$):

    A Marriages of Esau (26:34–35)
        B Blessing of Jacob (27:1–29)
            C Blessing of Esau (27:30–40)
        B₁ Blessing of Jacob (27:41–28:5)
    A₁ Marriages of Esau (28:6–9)

26:34–35. MARRIAGES OF ESAU

GEN 26:34–35 NKJV	GEN 26:34–35 ESV
34 When Esau was forty years old, he took as wives Judith the daughter of Beeri the Hittite, and Basemath the daughter of Elon the Hittite.	**34** When Esau was forty years old, he took Judith the daughter of Beeri the Hittite to be his wife, and Basemath the daughter of Elon the Hittite,
35 And they were a grief of mind to Isaac and Rebekah.	**35** and they made life bitter for Isaac and Rebekah.

Esau marries at the age of forty, similar to his father (25:20), who is then one hundred years old (25:26). However, unlike his father, Esau seeks his wife by himself without consulting his parents and chooses from among the women of the land. This information ties in with the preceding story of Isaac settling on the land. For Esau to marry native women is the logical continuation of his striving to settle and dig wells on that land. This connection between the two narratives is also suggested through the name *Beeri* "my well," father of Judith (Esau's wife, cf. 26:34), which resonates with the Hebrew word for "well" (*be'er*), a keyword in the preceding narrative. What appears to be a natural option poses a problem in regard to the spiritual perspective of the divine promise. The biblical writer notes that the Hittite women

---

579 See the commentary on 14:1–2.

were **a grief of mind to Isaac and Rebekah** (26:35). The Hebrew expression *merat ruakh* (lit. trans.: "bitterness of spirit") suggests that the parents were bitter and depressed (Prov 31:6). The Hittites' lifestyle, their moral corruption, and their idolatry (15:16; 18:19; Lev 20:23) were completely at odds with Isaac and Rebekah's ideals of holiness. This prelude about Esau's marriages reinforces his unworthiness and prepares for the forthcoming blessing of Jacob. Isaac and Rebekah share the same concern. Their profound harmony in regard to Esau's marriages (26:35) contrasts with their strong dissension regarding the blessing of the children. Rebekah remains consistent, not only with the moral evaluations she shares with her husband, but also with the divine plans (25:23).

27:1–29. BLESSING OF JACOB

The same introductory word *wayehi*, translated here **now it came to pass** (27:1), marks the new section, resuming the preceding line of thought. The plot leading to the actual blessing of Jacob by Isaac shares a number of significant themes with the story of Jacob and Esau around the meal of lentils (25:27–34): age (25:27; cf. 27:1–2), Esau as hunter (25:27; cf. 27:3), love, desire to eat a meal, game (25:28; cf. 27:3–4), and the prospect of death (25:32; cf. 27:2). The parallels between these two texts suggest that the deal between Jacob and Esau and the blessing of Jacob are related. This relationship somehow tempers the wrongdoing of Rebekah and Jacob in their attempt to deceive Isaac and Esau, for it reminds us that Jacob had earned his blessing, which Esau had despised. However, the behavior of Rebekah and Jacob is problematic because this blessing they worked for was, in fact, God's gift and did not depend on their human achievements and merits (25:23). This theology of grace conveys an irony: all these human efforts were not only ethically wrong, they were unnecessary. The process of the blessing of Jacob unfolds in three phases or three confrontations: Isaac asks Esau to cook a meal for him that he may bless him (27:1–4); Rebekah counsels Jacob to engage in a deceitful strategy to ensure the blessing of Jacob instead of Esau (27:5–17); Isaac is deceived by Jacob and gives his blessing to him in the place of Esau (27:18–29).

27:1–4. ISAAC AND ESAU

GEN 27:1–4 NKJV	GEN 27:1–4 ESV
1 Now it came to pass, when Isaac was old and his eyes were so dim that he could not see, that he called Esau his older son and said to him, "My son." And he answered him, "Here I am."	**1** When Isaac was old and his eyes were dim so that he could not see, he called Esau his older son and said to him, "My son"; and he answered, "Here I am."
2 Then he said, "Behold now, I am old. I do not know the day of my death.	**2** He said, "Behold, I am old; I do not know the day of my death.
3 Now therefore, please take your weapons, your quiver and your bow, and go out to the field and hunt game for me.	**3** Now then, take your weapons, your quiver and your bow, and go out to the field and hunt game for me,
4 And make me savory food, such as I love, and bring *it* to me that I may eat, that my soul may bless you before I die."	**4** and prepare for me delicious food, such as I love, and bring it to me so that I may eat, that my soul may bless you before I die."

Isaac's particular affinities toward Esau are noticeable from the early years: "Isaac loved Esau because he ate of his game" (25:28). Isaac and Esau have the same weakness, which affects their discernment and values. Just as Esau was willing to sacrifice his birthright as the elder brother for a meal, Isaac was ready, for a meal, to bless Esau instead of Jacob, against God's plans, and in spite of Esau's wrong choices.

27:1 When Isaac was old. Chronological computation indicates that Isaac must have been approximately 137 years of age at the time (25:26; 26:34);[580] yet, he lives until the age of 180 years (35:28), which suggests he was strong.

He could not see. Isaac's vigor suggests that his blindness is not merely a physical effect caused by old age; it also has spiritual significance because Isaac refuses to see Esau's iniquities and Jacob's righteousness. Ironically, it is his blindness that will lead to the blessing of Jacob.

He called Esau his older son. Although God's prophecy had prioritized the younger over the older (25:23), Isaac insists on using the custom of primogeniture that favors the "older son" in order to justify his intention to bless him instead of Jacob.

My son … here I am. The initiated dialogue reflects the dramatic dialogues of the *'aqedah* between God and Abraham (22:1), Abraham and Isaac (22:7), and the Angel of the Lord and Abraham (22:11). Although this parallel suggests the quality of Esau's obedience to his father, it is an oblique critique of Isaac, who is reminded that human obedience should be dependent on obedience to God. Isaac ignores the vertical requirement and behaves as if God did not speak (25:23) and as if he did not know about Esau's misbehavior (26:34–35).

27:2 I do not know the day of my death. In this statement, Isaac recognizes God's sovereignty (Eccl 6:12; 8:7; Jas 4:13–15), which contradicts his present behavior. Isaac maneuvers to bless Esau, thus ignoring God's prophecy while simultaneously recognizing God's providence in his life.

27:3–4 Take your weapons. The list of hunting instruments (27:3) suggests Esau's professional skills and denotes his violent character. Thus, the act of blessing, which belongs to the spiritual world, is here related to Esau's violence and Isaac's sensuality. The verb "love" often refers to the human love of God (Exod 20:8; 26:8; Pss 119:47–48, 97, 113, etc.), and the Hebrew phrase *'asher 'ahabti* **as I love** is used only in relation to God (Ps 119:47–48). Isaac's theology is thus determined by his appetite.

27:5–17. REBEKAH AND JACOB

GEN 27:5–17 NKJV	GEN 27:5–17 ESV
5 Now Rebekah was listening when Isaac spoke to Esau his son. And Esau went to the field to hunt game and to bring *it*.	**5** Now Rebekah was listening when Isaac spoke to his son Esau. So when Esau went to the field to hunt for game and bring it,
6 So Rebekah spoke to Jacob her son, saying, "Indeed I heard your father speak to Esau your brother, saying,	**6** Rebekah said to her son Jacob, "I heard your father speak to your brother Esau,

---

580 See SDABC 1:376.

7 'Bring me game and make savory food for me, that I may eat it and bless you in the presence of the Lᴏʀᴅ before my death.'

7 'Bring me game and prepare for me delicious food, that I may eat it and bless you before the Lᴏʀᴅ before I die.'

8 Now therefore, my son, obey my voice according to what I command you.

8 Now therefore, my son, obey my voice as I command you.

9 Go now to the flock and bring me from there two choice kids of the goats, and I will make savory food from them for your father, such as he loves.

9 Go to the flock and bring me two good young goats, so that I may prepare from them delicious food for your father, such as he loves.

10 Then you shall take *it* to your father, that he may eat *it*, and that he may bless you before his death."

10 And you shall bring it to your father to eat, so that he may bless you before he dies."

11 And Jacob said to Rebekah his mother, "Look, Esau my brother *is* a hairy man, and I *am* a smooth-*skinned* man.

11 But Jacob said to Rebekah his mother, "Behold, my brother Esau is a hairy man, and I am a smooth man.

12 Perhaps my father will feel me, and I shall seem to be a deceiver to him; and I shall bring a curse on myself and not a blessing."

12 Perhaps my father will feel me, and I shall seem to be mocking him and bring a curse upon myself and not a blessing."

13 But his mother said to him, "*Let* your curse *be* on me, my son; only obey my voice, and go, get *them* for me."

13 His mother said to him, "Let your curse be on me, my son; only obey my voice, and go, bring them to me."

14 And he went and got *them* and brought *them* to his mother, and his mother made savory food, such as his father loved.

14 So he went and took them and brought them to his mother, and his mother prepared delicious food, such as his father loved.

15 Then Rebekah took the choice clothes of her elder son Esau, which *were* with her in the house, and put them on Jacob her younger son.

15 Then Rebekah took the best garments of Esau her older son, which were with her in the house, and put them on Jacob her younger son.

16 And she put the skins of the kids of the goats on his hands and on the smooth part of his neck.

16 And the skins of the young goats she put on his hands and on the smooth part of his neck.

17 Then she gave the savory food and the bread, which she had prepared, into the hand of her son Jacob.

17 And she put the delicious food and the bread, which she had prepared, into the hand of her son Jacob.

The family rivalry is highlighted. The previous camp of Isaac and Esau (27:1–4), who is designated as Isaac's son (27:1), is now opposed to the camp of Rebekah and Jacob, who is designated as Rebekah's son (27:6, 8, 13). Rebekah reacts immediately to Isaac's moves and initiates controlling and changing the course of events, as planned by Isaac.

27:5–7 Rebekah was listening. Rebekah is present (compare Sarah in 18:10). She not only hears the conversation, but also observes Esau's implementation of Isaac's instruction. She immediately shares the relevant information with Jacob, focusing on what should concern him: Isaac intends to bless Esau, **in the presence of the Lord** (27:7). This reference to the divine Presence was absent in the preceding report of the actual event. Isaac merely stated, **before I die** (27:4). Rebekah's additional comment to Isaac's words indicates the blessing should be bestowed "in the presence of the Lord" and, therefore, with His approval. Thus, Rebekah implicitly condemns Isaac's intentions that ignore God's will and justifies her plot to counter

Isaac's plans. Rebekah's relation to Isaac's secular move is ironically of a similar vein. Similar to Isaac, Rebekah ignores "the presence of the Lord" and intends to take his place.

27:8 Obey my voice ... what I command you. Rebekah speaks with the authority of a prophet. Her language recalls God's commandment (2:16; Exod 12:28, 50) and Moses' admonitions to Israel (Deut 4:2; 11:13, 22, 27–28).

27:9 Two choice kids of the goats. The choice of two goats is puzzling. Not only would the two animals constitute too large a meal for one person, but they do not correspond to Isaac's expectation of wild game, which tastes quite different. The choice of the two goats has therefore been suggested to have sacrificial purposes (cf. Lev 16:8), in order to atone for the sin of dissension between the two brothers.[581] This interpretation may appear difficult, but Rebekah's allusion to an atoning sacrifice may well be intended for the following reasons. Rebekah may have been concerned with the forthcoming conflict that would put her two sons in opposition, both of whom she loved (27:45), and her in opposition to her husband (27:14, 46). She was also concerned with the curse such a deception would bring upon her and, therefore, needed forgiveness (27:13).

27:11–12 In response to his mother's argument, Jacob mentions potential problems with his brother (**Esau my brother**), his father (**my father will feel me ... deceiver to him**), and God (**a curse**). The lesson is that these three relationships are interdependent. The quality of our relationship with God is dependent on our relationship with our brother and vice versa. The quality of our relationship with our brother also depends on our relationship with our father and vice versa.

27:13 Let your curse be on me. To reassure Jacob of the rightness of her approach, Rebekah refers to her own conviction. According to God's prophecy, she knows that the blessing of Jacob is God's will. She thus uses God to justify her deceitful act and drag her son with her. She pressures him and identifies herself with God; she again appropriates the phrase **obey my voice** (cf. 27:8), which is generally used by God (22:18; 26:5; Exod 4:1; 18:19; 19:5; etc.). Rebekah similarly applies the phrase **go, get** (*lek qakh*), God's discourse in reverse "take, go" (*qakh lek*) (22:2), and orients this divine order to herself. She asks Jacob to obey **for me**.

27:14 And he went. In response to his mother's identification with God, Jacob obeys her in the same way as Abraham obeys God (12:1, 4; 22:2–3, 13). That Isaac is designated **his father**, in relation to Jacob, rather than "her husband," in relation to Rebekah, suggests a disruption in the couple's relationship.

27:15–17 Rebekah and Jacob are united in the same operation. The same verb "take" (*laqakh*) is used to describe their common action. Whereas Jacob went to "take" the animals, Rebekah went to "take" Esau's clothes (27:15). However, Jacob's participation is minimal; he is docile and does only what his mother tells him to do. Rebekah is the one who executes the entire operation. She resourcefully uses everything from the animals: the skin of the animals to cover Jacob's hands and neck (27:16) and the flesh of the animals for the meal (27:17). Jacob is described as passive. Not only does he not participate in any of the preparations, but he does not even gather the clothes or assist in cooking the meal. Rebekah is the one who puts the clothes and the goats' skins on him and who **gave the savory food ... into the hand**

---

581 See Rashi in Miqraot Gedolot on Genesis 27:9.

of her son Jacob (27:17). Jacob's passivity suggests his reluctance and lack of confidence in this deceitful enterprise. Jacob does not feel comfortable and may even feel guilty.

27:18–29. ISAAC AND JACOB

GEN 27:18–29 NKJV	GEN 27:18–29 ESV
18 So he went to his father and said, "My father." And he said, "Here I am. Who *are* you, my son?"	**18** So he went in to his father and said, "My father." And he said, "Here I am. Who are you, my son?"
19 Jacob said to his father, "I *am* Esau your firstborn; I have done just as you told me; please arise, sit and eat of my game, that your soul may bless me."	**19** Jacob said to his father, "I am Esau your firstborn. I have done as you told me; now sit up and eat of my game, that your soul may bless me."
20 But Isaac said to his son, "How *is it* that you have found *it* so quickly, my son?" And he said, "Because the Lord your God brought *it* to me."	**20** But Isaac said to his son, "How is it that you have found it so quickly, my son?" He answered, "Because the Lord your God granted me success."
21 Isaac said to Jacob, "Please come near, that I may feel you, my son, whether you *are* really my son Esau or not."	**21** Then Isaac said to Jacob, "Please come near, that I may feel you, my son, to know whether you are really my son Esau or not."
22 So Jacob went near to Isaac his father, and he felt him and said, "The voice *is* Jacob's voice, but the hands *are* the hands of Esau."	**22** So Jacob went near to Isaac his father, who felt him and said, "The voice is Jacob's voice, but the hands are the hands of Esau."
23 And he did not recognize him, because his hands were hairy like his brother Esau's hands; so he blessed him.	**23** And he did not recognize him, because his hands were hairy like his brother Esau's hands. So he blessed him.
24 Then he said, "*Are* you really my son Esau?" He said, "I *am*."	**24** He said, "Are you really my son Esau?" He answered, "I am."
25 He said, "Bring *it* near to me, and I will eat of my son's game, so that my soul may bless you." So he brought *it* near to him, and he ate; and he brought him wine, and he drank.	**25** Then he said, "Bring it near to me, that I may eat of my son's game and bless you." So he brought it near to him, and he ate; and he brought him wine, and he drank.
26 Then his father Isaac said to him, "Come near now and kiss me, my son."	**26** Then his father Isaac said to him, "Come near and kiss me, my son."
27 And he came near and kissed him; and he smelled the smell of his clothing, and blessed him and said: "Surely, the smell of my son *is* like the smell of a field which the Lord has blessed.	**27** So he came near and kissed him. And Isaac smelled the smell of his garments and blessed him and said, "See, the smell of my son is as the smell of a field that the Lord has blessed!
28 Therefore may God give you of the dew of heaven, of the fatness of the earth, and plenty of grain and wine.	**28** May God give you of the dew of heaven and of the fatness of the earth and plenty of grain and wine.
29 Let peoples serve you, and nations bow down to you. Be master over your brethren, And let your mother's sons bow down to you. Cursed *be* everyone who curses you, and blessed *be* those who bless you!"	**29** Let peoples serve you, and nations bow down to you. Be lord over your brothers, and may your mother's sons bow down to you. Cursed be everyone who curses you, and blessed be everyone who blesses you!"

This is the only time when the camps are crossed over, but this is done without the knowledge of the other camp. Jacob presents himself to Isaac as "his son" Esau. Only after having doubted seven times (27:18, 20–22, 24–27) does Isaac finally bless Jacob, thinking he was Esau.

27:18 So he went. Whereas the verb *wayyelek* "and he went" was used (27:14) in response to the mother's command, the verb *wayyabo'* "and he came" (JPS) is now used (the NKJV translates the two verbs with the same words: "he went"). The first verb denotes Jacob's resolution, whereas the second verb suggests his hesitation and fear, because he has penetrated the other camp.

My father. Jacob addresses his father with only one word, the same word Isaac used when he addressed his father: *'abi* "my father" (cf. 22:7). This echo suggests that Jacob approaches his father Isaac with the same timidity and sentiments of fear as Isaac did when he approached his father Abraham. Isaac responds to his son with the same word that Abraham had used to reassure his son, *hinneni* "here I am" (22:7). But while Abraham had only said "my son," Isaac asks a longer question: **who are you, my son?** Isaac knows that this is his son but is not sure which son it is (first doubt). He may even have recognized Jacob's voice (27:22).

27:19 Jacob identifies himself explicitly as **Esau your firstborn** and uses the very word "firstborn," which is in Isaac's mind while he prepares to bless Esau (27:1). He also repeats verbatim the words that Isaac had pronounced in his instruction **as you told me**, words he must have learned from his mother who had heard them because of her eavesdropping: **that your soul may bless me** (cf. 27:4). The similarity between his response and Esau's (27:31) also suggests that Jacob must have had some inkling of how Esau would have responded.

27:20–21 Isaac remains skeptical, considering the short time Jacob took to bring the game (second doubt). Jacob uses the supernatural argument to explain the abnormality of his hunting success. Jacob's answer is blasphemous (Exod 20:7) because he refers to God to support his lie (Exod 20:7). However, in a certain sense, Jacob interprets all that his mother does as God's hand: **the Lord your God brought it to me** (27:20). The reference to "your God," who is behind all this, is a way of reminding himself that he is simply fulfilling God's will, in spite of the dubious maneuver. Jacob's religious language does not fit Esau's nonreligious nature; it therefore triggers Isaac's suspicion: **whether you are really my son Esau or not** (27:21). This is the first and only time that Isaac expresses his doubt so explicitly and with so many words (third doubt). Isaac now wants to touch his son to verify with his own hand.

27:22 Even when Jacob comes near and Isaac touches him, he still doubts because he identifies the voice as **Jacob's voice** (fourth doubt). That Rebekah had not taken care of this potential problem may be due to the fact that Esau and Jacob, being twins, may have sounded alike to her. Isaac, however, who is blind, is endowed with more acute hearing and is therefore capable of distinguishing between the two voices. Isaac is confused by this contradiction; with his ears, he hears the voice of Jacob, but with his fingers, he feels the skin of Esau.

27:23 Because Isaac is unable to **recognize him … he blessed him**. The phrase is ambiguous. Whether the first pronoun "him" refers to Esau (most immediate antecedent) or to Jacob (the son in presence) is unclear. The second "him" refers to Jacob, since this is the very blessing that is being considered (27:19). Isaac remains uncertain about his blessing. This hesitancy is revealed by the fact that this first reference to blessing is not actualized; it is not followed by the words of blessing, as it will be in the second reference to blessing (27:27).[582] In the first reference to blessing, the verb *wayyoʾmer*, which is supposed to introduce the actual blessing, is disrupted by Isaac's new question. Isaac refrains from proceeding to the blessing. Only in the second reference to blessing does the verb *wayyoʾmer* open to the actual blessing.[583]

27:24 Isaac now appeals to Jacob's honesty; he asks him directly whether he is Esau and wants to hear Jacob speak to verify he is, once again, by the sound of his voice (fifth doubt). Jacob's strong affirmative response should be convincing; Jacob is also sufficiently prudent to limit his final speech to one single short word, *ʾani* "I" so Isaac will not notice the difference.

27:25 Isaac remains suspicious and wants, therefore, to eat the meal as a supplementary test to check if the food tastes like Esau's recipe, the way Isaac loved it (sixth doubt).

27:26–27a As Isaac finishes eating, he remains doubtful and wants to use another sense to again verify whether this is actually Esau. Isaac wants to smell the son (seventh doubt). Therefore, he asks him to come even nearer and kiss him. Then, after Isaac smells the personal scent of Esau's clothing, he **blessed him and said …**

27:27b–29 The narrative now shifts from prose to poetry and takes the form of a prophecy. The blessing is composed of three parts: intended for Esau, it begins with him (27:27b–28); it proceeds with the appropriation of the blessing destined for Jacob (27:29a; cf. 25:23); and it concludes with the Abrahamic promise (27:29b). Isaac's prophetic blessing, which begins only after the evocation of Esau (27:27), is ominously articulated in seven verbs—**give you … serve you … bow down … master over … bow down … cursed … blessed**—in a rhythm that echoes the rhythm of creation.

27:27b–28 Isaac moves from the smell of Esau to the smell of the field (27:27b), which reinforces the evocation of Esau, a "man of the field" (25:27; cf. 25:29; 27:3). Yet, the blessing will benefit Jacob, since the field is then no longer interpreted as a hunting place but as an agricultural resource, pointing to the benefit of the Promised Land. The language of the blessing indeed belongs to the evocation of the Promised Land. The phrase **may God give you** recalls the land that God has promised to **give** to the posterity of Abraham (12:7; 15:7, 18), of Isaac (26:4), and of Jacob (35:12). Likewise, the way this land is qualified as having **plenty of grain and wine** (27:28) coincides with the way the Promised Land is qualified (Deut 33:28).

27:29a Isaac deliberately applies the blessing that was originally destined for Jacob (25:23), whom he believes is Esau. In so doing, Isaac distorts God's blessing. The part that specified "the older shall serve the younger" is changed into a more universal statement: **let peoples serve you, and nations bow down to you**. The new blessing is sufficiently vague to avoid specifically harming Jacob. However, the remaining blessing includes Jacob, without mentioning him explicitly: **let your mother's sons bow down to you**. The plural used by Isaac allows him to refer to Jacob ("your mother's sons") in a more general way.

---

582 Note also the subtle variation of the Massoretic reading of the same word "and he blessed." The first *wayebar-khehu* is read with *shewa* under *resh* for the first blessing, whereas the second *wayebarakhehu* is read with *patakh shewa* under *resh*. This slight lengthening of the vowel suggests that only at the second step is the blessing formalized and is actually occurring.

583 It has also been suggested that "it could also be interpreted as an ingressive: 'he began to give him the blessing' " (*IBHS*, 33.3.1a).

27:29b Isaac applies the terms of the Abrahamic blessing (12:3) to the person he blesses (in his mind, Esau). For Isaac, Esau (not Jacob) should become the ancestor of the Messiah from whom the nations will obtain their blessing. Isaac attempts to change the prophetic course of events as planned by God.

27:30–40. BLESSING OF ESAU

GEN 27:30–40 NKJV	GEN 27:30–40 ESV
30 Now it happened, as soon as Isaac had finished blessing Jacob, and Jacob had scarcely gone out from the presence of Isaac his father, that Esau his brother came in from his hunting.	**30** As soon as Isaac had finished blessing Jacob, when Jacob had scarcely gone out from the presence of Isaac his father, Esau his brother came in from his hunting.
31 He also had made savory food, and brought it to his father, and said to his father, "Let my father arise and eat of his son's game, that your soul may bless me."	**31** He also prepared delicious food and brought it to his father. And he said to his father, "Let my father arise and eat of his son's game, that you may bless me."
32 And his father Isaac said to him, "Who *are* you?" So he said, "I *am* your son, your firstborn, Esau."	**32** His father Isaac said to him, "Who are you?" He answered, "I am your son, your firstborn, Esau."
33 Then Isaac trembled exceedingly, and said, "Who? Where *is* the one who hunted game and brought *it* to me? I ate all *of it* before you came, and I have blessed him—*and* indeed he shall be blessed."	**33** Then Isaac trembled very violently and said, "Who was it then that hunted game and brought it to me, and I ate it all before you came, and I have blessed him? Yes, and he shall be blessed."
34 When Esau heard the words of his father, he cried with an exceedingly great and bitter cry, and said to his father, "Bless me—me also, O my father!"	**34** As soon as Esau heard the words of his father, he cried out with an exceedingly great and bitter cry and said to his father, "Bless me, even me also, O my father!"
35 But he said, "Your brother came with deceit and has taken away your blessing."	**35** But he said, "Your brother came deceitfully, and he has taken away your blessing."
36 And *Esau* said, "Is he not rightly named Jacob? For he has supplanted me these two times. He took away my birthright, and now look, he has taken away my blessing!" And he said, "Have you not reserved a blessing for me?"	**36** Esau said, "Is he not rightly named Jacob? For he has cheated me these two times. He took away my birthright, and behold, now he has taken away my blessing." Then he said, "Have you not reserved a blessing for me?"
37 Then Isaac answered and said to Esau, "Indeed I have made him your master, and all his brethren I have given to him as servants; with grain and wine I have sustained him. What shall I do now for you, my son?"	**37** Isaac answered and said to Esau, "Behold, I have made him lord over you, and all his brothers I have given to him for servants, and with grain and wine I have sustained him. What then can I do for you, my son?"
38 And Esau said to his father, "Have you only one blessing, my father? Bless me—me also, O my father!" And Esau lifted up his voice and wept.	**38** Esau said to his father, "Have you but one blessing, my father? Bless me, even me also, O my father." And Esau lifted up his voice and wept.
39 Then Isaac his father answered and said to him: "Behold, your dwelling shall be of the fatness of the earth, and of the dew of heaven from above.	**39** Then Isaac his father answered and said to him: "Behold, away from the fatness of the earth shall your dwelling be, and away from the dew of heaven on high.

40 By your sword you shall live, and you shall serve your brother; and it shall come to pass, when you become restless, that you shall break his yoke from your neck."

40 By your sword you shall live, and you shall serve your brother; but when you grow restless you shall break his yoke from your neck."

When Isaac encounters the true Esau, he realizes with great distress (regret might be better) that he has been deceived and that the blessing is irrevocable. In this section, the word "father" appears twelve times. The same word had occurred only five times in the encounter between Isaac and Jacob. This repetition of the word "father" speaks loudly of the intense relationship Esau maintained with "his father." However, despite his closer relationship with his father, Esau does not receive the blessing he believes he deserves as the firstborn. He will instead receive the reverse of the blessing Jacob obtained, an antiblessing.

27:30 The narrative underscores the fact that Esau barely misses Jacob. When Esau **came in,** the blessing had just **finished** and **Jacob had scarcely gone out.** The short word *'akh*, an emphatic adverb (not rendered in the translation), and the repetition of action verbs suggest the emotional stress associated with this incident. Had Esau arrived a moment before he would have had a surprise encounter with his brother; not only would Jacob not have been blessed, he would have been killed by his brother (27:41).

27:31 Esau invites his father to eat of his meal with nearly the same words as Jacob's. However, the style of his address is slightly different. Whereas Jacob addresses his father in the second person, **please arise, sit and eat of my game** (27:19), Esau uses the third person, **let my father arise and eat of his son's game.** Not only is the father-son relationship emphasized here, but the third person address expresses greater reverence. Note that Esau begins his address with a long sentence, whereas Jacob uses only one word, *'abi* "my father." Esau is self-confident, whereas Jacob is unsure of himself.

27:32 I am your son. To Isaac's same question **who are you?** Esau's answer is also different. Whereas Jacob begins by identifying himself as Esau: *'anokhi 'esaw bechorkha* "I am Esau your firstborn" (lit. trans.) (27:19; cf. 27:32 NKJV: "your firstborn, Esau"), Esau begins by identifying himself simply as Isaac's son: "I am your son, your firstborn Esau" (lit. trans.). For Jacob, it is important to highlight Esau because he is not Esau. For Esau, it is important to highlight the particular filial bond that unites them.

27:33–38 The following scenes are poignant. The intense emotional state is rendered explicit by the description of feelings, a rare feature in biblical Hebrew literature: **Isaac trembled exceedingly** (27:33). As for Esau, when he **heard the words of his father, he cried with an exceedingly great and bitter cry.** Again, later **Esau lifted up his voice and wept** (27:38).

The emotional turmoil is also suggested by the multiple questions, sometimes the same questions, indicating their confusion before the unsolvable condition. Isaac twice asks questions: **Who? Where is the one who hunted game … ?** (27:33). **What shall I do now for you, my son?** (27:37). Similar to Isaac, Esau asks questions: **Is he not rightly named Jacob?** (27:36). **Have you not reserved a blessing for me?** (27:36). **Have you only one blessing, my father?** (27:38).

What is indeed disturbing for Isaac and Esau is not so much that they have been deceived, but the realization that they can do nothing about it. The course cannot be reversed. Isaac emphasizes this fact, using the emphatic adverb *gam* "indeed" (ESV: "yes") in the introduction to his assertion, **Indeed he shall be blessed** (27:33). The reason Isaac understands the blessing cannot be changed is that he knows at a deep level that this blessing was according to God's plan and that "the older shall serve the younger" (25:23). He also knows Esau's priorities regarding his birthright, which he despised (25:34), as well as his marital choices, which would compromise the holiness of God's people (26:34–35). Isaac recognizes God's hand in the turn of events. He had attempted to change God's design but failed. Isaac realizes that God is in control, despite his own maneuvers. Responding to his father, who informed him that the blessing was already given and will be fulfilled, Esau understands that the blessing cannot be transferred and insists that he **also** obtain a blessing (27:34, 38; cf. 27:36). The definitive character of the curse and blessing is difficult for us to understand.

27:36 Jacob … he has supplanted me these two times. Esau plays on the name "Jacob" (*Ya'aqob*), which has already been explained from its root *'aqeb*, meaning "heel," referring to Jacob's grasp of Esau's heel at the moment of their birth (25:26). Esau bitterly complains that this is the second time Jacob has grasped his heel. The first time Jacob caught Esau's heel in an attempt to supersede him. The second time Jacob usurped Esau's place, disguising himself as Esau and thus stealing the blessing that was destined for him. Attacking the heel also connotes deception and fatal aggression (3:15; 49:17, 19; Job 18:9; Ps 41:9 [10]). According to Esau, Jacob's intents are deceptive and criminal.

27:39–40 What Isaac can give to Esau is not qualified as a blessing. Whereas the word "bless" is used in the introduction to characterize Isaac's blessing on Jacob (27:27), it is not used in the introduction to Isaac's blessing on Esau. Isaac is simply responding to Esau: **Isaac his father answered and said** (27:39). Isaac's blessing on Esau reverses Isaac's blessing on Jacob; it is an antiblessing. Whereas Jacob will receive from God the resources of the Promised Land, "May God give you of the dew of heaven, of the fatness of the earth" (27:28), Esau will be deprived **of the fatness of the earth, and of the dew of heaven** (27:39) The preposition *min* (often translated "from" or "of") has here a privative sense, meaning "away from."[584] Note also that the blessing of Jacob, which prioritizes "heaven" (heaven-earth), has been reversed in the curse of Esau, which prioritizes "earth" (earth-heaven). Esau is thus placed outside of the divine influence. Consequently, all that Esau will obtain will be from his own strength, by his **sword** (27:40a). Yet, Esau is destined to serve his brother (27:40b), thus inverting the blessing pronounced for Jacob (27:29). This prophecy will be fulfilled. Although Edom will appear as an aggressive and hostile nation throughout biblical history, it will submit to Israel and even become a part of the Davidic kingdom (1 Sam 14:47; 2 Sam 8:12, 14; 1 Kgs 11:14–16). The same prophetic vision will resonate again in Balaam's prophecies (Num 24:18; cf. 1 Sam 14:47; 2 Sam 8:12, 14). The last line predicts that Edom will ultimately **break his yoke** (27:40c). Edom will regain its independence (2 Kgs 8:20–22). Although this last prophecy brings a note of hope for Edom, it remains that this deliverance is not given as a result of a supernatural process. Edom will obtain its freedom by its own human

---

584 See Wenham, *Genesis 16–50*, 212.

efforts. Unlike Jacob's destiny, which is in God's hands, Edom's history belongs to the mere political domain.

27:41–28:5. BLESSING OF JACOB

GEN 27:41–28:5 NKJV	GEN 27:41–28:5 ESV
41 So Esau hated Jacob because of the blessing with which his father blessed him, and Esau said in his heart, "The days of mourning for my father are at hand; then I will kill my brother Jacob."	**41** Now Esau hated Jacob because of the blessing with which his father had blessed him, and Esau said to himself, "The days of mourning for my father are approaching; then I will kill my brother Jacob."
42 And the words of Esau her older son were told to Rebekah. So she sent and called Jacob her younger son, and said to him, "Surely your brother Esau comforts himself concerning you *by intending* to kill you.	**42** But the words of Esau her older son were told to Rebekah. So she sent and called Jacob her younger son and said to him, "Behold, your brother Esau comforts himself about you by planning to kill you.
43 Now therefore, my son, obey my voice: arise, flee to my brother Laban in Haran.	**43** Now therefore, my son, obey my voice. Arise, flee to Laban my brother in Haran
44 And stay with him a few days, until your brother's fury turns away,	**44** and stay with him a while, until your brother's fury turns away—
45 until your brother's anger turns away from you, and he forgets what you have done to him; then I will send and bring you from there. Why should I be bereaved also of you both in one day?"	**45** until your brother's anger turns away from you, and he forgets what you have done to him. Then I will send and bring you from there. Why should I be bereft of you both in one day?"
46 And Rebekah said to Isaac, "I am weary of my life because of the daughters of Heth; if Jacob takes a wife of the daughters of Heth, like these *who are* the daughters of the land, what good will my life be to me?"	**46** Then Rebekah said to Isaac, "I loathe my life because of the Hittite women. If Jacob marries one of the Hittite women like these, one of the women of the land, what good will my life be to me?"
28:1 Then Isaac called Jacob and blessed him, and charged him, and said to him: "You shall not take a wife from the daughters of Canaan.	**28:1** Then Isaac called Jacob and blessed him and directed him, "You must not take a wife from the Canaanite women.
2 Arise, go to Padan Aram, to the house of Bethuel your mother's father; and take yourself a wife from there of the daughters of Laban your mother's brother.	**2** Arise, go to Paddan-aram to the house of Bethuel your mother's father, and take as your wife from there one of the daughters of Laban your mother's brother.
3 "May God Almighty bless you, and make you fruitful and multiply you, that you may be an assembly of peoples;	**3** God Almighty bless you and make you fruitful and multiply you, that you may become a company of peoples.
4 and give you the blessing of Abraham, to you and your descendants with you, that you may inherit the land in which you are a stranger, which God gave to Abraham."	**4** May he give the blessing of Abraham to you and to your offspring with you, that you may take possession of the land of your sojournings that God gave to Abraham!"
5 So Isaac sent Jacob away, and he went to Padan Aram, to Laban the son of Bethuel the Syrian, the brother of Rebekah, the mother of Jacob and Esau.	**5** Thus Isaac sent Jacob away. And he went to Paddan-aram, to Laban, the son of Bethuel the Aramean, the brother of Rebekah, Jacob's and Esau's mother.

The structure of the text containing the second blessing of Jacob parallels the structure of the text containing the first blessing of Jacob. Similar to the first blessing, the second blessing begins with Esau and the prospect of Isaac's death (27:41; cf. 27:1–4), continues with Rebekah and Jacob (27:42–45; cf. 27:6–17), Rebekah's encounter with Isaac (27:46; unparalleled), and concludes with the blessing of Jacob by Isaac (28:1–5; cf. 27:28–29).

27:41 The description of Esau's hatred and of his plans to kill Jacob is consistent with the report that has just presented him as a violent character living by his sword and hostile to Jacob (27:40). Out of reverence for his father, Esau decides, however, not to harm Jacob as long as his father is alive.

27:42 Esau's secret plans to kill Jacob are now expressed in words. Esau must have shared his criminal intentions with someone and **the words of Esau** were reported to Rebekah (27:42). The qualification of **Esau her older son** in parallel to **Jacob her younger son** reminds her of her motherly relationship to both of them. Rebekah loves them both and suffers from this dilemma (see 27:45). As a mother, Rebekah must have sensed all the intensity of her son's anger and frustration. She was still aware that, as the **older son** (27:42), Esau was entitled to the blessing of his father. This explains Rebekah's observation that Esau **comforts himself** with his criminal schemes. Knowing that he will kill Jacob comforts him for having lost the blessing, either because, in Jacob's death, he would inherit his rights, or because the simple thought of killing Jacob and the prospect of revenge for what he had done to him is comforting to him, a simple emotional relief.

27:43 Rebekah again speaks with the authority of a prophet and invites her son to religious obedience: **obey my voice** (27:43; cf. 27:13). Rebekah counsels Jacob to **flee** (*barakh*) far away to her **brother Laban in Haran** (27:43), a place from where he will also have to **flee** (*barakh*) later (31:21). Rebekah surmises he will stay there **a few days** (27:44), an expression that Jacob will use later to characterize his stay there (29:20). These verbal echoes between the two stories suggest that Rebekah may have had some prophetic intuition or at least some wish that Jacob would marry there, as implied in her following plea to Isaac.

27:45 **Why should I be bereaved also of you both in one day?** Rebekah, who knows her son Esau's temperament, is perceptive enough to foresee the nature of his anger; she therefore fears for Jacob's life. But she not only fears for Jacob's life, but also for Esau's life, having probably in mind the possibility of retaliation by the avenger of blood (cf. 4:14).

27:46 Compared with the parallel blessing of Jacob, this verse seemingly interferes with the flow of the story. However, this passage functions as a transition between the two stories; it concludes the section addressing Rebekah's intent to send Jacob away from Esau to Laban and introduces the actual blessing of Jacob by Isaac, because Jacob's departure will oblige his father to bless him. Diplomatically, Rebekah does not refer to Jacob's plight in fleeing from Esau's just anger, which would have reminded Isaac of Jacob's deceptive act. Instead, she refers to Esau's marriages with **the daughters of Heth**. While implicitly justifying the blessing of Jacob by Isaac instead of Esau, this strategy serves as an ideal pretext for sending Jacob away to Padan Aram in order to find a wife. In so doing, Rebekah relates to Abraham, who had sent his servant there to find the chosen wife for his son Isaac. For Rebekah, this is a matter of life and death. Whereas she was disgusted with life because of Esau's wives, she complains that she would lose her desire for life if Jacob were to take **the daughters of the land**. This constitutes Rebekah's last act that is recorded in the Hebrew Scriptures, an incident that marks her final appearance in the entire Bible.

28:1–2 Isaac is now the one who initiates calling and blessing Jacob. Once again, the intention of "blessing" is indicated explicitly (cf. 27:27). As a prelude to his blessing, Isaac commands Jacob: **you shall not take a wife from the daughters of Canaan** (28:1). The Hebrew verb *tsawah* for "command" (NKJV: "charged") has a religious connotation and denotes divine instruction. Similar to Rebekah, Isaac speaks with the authority of a prophet (cf. 27:8) and urges Jacob to go to his mother's brother but specifically adds that he must find a wife only within the limits of this family, a recommendation that was not included in Rebekah's instruction (28:2; cf. 27:43).

28:3–4 Isaac's blessing on Jacob is based on creation and Abraham. The first part of the blessing uses the language of creation (28:3; cf. 1:22, 28; 9:1, 7). It is the blessing of fruitfulness that leads to the formation of the worshipping *qahal* **assembly** (28:3; cf. Lev 16:17; 1 Kgs 8:55). The second part twice refers to Abraham (28:4), which leads to the inheritance of the Promised Land. Isaac's blessing relates to his preceding blessing in a chiastic fashion (ABB_1A_1): The fatness of the earth, A (*'erets*) (27:28), corresponds to the Promised Land, A_1 (*'erets*) (28:4), and the serving peoples, B (27:29), correspond to the worshipping peoples, B_1 (28:3). The **blessing of Abraham** (28:4) points to the blessing that Abraham received when he left Ur of the Chaldeans, which is repeated in Isaac's preceding blessing (12:3; 27:29). In other words, Isaac pronounces the same blessing on Jacob but in more explicit terms. Isaac had previously spoken in a veiled language because he felt guilty, thinking that he was blessing Esau while knowing that he should have blessed Jacob. Isaac now knows that he is blessing Jacob and is also aware that this blessing receives God's approval. Therefore, he can bless more openly, more freely, and in good conscience.

28:5 Jacob notably departs to Padan Aram, not on his mothers' instructions, but on his father's order. Now that Isaac has blessed Jacob, the father-son relationship has been restored.

28:6–9. MARRIAGES OF ESAU

GEN 28:6–9 NKJV	GEN 28:6–9 ESV
6 Esau saw that Isaac had blessed Jacob and sent him away to Padan Aram to take himself a wife from there, *and that* as he blessed him he gave him a charge, saying, "You shall not take a wife from the daughters of Canaan,"	**6** Now Esau saw that Isaac had blessed Jacob and sent him away to Paddan-aram to take a wife from there, and that as he blessed him he directed him, "You must not take a wife from the Canaanite women,"
7 and that Jacob had obeyed his father and his mother and had gone to Padan Aram.	**7** and that Jacob had obeyed his father and his mother and gone to Paddan-aram.
8 Also Esau saw that the daughters of Canaan did not please his father Isaac.	**8** So when Esau saw that the Canaanite women did not please Isaac his father,
9 So Esau went to Ishmael and took Mahalath the daughter of Ishmael, Abraham's son, the sister of Nebajoth, to be his wife in addition to the wives he had.	**9** Esau went to Ishmael and took as his wife, besides the wives he had, Mahalath the daughter of Ishmael, Abraham's son, the sister of Nebaioth.

The blessing of Jacob by Isaac conveys a crucial lesson for Esau, who finally understands that a connection exists between the blessing and the marital situation. Esau observes that Isaac's blessing of Jacob is indeed related to his instruction not to marry a Canaanite woman (28:6) and to Jacob obeying his father in this matter (28:7). Noting also that Esau's choices did not please his father (28:8), Esau decides to take a wife according to his father's wishes and chooses Mahalath. That she is **the daughter of Ishmael**, **Abraham's son** (28:9), and hence a member of Isaac's side of the family, suggests that Esau surmises that he will please his father and perhaps obtain a blessing from him.

ENCOUNTERING GOD AT BETHEL (28:10–22)

On his way to Haran (28:10), the place that his grandfather Abraham had left (11:31), Jacob encounters God at Bethel, the "house of God," "the gate of heaven" (28:17). The episode at Bethel is a reminder of the tragedy of Babel, where God had confused the men eager to reach the gate of God (11:4, 9), and anticipates the drama of Peniel, where God will wrestle with Jacob (32:22–32). The echoes between the account of Bethel and the accounts of Babel and Peniel are significant. Bethel stands between Babel and Peniel. The dream at Bethel develops in three phases. In the first phase (28:10–12), Jacob comes to a place where he sleeps and dreams of a ladder reaching to heaven, with angels going up and down. This unit is characterized by the keyword *maqom* "place," which is used three times in the same verse (28:11). In the second phase (28:13–19), Jacob is confronted with God Himself, an experience that will determine the name he gives to that place—"Bethel," which means "the House of God." The word *maqom* "place" occurs again three times (28:16–17, and 19). In the third phase (28:20–22), Jacob is concerned about the future and makes a vow of commitment to God.

28:10–12. THE LADDER OF THE PLACE

GEN 28:10–12 NKJV	GEN 28:10–12 ESV
10 Now Jacob went out from Beersheba and went toward Haran.	**10** Jacob left Beersheba and went toward Haran.
11 So he came to a certain place and stayed there all night, because the sun had set. And he took one of the stones of that place and put it at his head, and he lay down in that place to sleep.	**11** And he came to a certain place and stayed there that night, because the sun had set. Taking one of the stones of the place, he put it under his head and lay down in that place to sleep.
12 Then he dreamed, and behold, a ladder *was* set up on the earth, and its top reached to heaven; and there the angels of God were ascending and descending on it.	**12** And he dreamed, and behold, there was a ladder set up on the earth, and the top of it reached to heaven. And behold, the angels of God were ascending and descending on it!

28:10–11 Soon after Jacob leaves his home, Beersheba (28:10), he stumbles onto **the place** (lit. trans., see JPS; NKJV: "a certain place"). The verb *paga'* (translated **he came** in the NKJV) suggests the intensity of a surprise, such as an attack (1 Kgs 2:25). The same verb describes the surprise encounter with the angels at Mahanaim (32:1

[2]). The use of the definite article "*the* place" suggests that it is a special place, with particular significance. The phrase *hammaqom* "the place" refers to the place where God dwells, the sanctuary (Exod 15:7) or the temple (1 Chr 15:3; cf. 22:9); it also designates Peniel (32:30 [31]). Similar to the future experience at Peniel (32:22, 24), the experience at Bethel will take place at night, a propitious time for theophanies (15:12, 17).

At his head. Whether Jacob placed one of the stones under his head as a pillow or arranged the stones around his head as a protection is unclear (1 Sam 26:11–12; 1 Kgs 19:6). However, the word *mera'sh* "head" is echoed in the word *r'osh* **top** (28:12), referring to the "top" of the ladder where God is standing (28:13). This echo suggests that Jacob's dream of God takes place inside his head (cf. Dan 7:1). What Jacob sees belongs more to the subjective experience of his dream than to the objective reality and is therefore to be interpreted in symbolic terms.

28:12 A ladder. The imagery of a ladder reaching heaven recalls the scenario of Babel, where the men intended to build a tower to reach to heaven. The ancient Babylonian ziggurats as well as the ancient Egyptian pyramids were designed as stairways to allow humans on earth to elevate themselves to the divine sphere.

Set up. The Hebrew verb *mutsab* "set up," referring to the ladder standing up on the earth, is notably echoed in the verb *nitsab* "stood," referring to God's situation. This linguistic echo suggests the connective mechanism between the heavenly and the earthly sphere. The ladder contradicts the attempts of Babel. Whereas the men of Babel were planning to reach God by themselves, Jacob's ladder teaches that only God can provide that process (see John 1:51). The ladder is identified with God Himself.

Ascending and descending. The Babel process involved human effort ascending to the door of God. The lesson of Bethel is that human ascending is responded to by divine descending. Bethel refers to two camps of messengers or angels: the human messenger who reaches out to God, representing the human prayer and search for God; and the divine messenger outside of the human sphere, who responds from heaven and comes down to earth. The ascending and descending process belongs to the heavenly order and not to human effort and ambition.

28:13–19. THE HOUSE OF GOD

GEN 28:13–19 NKJV	GEN 28:13–19 ESV
13 And behold, the Lord stood above it and said: "I *am* the Lord God of Abraham your father and the God of Isaac; the land on which you lie I will give to you and your descendants.	**13** And behold, the Lord stood above it and said, "I am the Lord, the God of Abraham your father and the God of Isaac. The land on which you lie I will give to you and to your offspring.
14 Also your descendants shall be as the dust of the earth; you shall spread abroad to the west and the east, to the north and the south; and in you and in your seed all the families of the earth shall be blessed.	**14** Your offspring shall be like the dust of the earth, and you shall spread abroad to the west and to the east and to the north and to the south, and in you and your offspring shall all the families of the earth be blessed.
15 Behold, I *am* with you and will keep you wherever you go, and will bring you back to this land; for I will not leave you until I have done what I have spoken to you."	**15** Behold, I am with you and will keep you wherever you go, and will bring you back to this land. For I will not leave you until I have done what I have promised you."

16 Then Jacob awoke from his sleep and said, "Surely the Lᴏʀᴅ is in this place, and I did not know *it*."	**16** Then Jacob awoke from his sleep and said, "Surely the Lᴏʀᴅ is in this place, and I did not know it."
17 And he was afraid and said, "How awesome *is* this place! This *is* none other than the house of God, and this *is* the gate of heaven!"	**17** And he was afraid and said, "How awesome is this place! This is none other than the house of God, and this is the gate of heaven."
18 Then Jacob rose early in the morning, and took the stone that he had put at his head, set it up as a pillar, and poured oil on top of it.	**18** So early in the morning Jacob took the stone that he had put under his head and set it up for a pillar and poured oil on the top of it.
19 And he called the name of that place Bethel; but the name of that city had been Luz previously.	**19** He called the name of that place Bethel, but the name of the city was Luz at the first.

28:13–15 God identifies Himself as the God of past experiences: **The Lord God of Abraham your father and the God of Isaac** (28:13). Note that the qualification "your father" is unexpectedly related to Abraham and not to Isaac, a means of emphasizing the continuing line between the first call to Isaac and now to Jacob. This God of the past is also the God who will ensure the future. Three promises are laid down. The first promise concerns the Promised Land, **the land on which you lie** (28:13). The second promise concerns the descendants, who will be as numerous **as the dust of the earth** (28:14). The third and last promise carries a cosmic scope and concerns **all the families of the earth**, who will be blessed by the **seed** of Jacob (see 12:3). The messianic hope is thus outlined. God's attention then shifts to Jacob's near future, promising His presence and care until he returns safely to the land of his father and mother (28:15). The God of the distant past and of the distant future is also the God who cares for us in our present existence.

28:16 Ironically, Jacob's sleep arouses his awareness of the reality he **did not know** of when he was awake (28:16).

28:17 Upon awakening, Jacob understands that his dream has implications beyond himself. The phrase **gate of heaven**, which occurs only here in the entire Hebrew Bible, is reminiscent of the name *Bab-El* "gate of God" and thus of the vain enterprise of the men of Babel who never reached the "gate of heaven." The phrase **the gate of heaven** parallels the phrase **the house of God**, which refers to **this place** (*hammaqom*), that is, "the stone" (28:18–19), which is the earthly spot of "the ladder" (28:12). Therefore, as the heavenly counterpart of the earthly "house of God," "the gate of heaven" points to the heavenly abode or temple sanctuary.[585] The lesson of Bethel is that a connection exists between heaven and earth and that this connection is Jacob's ladder, which is God Himself.

28:18–19 To this point, Jacob has been lying down. He now stands up and responds to the lessons he has meditated on and understood. First, he takes one of the stones he had placed around (or under) his head, a stone that was associated with his extraordinary dream, and erects **a pillar** from it. The Hebrew word for "pillar," *matseba* "standing," which refers to the "standing" stone, echoes the words *mutsab* and *nitsab*, which designate, respectively, the "standing" ladder and the "standing" God. The erected pillar is not a repository of the spirit of gods or a representation of God's fertility, as was the case in ancient Canaanite cults. Jacob anoints the stone to

---

585 See Elias Brasil de Souza, "The Heavenly Sanctuary/Temple Motif in the Hebrew Bible: Function and Relationship to the Earthly Counterparts" (PhD diss., Andrews University, 2005), 121.

signify its consecration as a monument conveying a spiritual lesson. This stone recalls the lessons of Jacob's ladder, the heaven-earth connection.

Bethel. In contrast to the name "Babel," which recalls the vain attempt of the men who never reached the door of God, Bethel affirms that we are in the "house of God." The men of Bab-El entertained the ambition to reach and penetrate the place of God in order to take God's place. The lesson of Bethel is that access to God can only be achieved through God's gift, through His grace and incarnation, through the Ladder. The prior (profane) name of Luz indicates the intention of the author to emphasize the historical reality of the experience Jacob had just undergone. In the biblical worldview, the spiritual lesson is rooted in history.

28:20-22. JACOB'S VOW

GEN 28:20-22 NKJV	GEN 28:20-22 ESV
20 Then Jacob made a vow, saying, "If God will be with me, and keep me in this way that I am going, and give me bread to eat and clothing to put on,	**20** Then Jacob made a vow, saying, "If God will be with me and will keep me in this way that I go, and will give me bread to eat and clothing to wear,
21 so that I come back to my father's house in peace, then the LORD shall be my God.	**21** so that I come again to my father's house in peace, then the LORD shall be my God,
22 And this stone which I have set as a pillar shall be God's house, and of all that You give me I will surely give a tenth to You."	**22** and this stone, which I have set up for a pillar, shall be God's house. And of all that you give me I will give a full tenth to you."

Jacob's vow to God is based on two conditions. First, God should be with him, which means that He should keep him physically, provide him with bread and clothing (28:20), and ensure his safe return home (28:21a). Second, God should be his God, which means that He should keep him spiritually and prevent him from worshipping another god (28:21b). Note that the first request is not a condition for the second one, as if Jacob's spiritual commitment to God would be conditioned by God's physical protection. Both are Jacob's requests to God. If God meets these two conditions, Jacob will commit himself to the following two vows that echo the two conditions in a reverse structure (chiastic). The first vow, **this stone ... shall be God's house** (28:22), responds to the spiritual condition of God keeping Jacob from worshipping other gods (idolatry). The "stone" refers to the stone on which he had the dream of the ladder (28:11). The stone means the assurance of the connection between heaven and earth (28:12). Jacob commits to build a place of worship, a sanctuary that will testify to this truth. The second vow, **of all that You give me I will surely give a tenth to You** (28:22), responds to the material condition of God keeping Jacob physically safe. This vow refers to Jacob's recognition of the historical and physical presence of God in his material and physical life. The tithe signifies, on the side of worshipping and spiritual activities, the faith of a real God who is also involved in the benefits of our concrete existence—our health, our security, and our wealth. Jacob's religion, his worship, and his faithfulness are thus described as a response to God's acts of grace and not as a means to obtain God's favors. Because God is the personal God of Jacob, because the heavenly God has come down and connected with the earth, Jacob responds through worship. Because God is the God who cares about and takes care of Jacob's physical needs, because God is the source of all he has, **of all that You give me** (28:22), Jacob responds through the giving of his tithe to God. Significantly, the one-time "give" from Jacob (28:22) responds to the two "gives" from God (28:20, 22).

That Jacob fulfilled his two vows is not explicitly indicated in the biblical text. Only God's part of the deal has been recorded in the book of Genesis. Jacob will acknowledge God's part when he refers to his experience of God's protection: "God … who answered me in the day of my distress and has been with me in the way which I have gone" (35:3; cf. 46:3–4). On the horizon of Jacob's commitment, the building of the sanctuary, a sign of the worship of the God of heaven, and the institution of the tithe, a sign of the recognition of the God of the earth, suggest that Jacob's vows were also fulfilled on his level.

JACOB ARRIVES AT LABAN'S HOUSE (29:1–14)

The preceding account reported the beginning of Jacob's journey. The following account reports his arrival at the destination. The first verbs **went** (*wayyissa'*) and **came** (*wayyelek*), which describe his arrival at the land (29:1), and the last verb **stayed** (*wayyesheb*), which describes his settling at Laban's house (29:14), mark the boundaries of the passage, which fall into two scenes and two encounters. First, Jacob meets with foreigners, the people of the land, around the stone of a well. Jacob confronts the three eastern shepherds on the issue of rolling the stone in order to care for the sheep (29:1–9). Jacob then meets with his relatives, Rachel and Laban. This is the occasion for Jacob to demonstrate his character and his strength. Jacob rolls the stone from the well, kisses Rachel and Laban, and settles in Laban's house (29:10–14).

29:1–9. JACOB AND THE PEOPLE OF THE EAST

GEN 29:1–9 NKJV	GEN 29:1–9 ESV
1 So Jacob went on his journey and came to the land of the people of the East.	**1** Then Jacob went on his journey and came to the land of the people of the east.
2 And he looked, and saw a well in the field; and behold, there *were* three flocks of sheep lying by it; for out of that well they watered the flocks. A large stone *was* on the well's mouth.	**2** As he looked, he saw a well in the field, and behold, three flocks of sheep lying beside it, for out of that well the flocks were watered. The stone on the well's mouth was large,
3 Now all the flocks would be gathered there; and they would roll the stone from the well's mouth, water the sheep, and put the stone back in its place on the well's mouth.	**3** and when all the flocks were gathered there, the shepherds would roll the stone from the mouth of the well and water the sheep, and put the stone back in its place over the mouth of the well.
4 And Jacob said to them, "My brethren, where *are* you from?" And they said, "We *are* from Haran."	**4** Jacob said to them, "My brothers, where do you come from?" They said, "We are from Haran."
5 Then he said to them, "Do you know Laban the son of Nahor?" And they said, "We know him."	**5** He said to them, "Do you know Laban the son of Nahor?" They said, "We know him."
6 So he said to them, "Is he well?" And they said, "*He is* well. And look, his daughter Rachel is coming with the sheep."	**6** He said to them, "Is it well with him?" They said, "It is well; and see, Rachel his daughter is coming with the sheep!"

7 Then he said, "Look, *it is* still high day; *it is* not time for the cattle to be gathered together. Water the sheep, and go and feed t*hem*."

7 He said, "Behold, it is still high day; it is not time for the livestock to be gathered together. Water the sheep and go, pasture them."

8 But they said, "We cannot until all the flocks are gathered together, and they have rolled the stone from the well's mouth; then we water the sheep."

8 But they said, "We cannot until all the flocks are gathered together and the stone is rolled from the mouth of the well; then we water the sheep."

9 Now while he was still speaking with them, Rachel came with her father's sheep, for she was a shepherdess.

9 While he was still speaking with them, Rachel came with her father's sheep, for she was a shepherdess.

29:1 Again, the verb "went" (*wayyelek*) is used to express Jacob's response to his parents' instruction to leave (28:10; cf. 28:2), just as his grandfather Abram responded to God's call (12:1, 4). Jacob has now reached the final stage of his journey.

People of the East. The phrase *beney qedem* "sons of the east" refers generally to the territory east of Canaan, Padan Aram (25:20; 28:7) or Aram (Hos 12:12 [13]). The reference to the "east" (*qedem*) could also possibly contain a veiled threat, as the word often has a pejorative connotation in the book of Genesis, referring to a place of alienation (3:24; 4:14; 25:6) or vanity (11:2; 13:11). This language anticipates Jacob's forthcoming experiences in the new land.

29:2–3 Jacob first notices a well, particularly the stone on the well, and the three flocks of sheep lying beside it. The motif of "the stone" appears again (29:2), pointing to the stone that Jacob placed under (or near) his head when he slept and dreamed of the ladder, witnessing to God's presence (28:11) and to the stone that was subsequently erected in memory of that event (28:18). This time the stone provides Jacob with the opportunity to demonstrate the effect of God's presence with him. The stone is large, suggesting that it is heavy and therefore difficult to move. Therefore, the stone could only be moved when all three of the flocks, and hence the three shepherds, are together (29:3; cf. 29:8).

29:4–6 Although Jacob is concerned about this stone, which keeps the sheep from drinking water, he first engages in a friendly conversation with the shepherds (29:4). He calls them **my brethren** (29:4), a generic term to designate close friends. When he hears that these men are from Haran, he asks if they know Laban, since he is from there. Learning that they do know him, Jacob inquires about his *shalom*: **is he well?** (29:6). The word *shalom* means more than the mere notion of "peace"; derived from the root *shalem* "complete," it also expresses the ideas of "health," "safeness," and "happiness." Jacob's question is the equivalent of our polite "How are you?" preliminary to further, more substantial conversation (cf. 43:27). At that very moment, Rachel providentially appears, in the same manner that Rebekah had arrived (24:15). The added wording of **coming with the sheep** (29:6) explains her appearance (she is a shepherdess; cf. 29:9) and prepares for Jacob's next question and behavior.

29:7–9 Rachel's arrival (29:6) triggers an emotional reaction in Jacob. Until now, Jacob has remained calm and polite. However, he now suddenly becomes zealous and somewhat intrusive; although the sheep are not his, Jacob urges the shepherds to move quickly and water their sheep (29:7). The shepherds' explanation that they must wait until more shepherds arrive to roll the stone (29:8) suggests their inability to perform the task by themselves, implying it is too heavy, or they have already watered their own flocks (before Jacob's arrival) and do not want to roll the stone again for Rachel. This is why Jacob resorts to moving the stone by himself when Rachel arrives with her flock.

29:10–14. JACOB, RACHEL, AND LABAN

GEN 29:10–14 NKJV	GEN 29:10–14 ESV
10 And it came to pass, when Jacob saw Rachel the daughter of Laban his mother's brother, and the sheep of Laban his mother's brother, that Jacob went near and rolled the stone from the well's mouth, and watered the flock of Laban his mother's brother.	**10** Now as soon as Jacob saw Rachel the daughter of Laban his mother's brother, and the sheep of Laban his mother's brother, Jacob came near and rolled the stone from the well's mouth and watered the flock of Laban his mother's brother.
11 Then Jacob kissed Rachel, and lifted up his voice and wept.	**11** Then Jacob kissed Rachel and wept aloud.
12 And Jacob told Rachel that he *was* her father's relative and that he *was* Rebekah's son. So she ran and told her father.	**12** And Jacob told Rachel that he was her father's kinsman, and that he was Rebekah's son, and she ran and told her father.
13 Then it came to pass, when Laban heard the report about Jacob his sister's son, that he ran to meet him, and embraced him and kissed him, and brought him to his house. So he told Laban all these things.	**13** As soon as Laban heard the news about Jacob, his sister's son, he ran to meet him and embraced him and kissed him and brought him to his house. Jacob told Laban all these things,
14 And Laban said to him, "Surely you *are* my bone and my flesh." And he stayed with him for a month.	**14** and Laban said to him, "Surely you are my bone and my flesh!" And he stayed with him a month.

29:10 The mention that the flock Jacob watered was of **his mother's brother** suggests that the thought of his mother, Rebekah, may have motivated his heroic act. The evocation of Rebekah by the well at this juncture is a flashback to that particular incident that led to the marriage of Isaac and Rebekah (24:13–67), and this parallel anticipates the future marriage between Jacob and Rachel.

29:11 Jacob's subsequent move and behavior contrasts with his preceding acts of brute action and arrogant reaction toward the shepherds. Confronted with Rachel, Jacob softens: **Jacob kissed Rachel, and lifted up his voice and wept**. Note the difference of reaction in similar circumstances by Abraham's servant when encountering Rebekah. Whereas the servant respectfully bows before Rebekah, Jacob kisses Rachel. Whereas the servant prays silently, Jacob weeps aloud. Jacob's youth and close relation to his cousin explains this difference of behavior.

29:12–14 Rachel does not respond to Jacob's emotional outburst. Instead, she runs to report her encounter to her father (29:12), who, in his turn, runs to meet Jacob and kiss him (29:13). They both run, showing the same zeal of hospitality demonstrated by Abraham toward the visiting angels (18:2, 7) and by Rebekah and Laban toward the servant of Abraham (24:28–29). Having been brought into Laban's house, Jacob finally addresses Laban, **he told Laban all these things** (29:13). The text does not say what things Jacob told Laban. The demonstrative pronoun *'elleh* refers to the most recent events that took place by the well (cf. 24:28) but may also include stories from home, which could explain his coming to Padan Aram. After hearing Jacob's family report and of his intervention on behalf of his daughter and the account of his prowess at the stone of the well, Laban concludes that Jacob is part of the family. Laban's phrase **you are my bone and my flesh** (29:14) is reminiscent of Adam's exclamation expressing his intimate conjugal closeness with his wife (2:23) and thus anticipates the forthcoming marriage that will unite the two families. The mention that Jacob **stayed with him for a month** (29:14) signals the end of Jacob's journey. The Hebrew verb *wayyesheb* "stayed" expresses the idea of settling. However, the fact that Jacob resided there for one month suggests that the settling ends after that short time and anticipates further events, which indicate the opposite of settling.

LABAN DECEIVES JACOB (29:15–30)

The Laban who receives Jacob is the same the Laban who received Abraham's servant, still greedy and deceitful (cf. 24:29–33). His zealous hospitality and words of welcome are meant to gain Jacob's confidence in order to take advantage of him. Laban's first moves are indeed indicative of his intentions to exploit him as a worker and to deceive him as his son-in-law. Laban's deception will proceed in two steps over two seven-year periods. First, Jacob will work for Laban for seven years in exchange for Rachel (29:15–21). Second, after having been deceived into marrying Leah, Jacob will work for another seven years for Rachel (29:22–30).

29:15–21. JACOB SERVES SEVEN YEARS

GEN 29:15–21 NKJV	GEN 29:15–21 ESV
15 Then Laban said to Jacob, "Because you *are* my relative, should you therefore serve me for nothing? Tell me, what *should* your wages be?"	**15** Then Laban said to Jacob, "Because you are my kinsman, should you therefore serve me for nothing? Tell me, what shall your wages be?"
16 Now Laban had two daughters: the name of the elder *was* Leah, and the name of the younger *was* Rachel.	**16** Now Laban had two daughters. The name of the older was Leah, and the name of the younger was Rachel.
17 Leah's eyes *were* delicate, but Rachel was beautiful of form and appearance.	**17** Leah's eyes were weak, but Rachel was beautiful in form and appearance.
18 Now Jacob loved Rachel; so he said, "I will serve you seven years for Rachel your younger daughter."	**18** Jacob loved Rachel. And he said, "I will serve you seven years for your younger daughter Rachel."
19 And Laban said, "*It is* better that I give her to you than that I should give her to another man. Stay with me."	**19** Laban said, "It is better that I give her to you than that I should give her to any other man; stay with me."
20 So Jacob served seven years for Rachel, and they seemed *only* a few days to him because of the love he had for her.	**20** So Jacob served seven years for Rachel, and they seemed to him but a few days because of the love he had for her.
21 Then Jacob said to Laban, "Give *me* my wife, for my days are fulfilled, that I may go in to her."	**21** Then Jacob said to Laban, "Give me my wife that I may go in to her, for my time is completed."

29:15 Laban uses the pretense of caring for Jacob because he is his relative as a justification for his intention to hire him as his regular worker. His first question is rhetorical, which implies that, thus far, Jacob has been working for free: **should you therefore serve me for nothing?** Laban, who had noticed Jacob's industrious qualities, is interested in hiring him for good. However, he does not want to pay him for his work. Asking Jacob to tell him the price of his wages is a means of suggesting to Jacob that, as a relative, Jacob would not ask for wages and would work for free. Jacob understands the suggestion because he proposes the deal of working for a wife.

29:16 **The name of the elder was Leah.** The reference to the "elder" and the "younger" daughters recalls the Genesis paradigm (25:23) and suggests that the younger is the one who should be chosen. Note that both Leah and Rachel have names reflecting the shepherds' environment. *Leah* means "cow" and *Rachel* means "ewe." The larger value of the cow over the ewe corresponds to that of the elder daughter over the younger one.

29:17 **Leah's eyes were delicate.** The Hebrew word *rakh* for "delicate" means that Leah's eyes were weak. The contrast between this particular characteristic of Leah's eyes with the beauty of Rachel suggests a negative connotation. Leah's soft eyes do not have the sparkling quality that Rachel's have.

29:18–21 **Jacob loved Rachel.** The previous information leads to the conclusion of Jacob's love for Rachel. Jacob's love was not a superficial, momentary whim, as evidenced by his willingness to wait seven years and work hard in order to marry Rachel. Jacob's added specification **your younger daughter** (29:18) suggests that Jacob may have heard or had some inkling of Laban's intention. Laban pretends to be favorable to Jacob's request (29:19) while he secretly intends to give his older daughter to Jacob. Laban's comment **stay with me** betrays his personal advantage. Laban is more interested in keeping Jacob nearby for the benefit of his work than he is in making his daughters happy. The terse observation that **Jacob served seven years for Rachel** (29:20), without any other comment about the content of these years, corresponds to Jacob's impression that they were but **a few days to him**, which constitutes a supplementary evidence of Jacob's love for Rachel (29:20). When the seven years are fulfilled, Jacob immediately makes his demand to Laban to marry Rachel.

29:22–30. JACOB SERVES ANOTHER SEVEN YEARS

GEN 29:22–30 NKJV	GEN 29:22–30 ESV
22 And Laban gathered together all the men of the place and made a feast.	**22** So Laban gathered together all the people of the place and made a feast.
23 Now it came to pass in the evening, that he took Leah his daughter and brought her to Jacob; and he went in to her.	**23** But in the evening he took his daughter Leah and brought her to Jacob, and he went in to her.
24 And Laban gave his maid Zilpah to his daughter Leah *as* a maid.	**24** (Laban gave his female servant Zilpah to his daughter Leah to be her servant.)
25 So it came to pass in the morning, that behold, it *was* Leah. And he said to Laban, "What is this you have done to me? Was it not for Rachel that I served you? Why then have you deceived me?"	**25** And in the morning, behold, it was Leah! And Jacob said to Laban, "What is this you have done to me? Did I not serve with you for Rachel? Why then have you deceived me?"

26 And Laban said, "It must not be done so in our country, to give the younger before the firstborn.	**26** Laban said, "It is not so done in our country, to give the younger before the firstborn.
27 Fulfill her week, and we will give you this one also for the service which you will serve with me still another seven years."	**27** Complete the week of this one, and we will give you the other also in return for serving me another seven years."
28 Then Jacob did so and fulfilled her week. So he gave him his daughter Rachel as wife also.	**28** Jacob did so, and completed her week. Then Laban gave him his daughter Rachel to be his wife.
29 And Laban gave his maid Bilhah to his daughter Rachel as a maid.	**29** (Laban gave his female servant Bilhah to his daughter Rachel to be her servant.)
30 Then *Jacob* also went in to Rachel, and he also loved Rachel more than Leah. And he served with Laban still another seven years.	**30** So Jacob went in to Rachel also, and he loved Rachel more than Leah, and served Laban for another seven years.

Laban takes it upon himself to organize a great wedding feast. The wedding involves a series of ceremonials: processions from and to the bride's house, the reading of the wedding contract, and a large meal offered to the family members and other guests.[586] The precision with which Laban has invited **all the men of the place** (29:22) is surprising, considering his reluctance for this marriage and his greedy temperament. This measure suggests that Laban purposely organized the wedding with the intention of producing an important gathering and, hence, enough confusion to allow him to implement his scheme. The brief comment reporting Jacob's immediate response **and he went in to her** (29:23) suggests the rapidity of the operation and Jacob's impatience, as he has been waiting for this moment for seven years. Resorting to the effect of wine is unnecessary to explain Jacob's aptitude to be deceived, as was Lot by his daughters (19:30–38). The cultural custom of veiling the bride (cf. 24:65), the darkness of the night, Leah's anguished silence, and Jacob's emotion—these elements all play a role in the efficiency of the deception. Nothing in the biblical text suggests Jacob was drunk. Jacob simply trusts his mother's brother and is completely vulnerable, all the more so because he has no family member to watch over him.

29:24–25 Laban gives his maid to Leah, as was the custom, and the marriage proceeds according to the rules (29:24). Only in the morning does Jacob discover that it is Leah. The word *wehinneh* "behold" (29:25) denotes Jacob's surprise because he expected to see Rachel and instead saw Leah. Jacob's three questions to Laban the next morning suggest his great naïvety as the main reason why he was deceived.

29:26–27 Laban's reference to tradition (29:26) to justify his act is a weak excuse and shows that he does not really care about what Jacob thinks. Laban's resort to tradition may, in fact, allude to Jacob's act of deception when he, the younger, superseded his older brother. Laban holds strongly to his position and insists that Jacob **fulfill her week** (29:27), thus referring to the weeklong celebration of the wedding (Judg 14:12, 17). Laban goes so far as to present his deception as a generous act: **we will give you this one also** (29:27). In reality, what appears to be an act of generosity hides another aspect of Laban's scheme: Jacob will have to work seven more years for the price of Rachel.

---

586 Regarding the ceremonials involved in weddings in biblical times, see G. J. Wenham, "Weddings," in *Oxford Companion to the Bible*, eds. B. M. Metzger and M. D. Coogan (Oxford: Oxford University Press, 1993), 794–795.

29:28–30 The remaining events unfold mechanically. Jacob does as instructed by Laban; he completes Leah's week, and then Laban gives him Rachel **also** (29:28). The word "also" is repeated to ironically underscore Laban's generosity. Laban then proceeds to give his maid Bilhah to his daughter Rachel (29:29), just as he did for Leah. Laban, who is not so concerned with ethics, feels strongly, however, about the rules of tradition. The word **also** appears again, this time in connection with Jacob, who *also* **went in to Rachel, and he** *also* **loved Rachel** (29:30). The repetition of the adverb "also" suggests the irony of Laban, who pretends to be generous while cheating, and the naïvety of Jacob, who reacts like an automaton and has lost all his initiative. Jacob will now have to work for seven more years. Unlike the preceding seven years, which are characterized as "a few days" (29:20), these next seven years are simply mentioned with no comment. They will be lived as a burden for Jacob. Yet, these years of unwanted exile will be the most crucial years of Jacob's life. During these years, Jacob will father most of his children (eleven of twelve), the ancestors of the future people of Israel.

BIRTH OF JACOB'S CHILDREN (29:31–30:24)

This section constitutes the apex of the chiasm, the center of the whole Jacob cycle, climaxing with the birth of Joseph (30:24). The success of the unloved Leah, who gives birth immediately to four sons, contrasts with the failure and frustration of the loved, yet barren, Rachel. For the first time since Bethel, God intervenes; this reference to God envelops the whole section, suggesting that the entire process is under God's control. Thus, the section begins with the Lord (*YHWH*) who **saw that Leah was unloved**, and **He opened her womb** (29:31) and ends with God who **listened to Leah** (30:17) and **remembered Rachel ... and opened her womb** (30:22). Each divine intervention brings the birth of children. Leah gives birth to six sons and one daughter, and Rachel gives birth to one son. Between these two divine interventions, God is absent and the two women resort to their own human resources, including magic (mandrakes) to achieve their ends. First, Rachel and then Leah use their respective maids as surrogates to give birth, each one having two sons. Each operation is regularly introduced by the reference to the women's observation, **when Rachel saw** (30:1), **when Leah saw** (30:9), thus suggesting the following structure:

When the Lord saw ... Leah ... He opened her womb (29:31): four sons (29:31–35)
When Rachel saw (30:1) ... (Bilhah): two sons (30:1–8)
When Leah saw (30:9) ... (Zilpah): two sons (30:9–16)
God listened to Leah (30:17): two sons and one daughter (30:17–21)
God remembered Rachel, and God listened to her and opened her womb (30:22–24)

29:31–35. LEAH BEARS FOUR SONS

GEN 29:31–35 NKJV	GEN 29:31–35 ESV
31 When the LORD saw that Leah *was* unloved, He opened her womb; but Rachel *was* barren.	**31** When the LORD saw that Leah was hated, he opened her womb, but Rachel was barren.

32 So Leah conceived and bore a son, and she called his name Reuben; for she said, "The Lᴏʀᴅ has surely looked on my affliction. Now therefore, my husband will love me."

33 Then she conceived again and bore a son, and said, "Because the Lᴏʀᴅ has heard that I *am* unloved, He has therefore given me this *son* also." And she called his name Simeon.

34 She conceived again and bore a son, and said, "Now this time my husband will become attached to me, because I have borne him three sons." Therefore his name was called Levi.

35 And she conceived again and bore a son, and said, "Now I will praise the Lᴏʀᴅ." Therefore she called his name Judah. Then she stopped bearing.

32 And Leah conceived and bore a son, and she called his name Reuben, for she said, "Because the Lᴏʀᴅ has looked upon my affliction; for now my husband will love me."

33 She conceived again and bore a son, and said, "Because the Lᴏʀᴅ has heard that I am hated, he has given me this son also." And she called his name Simeon.

34 Again she conceived and bore a son, and said, "Now this time my husband will be attached to me, because I have borne him three sons." Therefore his name was called Levi.

35 And she conceived again and bore a son, and said, "This time I will praise the Lᴏʀᴅ." Therefore she called his name Judah. Then she ceased bearing.

29:31 That God's intervention on behalf of Leah is associated with the fact that she is unloved, whereas the loved Rachel is barren, suggests "the Lord's compassion for the neglected wife"[587] but also His concern for the balance of justice. The Hebrew verb *sn'* for **unloved**, also translated "hated" (ESV), designates the unloved wife of a man who has two wives (Deut 21:15, 17), a way of suggesting the husband's preference and does not imply "hatred" as we understand it. Rachel was Jacob's first (unique) choice from the beginning. Leah's status as "unloved" (29:31) was conferred after the first encounter (29:23, 25). Yet, God "saw" Leah's condition. Seeing her sorrow and her innocence, God did not penalize her for her father's wickedness. Although Leah became Jacob's wife as a result of Laban's deception, God blessed her. Ironically, she will become, through Judah, the ancestor of the Messiah, the Savior of the world.

29:32–35 Leah gives birth successively to four sons. The names she gives to her first three sons express her frustration as "unloved." Leah explains the name of **Reuben**, which contains the verb *ra'ah* "see," by the fact that God "saw" (*ra'ah*) her "affliction," that is, her condition of being hated by her husband. She then concludes that his birth will make her husband love her (29:32). The name of the second, **Simeon**, which contains the verb *shama'* "hear," is explained by the fact that God "heard" that she was unloved, just as God "heard" Hagar's affliction (16:11). God was sensitive to the injustice and oppression that was perpetrated against Leah, just as He was for Hagar. Likewise, the name of the third son, **Levi**, which contains the verb *lawah* "attach," expresses Leah's assurance that now her husband will not just love her or care for her, as implied respectively in the first and the second names, he will now **become attached** to her (29:34). Only with the third son, after God "saw" and "heard," does Leah finally reach the stage she has been hoping for, namely, that her husband clings to her for good. When Leah gives birth to her fourth son, Judah, she does not care for herself anymore, she only thinks of praising God. The name **Judah** does not refer to her affliction or to her happiness, or to anything God did to her.

---

587 Mathews, *Genesis 11:27–50:26*, 479.

The name "Judah," which contains the verb *hud* "give thanks," refers only to God Himself. This verb appears often in the Psalms, always directed to God to express thanksgiving (Pss 7:17 [18]; 9:1 [2]) and in parallel with the verb *halal* "praise" (Ps 111:1). The tribe of Judah will indeed produce the greatest praise chanter of all time, David. Ironically, when Leah is loved, she becomes like Rachel and cannot bear children anymore (29:35).

30:1–8. RACHEL (BILHAH) BEARS TWO SONS

GEN 30:1–8 NKJV	GEN 30:1–8 ESV
1 Now when Rachel saw that she bore Jacob no children, Rachel envied her sister, and said to Jacob, "Give me children, or else I die!"	**1** When Rachel saw that she bore Jacob no children, she envied her sister. She said to Jacob, "Give me children, or I shall die!"
2 And Jacob's anger was aroused against Rachel, and he said, "*Am* I in the place of God, who has withheld from you the fruit of the womb?"	**2** Jacob's anger was kindled against Rachel, and he said, "Am I in the place of God, who has withheld from you the fruit of the womb?"
3 So she said, "Here is my maid Bilhah; go in to her, and she will bear *a child* on my knees, that I also may have children by her."	**3** Then she said, "Here is my servant Bilhah; go in to her, so that she may give birth on my behalf, that even I may have children through her."
4 Then she gave him Bilhah her maid as wife, and Jacob went in to her.	**4** So she gave him her servant Bilhah as a wife, and Jacob went in to her.
5 And Bilhah conceived and bore Jacob a son.	**5** And Bilhah conceived and bore Jacob a son.
6 Then Rachel said, "God has judged my case; and He has also heard my voice and given me a son." Therefore she called his name Dan.	**6** Then Rachel said, "God has judged me, and has also heard my voice and given me a son." Therefore she called his name Dan.
7 And Rachel's maid Bilhah conceived again and bore Jacob a second son.	**7** Rachel's servant Bilhah conceived again and bore Jacob a second son.
8 Then Rachel said, "With great wrestlings I have wrestled with my sister, *and* indeed I have prevailed." So she called his name Naphtali.	**8** Then Rachel said, "With mighty wrestlings I have wrestled with my sister and have prevailed." So she called his name Naphtali.

At the very moment when Leah became unable to bear children (29:35) and could identify with Rachel's misery, **Rachel envied her sister** (30:1). Rachel's jealousy is out of place. She blames both Jacob and God for her condition. She blames Jacob when she demands that he give her children and blames God when she threatens to kill herself. Jacob answers her accordingly: **Am I in the place of God?** (30:2). It is this argument that triggers Rachel's reaction. Since God is not doing anything to solve the problem, Rachel decides to take the place of God and adopts Sarah's procedure in the same circumstance (16:2–4). She gives her maid Bilhah to Jacob twice as wife, and she has two sons (30:3–7). Rachel, not Bilhah, names the sons as a clear indication that she considers them to be her own sons. Both names refer to God. The first name, **Dan**, means "He judged," referring to God who **judged me** (30:6 ESV). The second name, **Naphtali**, means "my wrestling," referring to what Rachel calls, literally, "the wrestling of God" (translated **great wrestlings** by the NKJV). The word *'Elohim* is understood as an intensive by most commentators, meaning "great"

(NKJV) or "mighty" (ESV, NASB, NRSV). Rachel's explanation of this second name **I have wrestled with my sister, and indeed have prevailed** (30:8) recalls God's explanation of Jacob's new name "Israel" when he wrestles with God: **you have struggled with God and with men, and have prevailed** (32:28 [29]). Although the verbs *patal* "wrestle" and *sarah* "struggle," which are synonyms, are not the same words, the verb explaining both names is the same, *yakol* "prevail." Both names also reflect the same "double interest"[588] in relationship with God and men: Rachel's wrestling with God and her sister, anticipating Jacob's future struggle with God. Yet, the two experiences are fundamentally different. Although Rachel is the one who gives the name "Naphtali," it is God who gives the name "Israel" (32:28 [29]). Whereas Rachel initiates the struggle with God, it is God who initiates the attack on Jacob (32:24). Although Rachel, experiencing God's absence, intends to replace God, Jacob, being confronted with God's presence, wants to be blessed by God (32:26).

30:9–16. LEAH (ZILPAH) BEARS TWO SONS

GEN 30:9–16 NKJV	GEN 30:9–16 ESV
9 When Leah saw that she had stopped bearing, she took Zilpah her maid and gave her to Jacob as wife.	**9** When Leah saw that she had ceased bearing children, she took her servant Zilpah and gave her to Jacob as a wife.
10 And Leah's maid Zilpah bore Jacob a son.	**10** Then Leah's servant Zilpah bore Jacob a son.
11 Then Leah said, "A troop comes!" So she called his name Gad.	**11** And Leah said, "Good fortune has come!" so she called his name Gad.
12 And Leah's maid Zilpah bore Jacob a second son.	**12** Leah's servant Zilpah bore Jacob a second son.
13 Then Leah said, "I am happy, for the daughters will call me blessed." So she called his name Asher.	**13** And Leah said, "Happy am I! For women have called me happy." So she called his name Asher.
14 Now Reuben went in the days of wheat harvest and found mandrakes in the field, and brought them to his mother Leah. Then Rachel said to Leah, "Please give me *some* of your son's mandrakes."	**14** In the days of wheat harvest Reuben went and found mandrakes in the field and brought them to his mother Leah. Then Rachel said to Leah, "Please give me some of your son's mandrakes."
15 But she said to her, "*Is it* a small matter that you have taken away my husband? Would you take away my son's mandrakes also?" And Rachel said, "Therefore he will lie with you tonight for your son's mandrakes."	**15** But she said to her, "Is it a small matter that you have taken away my husband? Would you take away my son's mandrakes also?" Rachel said, "Then he may lie with you tonight in exchange for your son's mandrakes."
16 When Jacob came out of the field in the evening, Leah went out to meet him and said, "You must come in to me, for I have surely hired you with my son's mandrakes." And he lay with her that night.	**16** When Jacob came from the field in the evening, Leah went out to meet him and said, "You must come in to me, for I have hired you with my son's mandrakes." So he lay with her that night.

Similar to Rachel, Leah gives her maid to Jacob in order to have children from him (30:9–10). However, she differs from Rachel in that she gives names to her sons that contain no reference to God and only reflect her human impression. The name of her first son, **Gad** "luck" (30:11), expresses her belief that he is the mere product

---

588 Wenham, *Genesis 16–50*, 245.

of "good fortune" (ESV, NIV) or "luck" (TNK); the name of the second son, **Asher** "happiness," expresses the happiness she enjoys, which she attributes to her fellow women, perhaps a hint at her sister's jealousy (30:13).

30:14 Mandrakes. The next episode corresponds to the same line of thought, replacing or ignoring God. The Hebrew word *duda'im* for "mandrakes" sounds like *dodim* "love" (Ezek 16:8; Song 5:1). The mandrake was an odiferous plant (Song 7:13 [14]), the roots of which evoked the form of the lower human torso. It was thus used in the ancient Mediterranean world as an aphrodisiac or as a means to enhance fertility. The mandrakes become the object of contest between Leah and Rachel. That it is Leah's eldest son, Reuben, the first manifestation of birth success, who finds the mandrakes, is no accident. Whether he was searching for them or found them by chance is unclear. The fact is that both women are interested in the plant: Rachel because she is barren, and Leah because she has become barren.

30:14–15 These mandrakes are first destined for Leah (30:14), but Rachel obtains them from Leah in exchange for a night with her husband (30:15). The bargain between the two women suggests that Jacob was not sleeping with Leah anymore and preferred to go to Rachel instead. That Rachel allows Leah to sleep with her husband as the price for the mandrakes suggests that she attaches more importance to the prospect of giving birth than to the love of her husband, which she already possessed. However, Leah prefers sleeping with Jacob over the benefit of the mandrakes because she already has sons of her own and is only concerned with the love of Jacob (30:15).

30:16 Leah went out to meet him. Leah, who is normally pictured as passive (29:23), has now become aggressive toward Jacob, a reaction that is consistent with her angry mood a few hours before, because she feels cheated by Jacob's love for Rachel (30:15). Leah goes to meet Jacob in the field in order to prevent him from reaching the place of Rachel, which would oblige Leah to approach Jacob in Rachel's presence. Jacob's immediate response fits with his previous passive and automatic response (29:28). Jacob does not even discuss Leah's request and does not offer any resistance; he submits himself immediately: **and he lay with her that night**. The man who fought to obtain his birthright (25:29–34), cheated and risked his life to gain the blessing of his father (27:18–27), who will wrestle with God in order to force Him to bless him, has lost all his volition before the women.

30:17–21. LEAH BEARS TWO ADDITIONAL SONS AND A DAUGHTER

GEN 30:17–21 NKJV	GEN 30:17–21 ESV
17 And God listened to Leah, and she conceived and bore Jacob a fifth son.	**17** And God listened to Leah, and she conceived and bore Jacob a fifth son.
18 Leah said, "God has given me my wages, because I have given my maid to my husband." So she called his name Issachar.	**18** Leah said, "God has given me my wages because I gave my servant to my husband." So she called his name Issachar.
19 Then Leah conceived again and bore Jacob a sixth son.	**19** And Leah conceived again, and she bore Jacob a sixth son.

20 And Leah said, "God has endowed me *with a good endowment*; now my husband will dwell with me, because I have borne him six sons." So she called his name Zebulun.	**20** Then Leah said, "God has endowed me with a good endowment; now my husband will honor me, because I have borne him six sons." So she called his name Zebulun.
21 Afterward she bore a daughter, and called her name Dinah.	**21** Afterward she bore a daughter and called her name Dinah.

Although no mention is made of Leah speaking to God, the author notes that **God listened to Leah** (30:17). God hears the wishes of Leah's heart. God sees that Leah is more interested in the love of her husband than in the reward of a son, and she does not care for the virtue of the magic mandrake, nor even believe in it. God responds to Leah's love for Jacob and to her faith in Him. Leah goes to her husband thinking that this night will be unfruitful; she goes with no power of her own because she has relinquished the mandrakes and now relies only on God. She therefore obtains a son in response to her faith. The name of the two sons she obtains reflects Leah's experience of the grace of God. The name **Issachar** is derived from the word *sakar*, meaning "hire" (2 Kgs 7:6), "reward" (Ps 127:3), and refers to the deal concluded between the two sisters (30:16). Leah is rewarded (*sakar*) with the benefit of the son she had relinquished. Note that the word *sakar* "hire," "reward" is a keyword in the Jacob cycle (29:15; 30:18, 28, 32–33; 31:7–8, 41). Leah likewise explains the name of her next son, **Zebulun**, in reference to the grace of God, based on the phonetic connection between *zabad* and *zabal*. The name "Zebulun" contains both the notion of "gift," *zabad* **good endowment** (30:20a), evoking the grace of God, and the idea of "dwelling" (*zabal*), referring to the fact that her husband will now attach to her (30:20b; cf. 29:34). Because of this son, a manifestation of God's grace, Leah asserts that **my husband will dwell with me** (30:20). The next child is a daughter, **Dinah**, whose name is not explained, but is a reminder of Rachel's first son Dan (30:6). Both names are constructed on the same verb *din* "to judge." Leah's last child corresponds to Rachel's first child, with the same reference to "judgment" and "vindication."

30:22–24. RACHEL BEARS A SON

GEN 30:22–24 NKJV	GEN 30:22–24 ESV
22 Then God remembered Rachel, and God listened to her and opened her womb.	**22** Then God remembered Rachel, and God listened to her and opened her womb.
23 And she conceived and bore a son, and said, "God has taken away my reproach."	**23** She conceived and bore a son and said, "God has taken away my reproach."
24 So she called his name Joseph, and said, "The Lord shall add to me another son."	**24** And she called his name Joseph, saying, "May the Lord add to me another son!"

30:22 God remembered as He remembered Noah after the destruction of the flood (8:1) and as He remembered Abraham after the destruction of Sodom and Gomorrah (19:29). The same introductory phrase, *wayyizkor 'Elohim* "God remembered," is used in all of these cases. Rachel receives God's redemption as Noah and

Abraham did after their long night of destruction. Rachel had to wait seven years after her marriage and fourteen years after her betrothal to bear her first child (29:18, 27; cf. 30:25). Just as God "listened to Leah" (30:17), **God listened to Rachel**, implying that Rachel's conception, like Leah's conception, was due to her prayer to God and not to the mandrakes. This notion is reinforced by the specific wording that He **opened her womb**, echoing as an inclusio God's intervention on behalf of the unloved Leah at the onset of the birth process (29:31). Rachel's first son corresponds to Leah's first son. Rachel signifies her emotions in the name she gives to her son. The name of Joseph receives two meanings based on a pun between the word *'asaf* "take away" and the word *yasaf* "add."

30:23–24 Rachel's first statement looks back to the past, referring to her **reproach** (30:23), because of her barrenness; her second statement looks forward to the future, referring to her hope for **another son** (30:24). That the birth of this future son will occur on their way to Bethlehem is intriguing (35:17–19). The hope of this last son is thus associated with the hope of the return to the Promised Land.

JACOB DECEIVES LABAN (30:25–31:2)

Following the emphasis on Leah and Rachel, the focus now shifts back to Jacob and Laban. At the birth of Joseph (30:25), Jacob has completed his fourteen years of labor for Laban to earn his wives and now wants to return home (30:26). When Laban objects (30:27) and asks Jacob what wages he should give him (30:28), Jacob makes an offer to take a special breed of sheep (30:29–33), to which Laban agrees (30:34). This section comprises the dialogue between Jacob and Laban discussing the agreement about the sheep (30:25–34), followed by a narrative reporting Jacob's and Laban's competitive action to manage that deal, ending with the prosperity of Jacob (30:35–43), and concluding with Jacob's observation of jealousy and hostility on the part of Laban and his sons (31:1–2).

30:25–34. CONTRACT FOR THE SHEEP

GEN 30:25–34 NKJV	GEN 30:25–34 ESV
25 And it came to pass, when Rachel had borne Joseph, that Jacob said to Laban, "Send me away, that I may go to my own place and to my country.	**25** As soon as Rachel had borne Joseph, Jacob said to Laban, "Send me away, that I may go to my own home and country.
26 Give *me* my wives and my children for whom I have served you, and let me go; for you know my service which I have done for you."	**26** Give me my wives and my children for whom I have served you, that I may go, for you know the service that I have given you."
27 And Laban said to him, "Please *stay*, if I have found favor in your eyes, *for* I have learned by experience that the Lᴏʀᴅ has blessed me for your sake."	**27** But Laban said to him, "If I have found favor in your sight, I have learned by divination that the Lᴏʀᴅ has blessed me because of you.
28 Then he said, "Name me your wages, and I will give *it*."	**28** Name your wages, and I will give it."

29 So *Jacob* said to him, "You know how I have served you and how your livestock has been with me.

30 For what you had before I *came was* little, and it has increased to a great amount; the Lᴏʀᴅ has blessed you since my coming. And now, when shall I also provide for my own house?"

31 So he said, "What shall I give you?" And Jacob said, "You shall not give me anything. If you will do this thing for me, I will again feed and keep your flocks:

32 Let me pass through all your flock today, removing from there all the speckled and spotted sheep, and all the brown ones among the lambs, and the spotted and speckled among the goats; and *these* shall be my wages.

33 So my righteousness will answer for me in time to come, when the subject of my wages comes before you: every one that *is* not speckled and spotted among the goats, and brown among the lambs, will be considered stolen, if *it is* with me."

34 And Laban said, "Oh that it were according to your word!"

29 Jacob said to him, "You yourself know how I have served you, and how your livestock has fared with me.

30 For you had little before I came, and it has increased abundantly, and the Lᴏʀᴅ has blessed you wherever I turned. But now when shall I provide for my own household also?"

31 He said, "What shall I give you?" Jacob said, "You shall not give me anything. If you will do this for me, I will again pasture your flock and keep it:

32 let me pass through all your flock today, removing from it every speckled and spotted sheep and every black lamb, and the spotted and speckled among the goats, and they shall be my wages.

33 So my honesty will answer for me later, when you come to look into my wages with you. Every one that is not speckled and spotted among the goats and black among the lambs, if found with me, shall be counted stolen."

34 Laban said, "Good! Let it be as you have said."

30:25–26 The birth of Joseph prompts Jacob to consider returning home. The fact that Joseph is Jacob's first son by Rachel, and the prospect of a future and last son (Benjamin), may have played a role in his decision. From the viewpoint of the author of Genesis, Joseph is also the one who will mark the last step in the book of Genesis (50:22–26). The Promised Land is thus once again associated with the birth of Jacob's sons. The messianic hope explains this connection. The hope of the Messiah is related to the hope of the Promised Land, for it is the messianic seed that will ensure the recovery of the lost Garden of Eden. Jacob feels obliged to ask Laban for his authorization (30:25), not only out of respect for him as his uncle, but also because of his wives, who are Laban's daughters and are still living under his roof and therefore, to a certain extent, subject to his control (31:43). Jacob's argument is that he has earned his independence and his right to his wives and, hence, to the children he has begotten with them, through his fourteen years of service to Laban (30:26). Jacob describes himself as a slave: **I have served you** (30:26). Three times Jacob uses the verb *'abad* "serve," which characterizes the condition of slavery (Exod 1:13–14).

30:27–28 Laban knows that Jacob is right and wants to take advantage of this free service. However, instead of confessing his wrongdoing, he attributes his benefit to God, using religion to justify his abuse: **the Lord has blessed me for your sake** (30:27). He also implicitly recognizes that Jacob had worked for free, since he now asks him to propose his price (30:28).

30:29–30 Jacob does not confront Laban and does not complain against him.

Instead, he diplomatically uses Laban's arguments as a basis for his proposal. Referring back to Laban's mention of his **wages**, Jacob reminds Laban of the nature of his service, which concerned his flock: **your livestock** (30:29). This prepares Laban to accept his proposal, which will also concern **your flocks** (30:31). Whereas Laban used the argument of God's blessing to support his deception, Jacob refers to the same argument to insist that all that Laban has acquired he owes to God's blessing that is attributed to him, Jacob; for before Jacob's coming, Laban had little and now it is much (30:30): **little** (*me'at*) has become **a great amount** (*rob*). The words Jacob uses are strong. The Hebrew verb *parats* "increase" evokes the effect of a breakthrough (38:29) or of an overflow (Prov 3:10). Laban's wealth did not develop gradually and naturally, but suddenly and unexpectedly, suggesting an external intervention. Jacob ends his plea with a rhetorical question, implying that he has nothing and inviting Laban to consider the notion that it is time for him to work for the benefit of his **own house** (30:30).

30:31 Laban reluctantly asks **what shall I give you?** The question is short (in Hebrew three brief words) and exceeds the wage agreement (cf. 30:28). This is indeed the first time that Laban considers giving. Jacob knows how difficult it is for Laban to "give." He immediately reassures him that he does not have to give anything (30:31). He is even willing to work for him. Jacob will proceed to work for Laban six more years (31:41). However, Jacob does not qualify his new service for Laban as the work of a slave. Jacob contents himself to objectively describe the actual work: **feed and keep your flocks.**

30:32–34 Jacob proposes to Laban that **all the speckled and spotted sheep** (30:32a), which could be identified as **all the brown ones,**[589] **and the spotted and speckled among the goats** (30:32b) be removed and considered as his wages. Jacob's proposal is odd, for these breeds are rare in the Middle East, where goats are typically completely dark (Song 4:1), whereas sheep are typically completely white (Song 4:2). In other words, any white sheep or any brown goat (which is the norm) will be Laban's property, and any multicolored animal (which is unusual) will be Jacob's property. Jacob reinforces the deal with a legal clause. Jacob engages the righteousness of his character in the deal: any nonmulticolored animal found in his flock should be considered as stolen (30:33). This proposal appears as though Jacob is not asking for anything (30:31). Therefore, it is little wonder that the avaricious Laban agrees immediately and supports this contract according to Jacob's terms (30:34).

30:35–43. JACOB'S PROSPERITY

GEN 30:35–43 NKJV	GEN 30:35–43 ESV
35 So he removed that day the male goats that were speckled and spotted, all the female goats that were speckled and spotted, every one that had *some* white in it, and all the brown ones among the lambs, and gave *them* into the hand of his sons.	**35** But that day Laban removed the male goats that were striped and spotted, and all the female goats that were speckled and spotted, every one that had white on it, and every lamb that was black, and put them in the charge of his sons.

---

589 The *waw* introducing the qualification "brown ones" in the phrase "and all the brown ones" (30:32) is a *waw* of explanation, which should be translated "namely," or "that is," or simply rendered by a comma or a hyphen (see NIV, TNK).

36 Then he put three days' journey between himself and Jacob, and Jacob fed the rest of Laban's flocks.

37 Now Jacob took for himself rods of green poplar and of the almond and chestnut trees, peeled white strips in them, and exposed the white which *was* in the rods.

38 And the rods which he had peeled, he set before the flocks in the gutters, in the watering troughs where the flocks came to drink, so that they should conceive when they came to drink.

39 So the flocks conceived before the rods, and the flocks brought forth streaked, speckled, and spotted.

40 Then Jacob separated the lambs, and made the flocks face toward the streaked and all the brown in the flock of Laban; but he put his own flocks by themselves and did not put them with Laban's flock.

41 And it came to pass, whenever the stronger livestock conceived, that Jacob placed the rods before the eyes of the livestock in the gutters, that they might conceive among the rods.

42 But when the flocks were feeble, he did not put *them* in; so the feebler were Laban's and the stronger Jacob's.

43 Thus the man became exceedingly prosperous, and had large flocks, female and male servants, and camels and donkeys.

36 And he set a distance of three days' journey between himself and Jacob, and Jacob pastured the rest of Laban's flock.

37 Then Jacob took fresh sticks of poplar and almond and plane trees, and peeled white streaks in them, exposing the white of the sticks.

38 He set the sticks that he had peeled in front of the flocks in the troughs, that is, the watering places, where the flocks came to drink. And since they bred when they came to drink,

39 the flocks bred in front of the sticks and so the flocks brought forth striped, speckled, and spotted.

40 And Jacob separated the lambs and set the faces of the flocks toward the striped and all the black in the flock of Laban. He put his own droves apart and did not put them with Laban's flock.

41 Whenever the stronger of the flock were breeding, Jacob would lay the sticks in the troughs before the eyes of the flock, that they might breed among the sticks,

42 but for the feebler of the flock he would not lay them there. So the feebler would be Laban's, and the stronger Jacob's.

43 Thus the man increased greatly and had large flocks, female servants and male servants, and camels and donkeys.

30:35–36 Laban does not content himself with the status quo. He takes measures to ensure that Jacob gets nothing. Although Jacob had volunteered to proceed with the removal, Laban takes this assignment upon himself and is the one who removes all the multicolored animals. However, instead of leaving them to Jacob, according to the agreement, he cheats and gives them to his sons (30:35). Furthermore, to ensure that they will not mate with the animals of the flock of Jacob, he puts three days' distance between the two flocks (30:36). This precaution will ironically turn to Jacob's advantage, for it will allow him the freedom to apply his own strategy and facilitate his later flight. By complicating the process and making it impossible for this breed to be produced, Laban unwittingly highlights the supernatural characteristic of the process (see Judg 6:36–40).

30:37–42 Jacob's method may seemingly pertain to superstitious magic, yet the biblical text informs us that Jacob proceeded under divine guidance (31:11–12). In addition, further scientific studies have indicated that Jacob's method could have been consistent with the law of modern genetics. Jacob's use of the poplar, almond, and chestnut trees (30:37) are not accidental, since these three trees contain chemical substances that have the effect of stimulating the readiness to copulate.[590] Because hybrid animals are naturally stronger than other breeds, by choosing the stronger ones (30:41), Jacob is, in fact (perhaps without knowing it), selecting those that are already the result of mixing. When hybrid animals are bred with each other, the recessive genes reappear in the next generation. Exposing those strong animals to the peeled rods (30:38–39) when they copulated may have had an effect on the unborn offspring. Using this method, Jacob is able to produce a large flock composed of sturdy multicolored sheep and goats. Jacob did not use weak animals for this operation, leaving them for Laban: **so the feebler were Laban's and the stronger Jacob's** (30:42). This contrast between the two flocks suggests potential rivalry between the two camps.

30:43 The reference to Jacob becoming **exceedingly prosperous** recalls Jacob's qualification of Laban's wealth (30:30). The same language is used. The same verb *parats* describes the sudden explosion of wealth; yet in this instance, the explosion is intensified by the two repetitions of the adverb *meʼod* "very," which is translated "exceedingly" (NKJV) or "greatly" (ESV). The same adjective, *rab* "large," is used but in the plural this time (*rabot*). This echo between these two evaluations of Jacob's and Laban's wealth suggests that Jacob has now become wealthier than Laban and that his prosperity has been acquired from Laban's prosperity.

31:1–2. JACOB PERCEIVES HOSTILITY

GEN 31:1–2 NKJV	GEN 31:1–2 ESV
1 Now *Jacob* heard the words of Laban's sons, saying, "Jacob has taken away all that was our father's, and from what was our father's he has acquired all this wealth."	**1** Now Jacob heard that the sons of Laban were saying, "Jacob has taken all that was our father's, and from what was our father's he has gained all this wealth."
2 And Jacob saw the countenance of Laban, and indeed it *was* not *favorable* toward him as before.	**2** And Jacob saw that Laban did not regard him with favor as before.

The lesson implied in the preceding verse (30:43) is explicitly verbalized by Laban's sons (31:1), who used such loud and clear expressions that **Jacob heard** their words. This is the second time that Laban's sons are mentioned; the first time was in connection to their involvement, and perhaps complicity, in Laban's cheating (30:35). Therefore, it is not surprising that they are bitter and angry at Jacob. They thought they would benefit from Jacob's work, only to find the contrary. They transfer their frustrations onto him and blame him. Although Laban may not have spoken out like his sons, **Jacob saw** the expression of his face, his body language, and his changed behavior toward him (31:2). Jacob perceives hostility in what he hears and sees. The "hearing" and "seeing" echo the experience associated with the birth of his first two sons, Reuben and Simeon (29:32–33). Jacob is fearful for his sons.

---

590 Sarna, *Genesis*, 212.

JACOB LEAVES LABAN (31:3–55)

The shift to a new section is indicated by God's word to Jacob for the first time since Bethel. God urges Jacob to return to the land of his fathers. Jacob then calls his wives and flees from Laban (31:3–21). When Laban reaches him after seven days of pursuit, they confront each other. Laban accuses Jacob of having stolen his gods, and Jacob accuses Laban of mistreating him (31:22–42). In the end, Laban and Jacob decide to make a covenant with each other, after which Laban departs (31:43–55). The new section consists of dialogues between Jacob and his wives (31:4–16) and between Laban and Jacob (31:26–32, 36–42, 43–53), which are intercalated with short narratives (31:17–25, 33–35, 54–55). This section is saturated with God's presence. It begins with God speaking to Jacob (31:3) and ends with Jacob worshipping his God (31:54). Each dialogue is prompted by a divine intervention or by a reference to a divine intervention (31:3, 24, 42). Everyone in this section refers to God in his or her speech: Jacob (31:5, 9, 11–13, 42, 49–50), Jacob's wives (31:16), and Laban (31:29, 49, 53). When they were settled at home, God did not speak to them and was rarely mentioned; however, as soon as they are uprooted and moving on their way to the Promised Land, they hear God speaking to them and He is part of their discourse.

31:3–21. JACOB'S FLIGHT

GEN 31:3–21 NKJV	GEN 31:3–21 ESV
3 Then the LORD said to Jacob, "Return to the land of your fathers and to your family, and I will be with you."	**3** Then the LORD said to Jacob, "Return to the land of your fathers and to your kindred, and I will be with you."
4 So Jacob sent and called Rachel and Leah to the field, to his flock,	**4** So Jacob sent and called Rachel and Leah into the field where his flock was
5 and said to them, "I see your father's countenance, that it *is* not *favorable* toward me as before; but the God of my father has been with me.	**5** and said to them, "I see that your father does not regard me with favor as he did before. But the God of my father has been with me.
6 And you know that with all my might I have served your father.	**6** You know that I have served your father with all my strength,
7 Yet your father has deceived me and changed my wages ten times, but God did not allow him to hurt me.	**7** yet your father has cheated me and changed my wages ten times. But God did not permit him to harm me.
8 If he said thus: 'The speckled shall be your wages,' then all the flocks bore speckled. And if he said thus: 'The streaked shall be your wages,' then all the flocks bore streaked.	**8** If he said, 'The spotted shall be your wages,' then all the flock bore spotted; and if he said, 'The striped shall be your wages,' then all the flock bore striped.
9 So God has taken away the livestock of your father and given *them* to me.	**9** Thus God has taken away the livestock of your father and given them to me.
10 "And it happened, at the time when the flocks conceived, that I lifted my eyes and saw in a dream, and behold, the rams which leaped upon the flocks *were* streaked, speckled, and gray-spotted.	**10** In the breeding season of the flock I lifted up my eyes and saw in a dream that the goats that mated with the flock were striped, spotted, and mottled.

359

11 Then the Angel of God spoke to me in a dream, saying, 'Jacob.' And I said, 'Here I am.'	**11** Then the angel of God said to me in the dream, 'Jacob,' and I said, 'Here I am!'
12 And He said, 'Lift your eyes now and see, all the rams which leap on the flocks *are* streaked, speckled, and gray-spotted; for I have seen all that Laban is doing to you.	**12** And he said, 'Lift up your eyes and see, all the goats that mate with the flock are striped, spotted, and mottled, for I have seen all that Laban is doing to you.
13 I *am* the God of Bethel, where you anointed the pillar *and* where you made a vow to Me. Now arise, get out of this land, and return to the land of your family.'"	**13** I am the God of Bethel, where you anointed a pillar and made a vow to me. Now arise, go out from this land and return to the land of your kindred.'"
14 Then Rachel and Leah answered and said to him, "Is there still any portion or inheritance for us in our father's house?	**14** Then Rachel and Leah answered and said to him, "Is there any portion or inheritance left to us in our father's house?
15 Are we not considered strangers by him? For he has sold us, and also completely consumed our money.	**15** Are we not regarded by him as foreigners? For he has sold us, and he has indeed devoured our money.
16 For all these riches which God has taken from our father are *really* ours and our children's; now then, whatever God has said to you, do it."	**16** All the wealth that God has taken away from our father belongs to us and to our children. Now then, whatever God has said to you, do."
17 Then Jacob rose and set his sons and his wives on camels.	**17** So Jacob arose and set his sons and his wives on camels.
18 And he carried away all his livestock and all his possessions which he had gained, his acquired livestock which he had gained in Padan Aram, to go to his father Isaac in the land of Canaan.	**18** He drove away all his livestock, all his property that he had gained, the livestock in his possession that he had acquired in Paddan-aram, to go to the land of Canaan to his father Isaac.
19 Now Laban had gone to shear his sheep, and Rachel had stolen the household idols that were her father's.	**19** Laban had gone to shear his sheep, and Rachel stole her father's household gods.
20 And Jacob stole away, unknown to Laban the Syrian, in that he did not tell him that he intended to flee.	**20** And Jacob tricked Laban the Aramean, by not telling him that he intended to flee.
21 So he fled with all that he had. He arose and crossed the river, and headed toward the mountains of Gilead.	**21** He fled with all that he had and arose and crossed the Euphrates, and set his face toward the hill country of Gilead.

31:3 Although the preceding verses emphasize Jacob's discomfort toward Laban and his sons, it is not Jacob's sentiments or Laban's threat that drives Jacob back to the country of his fathers but divine instruction. Jacob may have prolonged his sojourn in Laban's house had God not spoken to him. Jacob may have entertained the desire to leave; yet he waited for this signal from God before undertaking his journey. Despite the troubles he is beginning to sense and anticipate from Laban and his sons, Jacob remains anxious to return home, fearing Esau his brother. This is why God reassures him that He will be with him, a promise Jacob had already heard when he was fleeing Canaan (28:15).

31:4–9 Jacob responds immediately to God's instruction. He sends for his wives and calls them **to the field, to his flock** (31:4), far from Laban, to be able to speak freely to them. Jacob wants to ensure that his wives will follow him before he moves forward. Having heard God speaking to him, Jacob has reason to impose his decision upon his wives. Yet, he respectfully presents his case to them. The sequence of the names **Rachel and Leah** (31:4) is not merely an expression of his preference for Rachel over Leah. If Jacob is first concerned with Rachel, it is perhaps because she is the one who is the most reluctant to leave the country, as her attachment to the local religion suggests (31:34). To convince his wives of the rightness of his decision, Jacob refers to Laban's hostility (31:5) and deceitfulness (31:7) toward him, in contrast to the quality of his personal service on Laban's behalf (31:6). Mindful of the rumors he has heard from Laban's sons, his wives' brothers, Jacob explains that he did not become wealthy because he cheated their father. On the contrary, Laban cheated him and **changed** his **wages ten times** (31:7), a round number indicating the intensity of Laban's misbehavior. Jacob had been passive regarding his wages, allowing Laban to take the initiative. To illustrate his point, Jacob presents a short version of the preceding events. Laban determined that all speckled animals would be Jacob's wages, thinking that there would be no speckled animals; yet, all the animals of the flock became speckled. Laban subsequently changed and determined that all streaked animals would be Jacob's wages, believing that there would be no streaked animals; yet, all the animals of the flock became streaked (31:8). Jacob explains this consistent phenomenon by referring to God's saving activity. The Hebrew verb *wayyatsel* "had taken away" refers to God's act of salvation, when God saves Israel from slavery (Exod 3:8) or from the enemy (1 Sam 12:11). Jacob communicates to his wives that God has saved the sheep from Laban (just as He will save Israel in the Exodus). Under the shepherd Jacob, the sheep are now liberated and on their way home.

31:10–13 Jacob expands the argument, based on the supernatural, with the account of his prophetic dream. The Angel of the Lord controlled the entire breeding operation. The dialogue between Jacob and the Angel of the Lord echoes the dialogue between Abraham and the Angel of the Lord at the *'aqedah*. It is the same call by the Angel of the Lord and the same answer, **here I am** (31:11; cf. 22:11); the same appeal **lift your eyes … and see** and the same vision of **rams** (31:12; cf. 22:13). This God is also identified as **the God of Bethel**, the God who commanded Jacob: **return to the land of your family** (31:13).

31:14–16 Despite the previous conflict between them, Rachel and Leah now speak for the first time with one voice. The two wives respond to Jacob's plea with the same two arguments to support their leaving. Similar to Jacob, they refer to Laban who had not only disinherited them (31:14) according to the custom (Num 27:7–11), but had also sold them, keeping the money for himself (31:15). This last complaint suggests that Laban was obligated to return the bride's price, what they refer to as **our money** (31:15), instead of retaining it. Similar to Jacob, they refer to God to whom they owe **these riches which God has taken from our father** (31:16). They use the same verb *natsal* (31:9) that Jacob had used, implying the same recognition that these riches and their children were "rescued" from Laban. Therefore, they completely agree with Jacob and support his decision to follow God's instructions (31:16).

31:17–21 Jacob acts immediately and sets up his departure (31:17). Children, wives, and all of Jacob's possessions are loaded. The narrative insists on Jacob's ownership by repeating the word "all" (31:18 [2x]) and the pronoun "his": **his wives, all his livestock, all his possessions**. The point is that "all" that Jacob takes with him belongs to him. All except the **household idols**, which Rachel steals from her father (31:19). The Hebrew word *teraphim*, translated "household idols," refers to idols of various sizes used for diverse purposes. These idols were likely ancestor images, suggesting that Rachel was still attached to the religion of her father (30:14; 35:2) and was therefore not so confident about leaving home (see the commentary on 31:4). As also indicated in the Nuzi (Mesopotamian) tablets,[591] the possession of these household gods gave them the right to the inheritance of which they had been deprived (31:14). The mention of Laban's absence suggests that Rachel had taken advantage of this opportunity to steal the objects from him. The ceremony of shearing the sheep was around April or May (Deut 18:4) and was an occasion for family and friends to feast. That Jacob and his family are excluded from this party shows how the two clans are already separated and confirms the suspicion and hostility that prevailed between them. In that context, Jacob's departure is thus described as a "stealing away." Just as Rachel stole (*ganab*) the idols from her father, Jacob **stole away** (*ganab*) from Laban, meaning that he left the place without informing Laban (31:20). Jacob's departure is thus not qualified as a mere "going"; **he fled** (*barakh*) from Laban (31:21), just as he fled (*barakh*) from Esau (27:43). Jacob leaves Padan Aram with the same sentiments of fear and guilt he had when he left Canaan. However, the crossing of the Euphrates will remain associated in the memory of Israel with their fathers Jacob and Abraham (Josh 24:2). The mention of Gilead, the direction the caravans take, anticipates the next location where Laban and Jacob will meet (31:23) and ultimately make a covenant with each other (31:47).

31:22–42. JACOB ACCUSES LABAN

GEN 31:22–42 NKJV	GEN 31:22–42 ESV
22 And Laban was told on the third day that Jacob had fled.	**22** When it was told Laban on the third day that Jacob had fled,
23 Then he took his brethren with him and pursued him for seven days' journey, and he overtook him in the mountains of Gilead.	**23** he took his kinsmen with him and pursued him for seven days and followed close after him into the hill country of Gilead.
24 But God had come to Laban the Syrian in a dream by night, and said to him, "Be careful that you speak to Jacob neither good nor bad."	**24** But God came to Laban the Aramean in a dream by night and said to him, "Be careful not to say anything to Jacob, either good or bad."
25 So Laban overtook Jacob. Now Jacob had pitched his tent in the mountains, and Laban with his brethren pitched in the mountains of Gilead.	**25** And Laban overtook Jacob. Now Jacob had pitched his tent in the hill country, and Laban with his kinsmen pitched tents in the hill country of Gilead.
26 And Laban said to Jacob: "What have you done, that you have stolen away unknown to me, and carried away my daughters like captives *taken* with the sword?	**26** And Laban said to Jacob, "What have you done, that you have tricked me and driven away my daughters like captives of the sword?

---

591 *ANET*, 219–220. Nuzi is a city in Mesopotamia (approximately 150 miles north of Baghdad), which flourished in the middle of the second millennium BC and had a significant bearing on the patriarchal narratives of the Bible (see *IDB* 3:573–574).

27 Why did you flee away secretly, and steal away from me, and not tell me; for I might have sent you away with joy and songs, with timbrel and harp?

28 And you did not allow me to kiss my sons and my daughters. Now you have done foolishly in *so* doing.

29 It is in my power to do you harm, but the God of your father spoke to me last night, saying, 'Be careful that you speak to Jacob neither good nor bad.'

30 And now you have surely gone because you greatly long for your father's house, *but* why did you steal my gods?"

31 Then Jacob answered and said to Laban, "Because I was afraid, for I said, 'Perhaps you would take your daughters from me by force.'

32 With whomever you find your gods, do not let him live. In the presence of our brethren, identify what I have of yours and take *it* with you." For Jacob did not know that Rachel had stolen them.

33 And Laban went into Jacob's tent, into Leah's tent, and into the two maids' tents, but he did not find *them*. Then he went out of Leah's tent and entered Rachel's tent.

34 Now Rachel had taken the household idols, put them in the camel's saddle, and sat on them. And Laban searched all about the tent but did not find *them*.

35 And she said to her father, "Let it not displease my lord that I cannot rise before you, for the manner of women *is* with me." And he searched but did not find the household idols.

36 Then Jacob was angry and rebuked Laban, and Jacob answered and said to Laban: "What *is* my trespass? What *is* my sin, that you have so hotly pursued me?

37 Although you have searched all my things, what part of your household things have you found? Set *it* here before my brethren and your brethren, that they may judge between us both!

38 These twenty years I *have been* with you; your ewes and your female goats have not miscarried their young, and I have not eaten the rams of your flock.

39 That which was torn *by beasts* I did not bring to you; I bore the loss of it. You required it from my hand, *whether* stolen by day or stolen by night.

27 Why did you flee secretly and trick me, and did not tell me, so that I might have sent you away with mirth and songs, with tambourine and lyre?

28 And why did you not permit me to kiss my sons and my daughters farewell? Now you have done foolishly.

29 It is in my power to do you harm. But the God of your father spoke to me last night, saying, 'Be careful not to say anything to Jacob, either good or bad.'

30 And now you have gone away because you longed greatly for your father's house, but why did you steal my gods?"

31 Jacob answered and said to Laban, "Because I was afraid, for I thought that you would take your daughters from me by force.

32 Anyone with whom you find your gods shall not live. In the presence of our kinsmen point out what I have that is yours, and take it." Now Jacob did not know that Rachel had stolen them.

33 So Laban went into Jacob's tent and into Leah's tent and into the tent of the two female servants, but he did not find them. And he went out of Leah's tent and entered Rachel's.

34 Now Rachel had taken the household gods and put them in the camel's saddle and sat on them. Laban felt all about the tent, but did not find them.

35 And she said to her father, "Let not my lord be angry that I cannot rise before you, for the way of women is upon me." So he searched but did not find the household gods.

36 Then Jacob became angry and berated Laban. Jacob said to Laban, "What is my offense? What is my sin, that you have hotly pursued me?

37 For you have felt through all my goods; what have you found of all your household goods? Set it here before my kinsmen and your kinsmen, that they may decide between us two.

38 These twenty years I have been with you. Your ewes and your female goats have not miscarried, and I have not eaten the rams of your flocks.

39 What was torn by wild beasts I did not bring to you. I bore the loss of it myself. From my hand you required it, whether stolen by day or stolen by night.

40 *There* I was! In the day the drought consumed me, and the frost by night, and my sleep departed from my eyes.	**40** There I was: by day the heat consumed me, and the cold by night, and my sleep fled from my eyes.
41 Thus I have been in your house twenty years; I served you fourteen years for your two daughters, and six years for your flock, and you have changed my wages ten times.	**41** These twenty years I have been in your house. I served you fourteen years for your two daughters, and six years for your flock, and you have changed my wages ten times.
42 Unless the God of my father, the God of Abraham and the Fear of Isaac, had been with me, surely now you would have sent me away empty-handed. God has seen my affliction and the labor of my hands, and rebuked *you* last night."	**42** If the God of my father, the God of Abraham and the Fear of Isaac, had not been on my side, surely now you would have sent me away empty-handed. God saw my affliction and the labor of my hands and rebuked you last night."

31:22–23 Laban learns about Jacob's flight only three days after his departure (31:22). Because they were separated by three days' journey (30:36), someone must have gone to report to Laban as soon as Jacob had left. It took seven days for Laban to reach Jacob at Gilead, which means that Gilead was a ten-day journey from Padan Aram. The same association of the verbs *radaf* **pursue** (31:23) and *nsg* **overtake** (31:25) will reappear in connection to the pharaoh who "pursued" and "overtook" the Israelites with "his horsemen and his army" (Exod 14:9). This common language suggests that Laban's intentions are of the same nature as the future Egyptians and are not peaceful.

31:24–25 Laban's dream from God prevents him from harming Jacob. God's warning is similar to a threat. The same Hebrew idiom *hisshamer … pen* **be careful** is used by God to warn His people against idolatry (Exod 34:12) or against any wicked intention (Exod 15:9). The phrase **neither good nor bad** implies that Laban must not say or do anything that could appear unfavorable or harmful to Jacob. God knows that even Laban's good intentions on behalf of Jacob could hide a harmful design. Instead of encountering and attacking Jacob, Laban puts himself on a parallel course; just as Jacob **had pitched his tent in the mountains … Laban with his brethren pitched in the mountains of Gilead** (31:25). Note the repetition of the "brethren," which designates the relatives, friends, and mercenaries constituting Laban's army.

31:26–30 Laban does not attack Jacob, but he speaks to him. He begins with an accusation, which echoes Jacob's initial accusation to Laban: **What have you done?** (31:26; cf. 29:25). Laban accuses Jacob of having taken his **daughters like captives taken with the sword** (31:26). Laban blames Jacob for the sin he had himself committed, since he is the one who had kept Jacob and his wives and forced Jacob to work for him for twenty years. Laban complains that he was deprived of the pleasure of organizing a feast for the occasion and of the opportunity to kiss his **sons and daughters** (31:28), referring to his grandsons and daughters. Note how he prioritizes his sons over his daughters and how he refers to them. They are not Jacob's wives or Jacob's sons but his own. Laban behaves as if he is the victim, even the victim of the God of Jacob, who has assailed and threatened him. Laban ironically emphasizes that Jacob has stolen his gods, thus implicitly recognizing the superiority of his gods over Jacob's God: "If your God is so awesome, why did you, then, steal my gods?" These images could not carry significant value for Laban, as their small size suggests (31:34); however, he capitalizes on them to use them as a pretext for pursuing Jacob and as a theological argument against Jacob.

31:31–32 Jacob responds directly to Laban, returning the accusation; he is the one who would indeed **take … by force** his daughters. The Hebrew verb *gazal* **take … by force**, which appears only once here to describe Laban's offense, contrasts with the seven occurrences of the Hebrew verb *ganab* "steal," which refers to Jacob or Rachel (31:19–20, 26–27, 30, 32, 39). The verb *ganab* describes a furtive or secret act (31:27; Josh 19:4; 2 Kgs 11:2), whereas the verb *gazal* describes the violent act of oppression (Ezek 18:18; Ps 62:10 [11]) that caused Jacob to be fearful (31:31). Jacob is so certain of his own innocence that, although he does not value this object, he is ready to use the price of a life as a pledge for his honesty (31:32; cf. 44:9). Of course, Jacob does not know that he is risking the life of his favorite wife (31:32), otherwise he would not have been so bold. This parenthetical information implies that Jacob was again deceived, this time by his wife. The deceiver continues to be deceived, even by those he trusts most. This is perhaps a reprobative hint at his former behavior.

31:33–34 Laban, who is untrustworthy, does not trust anyone, even his daughters. He immediately goes into the tent of Leah and those of the two maids. Rachel is the last one to be checked. Laban searches everywhere. The Hebrew verb *mashash* for "search" refers to thorough and careful activity; it is the same verb used to describe Isaac "searching" Jacob to verify if he was the correct son (27:21). Jacob is searched again, but this time the object of the search is hidden even to Jacob. Rachel had concealed it in the camel's saddle on which she was sitting (31:34). Rachel claims to have what she calls **the manner of women** (31:35), a discreet way of referring to her menstruation. Rachel's uncleanness prevents Laban from searching there. Rachel is saved by what makes her the most vulnerable, her femininity. Laban **searched but did not find** (31:35). The story ends leaving Laban powerless and ridiculously overcome by a woman, the very woman he had been able to deceive some twenty years before.

31:36–42 Jacob, who has sufficient reason to be angry, takes this opportunity to argue his entire case against Laban. Similar to Laban, he begins his plea of innocence with questions challenging Laban's suspicion in the presence of Laban's party and his own party (31:37). First, Jacob establishes his innocence. He reminds Laban of the quality of his service for the last twenty years: how he took care of the sheep beyond all measure (31:38), returning the hurt or stolen beasts (31:39) although it was not required by law (Exod 22:11, 13; Amos 3:12). According to ANE legislation, the shepherd was not responsible for the damage on the sheep if he could establish that he had not stolen the animal.[592] Jacob also reminds Laban how fully dedicated he was to his work, how he suffered in the drought of day and in the cold of night, with a loss of sleep (31:40). Jacob argues that it is Laban who should be charged, since he abused him and deceived him: he did not pay him for fourteen years of work; and for the next six years, he changed his wages ten times (31:41; cf. 31:7). In conclusion, Jacob refers to the very God Laban had evoked earlier, **the God of my father** (31:42; cf. 31:29). However, Jacob now expands the title and specifies the **God of Abraham and the Fear of Isaac** (31:42), implying that this God is not merely the God of *his* father but is, in fact, a God whom Laban should revere because He is also the God of Abraham, his grandfather's brother, and of Isaac, his brother-in-law. Jacob subtly reminds Laban of his sister. The expression "Fear of Isaac" adds to the mere

---

592 See Code of Hammurabi #266; *ANET*, 177.

reference to God the notion of "fear," which may have been implied in Laban's experience, since it is this fear that prevented Laban from harming Jacob (31:29).

31:43–55. A COVENANT BETWEEN JACOB AND LABAN

GEN 31:43–55 NKJV	GEN 31:43–55 ESV
43 And Laban answered and said to Jacob, "*These* daughters *are* my daughters, and *these* children *are* my children, and *this* flock *is* my flock; all that you see *is* mine. But what can I do this day to these my daughters or to their children whom they have borne?	**43** Then Laban answered and said to Jacob, "The daughters are my daughters, the children are my children, the flocks are my flocks, and all that you see is mine. But what can I do this day for these my daughters or for their children whom they have borne?
44 Now therefore, come, let us make a covenant, you and I, and let it be a witness between you and me."	**44** Come now, let us make a covenant, you and I. And let it be a witness between you and me."
45 So Jacob took a stone and set it up *as* a pillar.	**45** So Jacob took a stone and set it up as a pillar.
46 Then Jacob said to his brethren, "Gather stones." And they took stones and made a heap, and they ate there on the heap.	**46** And Jacob said to his kinsmen, "Gather stones." And they took stones and made a heap, and they ate there by the heap.
47 Laban called it Jegar Sahadutha, but Jacob called it Galeed.	**47** Laban called it Jegar-sahadutha, but Jacob called it Galeed.
48 And Laban said, "This heap *is* a witness between you and me this day." Therefore its name was called Galeed,	**48** Laban said, "This heap is a witness between you and me today." Therefore he named it Galeed,
49 also Mizpah, because he said, "May the Lᴏʀᴅ watch between you and me when we are absent one from another.	**49** and Mizpah, for he said, "The Lᴏʀᴅ watch between you and me, when we are out of one another's sight.
50 If you afflict my daughters, or if you take *other* wives besides my daughters, *although* no man *is* with us—see, God *is* witness between you and me!"	**50** If you oppress my daughters, or if you take wives besides my daughters, although no one is with us, see, God is witness between you and me."
51 Then Laban said to Jacob, "Here is this heap and here is this pillar, which I have placed between you and me.	**51** Then Laban said to Jacob, "See this heap and the pillar, which I have set between you and me.
52 This heap *is* a witness, and *this* pillar *is* a witness, that I will not pass beyond this heap to you, and you will not pass beyond this heap and this pillar to me, for harm.	**52** This heap is a witness, and the pillar is a witness, that I will not pass over this heap to you, and you will not pass over this heap and this pillar to me, to do harm.
53 The God of Abraham, the God of Nahor, and the God of their father judge between us." And Jacob swore by the Fear of his father Isaac.	**53** The God of Abraham and the God of Nahor, the God of their father, judge between us." So Jacob swore by the Fear of his father Isaac,
54 Then Jacob offered a sacrifice on the mountain, and called his brethren to eat bread. And they ate bread and stayed all night on the mountain.	**54** and Jacob offered a sacrifice in the hill country and called his kinsmen to eat bread. They ate bread and spent the night in the hill country.
55 And early in the morning Laban arose, and kissed his sons and daughters and blessed them. Then Laban departed and returned to his place.	**55** Early in the morning Laban arose and kissed his grandchildren and his daughters and blessed them. Then Laban departed and returned home.

31:43–44 Following Jacob's argument for his right to his wives, children, and his flocks, one would expect Laban to repent. Instead, countering Jacob's plea, Laban's first response to Jacob is to claim ownership of these, leaving nothing to Jacob: **all that you see is mine** (31:43). He then raises a rhetorical question that seems to indicate his paternal concern: **What can I do to these my daughters or to their children?** This question hides his fear from Jacob, the real reason for his need for a covenant with him. Similar to Abimelech, who saw that God was on the side of Isaac and was afraid and, therefore, initiated a covenant with Isaac (26:28), Laban is afraid but does not want to acknowledge it aloud and, therefore, asks for a covenant with Jacob.

31:45–47 Jacob does not speak to Laban. As at Bethel, **Jacob took a stone** (31:45; cf. 28:18). Instead of addressing Laban, he invites his brethren, that is, Laban's sons, to do the same, and they erect a pillar by which they share the covenant meal (31:46). Laban calls the place Jegar Sahadutha, an Aramaic expression that means "Heap of Witness," whereas Jacob calls it Galeed, which has the same meaning in Hebrew (31:47). This is the only passage in the Pentateuch containing an Aramaic phrase and its Hebrew translation. This linguistic distinction situates the two camps against each other, Jacob the Hebrew versus Laban the Aramean (cf. 31:20, 24).

31:48–53 Laban, who initiated the covenant, receives the honor of offering the first speech commenting on the meaning of that covenant.

31:48–50 Laban plays on the meaning of the Hebrew names "Galeed" and "Mizpah." **Galeed** refers to the human parties involved in that covenant: the heap (*gal/yegar*) will serve as a witness (*'ed/sahaduta*), a visible sign between the two parties to encourage remembrance and respect for each other (31:48). **Mizpah** refers to the divine presence to inspire fear from above in the absence of the other party (31:49). Laban only mentions *YHWH* **the Lord**, the God of Jacob, implying only Jacob's potential transgression. Laban ironically suggests the possibility that Jacob might **afflict** his daughters (31:50), when he was the one who had mistreated them (31:14–16), and that Jacob might **take other wives** (31:50), when he was the one who had forced Jacob into polygamy.

31:51–52 Laban clearly distinguishes between **the pillar** he set up and **the heap** set up by Jacob (31:51). Both monuments are visible signs functioning as witnesses that no one would pass them **for harm** (31:52). The place of the word "for harm" at the end of the phrase, in direct connection to Jacob, suggests that Laban hints rather at Jacob, as if the intention of harm would only or essentially apply to Jacob.

31:53 Laban identifies **the God of Abraham** with **the God of Nahor, and the God of their father**, suggesting that this god is a pagan Mesopotamian god. However, Jacob's specific mention of Isaac excludes any ambiguity. Jacob swears **by the Fear of Isaac his father** not only to remind Laban of the God who had revealed Himself in a dream to prevent him from harming Jacob, but also to clearly indicate that this is a different God, the God whom Laban himself had identified as "God of your father" (31:29).

31:54–55 Jacob has not spoken a word to Laban; he has only acted. He concludes the ceremony by offering a sacrifice. He then invites only his brethren, Laban's sons, to eat with him, as was the custom for a peace treaty (24:31–33; 26:30); Laban is not mentioned, similar to the previous case when they built the monument (31:46). Similarly, the next day when Laban leaves, he kisses only his daughters; nothing is mentioned in regard to Jacob. Laban returns **to his place**, a clear indication of the definitive separation. Laban will no longer interfere.

ENCOUNTERING GOD AT PENIEL (32:1–32)

Jacob's next encounter with God at Peniel corresponds to his Bethel encounter. The two accounts echo each other in words, structure, and themes. Both journeys emerge as a flight from a threatening relative. At Peniel, Jacob remembers Bethel and receives the promised blessing. Fearful of Esau, Jacob prays to God to deliver him from Esau (32:9 [10], 11 [12]) based on His promises at Bethel (28:13–15).[593] Bethel begins at sunset, anticipating darkness (28:11). Peniel ends at sunrise, anticipating the new day (32:31). Bethel, like Peniel, mingles human and divine encounters. At Bethel, Jacob sees a ladder connecting heaven to earth. At Peniel, the report of the human messengers Jacob sends to Esau parallel the section referring to the divine messengers he met. They are called by the same name, *mal'akh* "messenger, angel," and they both come in pairs (32:7–8). Like Bethel, the experience of Peniel develops in two phases: beginning with the meeting of two camps of messengers or angels, human and heavenly (32:1–21; cf. 28:12), and proceeding with Jacob wrestling with God Himself, which will determine the name of the place, Peniel (32:22–30; cf. 28:13–19), and ending with the prospect of a glorious future (32:31–32; cf. 28:20–22).

32:1–21. THE TWO CAMPS

GEN 32:1–21 NKJV	GEN 32:1–21 ESV
1 So Jacob went on his way, and the angels of God met him.	**1** Jacob went on his way, and the angels of God met him.
2 When Jacob saw them, he said, "This *is* God's camp." And he called the name of that place Mahanaim.	**2** And when Jacob saw them he said, "This is God's camp!" So he called the name of that place Mahanaim.
3 Then Jacob sent messengers before him to Esau his brother in the land of Seir, the country of Edom.	**3** And Jacob sent messengers before him to Esau his brother in the land of Seir, the country of Edom,
4 And he commanded them, saying, "Speak thus to my lord Esau, 'Thus your servant Jacob says: "I have dwelt with Laban and stayed there until now.	**4** instructing them, "Thus you shall say to my lord Esau: Thus says your servant Jacob, 'I have sojourned with Laban and stayed until now.
5 I have oxen, donkeys, flocks, and male and female servants; and I have sent to tell my lord, that I may find favor in your sight."'"	**5** I have oxen, donkeys, flocks, male servants, and female servants. I have sent to tell my lord, in order that I may find favor in your sight.'"
6 Then the messengers returned to Jacob, saying, "We came to your brother Esau, and he also is coming to meet you, and four hundred men *are* with him."	**6** And the messengers returned to Jacob, saying, "We came to your brother Esau, and he is coming to meet you, and there are four hundred men with him."
7 So Jacob was greatly afraid and distressed; and he divided the people that *were* with him, and the flocks and herds and camels, into two companies.	**7** Then Jacob was greatly afraid and distressed. He divided the people who were with him, and the flocks and herds and camels, into two camps,
8 And he said, "If Esau comes to the one company and attacks it, then the other company which is left will escape."	**8** thinking, "If Esau comes to the one camp and attacks it, then the camp that is left will escape."

---

593 See Mathews, *Genesis 11:27–50:26*, 536–537.

9 Then Jacob said, "O God of my father Abraham and God of my father Isaac, the Lord who said to me, 'Return to your country and to your family, and I will deal well with you':

10 I am not worthy of the least of all the mercies and of all the truth which You have shown Your servant; for I crossed over this Jordan with my staff, and now I have become two companies.

11 Deliver me, I pray, from the hand of my brother, from the hand of Esau; for I fear him, lest he come and attack me *and* the mother with the children.

12 For You said, 'I will surely treat you well, and make your descendants as the sand of the sea, which cannot be numbered for multitude.'"

13 So he lodged there that same night, and took what came to his hand as a present for Esau his brother:

14 two hundred female goats and twenty male goats, two hundred ewes and twenty rams,

15 thirty milk camels with their colts, forty cows and ten bulls, twenty female donkeys and ten foals.

16 Then he delivered *them* to the hand of his servants, every drove by itself, and said to his servants, "Pass over before me, and put some distance between successive droves."

17 And he commanded the first one, saying, "When Esau my brother meets you and asks you, saying, 'To whom do you belong, and where are you going? Whose *are* these in front of you?'

18 then you shall say, 'They *are* your servant Jacob's. It *is* a present sent to my lord Esau; and behold, he also *is* behind us.'"

19 So he commanded the second, the third, and all who followed the droves, saying, "In this manner you shall speak to Esau when you find him;

20 and also say, 'Behold, your servant Jacob *is* behind us.'" For he said, "I will appease him with the present that goes before me, and afterward I will see his face; perhaps he will accept me."

21 So the present went on over before him, but he himself lodged that night in the camp.

9 And Jacob said, "O God of my father Abraham and God of my father Isaac, O Lord who said to me, 'Return to your country and to your kindred, that I may do you good,'

10 I am not worthy of the least of all the deeds of steadfast love and all the faithfulness that you have shown to your servant, for with only my staff I crossed this Jordan, and now I have become two camps.

11 Please deliver me from the hand of my brother, from the hand of Esau, for I fear him, that he may come and attack me, the mothers with the children.

12 But you said, 'I will surely do you good, and make your offspring as the sand of the sea, which cannot be numbered for multitude.'"

13 So he stayed there that night, and from what he had with him he took a present for his brother Esau,

14 two hundred female goats and twenty male goats, two hundred ewes and twenty rams,

15 thirty milking camels and their calves, forty cows and ten bulls, twenty female donkeys and ten male donkeys.

16 These he handed over to his servants, every drove by itself, and said to his servants, "Pass on ahead of me and put a space between drove and drove."

17 He instructed the first, "When Esau my brother meets you and asks you, 'To whom do you belong? Where are you going? And whose are these ahead of you?'

18 then you shall say, 'They belong to your servant Jacob. They are a present sent to my lord Esau. And moreover, he is behind us.'"

19 He likewise instructed the second and the third and all who followed the droves, "You shall say the same thing to Esau when you find him,

20 and you shall say, 'Moreover, your servant Jacob is behind us.'" For he thought, "I may appease him with the present that goes ahead of me, and afterward I shall see his face. Perhaps he will accept me."

21 So the present passed on ahead of him, and he himself stayed that night in the camp.

32:1–2 The angels of God met him. The Hebrew verb *paga'* "met" indicates the surprising and aggressive character of an encounter (cf. Judg 8:21; 1 Sam 22:17–18; 1 Kgs 2:25) that Jacob did not expect, the same experience as at Bethel (see 28:11). The common language suggests that Jacob is confronted with the same two groups of "angels" he had seen in his dream at Bethel, "ascending and descending" (28:12), hence the name he gives to that place **Mahanaim**, meaning "two camps" (32:2). Mahanaim is situated at the east of the Jordan on the border between the territories of the half-tribe of Manasseh and the tribe of Gad (Josh 13:26–30). The place was used as a capital by Ishbosheth, Saul's son (2 Sam 2:8), and for a time by David (2 Sam 17:24, 27) and Solomon (1 Kgs 4:14). The word also refers to a mystical dance; its choreography may have evoked the "two camps" of Jacob's dream (Song 6:13 [7:1]).[594]

32:3–6 Jacob's first move is to send **messengers** (32:3)[595] to Esau with the intention of impressing him by displaying his wealth, thus gaining his favor (32:5). However, Esau is presented as ruling **the land of Seir, the country of Edom** (32:3 [4]), indicating that Esau had already begun to dispossess the Horites who previously dwelt there (Deut 2:12), suggesting his military power. The report Jacob receives from his messengers of Esau coming with **four hundred men** (32:6) confirms this notion of a mighty Esau and frightens Jacob (32:7).

32:7 Jacob was ... distressed. Jacob's distress (*tsarah*) inspires the prophet Jeremiah regarding the dreadful condition of Israel in exile (Jer 30:7). Yet, beyond this particular event, the language of the prophet clearly suggests that he views the future eschatological Day of the Lord (cf. Zeph 1:14–18).[596] Daniel also applies the same expression, referring to "distress," "trouble" (*tsarah*), to the time of the end (Dan 12:1; cf. Matt 24:15, 21). Jacob's distress derives from two causes. The first is horizontal and is related to his brother. The second is vertical and relates to God.

32:8 Jacob's first concern is with his brother, to whom he sends two companies of messengers. This initiative is a strategic operation to safeguard the second camp: in the event that the first camp is attacked, the second camp will have time to escape. This method also contains a profound lesson. In parallel to the "two camps of angels," whose function was to foster the relationship between earth and heaven, Jacob decides to send "two camps of messengers" to Esau. Jacob calls his two camps of human messengers by the same name "two camps" (32:7 [8] ESV), suggesting some type of connection between the angels he "met," who are the same as the angels of Bethel, and the messengers he "sent" to Esau. This connection teaches us that the vertical relationship (human-God) is related to the horizontal relationship (human-human). Jacob understands that, in order to recover his relationship with God, he must restore his relationship with his brother.

32:9–12 After performing his filial duty, Jacob turns to God and prays. Similar to his grandfather Abraham, Jacob implores God for help. Jacob directs his plea to God alone, for it is God who commanded that he should return to Canaan (32:9), the same God who promised to ensure his posterity (32:12). However, Jacob does not deserve God's attention and all that God has done on his behalf. Jacob refers to the

---

594 See Duane Garrett and Paul R. House, *Songs of Songs/Lamentations,* WBC 23B (Nashville: Thomas Nelson, 2004), 234.

595 These messengers are not the same as the heavenly messengers; otherwise the word would have been determined by the definite article ("the") implying the already mentioned "messengers" (32:1).

596 See G. L. Keown, P. J. Scalise, and T. G. Smothers, *Jeremiah 26–52,* WBC 27 (Dallas: Word Books Publisher, 1995), 93.

wonder of God's grace: **all the mercies and … all the truth … You have shown** (32:10). The two Hebrew words *khesed* "mercy" and *'emet* "truth" are the same words as those Abraham's servant used when he blessed God for having heard his prayer (24:17).

32:13–21 After praying, Jacob decides to **spend the night** there (32:13 [14] NIV). Jacob's experience at Mahanaim echoes his experience at Bethel. Both experiences occur at night. The same verb *lun* "lodged" will be used again at the end of this section, in inclusio (32:21 [22]). Following his prayer, Jacob is sufficiently confident to pause and camp for the night. However, before retiring, Jacob acts again. Thus, the text moves back and forth between prayer and action. Because Jacob is not naïve and his faith does not make him passive, he secures his camp. Jacob organizes wave after wave of gifts to be delivered to his brother Esau to **appease** him (32:20). The Hebrew verb *kpr* for "appease" means "to atone." The association with other words such as *minkhah* "present," a word referring to the offering (Lev 2:1–14), and *nasa' panim* "forgive" or "accept" attests to a religious perspective. The author suggests that Jacob has in mind his past reconciliation with God (32:22–32) as he attempts to reconcile himself with his brother (Matt 5:23).[597]

32:22–30 [23–31] The intriguing story of Jacob's encounter with God belongs to the account reporting the incident of Mahanaim and Jacob's preparation of the two camps (32:22–23 [23–24]). The encounter will occur suddenly and will evolve in three steps. Jacob is first confronted by a silent struggle with a mysterious man (32:24–25 [25–26]), followed by a dialogue between Jacob and this man in which the divine identity of the man is revealed (32:26–29 [27–30]), and concludes with Jacob alone, who applies the lesson of the encounter by naming the place and departing (32:30–32 [31–33]). The text reporting that story is shaped in the form of a chiastic structure (ABCB₁A₁):

A 32:22–23 [23–24]. Jacob crossed over (*'abar*), in the night, Jacob's children
   B 32:24–25 [25–26]. Jacob was left alone, encounter, see (*ra'ah*)
      C 32:26–29 [27–30]. Dialogue: "he said" (7x): Jacob
   B₁ 32:30 [32:31]. Jacob called, encounter, see (*ra'ah*)
A₁ 32:31–32 [32–33]. Jacob crossed over (*'abar*), sunrise, Israel's children

32:22–23 [23–24]. CROSSING THE JABBOK IN THE NIGHT

GEN 32:22–23 NKJV	GEN 32:22–23 ESV
22 And he arose that night and took his two wives, his two female servants, and his eleven sons, and crossed over the ford of Jabbok.	**22** The same night he arose and took his two wives, his two female servants, and his eleven children, and crossed the ford of the Jabbok.
23 He took them, sent them over the brook, and sent over what he had.	**23** He took them and sent them across the stream, and everything else that he had.

The note that Jacob **arose that night** (32:22) suggests that he was already in bed. Jacob decides to hide his family and separate them far from himself in order to keep them safe. Dinah is omitted because she will play no role in the genesis of the nation of Israel, which is the author's concern; note that she will not even be included in

---

597 See Wenham, *Genesis 16–50*, 292.

Jacob's benediction (49:1–27). The fact that Jacob sends his family over the river with **what he had** (32:23) indicates that he proceeds out of concern for his family, which he wants to spare in case of conflict with Esau. The Jabbok River, in eastern Canaan, which is currently called *Naher-es-Zerka* "blue river," flows into the Jordan, some twenty-five miles (forty kilometers) north of the Dead Sea.

32:24–25. WRESTLING WITH A MAN

GEN 32:24–25 NKJV	GEN 32:24–25 ESV
24 Then Jacob was left alone; and a Man wrestled with him until the breaking of day.	**24** And Jacob was left alone. And a man wrestled with him until the breaking of the day.
25 Now when He saw that He did not prevail against him, He touched the socket of his hip; and the socket of Jacob's hip was out of joint as He wrestled with him.	**25** When the man saw that he did not prevail against Jacob, he touched his hip socket, and Jacob's hip was put out of joint as he wrestled with him.

32:24 [25] Jacob remains alone because he wants to confront Esau alone, another strategy to prevent his brother from attacking him. Jacob surmises that the presence of his servants and the display of his wealth might have incited aggression and covetousness on the part of the men of Esau. However, Jacob's loneliness will serve the dramatic purpose of the next event. The story of the encounter begins with the phrase **a Man wrestled with him**, suggesting that it was the man who initiated the attack, which must have surprised Jacob. The anonymous qualification "a man" renders the mysterious identity of this person. No one knows who he is, including Jacob himself. This strange characteristic already suggests the transcendent nature of this man. Jacob will identify the man as God (32:30 [31]), as will the prophet Hosea (Hos 12:3–4). The simple qualification *'ish* "man" is a means of emphasizing his human individuality (cf. "each," 10:5 ESV) and functions as a contrast with divinity (32:28 [29]; cf. Isa 2:11, 17; Num 23:19; Hos 11:9). The same language will be used by Isaiah in his description of the Suffering Servant (Isa 53:3). That God takes human form to relate to humans is not unheard of (18:1, 17; Judg 6:11; 13:3). The same term, *'ish* is used by Daniel to designate the heavenly High Priest (Dan 10:5; cf. Dan 8:11) and the "commander of the army," (*sar hatsaba'*) (Dan 8:11), an expression that designates the Lord Himself (Josh 5:14–15). Therefore, it is not surprising that rabbinic interpretations have identified the man fighting Jacob as Michael,[598] the awaited Messiah and the High Priest officiating in the heavenly Zion.[599] Along the same lines, Christian tradition has viewed this Angel as a type of Christ,[600] or the Lord Jesus Christ Himself.[601] Note that it is "the man" who wrestles; nothing is mentioned about Jacob responding. Jacob must have been overwhelmed by the attack and completely unprepared. The man **wrestled with him until the breaking of the day**, a temporal indication that the attack lasted the entire night, as long as it was dark, a hint at Jacob's strength and endurance. The Hebrew verb for "wrestle" (*'abaq*) introduces and concludes the narrative section (32:25 [26]) and is part of a play on words with *yabbok* (Jabbok) and *Ya'aqob* (Jacob). Thus, the sound of

---

598 Gen. Rab. 78:1–3. Tg. Ps.-J., ad loc.

599 See Zevahim 62a; Menahot 110a.

600 Augustine, *City of God*, 16.39.

601 Ellen G. White, PP 197.

"wrestling" is heard in the name of Jacob and in the name of the river where the wrestling occurred. Note also that the Hebrew word *'abaq* "wrestle" means "dust" (Deut 28:24; Ezek 26:10), which suggests the dynamic of wrestling and rolling around in the dust. The wrestling event resonated in the name of Jacob, in the dust, and in the river, giving the impression of having a cosmic effect (cf. Josh 7:26; cf. Hos 2:15).

32:25 [26] The "man" continues to initiate the attack. All the verbs of the verse convey the "man" as a subject. The information that **He saw that He did not prevail** contains a crucial theological lesson about God in His relationship with humans. God's weakness in His confrontation with humans is an expression of His grace and love and of the mystery of His incarnation to reach out to humans and save them. This impression of weakness is immediately contradicted by the man's next move: **He touched the socket … and the socket … was out of joint**. A simple touch is sufficient to produce the dislocation, suggesting a superhuman power. The place of the blow, **the socket of Jacob's hip,** is also intended. The Hebrew word for "hip" (*yerek*) refers to the loin or the thigh (47:29), which is identified as "the general region of the body that constitutes the seat of the procreative power."[602] The divine touch is thus an implicit blessing pointing to Jacob's descendants (46:26; Exod 1:5).

32:26–29. DIALOGUE: FROM JACOB TO ISRAEL

GEN 32:26–29 NKJV	GEN 32:26–29 ESV
26 And He said, "Let Me go, for the day breaks." But he said, "I will not let You go unless You bless me!"	**26** Then he said, "Let me go, for the day has broken." But Jacob said, "I will not let you go unless you bless me."
27 So He said to him, "What *is* your name?" He said, "Jacob."	**27** And he said to him, "What is your name?" And he said, "Jacob."
28 And He said, "Your name shall no longer be called Jacob, but Israel; for you have struggled with God and with men, and have prevailed."	**28** Then he said, "Your name shall no longer be called Jacob, but Israel, for you have striven with God and with men, and have prevailed."
29 Then Jacob asked, saying, "Tell *me* Your name, I pray." And He said, "Why *is* it *that* you ask about My name?" And He blessed him there.	**29** Then Jacob asked him, "Please tell me your name." But he said, "Why is it that you ask my name?" And there he blessed him.

32:26 [27] The narrative now becomes a dialogue between the "man" and Jacob. Similar to the wrestling, the dialogue is initiated by the "man," who asks Jacob to let him go. The intensive form (*piel*) of the verb *shalakh* that is used here literally means "send me away." The same verb in the same intensive form (*piel*) is used in Genesis 3 concerning Adam when God "sent him out of the garden of Eden" (3:23). Jacob is not merely supposed to let Him go. He must push Him away with intensity. For it is in his vital interest that the "man" goes. The next words of the "man" explain this urgency: **for the day breaks**. The concern of the "man" is that the light of the day will expose His face to Jacob, which will subsequently endanger Jacob's life, for no man can see God and live (32:30 [31]; Exod 33:20). Instead, Jacob clings to Him and repeats the same words; he will not "send" Him away: **I will not let You go unless You bless me**

---

602 Davidson, *The Flame of Yahweh*, 8.

(32:26). The phrase translated "let You go" is the same word "send" (*shalakh*), which described Jacob's sending his messengers to Esau (32:3 [4], 5 [6], 18 [19]). The use of the same word suggests that the two acts of "sending" pertain to the same "distress" of Jacob. Yet, the two acts of "sending" are essentially different. Jacob's first sending was related to his fear of his brother's approach. Jacob's second sending is related to his fear of God leaving and his anguished yearning to be blessed and be forgiven. The prophet Hosea interprets Jacob's struggle with God as an experience of prayer: "he struggled with the Angel and prevailed; he wept and sought favor from Him" (Hos 12:4). It is Jacob's faith that inspires his tenacious insistence (Luke 11:5–8). Jacob's reaction is reminiscent of the baby Jacob, who forced his destiny and grabbed his brother's heel (25:26); of the young Jacob, who forced his brother to sell his birthright to him (25:31); and of the adult Jacob, who cheated his father to obtain a blessing from him (27:19). Jacob now fully understands that he is in God's presence; and with the same tenacity and the same frame of mind, he will not let Him go until he receives the divine blessing. All of these lessons apply to God's people at the end of time:

> Jacob's night of anguish, when he wrestled in prayer for deliverance from the hand of Esau (Genesis 32:24–30), represents the experience of God's people in the time of trouble. Because of the deception practiced to secure his father's blessing, intended for Esau, Jacob had fled for his life, alarmed by his brother's deadly threats. After remaining for many years an exile, he had set out, at God's command, to return with his wives and children, his flocks and herds, to his native country. On reaching the borders of the land, he was filled with terror by the tidings of Esau's approach at the head of a band of warriors, doubtless bent upon revenge. Jacob's company, unarmed and defenseless, seemed about to fall helpless victims of violence and slaughter. And to the burden of anxiety and fear was added the crushing weight of self-reproach, for it was his own sin that had brought this danger. His only hope was in the mercy of God; his only defense must be prayer. Yet he leaves nothing undone on his own part to atone for the wrong to his brother and to avert the threatened danger. So should the followers of Christ, as they approach the time of trouble, make every exertion to place themselves in a proper light before the people, to disarm prejudice, and to avert the danger which threatens liberty of conscience.[603]

32:27 [28] The man's question **what is your name?** puts the finger precisely on Jacob's problem, his character, which is capsulated in his name **Jacob**, the man of the heel and of cheating (27:36), who attempts to control his destiny. **He said, Jacob**. This line marks the center of the structure. This is the fourth "said" of the seven.

32:28 [29] The man's response *ki 'im* translated "but" echoes Jacob's last words *ki 'im* "unless," suggesting that what will follow is the answer to Jacob's tenacious prayer and anguish about his guilt. The man gives him a name, another indication of His divine origin (16:11; 17:19); in this instance, God changes the original name to a new one, just as He did to Abram-Abraham (17:5; cf. Isa 62:2; Rev 2:17). In the Hebrew civilization, a name is supposed to express the identity of a person. Changing one's name means changing one's identity. Jacob's new name is **Israel**. This change of name is the sign that Jacob has been forgiven. The explanation of the "man" introduces a number of paradoxes: First, Jacob has wrestled with God and yet the "man" explains that Jacob wrestled also with men. Second, the name *Israel* literally means

---

603 Ellen G. White, GC 616.

"God fights," although His explanation affirms that it is Jacob who fights. Third, Jacob has just been hit by the "man," who dislocated his hip, and yet the narrative explains that it is Jacob who prevailed. All of these paradoxes convey important theological lessons. First, Jacob should understand that the quality of his relationship with God depends on the quality of his relationship with men (in this instance Esau) and vice versa. Second, the name "Israel," "God fights," reminds Jacob of his personal struggle, namely, that he must learn to let God fight for him, a lesson that will be repeated to Israel, "the Lord will fight for you" (Exod 14:13–14; Deut 1:30; Deut 3:22; Neh 4:20). Third, Jacob will prevail insofar as he will allow God to prevail over him, a principle that will be enunciated by Paul: "when I am weak, then I am strong" (2 Cor 12:10).

32:29 [30] Jacob must not have understood the meaning of God's message, since he returns to the same question, asking for the name of the "man." Asking for the name of the supernatural being amounts to asking for the control of His power. Ancient Egyptian myths recount the story of the goddess Isis who asked the secret name of the god *Re* in order to acquire control over him. Jacob's request for the name of God is therefore suspicious, just as was Moses' request for a name (Exod 3:13). In both cases, God responds by showing that the question is inappropriate. To Moses, who asks God to give His name, God ironically answers, "I will be who I will be" (Exod 3:14, lit. trans.), or "I am who I am" (the typical translation), a way of reminding Moses that it would be impossible to lock God in by a definition, for no one would be able to catch Him and control Him. Likewise, God dismisses Jacob's question and answers it with another question (see Matt 21:24; Luke 20:21). God subsequently blesses him anyway, thus responding to his more profound demand.

Jacob's present blessing experience with God parallels his early blessing experience with his father Isaac (27:18–29). On both occasions, Jacob forces the blessing; and on both occasions, Jacob experiences an identity crisis. The father asks, "Who are you?" (27:18), "Are you really my son?" (27:24), whereas the "man" asks, "What is your name?" (32:27). The father touches Jacob (27:21–22), the "man" touches Jacob (32:25). Both blessing stories involve food (27:2–14, 25; cf. 32:32). The stories are also presented in contrast to each other. In the story of his father's blessing, Jacob hides his identity (27:16, 19), whereas in this story, Jacob discloses his (32:27) and Jacob confronts his opponent (32:26). Jacob previously lied about his name and his intentions, whereas he now tells the truth and exposes himself. Whereas the Bethel experience fulfilled his name "Jacob" (27:36), he receives now a new name "Israel" (32:28). Whereas the story of his previous blessing began with the incapacity to "see" the visible (27:1), the Peniel experience ends with the capacity to "see" the invisible (32:30). Whereas the previous blessing story ends at sunset (28:11) and Jacob fleeing from home (28:5), the Peniel story ends with sunrise (32:26) and Jacob coming home (33:18–20). These parallels and contrasts convey a significant lesson: the same Jacob has become a new person and is headed for a new destiny.

32:30 [31]. PENIEL: FACE TO FACE

GEN 32:30 NKJV	GEN 32:30 ESV
30 So Jacob called the name of the place Peniel: "For I have seen God face to face, and my life is preserved."	**30** So Jacob called the name of the place Peniel, saying, "For I have seen God face to face, and yet my life has been delivered."

If Jacob cannot name God, he can at least name the place where God has appeared to him. **Peniel** means "the face of God," which does not identify this place as the "face of God" but Jacob's personal experience, namely, that he was confronted by God and survived. The use of the Hebrew expression *panim 'el panim* **face to face** does not mean that Jacob has actually seen the physical face of God. This expression is equivalent to seeing "the form of the Lord" (Num 12:8) and describes rather the experience of a direct encounter with God (Deut 5:4). Jacob associates his salvation to this encounter: **and my life is preserved**. The Hebrew verb *natsal* "preserve" refers to the deliverance from enemies and troubles (1 Sam 12:21; Prov 19:19) but may also have the connotation of a spiritual salvation from sin and guilt (Pss 39:9; 119:170).

32:31–32. JACOB-ISRAEL AT SUNRISE

GEN 32:31–32 NKJV	GEN 32:31–32 ESV
31 Just as he crossed over Penuel the sun rose on him, and he limped on his hip.	**31** The sun rose upon him as he passed Penuel, limping because of his hip.
32 Therefore to this day the children of Israel do not eat the muscle that shrank, which *is* on the hip socket, because He touched the socket of Jacob's hip in the muscle that shrank.	**32** Therefore to this day the people of Israel do not eat the sinew of the thigh that is on the hip socket, because he touched the socket of Jacob's hip on the sinew of the thigh.

32:31 [32] The last scene is grandiose and paradoxical. While the sun rises, a sign of victory over the night, a sign of the new day and a new era, Jacob limps on his hip. Jacob's wrestling ends with a final lesson: his victory lies in his being crippled.

"Not until he fell crippled and helpless upon the breast of the covenant angel did Jacob know the victory of conquering faith and receive the title of a prince with God."[604] While in the light the "man" is no longer present (cf. 32:26), Jacob being crippled is the only visible trace left of his passage. The story has eschatological overtones. The only other occurrences of the rare term *tsala'* "limp" appear are used again by the prophets to refer to the lame of the last days who will constitute God's remnant.

32:32 [33] That Jacob was hit at the organ generator of life serves as a reason for dietary prohibition. The children of Israel should not **eat the muscle that shrank, which is on the hip socket**. The meaning of the Hebrew expression *gid hannasheh* "muscle that shrank" or "the sinew of the thigh" (ESV) is unclear. Scholars have suggested that the word *nasheh* is related to the Akkadian *nishu*, meaning "human," "life." The phrase *gid hannasheh* "sinew of the thigh" (ESV) would, then, refer to the life-producing sinew.[605] This interpretation is consistent with other dietary restrictions that forbid the consumption of blood, for life is in the blood (9:4). This practice is therefore more than a mere reminder of the story of Jacob; whereas it recalls that biblical episode, and with it, its theological lessons, it also draws the meat eater's attention to the fundamental principle of the sacredness of life. The event at Peniel recalls an important theological lesson of the book of Genesis: the God who blesses is the God who creates (see 1:22, 28; 2:3).

---

604 Ellen G. White, MB 62.

605 Stanley Gervitz, "Of Patriarchs and Puns: Joseph at the Fountain, Jacob at the Ford," *HUCA* 46 (1975): 53; cf. S. H. Smith, "'Heel' and 'Thigh': The Concept of Sexuality in the Jacob-Esau Narratives," *VT* 40 (1990): 468.

JACOB RETURNS THE BLESSING TO ESAU (33:1–17)

From his encounter with God, Jacob moves to his encounter with his brother. After twenty years, Esau will finally meet with Jacob. Esau had certainly heard of Jacob's return, since he was heading in his direction along with four hundred men, obviously with the intention of fulfilling his oath to kill him (27:41). Yet, against all expectations, Esau runs to embrace Jacob and the two brothers reconcile. Esau accepts Jacob's gifts. They then depart from each other in peace and will not meet again, except for a brief moment at the burial of their father (35:29). Jacob's preceding encounter with God prepared him for his encounter with Esau. The three-part structure of the text reflects this intention to relate the two encounters. The central section (33:5–15) connects the face of God with the face of Esau (33:10) and God's grace to Jacob (33:5, 11) with Esau's grace to Jacob (33:8, 10, 15). This central section, which is composed of five rounds of dialogue between Jacob and Esau, is enveloped by two narrative sections: one in prelude, before telling the story of the encounter (33:1–5), and one in postlude, after telling the story of their separation from each other (33:16–17). Thus, we have the following structure:

Prelude
> Jacob lifted his eyes (33:1)
> Esau lifted his eyes (33:5a)

Dialogues
> Esau said (33:5b)—Jacob said (33:5c)
> Esau said (33:8)—Jacob said (33:8)
> **Esau said (33:9)—Jacob said (33:10–11)**
> Esau said (33:12)—Jacob said (33:13)
> Esau said (33:15)—Jacob said (33:15)

Postlude
> Esau returned (33:16)
> Jacob journeyed (33:17)

33:1–5A. PREPARING TO MEET

GEN 33:1–5A NKJV	GEN 33:1–5A ESV
1 Now Jacob lifted his eyes and looked, and there, Esau was coming, and with him were four hundred men. So he divided the children among Leah, Rachel, and the two maidservants.	**1** And Jacob lifted up his eyes and looked, and behold, Esau was coming, and four hundred men with him. So he divided the children among Leah and Rachel and the two female servants.
2 And he put the maidservants and their children in front, Leah and her children behind, and Rachel and Joseph last.	**2** And he put the servants with their children in front, then Leah with her children, and Rachel and Joseph last of all.
3 Then he crossed over before them and bowed himself to the ground seven times, until he came near to his brother.	**3** He himself went on before them, bowing himself to the ground seven times, until he came near to his brother.

4 But Esau ran to meet him, and embraced him, and fell on his neck and kissed him, and they wept.	4 But Esau ran to meet him and embraced him and fell on his neck and kissed him, and they wept.
5a And he lifted his eyes and saw the women and children,	5a And when Esau lifted up his eyes and saw the women and children,

33:1–2 The phrase **lifted his eyes and looked, and there** (*wayyiss'a … 'eynaw wayyar' wehinneh*) (33:1; cf. 33:5a) is typical for introducing the theophany (see the commentary on 18:2), thus anticipating the association of Esau with God, which will reach its climax in the central section. The vision of Esau's approach is therefore loaded with hopeful prospect. However, Esau is accompanied by four hundred men, a vision that contradicts the preceding impression. Jacob immediately separates his camp from himself and divides the camp into three groups, from the least cherished to the most cherished: the servants first, then Leah, then Rachel with Joseph, who is the only child whose name is mentioned.

33:3 This time, however, Jacob changes his strategy with regard to his position. Instead of putting himself behind the companies, as he did previously (32:17, 19, 21), Jacob decides to precede his camp (33:3a) and initiates approaching Esau. However, he does not immediately confront Esau. He approaches him progressively in a dramatic fashion. He bows himself to the ground seven times while moving forward, until he comes near Esau, but remains at a distance from him, still bowing to the ground. Jacob's present position ironically recalls his father's blessing, "nations bow down to you" (27:29). Jacob's seven genuflections echo the seven blessings he had received from his father (see 27:27b–29), as if he desired to repair history and return to Esau the blessing he had stolen from him. The Jacob after Peniel differs from the Jacob who had left Beersheba some twenty years before (28:10). Humbled by God at the ford of Jabbok, the limping Jacob has lost his arrogance and his ambition to be the greatest. Jacob has become Israel. He is no longer the legitimate heir, not even the brother, to Esau who calls him **my brother** (33:9). Jacob continues to call him **my lord** (33:8, 13–15; cf. 32:4–5, 18) and identifies himself as **his servant** (33:5; cf. 32:4, 18, 20).

33:4 Then Esau runs. The form of the Hebrew verb *wayyarots* **ran**, with its consecutive *waw*, suggests that Esau's reaction was prompted by the preceding scene. Four verbs describe Esau's movement to Jacob: **ran … embraced … fell … kissed**. The fifth verb, **wept**, reunites Esau and Jacob. No more pride, no more claim, only the emotion of love. Such a denouement was unexpected. Esau's tough soldiers and Jacob's trembling servants do not understand. No one can make sense of this dramatically sudden turn of events. However, God may have forewarned Esau in a dream, just as He did with Abimelech and Laban (20:3–7; cf. 31:24).[606]

---

606 Mathews, *Genesis 11:27–50:26*, 567. Cf. Ellen G. White, "While Jacob was wrestling with the Angel, another heavenly messenger was sent to Esau. In a dream, Esau beheld his brother for twenty years in exile from his father's house; he witnessed his grief at finding his mother dead; he saw him encompassed by the hosts of God. This dream was related by Esau to his soldiers, with the charge not to harm Jacob, for the God of his father was with him" (PP 198).

33:5B–15. SPEAKING TO EACH OTHER

GEN 33:5B–15 NKJV	GEN 33:5B–15 ESV
5b and said, "Who *are* these with you?" So he said, "The children whom God has graciously given your servant."	**5b** he said, "Who are these with you?" Jacob said, "The children whom God has graciously given your servant."
6 Then the maidservants came near, they and their children, and bowed down.	**6** Then the servants drew near, they and their children, and bowed down.
7 And Leah also came near with her children, and they bowed down. Afterward Joseph and Rachel came near, and they bowed down.	**7** Leah likewise and her children drew near and bowed down. And last Joseph and Rachel drew near, and they bowed down.
8 Then Esau said, "What *do* you *mean by* all this company which I met?" And he said, "*These are* to find favor in the sight of my lord."	**8** Esau said, "What do you mean by all this company that I met?" Jacob answered, "To find favor in the sight of my lord."
9 But Esau said, "I have enough, my brother; keep what you have for yourself."	**9** But Esau said, "I have enough, my brother; keep what you have for yourself."
10 And Jacob said, "No, please, if I have now found favor in your sight, then receive my present from my hand, inasmuch as I have seen your face as though I had seen the face of God, and you were pleased with me.	**10** Jacob said, "No, please, if I have found favor in your sight, then accept my present from my hand. For I have seen your face, which is like seeing the face of God, and you have accepted me.
11 Please, take my blessing that is brought to you, because God has dealt graciously with me, and because I have enough." So he urged him, and he took *it*.	**11** Please accept my blessing that is brought to you, because God has dealt graciously with me, and because I have enough." Thus he urged him, and he took it.
12 Then Esau said, "Let us take our journey; let us go, and I will go before you."	**12** Then Esau said, "Let us journey on our way, and I will go ahead of you."
13 But Jacob said to him, "My lord knows that the children *are* weak, and the flocks and herds which are nursing *are* with me. And if the men should drive them hard one day, all the flock will die.	**13** But Jacob said to him, "My lord knows that the children are frail, and that the nursing flocks and herds are a care to me. If they are driven hard for one day, all the flocks will die.
14 Please let my lord go on ahead before his servant. I will lead on slowly at a pace which the livestock that go before me, and the children, are able to endure, until I come to my lord in Seir."	**14** Let my lord pass on ahead of his servant, and I will lead on slowly, at the pace of the livestock that are ahead of me and at the pace of the children, until I come to my lord in Seir."
15 And Esau said, "Now let me leave with you *some* of the people who *are* with me." But he said, "What need is there? Let me find favor in the sight of my lord."	**15** So Esau said, "Let me leave with you some of the people who are with me." But he said, "What need is there? Let me find favor in the sight of my lord."

33:5b–8 Esau subsequently asks two questions regarding the companies that surround Jacob. Esau's first question concerns the newcomers who press around Jacob, his servants, his wives, and his children who arrive successively (33:5–7). Jacob limits his answer to his children, tactfully avoiding the reference to his wives from Padan Aram, who were associated with the reason for Jacob's flight from home (28:2). Jacob does not boast about his acquisitions, which he attributes to the grace of God

(33:5). Esau's second question concerns the company Jacob had sent before Peniel to Esau as a gift to him (32:18). Jacob's answer refers here also to grace. The intention of this **present** (*minkhah*) is "grace" (*khen*): **to find favor** (*khen*) **in the sight of my lord** (33:8). Note the play on words in *khen* "grace," which resonates in the word *minkhah* "present," and recalls what God has "graciously given" (*khanan*) to Jacob (33:5) and Jacob's experience at "God's camp" (*makhaneh*) (32:2). The grace Jacob is seeking from Esau is related to the grace he received from God.

33:9–11 We reach the center of the section, the third of the five rounds of dialogue; this literary feature signals that this section is the most important, the central one of the biblical passage. To Esau's reluctance to accept the present (33:9), Jacob responds by explicitly connecting his relationship with him to his relationship with God: **I have seen your face as though I had seen the face of God** (33:10). It is that argument that convinces Esau to accept Jacob's present (33:11), a sign that he is willing to reconcile with his brother. Jacob has seen the "face of God" (Peniel) in the face of Esau. Jacob's experience with Esau is a second Peniel, the first Peniel preparing for the second Peniel. This evocation of God is reinforced by the use of the verb *ratsah* **pleased**, a technical verb that belongs to religious language, referring to the sacrifice or the worship that is "pleased," "accepted," of God (Lev 22:27; Amos 5:22). Jacob's encounter with God has helped him in his encounter with his brother, and his reconciliation with his brother will affect his relationship with God. The chapter ends with the report that Jacob erected an altar, which he called **El Elohe Israel** (33:20), meaning "God, the God of Israel." For the first time, Jacob acknowledges El as his own God. Jacob had previously referred to God only as his fathers' God, never as his God.[607] Jacob has come to understand that his love of God and his love of his brother are dependent on each other. Jesus infers this unique theological lesson from the Scriptures: " 'You shall love the Lord your God with all your heart, with all your soul, and with all your mind.' This is the first and great commandment. And the second is like it: 'You shall love your neighbor as yourself.' On these two commandments hang all the Law and the Prophets" (Matt 22:37–40).

33:12–15 The fourth and fifth dialogues between Jacob and Esau focus on preparing for the departure, as the vocabulary attests: **take our journey ... let us go ... I will go ... drive ... go on ahead ... lead on ... pace ... come ... leave**. Again, it is Esau who engages the dialogue. Esau desires to help and graciously proposes to Jacob that he lead the way (33:12) and provides people to accompany and protect Jacob's companies (33:15). Yet, Jacob turns down both offers (33:13, 15). Jacob's last remark **let me find favor in the sight of my lord** (33:15) suggests that he is still not completely confident and fears potential mischief. However, he appeals for grace, "favor" (*khen*) on the part of Esau. The dialogue between the two brothers ends then, with this note of grace.

33:16–17. DEPARTING

GEN 33:16–17 NKJV	GEN 33:16–17 ESV
16 So Esau returned that day on his way to Seir.	**16** So Esau returned that day on his way to Seir.
17 And Jacob journeyed to Succoth, built himself a house, and made booths for his livestock. Therefore the name of the place is called Succoth.	**17** But Jacob journeyed to Succoth, and built himself a house and made booths for his livestock. Therefore the name of the place is called Succoth.

---

607 Cf. Borgman, *Genesis*, 150.

The two brothers depart from each other. The construction of the phrases and the vocabulary reporting the two moves suggest a stark contrast between the two departures. Whereas, for Esau, the verb precedes the subject, *wayyashob 'esaw* **Esau returned** (33:16), for Jacob, the subject precedes the verb, *wey'aqob nasa'* **Jacob journeyed** (33:17). The conjunction *waw* "and" preceding Jacob is also a *waw* of opposition (disjunctive *waw*), and the two propositions should therefore have been rendered: "Esau returned, but Jacob journeyed." This contrast is also present in the semantics of the verbs. Whereas Esau "returned" (*wayyashob*), implying a definite place of origin, Jacob "journeyed" (*nasa'*), implying an open direction. The same contrast appears in the names. The name **Seir**, meaning "hairy," is a familiar name for Esau: the "hairy" (25:25). Seir is well known as the place of Esau. However, **Succoth** is a new name invented by Jacob (33:17) and expresses a transitory condition. Similar to the Succoth of the Exodus route (Exod 12:37), of which it should not be confused, the Succoth of Jacob is a place that was not designed to be a permanent settlement for Jacob. The Hebrew word *sukkah* refers to a covered booth that serves temporary purposes (2 Sam 11:11; Jonah 4:5) and applies to the booths, the "tabernacles," Israel built in the wilderness, an event that was commemorated in the Feast of *Sukkot*, the Feast of Tabernacles (Lev 23:33–43). Furthermore, the two places indicate opposite directions. According to the findings of archaeological excavations, Succoth should be identified with the modern Tell Deir 'Alla,[608] which is located approximately two miles (three kilometers) north of the Jabbok River, whereas Seir is located in the south. Therefore, the two brothers head in two opposite directions. They will never reside together at the same place (36:6–7).

33:18–20. JACOB IN SHECHEM

GEN 33:18–20 NKJV	GEN 33:18–20 ESV
18 Then Jacob came safely to the city of Shechem, which *is* in the land of Canaan, when he came from Padan Aram; and he pitched his tent before the city.	**18** And Jacob came safely to the city of Shechem, which is in the land of Canaan, on his way from Paddan-aram, and he camped before the city.
19 And he bought the parcel of land, where he had pitched his tent, from the children of Hamor, Shechem's father, for one hundred pieces of money.	**19** And from the sons of Hamor, Shechem's father, he bought for a hundred pieces of money the piece of land on which he had pitched his tent.
20 Then he erected an altar there and called it El Elohe Israel.	**20** There he erected an altar and called it El-Elohe-Israel.

As soon as Jacob leaves Esau and his four hundred men and reaches his first place of destination, a new threat looms. To this point, Jacob has been struggling as an exile. Now, for the first time, Jacob is exposed to the troubles of settling. Similar to Isaac at Gerar with Abimelech (26:1–33), Jacob is tempted at Shechem to find accommodation with the natives of the land of Canaan. Following the tensions of exile, Jacob aspires for peace. The Hebrew word *shalem* **safely** (33:18), which marks his first step in the land, contains the idea of *shalom* "peace" (see JPS: "in peace"). Jacob is tempted by peace with the inhabitants of Canaan. He purchases a parcel of land from the inhabitants (33:19) and erects **an altar there** as if

---

608 See H. J. Franken, "The Excavation at Eeir 'Alla in Jordan With 16 Plates," *VT* 11 (1960): 361–372; cf. the testimony of the Jerusalem Talmud (*y. Sheb* 9.2).

he wanted to also secure his settling from a religious perspective. Yet this peace is dangerous.

34:1–31. THE RAPE OF DINAH

At the core of the text is one of the most sordid incidents of the Genesis stories. Dinah, Jacob's one-and-only daughter, is raped by the Hivite Shechem. Amidst her brothers' fury, Shechem and his father attempt to negotiate a marriage between Shechem and Dinah. Dinah's brothers pretend to agree to the marriage under the condition that all the males of the city become circumcised. Shechem and his father present the case to the men of the city, arguing that they will all benefit from the deal. After all of the men are circumcised, Dinah's brothers force their way into their homes, kill all of them, and plunder their houses. The narration of these events suggests ambivalence. The characters are ambiguous, not totally right or totally wicked. They all seemingly act out of good faith. Even their crimes are justified and appear to be acts of righteousness. The sensual Shechem, who violates Dinah, is also the loving man who wants to repair and is ready to undergo circumcision for love. Simeon and Levi who lie, kill, and plunder are also those who defend God's commandments, promote circumcision, and resist intermarriage. As for Jacob, he is troubled and frightened. Yet, he responds to his sons' crime with a puzzling and embarrassing silence. The ambivalence of the story has been reflected in Jewish and Christian interpretation and explained by the critics as an indication of different sources. However, this ambivalence is precisely the mark of authenticity of that story. Its actors are real and bring to the plot their own contradiction. God will find His way through the confusion. The problem is the same as in the troubling story of Jacob cheating for the blessing of his father, and its lesson still strikes today in the life of religious men and women. When humans take God's place and insist on shaping their existence with their own hands at the expense of God's commandments, the result is problematic, even if the will of God is ultimately fulfilled. The text ends significantly with a question posed by Dinah's brothers seeking justification for their crime, a question without answer and where God is absent: **should he treat our sister like a harlot?** (34:31). We may perform God's will and be zealous for Him, and yet be totally disconnected from Him. When the mission for God supersedes the reason for that mission—namely, the presence of God in our lives—then the end, the kingdom of God, is used to justify the means, our lies, and our crimes.

The narratives reporting the crimes, the rape of Dinah by Shechem the Hivite (34:1–7) and the killing by the sons of Jacob (34:24–29), interact with the dialogues (34:8–19, 20–23, 30–31).

34:1–7. THE SEDUCTION OF DINAH

GEN 34:1–7 NKJV	GEN 34:1–7 ESV
1 Now Dinah the daughter of Leah, whom she had borne to Jacob, went out to see the daughters of the land.	**1** Now Dinah the daughter of Leah, whom she had borne to Jacob, went out to see the women of the land.
2 And when Shechem the son of Hamor the Hivite, prince of the country, saw her, he took her and lay with her, and violated her.	**2** And when Shechem the son of Hamor the Hivite, the prince of the land, saw her, he seized her and lay with her and humiliated her.

3 His soul was strongly attracted to Dinah the daughter of Jacob, and he loved the young woman and spoke kindly to the young woman.

3 And his soul was drawn to Dinah the daughter of Jacob. He loved the young woman and spoke tenderly to her.

4 So Shechem spoke to his father Hamor, saying, "Get me this young woman as a wife."

4 So Shechem spoke to his father Hamor, saying, "Get me this girl for my wife."

5 And Jacob heard that he had defiled Dinah his daughter. Now his sons were with his livestock in the field; so Jacob held his peace until they came.

5 Now Jacob heard that he had defiled his daughter Dinah. But his sons were with his livestock in the field, so Jacob held his peace until they came.

6 Then Hamor the father of Shechem went out to Jacob to speak with him.

6 And Hamor the father of Shechem went out to Jacob to speak with him.

7 And the sons of Jacob came in from the field when they heard *it*; and the men were grieved and very angry, because he had done a disgraceful thing in Israel by lying with Jacob's daughter, a thing which ought not to be done.

7 The sons of Jacob had come in from the field as soon as they heard of it, and the men were indignant and very angry, because he had done an outrageous thing in Israel by lying with Jacob's daughter, for such a thing must not be done.

This is the only biblical passage that involves Dinah, who had only been mentioned briefly at birth and, unlike her brothers, did not receive any etymological explanation regarding her name (29:21). In addition, she was omitted from the eleven sons sent across the Jabbok (32:22 [23]). Therefore, the author was seemingly mindful of the following troubling story when referring to Dinah.

34:1 The author identifies Dinah as **the daughter of Leah** (34:1), a most peculiar way of introducing a woman (cf. 36:39), and not as **the daughter of Jacob**, as perceived by Shechem (34:3; cf. 34:5). This unusual introduction implies her connection with Levi and Simeon, her full-blooded brothers, and thus prepares the reader for the rest of the story, anticipating the violent reaction of her brothers. The word **daughter** reappears in the typical phrase **daughters of the land**, which denotes contempt and reprobation, designating the women Jacob was not supposed to associate with (27:46). That Dinah **went out to see** (34:1) is also laden with suspicion. The problem was not so much that Dinah "went out," for she was not confined to her home and was free to go out, as Rebekah was (24:16). The problem was her intention **to see**. In the text, this verb "see" by Dinah corresponds to the same verb "see" by Shechem the Hivite: "Dinah … went out to *see*" (34:1), "Shechem … *saw* her" (34:2). This echo between the two verbs "see" suggests that Dinah's excursion may have been more than an innocent promenade. The Hebrew expression *lir'ot* "to see" could also be read *lehira'ot* "to be seen," and thus contain the double sense of "seeing" and being "seen."[609] The similarity of language ("daughters," "saw," "took") between this passage and the Genesis account of the intermarriage between the "sons of men" and the "daughters of God" (6:2) anticipates the disapproved outcome of the plot. The verb "went out" also recalls Leah's approach to Jacob with the intention of sleeping with him (30:16).

34:2–3 The consequence of her move, her sexual encounter with Shechem, and the additional information that Shechem **loved the young woman and spoke kindly to the young woman** (34:3) may support the idea that their encounter was more

---

609 See b. Sanhedrin 4b.

than accidental and was even premeditated.[610] The date ended, however, as rape (34:2), as indicated by the verb *'anah* "humiliate" (ESV), which characterizes the shame following inappropriate sexual intercourse (Deut 22:23–24).

34:4 Shechem's brief and direct request denotes the impulsive character of a spoiled child who is accustomed to getting what he wants from his father. Note the contemptuous, anonymous *hayyaldah* **this young woman** (ESV, NIV: "this girl") to designate her, in contrast to the author, who calls her *na'arah* (34:3), also translated "young woman" (NKJV).

34:5–7 Jacob does not seemingly care about Dinah's safety, her personal pain, or even her moral guilt but instead has ceremonial concerns: **Jacob heard that he had defiled Dinah** (34:5). The Hebrew word *tame'* "defiled" refers to ceremonial uncleanness (Lev 15:32; Num 5:3). When Jacob learns of the incident, he is confused and stunned into silence: **Jacob held his peace** (34:5 NASB: **kept silent**), which contrasts with the reaction of the sons of Jacob, who **were grieved and very angry** (34:7). The author's viewpoint is clearly conveyed by qualifying the case as **a disgraceful thing in Israel … a thing which ought not to be done** (34:7). From the author's perspective, Jacob's sons are more sensitive to the evil action than is Jacob, who remains silent. Had Jacob responded adequately and joined his sons' indignation, he might have tempered their anger and perhaps avoided their crime. Jacob's silence is thus suspect, betraying cowardice, lack of conscience, or even indifference, since Dinah is only Leah's daughter.

34:8–19. THE AGREEMENT OF CIRCUMCISION

GEN 34:8–19 NKJV	GEN 34:8–19 ESV
8 But Hamor spoke with them, saying, "The soul of my son Shechem longs for your daughter. Please give her to him as a wife.	**8** But Hamor spoke with them, saying, "The soul of my son Shechem longs for your daughter. Please give her to him to be his wife.
9 And make marriages with us; give your daughters to us, and take our daughters to yourselves.	**9** Make marriages with us. Give your daughters to us, and take our daughters for yourselves.
10 So you shall dwell with us, and the land shall be before you. Dwell and trade in it, and acquire possessions for yourselves in it."	**10** You shall dwell with us, and the land shall be open to you. Dwell and trade in it, and get property in it."
11 Then Shechem said to her father and her brothers, "Let me find favor in your eyes, and whatever you say to me I will give.	**11** Shechem also said to her father and to her brothers, "Let me find favor in your eyes, and whatever you say to me I will give.
12 Ask me ever so much dowry and gift, and I will give according to what you say to me; but give me the young woman as a wife."	**12** Ask me for as great a bride price and gift as you will, and I will give whatever you say to me. Only give me the young woman to be my wife."
13 But the sons of Jacob answered Shechem and Hamor his father, and spoke deceitfully, because he had defiled Dinah their sister.	**13** The sons of Jacob answered Shechem and his father Hamor deceitfully, because he had defiled their sister Dinah.
14 And they said to them, "We cannot do this thing, to give our sister to one who is uncircumcised, for that *would be* a reproach to us.	**14** They said to them, "We cannot do this thing, to give our sister to one who is uncircumcised, for that would be a disgrace to us.

---

610 This thesis is suggested by the Midrash Gen. Rab. 80:1.

15 But on this *condition* we will consent to you: If you will become as we *are*, if every male of you is circumcised,

16 then we will give our daughters to you, and we will take your daughters to us; and we will dwell with you, and we will become one people.

17 But if you will not heed us and be circumcised, then we will take our daughter and be gone."

18 And their words pleased Hamor and Shechem, Hamor's son.

19 So the young man did not delay to do the thing, because he delighted in Jacob's daughter. He *was* more honorable than all the household of his father.

15 Only on this condition will we agree with you—that you will become as we are by every male among you being circumcised.

16 Then we will give our daughters to you, and we will take your daughters to ourselves, and we will dwell with you and become one people.

17 But if you will not listen to us and be circumcised, then we will take our daughter, and we will be gone."

18 Their words pleased Hamor and Hamor's son Shechem.

19 And the young man did not delay to do the thing, because he delighted in Jacob's daughter. Now he was the most honored of all his father's house.

Although no answer is recorded from Jacob to Hamor, who had approached him to speak to him (34:6), Hamor and Shechem speak to the sons of Jacob and hear from them.

34:8–12 Both Hamor and Shechem handle the marriage project as a business transaction. Whereas Hamor refers to the general advantage of intermarriage, which will boost trade between the two parties (34:9–10), Shechem focuses on the more particular interest of Jacob's family; in regard to the customary dowry (*mohar*) (Exod 22:17 [16]), he generously invites them to name their own price (34:11) and offers extra money as a gift (34:12).

34:13–19 Unlike Jacob, who is silent to Hamor's request, the sons of Jacob answer Shechem and Hamor. However, their answer is deceitful (34:13). Although they seemingly consent to the Hivites' proposal, they are, in fact, preparing a trap for them. First, they pretend that the only reason they cannot comply with them is their uncircumcised state (34:14). They notably never refer to the crime Hamor committed against their sister as a problem. In their argument, they resist Shechem's request not because he raped Dinah but because he is uncircumcised. The only obstacle they see is of a ritual order. Thus, they turn the Abrahamite ritual of circumcision, a sign of the covenant with God, into a tribal identification. They will give Dinah to Shechem only on the condition that all males are circumcised (34:15). The sons of Jacob establish a theology for these godless people. Of course, this nonreligious language fits the mentality of Hamor and Shechem, who do not feel religiously bound by this ritual (34:18). Shechem is particularly happy and wants to comply immediately (34:19). The comment that Shechem was **more honorable than all the household of his father** (34:19) is intriguing. Judah will use a similar language of appreciation regarding Tamar, "she has been more righteous than I" (38:26), and this language will characterize Noah who was "perfect in his generations" (6:9 KJV; cf. 1 Chr 4:9). This judgment from the author suggests that Shechem may have been redeemable or indicates the degree of depravity of the remaining population. That Shechem, who committed this iniquity, is deemed better than all the other men of the city suggests the gravity of the moral condition of its inhabitants, which may appeal for God's judgment, thus implicitly justifying the acts of chastisement by Jacob's sons.

34:20–23. THE AGREEMENT OF INTERMARRIAGE

GEN 34:20–23 NKJV	GEN 34:20–23 ESV
20 And Hamor and Shechem his son came to the gate of their city, and spoke with the men of their city, saying:	**20** So Hamor and his son Shechem came to the gate of their city and spoke to the men of their city, saying,
21 "These men *are* at peace with us. Therefore let them dwell in the land and trade in it. For indeed the land is large enough for them. Let us take their daughters to us as wives, and let us give them our daughters.	**21** "These men are at peace with us; let them dwell in the land and trade in it, for behold, the land is large enough for them. Let us take their daughters as wives, and let us give them our daughters.
22 Only on this *condition* will the men consent to dwell with us, to be one people: if every male among us is circumcised as they *are* circumcised.	**22** Only on this condition will the men agree to dwell with us to become one people—when every male among us is circumcised as they are circumcised.
23 *Will* not their livestock, their property, and every animal of theirs *be* ours? Only let us consent to them, and they will dwell with us."	**23** Will not their livestock, their property and all their beasts be ours? Only let us agree with them, and they will dwell with us."

Hamor and Shechem plead their case to the men of the city (34:20) and propose that they intermarry (34:21) and they be circumcised, without referring to the actual reason for their request (Shechem's desire and mistake); their only motivation is their economic interests and a one-way benefit. Hamor and Shechem suggest to the men of the city that, by undergoing such a procedure, they will be able to acquire all the possessions of Jacob's family (34:23).

34:24–29. THE SLAUGHTER OF SHECHEM

GEN 34:24–29 NKJV	GEN 34:24–29 ESV
24 And all who went out of the gate of his city heeded Hamor and Shechem his son; every male was circumcised, all who went out of the gate of his city.	**24** And all who went out of the gate of his city listened to Hamor and his son Shechem, and every male was circumcised, all who went out of the gate of his city.
25 Now it came to pass on the third day, when they were in pain, that two of the sons of Jacob, Simeon and Levi, Dinah's brothers, each took his sword and came boldly upon the city and killed all the males.	**25** On the third day, when they were sore, two of the sons of Jacob, Simeon and Levi, Dinah's brothers, took their swords and came against the city while it felt secure and killed all the males.
26 And they killed Hamor and Shechem his son with the edge of the sword, and took Dinah from Shechem's house, and went out.	**26** They killed Hamor and his son Shechem with the sword and took Dinah out of Shechem's house and went away.
27 The sons of Jacob came upon the slain, and plundered the city, because their sister had been defiled.	**27** The sons of Jacob came upon the slain and plundered the city, because they had defiled their sister.
28 They took their sheep, their oxen, and their donkeys, what *was* in the city and what *was* in the field,	**28** They took their flocks and their herds, their donkeys, and whatever was in the city and in the field.

29 and all their wealth. All their little ones and their wives they took captive; and they plundered even all that *was* in the houses.

29 All their wealth, all their little ones and their wives, all that was in the houses, they captured and plundered.

34:24 The men of the city naïvely agree to circumcision and obediently do as recommended by Hamor, the chief of the tribe. The expression that refers to them, **all who went out of the gate of his city**, which is used twice in the verse (34:24), indicates their profession; as farmers, they would "go out of the city" to work in the fields. Hamor and Shechem would then be the lords of the district, whom the men of the city were to serve and obey. The memory of this peculiar demand has been preserved in the folklore of Israel and has inspired a humorous proverb: "Shechem falls in love and the peasant gets circumcised."[611]

34:25 The third day after circumcision is considered by Jewish tradition to be the most delicate moment of the wound.[612] This is precisely the day Simeon and Levi chose to attack the men of the city, who were, then, the most vulnerable (cf. Josh 5:8). Exactly why only Simeon and Levi, who were not the only full-blooded brothers born of Leah, were involved in the aggression is unclear. What about Reuben and Judah, who were born of the same mother and belonged to the same first series of births (29:31–35)? This is not the only instance when the brothers disagree. Another incident will ally Judah and Reuben against the other brothers to defend Joseph (37:21, 26; 42:22). However, the cruel temperament of Simeon (42:24) and the zealous character of the tribe of Levi (Exod 32:26–28), which will be manifested in later stories, may explain their association in this massacre. The "going out" (*yatsa'*) of the attackers responds to the "going out" (*yatsa'*) of Dinah, just as the "taking" (*laqakh*) of the swords and of Dinah by Simeon and Levi responds to the "taking" (*laqakh*) of Dinah by Shechem (34:2), suggesting the spirit of "eye for eye, tooth for tooth" (Exod 21:24) that inspired the revenge.

34:26 The special mention of Hamor and Shechem indicates the focus of the aggression. The information that Dinah was taken from Shechem's house suggests that either Dinah had chosen to take refuge in his house, fearing her family's anger, or that she was sequestered. In either case, her being there was inappropriate and justified the family's reaction.

34:27–29 The mention of **the sons of Jacob** instead of the specific "Simeon and Levi" suggests that these are more than the two brothers, as was the case previously (34:7, 11, 13). The fact that their coming is described as intervening **upon the slain** (34:27), that is, after the killing, reinforces that impression because it implies that not all the sons of Jacob were the direct agents of the slaughter. The plunder of the city is therefore a combined act of all the brothers. The irony is that the desire expressed by the men of the city, namely, that all the livestock and property of Jacob's family will be theirs (34:23), is now reversed (34:28). Instead of Jacob's women being theirs, as planned, and already implemented in Dinah, it is now their wives who are taken captive (34:29).

611 Gen. Rab. 80:8.
612 y. Shabbat 19:4; Gen. Rab. 80:9.

34:30–31. JACOB'S TROUBLE

GEN 34:30–31 NKJV	GEN 34:30–31 ESV
30 Then Jacob said to Simeon and Levi, "You have troubled me by making me obnoxious among the inhabitants of the land, among the Canaanites and the Perizzites; and since I *am* few in number, they will gather themselves together against me and kill me. I shall be destroyed, my household and I."	**30** Then Jacob said to Simeon and Levi, "You have brought trouble on me by making me stink to the inhabitants of the land, the Canaanites and the Perizzites. My numbers are few, and if they gather themselves against me and attack me, I shall be destroyed, both I and my household."
31 But they said, "Should he treat our sister like a harlot?"	**31** But they said, "Should he treat our sister like a prostitute?"

This is the first dialogue that is reported between Jacob and his sons. Jacob specifically addresses Simeon and Levi and blames them for the **trouble** they brought to his family and himself (34:30). The same Hebrew word *'akhor* "trouble" is used to characterize the trouble generated by the sin of Achan (Josh 7:24–26; cf. Hos 2:15 [17]). Jacob is concerned about his safety and worries that the entire clan will be annihilated by the very population he was supposed to replace (2 Sam 21:5), which may compromise the inheritance of the Promised Land (Lev 18:26–28). Jacob complains that he cannot live "in peace" with his neighbors, the Canaanites, as he longed for upon his arrival (33:18). This is precisely the problem that angers Simeon and Levi. The elect people are not supposed to compromise with the customs of their neighbors, to make covenants and intermarry with them (Deut 7:1–6). Jacob is ready to compromise with the inhabitants of Shechem and settle in the land at the expense of the Law of God, whereas Dinah is treated as a harlot. The Levitical principle may be implied in the brothers' charge against their father: "Do not prostitute your daughter, to cause her to be a harlot, lest the land fall into harlotry, and the land become full of wickedness" (Lev 19:29). The manner in which the two brothers insist on **our sister** (34:31) instead of "your daughter" is a veiled reproach to Jacob, emphasizing their parental relation with Dinah in contrast to his own. Jacob's bias against Leah's daughter is thus subtly denounced by her brothers. Jacob is threatened by potential conflicts from outside, from the surrounding peoples, and inside, by his own fractured family.

JACOB'S SONS, STRUGGLE AT BIRTH (35:1–26)

The background of recent events reveals a great need of repair. Jacob's faith in God and his hope in the Promised Land as well as the fruitfulness of his seed have been shaken. God speaks to Jacob. Until now, God was only briefly evoked (33:10) and worshipped (33:20) and was totally absent during the Dinah episode. This is the first time Jacob hears God speaking to him since his experience at Peniel (cf. 32:22–32). Although Jacob dwells in Bethel, God reminds him of his two dramatic encounters with Him, Bethel and Peniel. The evocation of Bethel reminds Jacob of the God who answered him in the day of distress and prompted him to eliminate idolatry in his camp. In response to this revelation, Jacob builds an altar (35:1–7). The evocation of Peniel reminds Jacob of his new name, Israel, and reinforces the divine promise of fruitfulness and of the inheritance of the Promised Land. Also in response to this theophany, Jacob erects a pillar and renews the Bethel covenant (35:9–15). When Jacob leaves Bethel, a new son is born to him (35:16–20), thus completing the twelve sons who founded the twelve tribes of Israel (35:22b–26). The positive reports of theophanies and births alternate with the negative reports of deaths and evil (indicated in italics in the structure below): the death of Deborah, Rebekah's nurse (35:8); the death of Rachel, while giving birth to Jacob's last son (35:19–20); and, coincidently, the shameful act of Jacob's first son (35:21–22a), which entailed his name being stricken from the genealogical record (1 Chr 5:1). The structure of this passage, which is sandwiched between the slaughter of Shechem (34:25–31), concluding the preceding section, and the death of Isaac (35:27–29), introduces the following section, as follows:

(*Slaughter of Shechem* [34:25–31])
Evocation of Bethel: Burying of idols, building of altar (35:1–7)
Death of Deborah (35:8)
Evocation of Peniel (35:9–15)
Death of Rachel/Birth of Jacob's last son (35:16–20)
Shameful act of Jacob's first son (35:21–22a)
List of Jacob's twelve sons (35:22b–26)
(*Death of Isaac* [35:27–29])

35:1–7. EVOCATION OF BETHEL

GEN 35:1–7 NKJV	GEN 35:1–7 ESV
1 Then God said to Jacob, "Arise, go up to Bethel and dwell there; and make an altar there to God, who appeared to you when you fled from the face of Esau your brother."	**1** God said to Jacob, "Arise, go up to Bethel and dwell there. Make an altar there to the God who appeared to you when you fled from your brother Esau."
2 And Jacob said to his household and to all who *were* with him, "Put away the foreign gods that *are* among you, purify yourselves, and change your garments.	**2** So Jacob said to his household and to all who were with him, "Put away the foreign gods that are among you and purify yourselves and change your garments.
3 Then let us arise and go up to Bethel; and I will make an altar there to God, who answered me in the day of my distress and has been with me in the way which I have gone."	**3** Then let us arise and go up to Bethel, so that I may make there an altar to the God who answers me in the day of my distress and has been with me wherever I have gone."
4 So they gave Jacob all the foreign gods which *were* in their hands, and the earrings which *were* in their ears; and Jacob hid them under the terebinth tree which *was* by Shechem.	**4** So they gave to Jacob all the foreign gods that they had, and the rings that were in their ears. Jacob hid them under the terebinth tree that was near Shechem.
5 And they journeyed, and the terror of God was upon the cities that *were* all around them, and they did not pursue the sons of Jacob.	**5** And as they journeyed, a terror from God fell upon the cities that were around them, so that they did not pursue the sons of Jacob.
6 So Jacob came to Luz (that *is*, Bethel), which *is* in the land of Canaan, he and all the people who *were* with him.	**6** And Jacob came to Luz (that is, Bethel), which is in the land of Canaan, he and all the people who were with him,

7 And he built an altar there and called the place El Bethel, because there God appeared to him when he fled from the face of his brother.	**7** and there he built an altar and called the place El-bethel, because there God had revealed himself to him when he fled from his brother.

The voice of God resonates with the tone of the two sons' rebuke: a**rise, go up to Bethel and dwell there** (35:1). Jacob should not have dwelt at Shechem among the Canaanites. Twice Jacob is urged to get up, just as Lot was twice urged to "escape" (19:17). The verb "arise" (*qum*) is reinforced by the verb "go up" (*'lh*). Jacob must return to Bethel, where he encountered the God who reassured him when he fled from Esau and taught him the lesson from the idolaters of Babel who sought to replace God with themselves. God urges Jacob and his family to **put away the foreign gods** (35:2). These were idols and other religious articles that had been taken in the plunder of the Shechemites, in addition to the household gods stolen by Rachel (31:19, 32). In a highly symbolic gesture, Jacob buries them under the terebinth of Shechem (35:4). Shechem becomes, then, a place of death. The Shechemites are buried with their gods. Jacob's family subsequently purifies itself. The camp, contaminated from the defilement (*tame'*) of Dinah (34:5, 13, 27) and the defilement of the slaughter (cf. Num 31:19–20), is now purified (*tahar*). As a result, Jacob is protected by God. Immediately following the massacre of Shechem, the people of the **cities that were all around them** (35:5b), who might have been tempted to retaliate, are neutralized by God. Because of **the terror of God**, no one dares attack Jacob (35:5a). The language points to the holy war that characterizes the possession of the Promised Land (Exod 23:27; Deut 2:25; Josh 2:9) and is indicative of God's awful presence. Jacob is now ready to approach God and worship Him. When Jacob arrives at Bethel, everyone is with him. The mention that **he and all the people who were with him** emphasizes the restored unity of the camp that had been disrupted by the Dinah incident. At Bethel, Jacob builds an altar and worships the God of Bethel (35:7). The new name **El Bethel** "God of Bethel" that he gives to the place emphasizes more the God who revealed Himself than the place where God was revealed.

35:8. DEATH OF DEBORAH

GEN 35:8 NKJV	**GEN 35:8 ESV**
8 Now Deborah, Rebekah's nurse, died, and she was buried below Bethel under the terebinth tree. So the name of it was called Allon Bachuth.	**8** And Deborah, Rebekah's nurse, died, and she was buried under an oak below Bethel. So he called its name Allon-bacuth.

Deborah, Rebekah's nurse, must have been sent to Jacob by Rebekah to encourage him to leave Padan Aram (cf. 27:45).[613] The name given to the site of her burial **Allon Bachuth** means "oak of weeping," testifying to Jacob's pain and mourning at the death of the nursemaid who took care of him as a child.

That Deborah's death is noted, whereas the death of Rebekah, her mistress, is omitted, is surprising to most commentators, who attribute this anomaly to Rebekah's deceptive act against Isaac. However, this argument is undermined with the observation that Rebekah is not the only one whose death is overlooked. The Scriptures

---

613 See Rashi in Miqraot Gedolot, ad loc.

are also silent about Leah's death, although she gave birth to the most spiritually important tribes of Israel (Judah, Levi), whereas Rachel's death is emphasized (35:18–20). In fact, the author elucidates the deaths of both Deborah and Rachel because both deaths took place in the course of Jacob's journey to the Promised Land. These intentional pauses mark the turning point, the transition from the past life in exile to the future prospects of the Promised Land.

35:9–15. EVOCATION OF PENIEL

GEN 35:9–15 NKJV	GEN 35:9–15 ESV
9 Then God appeared to Jacob again, when he came from Padan Aram, and blessed him.	**9** God appeared to Jacob again, when he came from Paddan-aram, and blessed him.
10 And God said to him, "Your name *is* Jacob; your name shall not be called Jacob anymore, but Israel shall be your name." So He called his name Israel.	**10** And God said to him, "Your name is Jacob; no longer shall your name be called Jacob, but Israel shall be your name." So he called his name Israel.
11 Also God said to him: "I *am* God Almighty. Be fruitful and multiply; a nation and a company of nations shall proceed from you, and kings shall come from your body.	**11** And God said to him, "I am God Almighty: be fruitful and multiply. A nation and a company of nations shall come from you, and kings shall come from your own body.
12 The land which I gave Abraham and Isaac I give to you; and to your descendants after you I give this land."	**12** The land that I gave to Abraham and Isaac I will give to you, and I will give the land to your offspring after you."
13 Then God went up from him in the place where He talked with him.	**13** Then God went up from him in the place where he had spoken with him.
14 So Jacob set up a pillar in the place where He talked with him, a pillar of stone; and he poured a drink offering on it, and he poured oil on it.	**14** And Jacob set up a pillar in the place where he had spoken with him, a pillar of stone. He poured out a drink offering on it and poured oil on it.
15 And Jacob called the name of the place where God spoke with him, Bethel.	**15** So Jacob called the name of the place where God had spoken with him Bethel.

35:9–12 Jacob had heard God speaking to him, reminding him of the lesson of Bethel, the occasion for Jacob to recommit to the God who had **appeared** to him at Bethel (35:1). Jacob is now confronted **again** (35:9) with God appearing to him after the Bethel experience. This time, God situates Himself along the lines of the Peniel experience: God blesses Jacob and reminds him of his new name, Israel (35:9–10; cf. 32:28–29). God then unfolds the double promise that is inherent in Jacob's blessing. First, Jacob is blessed with the blessing of Abraham: he will be fruitful and will generate many nations (35:11; cf. 12:2–3; 17:6). Second, Jacob will inherit the land that was promised to Abraham and Isaac (35:12; cf. 12:7; 26:3).

35:13 The observation that **God went up from him in the place** suggests that Jacob's encounter with the Divine was not a subjective experience that had only taken place in his mind. The fact that God had to "go up from the place" implies that the coming down of God to Jacob and to this place was an objective and historical reality, just as it was in the case of Abraham (17:22). That God "went up" implies also that God came down, which is the prerequisite for human worship. Reversing the views of Babel, which promoted the upward movement of man to reach the divine status,

Bethel reminds us that, unless God comes down, humans will not meet Him.

35:14–15 The pillar that Jacob erects recalls the ladder he saw at Bethel. The verbs *yatsab* **set up** and the related word *matsebah* **pillar** echo the verbs *mutsab* "set up" and *nitsab* "stood," describing, respectively, the position of the ladder (28:12) and of God at its top (28:13). When Jacob builds this monument, which he calls Bethel (35:14), he considers Bethel; more precisely, he intends to fulfill the vow he had formulated some twenty-two years before while fleeing his father's house (28:22). The pouring of the drink offering (probably grape juice)[614] and of the oil was often associated with the burnt offering and the sacrifices as a worship and consecration ritual (Exod 29:38–41; Lev 23:12–13, 18; Num 6:13, 15, 17; 28:6–7). The grape juice symbolizes the blood of the sacrifice (Deut 32:14) and the oil symbolizes the Holy Spirit (1 Sam 10:1–6; Isa 61:1). Both symbols reflect the fundamental truth of Bethel, namely, that worship is made possible only through God's descent and incarnation.

35:16–20. DEATH OF RACHEL

GEN 35:16–20 NKJV	GEN 35:16–20 ESV
16 Then they journeyed from Bethel. And when there was but a little distance to go to Ephrath, Rachel labored *in childbirth*, and she had hard labor.	**16** Then they journeyed from Bethel. When they were still some distance from Ephrath, Rachel went into labor, and she had hard labor.
17 Now it came to pass, when she was in hard labor, that the midwife said to her, "Do not fear; you will have this son also."	**17** And when her labor was at its hardest, the midwife said to her, "Do not fear, for you have another son."
18 And so it was, as her soul was departing (for she died), that she called his name Ben-Oni; but his father called him Benjamin.	**18** And as her soul was departing (for she was dying), she called his name Ben-oni; but his father called him Benjamin.
19 So Rachel died and was buried on the way to Ephrath (that *is*, Bethlehem).	**19** So Rachel died, and she was buried on the way to Ephrath (that is, Bethlehem),
20 And Jacob set a pillar on her grave, which *is* the pillar of Rachel's grave to this day.	**20** and Jacob set up a pillar over her tomb. It is the pillar of Rachel's tomb, which is there to this day.

Immediately after God's departure from Bethel, Jacob left the place, heading to his father's house in Hebron. Three interrelated events mark this last step of his journey: the birth of his last son, the death of his wife while giving birth, and the shameful act of his first son.

The geographical location of the next event is precisely located a short distance from Ephrath (35:16), **that is, Bethlehem** (35:19; cf. Ruth 1:2; 4:11; 1 Sam 17:12; Matt 2:18), which is approximately five miles (eight kilometers) south of Jerusalem. This precise location emphasizes that this event occurred within the confines of the Promised Land. The birth of Jacob's last son was, then, lived as the first fulfillment of God's promise and the first sign of the promising future. The midwife's reassuring observation points strongly in that direction. Her words **do not fear** (*'al tir'y*) are the

---

614 Although the word *shekar* generally means "strong drink," it has been suggested that in particular cases, such as Deuteronomy 29:6 [5], Numbers 28:7, and Exodus 29:40, the word carries the idea of abundance rather than that of drunkenness (Song 5:1; cf. Hag 1:5–6) and refers therefore to "satisfying grape juice" rather than to fermented alcoholic drinks. See Robert P. Teachout, "The Use of 'Wine' in the Old Testament" (ThD diss., Dallas Theological Seminary, 1979), 213–214, 338–340.

same as God's reassuring words to Abraham "do not be afraid" (*'al tir'*), which also concern the future birth of a son (15:1; cf. 15:4–5). This is precisely the message that Jacob registered in the new name he gave to his son. Whereas the name Rachel gives to her son refers to her present sorrow, **Ben Oni** (*ben 'oni*, "son of my sorrow"), the name Jacob gives refers to the future. **Benjamin** (*ben yamin*) means more than "son of the right." Because the ancient Hebrews oriented the cardinal points while looking east (the place of their origin),[615] the word *yamin* "right" referred to the south (Ps 89:12 [13]). Therefore, the expression "son of the south" refers to Jacob's future arrival in the south and alludes to the fact that Benjamin is the only son of Jacob who was born in Canaan, which is located in the south when coming from Aram.[616] Rachel dies while giving birth to Benjamin (35:18) and is buried on the way to Ephrath (35:19); her tomb may be found "in the territory of Benjamin at Zelzah" (1 Sam 10:2). Jacob erects a pillar, in which the Hebrew phrase *'ad hayyom* **to this day** (35:20) implies the later time of the Exodus. For the people of that time, Rachel's tomb will serve as a sign testifying to the first possession of the land by Jacob.

35:21–22A. SHAMEFUL ACT OF JACOB'S FIRST SON

GEN 35:21–22A NKJV	GEN 35:21–22A ESV
21 Then Israel journeyed and pitched his tent beyond the tower of Eder.	**21** Israel journeyed on and pitched his tent beyond the tower of Eder.
22a And it happened, when Israel dwelt in that land, that Reuben went and lay with Bilhah his father's concubine; and Israel heard *about it*.	**22a** While Israel lived in that land, Reuben went and lay with Bilhah his father's concubine. And Israel heard of it.

35:21 The place of **the tower of Eder** seems to be synonymous with Mount Zion and Jerusalem (Mic 4:7–8), the place of Moriah where Abraham offered his son and where he received God's blessing and the promise of fruitfulness (22:17–18). This geographical precision should have refreshed Jacob's hope. Given this last son, Jacob has now reached the time of the fulfillment of God's promise.

35:22a That Reuben chooses this particular moment of the birth of Benjamin and the erection of the monument to Rachel to sleep with Bilhah, his father's concubine and the maidservant of Rachel (35:25; 30:3), is not an accident. Reuben's outrageous act resonates with the arrogant reaction of his two brothers toward their father Jacob on account of Dinah their sister (34:31). Reuben's shameful act aims to not only humiliate his father, with the implied intention to claim his leadership and thus to claim the inheritance (2 Sam 12:8, 11; 16:21–22), but to also defile the memory of Rachel and the birth of Benjamin as revenge for the contempt endured by his mother, Leah, because of Rachel (29:30–31), and the humiliation of his sister, Dinah. That Reuben is Jacob's and Leah's first son and that Dinah is Leah's last child may unconsciously also play a role in Reuben's resentment against Benjamin, Rachel's last son. Note that Reuben seems to repent later, evidenced by his concern about Joseph and his attempt to save him from his brothers (37:29–30). However, because of his sin, he will lose his leadership right as the firstborn (49:3–4). Because his second and third

---

615 Compare this with the Egyptians, who oriented the cardinal points while looking at the south, the place they believed to be their origin, and thus called the west *imn*, indicated by their right hand.

616 See Rashi in Miqraot Gedolot, ad loc.

brothers, Simeon and Levi, are also discounted from leadership because of their crime, this privilege and blessing will be inherited by their fourth brother, Judah (49:8–10). As for Jacob's reaction to the incident, the author limits his report to the simple note that **Israel heard about it** (35:22). Although Jacob is overwhelmed and distraught with pain and profound anger, he chooses not to retaliate. Jacob's apparent passivity is the paradoxical expression of his faith. Jacob trusts God that, despite this terrible attempt from his son to disturb the course of history, God's promise will be fulfilled. Jacob, who would have previously responded by fighting to subdue others, behaves now as if he is defeated, allowing God to fight for him. Thus, Jacob's new name, **Israel**.

35:22B–26. THE SONS OF JACOB

GEN 35:22B–26 NKJV	GEN 35:22B–26 ESV
22b Now the sons of Jacob were twelve:	**22b** Now the sons of Jacob were twelve.
23 the sons of Leah *were* Reuben, Jacob's firstborn, and Simeon, Levi, Judah, Issachar, and Zebulun;	**23** The sons of Leah: Reuben (Jacob's firstborn), Simeon, Levi, Judah, Issachar, and Zebulun.
24 the sons of Rachel *were* Joseph and Benjamin;	**24** The sons of Rachel: Joseph and Benjamin.
25 the sons of Bilhah, Rachel's maidservant, *were* Dan and Naphtali;	**25** The sons of Bilhah, Rachel's servant: Dan and Naphtali.
26 and the sons of Zilpah, Leah's maidservant, *were* Gad and Asher. These were the sons of Jacob who were born to him in Padan Aram.	**26** The sons of Zilpah, Leah's servant: Gad and Asher. These were the sons of Jacob who were born to him in Paddan-aram.

This lesson of faith reappears in the listing of the sons of Jacob. This listing of the sons according to their mother and the additional comment of **Reuben** as **Jacob's firstborn** (35:23) manifests the tension between the two lines of brothers. However, the precision of **twelve** (35:22b), which includes Benjamin and omits Dinah, transcends the recent troubles and affirms, instead, the twofold fulfillment of God's promise. The sons who were born in exile have all survived and finally reached their destination in the Promised Land. Benjamin is unexpectedly included among the twelve sons who were born in Padan Aram (35:26), although he was born near Ephrath (35:16–18), because he was still considered the result of the exilic condition: conceived in exile and born during the painful course of the journey.

DEATH OF ISAAC (35:27–29)

35:27–29. DEATH OF ISAAC

GEN 35:27–29 NKJV	GEN 35:27–29 ESV
27 Then Jacob came to his father Isaac at Mamre, or Kirjath Arba (that *is*, Hebron), where Abraham and Isaac had dwelt.	**27** And Jacob came to his father Isaac at Mamre, or Kiriath-arba (that is, Hebron), where Abraham and Isaac had sojourned.
28 Now the days of Isaac were one hundred and eighty years.	**28** Now the days of Isaac were 180 years.

29 So Isaac breathed his last and died, and was gathered to his people, *being* old and full of days. And his sons Esau and Jacob buried him.	**29** And Isaac breathed his last, and he died and was gathered to his people, old and full of days. And his sons Esau and Jacob buried him.

The report of the death of Isaac here, although the event will occur chronologically much later, plays a double function. First, it allows for the presence of Esau alongside Jacob, implying that the reconciliation between the two brothers did take place (cf. 25:7–9). Second, it serves as the introduction to the genealogy of Esau in order to remind us that Esau still remains Isaac's son, despite his disconnection from the messianic line.

35:27 Jacob's return to his father comes after thirty-six years of separation. Jacob lives twenty more years with his father until Isaac's death when Jacob is 120 years old (25:26).

Mamre. The addition of **Kirjath Arba (Hebron)** implies that Jacob's place of settlement is not precisely situated in those towns and suggests that the meditative Jacob prefers to settle somewhere far from the hustle and bustle of city life (cf. 25:27). The preeminence of the name "Mamre" before all others confirms that intention, since it elicits the religious memory of Abraham (13:18; 18:1).

35:28 At one hundred and eighty years, Isaac is the longest living patriarch. He lived longer than did his father Abraham, who died at the age of 175 years (25:7), and longer than did his son Jacob, who died at the age of 147 years (47:28). Isaac was still alive when, eight years after Jacob's arrival, he heard of the disappearance (or death) of Joseph. He died twelve years after that event.

35:29 The account of Isaac's death in many ways echoes that of his father. In both cases, the age at death is given (25:7; 35:28). The words describing their deaths are the same: *wayyigwa' wayyamot 'abraham* "Abraham breathed his last and died" (25:8); *wayyigwa' yitskhaq wayyamot* **Isaac breathed his last and died** (35:29). The same expression refers to their **old** age when they died: *zaqen usabea'* for Abraham (25:8), *zaqen usba'* for Isaac (35:29). For Abraham, as for Isaac, two sons bury them (25:9; 35:29). Both deaths take place near Mamre (25:9; 35:27–29), and both are characterized by the idiomatic expression **gathered to his people** (35:29b). All of these echoes suggest Isaac was buried at Machpelah, similar to his father and mother, although this detail is not recorded here (see though 49:31). Within these parallels, one distinct feature is apparent: the expression *besebah tobah* that describes Abraham as "contented" (TNK) when he dies (NKJV: "good old age") is absent for Isaac. This slight but significant difference may account for the fact that Isaac died without having heard of Joseph's survival.

THE GENEALOGY OF ESAU (36:1–43)

Just as the death of Abraham is followed by the genealogy of the other son, Ishmael (25:7–18), and then by the cycle of Jacob (25:19–35:26), the death of Isaac (35:27–29) is followed by the genealogy of the other son, Esau (36:1–43), and then by the cycle of Joseph (37:1–48:20). Similar to the line of Jacob/Israel (35:22–26), both lines of Ishmael and Esau branch out into twelve sons and tribes (17:20; 25:13–16; cf. 22:20–24). These parallels between the genealogical record of Israel and that of the two other brothers shows that both Ishmael and Esau have benefited from the Abrahamic blessing, thus anticipating the promise of the blessing of the nations through Abraham (12:3; 26:4). However, these genealogies are clearly distinct from the genealogies of the elect lines of Jacob and Isaac and belong to different literary sections. In addition, the genealogies of Ishmael and Esau develop outside the Promised Land, without any reference to divine involvement, whereas the genealogies of the elect line develop inside the Promised Land and are a part of God's salvation history (36:8; 37:1). These parallels and contrasts between the two destinies carry a crucial theological lesson: the particular history of God's people and the universal history of the nations are mysteriously related and both unfold under God's control.

GENEALOGY OF ESAU/EDOM: HISTORY, GEOGRAPHY, AND ARCHAEOLOGY
BY PAUL Z. GREGOR

STRUCTURE OF THE GENEALOGY OF ESAU

Esau's descendants (36:1–19)
    36:1–5. Esau's descendants in Canaan
    36:6–8. Esau's move out of Canaan
    36:9–14. Esau's descendants to third generation
    36:15–19. Chiefs of Edom
Seir's descendants (36:20–30)
Kings of Edom (36:31–43)

The genealogy of Edom (Esau) is recorded in two locations, one here (36:1–43), and another shorter version in 1 Chronicles 1:35–54. In both biblical passages, the information is similarly presented. The author of Genesis first provides a short account of what occurred at the time when Esau was in the land of Canaan (36:1–5), after which the reason for departure is presented (36:6–8). Verses 9–14 provide information on Esau's descendants up to the third generation. The first section ends with the list of chiefs who are already listed as Esau's grandsons in earlier verses. The second section of this chapter displays the genealogy of Seir the Horite (36:20–30) who lived in the land before Esau. The last section of this chapter provides an Edomite King List who reigned in that particular territory (36:31–43).

ESAU'S DESCENDANTS (36:1–19)

Based on wording found in the first and last verses of this section, it is obvious that this section should be regarded as one literary unit, even though the last line is slightly different from the first. While the first line opens with "These are the generations of Esau" (ESV), the last line starts with "These are the sons of Esau" (ESV). Both lines end with the same phrase "who is Edom."

36:1–5. ESAU'S DESCENDANTS IN CANAAN

GEN 36:1–5 NKJV	GEN 36:1–5 ESV
1 Now this *is* the genealogy of Esau, who is Edom.	**1** These are the generations of Esau (that is, Edom).
2 Esau took his wives from the daughters of Canaan: Adah the daughter of Elon the Hittite; Aholibamah the daughter of Anah, the daughter of Zibeon the Hivite;	**2** Esau took his wives from the Canaanites: Adah the daughter of Elon the Hittite, Oholibamah the daughter of Anah the daughter of Zibeon the Hivite,
3 and Basemath, Ishmael's daughter, sister of Nebajoth.	**3** and Basemath, Ishmael's daughter, the sister of Nebaioth.
4 Now Adah bore Eliphaz to Esau, and Basemath bore Reuel.	**4** And Adah bore to Esau, Eliphaz; Basemath bore Reuel;
5 And Aholibamah bore Jeush, Jaalam, and Korah. These *were* the sons of Esau who were born to him in the land of Canaan.	**5** and Oholibamah bore Jeush, Jalam, and Korah. These are the sons of Esau who were born to him in the land of Canaan.

36:1 The first line opens up with a clear statement that Esau and Edom should be considered as one entity. This motion is supported three more times in this chapter (36:8, 19, 43). The text is not clear as to when the identification of Esau with Edom came into existence, but it may have to do with something related to his unfortunate trade with Jacob for a bowl of red lentil stew.[617]

36:2–3 Here the text displays the names of Esau's three wives and also their origin. All three are labeled as Canaanite women, which reminds readers of Isaac's rejection of the local Canaanite girls as candidates to become Jacob's wife (28:1). Esau's choice of wives seems to have been purposely used to agonize his parents (26:34; 28:6). It is to be assumed the list provides the names of his wives as they were married to him.

Esau

Adah	Aholibamah	Basemath
Eliphaz	*Jeush, Jalam, Korah*	*Reuel*
Teman		*Nahath*
Omar		*Zerah*
Zepho		*Shammah*
Gatam		*Mizzah*
Kenaz		
Amalek		

36:2 **Adah** is the first wife of Esau. This name should not be confused with another lady with the same name who was the wife of Lamech (4:19), since Adah was a very common name throughout the ancient Middle East.[618] She was born to Elon the Hittite. Earlier, we are informed of a Hittite presence in the area (23:3–16). Whether they lived as a group settled in the land of Canaan or scattered as individual families among other tribes is not clear, but their presence in the land was

---

617 Mathews, *Genesis 11:27–50:26*, 640.

618 U. Hubner, "Adah," *ABD* 1:60.

unmistakable.

Aholibamah is the second wife of Esau and was the daughter of Anah and the granddaughter of Zibeon. Even though the text indicates that they were of Hivite origin, the same names with the same relations are presented to be of Horite origin (36:24). In fact, the Greek translation (Septuagint) uses the word "Horite" instead of "Hivite" for all three individuals here (36:2). Most likely a scribal error resulted in this confusion, but the author wanted to make it clear who she was since her father and grandfather were mentioned in relation to her origin. Therefore, Zibeon in verse 2 is the same Zibeon of verse 24 who was of Horite origin and lived in the area. Not much is known about this group of people. The biblical text is very sporadic, mentioning them from time to time but not to any extent to help in their identification. In addition to this, extrabiblical material is even less useful.[619]

36:3 Basemath is the third wife of Esau who was the daughter of Ishmael, Abraham's firstborn son by Hagar the Egyptian. Even though Ishmael was married to an Egyptian girl (21:21), it is also probable that he had other wives from Canaan, and it is through this line that Basemath was considered to be in the same category of "Canaanite women." To make sure that the reader is not confused about her origin, her brother's name is also mentioned, who was the firstborn of Ishmael (25:13).

The names of Esau's three wives in this list do not correspond entirely with already existing lists found in earlier texts. Names and origins of the first two wives of Esau were recorded in 26:34, while the last one was mentioned in 28:9. The list in chapter 36 gives the names of Esau's wives in this order: Adah/Aholibamah/Basemath, while in earlier texts these names are used: Judith/Basemath/Mahalath. It seems that only Basemath belonged to both lists while the others are different. The complication is even more evident when their origin is compared. While Adah was the daughter of Elon, Aholibamah was the daughter of Anah, and Basemath was the daughter of Ishmael. The earlier list indicates that Judith was the daughter of Beeri, Basemath was the daughter of Elon, and Mahalath was the daughter of Ishmael. It seems that Adah and Basemath have the same father (Elon), and they may be the same individual. Basemath and Mahalath also have the same father (Ishmael), so they too might be the same person. Aholibamah from the first list and Judith from the second have different fathers altogether.[620] The Scripture is full of references indicating individuals with two different names, such as Abraham/Abram, Jacob/Israel, Jethro/Reuel, to mention a few. In the same way, it is quite possible that Esau's wives and their fathers were known by two different names that were used in different lists for different purposes.

36:4 Eliphaz. Adah is listed as the first wife of Esau who provided him with his firstborn son Eliphaz (cf. 36:15). The most probable meaning of this name is "my god is Paz/strong."[621] One of Job's "counselors" was also named Eliphaz (Job 2:11).

Reuel. Even though Basemath/Mahalath was Esau's third wife, she bore him his second son Reuel, which means "friend of God." The name was popular in the Middle East and within Israel as well. A Gadite was named with the same name (Num 2:14) as well as a Benjamite (1 Chr 9:8). Moses' father-in-law had the same name (Exod 2:18).

---

619 To learn more about Horites, see F. W. Bush, "Horites," *ISBE* 2:756–757.

620 To find more information on a possible solution to this problem, see Hamilton, *Genesis 18–50*, 392.

621 Wenham, *Genesis 16–50*, 337. For further study on meaning of this name, see U. Hubner, "Eliphaz," *ABD* 2:471.

36:5 The second wife, Aholibamah, bore Esau three sons: Jeush, Jaalam, and Korah.

Jeush. The etymology of this word is uncertain, but it may derive from the verb *'eush* meaning "may (God) help/protect."[622] The name was well used among different tribes of Israel as well (1 Chr 7:10; 8:39; 23:10–11; 2 Chr 11:19).

Jaalam. This is a rare name with uncertain origins. No other individual was named with this name. It may be derived from *ya'el,* which refers to a mountain goat (Ps 104:18).[623]

Korah. This is the third son of Aholibamah and the fifth son of Esau. Its meaning "baldhead" is generally accepted among most scholars. It was a popular name among Israelites and used by different individuals (1 Chr 2:43; Ps 42:1). The most infamous one was a Levite who stirred up a rebellion against Moses and Aaron in the wilderness (Num 16–17).

These were the sons of Esau who were born in the land of Canaan before he moved to the country of Seir. It was a company of five sons, three wives, and Esau himself. Further, the text also suggests that Esau had daughters, but it does not indicate their number or their names. It is to be assumed that he had an abundant number of servants in his household since he inherited all the wealth from his father Isaac.

36:6-8. ESAU'S MOVE OUT OF CANAAN

GEN 36:6-8 NKJV	GEN 36:6-8 ESV
6 Then Esau took his wives, his sons, his daughters, and all the persons of his household, his cattle and all his animals, and all his goods which he had gained in the land of Canaan, and went to a country away from the presence of his brother Jacob.	**6** Then Esau took his wives, his sons, his daughters, and all the members of his household, his livestock, all his beasts, and all his property that he had acquired in the land of Canaan. He went into a land away from his brother Jacob.
7 For their possessions were too great for them to dwell together, and the land where they were strangers could not support them because of their livestock.	**7** For their possessions were too great for them to dwell together. The land of their sojournings could not support them because of their livestock.
8 So Esau dwelt in Mount Seir. Esau *is* Edom.	**8** So Esau settled in the hill country of Seir. (Esau is Edom.)

36:6-7 Although Esau vowed to kill his brother Jacob (27:41), he reconciled with him upon Jacob's return from Haran (33:4). This reconciliation resulted in a friendlier relationship between Israel and Edom. Although Moabites and Ammonites could not be included as part of Israel's assembly, even to the tenth generation (Deut 23:3), Edomites are viewed as Israel's brothers (Num 20:14; Deut 23:7). This friendly relationship might have been why the author of Genesis dedicated the entire chapter to the genealogy of Esau.

The reference to wives, children, members of his household, cattle, beasts, and property suggests that the separation will be complete without the possibility of returning. The land of Canaan is to be left forever, to leave room for his brother Jacob who will stay in the Promised Land. The departure seems to be voluntary where the

---

622 D. F. Roberts, "Jeush," *ISBE* 2:1056, and also E. A. Knauf, "Jeush," *ABD* 3:882.

623 *HALOT* 2:420.

two brothers departed from each other forever. Again the reader is reminded that Esau and Edom are the same individual and his new territory is now in Seir, which is later known in the text as the land of Edom.

36:8 Mount Seir. The Edomite mainland was located on an elevated plateau, which the Hebrew prophets described as a place where eagles built their nests (Jer 49:16; Obad 4). Its eastern and southern borders were never clear, although it has been suggested that Ras en-Naqb might have been the marker of its southern border,[624] whereas the Arabian Desert marked its eastern boundary. The northern border is much clearer and is traditionally understood to be Wadi el Hasa, or the biblical brook Zered, which marked the borderline between Moab and Edom. The western border was Wadi Araba, which separated Edom from Israel.

Because of its desert climate, rainfall is scarce, apart from the northernmost part of the Edomite territory around the brook Zered. This type of climate would encourage a nomadic lifestyle supported by sheep and goat herding. The main, and likely the only, significant trade route was the King's Highway (Num 20:17) connecting its northern and southern sections.[625] This was a lifeline that provided the Edomites with trade opportunities where they could exchange their goods with the caravans that moved up and down the territory.

36:9–14. ESAU'S DESCENDANTS TO THE THIRD GENERATION

GEN 36:9–14 NKJV	GEN 36:9–14 ESV
9 And this *is* the genealogy of Esau the father of the Edomites in Mount Seir.	**9** These are the generations of Esau the father of the Edomites in the hill country of Seir.
10 These *were* the names of Esau's sons: Eliphaz the son of Adah the wife of Esau, and Reuel the son of Basemath the wife of Esau.	**10** These are the names of Esau's sons: Eliphaz the son of Adah the wife of Esau, Reuel the son of Basemath the wife of Esau.
11 And the sons of Eliphaz were Teman, Omar, Zepho, Gatam, and Kenaz.	**11** The sons of Eliphaz were Teman, Omar, Zepho, Gatam, and Kenaz.
12 Now Timna was the concubine of Eliphaz, Esau's son, and she bore Amalek to Eliphaz. These *were* the sons of Adah, Esau's wife.	**12** (Timna was a concubine of Eliphaz, Esau's son; she bore Amalek to Eliphaz.) These are the sons of Adah, Esau's wife.
13 These *were* the sons of Reuel: Nahath, Zerah, Shammah, and Mizzah. These were the sons of Basemath, Esau's wife.	**13** These are the sons of Reuel: Nahath, Zerah, Shammah, and Mizzah. These are the sons of Basemath, Esau's wife.
14 These were the sons of Aholibamah, Esau's wife, the daughter of Anah, the daughter of Zibeon. And she bore to Esau: Jeush, Jaalam, and Korah.	**14** These are the sons of Oholibamah the daughter of Anah the daughter of Zibeon, Esau's wife: she bore to Esau Jeush, Jalam, and Korah.

36:9 The Edomites in Mount Seir. Not much is known about the Edomites outside of biblical records. No surviving written documents of any form are directly available from the Edomites to reflect their history and location. In addition to biblical texts, the Egyptians were seemingly interested in the region and made sporadic references to the people who occupied the land.

---

624 Mathews, *Genesis 11:27–50:26*, 639.

625 Yohanan Aharoni, *The Land of the Bible: A Historical Geography* (Philadelphia: Westminster, 1979), 54–57.

The earliest reference to Edom might have been found in *The Story of Sinuhe*, which came into existence during the nineteenth century BC.[626] In the story, Sinuhe was met by Ya'ush from the land of Kushu as he traveled from Egypt to Syria. Because the land of Kushu is generally understood to be located in the Transjordan, south of Moabite territory,[627] it is tempting to associate Ya'ush with Je'ush, who was one of the chiefs born to Esau by Aholibamah (36:5). Another reference to the land of Kushu (Edom) appears on a document known as the Brussels texts, which was composed one century after the Sinuhe text. The value of this document is that it speaks of chiefs of Kushu rather than of rulers or kings. However, the names found on this document are corrupted, and no connection could be made with any of the names found in the chapter.

Both documents suggest the land was occupied by pastoral nomads who were not ruled by a monarch, but rather by chiefs of clans. This is in harmony with the biblical text, which suggests that the Edomite society was based on clans and tribes.

Later, Egyptian records refer to the Edomite territory as the land of Shasu instead of the land of Kushu. Reference to the Shasu land and Seir might appear in the list of names found in a temple of Amenhotep III at Soleb but without certainty. In addition, Amarna correspondence may have reference to Seir.[628] More impressive reference to Edom comes from the nineteenth dynasty, which ruled Egypt between the thirteenth and eleventh centuries BC. Several inscriptions are undoubtedly dated to the time of Ramesses II. Of special interest is a stele found at Tell er-Ratâba in the eastern delta. In this stele, Ramesses claims the following:

> Making great slaughter in the land of Shasu
> He plunders their tells
> Slaying their (people) and building with towns bearing his name.[629]

The second line might give the impression that ancient cities were located in the land of Edom. Since no large centers can be dated to this period, it has been concluded that this inscription cannot refer to the land of Edom.[630] However, Kitchen's correction offers a new translation: "he plunders their (mountain) ridges."[631]

A second inscription has been found at Tanis on an obelisk where "Shasu land" is paralleled with the "mountain of Seir." A similar expression is found on a stela from Gebel Shaluf, which indicates a close relationship between Shasu and Seir.

In the Papyrus Anastasi VI document, the term "Edom" appears for the first time. The Edomites are again represented as a nomadic society coming to Egypt with their livestock. "We have finished with allowing the Shasu clansfolk of Edom to pass the fort of Merenptah … to keep them alive and to keep alive their livestock."[632]

---

626 By that time, Jacob had already returned from Haran to the land of Canaan and reconciled with his brother Esau. Soon after, Esau moved to Transjordan with his family, where his sons and grandsons were considered to be *chiefs* (36:9–19).

627 K. A. Kitchen, "The Egyptian Evidence on Ancient Jordan," in *Early Edom and Moab: The Beginning of the Iron Age in Southern Jordan,* ed. P. Bienkowski, SAM 7 (Sheffield: J. R. Collis, 1992), 21.

628 Letter 288:26.

629 Translation from K. A. Kitchen, "Some New Light on the Asiatic Wars of Ramesses II," *Journal of Egyptian Archaeology* 50 (1964): 66–67. The other two translations from the monuments of Ramesses II are from the same translator.

630 Kitchen, "Some New Light on the Asiatic Wars of Ramesses II," 66.

631 Kitchen, "The Egyptian Evidence on Ancient Jordan," 27.

632 *ANET*, 259.

The relationship between Egypt and the Edomites during the New Kingdom (eighteenth and nineteenth dynasties) was extremely hostile.[633] During the time of Merneptah, the hostility ceased to a certain degree because the Egyptians offered them shelter.

During the reign of Ramesses III, hostility seems to have existed again between the Edomites and the Egyptians, as attested by Papyrus Harris I. Apparently, the pharaoh plundered the territory, once again leaving the land waste. The text reads: "I destroyed the people of Seir among the Bedouin tribes. I razed their tents: their people, their property, and their cattle as well, without number, pinioned and carried away in captivity, as the tribute of Egypt."[634] These raids might have been the result of the Egyptian mining interest in the Wadi Arabah and Feinan area.[635]

The importance of these Egyptian documents shows the presence of Edomites in the land and that the population of the region was nomadic dwellers, living in tents. Even when kings are mentioned, they are actually tribal chiefs reigning over tribal entities rather than kings of a unified monarchy. Egyptian interest in the region throughout the centuries confirms the fact that the Edomite region was not a deserted wilderness prior to the Iron I period (1200 BC). Because of the nomadic structure of the society, few architectural remains are expected to be extant, which would pose a problem for this interpretation. Moreover, frequent military interventions support the assumption that the bonds of a tribal society might create adequate opposition and danger to the interests of Egypt.

36:10–14 The following verses provide the names of Esau's grandchildren through Eliphaz and Reuel (36:10). It seems that the sons of Jeush, Jaalam, and Korah, who were born to Esau by Aholibamah, are without descendants since they are not listed here. Later, we see that they were listed as "chiefs" (36:18), which clearly indicates that they were heads of their clans. The reason for not listing their children is not given in the text.

36:11 Teman is the first of five sons born to Eliphaz. While the name's etymology is not certain, its meaning is "south." The name may refer to a person, as is the case here, or a region that is recognized for its wisdom (Jer 49:7). Husham, the Edomite king, ruled in the region of the Temanites (36:34). Teman may also be associated with an important city, maybe even the capital of Edom,[636] which is identified by some to be Tawilan.[637] Eliphaz, one of Job's friends, resided in Teman (Job 2:11).[638]

Omar is a name that is basically unknown. It may mean "eloquent" or "lamb," and it may have derived from 'amar "to speak." The name was never used by any biblical personage.

Zepho, Gatam. Both names are not known outside this genealogy list. *Zepho* may mean, "view," "fortune," or possibly "ram." On the other side, *Gatam* may refer to "thin."

---

633 D. Redford, "Contact Between Egypt and Jordan in the New Kingdom: Some Comments on Sources," in *Studies in the History and Archaeology of Jordan* (Amman: Department of Antiquities of Jordan, 1982), 115–119.

634 *ANET*, 262.

635 E. A. Knauf, "Cultural Impact of Secondary State Formation: The Cases of the Edomites and Moabites," in *Early Edom and Moab: The Beginning of the Iron Age in Southern Jordan* ed. P. Bienkowski, SAM 7 (Sheffield: J. R. Collis, 1992), 49.

636 Roland de Vaux, "Temman, ville ou region d'Edom?" *RB* 76 (1969): 379–385.

637 E. A. Knauf, "Teman," *ABD* 6:347–348; P. Bienkowski, "Tawilan," *NEAEHL* 4:1446–1447.

638 It is not clear from the text if Teman in Job's case was a town or region.

Kenaz. It is not certain if this name refers to Kenizzite (15:9) or to a clan from Judah (Num 32:12). Reference to Kenizzites was found earlier in respect to their land, which will be taken away from them for the benefit of Abraham (15:19). It is possible that the Kenizzites were a group of people from Edom who joined with the tribe of Judah.[639]

36:12 Timna was a concubine of Eliphaz, and she gave birth to Amalek. She was the daughter of Seir the Horite and sister of Lotan (36:22). Timna is also the name of a region located in the southern section of Wadi Arabah. The area was very rich in copper. Evidence of copper mines is recorded in archaeological records and dates to the beginning of the Late Bronze period (ca. 1550 BC).[640] Additionally, Timna refers to a city known as Tel Batash.[641]

Amalek, born to Eliphaz by his concubine Timna, is the sixth and the last son of Eliphaz. The fact that Timna was only a concubine should disqualify Amalek from his ancestry.[642] The Amalekites were purely nomadic tribes mentioned numerous times in the Scriptures (Exod 17:8–16; Num 14:39–45; Deut 25:17–19; 1 Sam 15) as opposed to the Edomites who had a sedentary or seminomadic lifestyle.[643] The Amalekites constantly harassed the Israelites on their wilderness journey (Exod 17:8–16). Animosity between them and Israel almost brought them to extinction (1 Sam 15).

36:13 Nahath may mean "pure" or "rest."[644] It was used several times by the Levites (1 Chr 6:26; 2 Chr 31:13).

Zerah is the second son of Reuel, and his name means "dawning, shining." The same name is used in the Edomite King List (36:33) and also refers to a Cushite ruler (2 Chr 4:9). The name was popular among Israelites (Josh 7:1; Neh 11:24). Judah named one of his sons with the same name (38:30; 46:12). Clans among the tribes of Judah, Simeon, and Levi were recognized by the same name (Num 26:13, 20; 1 Chr 4:24; 6:21, 41). It is suggested that the name could be associated with an agricultural settlement in the land of Edom.[645]

Shammah. There have been many attempts to establish the origin of this name.[646] It may have derived from the verbs *shama'* "to hear" or *shamar* "to keep." The name was accepted in Israel, especially during the reign of King David. One of David's brothers was given such a name (1 Sam 16:9; 17:13) and so were two of his military heroes (2 Sam 23:11, 25).

Mizzah. This name is obscure and virtually unknown in biblical literature.

639 Jacob Milgrom, *Numbers* (Philadelphia: Jewish Publication Society, 1990), 391–392.

640 Ben-Yosef Erez et al., "A New Chronological Framework for Iron Age Copper Production at Timna (Israel)," *BASOR* 367 (2012): 31–71.

641 G. L. Kelm and A. Mazar, *Timnah: A Biblical City in Sorek Valley* (Winona Lake: Eisenbrauns, 1995); N. Paintz-Cohen and A. Mazar, *Timnah (Tel Batash) III: The Finds From the Second Millennium BCE* (Jerusalem: Institute of Archaeology, Hebrew University of Jerusalem, 2006).

642 Mathews, *Genesis 11:27–50:26*, 650.

643 For more information on the Amalekites, see. Paul Z. Gregor, "In Search of an Amalekite City," *NEASB* 55 (2010): 17–25.

644 Wenham, *Genesis 16–50*, 338.

645 E. A. Knauf and S. Maani, "On the Phonemes of Fringe Canaanite: The Case of Zerah-Udruh and Kamashalta," *UF* 19 (1987): 91–93.

646 *HALOT* 4:1554.

36:15–19. CHIEFS OF EDOM

GEN 36:15–19 NKJV	GEN 36:15–19 ESV
15 These *were* the chiefs of the sons of Esau. The sons of Eliphaz, the firstborn *son* of Esau, were Chief Teman, Chief Omar, Chief Zepho, Chief Kenaz,	**15** These are the chiefs of the sons of Esau. The sons of Eliphaz the firstborn of Esau: the chiefs Teman, Omar, Zepho, Kenaz,
16 Chief Korah, Chief Gatam, *and* Chief Amalek. These *were* the chiefs of Eliphaz in the land of Edom. They *were* the sons of Adah.	**16** Korah, Gatam, and Amalek; these are the chiefs of Eliphaz in the land of Edom; these are the sons of Adah.
17 These *were* the sons of Reuel, Esau's son: Chief Nahath, Chief Zerah, Chief Shammah, and Chief Mizzah. These *were* the chiefs of Reuel in the land of Edom. These *were* the sons of Basemath, Esau's wife.	**17** These are the sons of Reuel, Esau's son: the chiefs Nahath, Zerah, Shammah, and Mizzah; these are the chiefs of Reuel in the land of Edom; these are the sons of Basemath, Esau's wife.
18 And these *were* the sons of Aholibamah, Esau's wife: Chief Jeush, Chief Jaalam, and Chief Korah. These *were* the chiefs *who descended* from Aholibamah, Esau's wife, the daughter of Anah.	**18** These are the sons of Oholibamah, Esau's wife: the chiefs Jeush, Jalam, and Korah; these are the chiefs born of Oholibamah the daughter of Anah, Esau's wife.
19 These *were* the sons of Esau, who is Edom, and these *were* their chiefs.	**19** These are the sons of Esau (that is, Edom), and these are their chiefs.

Attempts were made to show that Amalek should be deprived of the privilege to be named as a "chief."[647] Justification for such attempts is mainly seen to show that there are twelve chiefs of Edom to match the twelve tribes of Jacob. However, the list names fourteen individuals with the role of "chief." One name, Korah, is mentioned twice and most likely is some kind of error. Then, to reduce the list from thirteen to twelve, it is convenient to eliminate Amalek due to his origin, since his mother was Timna, Eliphaz's concubine. Nevertheless, Amalek is named as a "chief" and indeed his clan continued to be recognized as such for a long time, while other chiefs were lost in time and erased from memory.

It is interesting to notice that there were ten chiefs coming from Esau's grandsons; six from his firstborn son Eliphaz and four from Reuel, his second son. Three other chiefs on the list come from his three sons who were born by his wife Aholibamah. The fact is that she was of Horite origin; and according to the Horite list, only sons of Seir were listed as chiefs, not his grandsons.

36:15 **These were the chiefs …** The word *'aluf* **chief(s)** is used forty-three times in this chapter alone, and its frequent usage is of striking importance. Its denominative form refers to heads of a family or tribe and particularly, in this chapter, to the heads of the Edomites. The same word appears in Exodus 15:15 and is parallel to *'eyley*, which carries a similar meaning; it may be related to the Ugaritic or Northwest Semitic *'elef*, meaning "prince" or "thousand," respectively.[648] In addition, *'elef* may also mean a "tent group," "family,"[649] or "clan."[650] W. F. Petrie, who was followed by Mendenhall, expanded the meaning to a "sub-section of a tribe," used in the Old

---

647 Mathews, *Genesis 11:27–50:26*, 647–648.

648 J. R. Bartlett, *Edom and Edomites* (Sheffield: JSOT Press, 1989), 90.

649 W. F. M. Petrie, *Egypt and Israel* (London: SPCK, 1911), 43.

650 Sarna, *Genesis*, 250.

Testament (Mic 5:1), and may even mean a "contingent of troops" sent to war on specific occasions (Num 1:16; 10:4; Josh 22:21).[651] Nevertheless, the context of this chapter strongly suggests that the word *ʾaluf* "chief" should be understood as the "chief" or "head" of a clan or family—a conclusion that is accepted by most translators. With this understanding, it is evident that the term *ʾaluf* refers to a ruler of several extended families or a clan.

SEIR'S DESCENDANTS (36:20–30)

GEN 36:20–30 NKJV	GEN 36:20–30 ESV
20 These *were* the sons of Seir the Horite who inhabited the land: Lotan, Shobal, Zibeon, Anah,	**20** These are the sons of Seir the Horite, the inhabitants of the land: Lotan, Shobal, Zibeon, Anah,
21 Dishon, Ezer, and Dishan. These *were* the chiefs of the Horites, the sons of Seir, in the land of Edom.	**21** Dishon, Ezer, and Dishan; these are the chiefs of the Horites, the sons of Seir in the land of Edom.
22 And the sons of Lotan were Hori and Hemam. Lotan's sister *was* Timna.	**22** The sons of Lotan were Hori and Hemam; and Lotan's sister was Timna.
23 These *were* the sons of Shobal: Alvan, Manahath, Ebal, Shepho, and Onam.	**23** These are the sons of Shobal: Alvan, Manahath, Ebal, Shepho, and Onam.
24 These *were* the sons of Zibeon: both Ajah and Anah. This *was the* Anah who found the water in the wilderness as he pastured the donkeys of his father Zibeon.	**24** These are the sons of Zibeon: Aiah and Anah; he is the Anah who found the hot springs in the wilderness, as he pastured the donkeys of Zibeon his father.
25 These *were* the children of Anah: Dishon and Aholibamah the daughter of Anah.	**25** These are the children of Anah: Dishon and Oholibamah the daughter of Anah.
26 These *were* the sons of Dishon: Hemdan, Eshban, Ithran, and Cheran.	**26** These are the sons of Dishon: Hemdan, Eshban, Ithran, and Cheran.
27 These *were* the sons of Ezer: Bilhan, Zaavan, and Akan.	**27** These are the sons of Ezer: Bilhan, Zaavan, and Akan.
28 These *were* the sons of Dishan: Uz and Aran.	**28** These are the sons of Dishan: Uz and Aran.
29 These *were* the chiefs of the Horites: Chief Lotan, Chief Shobal, Chief Zibeon, Chief Anah,	**29** These are the chiefs of the Horites: the chiefs Lotan, Shobal, Zibeon, Anah,
30 Chief Dishon, Chief Ezer, and Chief Dishan. These *were* the chiefs of the Horites, according to their chiefs in the land of Seir.	**30** Dishon, Ezer, and Dishan; these are the chiefs of the Horites, chief by chief in the land of Seir.

Esau and his family settled in the land of the Horites, which would later become the land of Edom. The reference to Horites is scarce in biblical texts. They appear only in the context of Esau's settlement in their territory. The author of Genesis does not discuss how Esau and his family conquered the land. However, the book of Deuteronomy indicates that the Horites were destroyed and dispossessed by the will of God (Deut 2:12, 22). The descendants of Esau settled in their land, and the Horites

---

651 G. E. Mendenhall, "The Census List of Numbers 1 and 26," *JBL* 77 (1958): 52–66.

continued to occupy the same territory throughout New Testament times, when they were known as the Idumeans.

The text introduces seven sons of Seir the Horite (36:20–21); the sons fathered nineteen sons (36:22–28). Since the text does not produce any daughters except Timna (36:22) and Aholibamah (36:25), the complete number of Seir's children and grandchildren is not known. It is probable that Timna and Aholibamah were mentioned to indicate a link between Esau's and Seir's bloodlines.

36:20 Lotan, Shobal, Zibeon, Anah are listed as the first four sons of Seir. While the names of Lotan, Zibeon, and Anah are virtually unknown, Shobal is found elsewhere in the Scriptures as a name for an individual coming from the tribe of Judah (1 Chr 4:1) and another from the clan of Caleb (1 Chr 2:50).

36:21 Dishon, Ezer, and Dishan are the last three sons of Seir. Dishan and Dishon are very similar names and are not used in other biblical texts. Dishon is also the name of Anah's son (36:25). Ezer, on the other hand, is a widely used name. It is found in the tribes of Judah (1 Chr 4:4), Ephraim (1 Chr 7:21), and Gad (1 Chr 12:9). It is also the name of a ruler of Mizpah (Neh 3:19) and of a priest (Neh 12:42).

36:22 Hori and Hemam were two sons of Lotan, the firstborn of Seir. While the name of Hemam does not exist outside the list, Hori was also the name of one of the twelve spies sent by Moses to investigate Canaan prior to Israel's entrance into the land (Num 13:5).

36:23 Alvan, Manahath, Ebal, Shepho, and Onam were the sons of Shobal. While Alvan and Shepho are unknown names, Onam is found among the men of Judah (1 Chr 2:26, 28). Manahath may be associated with the word *Manoah* meaning "resting place."[652] Ebal was also the son of Joktan (1 Chr 1:22–23), and it was the name for the geographical region known as Mount Ebal (Deut 11:29), which was located in the hill country controlled by the tribe of Ephraim.

36:24 Ajah and Anah were the two sons of Zibeon, the third son of Seir. In addition to a personal name, "Ajah" is also the name of an unclean bird of prey, translated as "kite" (Lev 11:14). Unlike all the other names on the list, information about the unusual discovery of water was provided to distinguish Anah, the son of Zibeon, from Anah who was the fourth son of Seir. The mention of a herd of donkeys is an important remark to indicate the wealth of Zibeon. Discovering water in the desertlike area was also worthy of notice. Whether the word *hayyemim* should indicate "hot springs" or just "water" is hard to know since the word is used only here.[653]

36:25 Dishon and Aholibamah were the son and daughter of Anah, the fourth son of Seir on the list (see the comments on 36:2 and 36:20).

36:26 Hemdan, Eshban, Ithran, and Cheran were the four sons of Dishon. While the names of Hemdan, Eshban, and Cheran are virtually unknown, the name of Ithran was found one more time and was associated with a man coming from the tribe of Asher (1 Chr 7:37).

36:27 Bilhan, Zaavan, and Akan were the sons of Ezer. Bilhan was the name of a man who comes from the tribe of Benjamin (1 Chr 7:10). Zaavan is an unknown name. Akan may be associated with "Jaakan," which is the name of two geographical locations found in Edom. The first one listed is "Bene Jaakan" (Num 33:31–32), and the other is "Beeroth Bene-jaakan" (Deut 10:6 ESV).

---

652 *HALOT* 2:602, and also E. A. Knauf, *ABD* 4:493.
653 Mathews, *Genesis 11:27–50:26*, 655.

36:28 Uz and Aran were the two last grandsons of Seir, by his youngest son Dishan. Uz was also the name of Shem's grandson (10:23). Abraham's nephew (son of Nahor) carried the same name (22:20–21). Uz may indicate the name of a place, since Job's home was located there.[654] Aran is unknown.

KINGS OF EDOM (36:31–43)

GEN 36:31–43 NKJV	GEN 36:31–43 ESV
31 Now these *were* the kings who reigned in the land of Edom before any king reigned over the children of Israel:	**31** These are the kings who reigned in the land of Edom, before any king reigned over the Israelites.
32 Bela the son of Beor reigned in Edom, and the name of his city *was* Dinhabah.	**32** Bela the son of Beor reigned in Edom, the name of his city being Dinhabah.
33 And when Bela died, Jobab the son of Zerah of Bozrah reigned in his place.	**33** Bela died, and Jobab the son of Zerah of Bozrah reigned in his place.
34 When Jobab died, Husham of the land of the Temanites reigned in his place.	**34** Jobab died, and Husham of the land of the Temanites reigned in his place.
35 And when Husham died, Hadad the son of Bedad, who attacked Midian in the field of Moab, reigned in his place. And the name of his city *was* Avith.	**35** Husham died, and Hadad the son of Bedad, who defeated Midian in the country of Moab, reigned in his place, the name of his city being Avith.
36 When Hadad died, Samlah of Masrekah reigned in his place.	**36** Hadad died, and Samlah of Masrekah reigned in his place.
37 And when Samlah died, Saul of Rehoboth-*by*-the-River reigned in his place.	**37** Samlah died, and Shaul of Rehoboth on the Euphrates reigned in his place.
38 When Saul died, Baal-Hanan the son of Achbor reigned in his place.	**38** Shaul died, and Baal-hanan the son of Achbor reigned in his place.
39 And when Baal-Hanan the son of Achbor died, Hadar reigned in his place; and the name of his city *was* Pau. His wife's name *was* Mehetabel, the daughter of Matred, the daughter of Mezahab.	**39** Baal-hanan the son of Achbor died, and Hadar reigned in his place, the name of his city being Pau; his wife's name was Mehetabel, the daughter of Matred, daughter of Mezahab.
40 And these *were* the names of the chiefs of Esau, according to their families and their places, by their names: Chief Timnah, Chief Alvah, Chief Jetheth,	**40** These are the names of the chiefs of Esau, according to their clans and their dwelling places, by their names: the chiefs Timna, Alvah, Jetheth,
41 Chief Aholibamah, Chief Elah, Chief Pinon,	**41** Oholibamah, Elah, Pinon,
42 Chief Kenaz, Chief Teman, Chief Mibzar,	**42** Kenaz, Teman, Mibzar,
43 Chief Magdiel, and Chief Iram. These *were* the chiefs of Edom, according to their dwelling places in the land of their possession. Esau *was* the father of the Edomites.	**43** Magdiel, and Iram; these are the chiefs of Edom (that is, Esau, the father of Edom), according to their dwelling places in the land of their possession.

---

654 John Day, "How Could Job Be an Edomite?" in *The Book of Job*, ed. W. A. M. Beuken (Leuven: Leuven University Press, 1994), 392–399.

The Hebrew word *melek* **king** (36:31) is one of the most commonly used nouns in the Bible, which might be translated as "counselor." The root *malak* means "to advise," "to counsel," as testified in the Akkadian cognate *milku*, a meaning that has survived in Aramaic (Dan 4:24). Thus, the word *melek*, which is most commonly translated as "king," certainly has a wider range.[655] This word is used in the Bible and other literature to designate Hebrew and Gentile rulers as well as a title for the Divinity. The title is given to various rulers in the Bible. Although its meaning in antiquity is similar to the current-day meaning, its application is significantly different. The word might apply to an emperor (such as Nebuchadnezzar; Jer 46:2), an emperor's vassal (such as Jehoiakim, king of Judah; Jer 46:2), or even to a chieftain of a small city-state (such as the Canaanite and Philistine towns; 14:2–8; 20:2; 26:1, 8; Josh 10:1–3). The word might also be used to denote joint rulership, triumvirate (Belshazzar; Dan 5:11), or a subordinate governor of a province (Gubaru was governor of Babylon under Cyrus, emperor of Persia; Dan 5:30).[656]

According to the discussion above, the word "king" (*melek*) would apply to more than a ruler of a settled, unified, national monarchy. The probability that the "kings" did not rule over all Edom elicits a new understanding of the title "king." The phenomenon of tribal "kings" or "chiefs" was well known and documented in the ancient world. For example, the Assyrian King Lists mention seventeen kings who dwelt in tents.[657] Further, the royal archives from Mari discuss the defeat of several seminomadic tribal kings.[658] The Mari texts also describe people groups such as the Haneans and Yaminites, who were known as seminomadic people, having kings.[659]

The Bible writers also occasionally use "king" in this restricted tribal sense, supported by a nomadic lifestyle. The five defeated Midian leaders are called the "kings of Midian" and mentioned by name (Num 31:8), whereas the same persons are also known as the **princes of Midian** (Josh 13:21). That the land of Midian was occupied by five tribes is apparently not a coincidence (25:4).

Therefore, the king list included in this chapter (36) does not require a settled, unified, national monarchy under a strong centralized bureaucracy. Those rulers were nothing more than local tribal leaders who might have lived in tent encampments, which is why every king was assigned to a different territory without leaving any dynasty after them, similar to the appointed judges of Israel.

Throughout the last two centuries, numerous attempts have been made to identify certain names mentioned in Genesis 36.[660] The text states that these are the kings

---

655 A. R. Millard and P. Bordreuil, "A Statue From Syria With Assyrian and Aramaic Inscriptions," *BA* 45 (1982): 139.

656 R. R. Culver, "Melek, King," *TWOT* 1:508; D. F. Payne, "King; Kingdom," *ISBE* 3:21.

657 I. J. Gelb, "Two Assyrian King Lists," *JNES* 13 (1954): 223. Two nearly identical Assyrian King Lists exist. One is known as the Khorsabad King List (Khors list), and the other as the Seventh-day Adventist Seminary List (SDAS list). In the first nine lines on the Khors list and the first eight lines on the SDAS list, there are seventeen names as follows: Tudija, Adamu, Jangi, Kitlamu, Harharu, Mandaru, Imsu, Harsu, Didanu, Hanu, Zuabu, Nuabu, Abazu, Belu, Azarah, Ušpia, and Apiašal. The tenth line on the Khors list and the ninth on the SDAS list state the following: "PAB 17 LUGAL.MEŠ-a-ni a-ši-bu-tu kul-ta-ri" meaning "Total of 17 kings who dwelled in tents."

658 Sarna, *Genesis*, 409. Unfortunately, Sarna does not give any primary data to support his statement.

659 A. Malamat, "History of the Prophetic Vision in a Mari Letter," *ErIsr* 5 (1959): 67. In his dedication of the Shamash temple, Yahdun-Lim speaks of his military success over the Haneans, whose rulers built a city called Haman. Five tablets were found by A. Parrot in 1953, and the reference to Hanean rulers appears at the end of the fourth tablet. Later, during the reign of his son Zimri-Lim, a letter was written by the governor of Nahur. Line 35 of the letter states: "Se[nd] me your messengers and lay your full report before me, and then I will have the kings of Yaminites [coo]ked."

660 Julius Wellhausen, *De Gentibus et familiis Judaeis Quae 1 Chr. 2.4 Enumarantur* (Göttingen: Deitrich, 1870), 28–30; B. Moritz, "Edomitische Genealogien 1," *ZAW* 44 (1926): 81–92; William F. Albright, *From Stone Age to Chris-*

who reigned in the land of Edom before any king reigned over the children of Israel (36:31). Most scholars concur this could simply refer to the period before the monarchy of Israel was established, and thus to King Saul. Others suggest this refers to the period before any Israelite king ruled over Edom, which implies King David. Either way, Westermann indicates that this may have been an insertion by the court of David or Solomon,[661] and Morris suggests that it was the prophetic expression of the author, based on Deuteronomy 17:14–20.[662]

An analysis of the king list indicates that two formulas were used: (1) **and the name of his city was** (Bela, Hadad, Hadar) (36:32, 35, 39), and (2) the use of the Hebrew preposition *mi* **of**, **from** (Jobab, Husham, Samlah, Saul) (36:33–34, 36–37). Scholars have struggled to identify whether these names were personal names or place names.

Furthermore, according to the list, the first, fourth, and seventh kings with their cities belong to the first "formula," whereas the second, third, fifth, and sixth kings belong to the second "formula." This creates a perfect structure, as follows:

> **A** Bela (1)
>   **B** Jobab (2)
>   **B** Husham (3)
> **A** Hadad (4)
>   **B** Samlah (5)
>   **B** Saul (6)
> **A** Hadar (7)

Moreover, the change in the "formula" may be nothing more than the artistic literary ability of the author, who sets the text in such a way that the reader may enjoy it to the fullest extent. The presence of the formula **when … died, then … reigned after him** that is found in connection with every king in the list, but the last one (who may have been alive at the author's time), further supports the unity of the list.

Determining whether the list is arranged by the location of places (east-west or north-south) exceeds the available data, and any suggestion would be highly speculative. Most of the names, whether person or place, are generally not mentioned in the Old Testament outside of the list, with a few exceptions. This, however, cannot be understood as a denial that the list is "an historical document in the strict sense."[663] Because none of the "kings" established a dynasty, the list suggests succession through election or by the power of arms, where the chief of the strongest clan took precedence, rather than dynastic kingship; although some have strongly proposed dynastic lineage through the daughters of the kings. Traditionally, the list represents a chronological succession, giving every king approximately twenty to twenty-five years of their reign. Although the text strongly suggests that the succession is chronological, any proposal concerning their years of reign is highly speculative and should not be accepted as fact. The biblical judges were appointed to rule over smaller territories from the center or city in which they were born. Similarly, the kings of

---

tianity: Monotheism and Historical Process (Garden City, NJ: Doubleday, 1957), 126–128, 210.

661 Westermann, *Genesis 12–36*, 251.

662 Morris, *The Genesis Record*, 530.

663 Westermann, *Genesis 12–36*, 251.

Edom ruled from the cities of their birth, which were also the centers of their clan or tribe.

36:32 The meaning of **Bela** is not certain, but it may mean "to announce, to report." The same name was given to Benjamin's firstborn son (46:21). Also, it was the name of a Reubenite clan (1 Chr 5:8). The same name was used for a city also known as Zoar (14:2, 8). Most likely Bela has been identified as referring to Balaam. This comparison is reasonable, since his city, **Dinhabah**, is identified by Jerome and Eusebius either with Dannaia, located about eight miles north of Aeropolis toward the Arnon, or with Dannaba, located in the hill country west of Hisban, north of Arnon.[664] If this identification is correct, then Dinhabah is deep in Moabite territory.

His city. The Edomite King List also employs the term *'ir* "city," referring to the three kings (36:32, 35, 39) who reigned from their designated cities. Although the term *'ir* is typically related to walled or fortified places, its application must not be restricted to strong fortified centers because it may also indicate any form of enclosure formed by a ring of adjoining houses. In addition to walled cities and towns, the term *'ir* is also used together with the term *perazi* "unwalled," indicating the existence of unwalled cities (Deut 3:5).

36:33 **Jobab.** This name appears several more times in the Bible attached to different individuals (10:29; Josh 1:11; 1 Chr 8:9, 18). The identification of his city **Bozrah** is universally accepted among scholars as Buseira, located some twenty-two miles (thirty-five kilometers) south of the Dead Sea.[665]

36:34 The name **Husham** is unknown; it is only used here in connection to this king. **The land of the Temanites** may be identified as Wadi Hisma or an oasis of Teima toward northwest Arabia.[666] Nelson Glueck suggests that Tawilan is ancient Teman; yet others consider it to be Shobek.[667] In any case, the southern region of Edom is generally accepted as the land of the Temanites.[668]

36:35 The name **Hadad** may refer to an individual (25:15; 1 Kgs 11:14–22, 25; 15:18) or to a well-known Canaanite deity.[669] Hadad's city, **Avith**, has been associated with certain hills known as el-Ghoweythe.[670] These hills are also located in Moab.

36:36 The name **Samlah** is virtually unknown; it is used only here in association with the king list. It may mean "garment, cloak." **Masrekah**, the city of Samlah, is etymologically connected to a vine-growing region in northern Edom or, to be more precise, in Gebalene.[671] According to B. Moritz and J. Simons, the region of modern Jebel Mishraq, between Ma'an and Aqaba, is the most plausible territory for the biblical Masrekah.[672]

---

664 E. Klostermann, ed., *Das Onomasticon der Biblischen Ortsnamen* (Leipzig: Hinrichs, 1904), 76.

665 Bartlett, *Edom and Edomites*, 98.

666 E. A. Knauf, "Alter und Herkunft der Edomitischen Königsliste Gen 36: 31–39," *ZAW* 39 (1985): 249–250.

667 Klostermann, *Das Onomasticon der Biblischen Ortsnamen*, 96; J. Simons, *The Geographical and Topographical Texts of the Old Testament* (Leiden: Brill, 1959), 404; Buhl, "Hamath," 31.

668 Bartlett, *Edom and Edomites*, 40, 99.

669 Walter A. Maier III, "Hadad (Deity)," *ABD* 3:11.

670 J. Burckhardt, *Travels in Syria and the Holy Land* (London: John Murray, 1983), 375; L. Desnoyers, *L'Histoire du Peuple Hébreu des Juges á la Captivité* (Paris: A. Picard, 1922), 70; H. Gunkel, *Genesis* (Gottingen: Vandenhoeck & Ruprecht, 1966), 394; Bartlett, *Edom and Edomites*, 97; J. Lury, *Geschichte der Edomite rim Biblischen Zeitalter* (Berlin: Weschselmann, 1896), 26.

671 Klostermann, *Das Onomasticon der Biblischen Ortsnamen*, 124.

672 B. Moritz, "Die Konige von Edom," *Museon* 50 (1937): 101; Simons, *Geographical and Topographical Texts*, 390.

36:37 The name **Saul** was used several times in the biblical text. The best known one is the name of the first king of Israel (1 Sam 9:2). It is also associated with one Simeonite clan and one individual coming from the Levite tribe (1 Chr 6:24). **Rehoboth**, the realm of Saul, is placed in the northwest corner of Edom or, more accurately, near modern Khirbet Rihab, immediately south of Wadi el-Hesa. Even though some translations may suggest that Rehoboth was located on the river Euphrates, the Hebrew text indicates that the city is located "on the river."

36:38 Whether the tradition concerning **Baal-Hanan** is an isolated fragment inserted later in the list, as suggested by Bartlett,[673] or whether his city was Rehoboth, the same as Saul's, is impossible to determine at this time. The name means "Baal is gracious," and it is used by another person who was in charge of Sycamore trees during the time of David (1 Chr 27:28). Baal-Hanan was son of Achbor, who appears to be a high official in Josiah's court (1 Chr 1:49; 2 Kgs 22:12, 14).

36:39 **Hadar** is the last king of Edom mentioned on this list. According to the Chronicler (1 Chr 1:50), the name of this king was "Hadad." Whether this king's name was "Hadar" or "Hadad" makes no difference since they are different individuals, married to two different persons. His city was **Pau** (Pai in 1 Chr 1:50). The Septuagint version replaced Pau with Phogor, which is also found in Numbers 23:28 and is known to be in Moab. Eusebius follows this version and suggests that its location is to be found in the mountains of Moab.[674] Certain other vague speculations exist regarding the name "Mezahab," grandmother of Hadar's wife. Scholars have suggested that Mezahab is a place rather than a personal name. Following this hypothesis, Hadar and his city would certainly be placed in the territory of Moab.

36:40–43 **Chiefs of Edom.** The list ends with eleven names who are designated as "chiefs of Edom." It contains the names of individuals who were found on previous lists of Edomite and Horite chiefs, and there are also a few names that are mentioned for the first time. Even though some names are mentioned earlier, it is possible that these are different individuals who were chiefs of clans of Edom during or after the reign of certain kings of Edom.

THE CYCLE OF JOSEPH (37:1–48:20)

The next section (37:1–48:20) covers the life of Joseph, who, although he is one of the sons of Jacob, stands out as a great patriarchal figure, similar to Abraham, Isaac, and Jacob. In fact, he occupies more space in the book of Genesis than any of the three patriarchs.[675] His two sons receive equal status with the other sons of Jacob; they will generate two of the twelve tribes of Israel. The theological intention of this emphasis is twofold. First, Joseph incarnates one of the main theological motifs of the Pentateuch, namely, the promise-fulfillment motif, the hope that evil will turn into good. What he hears from God in his prophetic dreams during the first part of his existence is fulfilled in the second part of his existence. Through Joseph's leadership in Egypt, the blessing of Abraham to the nations is already fulfilled. The salvation of his brothers and of his father, Israel, also take place through Joseph, anticipating

---

673 J. R. Bartlett, "The Edomite King List of Genesis xxxvi 31–39 and 1 Chr i 43–50," *JTS* 16 (1965): 309.

674 Klostermann, *Das Onomasticon der Biblischen Ortsnamen,* 168.

675 Compare Abraham (12:1–22:19); Isaac (22:20–25:18); Jacob (25:19–35:29); Joseph (37:1–48:20).

the return of Israel to the Promised Land. The structure of the section reflects these theological lessons.

A Jacob loves Joseph (37:1–11)
    B Joseph and his brothers (37:12–36)
        C God saves Tamar through Judah (38:1–30)
        C₁ God saves Egypt through Joseph (39:1–41:57)
    B₁ Joseph and his brothers (42:1–47:31)
A₁ Jacob blesses Joseph' sons (48:1–20)

37:1–11. JACOB LOVES JOSEPH

GEN 37:1–11 NKJV	GEN 37:1–11 ESV
1 Now Jacob dwelt in the land where his father was a stranger, in the land of Canaan.	**1** Jacob lived in the land of his father's sojournings, in the land of Canaan.
2 This *is* the history of Jacob. Joseph, *being* seventeen years old, was feeding the flock with his brothers. And the lad *was* with the sons of Bilhah and the sons of Zilpah, his father's wives; and Joseph brought a bad report of them to his father.	**2** These are the generations of Jacob. Joseph, being seventeen years old, was pasturing the flock with his brothers. He was a boy with the sons of Bilhah and Zilpah, his father's wives. And Joseph brought a bad report of them to their father.
3 Now Israel loved Joseph more than all his children, because he *was* the son of his old age. Also he made him a tunic of *many* colors.	**3** Now Israel loved Joseph more than any other of his sons, because he was the son of his old age. And he made him a robe of many colors.
4 But when his brothers saw that their father loved him more than all his brothers, they hated him and could not speak peaceably to him.	**4** But when his brothers saw that their father loved him more than all his brothers, they hated him and could not speak peacefully to him.
5 Now Joseph had a dream, and he told *it* to his brothers; and they hated him even more.	**5** Now Joseph had a dream, and when he told it to his brothers they hated him even more.
6 So he said to them, "Please hear this dream which I have dreamed:	**6** He said to them, "Hear this dream that I have dreamed:
7 There we were, binding sheaves in the field. Then behold, my sheaf arose and also stood upright; and indeed your sheaves stood all around and bowed down to my sheaf."	**7** Behold, we were binding sheaves in the field, and behold, my sheaf arose and stood upright. And behold, your sheaves gathered around it and bowed down to my sheaf."
8 And his brothers said to him, "Shall you indeed reign over us? Or shall you indeed have dominion over us?" So they hated him even more for his dreams and for his words.	**8** His brothers said to him, "Are you indeed to reign over us? Or are you indeed to rule over us?" So they hated him even more for his dreams and for his words.
9 Then he dreamed still another dream and told it to his brothers, and said, "Look, I have dreamed another dream. And this time, the sun, the moon, and the eleven stars bowed down to me."	**9** Then he dreamed another dream and told it to his brothers and said, "Behold, I have dreamed another dream. Behold, the sun, the moon, and eleven stars were bowing down to me."

10 So he told *it* to his father and his brothers; and his father rebuked him and said to him, "What *is* this dream that you have dreamed? Shall your mother and I and your brothers indeed come to bow down to the earth before you?"

11 And his brothers envied him, but his father kept the matter *in mind.*

10 But when he told it to his father and to his brothers, his father rebuked him and said to him, "What is this dream that you have dreamed? Shall I and your mother and your brothers indeed come to bow ourselves to the ground before you?"

11 And his brothers were jealous of him, but his father kept the saying in mind.

Jacob's close ties with his favorite son, Joseph, trigger the rest of the story; it is the brothers' sentiments of jealousy toward Joseph as well as their reaction to his dreams that will bring the whole family to Egypt.

37:1 For the first time, the patriarch **dwelt**. For Jacob's father, Isaac, Canaan was merely a land for sojourning as **a stranger** (*gur*). For Jacob, it is now a dwelling place (*yashab*). Perhaps Jacob begins to think of definitively settling in the Promised Land.

37:2 Jacob's need to settle may be related to the particular bond he shares with his son, Joseph. The old Jacob aspires to some stability to enjoy his relationship with his favorite son. This is why verse 1 belongs to the stories of chapter 37, which it introduces, rather than to the preceding chapter. Jacob's unique connection with his son Joseph is subtly alluded to through the echo on the number **seventeen**. The first seventeen years of Joseph with his father Jacob will be echoed in the last seventeen years of Jacob in Egypt with his son Joseph (47:28).

This particular attention to Joseph is reflected in **the genealogy of Jacob**, which concerns only Joseph (37:2), and in the fact that Joseph is associated with the sons of the maidservants Bilhah and Zilpah, who are called **his father's wives**, rather than with his other brothers, the sons of Leah. Joseph also feels more comfortable with these brothers who, as the concubines' sons, may be despised by the sons of Leah, the legitimate wife. The enemies of his enemies are his friends. However, the reference to **his brothers**, which distinguishes them from the sons of Bilhah and the sons of Zilpah, suggests that, while it includes them, it is not limited to them. These are all "his brothers."

Joseph brought a bad report of them to his father. Joseph's "report of them" concerns all of his brothers and not just the maidservants' sons. Joseph reports to "his father" and not to "their father," as if Joseph was more his son than they, if not his only son. The Hebrew word *dibbah*, here translated "report," is often used in a pejorative sense and implies a reprehensible behavior, designating the wicked act of slandering and even making false reports (Prov 10:18; Num 14:36–37). Considering what we know of the brothers' behavior and of Joseph's behavior, the brothers were likely behaving wrongly, and Joseph's report was a righteous one. The author's use of the negative *dibbah* does not apply so much to Joseph's report per se as to the perspective of his brothers, who must have claimed that his report was all lies (*dibbah*).

37:3–4 What was only previously implicit is now unveiled, namely, that **Israel loved Joseph more than all his children** (37:3–4). The language is reminiscent of Jacob, who "loved Rachel more than Leah" and that Leah was "unloved" (29:30–31). The same association of verbs *'hb* "love" and *sn'* "hate, unloved" is used in both passages. The echo between the two texts suggests the internal process of Jacob's sentiments. Jacob's love for Joseph recalls Jacob's love for Rachel. The author refers to

Joseph as **the son of his old age** (37:3); although Benjamin, having come later, would fit better in that category (44:20), because Joseph was Rachel's first son after a long waiting time (30:22–24), and this birth also implied the next one of Benjamin (30:24). Jacob does not merely love Joseph in his heart; he shows his sentiments concretely: **he made him a tunic of many colors** (37:3), an expression that is used elsewhere in the Scriptures to designate a prince's garment (2 Sam 13:18–19). The Hebrew phrase *ketonet passim* also recalls the Akkadian *kitu pishannu*, which designates the ceremonial robe of a goddess, with gold ornaments.[676] This background suggests that this tunic had special significance, perhaps indicating Jacob's secret intention to make Joseph, the firstborn from Rachel, his firstborn, thus ignoring his other sons from Leah, a way of repairing and taking revenge on Laban's deception. Joseph eventually will receive the rights of the firstborn (1 Chr 5:2) and hence the double portion of the inheritance (48:5). No wonder, then, that his brothers **hated him and could not speak peaceably to him** (37:4). The Hebrew word *shalom* "peace" that is used here suggests that, in their conversations with him, they meant war and conflict with him.

37:5–8 His brothers' hatred is exacerbated by Joseph's dreams and the fact that he shares these dreams with them. The verb expressing the additional hatred *yasaf* "add" is a play on words of the name "Joseph" (*Yosef*). This observation occurs twice—in the beginning and at the end of the passage—in inclusio (37:5, 8), a literary way of emphasizing this information. The fact that Joseph has dreams is humiliating for the brothers, since this is a divine sign of his "spiritual" superiority. When Joseph tells his dreams to his brothers out of his naïve desire to share his puzzling revelation with them, they are irritated and hate him even more. The reason for their increased anger is that they have understood the meaning of the dream (37:8), perhaps even more than he has. As shepherds and people living from the land, the picture of sheaves evokes the production of basic food. The fact that their sheaves bow before their brother's sheaf (37:7) suggests that they will someday be economically dependent on him and even behave as servants to him for that purpose. At the same time, the sheaves point to the "heads" of grain in Pharaoh's dream (41:22) and the grain that will be stored according to Joseph's recommendation (41:36).

37:9–11 The repetition of dreams with the same message confirms the truth of the message and is a sign that these dreams come from God (41:32). Again, the same prediction concerning his family bowing before him is intended. Jacob interprets the symbols of the sun, the moon, and the eleven stars as referring respectively to the father (himself), the mother (his wife), and his eleven sons (37:10). Because Joseph was only six or seven years old when Rachel died, either Leah (as the principal wife) or Bilhah (Rachel's maidservant)[677] must have become his surrogate mother and therefore is hinted at (as the moon) by Jacob. Although Jacob rebukes (37:10), or pretends to rebuke (because he is in the presence of the rest of his family), the meaning of the dream, he secretly ponders the dream (37:11), implying that he intends to wait to see its fulfillment. However, the brothers are depicted as jealous (37:11), which suggests that they also realize the truth of the dream and is, therefore, threatening to them.

---

676 See Speiser, *Genesis*, 290.
677 Gen. Rab. 84:11.

JOSEPH AND HIS BROTHERS (37:12–36)

J oseph's brothers take the first opportunity to eliminate the dreamer. The occasion presents when Jacob sends Joseph to visit his brothers in the fields. Although Joseph is alone and facing danger, at each step of his troubles someone unexpectedly intervenes on his behalf. When the brothers plot to kill him, Reuben persuades his brothers to cast him into a pit instead. When he is cast into the pit, waiting to be killed, Judah convinces his brothers to sell him to a passing caravan instead. When Joseph is sold to the Midianites, Reuben tears his clothes and Joseph's tunic is then shown to Jacob, who also tears his clothes. The story begins with Jacob, who sends away his son, and ends with Jacob mourning his son. Between these two references to Jacob, which echo each other in inclusio, Reuben, Judah, and again Reuben, stand up to save Joseph. These two brothers are, intriguingly, the ones who have a claim to the birthright, the very birthright that Jacob wants to pass to Joseph. Judah occupies the center (apex) in the chiastic structure that is suggested by Joseph's supporters:

> **A** Jacob sends Joseph (37:12–17)
> > **B** Reuben defends Joseph (37:18–24)
> > > **C Judah rescues Joseph (37:25–28)**
> > **B₁** Reuben misses Joseph (37:29–32)
> **A₁** Jacob mourns Joseph (37:33–36)

37:12–17. JACOB SENDS JOSEPH

GEN 37:12–17 NKJV	GEN 37:12–17 ESV
12 Then his brothers went to feed their father's flock in Shechem.	**12** Now his brothers went to pasture their father's flock near Shechem.
13 And Israel said to Joseph, "Are not your brothers feeding *the flock* in Shechem? Come, I will send you to them." So he said to him, "Here I am."	**13** And Israel said to Joseph, "Are not your brothers pasturing the flock at Shechem? Come, I will send you to them." And he said to him, "Here I am."
14 Then he said to him, "Please go and see if it is well with your brothers and well with the flocks, and bring back word to me." So he sent him out of the Valley of Hebron, and he went to Shechem.	**14** So he said to him, "Go now, see if it is well with your brothers and with the flock, and bring me word." So he sent him from the Valley of Hebron, and he came to Shechem.
15 Now a certain man found him, and there he was, wandering in the field. And the man asked him, saying, "What are you seeking?"	**15** And a man found him wandering in the fields. And the man asked him, "What are you seeking?"
16 So he said, "I am seeking my brothers. Please tell me where they are feeding *their flocks*."	**16** "I am seeking my brothers," he said. "Tell me, please, where they are pasturing the flock."
17 And the man said, "They have departed from here, for I heard them say, 'Let us go to Dothan.'" So Joseph went after his brothers and found them in Dothan.	**17** And the man said, "They have gone away, for I heard them say, 'Let us go to Dothan.'" So Joseph went after his brothers and found them at Dothan.

That Jacob's sons went to Shechem, which is so far north from Hebron where Jacob dwelt, is surprising (37:14). However, because it was the dry season, as suggested by the empty well (37:24), this choice can be explained by the need for the green pastures of the north during that time (April–October). Besides, Jacob had properties in that region (33:19). That Jacob sends Joseph to inquire about his brothers and to report to him (37:13–14) is consistent with the habit he had acquired on that matter (37:2). Yet, Jacob did not intend to spy on his sons. The memory of the Dinah incident only two years earlier (34:2–26) must have been the cause for Jacob's concern for his sons (37:14). The Hebrew word *shalom* "peace" (translated by the word "well") suggests that Jacob has more in mind than their simple welfare; given their previous troubles, Jacob may be concerned about possible conflicts with the population of Shechem. The repetition of the name "Shechem," although the brothers are not even there, evokes the previous crime of the brothers (34:25–31) and prepares the reader for their forthcoming treachery (37:19–36). The presence of **a certain man** (*'ish*) (37:15) at this juncture is providential. The same term is used to designate the "man" (*'ish*) who attacked Jacob at the ford of Jabbok (32:24) and to whom Jacob owes his new name "Israel" (32:28). This evocation may explain the use of the name "Israel" to refer to Jacob in the present context (37:13). This man who finds Joseph (37:15) as he is **wandering in the field** and correctly guides him to his brothers, knowing the content of their conversations (37:17), may have something to do with that extraordinary Being who also found Jacob (32:24) and responded to his anxiety.[678] The phrase **Joseph ... found them** (37:17) echoes **a certain man found him**. Joseph finds his brothers because the man had found him.

37:18–24. REUBEN DEFENDS JOSEPH

GEN 37:18–24 NKJV	GEN 37:18–24 ESV
18 Now when they saw him afar off, even before he came near them, they conspired against him to kill him.	**18** They saw him from afar, and before he came near to them they conspired against him to kill him.
19 Then they said to one another, "Look, this dreamer is coming!	**19** They said to one another, "Here comes this dreamer.
20 Come therefore, let us now kill him and cast him into some pit; and we shall say, 'Some wild beast has devoured him.' We shall see what will become of his dreams!"	**20** Come now, let us kill him and throw him into one of the pits. Then we will say that a fierce animal has devoured him, and we will see what will become of his dreams."
21 But Reuben heard *it*, and he delivered him out of their hands, and said, "Let us not kill him."	**21** But when Reuben heard it, he rescued him out of their hands, saying, "Let us not take his life."
22 And Reuben said to them, "Shed no blood, *but* cast him into this pit which *is* in the wilderness, and do not lay a hand on him"—that he might deliver him out of their hands, and bring him back to his father.	**22** And Reuben said to them, "Shed no blood; throw him into this pit here in the wilderness, but do not lay a hand on him"—that he might rescue him out of their hand to restore him to his father.
23 So it came to pass, when Joseph had come to his brothers, that they stripped Joseph of his tunic, the tunic of *many* colors that *was* on him.	**23** So when Joseph came to his brothers, they stripped him of his robe, the robe of many colors that he wore.
24 Then they took him and cast him into a pit. And the pit *was* empty; *there was* no water in it.	**24** And they took him and threw him into a pit. The pit was empty; there was no water in it.

678 See Rashi in Miqraot Gedolot, ad loc; cf. Gen. Rab. 84:14.

Joseph is pleased to see them, even from afar, because it was a long and painful journey and because he feels relieved to find them in peace. They are also happy and excited to see him, **even before he came near**, because they realize this is their opportunity to kill him (37:18). The plural exhortations of the brothers (37:20): **come … let us kill now him and cast him … and we shall say** (*leku wenahargehu wenash-likhehu … we'amarnu*) recalls the plural exhortations of the men of Babel: "they said: 'Come, let us make bricks and bake them … let us build … let us make'" (*wayyo'meru … habah nilbenah lebenim, we nisrefah … nibneh … wena'aseh*) (11:3–4). The parallel language suggests a similar mentality and attitude. Similar to the men of Babel, the brothers have taken God's place and intend to determine their own destiny and that of their brother. They are anxious to kill him, not because he reports to his father or that they are jealous of him; the only blame they retain against him is his dreams. The Hebrew expression they use to qualify him is ironic: *ba'al hakhalomot*, which literally means "Master of dreams." What they intended as a mockery will become prophetic, since Joseph will excel in the interpretation of dreams (41:15). They want to kill him because they feel threatened by his dreams (37:20). Their plan is to kill him and then cast his corpse into a pit (37:20). Reuben must not have participated in that conversation, since he **heard it** (37:21). Reuben is described as the one who defends Joseph. The Hebrew verb *natsal* "deliver, defend" is used twice in the beginning and at the end of the paragraph (37:21–22). The first occurrence refers to Reuben's first attempt to defend Joseph and rescue him from his brothers' hands when they are about to kill him (37:21). The second occurrence refers to his plan of bringing Joseph back to his father (37:22). The causative form of the verb (*hiphil*) conveys the idea of "defending" rather than the actual act of saving.[679] Whereas the verb *natsal* refers to the attempt to save, the verb *yasha'* refers to the realization of saving (see NIV: "to rescue him"; cf. TNK: "tried to save him").

37:25–28. JUDAH RESCUES JOSEPH

GEN 37:25–28 NKJV	GEN 37:25–28 ESV
25 And they sat down to eat a meal. Then they lifted their eyes and looked, and there was a company of Ishmaelites, coming from Gilead with their camels, bearing spices, balm, and myrrh, on their way to carry *them* down to Egypt.	**25** Then they sat down to eat. And looking up they saw a caravan of Ishmaelites coming from Gilead, with their camels bearing gum, balm, and myrrh, on their way to carry it down to Egypt.
26 So Judah said to his brothers, "What profit *is there* if we kill our brother and conceal his blood?	**26** Then Judah said to his brothers, "What profit is it if we kill our brother and conceal his blood?
27 Come and let us sell him to the Ishmaelites, and let not our hand be upon him, for he *is* our brother *and* our flesh." And his brothers listened.	**27** Come, let us sell him to the Ishmaelites, and let not our hand be upon him, for he is our brother, our own flesh." And his brothers listened to him.
28 Then Midianite traders passed by; so *the brothers* pulled Joseph up and lifted him out of the pit, and sold him to the Ishmaelites for twenty *shekels* of silver. And they took Joseph to Egypt.	**28** Then Midianite traders passed by. And they drew Joseph up and lifted him out of the pit, and sold him to the Ishmaelites for twenty shekels of silver. They took Joseph to Egypt.

---

679 See 1 Chr 11:14 where the verb *ntsl*, translated there "defend" is distinct from the idea of "save" (*ysh'*); cf. 2 Sam 23:12.

The scene of the brothers sitting down to enjoy their meal (37:25) while the naked Joseph lies in an empty pit without water (37:24) anticipates, ironically, the reverse situation when the well-fed Joseph will save his brothers from starvation (42:2, 33; 43:1–2; 44:1; 45:17–18). The technical expression **they lifted their eyes and looked, and there** (*wayyis'u 'eyneyhem wayyir'u wehinneh*) (37:25) marks the anticipation of God's intervention to save (see the commentary on 18:2; cf. 22:13). The vision of the caravan anticipates the salvation of Joseph. That the caravan appears at that precise moment is indeed providential. Judah is the only one who acts successfully on behalf of Joseph against his brothers. Whereas Reuben can only "hear" his brothers plotting to kill Joseph, Judah is "heard" by his brothers, who are then convinced by his arguments. Whereas Reuben can only delay the killing, Judah is able to save Joseph for good from his brothers' hands and trigger the process that will lead not only to the present rescue of Joseph, but also to the future salvation of Jacob's family and Egypt. Two details of the story are evidence of its historical authenticity: the identification of the Ishmaelites with the Midianites, and the price of twenty shekels.

The designations **Ishmaelites** (37:25, 27) and **Midianites** (37:28) refer to the same group of peoples, since they were related by marriage and profession (25:2, 17–18; 29:9). The term "Midianite" has been suggested to refer to the ethnic origin of the people, whereas the term "Ishmaelite" refers to their nomadic condition.[680]

37:28 **Twenty shekels** was the minimum rate for a male slave in Old Babylonian times (first half of the second millennium). Considering that the average price was typically thirty shekels (Exod 21:32), the Ishmaelites were clearly taking advantage of the brothers. The brothers' strong desire to sell Joseph does not position them well in the bargaining discussion. Because these men, who are trying to sell their brother, also look suspicious, it is easy for the Ishmaelites to bargain for the minimal payment. The same brothers will later ironically offer the maximal price to obtain favor from Joseph and save Benjamin from slavery (43:11–44:33). The slave trade is well documented in ancient Egypt during the time of Joseph.[681]

37:29–32. REUBEN MISSES JOSEPH

GEN 37:29–32 NKJV	GEN 37:29–32 ESV
29 Then Reuben returned to the pit, and indeed Joseph *was* not in the pit; and he tore his clothes.	**29** When Reuben returned to the pit and saw that Joseph was not in the pit, he tore his clothes
30 And he returned to his brothers and said, "The lad *is* no *more*; and I, where shall I go?"	**30** and returned to his brothers and said, "The boy is gone, and I, where shall I go?"
31 So they took Joseph's tunic, killed a kid of the goats, and dipped the tunic in the blood.	**31** Then they took Joseph's robe and slaughtered a goat and dipped the robe in the blood.
32 Then they sent the tunic of *many* colors, and they brought *it* to their father and said, "We have found this. Do you know whether it *is* your son's tunic or not?"	**32** And they sent the robe of many colors and brought it to their father and said, "This we have found; please identify whether it is your son's robe or not."

---

680 Hamilton, *Genesis 18–50*, 423.

681 See Brooklyn Museum, "Wilbour Papyrus" (under the reign of Sobekhotep III, 1743–1740 BC), which lists seventy-nine slaves, forty-five of whom are Semites.

The note that **Reuben returned to the pit** (37:29) indicates that Reuben was not present during the negotiation with the Ishmaelites, and his surprise not to see Joseph in the pit (37:29–30) shows that he was completely unaware of the selling of Joseph. His immediate reaction of tearing his clothes (37:29) is an expression of his sentiment of devastation and clearly conveys to his brothers that he dissociates himself from their action. Furthermore, Reuben behaves as the firstborn and identifies with his father, who will also tear his clothes (37:34). However, unlike Judah, Reuben's response goes unnoticed. His brothers do not care to answer their brother's question, at least verbally and explicitly; however, as indicated by the form of the verb, their silent action is intended to respond to his question: **so they took Joseph's tunic, killed a kid of the goats** (37:31). This gesture is highly significant. The very tunic that had so irritated his brothers is now used as evidence for Joseph's death. The brothers' gesture is reminiscent of Jacob's gesture. The brothers use a kid to deceive their father, similarly as Jacob did with his father (27:16, 23). In their cowardice, they do not face their father when they share the bad news. They send the tunic to Hebron, to their father without any explanation; their only comment is a question: **Do you know whether it is your son's tunic or not?** (37:32). They pretend to be ignorant of what happened, allowing Jacob to solely infer that Joseph had been killed by an animal, a strategy they had already conceived (37:20). Note how they refer to Joseph as "your son" rather than as "our brother." Joseph is more Jacob's son than he is their brother.

37:33–36. JACOB MOURNS JOSEPH

GEN 37:33–36 NKJV	GEN 37:33–36 ESV
33 And he recognized it and said, "*It is* my son's tunic. A wild beast has devoured him. Without doubt Joseph is torn to pieces."	**33** And he identified it and said, "It is my son's robe. A fierce animal has devoured him. Joseph is without doubt torn to pieces."
34 Then Jacob tore his clothes, put sackcloth on his waist, and mourned for his son many days.	**34** Then Jacob tore his garments and put sackcloth on his loins and mourned for his son many days.
35 And all his sons and all his daughters arose to comfort him; but he refused to be comforted, and he said, "For I shall go down into the grave to my son in mourning." Thus his father wept for him.	**35** All his sons and all his daughters rose up to comfort him, but he refused to be comforted and said, "No, I shall go down to Sheol to my son, mourning." Thus his father wept for him.
36 Now the Midianites had sold him in Egypt to Potiphar, an officer of Pharaoh *and* captain of the guard.	**36** Meanwhile the Midianites had sold him in Egypt to Potiphar, an officer of Pharaoh, the captain of the guard.

As expected, the ingeniously crafted plan succeeds. Jacob deduces from the evidence the unavoidable conclusion that **a wild beast has devoured him** (37:33). The state of the tunic is such that **without doubt Joseph is torn to pieces** (37:33). Jacob's tearing his clothes responds to the tearing of Joseph and the tearing of the tunic. Jacob's mourning is more dramatic and more genuine than is Reuben's. Unlike Reuben, who only tears his clothes, Jacob fulfills the entire mourning ceremonial; in addition to tearing his clothes, he puts sackcloth on his waist and mourns his son many days (37:34). Jacob decides to mourn his son until his death and refuses to be comforted by **all his sons and all his daughters**, the daughters referring to the brothers' wives (37:35).

These scenes of death and mourning are immediately contradicted by the information that Joseph is alive and well. Joseph has been sold to a high Egyptian officer, **Potiphar** (37:36), a shortened form of *Potiphera*, which means "he whom Ra has given" (*Pa-di-Pa-R'*). This conclusion, which anticipates the success of Joseph and ultimately the salvation of Israel and Egypt, is an implicit recognition of Judah's positive role in selling Joseph. Judah has saved Joseph and, consequently, the country, without knowing it. Judah's evil act of selling Joseph will thus be transformed into an act of salvation, the very lesson Joseph will draw later: "you meant evil against me; but God meant it for good, in order to bring it about as it is this day, to save many people alive" (50:20).

GOD SAVES TAMAR THROUGH JUDAH (38:1–30)

The story of Judah's incident with his daughter-in-law Tamar, which follows immediately after the sale of Joseph and his arrival in the Egyptian house of Potiphar, seems to be misplaced at this point in time. Yet, chapter 38 fits very well here. Not only does it follow chronologically chapter 37, as clearly indicated in the introductory formula, **at that time** (38:1), it also shares linguistic and thematic parallels with that chapter: the same words *haker na'* "know" (37:32), "determine" (38:25); the same reference to a *se'ir izzim* or *gedi 'izzim* "young goat" (37:31; 38:17). More importantly, the two texts convey the same fundamental theological lesson; they testify to the same providential work in the sinful flesh of human history. Once again, Judah's evil act is turned into a positive event leading to the salvation of Israel. The chiastic structure (ABA₁) evidences that particular lesson, highlighting in its apex the sordid sexual encounter between Judah and Tamar, which will not only end up with the redemption of the childless Tamar, but also produce the birth of the ancestor of David and hence of the Messiah of Israel, the Savior of the world.

A Judah's sons and Tamar (38:1–11)
   B Tamar's prostitution with Judah (38:12–26)
A₁ Judah's sons with Tamar (38:27–30)

Each section is marked with a reference to time in its introduction:

A "it came to pass at that time" (*wayehi . . . 'et*) (38:1)
   B "in the process of time" (*wayyirbu hayyamim*; lit. trans.: "after many days") (38:12)
   B₁ "and it came to pass . . . three months after" (*wayehi . . . shelosh khodashim*) (38:24)
A₁ "and it came to pass at the time" (*wayehi . . . 'et*) (38:27)

Note the parallel between A and A₁—both are introduced with the same phrase indicating a vague span of time *wayehi . . . 'et*—whereas B is introduced in its two subsections with a more specific reference to time, "days" (*yamim*) and "months" (*khodashim*).

38:1–11. JUDAH'S SONS AND TAMAR

GEN 38:1–11 NKJV	GEN 38:1–11 ESV
1 It came to pass at that time that Judah departed from his brothers, and visited a certain Adullamite whose name *was* Hirah.	**1** It happened at that time that Judah went down from his brothers and turned aside to a certain Adullamite, whose name was Hirah.
2 And Judah saw there a daughter of a certain Canaanite whose name *was* Shua, and he married her and went in to her.	**2** There Judah saw the daughter of a certain Canaanite whose name was Shua. He took her and went in to her,
3 So she conceived and bore a son, and he called his name Er.	**3** and she conceived and bore a son, and he called his name Er.
4 She conceived again and bore a son, and she called his name Onan.	**4** She conceived again and bore a son, and she called his name Onan.
5 And she conceived yet again and bore a son, and called his name Shelah. He was at Chezib when she bore him.	**5** Yet again she bore a son, and she called his name Shelah. Judah was in Chezib when she bore him.
6 Then Judah took a wife for Er his firstborn, and her name *was* Tamar.	**6** And Judah took a wife for Er his firstborn, and her name was Tamar.
7 But Er, Judah's firstborn, was wicked in the sight of the Lord, and the Lord killed him.	**7** But Er, Judah's firstborn, was wicked in the sight of the Lord, and the Lord put him to death.
8 And Judah said to Onan, "Go in to your brother's wife and marry her, and raise up an heir to your brother."	**8** Then Judah said to Onan, "Go in to your brother's wife and perform the duty of a brother-in-law to her, and raise up offspring for your brother."
9 But Onan knew that the heir would not be his; and it came to pass, when he went in to his brother's wife, that he emitted on the ground, lest he should give an heir to his brother.	**9** But Onan knew that the offspring would not be his. So whenever he went in to his brother's wife he would waste the semen on the ground, so as not to give offspring to his brother.
10 And the thing which he did displeased the Lord; therefore He killed him also.	**10** And what he did was wicked in the sight of the Lord, and he put him to death also.
11 Then Judah said to Tamar his daughter-in-law, "Remain a widow in your father's house till my son Shelah is grown." For he said, "Lest he also die like his brothers." And Tamar went and dwelt in her father's house.	**11** Then Judah said to Tamar his daughter-in-law, "Remain a widow in your father's house, till Shelah my son grows up"—for he feared that he would die, like his brothers. So Tamar went and remained in her father's house.

Judah marries a Canaanite with whom he has three sons and then arranges the marriages of his three sons to Tamar with whom they cannot have children because the first two die prematurely and the third one is too young.

38:1–2 That Judah leaves his brothers at this juncture (38:1) suggests his disagreement with them, which must have begun earlier when he used the argument of kinship against his brothers ("he is our brother and our flesh") to prevent them from killing Joseph (37:27). After the sale of Joseph, Judah does not feel comfortable living with his brothers any longer and prefers to dissociate himself from them. Judah's conscience is stirring, as evidenced later in his plea for Benjamin (44:18–34). Judah, who "went down" (*yarad*) (38:1 ESV, NIV), echoes Joseph who "went down" (*yarad*) to Egypt (37:25, 35; 39:1), suggesting that Judah's move down is somehow sympathetic to Joseph's move down to Egypt. Having left the company of his brothers, Judah now joins the natives of Canaan. Jacob's family has lost its status as a separate and holy people. Judah will subsequently engage in his dubious acts with the support and complicity of his Canaanite friend Hirah (38:12, 20) who comes from Adullam (presently Tell esh-Madhkur), a Canaanite city that is located about three miles (five kilometers) southwest of Bethlehem, and whose king will be defeated by Joshua (Josh 12:15). It is from this Canaanite association that Judah finds his Canaanite wife, whose name remains unknown in the Scripture (38:2).

38:3–5 With this anonymous wife Judah has three sons, Er, Onan, and Shelah. The name of the first son Er, is given by his father (38:3), whereas the names of the two other sons, Onan and Shelah, are given by his wife (38:4–5), an indication of the preeminence of the first son over the others. When the third son is born, the localization of these events is unveiled: Chezib (38:5), a nearby city, three miles (five kilometers) west of Adullam.

38:6 For his firstborn, Er, Judah finds a wife whose name is *Tamar*, meaning "palm tree." The fact that Judah initiates finding a wife for his son indicates his concern for proper genealogy. The text does not disclose Tamar's origin, but this silence suggests that she is not considered Canaanite; however, when it is determined to be the case, this fact is specified (38:2; cf. 26:34–35). Although Judah's wife is never called by her name, Judah's daughter-in-law is known only by her name Tamar. Jewish tradition reports that Tamar was originally a Gentile but, like Ruth, had converted to the God of Israel.[682]

38:7 Er is called the firstborn (*bekhor*) twice (38:6–7) emphasizing Judah's spiritual expectation for his son. However, this ends in a tragic disappointment. Er is "evil." The name "Er" (*'er*) is a play on words, and the adjective "wicked" (*r'*) is made of the reverse letters (anagram). Er is thus qualified as essentially wicked; he is "radical evil," so much so that **the Lord killed him**. This is the first time the Scriptures explicitly state that God killed someone.

38:8–10 Judah subsequently enjoins Onan, the next son in line, to marry Tamar to provide an heir to his dead brother. Although this custom of "levirate" marriage was common practice in the ANE, in this particular case, this necessity had an additional significance because it is from the seed of Judah that the Davidic Messiah would come. Thus, Onan's deliberate wasting of his seed implies more than a mere temperamental reaction. Onan does this systematically with Tamar, and his unwillingness to give an heir to his brother amounts to refusing to transmit the messianic seed (cf. Isa 7:10–14). The language describing Onan's action is of cosmic proportion. The Hebrew phrase translated **emitted on the ground** (38:9) could be literally translated: "he destroyed to the earth." This action is deemed as "evil" by the Lord. The same word *r'*, "wicked," "evil," that qualified Er is now applied to Onan. Therefore, Onan faces the same destiny as his brother. God kills him also (38:10).

38:11 After his first two sons die (killed by God because of their wickedness), Judah turns to Tamar and sends her away to her father's house as a widow. Judah seemingly blames Tamar for all these tragedies, ignoring the real cause of his sons' death. Although he promises Tamar his son Shelah when Shelah is grown, his

---

682 Sotah 10a.

behavior suggests that he does not intend to fulfill his word. Tamar has no choice but to return to her father's house without hope.

38:12–26. TAMAR'S PROSTITUTION WITH JUDAH

GEN 38:12–26 NKJV	GEN 38:12–26 ESV
12 Now in the process of time the daughter of Shua, Judah's wife, died; and Judah was comforted, and went up to his sheepshearers at Timnah, he and his friend Hirah the Adullamite.	**12** In the course of time the wife of Judah, Shua's daughter, died. When Judah was comforted, he went up to Timnah to his sheepshearers, he and his friend Hirah the Adullamite.
13 And it was told Tamar, saying, "Look, your father-in-law is going up to Timnah to shear his sheep."	**13** And when Tamar was told, "Your father-in-law is going up to Timnah to shear his sheep,"
14 So she took off her widow's garments, covered *herself* with a veil and wrapped herself, and sat in an open place which *was* on the way to Timnah; for she saw that Shelah was grown, and she was not given to him as a wife.	**14** she took off her widow's garments and covered herself with a veil, wrapping herself up, and sat at the entrance to Enaim, which is on the road to Timnah. For she saw that Shelah was grown up, and she had not been given to him in marriage.
15 When Judah saw her, he thought she *was* a harlot, because she had covered her face.	**15** When Judah saw her, he thought she was a prostitute, for she had covered her face.
16 Then he turned to her by the way, and said, "Please let me come in to you"; for he did not know that she *was* his daughter-in-law. So she said, "What will you give me, that you may come in to me?"	**16** He turned to her at the roadside and said, "Come, let me come in to you," for he did not know that she was his daughter-in-law. She said, "What will you give me, that you may come in to me?"
17 And he said, "I will send a young goat from the flock." So she said, "Will you give *me* a pledge till you send *it?*"	**17** He answered, "I will send you a young goat from the flock." And she said, "If you give me a pledge, until you send it—"
18 Then he said, "What pledge shall I give you?" So she said, "Your signet and cord, and your staff that *is* in your hand." Then he gave *them* to her, and went in to her, and she conceived by him.	**18** He said, "What pledge shall I give you?" She replied, "Your signet and your cord and your staff that is in your hand." So he gave them to her and went in to her, and she conceived by him.
19 So she arose and went away, and laid aside her veil and put on the garments of her widowhood.	**19** Then she arose and went away, and taking off her veil she put on the garments of her widowhood.
20 And Judah sent the young goat by the hand of his friend the Adullamite, to receive *his* pledge from the woman's hand, but he did not find her.	**20** When Judah sent the young goat by his friend the Adullamite to take back the pledge from the woman's hand, he did not find her.
21 Then he asked the men of that place, saying, "Where is the harlot who *was* openly by the roadside?" And they said, "There was no harlot in this *place.*"	**21** And he asked the men of the place, "Where is the cult prostitute who was at Enaim at the roadside?" And they said, "No cult prostitute has been here."
22 So he returned to Judah and said, "I cannot find her. Also, the men of the place said there was no harlot in this *place.*"	**22** So he returned to Judah and said, "I have not found her. Also, the men of the place said, 'No cult prostitute has been here.'"

23 Then Judah said, "Let her take *them* for herself, lest we be shamed; for I sent this young goat and you have not found her."	**23** And Judah replied, "Let her keep the things as her own, or we shall be laughed at. You see, I sent this young goat, and you did not find her."
24 And it came to pass, about three months after, that Judah was told, saying, "Tamar your daughter-in-law has played the harlot; furthermore she *is* with child by harlotry." So Judah said, "Bring her out and let her be burned!"	**24** About three months later Judah was told, "Tamar your daughter-in-law has been immoral. Moreover, she is pregnant by immorality." And Judah said, "Bring her out, and let her be burned."
25 When she *was* brought out, she sent to her father-in-law, saying, "By the man to whom these belong, I *am* with child." And she said, "Please determine whose these *are*—the signet and cord, and staff."	**25** As she was being brought out, she sent word to her father-in-law, "By the man to whom these belong, I am pregnant." And she said, "Please identify whose these are, the signet and the cord and the staff."
26 So Judah acknowledged *them* and said, "She has been more righteous than I, because I did not give her to Shelah my son." And he never knew her again.	**26** Then Judah identified them and said, "She is more righteous than I, since I did not give her to my son Shelah." And he did not know her again.

Tamar's desperate condition leads her to embrace desperate measures. Because Judah does not fulfill his promise after Shelah is grown, Tamar takes the initiative and resorts to prostitution to thus trap Judah into having intercourse with her.

38:12 The Hebrew phrase *wayyirbu hayyamim* (lit. trans: "and the days are many") **in the process of time** indicates that the next events occur "after a long time" (NIV; cf. TNK: "a long time afterward"), allowing sufficient time for Shelah to grow and reach marriageable age (38:14b). Another death strikes Judah's family: this time it is Judah's wife who dies. After having secretly blamed Tamar for the death of his two sons, Judah should now understand, after the death of his wife, that Tamar had nothing to do with the death of his children. Judah mourns his wife and seeks comfort, something he did not do for the death of his sons. The mention of Judah's trip to Timnah with his Canaanite friend at that crucial moment suggests that this particular excursion may be intended to play a role in the comforting process. Sheep shearing was an occasion for partying (1 Sam 25:2–37; 2 Sam 13:23–28) and was even associated in Canaanite religion with the rituals of sacred prostitution (Hos 4:13–14; 9:1–2).

38:13–14 This particular context explains why, when Tamar hears that Judah **is going up to Timnah to shear his sheep** (38:13), she decides to play the prostitute (38:14). She takes off **her widow's garments,** which distinctively suggest that she has lost her husband (2 Sam 14:2), and instead covers herself with a veil, which suggests that she is promised to a husband (24:65; 29:21–25).[683] The reason for this behavior is that she had been promised to Shelah and **she saw that Shelah was grown, and she was not given to him as a wife** (38:14b). Her intention is to make herself visible to everyone, as implied in the Hebrew expression *be petakh 'eynayim* (lit. trans.: "in the open of eyes"; cf. 38:14 NKJV: **in an open place**), and more particularly to Judah, since she chooses to sit **on the way to Timnah,** which will be taken by Judah.

38:15 Judah ironically misinterprets her acts. Although she puts on a veil to

---

683 For the significance of "garment," see Wilfried Warning, "Terminological Patterns and Genesis 38," *AUSS* 38, no. 2 (2000): 302–304.

signify her condition as betrothed, he thinks that she has a veil because she is a cult prostitute. The Hebrew word *qedeshah*, which will be used later by the Adullamite to refer to her, is the technical term for the sacred prostitute (38:21; Deut 23:17 [18]; Hos 4:14). According to Assyrian law, only sacred prostitutes had to be veiled in public; regular prostitutes were forbidden to wear a veil.[684] That Judah engages with a sacred prostitute worsens his case. He is not simply satisfying his sexual frustration due to the loss of his wife but involves himself in a Canaanite cult.

38:16–18 The irony is that although she is exposed to all eyes, Judah does not see her; he cannot recognize her because of her veil. He is thus not even aware of the sins of adultery and incest he is about to commit. Tamar is not only still betrothed to Shelah (cf. Deut 22:23), she is also his daughter-in-law (cf. Lev 18:15). Judah does not see her, nor does he see himself. Whereas Judah has lost his lucidity and self-control, Tamar behaves as a shrewd businesswoman and is in full control of the situation. She likely knows that Judah is taken by surprise and did not prepare for such an encounter; she knows that he will not be able to pay cash. Therefore, when Judah promises that he will later send **a young goat from the flock** (38:17a), a precious gift (Judg 13:15), she is prudent, considering her own experience with him, and requires an immediate guarantee (38:17b); she chooses an object that will prove his identity: **your signet and cord, and your staff that is in your hand** (38:18). The "signet" (*khotam*) referred to a seal made of an engraved stone that was rolled on soft clay to leave the print of the distinctive design that was characteristic of its owner (Exod 28:11; 1 Kgs 21:8). The signet was attached to a rope, which was worn around the neck. The "staff" (*mateh*) was a stick, representing the authority of its owner (Num 17:3). The word also means "tribe" (Num 2:7, 12). The holder of the *mateh* would represent the tribe, as its leader; thus the *mateh* became the ensign of royalty, the scepter (Ezek 19:11, 14), with a messianic connotation (Ps 110:2). In our text, Judah's staff may be an allusion to the messianic destiny associated to the tribe of Judah (49:10; Num 24:17).[685] This allusion is all the more significant in our context because it is from this first and unique sexual encounter with Judah that Tamar will become pregnant (38:18) and give birth to the ancestor of the Davidic Messiah (see the commentary on 38:29; cf. Ruth 4:18–22). It is on this note of immediate success, a sign of the involvement of divine providence, that Tamar **arose and went away, and laid aside her veil and put on the garments of her widowhood** (38:19). Mission accomplished, Tamar returns to her previous condition and place, yet secretly holds in her hand the pledge of Judah.

38:20–23 When Judah's friend, the Adullamite, comes to the specific place with the promised young goat in order to receive back his pledge, he finds no woman there (38:20). Note that Judah does not come himself; he sends his Canaanite friend for this task. Judah does not want to compromise himself and prefers to hide. When Judah's friend shares the result of his inquiry with Judah, namely, that there was never a prostitute at that place, Judah is confused and prefers not to pursue the matter further. Judah fears for his reputation: **lest we be shamed** (38:23), "or we shall be laughed at" (ESV); we will "become a laughingstock" (NIV, TNK). The Hebrew word *buz* translated "shamed" (NKJV) means to be ridiculed (Job 31:34).

---

684 *ANET*, 183 #40.

685 Although these passages use another Hebrew word for "scepter" (*shebet*), the messianic allusion may still hold inasmuch as this word is a synonym that is associated with the word *mateh* (Ezek 19:14).

38:24 After three months, when Tamar's pregnancy becomes apparent, the fact is immediately reported to Judah. Tamar is accused of having **played the harlot** and that **she is with child by harlotry**; it is then recommended that she **be burned**. Note that the accusation is correct. Tamar is not charged with simple adultery; knowing the customs of the land, they suppose that Tamar had acted as a prostitute. Ironically, Judah, who has recently been involved with a harlot, is ready to apply the punishment. His words **bring her out** resonate with the legislation of the Torah, which will be later prescribed for that case: "they shall bring out the young woman to the door of the father's house, and the men of the city shall stone her to death" (Deut 22:21).

38:25 Tamar submits herself to the disciplinary measure: **when she was brought out**. However, she immediately presents her assets—Judah's pledge, his staff, and his signet—although she does not accuse. She simply allows Judah to conclude the identity of the man who involved himself with her as prostitute. Tamar's strategy recalls Nathan the prophet who allowed David to discover that he was the guilty one: "you are the man" (2 Sam 12:7). Tamar's words *haker na'* "determine" are curiously the same words that Judah and his brothers used when they deceitfully reported to Jacob the death of Joseph: "Do you know [*haker na'*] whether it is your son's tunic or not?" (37:32), which was perhaps a subtle way of reminding Judah of his sin and awakening his guilty conscience.

38:26 Similar to his descendant David, Judah humbly and courageously acknowledges the pledge. He even recognizes his misery and, compared to Tamar, realizes that she had been **more righteous** than he was. Judah does not refer here to her behavior as a prostitute but to his behavior as a father-in-law. What makes Tamar "more righteous" is not what she did, her deception, her prostitution. What makes Tamar "more righteous" is what Judah did: **because I did not give her to Shelah my son**. Judah remembers and confesses his duplicity, his cowardice; but, more importantly, he realizes that for a moment he had compromised the hope of the messianic seed. The fact that **he never knew her again** indicates that this unique encounter was special, that it carried a certain messianic significance.

38:27–30. JUDAH'S SONS WITH TAMAR

GEN 38:27–30 NKJV	GEN 38:27–30 ESV
27 Now it came to pass, at the time for giving birth, that behold, twins *were* in her womb.	**27** When the time of her labor came, there were twins in her womb.
28 And so it was, when she was giving birth, that *the one* put out *his* hand; and the midwife took a scarlet *thread* and bound it on his hand, saying, "This one came out first."	**28** And when she was in labor, one put out a hand, and the midwife took and tied a scarlet thread on his hand, saying, "This one came out first."
29 Then it happened, as he drew back his hand, that his brother came out unexpectedly; and she said, "How did you break through? *This* breach *be* upon you!" Therefore his name was called Perez.	**29** But as he drew back his hand, behold, his brother came out. And she said, "What a breach you have made for yourself!" Therefore his name was called Perez.
30 Afterward his brother came out who had the scarlet *thread* on his hand. And his name was called Zerah.	**30** Afterward his brother came out with the scarlet thread on his hand, and his name was called Zerah.

We reach now the climax of the story. In the book of Genesis, stories always end with a birth. The particular nature of that birth, which is reminiscent of the births of Jacob and Esau, reinforces its providential character.

38:27 At the time for giving birth. The word "time" (*'et*), which introduces the birth event, echoes the word "time" (*'et*), which introduces Judah's departure from his brothers; as if the two events were related. For Judah to produce that birth necessitated that he distance himself from his brothers after the crime committed against Joseph.

Behold, twins were in her womb. This is the same phrase that describes the birth of Jacob and Esau (25:24), denoting the same feeling of wonder through the same introductory word *hinneh* "behold."

38:28–30 The parallel is not limited to their condition as twins. They behave in the same manner. Similar to Jacob and Esau, the first one to emerge, and who is marked with a scarlet thread on his hand by the midwife (38:28), is actually born second, and the "second" forces his way through **unexpectedly** (38:29) and is born first. The names of the twins signify each case. Although he presented first, the child whose hand has a scarlet thread is called second (38:30), and his name is simply an objective observation of that scarlet thread. The name **Zerah** (38:30) means "shining," evoking the brilliant rising of the sun (Eccl 1:5; Isa 60:3). Although he is presented second, the child who broke through is born and named first (38:29), and his name is an aspect of the exclaiming question: **how did you break through?** (38:29). The name **Perez** means "break through." The story of Tamar "unexpectedly" ends with the birth of the one who "breaks through." This second who became first is the one that is retained in salvation history, in the genealogy of David (Ruth 4:18–22), and ultimately in the genealogy of Jesus Christ (Matt 1:3). In the New Testament genealogy, Tamar is the first of four women, followed by Rahab (Matt 1:5), Ruth (Matt 1:6), and the "wife of Uriah" (Matt 1:6) who preceded Mary the mother of Jesus (Matt 1:16). These are the only ancestresses of the Old Testament who are mentioned in the genealogy, a record that is all the more significant because it excludes the great matriarchs Sarah, Rebekah, Rachel, and Leah. The connection between these four women could be explained by the fact that all of them had a highly irregular, even suspicious marital relationship, thus preparing the way for Mary, who presented a similarly suspicious case, being pregnant and yet unmarried to her husband. Thus, the story of the prostitution of Tamar, similar to the stories of all these other women, evidences the paradigm that underlies the story of Joseph, namely, that the suspicious and evil will be turned into good and will lead to deliverance (50:20). Just as God delivered Tamar through Judah's dubious relation with her, God delivered Joseph and, ultimately, the land through Judah's sale of Joseph.

FROM SLAVE TO MANAGER (39:1–23)

The deliverance of Egypt (39:1–41:57) proceeds according to the previously mentioned principle: evil will turn into good. This principle will be verified in three phases. First, it appears in a private house (39:1–23); second, in a state prison (40:1–23); and third, it works on a cosmic scale, extending to the entire country and the entire world (41:1–57).

After having been sold by his brothers, Joseph becomes the overseer of the house of Potiphar, an Egyptian high officer (39:4) and the overseer of the prison (39:22).

Between these two stations Joseph is confronted by Potiphar's wife, who tries to seduce him. The first and third sections echo each other. What characterizes Joseph in these two sections (39:1–6a; 39:20–23) in Egypt is "success." The keyword *hatsliakh* "succeed" is repeated twice in the beginning of the story (39:2–3) and once at the end of the story, as the last word in the Hebrew sentence (39:23). What characterizes Joseph in the second station of the middle (39:6b–19) is his innocence. The keyword *beged* "garment" is repeated six times in that section, alluding to another meaning of the root *bagad* "to deceive" or "to lie" (cf. Isa 24:16).

The passage consists, then, of a chiastic structure:

A Joseph succeeds in Potiphar's house (39:1–6a)
    B Joseph is innocent (39:6b–19)
A₁ Joseph succeeds in prison (39:20–23)

39:1–6A. JOSEPH SUCCEEDS IN POTIPHAR'S HOUSE

GEN 39:1–6A NKJV	GEN 39:1–6A ESV
1 Now Joseph had been taken down to Egypt. And Potiphar, an officer of Pharaoh, captain of the guard, an Egyptian, bought him from the Ishmaelites who had taken him down there.	**1** Now Joseph had been brought down to Egypt, and Potiphar, an officer of Pharaoh, the captain of the guard, an Egyptian, had bought him from the Ishmaelites who had brought him down there.
2 The LORD was with Joseph, and he was a successful man; and he was in the house of his master the Egyptian.	**2** The LORD was with Joseph, and he became a successful man, and he was in the house of his Egyptian master.
3 And his master saw that the LORD *was* with him and that the LORD made all he did to prosper in his hand.	**3** His master saw that the LORD was with him and that the LORD caused all that he did to succeed in his hands.
4 So Joseph found favor in his sight, and served him. Then he made him overseer of his house, and all *that* he had he put under his authority.	**4** So Joseph found favor in his sight and attended him, and he made him overseer of his house and put him in charge of all that he had.
5 So it was, from the time *that* he had made him overseer of his house and all that he had, that the LORD blessed the Egyptian's house for Joseph's sake; and the blessing of the LORD was on all that he had in the house and in the field.	**5** From the time that he made him overseer in his house and over all that he had the LORD blessed the Egyptian's house for Joseph's sake; the blessing of the LORD was on all that he had, in house and field.
6a Thus he left all that he had in Joseph's hand, and he did not know what he had except for the bread which he ate.	**6a** So he left all that he had in Joseph's charge, and because of him he had no concern about anything but the food he ate.

39:1 The going down of Joseph to Egypt echoes the going down of Judah to Canaan, suggesting the former descent led to the latter one. The verse reporting the purchasing of Joseph from the Ishmaelites by the Egyptian Potiphar reconnects to the last verse of the preceding story of Joseph, which relates the selling of Joseph by the Ishmaelites to Potiphar (37:36), that had been interrupted by the sordid affair of Judah with Tamar (38:1–30). Potiphar is an **officer of Pharaoh, captain of the guard**. The term *saris* translated "officer," refers to the person in charge of the administration of the house, a court official (2 Kgs 18:17); it will later receive, by the turn of the millennium[686] and particularly in the Persian period, the narrower meaning of "eunuch" (Esth 2:3; 4:4), given the practice in the ANE to use castrated men in key administrative positions. The other title, "captain of the guard," refers to the person in charge of the prison for royal officials (40:3–4; 41:10–12; cf. 2 Kgs 25:8–12). To these two titles, which were previously mentioned in the report of the sale of Joseph (37:36), is added a third one, *hammitsri* "the Egyptian," which emphasizes the representative function of Potiphar who is identified with the land of Egypt; he is *the* Egyptian par excellence. This emphasis on the Egyptian identity of the officer may also be due to the non-Egyptian identity of the pharaohs of that time, the Hyksos dynasties (Second Intermediate period: 1674–1550 BC) and kings of Semitic origin. This accumulation of titles designating the highest authorities of the country suggests the proximity of the royal court and prepares for Joseph's next promotion as the highest officer of Pharaoh.

39:2–5 Just as Potiphar is the *'ish mitsri* "Egyptian man" (39:1), Joseph is the *'ish matsliakh* "successful man" (39:2). Success has become his identity, which is explicitly indicated through the word **success** (39:2–3), but is also strongly implied in the observation that God was with him (39:3) and that God blessed him (39:3, 5). The emphasis on the comprehensiveness of this success-blessing is expressed by the repetitive use of the word "all" "everything" (Heb. *kol*) that occurs five times in the passage (39:3–4, 5 [2x], 6). God's blessing on Joseph affects even the Egyptian: **his master saw that the Lord was with him**. We are not informed about what the master saw, but this note suggests an unusual experience, which may have inspired in him wonder and the awareness of the supernatural Presence. The master's discovery is not confined to the external observation; it becomes an existential experience for the Egyptian, who enjoys the beneficial effect of God's presence in his personal life. The Egyptian is blessed **for Joseph's sake** (39:5).

39:6a Because God blesses Joseph in "all," the master entrusts **all that he had**, all **except for the bread which he ate**. This phrase may be an idiomatic expression referring discretely to his wife (Prov 30:20), as the parallel language will suggest later in Joseph's response: **nor has he kept back anything from me but you, because you are his wife** (39:9). This allusion to the master's wife and the immediate reference to Joseph's handsome appearance anticipate the following events.

39:6B–19. JOSEPH IS INNOCENT

GEN 39:6B–19 NKJV	GEN 39:6B–19 ESV
6b Now Joseph was handsome in form and appearance.	**6b** Now Joseph was handsome in form and appearance.
7 And it came to pass after these things that his master's wife cast longing eyes on Joseph, and she said, "Lie with me."	**7** And after a time his master's wife cast her eyes on Joseph and said, "Lie with me."
8 But he refused and said to his master's wife, "Look, my master does not know what *is* with me in the house, and he has committed all that he has to my hand.	**8** But he refused and said to his master's wife, "Behold, because of me my master has no concern about anything in the house, and he has put everything that he has in my charge.

---

686 J. Vergote, "Joseph en Egypte: 25 ans après," in *Pharaonic Egypt: The Bible and Christianity*, ed. S. Israelit-Groll (Jerusalem: Magnes Press, 1985), 118.

9 *There is* no one greater in this house than I, nor has he kept back anything from me but you, because you *are* his wife. How then can I do this great wickedness, and sin against God?"

9 He is not greater in this house than I am, nor has he kept back anything from me except yourself, because you are his wife. How then can I do this great wickedness and sin against God?"

10 So it was, as she spoke to Joseph day by day, that he did not heed her, to lie with her *or* to be with her.

10 And as she spoke to Joseph day after day, he would not listen to her, to lie beside her or to be with her.

11 But it happened about this time, when Joseph went into the house to do his work, and none of the men of the house *was* inside,

11 But one day, when he went into the house to do his work and none of the men of the house was there in the house,

12 that she caught him by his garment, saying, "Lie with me." But he left his garment in her hand, and fled and ran outside.

12 she caught him by his garment, saying, "Lie with me." But he left his garment in her hand and fled and got out of the house.

13 And so it was, when she saw that he had left his garment in her hand and fled outside,

13 And as soon as she saw that he had left his garment in her hand and had fled out of the house,

14 that she called to the men of her house and spoke to them, saying, "See, he has brought in to us a Hebrew to mock us. He came in to me to lie with me, and I cried out with a loud voice.

14 she called to the men of her household and said to them, "See, he has brought among us a Hebrew to laugh at us. He came in to me to lie with me, and I cried out with a loud voice.

15 And it happened, when he heard that I lifted my voice and cried out, that he left his garment with me, and fled and went outside."

15 And as soon as he heard that I lifted up my voice and cried out, he left his garment beside me and fled and got out of the house."

16 So she kept his garment with her until his master came home.

16 Then she laid up his garment by her until his master came home,

17 Then she spoke to him with words like these, saying, "The Hebrew servant whom you brought to us came in to me to mock me;

17 and she told him the same story, saying, "The Hebrew servant, whom you have brought among us, came in to me to laugh at me.

18 so it happened, as I lifted my voice and cried out, that he left his garment with me and fled outside."

18 But as soon as I lifted up my voice and cried, he left his garment beside me and fled out of the house."

19 So it was, when his master heard the words which his wife spoke to him, saying, "Your servant did to me after this manner," that his anger was aroused.

19 As soon as his master heard the words that his wife spoke to him, "This is the way your servant treated me," his anger was kindled.

39:6b–7 The events precipitate and are initiated by the master's wife who "lifts up her eyes toward Joseph" (lit. trans.), which implies that she has noticed his handsome appearance (39:6b). The next step follows; she invites Joseph to sleep with her: **lie with me**. Her invitation is short (two Hebrew words), direct and explicit. This boldness suggests her arrogance; she is the mistress and is used to being obeyed. This direct and explicit language, which shows her familiarity with this type of situation, suggests that she has often been unfaithful to her husband, which may well explain the master's expressed concern and warning.

39:8–9 Joseph's response is unambiguous: **he refused** (39:8). However, unlike the master's wife, Joseph speaks at length. While the woman dehumanizes him and is only concerned with sex, without any consideration of what this may imply for herself and for the others, by contrast Joseph explains his response in regard to the others. Joseph cannot concur because of what the master has done: **he has commit-ted all that he has to my hand** (39:8), because of who the woman is: **you are his wife** (39:9a), and because of God: **how then can I do this great wickedness, and sin against God?** (39:9b). In this story, the mechanism of sin is unveiled and the resis-tance against sin is provided. Whereas sin only involves present enjoyment and ignores human reality, the best argument against sin is the future, the effect of sin on others, and the religious awareness that it goes against God.

39:10 Joseph's resistance is not confined to a single incident. The master's wife continues to tempt him each day, speaking to him, probably using more than two words. The woman's words are not reported. Joseph does not listen to her. Joseph not only refuses to sleep with her, he also refrains to be with her. Resisting sin on one occasion is not enough; we must persevere in that resistance (Eph 6:18). Abstain-ing from sin is not enough; we must not focus on it nor desire it (Matt 5:27–28). Moreover, we must prevent sin from occurring and avoid situations that could lead us to sin (2 Tim 2:22–23).

39:11–12 When the master's wife realizes that she can never be alone with Joseph and that her words go unheeded, she takes the opportunity with the absence of people in the house to take a further step and grabs Joseph's garment. The passive form (*niphal*) of the verb suggests that she hangs onto his garments and is therefore so tightly connected to him that in order to liberate himself from her, Joseph has no other choice but to leave his garment in her hands. Joseph does not even stay around but flees outside far from her.

39:13–15 The woman holding the empty garment not only feels rejected, as she will indicate later (cf. 39:14), but also powerless. She can no longer reach Joseph (39:13). Therefore, she resorts to malicious falsehood. The fact that she calls the men and that they respond immediately (39:14) suggests that she knew where they were during their absence from the house. These men were likely her servants and owed her obedience. Astutely, she includes them in her humiliation, with a veiled accusa-tion against the master: **see, he has brought in to us a Hebrew to mock us** (39:14). Joseph's garment is again used to support a lie against him. Similar to Joseph's broth-ers (37:32–33), the woman uses Joseph's garment as evidence for her innocence. The Hebrew word *bgd* for "garment," which is a recurring keyword in this passage (39:12 [2x], 13, 15–16, 18), hints at another meaning of the word *bgd,* that is, "to deceive," "to lie" (Isa 24:16). Her claim that she had **cried out with a loud voice** suggests that the men were too far (or too busy) to hear her cries (cf. Deut 22:22, 27).

39:16–19 Because the woman's stratagem successfully worked with her servants, she uses it again with her husband. Having kept Joseph's garment, she tells him the same lies (39:16–18) and subtly blames him for what happened: **the Hebrew servant whom you brought to us** (39:17), stressing *your* servant did to me (39:19). The master's reaction to his wife is different from Joseph's reaction to her. Whereas Joseph **did not heed her** (39:10), **his master heard the words which his wife spoke to him** (39:19). The same verb *shama'* "heed," "hear" is used in both cases. Whereas Joseph remains cool and never sins, the master becomes angry. However, the object of the master's anger is intriguingly not indicated, suggesting his ambivalent judgment.

39:20–23. JOSEPH SUCCEEDS IN PRISON

GEN 39:20–23 NKJV	GEN 39:20–23 ESV
20 Then Joseph's master took him and put him into the prison, a place where the king's prisoners *were* confined. And he was there in the prison.	**20** And Joseph's master took him and put him into the prison, the place where the king's prisoners were confined, and he was there in prison.
21 But the LORD was with Joseph and showed him mercy, and He gave him favor in the sight of the keeper of the prison.	**21** But the LORD was with Joseph and showed him steadfast love and gave him favor in the sight of the keeper of the prison.
22 And the keeper of the prison committed to Joseph's hand all the prisoners who *were* in the prison; whatever they did there, it was his doing.	**22** And the keeper of the prison put Joseph in charge of all the prisoners who were in the prison. Whatever was done there, he was the one who did it.
23 The keeper of the prison did not look into anything *that was* under *Joseph's* authority, because the LORD was with him; and whatever he did, the LORD made *it* prosper.	**23** The keeper of the prison paid no attention to anything that was in Joseph's charge, because the LORD was with him. And whatever he did, the LORD made it succeed.

39:20 Strangely, the master does not require the capital punishment that is normally expected for that type of crime (attempted rape). Instead, the master sends him to prison (39:20). The specific information, that this prison was **a place where the king's prisoners were confined**, prepares the reader for the next story, which will involve the butler and the baker of the king (40:1). This soft penalty suggests the master's ambivalence toward Joseph's crime. In one aspect, he wanted to please his wife; however, he may have doubted his wife's version of the facts. Secretly, he hopes to later save him from the prison (cf. 37:22; Dan 6:18–20), particularly because he has certain control over these institutions. The short mention of Joseph, **and he was there in the prison**, suggests a silent Joseph who has been abandoned in the prison, with no one to care for him. Either Potiphar had forgotten him, or he did not have the strength of character to save him.

39:21 When in prison, Joseph again faces the same fate. God will turn this sad and unjust condition into an opportunity for success. This is first of all true in the midst of trouble: **the Lord was with Joseph**. When God's children are in trouble, they experience God's proximity: "for You are with me" (Ps 23:4). The next remark is particularly reassuring because God does not content Himself with a "pastoral," sympathetic approach. God does not just **show him mercy**; He does not just provide us with an emotional and sentimental comfort. God affects the concrete and objective material of the event: God **gave him favor in the sight of the keeper of the prison**. God turns the enemy into a friend. This action is not only a message of hope for Joseph, anticipating the forthcoming success, it is also a lesson about our relationship with this enemy in the prison. The fact that Joseph is holy does not turn him into an angry saint. Thanks to God Joseph is able to entertain a relationship of grace and love with the wicked man of the world (cf. Dan 1:9).

39:22–23 Joseph is once again promoted as supervisor. The same language that described Joseph's success under Potiphar reappears in the context of Joseph in the prison: **the keeper of the prison committed to Joseph's hand all the prisoners** (39:22; cf. 39:5–6a). Similar to Potiphar (39:5–6), **the keeper of the prison** trusts Joseph completely. The text says that he **did not look into anything that was under**

Joseph's authority (39:23; cf. 39:6). The same supernatural reasons are given to explain this unexpected turn of events: **the Lord was with him** (39:23; cf. 39:2) **and whatever he did, the Lord made it prosper** (39:23 cf. 39:3). These parallels indicate God's consistent faithfulness and His creative capacity to change what is meant for evil into good (50:20). These recurring circumstances also testify to Joseph's persistent faith and stability despite repeated adversities.

TWO DREAMS IN PRISON (40:1–23)

Joseph is put in charge of the prisoners, Pharaoh's butler and baker, who are troubled by dreams they cannot understand (40:1–8). Joseph interprets the dreams as predictions of their opposite future fates beyond their present conditions: the butler's dream means he will be restored to his former position (40:9–15), whereas the baker's dream means he will be hanged (40:16–19). The chapter ends with the report of the fulfillment of these dreams (40:20–23), thus confirming the truth of the dreams and Joseph's correct interpretation.

40:1–8. JOSEPH IN CHARGE OF PRISONERS

GEN 40:1–8 NKJV	GEN 40:1–8 ESV
1 It came to pass after these things *that* the butler and the baker of the king of Egypt offended their lord, the king of Egypt.	**1** Some time after this, the cupbearer of the king of Egypt and his baker committed an offense against their lord the king of Egypt.
2 And Pharaoh was angry with his two officers, the chief butler and the chief baker.	**2** And Pharaoh was angry with his two officers, the chief cupbearer and the chief baker,
3 So he put them in custody in the house of the captain of the guard, in the prison, the place where Joseph *was* confined.	**3** and he put them in custody in the house of the captain of the guard, in the prison where Joseph was confined.
4 And the captain of the guard charged Joseph with them, and he served them; so they were in custody for a while.	**4** The captain of the guard appointed Joseph to be with them, and he attended them. They continued for some time in custody.
5 Then the butler and the baker of the king of Egypt, who *were* confined in the prison, had a dream, both of them, each man's dream in one night *and* each man's dream with its *own* interpretation.	**5** And one night they both dreamed—the cupbearer and the baker of the king of Egypt, who were confined in the prison—each his own dream, and each dream with its own interpretation.
6 And Joseph came in to them in the morning and looked at them, and saw that they *were* sad.	**6** When Joseph came to them in the morning, he saw that they were troubled.
7 So he asked Pharaoh's officers who *were* with him in the custody of his lord's house, saying, "Why do you look *so* sad today?"	**7** So he asked Pharaoh's officers who were with him in custody in his master's house, "Why are your faces downcast today?"
8 And they said to him, "We each have had a dream, and *there is* no interpreter of it." So Joseph said to them, "Do not interpretations belong to God? Tell *them* to me, please."	**8** They said to him, "We have had dreams, and there is no one to interpret them." And Joseph said to them, "Do not interpretations belong to God? Please tell them to me."

40:1–2 The presence of Pharaoh's two officers in the prison is set in contrast to Joseph. Whereas Joseph was innocent and was put into prison by Potiphar, although he had done nothing to deserve this punishment, the chief butler and the chief baker had offended the king (40:1). Although Potiphar's anger has no object (39:19), Pharaoh's anger is explicitly directed against his two officers (40:2).

40:3–4 The captain of the guard is none other than Potiphar himself, who has the same title "captain of the guard" (37:36; 39:1). Potiphar, who knows and trusts Joseph, decides to place the prisoners under his care (40:4). The fact that they were put into the same prison as Joseph (40:3) expresses the intention to underline the providential orientation of the events.

40:5–8 Note the parallel between the two officers who dreamed a dream **both of them … each man's dream in one night … each man's dream with its own interpretation** (40:5). The parallel is still obvious in the morning when Joseph observes the same expression of sadness on their faces (40:6). When Joseph asks them why they are so sad, they even speak together, giving the same answer (40:8). Joseph is not only perceptive in discerning their feelings, but also cares for them; he asks the reason for their sadness. Their trouble is not so much the dreams; they are intrigued by the exact similitude of their cases. This coincidence again suggests the mysterious work of Providence. They are particularly disturbed by their incapacity to decode their dreams, because **there is no interpreter** (40:8). Although their confession may refer to their former privilege in the royal court, which provided for the use of professional magicians, it is an implicit call for supernatural help. Joseph perceives this tone in their words and immediately takes the opportunity to witness for God. The best and most efficient testimony for God is the one that responds to an expressed need. Only after he reveals that the interpretation belongs to God does Joseph offer his help (40:8b).

40:9–15. THE BUTLER'S DREAM

GEN 40:9–15 NKJV	GEN 40:9–15 ESV
9 Then the chief butler told his dream to Joseph, and said to him, "Behold, in my dream a vine *was* before me,	9 So the chief cupbearer told his dream to Joseph and said to him, "In my dream there was a vine before me,
10 and in the vine *were* three branches; it *was* as though it budded, its blossoms shot forth, and its clusters brought forth ripe grapes.	10 and on the vine there were three branches. As soon as it budded, its blossoms shot forth, and the clusters ripened into grapes.
11 Then Pharaoh's cup *was* in my hand; and I took the grapes and pressed them into Pharaoh's cup, and placed the cup in Pharaoh's hand."	11 Pharaoh's cup was in my hand, and I took the grapes and pressed them into Pharaoh's cup and placed the cup in Pharaoh's hand."
12 And Joseph said to him, "This *is* the interpretation of it: The three branches *are* three days.	12 Then Joseph said to him, "This is its interpretation: the three branches are three days.
13 Now within three days Pharaoh will lift up your head and restore you to your place, and you will put Pharaoh's cup in his hand according to the former manner, when you were his butler.	13 In three days Pharaoh will lift up your head and restore you to your office, and you shall place Pharaoh's cup in his hand as formerly, when you were his cupbearer.

14 But remember me when it is well with you, and please show kindness to me; make mention of me to Pharaoh, and get me out of this house.
15 For indeed I was stolen away from the land of the Hebrews; and also I have done nothing here that they should put me into the dungeon."

14 Only remember me, when it is well with you, and please do me the kindness to mention me to Pharaoh, and so get me out of this house.
15 For I was indeed stolen out of the land of the Hebrews, and here also I have done nothing that they should put me into the pit."

40:9–11 That the butler, whose dream means good news, is the first to respond, prepares and encourages the baker to do the same. Had the baker responded first, the butler would have been discouraged to ask for an interpretation, and Joseph would have remained in prison. Even the butler-baker sequence is providential. The recurrence of the number three in the dream is also a sign of the divine control over the events. The vine has three branches (40:10), which grow in three stages (**budded … blossoms … ripe** [40:10]), and the butler performs three successive actions (**took the grapes … pressed them … placed the cup in Pharaoh's hand** [40:11]).

40:12–13 The interpretation of the dream matches the data of the dream, also following the rhythm of three. The growing of the three branches, which indicates the passing of time, refers to **three days** (40:12). The three successive actions of the dreaming butler refer to three successive actions in real life: **lift up … restore … put** (40:13).

40:14–15 As a messenger of good news, Joseph feels encouraged to ask for recognition and remembrance: **remember me when it is well with you** (40:14). When all goes well, it is easy to forget. The Hebrew verb *ytab* "it is well," which is related to the adjective *tob* "good," expresses the concept of happiness (Deut 5:16; Prov 15:13). We tend to take our happiness for granted and enjoy it as if it were something we naturally deserve, forgetting it has come by grace and that we owe it to someone. The reference to *khesed*, which means "grace" (NKJV: **kindness**) in this context (40:14), is not accidental. Joseph's reference to his case as someone who was **put into the dungeon** although he **did nothing** (40:15) is perfectly fitting; it conveys the same message of grace. Just as the butler's restoration is undeserved and he did nothing to receive a promotion, Joseph's imprisonment is undeserved and he did nothing to receive such a punishment. Joseph uses the same word *bor* **dungeon**, which referred to the **pit** (37:24) into which he was cast by his brothers, although he had done nothing. By using the same word, Joseph associates the two situations. Joseph confronts the butler with the argument of his repeated injustice to awaken in him the sense of grace, which could save him from the pit.

40:16–19. THE BAKER'S DREAM

GEN 40:16–19 NKJV	GEN 40:16–19 ESV
16 When the chief baker saw that the interpretation was good, he said to Joseph, "I also *was* in my dream, and there *were* three white baskets on my head.	**16** When the chief baker saw that the interpretation was favorable, he said to Joseph, "I also had a dream: there were three cake baskets on my head,
17 In the uppermost basket *were* all kinds of baked goods for Pharaoh, and the birds ate them out of the basket on my head."	**17** and in the uppermost basket there were all sorts of baked food for Pharaoh, but the birds were eating it out of the basket on my head."

18 So Joseph answered and said, "This *is* the interpretation of it: The three baskets *are* three days.	**18** And Joseph answered and said, "This is its interpretation: the three baskets are three days.
19 Within three days Pharaoh will lift off your head from you and hang you on a tree; and the birds will eat your flesh from you."	**19** In three days Pharaoh will lift up your head—from you!—and hang you on a tree. And the birds will eat the flesh from you."

40:16–17 Seeing that the butler's dream receives a positive interpretation, the baker is encouraged to present his dream for interpretation. The number three also marks the rhythm of the dream. The baker sees three things (**basket, baked goods,** and **birds**) three times.

40:18–19 The interpretation of the dream also fits its data. Three baskets, which are put on the head, one upon the other, suggest the passing of time, the three stages of baking, referring to three days (40:18). Similar to the butler, the historical fulfillment of the dream parallels the events of the dream: **lift off … hang … eat** (40:19). The suspense of the interpretation is suggested twice. First, when the baker starts speaking; the phrase **I also was in my dream** (40:16) clearly indicates that the baker expects, "he also," a good interpretation. Second, the interpretation begins with the same Hebrew expression *ns' ro'sh* for the baker as for the butler (**lift up [off] your head** [40:13; cf. 40:19]), implying the same expectation of restoration for the baker as for the butler. Only at the conclusion does the expression mean a different fate for each. For the butler, "lift up the head" means that he will be restored to his former position, whereas for the baker, it means that he will be hanged (40:19). The contrast between the two imageries in the respective dreams indicates the difference between the two destinies: whereas the butler places the cup in Pharaoh's hand (40:11), the baker has birds eating out of the basket on his head (40:17). In the butler's case, the actors (the butler and Pharaoh) are active: the butler gives a drink to Pharaoh who receives it in his hand. In the baker's case, the actors (the baker and Pharaoh) are passive: the birds eat the baked goods, and Pharaoh does not receive anything. The butler's dream ends with Pharaoh's open hand, a sign of his welcome, whereas the baker's dream ends with the baker's head, a sign of his hanging. Note also the color difference: the red of the grapes that are freshly pressed, signifying the flow of life, contrasts with the white of the breads, suggesting the paleness of death and shame (Isa 29:22).[687]

40:20–23. FULFILLMENT OF THE DREAMS

GEN 40:20–23 NKJV	GEN 40:20–23 ESV
20 Now it came to pass on the third day, *which was* Pharaoh's birthday, that he made a feast for all his servants; and he lifted up the head of the chief butler and of the chief baker among his servants.	**20** On the third day, which was Pharaoh's birthday, he made a feast for all his servants and lifted up the head of the chief cupbearer and the head of the chief baker among his servants.
21 Then he restored the chief butler to his butlership again, and he placed the cup in Pharaoh's hand.	**21** He restored the chief cupbearer to his position, and he placed the cup in Pharaoh's hand.
22 But he hanged the chief baker, as Joseph had interpreted to them.	**22** But he hanged the chief baker, as Joseph had interpreted to them.

---

687 On the meaning of the Hebrew word *khori*, from the root *khor* (cf. the Arabic *khuwarah*: "white," "pale"), refer-ring to the whiteness of the flour, see *HALOT* 1:299, 353.

23 Yet the chief butler did not remember Joseph, but forgot him.	**23** Yet the chief cupbearer did not remember Joseph, but forgot him.

40:20–22 **The third day** (40:20) connotes the idea of restoration and resurrection (Hos 6:2; Jonah 1:17; 1 Cor 15:4). **Pharaoh's birthday** (40:20) may refer to the celebration of his birth as the son of *Re*, and hence of his accession to the throne. This day was marked by banquets and served as an occasion for pardoning prisoners.[688] The historical fulfillment of the dreams matches the data of the dream—**the chief butler … placed the cup in Pharaoh's hand** (40:21; cf. 40:11)—and confirms the correctness of their interpretation, **as Joseph has interpreted to them** (40:22).

40:23 The first word **yet** translates the adversative *waw* marking the contrast between the fulfillments of the previous dreams for the butler and the baker and the nonfulfillment of Joseph's request (40:14). Whereas the prophetic dreams of the butler and the baker are fulfilled literally, according to their words, the opposite occurs to Joseph. He had asked the butler to remember him (40:14), and *yet* **the chief butler did not remember Joseph, but forgot him**. The repetition of the same idea in the two verbs ("did not remember"/"forgot") suggests that the butler forgot because he did not exert effort to remember. The verb "forgot" denotes Joseph's definitive condition: Joseph is bound to stay in the pit forever.

PHARAOH'S TWO DREAMS (41:1–57)

Following the two dreams of the high officers, Pharaoh also has two dreams, which no one can interpret (41:1–7). The butler, who suddenly remembers Joseph, recommends him to Pharaoh (41:8–13). Similar to the two preceding dreams, Pharaoh exposes his dreams to Joseph (41:14–24) who, then, interprets them as a message for the economic future of Egypt and counsels the king accordingly (41:25–36). Impressed by Joseph's wisdom, Pharaoh promotes Joseph and entrusts him with the administration of the country (41:37–46). Joseph manages the gathered grain (41:47–57).

41:1–7. COWS AND HEADS OF GRAIN

GEN 41:1–7 NKJV	GEN 41:1–7 ESV
1 Then it came to pass, at the end of two full years, that Pharaoh had a dream; and behold, he stood by the river.	**1** After two whole years, Pharaoh dreamed that he was standing by the Nile,
2 Suddenly there came up out of the river seven cows, fine looking and fat; and they fed in the meadow.	**2** and behold, there came up out of the Nile seven cows attractive and plump, and they fed in the reed grass.
3 Then behold, seven other cows came up after them out of the river, ugly and gaunt, and stood by the *other* cows on the bank of the river.	**3** And behold, seven other cows, ugly and thin, came up out of the Nile after them, and stood by the other cows on the bank of the Nile.

---

688 See James K. Hoffmeier, *Israel in Egypt* (New York: Oxford University Press, 1996), 89–91.

4 And the ugly and gaunt cows ate up the seven fine looking and fat cows. So Pharaoh awoke.	**4** And the ugly, thin cows ate up the seven attractive, plump cows. And Pharaoh awoke.
5 He slept and dreamed a second time; and suddenly seven heads of grain came up on one stalk, plump and good.	**5** And he fell asleep and dreamed a second time. And behold, seven ears of grain, plump and good, were growing on one stalk.
6 Then behold, seven thin heads, blighted by the east wind, sprang up after them.	**6** And behold, after them sprouted seven ears, thin and blighted by the east wind.
7 And the seven thin heads devoured the seven plump and full heads. So Pharaoh awoke, and indeed, *it was* a dream.	**7** And the thin ears swallowed up the seven plump, full ears. And Pharaoh awoke, and behold, it was a dream.

41:1 Two years pass until **Pharaoh had a dream**. The episode of the dream is given even before the pharaoh's report of his dream (41:15), following the chronological sequence of events. This time precision implicitly indicates that Joseph spent two full years in prison and that he had to wait until Pharaoh had a dream to be liberated. Joseph does not owe his salvation to the butler, who was supposed to remember him (40:14), but only to God.

He stood by the river. The name of the river *ye'or* (probably meaning "the seasonal one") is the Egyptian term for the Nile (Exod 2:3, 5; 7:15, etc.), which suggests that the prophetic events and the destiny of Egypt are related to that river. As the Greek writer Herodotus observed, "Egypt is the gift of the Nile," and the Romans stated, "*Aut Nilus, aut nihil*" (either the Nile or nothing). The agricultural fate of the country indeed depended on the flow of the Nile, so much so that even the taxes imposed on the peasants were evaluated according to the measure of the rise of the level of the river. This association was so powerful that Hapy, the god who personified the inundations of the Nile, was represented by an obese fecund figure with large breasts. In Pharaoh's dream, God was speaking the language Pharaoh could understand.

41:2–7 The two dreams are parallel. The **seven cows** parallel the seven heads of grain. The contrast between the first seven fat cows and the second thin cows parallels the co-contrast between the first seven plump heads of grain and the second thin heads of grain. All of these parallels suggest that **the dreams are one** (41:25); they refer to the same event. The figure of the cows was familiar to the pharaoh and was part of his mythological baggage. The motif of the "cows" is a typically Egyptian motif, attested on the tombs of El-Bersheh (between Beni Hassan and Tell-el-Amarna), where the skinny cows represent the country of Retenu (Canaan) and the fat cows represent Egypt. The "seven cows" motif is also present in chapter 148 of the *Book of the Dead*, where the seven cows provide the deceased with the necessary supplies to survive in the afterlife.[689] The image of the cows coming out of the Nile (41:2), the source of the Egyptian economy, carried a message about the economic condition of Egypt.

41:2 In the meadow. The Hebrew word *'akhu* is an Egyptian word, which designates the "reeds" (ESV, NIV) or the papyrus thicket related to the word *'akht* that refers to the "inundation season." The use of this Egyptian word suggests the flood of the Nile as the natural background of the fat cows.

---

689 See also the *Ramesside Dream Book* (recto 5. 16), where the dream of a cow is interpreted as a good omen (quoted in Kasia Szpakowska, *Behind Closed Eyes: Dreams and Nightmares in Ancient Egypt* [Swansea: Classical Press of Wales, 2003], 92).

41:6 **The east wind** is also a familiar element to Pharaoh; it refers to the hot *khamsin*, which blows from the desert and destroys all plants (Exod 14:21).

41:8–13. THE BUTLER REMEMBERS

GEN 41:8–13 NKJV	GEN 41:8–13 ESV
8 Now it came to pass in the morning that his spirit was troubled, and he sent and called for all the magicians of Egypt and all its wise men. And Pharaoh told them his dreams, but *there was* no one who could interpret them for Pharaoh.	8 So in the morning his spirit was troubled, and he sent and called for all the magicians of Egypt and all its wise men. Pharaoh told them his dreams, but there was none who could interpret them to Pharaoh.
9 Then the chief butler spoke to Pharaoh, saying: "I remember my faults this day.	9 Then the chief cupbearer said to Pharaoh, "I remember my offenses today.
10 When Pharaoh was angry with his servants, and put me in custody in the house of the captain of the guard, *both* me and the chief baker,	10 When Pharaoh was angry with his servants and put me and the chief baker in custody in the house of the captain of the guard,
11 we each had a dream in one night, he and I. Each of us dreamed according to the interpretation of his *own* dream.	11 we dreamed on the same night, he and I, each having a dream with its own interpretation.
12 Now there *was* a young Hebrew man with us there, a servant of the captain of the guard. And we told him, and he interpreted our dreams for us; to each man he interpreted according to his *own* dream.	12 A young Hebrew was there with us, a servant of the captain of the guard. When we told him, he interpreted our dreams to us, giving an interpretation to each man according to his dream.
13 And it came to pass, just as he interpreted for us, so it happened. He restored me to my office, and he hanged him."	13 And as he interpreted to us, so it came about. I was restored to my office, and the baker was hanged."

41:8 **His spirit was troubled.** The Hebrew verb *pa'am* (translated "trouble") refers to the step or the foot (Ps 57:6 [7]) or the anvil (1 Kgs 7:30). Pharaoh's heart beats like the hammering of the foot, thus suggesting the intensity of Pharaoh's emotion (cf. Dan 2:1, 3). Pharaoh is troubled only after the second dream when he realizes that the same features of the dream are repeated a second time, an indication of their divine origin, and hence of their significance. This is why he is so anxious for an explanation and, for that purpose, calls the magicians of Egypt.

Magicians. The Hebrew word for "magician" (*khartummim*) is borrowed from the Egyptian *kheri-tp* (lector priest), which refers to a class of priests whose functions included the reading of spells and the interpretation of dreams. Pharaoh experiences the same frustration as his officers, the butler and the baker; similar to them, he does not find anyone able to interpret his dreams (cf. 40:8).

41:9 The chief butler is present at court when all of this turmoil occurs, and all of these events cause him to **remember** (41:9) his own experience in prison. The Hebrew verb *mazkir* (translated "remember") is the causative form (*hiphil*) of the verb *zkr* "remember" and means "to cause to (to make) remember," "to remind." The butler is embarrassed because he will make the king remember his (the butler's) mistake. The butler risks awakening old memories, which may have a certain effect on the king's disposition toward him. However, the butler "remembers" (*zakar*)

Joseph and thus fulfills what Joseph had asked of him: "remember me" (*zekartani*) "make mention of me" (*wehizkirtani*) (40:14). Note that the second verb Joseph uses "make mention of me" (*wehizkirtani*) is the same causative form (*hiphil*) of the same verb *zakar*, which the butler uses (*mazkir*), a clear indication that the butler remembers Joseph's words.

41:10–13 The butler also repeats the same verb that characterized the pharaoh's anger (*qetsep*) in 40:2. The intention of this systematic evocation of the past is that all that was predicted in the past has now come true. The past has reappeared in the present: **it came to pass, just as he interpreted for us … so it happened** (41:13). The present observation **he restored me to my office, and he hanged him** is the palpable evidence of the truth of Joseph's interpretation of the dreams. This is enough to convince the pharaoh to call Joseph.

41:14–24. PHARAOH EXPOSES HIS DREAMS

GEN 41:14–24 NKJV	GEN 41:14–24 ESV
14 Then Pharaoh sent and called Joseph, and they brought him quickly out of the dungeon; and he shaved, changed his clothing, and came to Pharaoh.	**14** Then Pharaoh sent and called Joseph, and they quickly brought him out of the pit. And when he had shaved himself and changed his clothes, he came in before Pharaoh.
15 And Pharaoh said to Joseph, "I have had a dream, and *there is* no one who can interpret it. But I have heard it said of you *that* you can understand a dream, to interpret it."	**15** And Pharaoh said to Joseph, "I have had a dream, and there is no one who can interpret it. I have heard it said of you that when you hear a dream you can interpret it."
16 So Joseph answered Pharaoh, saying, "*It is* not in me; God will give Pharaoh an answer of peace."	**16** Joseph answered Pharaoh, "It is not in me; God will give Pharaoh a favorable answer."
17 Then Pharaoh said to Joseph: "Behold, in my dream I stood on the bank of the river.	**17** Then Pharaoh said to Joseph, "Behold, in my dream I was standing on the banks of the Nile.
18 Suddenly seven cows came up out of the river, fine looking and fat; and they fed in the meadow.	**18** Seven cows, plump and attractive, came up out of the Nile and fed in the reed grass.
19 Then behold, seven other cows came up after them, poor and very ugly and gaunt, such ugliness as I have never seen in all the land of Egypt.	**19** Seven other cows came up after them, poor and very ugly and thin, such as I had never seen in all the land of Egypt.
20 And the gaunt and ugly cows ate up the first seven, the fat cows.	**20** And the thin, ugly cows ate up the first seven plump cows,
21 When they had eaten them up, no one would have known that they had eaten them, for they *were* just as ugly as at the beginning. So I awoke.	**21** but when they had eaten them no one would have known that they had eaten them, for they were still as ugly as at the beginning. Then I awoke.
22 Also I saw in my dream, and suddenly seven heads came up on one stalk, full and good.	**22** I also saw in my dream seven ears growing on one stalk, full and good.
23 Then behold, seven heads, withered, thin, *and* blighted by the east wind, sprang up after them.	**23** Seven ears, withered, thin, and blighted by the east wind, sprouted after them,
24 And the thin heads devoured the seven good heads. So I told *this* to the magicians, but *there was* no one who could explain *it* to me."	**24** and the thin ears swallowed up the seven good ears. And I told it to the magicians, but there was no one who could explain it to me."

41:14 Pharaoh is immediately eager to meet Joseph: **they brought him hastily**. The Hebrew verb *wayirtsehu* means literally "they made him run." The notion is that Joseph is rushed out of the pit, not only because Pharaoh is anxious to have his dream interpreted, but also because people have begun to realize that he does not belong there. Joseph's first act is to assume an Egyptian appearance, **he shaved**, thus following the Egyptian requirement of the priest, versus the Hebrew usage of keeping the beard, and **changed his clothing**, probably a priestly robe. Joseph now appears as an Egyptian officer, perhaps even a priest.

41:15–16 The fact that Pharaoh does not need the help of an interpreter to communicate with Joseph, as was common practice in the royal court (42:23), suggests that Joseph was proficient in the Egyptian language. Joseph's adjustment contrasts with the pharaoh's uneasiness to adapt to his new and unusual situation as a Pharaoh; he is powerless in regard to his dream: **there is no one who can interpret it** (41:15). Pharaoh's awareness of his limitation becomes for Joseph the opportunity to witness to the only One who "can interpret it": **It is not in me; God will give … an answer of peace** (41:16). First, Joseph emphasizes that this has nothing to with him. His first word is a strong negation: *bil'adai* "not in me." Joseph then refers to God. Joseph's reference to "peace" (*shalom*) indicates that Pharaoh is deeply troubled by his dream; he has lost that "peace" that will return to him only by God through Joseph's interpretation of the dream.

41:17–24 Pharaoh is now confident and tells his dream to Joseph. A comparison of the pharaoh's version of the dream with the author's original account (41:1–7) reveals a number of significant differences. The pharaoh's version is more precise and more dramatic than the author's version. Whereas the author vaguely situates the pharaoh **by the river** (41:1), Pharaoh sees himself **on the bank of the river** (41:17). Whereas the author describes the second series of cows simply as **ugly and gaunt** (41:3), Pharaoh sees them as **very ugly and gaunt**, and insists, **such ugliness as I have never seen in all the land of Egypt** (41:19). Pharaoh also observes something strange that had not been indicated in the original narrative. The lean cows remain lean and ugly, even after eating the preceding cows (41:20–21). The cows are determined to be indefinitely ugly. Likewise, the pharaoh's report of his dream of the ear of grain is harsher than the author's report. Whereas the author simply observes that they are **blighted by the east wind** (41:6), Pharaoh elaborates and notes that they are **withered, thin, and blighted by the east wind** (41:23). This new emphasis reflects the pharaoh's anxiety and anguish. Another reason for the pharaoh's anguish is that **no one … could explain it** (41:24), an observation that both ends and begins the pharaoh's report (41:15).

41:25–36. JOSEPH INTERPRETS THE DREAMS

GEN 41:25–36 NKJV	GEN 41:25–36 ESV
25 Then Joseph said to Pharaoh, "The dreams of Pharaoh *are* one; God has shown Pharaoh what He *is* about to do:	**25** Then Joseph said to Pharaoh, "The dreams of Pharaoh are one; God has revealed to Pharaoh what he is about to do.
26 The seven good cows *are* seven years, and the seven good heads *are* seven years; the dreams *are* one.	**26** The seven good cows are seven years, and the seven good ears are seven years; the dreams are one.

27 And the seven thin and ugly cows which came up after them *are* seven years, and the seven empty heads blighted by the east wind are seven years of famine.	**27** The seven lean and ugly cows that came up after them are seven years, and the seven empty ears blighted by the east wind are also seven years of famine.
28 This *is* the thing which I have spoken to Pharaoh. God has shown Pharaoh what He *is* about to do.	**28** It is as I told Pharaoh; God has shown to Pharaoh what he is about to do.
29 Indeed seven years of great plenty will come throughout all the land of Egypt;	**29** There will come seven years of great plenty throughout all the land of Egypt,
30 but after them seven years of famine will arise, and all the plenty will be forgotten in the land of Egypt; and the famine will deplete the land.	**30** but after them there will arise seven years of famine, and all the plenty will be forgotten in the land of Egypt. The famine will consume the land,
31 So the plenty will not be known in the land because of the famine following, for it *will be* very severe.	**31** and the plenty will be unknown in the land by reason of the famine that will follow, for it will be very severe.
32 And the dream was repeated to Pharaoh twice because the thing *is* established by God, and God will shortly bring it to pass.	**32** And the doubling of Pharaoh's dream means that the thing is fixed by God, and God will shortly bring it about.
33 "Now therefore, let Pharaoh select a discerning and wise man, and set him over the land of Egypt.	**33** Now therefore let Pharaoh select a discerning and wise man, and set him over the land of Egypt.
34 Let Pharaoh do *this*, and let him appoint officers over the land, to collect one-fifth *of the produce* of the land of Egypt in the seven plentiful years.	**34** Let Pharaoh proceed to appoint overseers over the land and take one-fifth of the produce of the land of Egypt during the seven plentiful years.
35 And let them gather all the food of those good years that are coming, and store up grain under the authority of Pharaoh, and let them keep food in the cities.	**35** And let them gather all the food of these good years that are coming and store up grain under the authority of Pharaoh for food in the cities, and let them keep it.
36 Then that food shall be as a reserve for the land for the seven years of famine which shall be in the land of Egypt, that the land may not perish during the famine."	**36** That food shall be a reserve for the land against the seven years of famine that are to occur in the land of Egypt, so that the land may not perish through the famine."

41:25–28 Joseph interprets the dream: the two series of seven cows, as the two series of seven heads, refer to the same event (41:25); they represent two series of good and bad years, which will come on the country of Egypt. The memory of seven years of famine has been preserved in Egyptian tradition. The so-called "Famine Stela," a hieroglyphic inscription (from Ptolemy V, 187 BC) on a rock located at the top of Sehel Island in the Nile south of Aswan, reports that in the year 18 of the reign of Djoser (third dynasty, approximately 2700 BC), the entire country suffered seven years of famine.[690] The story of the famine is also associated with a dream that was given to the king, promising him good years of harvest to come.

41:28 God has shown Pharaoh what He is about to do. The dream is not simply a prediction of the future but reveals God's action. Joseph shares with the king his philosophy of history: God is in control and is the One who shapes the course of events.

---

690 See *AEL* 3:94–100.

Therefore, nothing that the pharaoh can do will prevent this from occurring.

41:29–32 The strange phenomenon of the lean cows that remain lean, although they had eaten the fat cows (41:21), illustrates the fact that the good years will be forgotten during the bad years. The literal fulfillment of the dreams again confirms the determining characteristic of the prophecy. The event will occur exactly as indicated. This assurance is reinforced by the repetition of the dreams, which means that **the thing is established by God** (41:32). The Hebrew participle *nakhon* "established" is derived from the verb *kun* "firm" and expresses the idea that it is "fixed, surely determined,"[691] and unavoidable "as the morning" after the night (Hos 6:3). The promptness of the divine action (**shortly**) is not necessarily temporal; it is a means of suggesting the surprising eruption of the event (Jer 48:16). The surprise is intensified because the bad years follow the good years and are therefore unexpected.

41:33–36 Joseph exceeds the pharaoh's request. He takes the initiative to advise him about what measures to take to manage the crisis. Joseph does not content himself with the revelation of God's plans nor is he passive, waiting for God to perform another miracle. Joseph's faith leads him to think and act boldly by suggesting that **a discerning and wise man** (*nabon wekhakam*) be appointed over the entire operation (41:33). In reverse order, the same words (*khakam wenabon*) are used to characterize the wisdom God gives to David (1 Kgs 3:12) to help him govern the country (1 Kgs 3:9). Only divine guidance could navigate the problem. In addition to this spiritual lesson, Joseph provides a course in economics. To help Egypt survive the famine, Joseph recommends that **one-fifth** (41:34) of the produce be collected during the seven plentiful years. Joseph's counsel fits the historical context of ancient Egypt, which was the first society to have adopted the system of taxation from the first dynasty (3000–2800 BC). In the Levitical system, the same quota of "one-fifth" (20%) was demanded of any person who had unintentionally eaten from a "holy offering" (Lev 22:14; cf. Lev 5:16). Joseph's measure of "one-fifth" may thus imply that the Egyptians, who were enjoying the good years, were in fact suspected of having unintentionally eaten from a "holy offering," a capital that they owed to God. The storage of the fifth will save Egypt in the years of famine (41:36).

41:37–46. JOSEPH IS PROMOTED

GEN 41:37–46 NKJV	GEN 41:37–46 ESV
37 So the advice was good in the eyes of Pharaoh and in the eyes of all his servants.	**37** This proposal pleased Pharaoh and all his servants.
38 And Pharaoh said to his servants, "Can we find *such a one* as this, a man in whom *is* the Spirit of God?"	**38** And Pharaoh said to his servants, "Can we find a man like this, in whom is the Spirit of God?"
39 Then Pharaoh said to Joseph, "Inasmuch as God has shown you all this, *there is* no one as discerning and wise as you.	**39** Then Pharaoh said to Joseph, "Since God has shown you all this, there is none so discerning and wise as you are.
40 You shall be over my house, and all my people shall be ruled according to your word; only in regard to the throne will I be greater than you."	**40** You shall be over my house, and all my people shall order themselves as you command. Only as regards the throne will I be greater than you."

---

691 BDB 465.

41 And Pharaoh said to Joseph, "See, I have set you over all the land of Egypt."	**41** And Pharaoh said to Joseph, "See, I have set you over all the land of Egypt."
42 Then Pharaoh took his signet ring off his hand and put it on Joseph's hand; and he clothed him in garments of fine linen and put a gold chain around his neck.	**42** Then Pharaoh took his signet ring from his hand and put it on Joseph's hand, and clothed him in garments of fine linen and put a gold chain about his neck.
43 And he had him ride in the second chariot which he had; and they cried out before him, "Bow the knee!" So he set him over all the land of Egypt.	**43** And he made him ride in his second chariot. And they called out before him, "Bow the knee!" Thus he set him over all the land of Egypt.
44 Pharaoh also said to Joseph, "I *am* Pharaoh, and without your consent no man may lift his hand or foot in all the land of Egypt."	**44** Moreover, Pharaoh said to Joseph, "I am Pharaoh, and without your consent no one shall lift up hand or foot in all the land of Egypt."
45 And Pharaoh called Joseph's name Zaphnath-Paaneah. And he gave him as a wife Asenath, the daughter of Poti-Pherah priest of On. So Joseph went out over *all* the land of Egypt.	**45** And Pharaoh called Joseph's name Zaphenath-paneah. And he gave him in marriage Asenath, the daughter of Potiphera priest of On. So Joseph went out over the land of Egypt.
46 Joseph was thirty years old when he stood before Pharaoh king of Egypt. And Joseph went out from the presence of Pharaoh, and went throughout all the land of Egypt.	**46** Joseph was thirty years old when he entered the service of Pharaoh king of Egypt. And Joseph went out from the presence of Pharaoh and went through all the land of Egypt.

41:37 From Joseph's long response, his interpretation of the dream, and his advice about its application, Pharaoh focuses on his advice as the most important words from Joseph. The pharaoh's main concern is not the meaning of the dream, of which he might have had some inkling, as much as it is the solution to the problem of which this dream is warning. The fact that Joseph impresses not only Pharaoh, but also **all his servants** (41:37), facilitates Pharaoh's decision to appoint him over **all the land of Egypt** (41:41). This echo on the word "all" suggests that the servants who are present are representatives of the entire country and are therefore ready to support the pharaoh's decision.

41:38–39 The pharaoh's decision to appoint Joseph is based on his two observations of the divine Presence in him: first, because "the advice was good" (41:37), he concludes that this is a man **in whom is the Spirit of God** (41:38); second, because Joseph is able to interpret the dream, **Since God has shown you all this, there is none so discerning and wise as you are** (41:39 ESV). Pharaoh uses the same expression "discerning and wise" (*nabon wekhakam*) that was used by Joseph and that implies the divine influence (see the commentary on 41:32). That Joseph's exceptional wisdom plays a part in Pharaoh's decision to appoint him as the vizier of the land is congruent with Egyptian custom to select the viziers preferably from among the wise men (see, for instance, the cases of Ptahotep and Kagemmi who were viziers and to whom are attributed great works of wisdom literature).[692]

41:40 Similar to Potiphar leaving all in Joseph's hand, except for his wife (39:6, 9), the pharaoh appoints Joseph over his house and all his people, except for the throne. This parallel suggests Joseph's ethics; similar to his practice in Potiphar's house, he will respect the limitation of his power.

---

692 See *AEL* 1:5–7, 59–63.

41:41 This is the third occurrence of the phrase **Pharaoh said** (cf. 41:38–39), and the third time that Pharaoh addresses Joseph, and yet Joseph does not reply, either out of respect, or simply because he is surprised and overwhelmed by the course of events and this extraordinary nomination. The scope of his rule, **over all the land of Egypt**, suggests that Joseph has been appointed as the new vizier (*tjaty* in Egyptian). Cases of foreign and even Hebrew viziers are attested throughout Egyptian history.[693] The vizier's responsibilities were considerable; he was "the administrative deputy of the king" in charge of legal justice and "the official entrusted with the management of the land."[694] The fact that Joseph is placed over the entire land confirms that this vizier could not belong to the New Kingdom period when there were generally two viziers, one for Lower Egypt and one for Upper Egypt. The fact that during the Old Kingdom the vizier was chosen among the sons or the grandsons of the king also excludes that period of time. This vizier should therefore belong to the Middle Kingdom (Theban period) or the Second Intermediate period when this official could be selected based on his wisdom qualities (41:39). In contrast to other periods, during the Second Intermediate period under the rule of the Hyksos, the viziers were most powerful and provided the most stability despite short reigns.

41:42–43 The pharaoh's investiture of Joseph fits the Egyptian context. The **signet ring** (41:42), which is called in the Hebrew text *tabba'at*, designates the Egyptian signet or seal *djeba'ot*, which is derived from the word *djeba'*, meaning "finger," by reference to its position around the finger. This signet ring extends full authority to Joseph to sign all official documents in the name of the king. The term designating the "linen" (*shes*) in the phrase **garments of fine linen** (41:42) is an Egyptian word referring to linen, which was the primary fabric used for clothing in ancient Egypt. This is the first biblical occurrence of this word, which constitutes a clue of the antiquity of this story, because in later texts it is the technical word *buts* that is used (2 Chr 3:14). The **gold chain around his neck** (41:42) refers to the collar on which hung the symbol of the Maat, symbol of equity, which characterized the function of the "vizier," a Turkish word (derived from the Arabic) for the chief minister of state. The rank of "**second**" (*mishneh*) (41:43) is attested in ancient Egypt as the title of the vizier who was called "the second of the king" (*sn.nw n(y)sw.t*). The vizier ceremony involving someone riding on a chariot, preceded by people calling out to invite attention to his passing (41:43), is also an Egyptian custom. The word *'abrek* (generally translated "bow the knee") that is used in our text[695] is not Hebrew but Egyptian. In Egyptian, the word *'abrek* means "attention," "make way" (NIV).

41:44–46 The pharaoh concludes his honoring ceremony by affirming who he is and thus guaranteeing that, as the pharaoh, he confers upon Joseph all power over the entire land (41:44). Furthermore, the pharaoh gives Joseph an honorific name, not only to give him, as a foreigner, the characteristic of an Egyptian official, but also to mark the special distinction that is attached to his new function. The Egyptian

---

693 See for instance the case of a Semitic vizier, Aper-El (around 1350 BC), who supervised the king's affairs during the reigns of Amenhotep III and Akhenaten (Alain-Pierre Zivie, *Découverte à Saqqarah: Le vizir oublié* [Paris: Seuil, 1990]; Alain-Pierre Zivie, "Tombes rupestres de la falaise du Bubasteion à Saqqara," *ASAE* 68 [1982]: 63–68). See also under Merneptah (1235–1224 BC) the case of Ben-Azen, originally from the east of the lake of Tiberiad. Joseph M. Modrzejewski, *The Jews of Egypt: From Rameses II to Emperor Hadrian* (Philadelphia: Jewish Publication Society, 1995), 10, 30.

694 David A. Warburton, "Officials," *OEAE* 2:579.

695 See Kurt Sethe, *Urkunden der 18. Dymastie*, vol. 3 (Berlin: Akademie-Verlag, 1961), IV, 1072, line 10.

name that Joseph receives, **Zaphnath-Paaneah** (41:45), may be analyzed according to the following Egyptian transliteration: *djf n t' pw 'nkh*, meaning, "food of the land, this is life." This reading not only resonates with the present situation, but also fits the historical context of ancient Egypt at that time because the use of the introductory component *djf* (food) is attested in names of high officials of the thirteenth and fourteenth dynasties, immediately preceding Hyksos rule.[696] The pharaoh also gives Joseph an Egyptian wife, whose name, **Asenath** (41:45), has variably been deciphered as meaning either "she belongs to Neith" (*Iw.s-(n)-Nt*), a goddess of the city of Sais in the delta, or "she belongs to father" (*Iw.s-n-'t*). However, the fact that the "she belongs to Neith" interpretation requires supplying the missing conjunction *n* "belong to," whereas the "she belongs to father" interpretation does not require any addition may support this interpretation. Her father's name **Poti-Pherah** (41:45) is likely the longer form of the name "Potiphar" (37:36), which means "he whom R' has given." All these Egyptian names are well attested in the Middle Kingdom and the Hyksos periods (2000–1550 BC) and fit, therefore, in the time of Joseph. The name "Poti-Pherah" renders his origin and function as priest of the city of **On**. The name "On" is the Egyptian *Iwnw* "pillar," resembling an obelisk, which in Egyptian mythology refers to the primordial mound on which the sun god arose from the primordial waters. Its Greek name *Heliopolis* "city of the sun," which occurs in classical sources from the time of Herodotus (450 BC), reflects the city's association with solar theology. This particular connection with the sun god Re, which is not only present in the name of Asenath's father Poti-Pherah, but also in the city of On (Heliopolis), further supports the interpretation of her name as "belonging to father," since Re is traditionally identified as "father." The interpretation "belong to Neith" suggests another geographical and cultural setting (41:45).

Married to the daughter of one of the most prestigious religious figures in Egypt, the **priest of On** (41:45) also called "the greatest seer" (*wr ma3w*), and identified with an Egyptian name of good omen, Joseph is now well accepted in all Egyptian societies and can visit **all the land of Egypt** (41:45–46).

41:47–57. JOSEPH MANAGES THE GRAIN

GEN 41:47–57 NKJV	GEN 41:47–57 ESV
47 Now in the seven plentiful years the ground brought forth abundantly.	**47** During the seven plentiful years the earth produced abundantly,
48 So he gathered up all the food of the seven years which were in the land of Egypt, and laid up the food in the cities; he laid up in every city the food of the fields which surrounded them.	**48** and he gathered up all the food of these seven years, which occurred in the land of Egypt, and put the food in the cities. He put in every city the food from the fields around it.
49 Joseph gathered very much grain, as the sand of the sea, until he stopped counting, for *it was* immeasurable.	**49** And Joseph stored up grain in great abundance, like the sand of the sea, until he ceased to measure it, for it could not be measured.
50 And to Joseph were born two sons before the years of famine came, whom Asenath, the daughter of Poti-Pherah priest of On, bore to him.	**50** Before the year of famine came, two sons were born to Joseph. Asenath, the daughter of Potiphera priest of On, bore them to him.

---

696 See Yahuda, *Language of the Pentateuch*, 31–35.

51 Joseph called the name of the firstborn Manasseh: "For God has made me forget all my toil and all my father's house."	**51** Joseph called the name of the firstborn Manasseh. "For," he said, "God has made me forget all my hardship and all my father's house."
52 And the name of the second he called Ephraim: "For God has caused me to be fruitful in the land of my affliction."	**52** The name of the second he called Ephraim, "For God has made me fruitful in the land of my affliction."
53 Then the seven years of plenty which were in the land of Egypt ended,	**53** The seven years of plenty that occurred in the land of Egypt came to an end,
54 and the seven years of famine began to come, as Joseph had said. The famine was in all lands, but in all the land of Egypt there was bread.	**54** and the seven years of famine began to come, as Joseph had said. There was famine in all lands, but in all the land of Egypt there was bread.
55 So when all the land of Egypt was famished, the people cried to Pharaoh for bread. Then Pharaoh said to all the Egyptians, "Go to Joseph; whatever he says to you, do."	**55** When all the land of Egypt was famished, the people cried to Pharaoh for bread. Pharaoh said to all the Egyptians, "Go to Joseph. What he says to you, do."
56 The famine was over all the face of the earth, and Joseph opened all the storehouses and sold to the Egyptians. And the famine became severe in the land of Egypt.	**56** So when the famine had spread over all the land, Joseph opened all the storehouses and sold to the Egyptians, for the famine was severe in the land of Egypt.
57 So all countries came to Joseph in Egypt to buy *grain*, because the famine was severe in all lands.	**57** Moreover, all the earth came to Egypt to Joseph to buy grain, because the famine was severe over all the earth.

41:47–49 The next seven years are years of abundance across the land (41:47). Joseph's management strategy is comprehensive: he organizes the stockpiling of the grain **in every city** (41:48). However, the grain production is such that it becomes "immeasurable" (41:49), an evidence that it has reached the stage beyond human control and is a sign of supernatural providence. The author attributes the benefit of the grain to Joseph. He is the one who **gathered very much grain**, and the one who **stopped counting** (41:49). The imagery used to characterize the extraordinary fruitfulness of the land is the same as that referring to the human fruitfulness that resulted from divine blessing; it is compared to **the sand of the sea** (41:49; cf. 22:17).

41:50–52 The news of Joseph's fruitfulness following the description of the fruitfulness of the land at that time (41:50) conveys the message that the same God is behind both events. The God who governs nature and creation is the same as the personal God who cares for our existence. The names of Joseph's two sons record this acknowledgment of God's presence in Joseph's life. Both testify to the miraculous operation of God who turns evil into good, the very principle that underlies Joseph's journey (50:20).

41:51 Manasseh. The name of Joseph's first son, "Manasseh" (meaning "making forget"), emphasizes the idea that God has turned Joseph's **toil** in his father's house into such happiness that he has forgotten his past pain. Joy has replaced misery. This transforming experience, which erases the memory of his suffering, prepares Joseph to forgive. This does not mean that Joseph has forgotten his father and his family. The story will later clearly indicate that Joseph remembers his father and his family (43:7, 27, 29; 44:19; 45:3, 9). First as a servant and then as a prisoner, Joseph did not have the freedom to communicate with his family. As soon as Joseph comes to power, God fulfills the warning of the prophetic dreams (42:9) and guides the course of events to produce that opportunity (45:5–8).

41:52 Ephraim. The name of Joseph's second son conveys the idea that God has turned Egypt, which Joseph calls **the land of my affliction**, into an experience of fruitfulness. The name "Ephraim" is derived from the verb *parah* "to bear fruit" (1:22, 28). By "land of my affliction," Joseph implies the land of Egypt where he endured oppression and injustice as a result of the actions of his brothers and Potiphar's wife. The word for "affliction" (*'ani*) is the same word that describes the "oppression" of Israel in Egypt (Exod 3:7, 17; 4:31). As far as Joseph is concerned, God has turned this affliction into fruitfulness. This echo between the two experiences suggests an intended parallel between them. That Joseph's misery in Egypt has been turned into glory is to be understood as a sign of hope for the future misery of Israel in Egypt.

41:53–55 The seven years of abundance end (41:53) and are followed by a time of famine, just **as Joseph had said** (41:54). The course of events confirms, then, Joseph's prophetic gift, and the pharaoh's response to his people's needs is founded on that observation. The "say" of Pharaoh's phrase **whatever he *says* to you, do** echoes the "say" that records Joseph's prophetic word in the phrase **as Joseph had *said*** (41:54). Because Joseph was the only one who was able to predict the coming famine, he was also the only one in the world at that time who was able to take measures against it. Consequently, Egypt is now the only country with bread (41:54).

41:56–57 The language that describes the scope of the famine, *'al kol pney ha-'erets* **over all the face of the earth** (41:56), is reminiscent of the language describing the pre-creation stage, *'al pney ha-khoshek* "darkness was on the face of the deep" (1:2). The salvation of Egypt by Joseph takes, then, a universal proportion. Joseph does not merely provide food for Egypt but for **all the earth** (41:57 ESV), thus fulfilling again the promise that through the blessing of Abraham "all the families of the earth" will be blessed (12:3).

FROM JACOB TO JOSEPH (42:1–24)

After twenty years, Joseph again meets his brothers. Joseph was seventeen years of age when he last saw his brothers (37:2) and thirty years of age when he became vizier of Egypt (41:46), and now, seven years later, at the onset of the famine, he is thirty-seven years of age. This is the time when his dreams about his father and his brothers bowing before him (37:7–10) will be fulfilled. The section (42:1–47:31) covers this event and will therefore respond to its parallel section (37:12–30). The fulfillment of Joseph's dreams develops in three steps, as Joseph's brothers will visit Egypt and will thus meet with Joseph three times. The first meeting occurs with only ten of Joseph's brothers (42:1–38), those who questioned his dreams and hated him because of these dreams (37:8, 19). They now bow before Joseph for the first time (42:6). The second meeting occurs with Joseph's ten brothers and with Joseph's younger brother Benjamin (43:1–45:28); they all bow before Joseph twice (43:26, 28). On this occasion, the ten brothers will again bow before Joseph a fourth time on account of Benjamin (44:14). The third meeting occurs with Jacob, who comes for the first time to Egypt (46:1–47:31). Jacob also bows before Joseph (47:31); unlike his sons, it is not because Joseph is the governor of Egypt that he bows before him, but because Joseph promises to carry him "out of Egypt" when he dies (47:29–31).

42:1–38 Joseph meets with his ten brothers. The story of the meeting between Joseph and his brothers unfolds in two phases. The first phase (42:1–20) covers the move of the brothers from Jacob to Joseph. The second phase (42:21–38) covers their move back from Joseph to Jacob. These two moves encompass five scenes according to the following chiastic structure (ABCB₁A₁):

> **A** Jacob sends his sons to Egypt (42:1–5)
> > **B** Joseph sells food to all people (42:6)
> > > **C Joseph and his brothers (42:7–24)**
> > **B₁** Joseph gives food to his brothers (42:25–28)
> **A₁** Return of the brothers to Jacob: Joseph under a mask of cruelty (42:29–38)

The famine obliges Jacob to send his sons to Egypt to buy grain. When they arrive in Egypt they are immediately recognized by Joseph, who pretends not to recognize them, and speaks roughly to them. First, he questions their intentions and suspects them of having come as spies. When they describe their condition and refer to their family situation, mentioning among other things, the existence of their younger brother left in Canaan, Joseph pretends not to believe them and puts them in prison. As a test of their honesty, he takes one of them, Simeon, as hostage and demands they return with their younger brother Benjamin.

42:1–5. JACOB SENDS HIS SONS TO EGYPT

GEN 42:1–5 NKJV	GEN 42:1–5 ESV
1 When Jacob saw that there was grain in Egypt, Jacob said to his sons, "Why do you look at one another?"	**1** When Jacob learned that there was grain for sale in Egypt, he said to his sons, "Why do you look at one another?"
2 And he said, "Indeed I have heard that there is grain in Egypt; go down to that place and buy for us there, that we may live and not die."	**2** And he said, "Behold, I have heard that there is grain for sale in Egypt. Go down and buy grain for us there, that we may live and not die."
3 So Joseph's ten brothers went down to buy grain in Egypt.	**3** So ten of Joseph's brothers went down to buy grain in Egypt.
4 But Jacob did not send Joseph's brother Benjamin with his brothers, for he said, "Lest some calamity befall him."	**4** But Jacob did not send Benjamin, Joseph's brother, with his brothers, for he feared that harm might happen to him.
5 And the sons of Israel went to buy *grain* among those who journeyed, for the famine was in the land of Canaan.	**5** Thus the sons of Israel came to buy among the others who came, for the famine was in the land of Canaan.

42:1–2 Jacob is the one who initiates the operation. He is the one who **saw** and **heard** of the good situation in Egypt (42:1), who is informed that Egypt has grain (42:1–2), and who decides that his sons should travel there. This trip is a matter of life and death (42:2; cf. 42:8). Jacob's sons are seemingly at a loss in relating to Jacob's dismay, who reproaches them for their passivity: **Why do you look at one another?** (42:1). Those who were so ingenious in their plot against Joseph (37:20, 32) now stand numb before the calamity and have lost all their self-assurance. Jacob must twice repeat his information about Egypt (42:1–2) because they do not respond to Jacob's proposition, as they normally do (34:31; 43:3–10).

42:3–5 Their docile obedience is symptomatic of their nervousness in the matter (42:3). This hesitant attitude may reflect their guilty consciences about selling Joseph, especially after witnessing their father's pain. They do not dare question Jacob's preferential treatment toward Benjamin, who is the only son remaining at home (42:4), although he is no longer a child and must by then be in his twenties. The manner in which Joseph's brothers are depicted, **among those who journeyed** (42:5), reinforces the impression of weakness and lack of character.

42:6. JOSEPH SELLS FOOD TO ALL PEOPLE

GEN 42:6 NKJV	GEN 42:6 ESV
6 Now Joseph *was* governor over the land; and it was he who sold to all the people of the land. And Joseph's brothers came and bowed down before him with *their* faces to the earth.	6 Now Joseph was governor over the land. He was the one who sold to all the people of the land. And Joseph's brothers came and bowed themselves before him with their faces to the ground.

Joseph is identified as the **governor over the land** (42:6a). The Hebrew word *shalit* (see the cognate Arabic word "Sultan") for "governor" derives from the verb *shlt,* which means "to domineer," "to have power" (Neh 5:15; Esth 9:1), and is used as a generic word to designate the ruler who holds the power (Eccl 8:8). The Hebrew title refers to the Egyptian position of "vizier" to suggest the notion of power. Joseph stands as the powerful man who provides grain to **all the people of the land**. This description contrasts with his needy brothers who bow before him, with **their faces to the earth** (42:6). In the Hebrew verse, the same word *'erets* "land," "earth" is used to refer to Joseph as "governor over the land [*'erets*]," to "all the people of the land [*'erets*]," and to the brothers who prostrate themselves with "their faces to the earth [*'erets*]." This play on words suggests the superiority of Joseph, who is described as controlling "over" and providing "to" (preposition: *le* "for the benefit of"), whereas the brothers are described, as the termination *hey* indicates, lying on the earth, their "mouth in the dust" (Lam 3:29).

42:7–24. JOSEPH AND HIS BROTHERS

GEN 42:7–24 NKJV	GEN 42:7–24 ESV
7 Joseph saw his brothers and recognized them, but he acted as a stranger to them and spoke roughly to them. Then he said to them, "Where do you come from?" And they said, "From the land of Canaan to buy food."	7 Joseph saw his brothers and recognized them, but he treated them like strangers and spoke roughly to them. "Where do you come from?" he said. They said, "From the land of Canaan, to buy food."
8 So Joseph recognized his brothers, but they did not recognize him.	8 And Joseph recognized his brothers, but they did not recognize him.

9 Then Joseph remembered the dreams which he had dreamed about them, and said to them, "You *are* spies! You have come to see the nakedness of the land!"

10 And they said to him, "No, my lord, but your servants have come to buy food.

11 We *are* all one man's sons; we *are* honest *men*; your servants are not spies."

12 But he said to them, "No, but you have come to see the nakedness of the land."

13 And they said, "Your servants *are* twelve brothers, the sons of one man in the land of Canaan; and in fact, the youngest *is* with our father today, and one *is* no more."

14 But Joseph said to them, "It *is* as I spoke to you, saying, 'You *are* spies!'

15 In this *manner* you shall be tested: By the life of Pharaoh, you shall not leave this place unless your youngest brother comes here.

16 Send one of you, and let him bring your brother; and you shall be kept in prison, that your words may be tested to see whether *there is* any truth in you; or else, by the life of Pharaoh, surely you *are* spies!"

17 So he put them all together in prison three days.

18 Then Joseph said to them the third day, "Do this and live, *for* I fear God:

19 If you *are* honest *men*, let one of your brothers be confined to your prison house; but you, go and carry grain for the famine of your houses.

20 And bring your youngest brother to me; so your words will be verified, and you shall not die." And they did so.

21 Then they said to one another, "We *are* truly guilty concerning our brother, for we saw the anguish of his soul when he pleaded with us, and we would not hear; therefore this distress has come upon us."

22 And Reuben answered them, saying, "Did I not speak to you, saying, 'Do not sin against the boy'; and you would not listen? Therefore behold, his blood is now required of us."

9 And Joseph remembered the dreams that he had dreamed of them. And he said to them, "You are spies; you have come to see the nakedness of the land."

10 They said to him, "No, my lord, your servants have come to buy food.

11 We are all sons of one man. We are honest men. Your servants have never been spies."

12 He said to them, "No, it is the nakedness of the land that you have come to see."

13 And they said, "We, your servants, are twelve brothers, the sons of one man in the land of Canaan, and behold, the youngest is this day with our father, and one is no more."

14 But Joseph said to them, "It is as I said to you. You are spies.

15 By this you shall be tested: by the life of Pharaoh, you shall not go from this place unless your youngest brother comes here.

16 Send one of you, and let him bring your brother, while you remain confined, that your words may be tested, whether there is truth in you. Or else, by the life of Pharaoh, surely you are spies."

17 And he put them all together in custody for three days.

18 On the third day Joseph said to them, "Do this and you will live, for I fear God:

19 if you are honest men, let one of your brothers remain confined where you are in custody, and let the rest go and carry grain for the famine of your households,

20 and bring your youngest brother to me. So your words will be verified, and you shall not die." And they did so.

21 Then they said to one another, "In truth we are guilty concerning our brother, in that we saw the distress of his soul, when he begged us and we did not listen. That is why this distress has come upon us."

22 And Reuben answered them, "Did I not tell you not to sin against the boy? But you did not listen. So now there comes a reckoning for his blood."

23 But they did not know that Joseph understood them, for he spoke to them through an interpreter.	**23** They did not know that Joseph understood them, for there was an interpreter between them.
24 And he turned himself away from them and wept. Then he returned to them again, and talked with them. And he took Simeon from them and bound him before their eyes.	**24** Then he turned away from them and wept. And he returned to them and spoke to them. And he took Simeon from them and bound him before their eyes.

The meeting contains two dialogues. In the first dialogue, Joseph confronts his brothers (42:7–20), whereas the second dialogue is only among the brothers themselves (42:21–24).

42:7 Joseph recognizes his brothers twice (42:7–8). The first time, Joseph recognizes them when he sees them (42:7a) and engages in conversation with them. They do not recognize him simply because **he acted as a stranger** (42:7). Dressed and shaved as an Egyptian, speaking Egyptian, and communicating with them with the help of a translator (42:23), Joseph behaves like a stranger and cannot therefore be recognized by his brothers, not to mention the fact that the brothers are not expecting to meet Joseph in this environment. In addition, Joseph chooses to speak roughly with them, not only because this is the best way to dissipate any potential recognition on their part, but also as a personal psychological help to control his own emotions. Joseph exaggerates the tone of his voice to make it more authoritarian and angry (42:7). The Hebrew word *qashot* "harsh" is in the plural, expressing the intensity of the unusual harshness of his voice's tone.[697]

42:8 The second time he recognizes them is when he hears them speaking and explaining that they come **from the land of Canaan** (42:7b). This time, the text explicitly says that **they did not recognize him** (42:8). That Joseph is able to recognize his brothers in the large crowd of newcomers from all the countries should not be surprising. These ten men are conspicuously different from the Egyptians, with their beards and colored woolen clothing, and are bound to attract attention. Joseph's reference to spies, a real threat in these times of crisis, suggests a good net of information in place. The Egyptian intelligence services may have noticed these ten individuals and selected them to be presented to Joseph. Joseph may also have been particularly interested in that particular ethnic group, suspecting (hoping) that the famine would oblige members of his family to take the trip. He may even have given special instructions about them.

42:9 Only when they disclose their Canaanite origin does Joseph begin to identify them as his brothers, which triggers the remembrance of his dreams (42:9a). When it is clear that they do not recognize him, he proceeds and accuses them of being spies who came with the intention **to see the nakedness of the land** (42:9). By this expression, Joseph infers that the purpose of their visit is to detect the weak and vulnerable points of Egypt in order to be able to prepare raids against the country and eventually control it. In times of international economic crisis such as these, and with the overwhelming flux of emigrants, Joseph's point is justified.[698]

---

697 The only two occurrences of the Hebrew word *qashot* are found in this chapter (42:7, 30); all the other occurrences have the simpler form *qasheh* (1 Sam 20:10; 25:3; 1 Kgs 12:13; 2 Chr 10:13).

698 In the confusion caused by the flux of Canaanites who settled in the delta during the First Intermediate period (2181–2060 BC), see the testimonies of "The Instruction of Merikare," where these emigrants, the so-called "wretched Asiatics," are depicted as unstable, barbarous, and thieves (*ANET*, 416, lines 91–98). The memory of this turmoil is

42:10–12 To convince Joseph of their honesty and show him they are not spies (42:11), the brothers refer to their family situation: **we are all one man's sons** (42:11). This is a way of saying that they do not belong to some sort of political gang. To their emphatic **no, my lord** (42:10), Joseph opposes with another terse **no** (42:12), insisting they are indeed spies and implying they are lying.

42:13 The brothers expand their argument and become more specific in their report on their family situation. They now mention their younger brother (Benjamin) and the one who **is no more** (Joseph), who, ironically, is standing before them.

42:14 This mention precipitates the course of events. Joseph emphatically indicates to them that he does not believe them and definitely concludes they are spies (42:14). The discussion is closed, and the brothers do not speak anymore. Joseph decides to act and takes unilateral measures. He swears they will not leave that place until their youngest brother shows up and thus presents evidence that they did not lie.

42:15–16 To signify he is not bluffing, Joseph supports his statement with an oath, **by the life of Pharaoh**, which is well attested in ancient Egypt, as a means to prove that one is saying the truth.[699] Because in Egypt the pharaoh is god (son of *Re*), the oath is in fact an invocation of the divine agency to be the guarantor of the oath taker's honesty. The equivalent oath in Israel refers to God (1 Kgs 1:29). When it refers to the king, it is also associated with God (2 Sam 15:21). Joseph makes this oath twice. The first oath is intended to ensure that they will go bring their brother (42:15); the second oath is to ensure that, if they do not bring their brother, they will be considered spies and suffer the consequences (42:16). First, Joseph proposes to his brothers that one of them return to Canaan in order to fetch their younger brother, while the remaining brothers are kept in prison in Egypt (42:16).

42:17–18 The brothers apparently do not accept this initial deal because they are all put together in prison for **three days**. The wording of the passage reporting about the brothers' sojourn in prison echoes the passage reporting about Joseph's sojourn in prison with the two officers of the pharaoh:

So he put them all together in prison (*mishmar*) **three days** (. . . *yamim*) (42:17)
So he put them . . . they were in custody (*mishmar*) for a while (*yamim*) (40:3–4)

The two lines share the following Hebrew words: *yamim* "days," *mishmar* "prison," "custody." Note also the parallel sequence of the words: he-they-prison-days.

This significant parallel between the two passages suggests that the brothers' experience in prison is to be understood as a type of payback-revenge for Joseph's experience in prison. The brothers' trial is much softer, because Joseph and Pharaoh's officers remained in prison for several years, as indicated through the expression *yamim* (lit. trans.: "days,"), which is often used as an idiomatic expression referring to "years" (1 Sam 27:7; Lev 25:28; Exod 13:10). The brothers stayed in prison for only three days. Note that the expression *yamim* may even refer to three years (1 Kgs

. . .
still vivid one hundred years later during the Middle Kingdom (2060–1700 BC) in "the Prophecy of Neferty," which describes the same scenario. The eastern delta has become home to the Asiatics who are growing fast and intend to stay there permanently (*ANET*, 445, lines 25–40).

699 See, for instance, the stela of Sebek-Khu who lived under Senosret III (1887–1849 BC) where we have the following inscription: "as Senosret lives for me, I have spoken the truth." Alan Gardiner, *Egyptian Grammar*, 3rd ed. (Oxford: Griffith Institute, 1999), 164.

2:38–39), in which case, the echo between the two confinements would then be even more striking: three days for three years. This time should be sufficient for them to meditate and reflect on their evil action against Joseph. Suffering from the same suffering they had caused should bring them to repentance. Joseph's statement, **do this and live** (42:18) resonates with the Deuteronomic principle of exact retribution (Deut 30:19) and confirms the intention of the echo we noted between the two passages to bring out the contrast between them. Joseph emphasizes that he fears God (42:18), implying that he was unlike his brothers who did not fear God.

42:19–20 If you are honest men. The Hebrew word *ken* "honest" suggests the idea of certainty, "what is firm, upright, true."[700] Joseph questions their ethical character. Having been the victim of their duplicity and lies, Joseph's suspicion is well founded, and he treats them according to what they were. The only way to establish that they are true is for them to offer tangible proof supporting their claim. Joseph's brothers had shown duplicity in sending their brother Joseph to Egypt; they will now be required to bring their brother Benjamin to Egypt as evidence of their honesty.

42:21–22 Joseph's implicit message of payback must have been well understood by his brothers, since they immediately remember their wicked action and feel **truly guilty** about it (42:21b). The Hebrew word *'ashem* (translated "guilty") also conveys the idea of "punishment and its aftermath or, as an alternative, atonement."[701] Jerome, in the Latin translation of the Vulgate, interprets this word in those terms: "we deserve to suffer, because we have sinned." Note that this awakening of conscience concerns all of them. The expression **they said to one another** (42:21a) is the same as when they began to plot against Joseph (37:19). Those who "said to one another" then, when plotting against him, are the same as those who "said to one another" now, who are feeling guilty about it. The repentance process is thus clearly suggested. They even confess their sin: **we saw the anguish of his soul … and we would not hear** (42:21c). They conclude they are now justly paying for that fault: **therefore this distress has come upon us** (42:21d). They understand the payback effect, which was alluded to by Joseph. Reuben, who had tried to save Joseph and who, unlike his brothers, "heard" (37:21) when the others would not hear (42:21c, 22), reinforces this payback principle: **his blood is now required of us** (41:22). Reuben's words now echo his own words then, "shed no blood" (37:22), when he had tried to save Joseph. On both occasions, Reuben refers to Joseph's blood. Despite Reuben's opposition to the brothers' action, he still shares their guilt. Reuben's good intention was not enough. The objective facts still stand against him. Reuben's protest and action were not sufficiently strong and convincing. When he discovered Joseph's absence from the pit, he merely mumbled, thinking only of himself, "and I, where shall I go?" (37:30), and then no more is heard from him. He joins the group of brothers and shares their deceptive maneuvers against their father (37:31–35).

42:23–24 Because the brothers believe no one can understand them, especially not Joseph, who communicates with them through a translator (42:23), Joseph is able to probe their honesty. When Joseph hears his brothers' confession and detects genuine regret on their faces, he is so moved that he can no longer control himself and must turn away so they cannot see the tears in his eyes. His emotion is so powerful that he must temporarily leave: **he turned himself away from them and wept**

---

700 *"Ken,"* KBL.
701 *TWOT* 79.

(42:24). Joseph will weep seven times (cf. 43:30; 45:2, 14–15; 46:29; 50:1, 17). Power and the demands of administration have not turned him into a callous politician. Joseph is still moved; he is still the sensitive younger brother. However, he does not want to be governed by his feelings. Joseph's love for his brothers and the fact that he has been touched by their sincere repentance does not affect his scheme and his profound desire to redeem his brothers completely. Before they can fully enjoy mercy and grace, they must fully endure the effects of justice. Grace is experienced as grace only when it is received with the consciousness of sin and the expectation of justice.

After recovering his emotions, Joseph returns to his brothers and again speaks to them, as if nothing happened, with the same tone of voice as before. Furthermore, he grasps his older brother Simeon and binds him in front of them. The language that describes Simeon's trial in Joseph's hands echoes the language that describes Joseph's trial in his master's hands:

> **He took** (*wayyiqakh*) ... **bound** (*'sr*) **him** (*'oto*) (42:24)
> He took (*wayyiqakh*) ... him (*'oto*) ... prisoners (*'sr*) ... confined (*'sr*) (39:20)

Why Simeon? He likely played a predominant role in the plot to kill Joseph.[702] Simeon was also the toughest and cruelest of the brothers, as indicated in the Dinah incident (34:25, 30). In choosing Simeon, Joseph signified his power over all his brothers. Even if Simeon was able to stand up to his father (34:30–31), he could not stand before Joseph, who thus revealed himself as even more powerful than his father, again, a hint at his dream (37:10).

FROM JOSEPH TO JACOB (42:25–38)

Joseph commands his servant to fill the sacks of his brothers with grain and to secretly put the money they used to buy the grain into their sacks. On their return to Canaan, the brothers discover the money in their sacks and are confused and afraid. Thus, when the nine brothers inform Jacob of Joseph's request to bring Benjamin with them to Egypt, Jacob refuses and decides not to send them again.

42:25–28. JOSEPH FILLS THE SACKS OF HIS BROTHERS

GEN 42:25–28 NKJV	GEN 42:25–28 ESV
25 Then Joseph gave a command to fill their sacks with grain, to restore every man's money to his sack, and to give them provisions for the journey. Thus he did for them.	**25** And Joseph gave orders to fill their bags with grain, and to replace every man's money in his sack, and to give them provisions for the journey. This was done for them.
26 So they loaded their donkeys with the grain and departed from there.	**26** Then they loaded their donkeys with their grain and departed.

---

702 See Rashi in Miqraot Gedolot on 42:42 (cf. Tg. Ps.-J.); cf. also Ellen G. White, "In the cruel treatment of their brother, Simeon had been the instigator and chief actor, and it was for this reason that the choice fell upon him" (PP 226).

27 But as one *of them* opened his sack to give his donkey feed at the encampment, he saw his money; and there it was, in the mouth of his sack.	**27** And as one of them opened his sack to give his donkey fodder at the lodging place, he saw his money in the mouth of his sack.
28 So he said to his brothers, "My money has been restored, and there it is, in my sack!" Then their hearts failed *them* and they were afraid, saying to one another, "What *is* this *that* God has done to us?"	**28** He said to his brothers, "My money has been put back; here it is in the mouth of my sack!" At this their hearts failed them, and they turned trembling to one another, saying, "What is this that God has done to us?"

42:25 **Joseph gave a command.** The verb *wayetsaw* "gave command" (JPS: "commanded") suggests his sovereign power and authority; it is used with God or with the pharaoh as a subject (2:16; 12:20; Exod 1:22; 5:6). The same Hebrew word (*bar*) designates both the **grain** that is put into his brothers' sacks and the "grain" that was stored up for the benefit of Egypt. Thus, the food that was originally destined for the Egyptians is now given to his brothers.

Restore every man's money. Each brother carried two sacks, one of which contained grain for human consumption, and the other, food for their donkeys. Money was put into the second sack, probably because this was the sack that would be opened first in the course of the journey. The word *kesep* "money" is notably the same as the one that was used to designate what they had obtained from the Ishmaelites when they sold Joseph (37:28). The irony is that this money, which was supposed to make him a slave, has turned him into a prince. Thus, the money is returned to them.

As a bonus, Joseph provides food for their journey back to Canaan. All that he did was **for them**. In addition to testing the brothers,[703] Joseph's maneuver concealed the same profound lesson that was associated with Joseph's destiny: what was originally intended by them to be harmful has now returned to them as beneficial, even beyond measure, since the money they received is far more than the money they obtained from selling Joseph. Whereas they had sold Joseph at a lower price, twenty shekels (37:28), instead of the regular price of thirty shekels (Exod 21:32), they now earn more than what they had paid for since they do not pay anything for the grain. In Joseph's eyes, they have more value than he had in their eyes. Not only does Joseph return good for evil, the good he gives surpasses the evil they did.

While revenge often tends to demand more than the mere value of the loss, Joseph suggests the response of grace, that is, to give instead of being compensated, even more than the value of what has been lost. In practical and concrete terms, if someone has stolen five dollars from me, instead of demanding ten dollars from him as his punishment and my revenge (or compensation for my pain), I should give him one hundred. This is similar to the good priest in Victor Hugo's novel *Les Misérables*, who gives to the thief Jean Valjean not only the silver he had stolen from him, but also an additional precious candelabra. This is the same principle of grace that Jesus referred to in the Sermon on the Mount: "If anyone wants to sue you and take away your tunic, let him have your cloak also. And whoever compels you to go one mile, go with him two" (Matt 5:40–41). However, the brothers are described as passive and completely unaware of their situation. They load

---

703 See Mathews, *Genesis 11:27–50:26*, 781; cf. Ellen G. White, PP 225.

their donkeys and leave the place sad and worried, not knowing that they are, in fact, rich and forgiven (42:26).

42:27–28 Suddenly, one of the brothers opens his grain sack to give food to his donkey and discovers the money that was supposed to pay for the grain (42:27). Although the text does not reveal the identity of this brother, the adjective that qualifies him *'akhad* **one** suggests that he is by himself, implying that it is perhaps Levi who remained by himself without his brother Simeon, his regular companion (29:33–34; 34:25, 30), who remained in prison in Egypt.[704] The brother dares not touch nor take the money, which he shows to his brothers: **there it is, in my sack** (42:28). The brothers' reaction is unanimous and similar to when they were confronted by the governor of Egypt (42:21). The same phrase **saying to one another** reappears (42:21, 28). This echo suggests the nature of their fear; they sense that all of these events are the retribution from God for what they had done to Joseph. This time their anguish is even more intense than the first time. Before, they had acknowledged their guilt and admitted that their present experience was related to their wickedness against their brother (42:21–22). Now they are terribly afraid, for their fear is confirmed. For the first time, they recognize that God is behind all these events; for God is not only the God of justice, He is also the only One who knows what they did. Their question hangs without response: **What is this that God has done to us?** (42:28). They are so confused that not one of the other brothers has the presence of mind to open his sack to check and see if he is in the same situation.

42:29–38. RETURN OF THE BROTHERS TO JACOB

GEN 42:29–38 NKJV	GEN 42:29–38 ESV
29 Then they went to Jacob their father in the land of Canaan and told him all that had happened to them, saying:	**29** When they came to Jacob their father in the land of Canaan, they told him all that had happened to them, saying,
30 "The man *who is* lord of the land spoke roughly to us, and took us for spies of the country.	**30** "The man, the lord of the land, spoke roughly to us and took us to be spies of the land.
31 But we said to him, 'We *are* honest *men*; we are not spies.	**31** But we said to him, 'We are honest men; we have never been spies.
32 We *are* twelve brothers, sons of our father; one *is* no *more*, and the youngest *is* with our father this day in the land of Canaan.'	**32** We are twelve brothers, sons of our father. One is no more, and the youngest is this day with our father in the land of Canaan.'
33 Then the man, the lord of the country, said to us, 'By this I will know that you *are* honest *men*: Leave one of your brothers *here* with me, take *food for* the famine of your households, and be gone.	**33** Then the man, the lord of the land, said to us, 'By this I shall know that you are honest men: leave one of your brothers with me, and take grain for the famine of your households, and go your way.
34 And bring your youngest brother to me; so I shall know that you *are* not spies, but *that* you *are* honest *men*. I will grant your brother to you, and you may trade in the land.'"	**34** Bring your youngest brother to me. Then I shall know that you are not spies but honest men, and I will deliver your brother to you, and you shall trade in the land.'"

704 See Rashi in Miqraot Gedolot on 42:27.

35 Then it happened as they emptied their sacks, that surprisingly each man's bundle of money *was* in his sack; and when they and their father saw the bundles of money, they were afraid.	**35** As they emptied their sacks, behold, every man's bundle of money was in his sack. And when they and their father saw their bundles of money, they were afraid.
36 And Jacob their father said to them, "You have bereaved me: Joseph is no *more*, Simeon is no *more*, and you want to take Benjamin. All these things are against me."	**36** And Jacob their father said to them, "You have bereaved me of my children: Joseph is no more, and Simeon is no more, and now you would take Benjamin. All this has come against me."
37 Then Reuben spoke to his father, saying, "Kill my two sons if I do not bring him back to you; put him in my hands, and I will bring him *back* to you."	**37** Then Reuben said to his father, "Kill my two sons if I do not bring him back to you. Put him in my hands, and I will bring him back to you."
38 But he said, "My son shall not go down with you, for his brother is dead, and he is left alone. If any calamity should befall him along the way in which you go, then you would bring down my gray hair with sorrow to the grave."	**38** But he said, "My son shall not go down with you, for his brother is dead, and he is the only one left. If harm should happen to him on the journey that you are to make, you would bring down my gray hairs with sorrow to Sheol."

Joseph's brothers approach their father with skillful diplomacy. They first describe the lord of Egypt (Joseph) as a cruel and frightening master (42:29–34), then they present his request to bring Benjamin with them (42:35–38).

42:29–34 The author is silent as to the rest of the trip home (42:29a), suggesting the anguished mood of the brothers who could not speak anymore (cf. 22:8). The next step is with Jacob to whom they tell their story (42:29b). They begin with Joseph whom they anonymously call **the man** (42:30) as a way of blaming him for all that has happened to them. They insist on his power; they repeat twice that he is **lord of the land** (42:30, 33). They depict him as a wicked man; **he spoke roughly to us** (42:30). They accuse him of wrongly taking them as spies, although they are **honest men** (42:31). Note that they use the very same word *kenim* "honest," which was used by Joseph to express his suspicion of them (42:19). They cowardly respond to Joseph's accusation, although he is not present to hear. They argue to their father that in order to prove their honesty they must bring Benjamin as evidence that they had spoken truthfully. This is the only means for being allowed to **trade in the land** (42:34). As they implicitly proclaim their innocence to their father, they are ironically betrayed by their language, which recalls their guilt. The Hebrew word for "trade" (*sachar*), which they use to describe their operation in Egypt, is reminiscent of the "trade" (*sachar*) associated with the murder of the Shechemites by Simeon and Levi (34:10, 21) and of the Midianite "traders" (*sachar*) to whom Joseph was sold (37:28).

42:35–36 The next incident reveals their guilt. When they open their sacks, they all discover the extra money, evidence of their dishonesty. The text specifies that the brothers, along with their father, **saw** the shameful money and **they were afraid** (42:35). Jacob summarizes the tragedy and blames his sons, for **you have bereaved me of my children** (42:36a). Jacob explicitly refers to Joseph, Simeon, and Benjamin (42:36b). Jacob considers it to be a personal attack against him: **all these things are against me** (42:36c). Jacob is worried that, after having lost Joseph, he may now lose Benjamin. Jacob's attitude may reflect his suspicion. Seeing the money in the sacks, Jacob may have made a connection between this gain of money and the loss of

Simeon. Maybe Simeon was sold as a slave in Egypt. The memory of the loss of Joseph may have triggered his suspicion toward his sons.[705] Now, Jacob's suspicion meets Joseph's suspicion: they are not honest.

42:37–38 Reuben may have guessed his father's thoughts. Responding to Jacob's allusion to the loss of his two sons, Reuben offers the sacrifice of his two sons (42:37), which amounts to half the number of his sons, since he had four sons (1 Chr 5:3). Reuben's new formula does not satisfy Jacob; for under Reuben's new plan, this is not just one son who would be in peril but three: Simeon, Reuben, and Benjamin, not to mention Reuben's two sons, Jacob's grandsons, in case Reuben fails. No wonder Jacob refuses Reuben's offer, for this would mean, in case of failure, the loss of five sons. Jacob is untouched by Reuben's willingness to expose the lives of his two sons.

Reuben's reference to his two sons versus the loss of Joseph, and now the prospect of the loss of Benjamin, have refreshed the old wound and revived the old tension between the sons of Rachel and the sons of Leah. Jacob refers to Benjamin as **my son** (42:38), as if this were his only son, and not "your brother," and to Joseph as **his brother** (42:38), that is Benjamin's brother, and not "your brother." Jacob is more concerned about the loss of Rachel's two sons than about the loss of Leah's two sons. Losing Benjamin would be to him as it was when he lost Joseph and would bring him to his death (37:35). Jacob holds his sons responsible for his death: **you would bring down my gray hair … to the grave** (42:38).

For Jacob, the prospect of death is not positive. Jacob does not gladly expect to join the dead and does not hope to meet his dead sons there. The Hebrew word *she'ol* for "grave," which is derived from the root *sha'ah*, refers to a place of desolation, described as an empty pit (*bor*), with which it is often associated (Ps 30:4 [3]; Prov 1:12; Isa 14:15; etc.), and appears in parallel to the word "destruction" (*shakhat*) (Ps 16:10). Speaking to God, Isaiah refers to *she'ol* as a place where there is no life and where God is absent: "Sheol cannot thank You, Death cannot praise You; those who go down to the pit cannot hope for Your truth. The living, the living man, he shall praise You" (Isa 38:18–19). The word *yagon* **sorrow** (42:38), which describes Jacob's mental suffering, clearly reflects these views. This word is often used in laments (Ps 13:2 [3]; Lam 1:4–5; 3:31) and appears in parallel to synonyms such as "pain" or "suffering" (Ps 107:39). The section ends with the strong "no" of Jacob, which leaves Simeon in the Egyptian prison and suggests the precarious state of the economic future of Jacob's family.

43:1–45:28 The lack of food forces Jacob to consent to a second visit of the brothers to Egypt, although this means allowing Benjamin to go with his brothers. The entire cycle of Joseph reaches its climax when Joseph finally reveals his identity and welcomes his brothers. This narrative unit contains many echoes referring back to the previous journey,[706] thus suggesting the unity of that section, despite the chapter divisions. Even the progression of the stories goes in parallel, as indicated in the following chiastic structure ($ABCB_1A_1$):

---

705 This hypothesis is suggested by the Midrash (Gen. Rab. 91:9); cf. Rashi in Miqraot Gedolot on 42:35–36; cf. Calvin who also explains Jacob's suspicions in similar terms in his *Commentary on the First Book of Moses Called Genesis*, trans. J. King (Grand Rapids: Eerdmans, 1948), 348–349; cf. Mathews, *Genesis 11:27–50:26*, 783.

706 For a list of these echoes, see Mathews, *Genesis 11:27–50:26*, 771–772.

A Jacob sends his sons to Egypt (43:1–15; cf. 42:1–5)
    B Joseph welcomes his brothers (43:16–26; cf. 42:6)
        C Joseph recognizes his brothers (43:27–34; cf. 42:7–24)
    B₁ Joseph fills the sacks of his brothers (44:1–34; cf. 42:25–28)
A₁ Joseph reveals his identity: Return to Jacob (45:1–28; cf. 42:29–38)

JACOB SENDS HIS SONS TO EGYPT (43:1–15)

GEN 43:1–15 NKJV	GEN 43:1–15 ESV
1 Now the famine *was* severe in the land.	**1** Now the famine was severe in the land.
2 And it came to pass, when they had eaten up the grain which they had brought from Egypt, that their father said to them, "Go back, buy us a little food."	**2** And when they had eaten the grain that they had brought from Egypt, their father said to them, "Go again, buy us a little food."
3 But Judah spoke to him, saying, "The man solemnly warned us, saying, 'You shall not see my face unless your brother *is* with you.'"	**3** But Judah said to him, "The man solemnly warned us, saying, 'You shall not see my face unless your brother is with you.'
4 If you send our brother with us, we will go down and buy you food.	**4** If you will send our brother with us, we will go down and buy you food.
5 But if you will not send *him*, we will not go down; for the man said to us, 'You shall not see my face unless your brother *is* with you.'"	**5** But if you will not send him, we will not go down, for the man said to us, 'You shall not see my face, unless your brother is with you.'"
6 And Israel said, "Why did you deal *so* wrongfully with me *as* to tell the man whether you had still *another* brother?"	**6** Israel said, "Why did you treat me so badly as to tell the man that you had another brother?"
7 But they said, "The man asked us pointedly about ourselves and our family, saying, '*Is* your father still alive? Have you *another* brother?' And we told him according to these words. Could we possibly have known that he would say, 'Bring your brother down'?"	**7** They replied, "The man questioned us carefully about ourselves and our kindred, saying, 'Is your father still alive? Do you have another brother?' What we told him was in answer to these questions. Could we in any way know that he would say, 'Bring your brother down'?"
8 Then Judah said to Israel his father, "Send the lad with me, and we will arise and go, that we may live and not die, both we and you *and* also our little ones.	**8** And Judah said to Israel his father, "Send the boy with me, and we will arise and go, that we may live and not die, both we and you and also our little ones.
9 I myself will be surety for him; from my hand you shall require him. If I do not bring him *back* to you and set him before you, then let me bear the blame forever.	**9** I will be a pledge of his safety. From my hand you shall require him. If I do not bring him back to you and set him before you, then let me bear the blame forever.
10 For if we had not lingered, surely by now we would have returned this second time."	**10** If we had not delayed, we would now have returned twice."
11 And their father Israel said to them, "If *it must be* so, then do this: Take some of the best fruits of the land in your vessels and carry down a present for the man—a little balm and a little honey, spices and myrrh, pistachio nuts and almonds.	**11** Then their father Israel said to them, "If it must be so, then do this: take some of the choice fruits of the land in your bags, and carry a present down to the man, a little balm and a little honey, gum, myrrh, pistachio nuts, and almonds.

12 Take double money in your hand, and take back in your hand the money that was returned in the mouth of your sacks; perhaps it was an oversight.

13 Take your brother also, and arise, go back to the man.

14 And may God Almighty give you mercy before the man, that he may release your other brother and Benjamin. If I am bereaved, I am bereaved!"

15 So the men took that present and Benjamin, and they took double money in their hand, and arose and went down to Egypt; and they stood before Joseph.

12 Take double the money with you. Carry back with you the money that was returned in the mouth of your sacks. Perhaps it was an oversight.

13 Take also your brother, and arise, go again to the man.

14 May God Almighty grant you mercy before the man, and may he send back your other brother and Benjamin. And as for me, if I am bereaved of my children, I am bereaved."

15 So the men took this present, and they took double the money with them, and Benjamin. They arose and went down to Egypt and stood before Joseph.

43:1–2 The formula **famine was severe in the land** (43:1) is used to anticipate and justify the decision to leave that land (Canaan) to obtain food (cf. 12:10; 41:57) in order to survive (42:2). This famine condition is aggravated by the fact that Jacob and his family have consumed all their provisions: **they had eaten up the grain which they had brought from Egypt** (43:2). The lack of chronological precision and the absence of explicit identification of the subject of the verb ("*they* had eaten up") suggests that this crisis still belongs to the context of chapter 42 and occurred just a few months afterward. Again, it is the father who takes the initiative and calls for a new trip to Egypt. However, this time, Jacob's mood and tone of his address are different. Whereas in the first exchange Jacob had chided his sons and elaborated at length on the need to go to Egypt (42:1–2), Jacob's discourse is now much shorter and timid: **go back, buy us a little food** (43:2). Jacob does not even mention the problem of his sons, ignoring the previous conversation he had with them a short time ago. Jacob simply asks for "a little food," secretly hoping that his "little" request will not generate a big discussion, involving the departure of Benjamin.

43:3–5 However, it is Judah who dares to confront his father. Unlike Reuben, who was not heard by his brothers (37:30) or by his father (42:37–38), Judah is more respected (37:26–28). Yet, Judah opposes the authority of the governor of Egypt to the authority of his father: **the man solemnly warned us** (43:3). In a straightforward manner, Judah clearly reminds his father of the conditions of the man's warning: **You shall not see my face unless your brother is with you** (43:3), which he repeats a second time (43:5). Consequently, Judah informs his father that without Benjamin, they will not go (43:5). Judah's response to Jacob appears to be open disobedience, which is unusual (cf. 42:3).

43:6 Jacob does not respond directly to Judah but addresses all of his sons instead. Speaking in the second person plural, Jacob accuses his sons of causing evil. The verb translated **deal wrongfully** is the causative form of the Hebrew verb *r'*, which is related to the word *ra'ah* "evil." The brothers used the same word when they described the evil *ra'ah*[707] animal that had presumably killed Joseph (37:20, 33). Through that echo, Jacob implicitly blames his sons of doing to him with Benjamin what they had done to him with Joseph.

---

707 Translated "wild beast" (NKJV); "evil beast" (JPS).

43:7 For the first time, the sons speak to their father. They have perceived the sense of their father's charge against them and immediately respond to justify themselves. They explain how sincere and candid they were; they had acted in good faith and responded honestly to the man without knowing that he would have asked for Benjamin, implicitly blaming the man for that evil, just as was the case the last time (42:30). Unlike Judah, who was frank and firm, yet respectful to his father, the brothers' last response to their father borders on insolence; it is a rhetorical question, suggesting a veiled accusation to their father for his lack of sympathy and discernment (cf. 34:31).

43:8–10 Judah feels the inappropriateness of his brothers' response and fears that his brothers' words may irritate his father and ultimately lead to his suspicion and, hence, trigger a negative reaction from him. Judah assumes a personal stance on the matter and engages himself solely in that enterprise; note the emphasis on the first person, including the use of the Hebrew emphatic "I" (*'anokhi*, translated "I myself"): **with me ... I myself (*'anokhi*) ... my hand ... If I do not ... then let *me*** (43:8–9). Judah distances himself from his brothers and engages solely in this matter. Judah puts his own life at risk, unlike Reuben, who had put his two sons' lives on the line (42:37). Yet, instead of dramatically offering his death, he offers the service of his entire life: **let me bear the blame forever** (43:9). Thus, Judah puts himself as a guarantee: **I myself will be surety for him** (43:9). The Hebrew verb for "be surety" (*'arab*) refers to the pledge to guarantee repayment. Judah repeats here the related term "pledge" (*'erbon*) he had used with Tamar to gain her trust (38:18). Unlike his brothers, who are defensive, thinking only of themselves, Judah frames his plea with positive arguments. He begins his defense by focusing on the interest of everyone, including Jacob: **that we may live and not die, both we and you and also our little ones** (43:8). He ends by anticipating the successful outcome of the journey: **by now we would have returned this second time** (43:10).

43:11 Jacob flinches. Whereas he had been unconvinced by Reuben's dramatic and unrealistic offer (42:37–38), Jacob is now convinced by the more modest and genuine attitude of Judah. Jacob places more trust in Judah, whose behavior is characterized by honesty and righteousness (cf. 37:26–27) and who had honored his pledge with Tamar, which had just been alluded to. Judah's history of fathering twins also suggests the same supernatural Presence that had presided over Jacob's own providential birth (38:27–30; cf. 25:24–27). Jacob, then, again initiates the operation; he commands that they bring presents to the governor of Egypt. The same Hebrew word *minkhah* "present" refers to the present Jacob brought to his brother Esau to appease him and to obtain forgiveness from him (32:15–22; 33:8–11). Note that Jacob's suggestion includes the same products (gum, balm, and myrrh) brought by the Ishmaelites traveling down to Egypt (37:25), which were used by the Egyptians in their embalming practices. Jacob adds two more products, which were also precious for the ancient Egyptians. Honey was particularly important in Egyptian religion because the pharaoh liked to serve it as an offering to the gods; it was also used in daily life to sweeten food and even in the cure of diseases because of its natural antibacterial properties. Regarding almonds, the most ancient Egyptian evidence of their existence dates to the New Kingdom (1500–1000 BC). At the time of Joseph, almonds, although common in Canaan, were rare in Egypt. All of these products were familiar to Joseph and were likely to remind him of Canaan and of his childhood.

43:12 **Double money** refers to the returned money that was found in their sacks, plus the sum intended to buy new grain. Note the word **perhaps**, which suggests Jacob's doubt concerning the reason for the presence of that money. Was it an **oversight** (*mishgeh*), an unintentional act, as the root of the Hebrew word (*shagah*) suggests (Lev 4:2)? That Jacob questions the intentionality behind the presence of the money suggests that he is suspicious of his sons, for Jacob could not imagine that the Egyptian governor would intentionally put the money there.

43:13–14 Given these mixed feelings, and even suspicions, Jacob allows Benjamin to go with them. Note, however, how he refers to Benjamin, whom he had so far identified as "my son" (42:38): he now calls him **your brother** (43:13), thus appealing to their responsibility and family relation. Jacob, who does not trust his sons, is thus obliged to entrust the life of his son to **God Almighty**, that is, *'El Shaddai* (43:14), the God who protects and will save the future (see the commentary on 17:1). Out of his faith and trust in God's promise and protection, Jacob affirms his submission to God's will: **if I am bereaved, I am bereaved**. This was his way of saying that he was willing to accept the worst scenario.

43:15 The verbatim repetition of Jacob's commands **take … a present … take double money in your hand … arise, go back to the man** (cf. 43:11–13), with "they" as the subject of the verbs, suggests that Joseph's brothers obey their father and do exactly as he says. The sons leave at peace with their father and in a spirit of unity.

JOSEPH DINES WITH HIS BROTHERS (43:16–26)

GEN 43:16–26 NKJV	GEN 43:16–26 ESV
16 When Joseph saw Benjamin with them, he said to the steward of his house, "Take *these* men to my home, and slaughter an animal and make ready; for *these* men will dine with me at noon."	**16** When Joseph saw Benjamin with them, he said to the steward of his house, "Bring the men into the house, and slaughter an animal and make ready, for the men are to dine with me at noon."
17 Then the man did as Joseph ordered, and the man brought the men into Joseph's house.	**17** The man did as Joseph told him and brought the men to Joseph's house.
18 Now the men were afraid because they were brought into Joseph's house; and they said, "*It is* because of the money, which was returned in our sacks the first time, that we are brought in, so that he may make a case against us and fall upon us, to take us as slaves with our donkeys."	**18** And the men were afraid because they were brought to Joseph's house, and they said, "It is because of the money, which was replaced in our sacks the first time, that we are brought in, so that he may assault us and fall upon us to make us servants and seize our donkeys."
19 When they drew near to the steward of Joseph's house, they talked with him at the door of the house,	**19** So they went up to the steward of Joseph's house and spoke with him at the door of the house,
20 and said, "O sir, we indeed came down the first time to buy food;	**20** and said, "Oh, my lord, we came down the first time to buy food.
21 but it happened, when we came to the encampment, that we opened our sacks, and there, *each* man's money *was* in the mouth of his sack, our money in full weight; so we have brought it back in our hand.	**21** And when we came to the lodging place we opened our sacks, and there was each man's money in the mouth of his sack, our money in full weight. So we have brought it again with us,

22 And we have brought down other money in our hands to buy food. We do not know who put our money in our sacks."	**22** and we have brought other money down with us to buy food. We do not know who put our money in our sacks."
23 But he said, "Peace be with you, do not be afraid. Your God and the God of your father has given you treasure in your sacks; I had your money." Then he brought Simeon out to them.	**23** He replied, "Peace to you, do not be afraid. Your God and the God of your father has put treasure in your sacks for you. I received your money." Then he brought Simeon out to them.
24 So the man brought the men into Joseph's house and gave *them* water, and they washed their feet; and he gave their donkeys feed.	**24** And when the man had brought the men into Joseph's house and given them water, and they had washed their feet, and when he had given their donkeys fodder,
25 Then they made the present ready for Joseph's coming at noon, for they heard that they would eat bread there.	**25** they prepared the present for Joseph's coming at noon, for they heard that they should eat bread there.
26 And when Joseph came home, they brought him the present which *was* in their hand into the house, and bowed down before him to the earth.	**26** When Joseph came home, they brought into the house to him the present that they had with them and bowed down to him to the ground.

43:16 Once again, Joseph sees his brothers without them recognizing him (cf. 42:8). Joseph particularly notices Benjamin (43:16), while nearly ignoring the other brothers. The narrative notes that **Joseph saw Benjamin with them**. Whereas Benjamin is referred to by name, the other brothers are only identified anonymously, either by the personal pronoun **with them** or by the neutral phrase **these men** (NKJV) with the definite article *ha-ʾanashim*, meaning literally "the men" (ESV). This practice will govern the entire narrative, in which only Benjamin and Joseph are called by their names (43:24, 26, 29), whereas the brothers are always identified as *ha-ʾanashim* "the men" or by the personal pronoun. Joseph's particular interest for Benjamin causes him to invite the brothers for a meal: **when Joseph saw Benjamin … he said to the steward of his house … slaughter an animal … these men will dine with me.** The word for **slaughter** (*tabakh*) suggests the preparation for a banquet (Prov 9:2), likely involving the killing of an ox (Exod 22:1 [21:37]; Deut 28:31), which was in Egypt a very expensive treat, enjoyed only by the royal family,[708] particularly in these times of famine.

43:17–22 Joseph's brothers do not anticipate such an invitation; thus, they are afraid when they see they are brought to Joseph's house (43:17–18). The thought that they are being taken as his slaves in retaliation for stealing crosses their minds (43:18). Therefore, it is with apprehension that they approach the steward, even before entering the house, **at the door of the house** (43:19). They are eager to dissipate the misunderstanding; they prudently anticipate the accusation by explaining that their money had been put in their sacks. The evidence of their good faith is that they have brought the money back and **did not know who put** this money in their sacks (43:20–22).

43:23–26 The steward knows who has put this money in their sacks because he may have been the one who put it there (42:25). The steward, who sees they are afraid, reassures them and wishes them peace (*shalom*). He informs them that he has received the

---

708 Salima Ikra, "Diet," *OEAE* 1:394.

money; his accounting is balanced. To explain this anomaly, the steward resorts to supernatural intervention. Interestingly, he refers to the God of their father as the One who must have put that money in their sacks. The steward likely behaves and speaks according to Joseph's instructions, repeating his own words. Yet, instead of using the word "money" (*kesep*), the steward refers to a **treasure** (43:23). The Hebrew word for "treasure" (*matmun*), from the root *tmn* "hide" (35:4), suggests that a treasure is hidden there (see Job 3:21; Isa 45:3). The implicit lesson is that God is hidden beneath what may appear to be an evil operation (45:7–8; 50:19–20). The steward's subsequent moves confirm his good intentions. Simeon is immediately liberated (43:23), and Joseph's brothers are welcome in Joseph's house and enjoy the customary acts of hospitality; they are provided with water to wash their feet and with fodder for their donkeys (cf. 18:4; 19:2). They are now completely reassured, and all the more as they learn why they are in Joseph's house: **they heard that they would eat bread there** (43:25). In that mood, they prepare themselves to meet the master of the house and offer their gifts to him (43:26).

JOSEPH RECOGNIZES HIS BROTHERS (43:27–34)

GEN 43:27–34 NKJV	GEN 43:27–34 ESV
27 Then he asked them about *their* well-being, and said, "*Is* your father well, the old man of whom you spoke? *Is* he still alive?"	**27** And he inquired about their welfare and said, "Is your father well, the old man of whom you spoke? Is he still alive?"
28 And they answered, "Your servant our father *is* in good health; he *is* still alive." And they bowed their heads down and prostrated themselves.	**28** They said, "Your servant our father is well; he is still alive." And they bowed their heads and prostrated themselves.
29 Then he lifted his eyes and saw his brother Benjamin, his mother's son, and said, "*Is* this your younger brother of whom you spoke to me?" And he said, "God be gracious to you, my son."	**29** And he lifted up his eyes and saw his brother Benjamin, his mother's son, and said, "Is this your youngest brother, of whom you spoke to me? God be gracious to you, my son!"
30 Now his heart yearned for his brother; so Joseph made haste and sought *somewhere* to weep. And he went into *his* chamber and wept there.	**30** Then Joseph hurried out, for his compassion grew warm for his brother, and he sought a place to weep. And he entered his chamber and wept there.
31 Then he washed his face and came out; and he restrained himself, and said, "Serve the bread."	**31** Then he washed his face and came out. And controlling himself he said, "Serve the food."
32 So they set him a place by himself, and them by themselves, and the Egyptians who ate with him by themselves; because the Egyptians could not eat food with the Hebrews, for that *is* an abomination to the Egyptians.	**32** They served him by himself, and them by themselves, and the Egyptians who ate with him by themselves, because the Egyptians could not eat with the Hebrews, for that is an abomination to the Egyptians.
33 And they sat before him, the firstborn according to his birthright and the youngest according to his youth; and the men looked in astonishment at one another.	**33** And they sat before him, the firstborn according to his birthright and the youngest according to his youth. And the men looked at one another in amazement.
34 Then he took servings to them from before him, but Benjamin's serving was five times as much as any of theirs. So they drank and were merry with him.	**34** Portions were taken to them from Joseph's table, but Benjamin's portion was five times as much as any of theirs. And they drank and were merry with him.

43:27–28 Joseph initiates the conversation with a question about the well-being (*shalom*) of their father (43:27). He then refers to their words **of whom you spoke** (43:27) to justify his interest about him. Joseph's prudent specification intends to prevent the brothers' suspicion about the nature of his interest. Joseph would have them think his question about their father is due only to the fact that they mentioned him during the previous visit. This is the second time the word *shalom* is used (cf. 43:23), which will be repeated a third time by the brothers, confirming that their father is in *shalom* **in good health** (43:28). The entire family is now included and established in *shalom*. The primary meaning of the word *shalom*, "completeness," may be implied here, for it is the first time that the "complete" family is present, although the father is not physically present. Thus, when the eleven brothers bow and prostrate themselves before Joseph, reporting on the *shalom* of their father (43:28), they are again fulfilling the dream of Joseph (37:9).

43:29 Joseph's interest now shifts from his father to **his brother Benjamin** (43:29). The introductory expression **he lifted his eyes and saw** (43:29) marks a particular attention and anticipates a crucial observation (13:10; 22:4; etc.). This is the first and only time the family relationship is indicated. Whereas the brothers are identified only as "the men," Benjamin is twice called "brother" (the first time in relation to Joseph, and the second time in relation to the other ten brothers) and once "mother's son." Note that, once again, Joseph prudently explains his interest for this brother by referring to his brothers' report (**of whom you spoke to me**) to avoid their suspicion (cf. 43:27). Joseph even goes so far as to call him **my son** (*beni*), which is an affectionate way of addressing someone younger (1 Sam 3:16; 2 Sam 18:22). However, the use of this term in this unit may have an additional function, since it is associated only with Joseph or Benjamin (37:33; 42:38; 45:28; 48:19); this may then be a way of singling them out from the other brothers. Note also the qualification *beni* "my son," which is reminiscent of the name "Benjamin" (*ben yamin*), meaning "son of the right hand" (35:18). By calling Benjamin *beni* "my son," Joseph may well have been intentionally playing on his name.

God be gracious to you. Joseph is not simply expressing his particular relation with his brother; he is also extending to him a special blessing, wishing him the grace of God. This formula will become a part of the priestly blessing (Num 6:25). However, there is more; Joseph's use of the verb *khanan* "grace" ironically recalls Joseph's begging for grace (*behitkhanenu*), which was not heard (42:21). Joseph returns to Benjamin the "grace" he had not received from his other brothers.

43:30 Upon seeing Benjamin, Joseph is moved and weeps (43:30) just as he did when he saw his brothers for the first time (42:24). The Hebrew phrase *nikmeru rakhamayw* **his heart yearned**, meaning literally "his bowels/womb (compassion) grew hot," expresses the emotion of motherly attachment (1 Kgs 3:26; Hos 11:8), which relates to Joseph's address to Benjamin as "my son" (43:29). In his mother's absence, Joseph feels for his younger brother the sentiments of a mother. The emotion is so powerful that Joseph can scarcely control himself and must rush (*mhr*) out to another room where people cannot see him. Only after having recovered himself and washing his face does Joseph return and give the order to **serve** (*sim*) **the bread**, that is, to set up the table (43:31).

43:32 The same word *sim* is used to refer to the organization of the meals: **so they set (*sim*) him a place by himself**. Joseph still plays the Egyptian and, as such, cannot share the same meal with his brothers because this is considered **an abomination to the Egyptians**. The Hebrew word for "abomination" (*to'ebah*) may be a play on words, pointing to the Egyptian word *w'ab*, which is the typical word for "pure," and refers to the sacred and religious domain, including "priests," "libations," and "sacrifices." The "pure" Egyptian priests could not mix with the impure Hebrews, especially in relation to food. According to the testimony of Herodotus,[709] the Egyptians were forbidden to eat or sacrifice cows, which were considered sacred and pure (*w'b*); hence, their revulsion for shepherds (46:34).

43:33–34 Although Joseph eats at another table, he is still placed in front of them (43:33), so that he may watch their reaction to his arrangement. All the brothers are seated according to their ages, thus respecting the rules of honor, from the oldest to the youngest. The brothers are surprised and share their astonishment with each other, for no one is supposed to know so precisely their respective age and family ranking; and yet, when Benjamin is served five times more abundantly than all the other brothers, no reaction on their part is reported. This favoritism does not seem to bother them. On the contrary, they eat and drink and enjoy the moment with Benjamin (43:34). Joseph observes that his brothers have changed; they are not jealous of their brother Benjamin as they used to be of him, when he was his father's favorite (37:3–4).

JOSEPH FILLS THE SACKS OF HIS BROTHERS (44:1–34)

The following story parallels the previous similar incident (42:25–28). According to Joseph's specific instructions, the steward frames Benjamin, using Joseph's cup, and once again fills the men's sacks with food (44:1–6). The parallel emphasizes the contrast between the two endings. Whereas in the previous trip, the brothers returned to Canaan in order to obtain Benjamin, without whom they could not return to Egypt, now they are obliged to return to Egypt to account for their suspected crime. Two confrontations ensue. First, the brothers are confronted by the steward who had put Joseph's cup in Benjamin's sack and now accuses them of having stolen the cup (44:7–13). Judah then confronts Joseph who has decided to keep Benjamin as his slave in retaliation for their crime (44:14–34).

44:1–13. JOSEPH'S CUP

GEN 44:1–13 NKJV	GEN 44:1–13 ESV
1 And he commanded the steward of his house, saying, "Fill the men's sacks with food, as much as they can carry, and put each man's money in the mouth of his sack.	**1** Then he commanded the steward of his house, "Fill the men's sacks with food, as much as they can carry, and put each man's money in the mouth of his sack,
2 Also put my cup, the silver cup, in the mouth of the sack of the youngest, and his grain money." So he did according to the word that Joseph had spoken.	**2** and put my cup, the silver cup, in the mouth of the sack of the youngest, with his money for the grain." And he did as Joseph told him.
3 As soon as the morning dawned, the men were sent away, they and their donkeys.	**3** As soon as the morning was light, the men were sent away with their donkeys.

---

709 Herodotus, *Histories*, 2.18, 41; 2.42, 46.

4 When they had gone out of the city, *and* were not *yet* far off, Joseph said to his steward, "Get up, follow the men; and when you overtake them, say to them, 'Why have you repaid evil for good?

5 *Is* not this *the one* from which my lord drinks, and with which he indeed practices divination? You have done evil in so doing.'"

6 So he overtook them, and he spoke to them these same words.

7 And they said to him, "Why does my lord say these words? Far be it from us that your servants should do such a thing.

8 Look, we brought back to you from the land of Canaan the money which we found in the mouth of our sacks. How then could we steal silver or gold from your lord's house?

9 With whomever of your servants it is found, let him die, and we also will be my lord's slaves."

10 And he said, "Now also *let* it *be* according to your words; he with whom it is found shall be my slave, and you shall be blameless."

11 Then each man speedily let down his sack to the ground, and each opened his sack.

12 So he searched. He began with the oldest and left off with the youngest; and the cup was found in Benjamin's sack.

13 Then they tore their clothes, and each man loaded his donkey and returned to the city.

4 They had gone only a short distance from the city. Now Joseph said to his steward, "Up, follow after the men, and when you overtake them, say to them, 'Why have you repaid evil for good?

5 Is it not from this that my lord drinks, and by this that he practices divination? You have done evil in doing this.'"

6 When he overtook them, he spoke to them these words.

7 They said to him, "Why does my lord speak such words as these? Far be it from your servants to do such a thing!

8 Behold, the money that we found in the mouths of our sacks we brought back to you from the land of Canaan. How then could we steal silver or gold from your lord's house?

9 Whichever of your servants is found with it shall die, and we also will be my lord's servants."

10 He said, "Let it be as you say: he who is found with it shall be my servant, and the rest of you shall be innocent."

11 Then each man quickly lowered his sack to the ground, and each man opened his sack.

12 And he searched, beginning with the eldest and ending with the youngest. And the cup was found in Benjamin's sack.

13 Then they tore their clothes, and every man loaded his donkey, and they returned to the city.

44:1 Joseph again commands his steward to fill his brothers' sacks and to return their money, as he did in their previous journey (42:25). The new remark **as much as they can carry** (44:1) reflects the generosity of the gift, possibly implying that the second provision is even larger than the previous one.

44:2 Also put my cup. The reference to the cup at the beginning of the Hebrew sentence indicates that an emphasis is intended: "as for my cup, the silver cup, you will put it in the mouth of the sack of the youngest" (author's translation). This emphasis suggests that the cup had already been mentioned and that the preceding operation had, in fact, been designed in view of the cup. The repetition of the word **the cup** and its qualification as **silver** suggest its importance and its precious value. The Hebrew term for the cup (*gabi'a*) also designates the golden bowl of the lampstand in the tabernacle (Exod 25:31). This cup (*gabi'a*) is therefore not a ordinary "drinking cup" (*kos*); it refers instead to a specially ornamented vessel destined for extraordinary occasions (Jer 35:5). The cup may have been used during the banquet of the preceding day; and since Benjamin had been the guest of honor, he may have even had the privilege of drinking from it and probably admired it.

44:4–6 Therefore, when the cup is found in Benjamin's sack, the steward's comments make sense: **why have you repaid evil for good?** (44:4).

The fact that this cup has magical powers adds to the gravity of the felony. The word *ra'ah* **evil** is repeated once more, this time in connection with the magical power of the cup (cf. 44:4). The practice of using drinking cups for libation and magical purposes (scyphomancy) was current in ancient Egypt. People, typically the priest, would fill the cup with spiced beer and then pour out its content as a libation to the god. The examination of the sediment left in the bottom of the cup (ripples, designs) was then deciphered as a message from the god. The Hebrew verb *nakhash* for **divination** (44:5) occurs for the first time when Laban states that he has "learned by divination" (30:27 NIV) that he had enjoyed blessing for the sake of Jacob. The word *nakhash* reappears in Balaam's prophecy in parallel to the word *qesem* "divination," "magic" (Num 23:23; 24:1). The practice of divination was forbidden in Israel (Lev 19:26; Deut 18:10). That Joseph refers to it does not mean that he was using it. This was another strategy to cover up his identity before his brothers. The fact that Joseph pretends to use this magical practice, although he knows the events well, since he had himself orchestrated them, is a clear indication that he does not believe in the power of magic. The steward may also share Joseph's skepticism because he is his accomplice in the entire operation; he acts and speaks exactly according to Joseph's commands (44:6).

44:7–10 The brothers respond with vehement rhetoric: **Why? … Far … from us** (44:7). They subsequently argue on the basis of their past honesty: **we brought back … the money** (44:8); they are so self-confident that they are willing to die or become slaves if the cup is found in their sacks (44:9). The deal is that the one who has the cup will die, whereas the remaining brothers will serve as slaves. The steward plays the role of the righteous and turns down their request: only the guilty one should pay (44:10).

44:11 The intensity of the brothers' emotion is rendered through their rush. Just as Joseph "made haste" (*mahar*) to go somewhere to weep (43:30), the brothers **speedily** (*mahar*) open their sacks.

44:12–13 The steward's searching process follows the same order as when they were served at the table, from the oldest to the youngest (cf. 43:33). However, this time it is not to honor the youngest more than the others, but on the contrary, to dishonor him more than the others. The intention of the method is to increase the surprise. As the steward's search progresses, the brothers' assurance grows. Yet, when they least expect it, the cup is found in the end in the sack of the youngest brother, Benjamin, who is mentioned for the first time (44:12). The men do not speak anymore. They tear their clothes as a sign of mourning and despair (cf. 37:29, 34) and silently load their donkeys and return to the city (44:13). They are all united in the same pain, fearing for Benjamin, who will be lost like Joseph, and like him, become a slave in Egypt. The scenario is the same, resonating with the same fate. The situation is fundamentally different, though. Whereas they were previously guilty and indifferent to Joseph's anguish and to the pain of their father, now they are innocent and suffer on account of Benjamin and worry about their father, who they know will not survive this new trial. All of these sentiments and thoughts that assail them, but remain unexpressed, will later be revealed in Judah's words.

44:14–34. JUDAH STANDS FOR BENJAMIN

GEN 44:14–34 NKJV	GEN 44:14–34 ESV
14 So Judah and his brothers came to Joseph's house, and he *was* still there; and they fell before him on the ground.	**14** When Judah and his brothers came to Joseph's house, he was still there. They fell before him to the ground.
15 And Joseph said to them, "What deed *is* this you have done? Did you not know that such a man as I can certainly practice divination?"	**15** Joseph said to them, "What deed is this that you have done? Do you not know that a man like me can indeed practice divination?"
16 Then Judah said, "What shall we say to my lord? What shall we speak? Or how shall we clear ourselves? God has found out the iniquity of your servants; here we are, my lord's slaves, both we and *he* also with whom the cup was found."	**16** And Judah said, "What shall we say to my lord? What shall we speak? Or how can we clear ourselves? God has found out the guilt of your servants; behold, we are my lord's servants, both we and he also in whose hand the cup has been found."
17 But he said, "Far be it from me that I should do so; the man in whose hand the cup was found, he shall be my slave. And as for you, go up in peace to your father."	**17** But he said, "Far be it from me that I should do so! Only the man in whose hand the cup was found shall be my servant. But as for you, go up in peace to your father."
18 Then Judah came near to him and said: "O my lord, please let your servant speak a word in my lord's hearing, and do not let your anger burn against your servant; for you *are* even like Pharaoh.	**18** Then Judah went up to him and said, "Oh, my lord, please let your servant speak a word in my lord's ears, and let not your anger burn against your servant, for you are like Pharaoh himself.
19 My lord asked his servants, saying, 'Have you a father or a brother?'	**19** My lord asked his servants, saying, 'Have you a father, or a brother?'
20 And we said to my lord, 'We have a father, an old man, and a child of *his* old age, *who is* young; his brother is dead, and he alone is left of his mother's children, and his father loves him.'	**20** And we said to my lord, 'We have a father, an old man, and a young brother, the child of his old age. His brother is dead, and he alone is left of his mother's children, and his father loves him.'
21 Then you said to your servants, 'Bring him down to me, that I may set my eyes on him.'	**21** Then you said to your servants, 'Bring him down to me, that I may set my eyes on him.'
22 And we said to my lord, 'The lad cannot leave his father, for *if* he should leave his father, *his father* would die.'	**22** We said to my lord, 'The boy cannot leave his father, for if he should leave his father, his father would die.'
23 But you said to your servants, 'Unless your youngest brother comes down with you, you shall see my face no more.'	**23** Then you said to your servants, 'Unless your youngest brother comes down with you, you shall not see my face again.'
24 "So it was, when we went up to your servant my father, that we told him the words of my lord.	**24** "When we went back to your servant my father, we told him the words of my lord.
25 And our father said, 'Go back *and* buy us a little food.'	**25** And when our father said, 'Go again, buy us a little food,'
26 But we said, 'We cannot go down; if our youngest brother is with us, then we will go down; for we may not see the man's face unless our youngest brother *is* with us.'	**26** we said, 'We cannot go down. If our youngest brother goes with us, then we will go down. For we cannot see the man's face unless our youngest brother is with us.'

27 Then your servant my father said to us, 'You know that my wife bore me two sons;	**27** Then your servant my father said to us, 'You know that my wife bore me two sons.
28 and the one went out from me, and I said, "Surely he is torn to pieces"; and I have not seen him since.	**28** One left me, and I said, Surely he has been torn to pieces, and I have never seen him since.
29 But if you take this one also from me, and calamity befalls him, you shall bring down my gray hair with sorrow to the grave.'	**29** If you take this one also from me, and harm happens to him, you will bring down my gray hairs in evil to Sheol.'
30 "Now therefore, when I come to your servant my father, and the lad *is* not with us, since his life is bound up in the lad's life,	**30** "Now therefore, as soon as I come to your servant my father, and the boy is not with us, then, as his life is bound up in the boy's life,
31 it will happen, when he sees that the lad *is* not *with us*, that he will die. So your servants will bring down the gray hair of your servant our father with sorrow to the grave.	**31** as soon as he sees that the boy is not with us, he will die, and your servants will bring down the gray hairs of your servant our father with sorrow to Sheol.
32 For your servant became surety for the lad to my father, saying, 'If I do not bring him *back* to you, then I shall bear the blame before my father forever.'	**32** For your servant became a pledge of safety for the boy to my father, saying, 'If I do not bring him back to you, then I shall bear the blame before my father all my life.'
33 Now therefore, please let your servant remain instead of the lad as a slave to my lord, and let the lad go up with his brothers.	**33** Now therefore, please let your servant remain instead of the boy as a servant to my lord, and let the boy go back with his brothers.
34 For how shall I go up to my father if the lad *is* not with me, lest perhaps I see the evil that would come upon my father?"	**34** For how can I go back to my father if the boy is not with me? I fear to see the evil that would find my father."

44:14 Judah emerges as the leader of his brothers; he is the first and only brother that is named among his brothers: **Judah and his brothers** (44:14). The construction of the sentence not only suggests that the brothers follow him, but that he is also determined. The note that Joseph **was still there** indicates that he has been waiting for them. Again, the brothers prostrate themselves before him; this is the fourth and last time they bow down before him (42:6; 43:26, 28; 44:14; cf. 37:7, 9–10).

44:15–17 Joseph, as the superior, initiates the dialogue. He again refers to his magical power to justify his capacity to have guessed their crime. This is also another subtle way to imply the supernatural domain, which means for the brothers the divine order. This is how Judah interprets Joseph's implied message because he (Judah) refers to God (44:16). For Judah, however, this turn of events is due to their own iniquity, that is, the selling of their brother Joseph, a crime the brothers still carry on their consciences (42:22). Judah proposes that he and all of his brothers, including their young brother, be taken as slaves. His request differs from the preceding one, when the brothers had called for the capital punishment of the guilty person (44:9). Judah does not differentiate among them and identifies with Benjamin, for he knows that he is innocent, as they are. Similar to the steward, Joseph insists that only the guilty one shall pay (44:17). Joseph concludes his words with the word *shalom* "peace": **go up in peace to your father**. The last time Joseph had used this term was also in connection to their father (43:27–28). The term in these circumstances is, then, full of cruel irony, for everyone knows (the brothers, Joseph, and the steward) that this decision of the governor of Egypt is not as a generator of peace; it is not so for the brothers and much less so for their father (cf. 42:38).

44:18-34 Judah's long and eloquent plea is particularly loaded with his concern for his father. The word **father** occurs fourteen times in the unit, which falls into two parts. From the review of past events, which took the brothers back and forth to their father (44:18–29), Judah draws a double lesson; each one is regularly introduced by the conjunction expressing the consequence in the present: we'atah **now therefore** (44:30, 33). The first lesson applies to the fate of his father (44:30–32), and the second lesson applies to his own fate (44:33–34).

44:18-29 Prudently and reverently, Judah approaches Joseph, whom he addresses on the same level as the pharaoh (44:18). Judah then proceeds to report on previous conversations that he had had with Joseph (44:19–23) and with his father (44:24–29). Judah does not use his own arguments to convince Joseph. Instead, he diplomatically bases his plea on the words of Joseph and his father.

44:27 **My wife bore me two sons.** Whereas the reference to Rachel as "my wife" in Jacob's speech may reflect his particular concern about his two sons Joseph and Benjamin, this title also indicates Jacob's unique relationship with "his wife" Rachel. In the last section of the book of Genesis, it is indeed significant that only Rachel is retained as Jacob's wife. Whereas in the past, Jacob previously called both Leah and Rachel "my wives" (30:26; 31:50), he now reserves this title strictly for Rachel. This emphasis is consistent with Jacob's language at the end of his life. When he discusses his future burial with his sons, Jacob uses the term "wife" for Sarah and Rebekah, whereas he refers to Leah simply as "Leah" (49:31). The biblical author refers specifically to Rachel as "Jacob's wife" (46:19), whereas he only refers to Leah, Zilpah, and Bilhah simply as women who "bore to Jacob" children (46:15, 18, 25). This systematic distinction suggests the biblical author's intention to underscore Jacob's monogamous relation in the last years of his life, in contrast to his polygamous ways in the early part of his life. That this shift in language occurs immediately after Jacob's encounter at the Jabbok suggests that Jacob's monogamous commitment is related to that conversion experience.[710]

44:30-32 Judah infers from his father's words and condition that this decision of putting Benjamin in prison will be fatal to his father; for **his life is bound up in the lad's life** (44:30). Judah specifies that, by returning to their father without Benjamin, the brothers (**your servants**) will kill their father; Judah here uses his father's own words: **bring down the gray hair of your servant** (44:31; cf. 44:29; 42:38). Judah relates his responsibility in that matter, repeating the same words he used when he spoke to his father: **I shall bear the blame before my father forever** (44:32; cf. 43:9).

44:33-34 Judah subsequently comes to the ultimate conclusion that he should go to prison **instead** (*takhat*) of Benjamin (44:33). The same language had been used to describe the offering of the ram "instead" (*takhat*) of Isaac (22:13). Judah identifies himself with the substitutionary sacrifice, whose purpose is to atone and turn evil into good. Judah's further reference to "evil" may well suggest the same line of thought. The reason Judah gives to justify his request is that he cannot **see the evil that would come upon his father** (44:34). The word **evil** (*ra'*) has been a keyword

---

710 For this analysis, see Davidson, *The Flame of Yahweh*, 188–189.

in the unit, which was used to refer to the beast that would have killed Joseph (37:20, 33), the "evil" (*ra*ʿ) that Jacob accused his sons to have caused to come upon him when they mentioned their other brother (43:6), and even the "evil" they had been accused to have committed in response to the "good" they had received (44:4–5). The repetition of the word "evil" anticipates the imminent unveiling of Joseph who will reveal that behind this evil, God was working for the purpose of good (45:5–8; cf. 50:20). The thought that by taking the place of the guilty, the innocent Judah turns the good into evil is related to the thought that God will turn evil into good. All of these associations of ideas denote a theology of salvation: the solution to the problem of evil pertains to God's creative action that changes evil into good, and this operation is mysteriously dependent on the process of substitution.

JOSEPH REVEALS HIS IDENTITY: RETURN TO CANAAN (45:1–28)

Twenty-two years have elapsed from the time the seventeen-year-old Joseph tells his dreams to his brothers and father (37:1–11) to the time when the thirty-nine-year-old Joseph (41:46; cf. 45:6) makes himself known to his brothers. The story of Joseph now reaches its climax and meets its full significance. Finally, Joseph's brothers understand the fulfillment of his dreams and understand their meaning. Joseph is the only hero of this unit, and the only one who speaks. Joseph's speech is introduced and concluded with his weeping (45:2, 14–15). The entire episode is bordered by a reference to Pharaoh, who hears of the strange incident at the onset (45:2) and at the end (45:16–20), a reminder that the family reunion occurs in exile. The loud and emotional incident of Joseph weeping (45:1–15) is then followed by Pharaoh's instructions to go to Canaan to bring their father to the land of Egypt (45:16–28).

45:1–15. SEVEN DECLARATIONS OF GOD'S WORKS

GEN 45:1–15 NKJV	GEN 45:1–15 ESV
1 Then Joseph could not restrain himself before all those who stood by him, and he cried out, "Make everyone go out from me!" So no one stood with him while Joseph made himself known to his brothers.	**1** Then Joseph could not control himself before all those who stood by him. He cried, "Make everyone go out from me." So no one stayed with him when Joseph made himself known to his brothers.
2 And he wept aloud, and the Egyptians and the house of Pharaoh heard *it*.	**2** And he wept aloud, so that the Egyptians heard it, and the household of Pharaoh heard it.
3 Then Joseph said to his brothers, "I *am* Joseph; does my father still live?" But his brothers could not answer him, for they were dismayed in his presence.	**3** And Joseph said to his brothers, "I am Joseph! Is my father still alive?" But his brothers could not answer him, for they were dismayed at his presence.
4 And Joseph said to his brothers, "Please come near to me." So they came near. Then he said: "I *am* Joseph your brother, whom you sold into Egypt.	**4** So Joseph said to his brothers, "Come near to me, please." And they came near. And he said, "I am your brother, Joseph, whom you sold into Egypt.
5 But now, do not therefore be grieved or angry with yourselves because you sold me here; for God sent me before you to preserve life.	**5** And now do not be distressed or angry with yourselves because you sold me here, for God sent me before you to preserve life.

6 For these two years the famine *has been* in the land, and *there are* still five years in which *there will be* neither plowing nor harvesting.	**6** For the famine has been in the land these two years, and there are yet five years in which there will be neither plowing nor harvest.
7 And God sent me before you to preserve a posterity for you in the earth, and to save your lives by a great deliverance.	**7** And God sent me before you to preserve for you a remnant on earth, and to keep alive for you many survivors.
8 So now *it was* not you *who* sent me here, but God; and He has made me a father to Pharaoh, and lord of all his house, and a ruler throughout all the land of Egypt.	**8** So it was not you who sent me here, but God. He has made me a father to Pharaoh, and lord of all his house and ruler over all the land of Egypt.
9 "Hurry and go up to my father, and say to him, 'Thus says your son Joseph:"God has made me lord of all Egypt; come down to me, do not tarry.	**9** Hurry and go up to my father and say to him, 'Thus says your son Joseph, God has made me lord of all Egypt. Come down to me; do not tarry.
10 You shall dwell in the land of Goshen, and you shall be near to me, you and your children, your children's children, your flocks and your herds, and all that you have.	**10** You shall dwell in the land of Goshen, and you shall be near me, you and your children and your children's children, and your flocks, your herds, and all that you have.
11 There I will provide for you, lest you and your household, and all that you have, come to poverty; for *there are* still five years of famine."'	**11** There I will provide for you, for there are yet five years of famine to come, so that you and your household, and all that you have, do not come to poverty.'
12 "And behold, your eyes and the eyes of my brother Benjamin see that *it is* my mouth that speaks to you.	**12** And now your eyes see, and the eyes of my brother Benjamin see, that it is my mouth that speaks to you.
13 So you shall tell my father of all my glory in Egypt, and of all that you have seen; and you shall hurry and bring my father down here."	**13** You must tell my father of all my honor in Egypt, and of all that you have seen. Hurry and bring my father down here."
14 Then he fell on his brother Benjamin's neck and wept, and Benjamin wept on his neck.	**14** Then he fell upon his brother Benjamin's neck and wept, and Benjamin wept upon his neck.
15 Moreover he kissed all his brothers and wept over them, and after that his brothers talked with him.	**15** And he kissed all his brothers and wept upon them. After that his brothers talked with him.

45:1 The last word Joseph heard from his brother's speech was *'abi*, **my father** (44:34). The affectionate title evoking a tender relation to the father moves Joseph (cf. 22:7). In addition, Judah's readiness to take Benjamin's place must take Joseph by surprise. Joseph discovers that Judah has dramatically changed. Judah is not only thoughtful toward his father and brother(s), but his language also reflects profound religious thinking; Judah is in touch with God. Joseph is at last overwhelmed by his emotions. Whereas he had been previously able to control himself (43:31), he cannot anymore. This is the third weeping of Joseph and the loudest. He cries and abruptly sends everyone away except for his brothers. This experience is too personal. For the first time, Joseph dissociates himself from the Egyptians who do not really know him. Only after all the Egyptians have left the place does Joseph make himself known to his brothers. The verb **made himself known** (*hitwada'*), the reflexive form (*hitpael*) from the root *yada'* "know," contains a veiled allusion to God. The only other occurrence of this verbal form in the Hebrew Scriptures refers to God's revelation of Himself to Moses (Num 12:6). The same verb in the *niphal* with a reflexive sense[711] describes God's self-revelation (Exod 6:3; Ezek 20:9; Pss 9:16 [17]; 76:1 [2]; etc.). The use of this form suggests that by making himself known to his brothers, Joseph will make God reveal Himself to them. Note that the verb does not refer to a contemporary situation; it is part of the introduction referring to the entire forthcoming episode.

45:2 The sound of Joseph's weeping is so loud that it is heard by **the house of Pharaoh**, a way of suggesting that Pharaoh himself heard it. Note that the Egyptian word *Pharaoh* means the "great house." The reference to "the house of Pharaoh" implies Pharaoh himself who identifies with it. All of the emotions Joseph had so far been able to suppress explode beyond all measure. The scene sounds and looks surreal for the group of Egyptians present; for the steward—he is close to the vizier and conspired with him against these Hebrews, now he has been rushed out of the presence of the vizier; for Pharaoh, who hears Joseph weeping from his palace. Such behavior is inconsistent with the typical image he has of the wise and self-controlled Joseph. The specific mention that Pharaoh hears Joseph's loud weeping suggests that this unusual show of emotion has taken him by surprise. More importantly, this manifestation sounds surreal for Joseph's brothers who are left alone with him, whom they perceived a short time ago to be the distant and contemptuous vizier of Egypt.

45:3–4 Joseph must have noticed their dismay, because he repeats a second time: **I am Joseph** (45:3–4). After Joseph said it the first time, he only inquires about his father, whether he is still alive (45:3a). The question is awkward because he had already asked that question and had received an answer from them about it (43:27–28). Joseph seems to be confused because of the intensity of his emotions. The brothers are perplexed and worried. They may even have certain doubts about Joseph's claim, since he does not provide any more information than what they had indicated to him. All of this appears suspicious, particularly considering the more recent experiences they have had with this man. Therefore, the brothers choose not to answer (45:3b). This is why Joseph repeats a second time "I am Joseph"; but this time, he is more precise and adds a piece of information no one knows, except the ten brothers (excluding Benjamin) and himself: **your brother, whom you sold into Egypt** (45:4).

45:5–9 The brothers' reaction is immediate and strong. Joseph detects in it a mixture of distress (ESV) and anger with themselves (45:5). The same pair of Hebrew words (*'atsab* "distress," and *khara* "anger") appear on two other occasions in the Scriptures, each time to characterize the mental state of people who are overwhelmed with the double emotion of sadness and anger: Dinah's brothers, when they heard of what had been done to their sister (34:7), and Jonathan, when he understood that his father was determined to kill his friend David (1 Sam 20:34). Joseph's response is framed with the same **now therefore** (*we'atah*) that, similarly, articulated Judah's discourse (45:5, 8; cf. 44:30, 33). Joseph's response addresses Judah's concern: he will now be able to go up to his father without the fear of seeing "the evil" (44:34).

To reassure his brothers, Joseph's argument is fundamental and pertains to the principle that underlies the entire story of Joseph. God is behind the course of events and turns evil into good. Joseph's plea consists of seven declarations that acknowledge

---

711 See *GKC* §51 c–e.

God's works of salvation (45:5, 7–9; 50:20, 24–25). These seven declarations regarding God's work that conclude the book of Genesis echo God's seven works of creation in its introduction, in inclusio.[712] Joseph's first four acknowledgments are found in this chapter; they refer to what God did for him, from the beginning of his journey (God sent Joseph, 45:5, 7) to its end (God made Joseph lord of Egypt, 45:8–9). The last three acknowledgments are found in the last chapter of Genesis; they refer to what God did and will do for his brothers, from the beginning of their evil to this day (God meant their evil for good, 50:20) and to the future (God will visit them, 50:24–25).

45:5 God sent me. It is God who "sent" him. The last time Joseph was sent, it was by Jacob, who had sent Joseph to inquire of their *shalom* (37:13–14). The verb "send" (*shalakh*) is used three times in this paragraph (45:5–8) to insist that God is the One who "sent." God sent him before his brothers for a specific purpose: **to preserve life.** The idiom for "preserve life" (*lemikhyeh*), related to the word *khayyim* "life," expresses the notion of life survival (cf. 2 Chr 14:13 [12]), as implied in its association with the word *she'arit* "remnant" (45:7 ESV).[713] Joseph suggests that it was necessary that they sell him to ensure their survival. Thus, the brothers thought *they* had sold their brother, whereas, in fact, it was God who was leading in that operation. The present situation of **famine ... in the land** (45:6a), which will last for another **five years** (45:6), is an implicit evidence of God's presence, since only God possesses this prescience (cf. 41:16).

45:7 To preserve a posterity ... to save your lives by a great deliverance. The association of the words **posterity** ("remnant") and **deliverance** (*pleytah*) conveys "a word of hope."[714] The same combination of the two words occurs elsewhere in the Scriptures to refer to the salvation of Israel (2 Kgs 19:31; Isa 37:32). This language points beyond the present family of Jacob to the future people of Israel "because in the preservation of a surviving remnant, the nucleus of a 'great people' (50:20) was preserved."[715]

45:8 A father to Pharaoh. This formula reflects the Egyptian title *itf-ntr*, meaning literally "father of God," which refers to Pharaoh as a god. Joseph would not use the expression as it was in the Egyptian language without sounding blasphemous to his brothers and father, so he simply said, "father of Pharaoh." This was a priestly title, which was borne by the highest officers, including viziers, such as Ptah-hotep, vizier of King Isesi (2675 BC).[716] The other title of Joseph, **ruler throughout all the land of Egypt,** refers to his rule over the entire country of the two lands (Upper and Lower Egypt) and reflects another Egyptian title, *nb t3.wy* "lord of the two lands," which was an official permanent title borne by the deputy of Pharaoh.[717] Note that the dual form of the Hebrew word *mitsrayim* for "Egypt," reflects the two divisions of Egypt. Joseph's emphasis on his status in Egypt is intentional to emphasize his extraordinary position, thereby reminding his brothers of the dream, which had portrayed him as ruler to whom all (including his father) would bow (37:9). Alluding to the dream, Joseph is using the fulfillment of that dream as an implicit argument for God's providence.

---

712 See Ostring, "The Theology of Human Work," 327–328.

713 This meaning of "survival" has been retained in the Qumran texts where it appears twice, each time associated, as in the passage here, with the word *she'arit* "remnant" (1QM 13:8; 1QH 6:8).

714 Von Rad, *Genesis*, 394.

715 Hasel, *The Remnant*, 158.

716 See *AEL* 1:62.

717 See Gardiner, *Egyptian Grammar*, 573.

45:9 **God has made me lord of all Egypt.** Joseph then urges his brothers to return promptly to their father. The word "hasten" (*mahar*) begins and concludes Joseph's speech, as an inclusio (45:9, 13), and is reinforced at the end of the verse by the injunction not to **tarry**. The purpose of this rush is to inform his father that it is God who made him lord of Egypt. Joseph emphasizes this point; the phrase "God has made me" stands at the head of the sentence. Joseph's strategy is designed to reassure his father and convince him to come quickly to Egypt.

45:10 Joseph promises to his father that he will **dwell in the land of Goshen** (45:10). This is the second time the verb "dwell" (*yashab*) is used in connection with Jacob (cf. 37:1). The preceding (and first) occurrence of this verb in relation to Jacob was to signify Jacob's first intention to settle in the Promised Land (37:1) versus the preceding patriarchs who had so far merely "sojourned" as strangers (*gur*) there (17:8; 23:4; 28:4; 36:7; cf. Heb 11:9). The prospect for Jacob is again to "dwell" but this time in Egypt, supported only by his faith in God's promise (cf. Heb 11:13). Joseph's use of the verb is intentional to suggest to Jacob that he will be safe and at home in Egypt and that he could settle there for good. The reference to **your children and your children's children** reinforces this affirmation because it brings a future perspective to this settling. As for "the land of Goshen," it is not to be confused with the Canaanite town of Goshen (Josh 15:51) or the other "land of Goshen" in the south of Judah (Josh 10:41; 11:16; 15:5). The "land of Goshen," here, refers to a place in the eastern delta area (identified as Wadi Tumilat in the ancient records), a territory that was controlled by the Hyksos pharaohs of that time. This area was so well known for its rich pastures that, by the time of Merneptah (1236–1223 BC), it had become a popular place for the Bedouin herdsmen of Sinai to come "to keep them alive and to keep their cattle alive."[718] According to Egyptologist Warburton, during the unproductive dry season when grain feeding was not possible, large herds were a means of ensuring survival after natural disasters, such as drought, and thus the Nile Delta, where enough moisture existed, was an ideal place for cattle to be kept.[719] Therefore, the mention of that location was intentional in an effort to encourage Jacob to come, because he had certainly heard of the pastoral quality of that land. That Joseph could make such a promise without consulting with the pharaoh suggests that he had received power over the distribution of the land (41:40–41; Ps 105:21).

45:11 However, during a time of famine and drought, grazing is problematic. Therefore, Joseph assures his father that he will care for the entire family: **I will provide for you … and your household** (45:11); otherwise, he warns, you will **come to poverty**, because there are **still five years of famine** to come. This last information, which implies his foreknowledge, should inspire even more trust from his father, since Joseph's prescience is an evidence of God's presence on his side.

45:12–13 Joseph's ultimate argument is the tangible testimony of his brothers. In addition to his hospitality and abundant provisions, Joseph presents to his brothers and, more specifically to Benjamin, the evidence of what they see: **it is my mouth that speaks to you** (45:12). Joseph urges them to report to his father what they have seen and thus testify to what he calls **all my glory in Egypt** (45:13a). The purpose of this plea is to bring **my father down here** (45:13b) as quickly as possible. Note how Joseph insists on calling his father "my father" rather than "our father," although

---

718 *ANET*, 259a.
719 See Douglas J. Brewer, "Cattle," *OEAE* 1:242–244.

he speaks to his brothers. This language suggests that Joseph still holds a special relation with his father, which he does not share with his other brothers (cf. 37:3–4).

45:14–15 Joseph also displays the same particular connection with his unique brother, the other son of his mother (cf. 45:9). Joseph weeps on his brother's neck, and Benjamin reciprocates (45:14). This is a moment of great emotion in which the other brothers do not partake. Only when he turns to them and kisses **all his brothers** (45:15a) do they finally speak to him for the first time (45:15b).

45:16–28. PHARAOH INVITES JACOB

GEN 45:16–28 NKJV	GEN 45:16–28 ESV
16 Now the report of it was heard in Pharaoh's house, saying, "Joseph's brothers have come." So it pleased Pharaoh and his servants well.	**16** When the report was heard in Pharaoh's house, "Joseph's brothers have come," it pleased Pharaoh and his servants.
17 And Pharaoh said to Joseph, "Say to your brothers, 'Do this: Load your animals and depart; go to the land of Canaan.	**17** And Pharaoh said to Joseph, "Say to your brothers, 'Do this: load your beasts and go back to the land of Canaan,
18 Bring your father and your households and come to me; I will give you the best of the land of Egypt, and you will eat the fat of the land.	**18** and take your father and your households, and come to me, and I will give you the best of the land of Egypt, and you shall eat the fat of the land.'
19 Now you are commanded—do this: Take carts out of the land of Egypt for your little ones and your wives; bring your father and come.	**19** And you, Joseph, are commanded to say, 'Do this: take wagons from the land of Egypt for your little ones and for your wives, and bring your father, and come.
20 Also do not be concerned about your goods, for the best of all the land of Egypt *is* yours.'"	**20** Have no concern for your goods, for the best of all the land of Egypt is yours.'"
21 Then the sons of Israel did so; and Joseph gave them carts, according to the command of Pharaoh, and he gave them provisions for the journey.	**21** The sons of Israel did so: and Joseph gave them wagons, according to the command of Pharaoh, and gave them provisions for the journey.
22 He gave to all of them, to each man, changes of garments; but to Benjamin he gave three hundred *pieces* of silver and five changes of garments.	**22** To each and all of them he gave a change of clothes, but to Benjamin he gave three hundred shekels of silver and five changes of clothes.
23 And he sent to his father these *things*: ten donkeys loaded with the good things of Egypt, and ten female donkeys loaded with grain, bread, and food for his father for the journey.	**23** To his father he sent as follows: ten donkeys loaded with the good things of Egypt, and ten female donkeys loaded with grain, bread, and provision for his father on the journey.
24 So he sent his brothers away, and they departed; and he said to them, "See that you do not become troubled along the way."	**24** Then he sent his brothers away, and as they departed, he said to them, "Do not quarrel on the way."
25 Then they went up out of Egypt, and came to the land of Canaan to Jacob their father.	**25** So they went up out of Egypt and came to the land of Canaan to their father Jacob.
26 And they told him, saying, "Joseph *is* still alive, and he *is* governor over all the land of Egypt." And Jacob's heart stood still, because he did not believe them.	**26** And they told him, "Joseph is still alive, and he is ruler over all the land of Egypt." And his heart became numb, for he did not believe them.

27 But when they told him all the words which Joseph had said to them, and when he saw the carts which Joseph had sent to carry him, the spirit of Jacob their father revived.

28 Then Israel said, "*It is* enough. Joseph my son *is* still alive. I will go and see him before I die."

27 But when they told him all the words of Joseph, which he had said to them, and when he saw the wagons that Joseph had sent to carry him, the spirit of their father Jacob revived.

28 And Israel said, "It is enough; Joseph my son is still alive. I will go and see him before I die."

45:16–20 When Pharaoh learns that Joseph's turmoil is due to a family reunion he is relieved: **it pleased Pharaoh** (45:16). The same Hebrew verb (*wayyitab*) is used to describe Pharaoh's reaction when he heard Joseph's proposal to save Egypt from the famine (41:37). In fact, the two Hebrew lines are identical:[720]

> *wayyitab haddabar be'eyney par'oh wbe'eyne kol 'abadaw* "So the advice was good in the eyes of Pharaoh and in the eyes of all his servants" (41:37)
> *wayyitab be'eyney par'oh wbe'eyney 'abadaw* "So it pleased Pharaoh and his servants well" (45:16)

This echo suggests that Pharaoh's satisfaction is related to the same issue regarding the threat of famine. When Pharaoh heard Joseph's intense weeping (45:2), he may have been concerned about Joseph's capacity to manage the Egyptian crisis. Now that he knows the real reason for Joseph's behavior, he is reassured. He is so relieved that he immediately confirms Joseph's invitation to his brothers and father and, in his enthusiasm, is even more generous than Joseph. Whereas Joseph had just promised "the land of Goshen," Pharaoh offers **the best of the land … the fat of the land** (45:18). The mention "best of the land" is repeated a second time (45:20). Pharaoh certainly has the land of Goshen in mind because he will later associate this description with the land of Goshen (47:4). Whereas Joseph had vaguely promised that he would provide for his family, Pharaoh is more concrete and presses for action—**do this: load your animals and depart; go to the land of Canaan** (45:17)—and gives them the means to accomplish this work; he gives them **carts out of the land of Egypt** (45:19) that they may transport the most fragile, the little ones, the wives, and the old father (45:19). Similar to Joseph, Pharaoh engages himself personally in the operation: **come to me** (45:18; cf. 45:9).

45:21–24 The return of the brothers progresses in two phases. First, Joseph organizes the journey. According to Pharaoh's orders (cf. 45:19), Joseph gives carts to his brothers to ensure the safe transport of their families back to Egypt. The mention of the other gifts as an afterthought suggests that the provisions for the journey (45:21b) and the changes of garments (45:22a) seem to have been done on his personal initiative, particularly in the case of Benjamin. Whereas Joseph gives only one change of garments to each of his ten brothers, to Benjamin he gives five times more changes of garments, in addition to a great sum of money. The association of the garments and the money hints at the episode when he was sold by his brothers. The same word for "garment" (*simlah*) is used to refer to Joseph's tunic that was supposedly torn by a beast (37:31–33), and the same word for "money" (*kesep*) designates

---

720 The word *haddabar* "the matter," "proposal," which does not occur in the second passage, and the word *kol* "all," which is also absent in the second occurrence suggests that, on that occasion, not "all" of the servants of Pharaoh are present.

the money that was received by the brothers for the sale of Joseph (37:28). This echo between the two passages suggests Joseph's intention to repair the past crime and again turn evil into good. The torn tunic has become five brand-new tunics and the miserable twenty shekels of silver have become the lavish sum of three hundred. The former episode has led to the latter: it is because Joseph's tunic was torn and because he was sold that he is now able to be so generous with his family and even save their lives (cf. 45:7). The same type of connection is suggested through the echo between the "five garments" (see also the five servings of food in 43:34) and the "five years of famine." Ironically, the famine that would otherwise impoverish has now enriched the family of Jacob. For the gift destined for his father, Joseph offers twice the value of the gift destined for Benjamin: the number five has become ten. Ten male donkeys are loaded with unidentified precious things of Egypt, and ten female donkeys are loaded with food (45:23). Benjamin and Jacob have received much more than the ten brothers, with Benjamin receiving five times more and Jacob ten times more. This particular gesture of favoritism could be sufficient to provoke jealousy among the brothers. Joseph, who knows his brothers well, adds the last recommendation as they depart: **do not quarrel on the way** (45:24b ESV; cf. NIV).[721]

45:25–28 The brothers leave for the land of Canaan and report to their father about Joseph. Apparently, the brothers' move is slow considering the number of verbs describing the process. After Joseph's act of "sending" them (45:24), three more verbs are mentioned (45:24–25): **they departed** (*wayyeleku*) **... they went up** (*way'alu*) **... and came** (*wayyabo'u*). These three verbs also suggest the three aspects of this journey. First, they "leave" (*halak*) the place; this is the same verb that is used for Abraham who leaves and goes to the Promised Land (12:1, 4). They "go up" (*'alah*) **to the land of Canaan** (45:25); one always goes up to Canaan (13:1; 46:4; 50:6; Num 13:21) because it is a mountainous place, in contrast to flat Egypt (Deut 11:11), but also in a spiritual sense, as one goes up to Jerusalem or to the house of the Lord to worship Him (Isa 2:3; 2 Chr 29:30; Jer 31:6). Finally, when they reach their destination, they "come" (*ba'*) to Canaan and to their father. They immediately speak about Joseph and limit their report to the mere information that he is **alive, and he is governor over all ... Egypt** (45:26). They do not elaborate on his glorious status in keeping with Joseph's specific request (45:13), nor do they tell about the nature of their encounter with him. Jacob's response to this news is both emotional and mental: **Jacob's heart stood still ... he did not believe them** (45:26). Jacob is stunned. The Hebrew verb *wayapog* "stood still" renders the idea of "ceasing" (Ps 77:3 [2]) or the notion of "powerlessness." Jacob is numb and shocked. Aaron displays the same reaction when he hears the news of the death of his two sons, killed by the heavenly fire: "Aaron remained silent" (Lev 10:3 NIV). He also refuses to be emotionally touched by such extraordinary news, lest he rejoice and later be disappointed. Jacob cannot believe. Only when his sons report the very words of Joseph and when he sees the carts Joseph has sent to him for his transportation does he breathe again. The reference to the **spirit** (*ruakh*) is ambiguous. The word means "spirit" (Ps 32:2) or "air for breathing" (Jer 14:6), which also refers to the principle of life, the *ruakh* of life (6:17; cf. Ps 104:29–30). Jacob comes back to life. The entire passage revolves around the issue of life and death (45:28). Jacob's life was dependent

---

721 This interpretation of the Hebrew verb *ragaz* (NKJV: "become troubled") is the one that has generally been retained in Jewish and Christian traditions.

on Joseph's life (37:35; cf. 44:29). For Jacob, the fact that Joseph was alive was enough to bring life to him. The word *rab*, translated **enough**, conveys the idea of abundance (6:5). Jacob is overwhelmed by all this information but makes the decision to go[722] to Egypt. Jacob is now called **Israel**; with all of his twelve sons, full of the promise of blessing, Jacob anticipates the future of the twelve tribes. Israel is on the horizon.

46:1–47:31. JACOB IN EGYPT

This is the final and third journey from Canaan to Egypt by Joseph's brothers. This time Jacob has joined his sons in Egypt with the intention of settling there. However, the unit ends with the prospect of returning from Egypt to the Promised Land. Between these two orientations, from Canaan to Egypt (46:1–27) and the anticipation of returning to Canaan (47:27–31), life is organized in Egypt: Joseph meets with his family and Pharaoh (46:28–47:6) and cares for both his family and Egypt (47:11–26). The unit reaches its climax at midpoint when Jacob meets with Pharaoh and blesses him (47:7–10). The unit is thus organized according to the following chiastic structure:

A From Canaan to Egypt (46:1–27)
    B Joseph meets with his family and Pharaoh (46:28–47:6)
        C Jacob meets and blesses Pharaoh (47:7–10)
    B₁ Joseph cares for his family and Egypt (47:11–26)
A₁ From Egypt to Canaan (47:27–31)

FROM CANAAN TO EGYPT (46:1–27)

Jacob's journey from Canaan to Egypt progresses in two steps. First, Jacob pauses at Beersheba where he offers a sacrifice and hears God's words of encouragement for his journey to Egypt (46:1–4); Jacob then departs from Beersheba (46:5–7). Afterward, a list of the names of all of the children of Israel who go to Egypt is given (46:8–27), anticipating the list of their descendants who will return to the Promised Land four hundred years later (Num 1:1–46).

46:1–4. PAUSE IN BEERSHEBA

GEN 46:1–4 NKJV	GEN 46:1–4 ESV
1 So Israel took his journey with all that he had, and came to Beersheba, and offered sacrifices to the God of his father Isaac.	**1** So Israel took his journey with all that he had and came to Beersheba, and offered sacrifices to the God of his father Isaac.
2 Then God spoke to Israel in the visions of the night, and said, "Jacob, Jacob!" And he said, "Here I am."	**2** And God spoke to Israel in visions of the night and said, "Jacob, Jacob." And he said, "Here am I."
3 So He said, "I *am* God, the God of your father; do not fear to go down to Egypt, for I will make of you a great nation there.	**3** Then he said, "I am God, the God of your father. Do not be afraid to go down to Egypt, for there I will make you into a great nation.

---

722 The form of the Hebrew verb *'elkha* "I will go" is a cohortative statement suggesting his determination to go.

4 I will go down with you to Egypt, and I will also surely bring you up *again*; and Joseph will put his hand on your eyes."	4 I myself will go down with you to Egypt, and I will also bring you up again, and Joseph's hand shall close your eyes."

Jacob is likely residing in Hebron (37:14; 35:27). His departure to Egypt is reminiscent of the Abrahamic stories and recalls Abram's departure to Egypt (12:10). Both Jacob and Abram leave Canaan because of famine, and both moves are rendered by the same verbal form *wayyisa* **took his journey** (46:1), which was used with Abram for the first time. However, a fundamental difference exists between the two journeys. Whereas Abram went to Egypt without seeking the support of his God, Jacob preludes his journey by an intense moment of worship. The manner in which God addresses Jacob recalls how He called Abraham on Moriah, repeating his name twice: **Jacob, Jacob!** (46:2; cf. 22:11a). Jacob responds with the same words: *hinneni* **here I am** (46:2; cf. 22:11b). Likewise, in both texts, the same divine promise to Abram reappears to Jacob: God will make of him **a great nation** (*goy gadol*) (46:3; cf. 12:2). The passage is also reminiscent of the account of the covenant with Abram. There also, God strengthens Abram with the same reassuring words: **do not fear** (46:3a; cf. 15:1) and provides him with the same promise of descendants (46:3b; 15:4–5). The experience of the two patriarchs is similar. Both have visions in the night (46:2; cf. 15:5) and are involved in sacrificial activities (46:1; cf.15:9–10). Both receive the same prophecy about the future condition of Israel as slaves and strangers in a foreign land for four hundred years, after which they will come out (46:3–4; cf. 15:13–14). For Jacob as for Abram/Abraham, the promise of fruitfulness is associated with the same prospect of the Promised Land (46:4a; cf. 12:1; 15:18; 22:17). Jacob is thus depicted as a second Abraham. God will not only accompany Jacob to Egypt, he will also bring him back to the Promised Land. God's promise of the future is supported by a confirmation that Joseph is indeed alive, and he will be the one who will **put his hand on your eyes** (46:4). This last information anticipates the close of this literary unit, which ends with Jacob making Joseph swear that he will bring him back to Canaan and bury him with his fathers (47:29–31). Thus, the introduction and the conclusion of this unit echo each other in inclusio.

46:5–7. DEPARTURE FROM BEERSHEBA

GEN 46:5–7 NKJV	GEN 46:5–7 ESV
5 Then Jacob arose from Beersheba; and the sons of Israel carried their father Jacob, their little ones, and their wives, in the carts which Pharaoh had sent to carry him.	5 Then Jacob set out from Beersheba. The sons of Israel carried Jacob their father, their little ones, and their wives, in the wagons that Pharaoh had sent to carry him.
6 So they took their livestock and their goods, which they had acquired in the land of Canaan, and went to Egypt, Jacob and all his descendants with him.	6 They also took their livestock and their goods, which they had gained in the land of Canaan, and came into Egypt, Jacob and all his offspring with him,
7 His sons and his sons' sons, his daughters and his sons' daughters, and all his descendants he brought with him to Egypt.	7 his sons, and his sons' sons with him, his daughters, and his sons' daughters. All his offspring he brought with him into Egypt.

Jacob will finally depart for Egypt from Beersheba (46:5a). The specification of the sons of Israel (NIV) following the reference to **Jacob** alludes to the potential nation of Israel (cf. 46:8). The first consideration is for the most delicate ones, the old Jacob, the little ones, and the wives who take their places in the carts provided by Pharaoh (46:5). The report emphasizes the comprehensiveness of Jacob's expedition, an indication of his intention to settle in Egypt. They take with them everything they own, **their livestock and their goods** (46:6), language that recalls again the experience of Abraham (31:18; cf. 46:1; 12:20; 13:1); and the trip involves everyone: **Jacob and all his descendants with him** (46:6; cf. 46:7). The next verse refers not only to **his sons and his son's sons**, but adds a special mention of **his daughters, and his son's daughters** (46:7). Dinah and other unidentified daughters (cf. 34:9, 16, 21) are thus included.

46:8–27. THE SEVENTY CHILDREN OF ISRAEL

GEN 46:8–27 NKJV	GEN 46:8–27 ESV
8 Now these *were* the names of the children of Israel, Jacob and his sons, who went to Egypt: Reuben *was* Jacob's firstborn.	**8** Now these are the names of the descendants of Israel, who came into Egypt, Jacob and his sons. Reuben, Jacob's firstborn,
9 The sons of Reuben *were* Hanoch, Pallu, Hezron, and Carmi.	**9** and the sons of Reuben: Hanoch, Pallu, Hezron, and Carmi.
10 The sons of Simeon *were* Jemuel, Jamin, Ohad, Jachin, Zohar, and Shaul, the son of a Canaanite woman.	**10** The sons of Simeon: Jemuel, Jamin, Ohad, Jachin, Zohar, and Shaul, the son of a Canaanite woman.
11 The sons of Levi *were* Gershon, Kohath, and Merari.	**11** The sons of Levi: Gershon, Kohath, and Merari.
12 The sons of Judah *were* Er, Onan, Shelah, Perez, and Zerah (but Er and Onan died in the land of Canaan). The sons of Perez were Hezron and Hamul.	**12** The sons of Judah: Er, Onan, Shelah, Perez, and Zerah (but Er and Onan died in the land of Canaan); and the sons of Perez were Hezron and Hamul.
13 The sons of Issachar *were* Tola, Puvah, Job, and Shimron.	**13** The sons of Issachar: Tola, Puvah, Yob, and Shimron.
14 The sons of Zebulun *were* Sered, Elon, and Jahleel.	**14** The sons of Zebulun: Sered, Elon, and Jahleel.
15 These *were* the sons of Leah, whom she bore to Jacob in Padan Aram, with his daughter Dinah. All the persons, his sons and his daughters, *were* thirty-three.	**15** These are the sons of Leah, whom she bore to Jacob in Paddan-aram, together with his daughter Dinah; altogether his sons and his daughters numbered thirty-three.
16 The sons of Gad *were* Ziphion, Haggi, Shuni, Ezbon, Eri, Arodi, and Areli.	**16** The sons of Gad: Ziphion, Haggi, Shuni, Ezbon, Eri, Arodi, and Areli.
17 The sons of Asher *were* Jimnah, Ishuah, Isui, Beriah, and Serah, their sister. And the sons of Beriah *were* Heber and Malchiel.	**17** The sons of Asher: Imnah, Ishvah, Ishvi, Beriah, with Serah their sister. And the sons of Beriah: Heber and Malchiel.
18 These *were* the sons of Zilpah, whom Laban gave to Leah his daughter; and these she bore to Jacob: sixteen persons.	**18** These are the sons of Zilpah, whom Laban gave to Leah his daughter; and these she bore to Jacob—sixteen persons.

19 The sons of Rachel, Jacob's wife, *were* Joseph and Benjamin.	**19** The sons of Rachel, Jacob's wife: Joseph and Benjamin.
20 And to Joseph in the land of Egypt were born Manasseh and Ephraim, whom Asenath, the daughter of Poti-Pherah priest of On, bore to him.	**20** And to Joseph in the land of Egypt were born Manasseh and Ephraim, whom Asenath, the daughter of Potiphera the priest of On, bore to him.
21 The sons of Benjamin *were* Belah, Becher, Ashbel, Gera, Naaman, Ehi, Rosh, Muppim, Huppim, and Ard.	**21** And the sons of Benjamin: Bela, Becher, Ashbel, Gera, Naaman, Ehi, Rosh, Muppim, Huppim, and Ard.
22 These *were* the sons of Rachel, who were born to Jacob: fourteen persons in all.	**22** These are the sons of Rachel, who were born to Jacob—fourteen persons in all.
23 The son of Dan *was* Hushim.	**23** The sons of Dan: Hushim.
24 The sons of Naphtali *were* Jahzeel, Guni, Jezer, and Shillem.	**24** The sons of Naphtali: Jahzeel, Guni, Jezer, and Shillem.
25 These *were* the sons of Bilhah, whom Laban gave to Rachel his daughter, and she bore these to Jacob: seven persons in all.	**25** These are the sons of Bilhah, whom Laban gave to Rachel his daughter, and these she bore to Jacob—seven persons in all.
26 All the persons who went with Jacob to Egypt, who came from his body, besides Jacob's sons' wives, *were* sixty-six persons in all.	**26** All the persons belonging to Jacob who came into Egypt, who were his own descendants, not including Jacob's sons' wives, were sixty-six persons in all.
27 And the sons of Joseph who were born to him in Egypt *were* two persons. All the persons of the house of Jacob who went to Egypt were seventy.	**27** And the sons of Joseph, who were born to him in Egypt, were two. All the persons of the house of Jacob who came into Egypt were seventy.

The listing of the names of the children of Israel who went to Egypt not only recalls the fulfillment of God's promise, but reinforces the historical characteristic of the journey. The list of names is structured around Jacob's wives and their respective maids (Leah and Zilpah, and then Rachel and Bilhah), thus forming a four-part arrangement:

> **Leah:** Thirty-three children (46:8–15)
> **Zilpah:** Sixteen children (46:16–18)
> **Rachel:** Fourteen children (46:19–22)
> **Bilhah:** Seven children (46:23–25)

Note that each maid has half the number of children as her mistress (33/16; 14/7). The addition of the number of children makes a total of seventy. At the conclusion of the list, two numbers (sixty-six and seventy) are given, suggesting two different ways of counting. The number **sixty-six** refers to Jacob's direct descendants (46:26) who went to Egypt with Jacob, hence the use of the preposition *le* "to," "in connection to" in the Hebrew phrase *leya'aqob* translated **with Jacob** (NKJV) or **belonging to Jacob** (46:26 ESV). Jacob is obviously not counted among his descendants, and Joseph and his two sons were not part of the journey. The number **seventy** includes Jacob and Joseph and his two sons, hence the use of the expression **the house of Jacob** (*beyt ya'aqob*) (46:27), which should include the head of the family as well as those of the family who are already in Egypt. The reminder of the "seventy" in the introduction to the Exodus account (Exod 1:5) resonates with our passage to signal the fulfillment of God's promise to return to the Promised Land. The number seventy may also convey a spiritual meaning; it expresses the idea of totality. It is "all Israel" that goes to Egypt and will return from there "as the stars of heaven in multitude" (Deut 10:22). The fact that the same number seventy characterizes the nations of the earth (10:1–32) suggests that Israel is viewed as "the family of man in microcosm."[723]

JOSEPH MEETS WITH HIS FAMILY AND PHARAOH (46:28–47:6)

Shortly after Jacob and his family arrive in Egypt, Joseph meets with them in Goshen to prepare them for their meeting with Pharaoh and to ensure a smooth adjustment in Egypt (46:28–34). The report of this first encounter between Joseph and his family significantly begins and ends with a reference to Goshen (46:28–29, 34). Joseph subsequently meets with Pharaoh to introduce his family and obtain from Pharaoh the formal authorization that they may settle in Goshen (47:1–6). The mention of Goshen here marks the beginning (47:1) and end of the unit (47:6).

46:28–34. MEETING IN GOSHEN

GEN 46:28–34 NKJV	GEN 46:28–34 ESV
28 Then he sent Judah before him to Joseph, to point out before him *the way* to Goshen. And they came to the land of Goshen.	**28** He had sent Judah ahead of him to Joseph to show the way before him in Goshen, and they came into the land of Goshen.
29 So Joseph made ready his chariot and went up to Goshen to meet his father Israel; and he presented himself to him, and fell on his neck and wept on his neck a good while.	**29** Then Joseph prepared his chariot and went up to meet Israel his father in Goshen. He presented himself to him and fell on his neck and wept on his neck a good while.
30 And Israel said to Joseph, "Now let me die, since I have seen your face, because you *are* still alive."	**30** Israel said to Joseph, "Now let me die, since I have seen your face and know that you are still alive."
31 Then Joseph said to his brothers and to his father's household, "I will go up and tell Pharaoh, and say to him, 'My brothers and those of my father's house, who *were* in the land of Canaan, have come to me.	**31** Joseph said to his brothers and to his father's household, "I will go up and tell Pharaoh and will say to him, 'My brothers and my father's household, who were in the land of Canaan, have come to me.
32 And the men *are* shepherds, for their occupation has been to feed livestock; and they have brought their flocks, their herds, and all that they have.'	**32** And the men are shepherds, for they have been keepers of livestock, and they have brought their flocks and their herds and all that they have.'
33 So it shall be, when Pharaoh calls you and says, 'What is your occupation?'	**33** When Pharaoh calls you and says, 'What is your occupation?'
34 that you shall say, 'Your servants' occupation has been with livestock from our youth even till now, both we *and* also our fathers,' that you may dwell in the land of Goshen; for every shepherd *is* an abomination to the Egyptians."	**34** you shall say, 'Your servants have been keepers of livestock from our youth even until now, both we and our fathers,' in order that you may dwell in the land of Goshen, for every shepherd is an abomination to the Egyptians."

---

723 Wenham, *Genesis 16–50*, 442.

46:28 **He sent Judah.** As is typical, Judah takes the lead. Jacob has chosen him and sent him, to Joseph to prepare the way to Goshen. The verb "send" (*shalakh*) is a reminder of the beginning of Joseph's adventures, when Jacob "sent" Joseph to his brothers (37:13). This is the second time that Jacob sends a son to the other brother. The first time Jacob sent Joseph to his brothers and was then sent by Judah to Egypt (37:27); now it is Judah who is sent to Joseph. This literary reversal suggests the repair of the link between Joseph and his family that was broken for so many years. The encounter will take place at Goshen, which is the prospective place where the family hopes to settle.

46:29–30 Although Judah was supposed to be the first to meet with Joseph, the author ignores this encounter and focuses instead on the meeting between Joseph and his father. The use of the verb **presented himself** (*wayyera'*) is intriguing. This verbal form normally applies to God who appears to humans (12:7; 17:1; 18:1; 26:2, 24; 35:9). This common language suggests that Jacob considers this encounter with Joseph, the son he had lost, as an experience with the divine, just as he did when he met again with Esau, the brother he had lost (33:10). On both occasions, the meeting is the occasion of a miracle. No one could have imagined such a turnabout of events that could be likened to a resurrection from the dead. Jacob thinks of resurrection as he refers to both categories of life and death (46:30). Joseph expresses the intensity of his emotion. He falls on his father's neck and weeps for **a good while** (NIV: "a long time"). The Hebrew word *'od*, normally expresses the notion of repetition and permanence (2 Sam 3:35). Joseph must have wept again and again. However, it is striking that Jacob remains mute. Perhaps he is paralyzed or overwhelmed by emotion. No words or body language could adequately express his sentiments.

46:31–34 Joseph's other brothers are likely present during this extraordinary encounter because Joseph immediately turns and speaks to them to prepare them for the next step, namely, their meeting with Pharaoh (46:31). Joseph informs them of what he will say to Pharaoh and advises them regarding how and what they should respond to Pharaoh. Joseph's instructions to his brothers are specific; he wants them to be honest in their testimony and not to hide their occupation. The explanative statement **for every shepherd is an abomination to the Egyptians** (46:34; cf. Exod 8:26 [22]) is a side comment by the author that concerns the native Egyptians and not the Hyksos pharaohs who are themselves shepherds. Joseph's strategy is twofold. Joseph wishes to reassure the pharaoh, playing on the common occupation shared by his family and the pharaoh; they are both shepherds. He knows that Goshen is located in the delta zone and is therefore under the supervision of the Hyksos pharaohs. However, Joseph is concerned about the comfort, security, and holiness of his family. By separating them from the traditional Egyptians, Joseph not only prevents them from the risk of provoking jealousy or hostility,[724] but also protects them from any idolatrous influence, thus preparing the ground for the birth of the future chosen people. This separation will even save them when Egypt suffers the plagues (cf. Exod 8:22–23).

---

724 The conflict during the reign of Darius II (425–424 BC) between the Jewish mercenaries of Elephantine who sacrificed their sheep or ram to their God (*YAO* alias *YHWH*) and the Egyptians who worshipped the ram-god Khnum perfectly illustrates Joseph's concern (see Modrzejewski, *The Jews of Egypt*, 37–40).

47:1–6. MEETING WITH PHARAOH

GEN 47:1–6 NKJV	GEN 47:1–6 ESV
1 Then Joseph went and told Pharaoh, and said, "My father and my brothers, their flocks and their herds and all that they possess, have come from the land of Canaan; and indeed they *are* in the land of Goshen."	**1** So Joseph went in and told Pharaoh, "My father and my brothers, with their flocks and herds and all that they possess, have come from the land of Canaan. They are now in the land of Goshen."
2 And he took five men from among his brothers and presented them to Pharaoh.	**2** And from among his brothers he took five men and presented them to Pharaoh.
3 Then Pharaoh said to his brothers, "What *is* your occupation?" And they said to Pharaoh, "Your servants *are* shepherds, both we *and* also our fathers."	**3** Pharaoh said to his brothers, "What is your occupation?" And they said to Pharaoh, "Your servants are shepherds, as our fathers were."
4 And they said to Pharaoh, "We have come to dwell in the land, because your servants have no pasture for their flocks, for the famine is severe in the land of Canaan. Now therefore, please let your servants dwell in the land of Goshen."	**4** They said to Pharaoh, "We have come to sojourn in the land, for there is no pasture for your servants' flocks, for the famine is severe in the land of Canaan. And now, please let your servants dwell in the land of Goshen."
5 Then Pharaoh spoke to Joseph, saying, "Your father and your brothers have come to you.	**5** Then Pharaoh said to Joseph, "Your father and your brothers have come to you.
6 The land of Egypt *is* before you. Have your father and brothers dwell in the best of the land; let them dwell in the land of Goshen. And if you know *any* competent men among them, then make them chief herdsmen over my livestock."	**6** The land of Egypt is before you. Settle your father and your brothers in the best of the land. Let them settle in the land of Goshen, and if you know any able men among them, put them in charge of my livestock."

The meeting between Joseph and Pharaoh begins with Joseph, who speaks to Pharaoh (47:1), and ends with Pharaoh, who speaks to Joseph (47:5–6). Between these two addresses, the dialogue shifts from Pharaoh to the brothers and then from the brothers to Pharaoh. The chain of the conversation follows this chiastic structure: $ABCB_1A_1$ (Joseph-Pharaoh-**brothers**-Pharaoh-Joseph).

47:1 They are in the land of Goshen. Joseph informs the pharaoh of the arrival of his father and brothers and specifies where they are: "the land of Goshen." Although Joseph had promised his father this was to be their future home (45:10), the pharaoh had also considered this place for Joseph's family. Pharaoh had promised Joseph he would give "the best of the land of Egypt" (45:18), an expression that he later applies to the land of Goshen (47:6). Joseph simply reports to the pharaoh that all is going as planned (implying the pharaoh's plans). His family is now waiting for further directions from the pharaoh.

47:2–4 Joseph selects five (less than half) of his brothers to present to Pharaoh (47:2). The brothers are unidentified and no reason is given for their selection, suggesting Joseph's lack of intention to impress the pharaoh.[725] This act of modesty inspires trust in Pharaoh, who desires to employ Joseph's brothers; hence, his interest to know their area of expertise: **What is your occupation?** (47:3a). Joseph's brothers consider this question as an opportunity to obtain from the pharaoh the optimal

---

725 A rabbinic tradition explains that Joseph picked the least impressive brothers so that the pharaoh may not be tempted to enroll them in his army (Gen. Rab. 95:4).

place to dwell in. Because they are shepherds (47:3b–4a), they ask for the land of Goshen (47:4b).

47:5–6 The pharaoh does not answer Joseph's brothers but turns to Joseph and responds to his former address (47:1) by informing him that now that his father and brothers have arrived (47:5) they should settle in the land of Goshen (47:6a). Anticipating the answer from Joseph's brothers, he further pursues his inquiry and suggests that they could serve as **chief herdsmen over** his **livestock** (47:6). This last detail about the pharaoh's interest in matters of livestock is congruent with archaeological evidence suggesting the Egyptian herds were very large and that cattle were herded to the Nile Delta, which was not as heavily cultivated as Upper Egypt.[726]

JACOB MEETS AND BLESSES PHARAOH (47:7–10)

GEN 47:7–10 NKJV	GEN 47:7–10 ESV
7 Then Joseph brought in his father Jacob and set him before Pharaoh; and Jacob blessed Pharaoh.	**7** Then Joseph brought in Jacob his father and stood him before Pharaoh, and Jacob blessed Pharaoh.
8 Pharaoh said to Jacob, "How old *are* you?"	**8** And Pharaoh said to Jacob, "How many are the days of the years of your life?"
9 And Jacob said to Pharaoh, "The days of the years of my pilgrimage *are* one hundred and thirty years; few and evil have been the days of the years of my life, and they have not attained to the days of the years of the life of my fathers in the days of their pilgrimage."	**9** And Jacob said to Pharaoh, "The days of the years of my sojourning are 130 years. Few and evil have been the days of the years of my life, and they have not attained to the days of the years of the life of my fathers in the days of their sojourning."
10 So Jacob blessed Pharaoh, and went out from before Pharaoh.	**10** And Jacob blessed Pharaoh and went out from the presence of Pharaoh.

The story of Jacob's encounter with the pharaoh marks the climax of Jacob's visit in Egypt (46:1–47:31) and forms the apex of the chiasm. After having presented his five brothers, Joseph introduces his father.

47:7 The contrast between the two meetings is striking, which is conveyed by the verb that describes the introduction. Whereas the brothers are simply "presented" (47:2), Jacob is **set … before**, a verbal form (*'amad lipney*) that normally occurs in priestly contexts (Lev 14:11; 16:7). The meeting is thus tinged with religious significance, an impression that is immediately reinforced by Jacob's formal blessing of the pharaoh at the opening (47:7b) and closure of the encounter (47:10). For Jacob, a blessing is more than a mere polite formality. From the early stages of his life, Jacob regarded a blessing highly. Jacob cheated his father (27:18–29) and risked his life for that blessing (27:41); he wrestled with the Lord to gain a blessing (32:26). When Jacob blesses Joseph and all his sons, it is with the prospect of divine visitation, and his blessing is pregnant with benevolent prophecy (48:15, 20; 49:1–28). Of high significance is the fact that this blessing of a patriarch on a foreigner is unique in the Scriptures. Furthermore, it is unusual that an inferior (Jacob) blesses a superior

---

726 Douglas Brewer, "Fauna," *OEAE* 1:510.

(Pharaoh). All these observations indicate the special nature of Jacob's blessing of the pharaoh. This extraordinary incident hints at the ancient promise of blessing for the nations (cf. 12:3; 22:18; 28:14). The content of the conversation that follows and precedes the blessing is coherent with the spiritual charge of the blessings.

47:8 How old are you? The pharaoh is intrigued by Jacob's old age, a sign of the supernatural. The man standing before him is the father of the one who decoded his dreams and holds great wisdom. The pharaoh's question denotes his perplexity before the mystery that confronts him. In ancient Egypt, 110 years old is considered the ideal age that the most blessed person could attain.[727] The pharaoh has a certain inkling that Jacob has exceeded that ideal age.

47:9 Jacob is **one hundred and thirty years** old and will live seventeen more years (47:28). Instead of receiving the compliment and boasting about his great age, Jacob humbly recognizes that not only have the days of his life been miserable, but they are **few** compared to his fathers (Abraham was 175 years [25:7] and Isaac was 180 years [35:28] when they died). This last information must have baffled the pharaoh, who does not respond.

47:10 Contrary to normal protocol, Jacob has the last word with another blessing for the silent pharaoh and then **went out from before Pharaoh**. A similar phrase will later be used to describe Moses leaving the pharaoh at the fourth plague: "went out from Pharaoh" (Exod 8:30 [26]). This Pharaoh is characterized as "a new king … who did not know Joseph" (Exod 1:8). In addition to the historical allusion to a new type of dynasty (the change from the Semitic Hyksos to the native Egyptians), this line may reflect a spiritual shift in the pharaoh himself, who will progressively pass from the stage of "hardened his heart" (Exod 7:13, 22; 8:15, 32; 9:7) to a point of no return: "the Lord hardened the heart of Pharaoh" (Exod 9:12; 10:1, 20, 27; 11:10). This last spiritual moment between the patriarch Jacob and the pharaoh witnesses to the universality of God's appeal. God is also interested in the salvation of the pharaoh.

JOSEPH CARES FOR HIS FAMILY AND EGYPT (47:11–26)

GEN 47:11–26 NKJV	GEN 47:11–26 ESV
11 And Joseph situated his father and his brothers, and gave them a possession in the land of Egypt, in the best of the land, in the land of Rameses, as Pharaoh had commanded.	**11** Then Joseph settled his father and his brothers and gave them a possession in the land of Egypt, in the best of the land, in the land of Rameses, as Pharaoh had commanded.
12 Then Joseph provided his father, his brothers, and all his father's household with bread, according to the number in *their* families.	**12** And Joseph provided his father, his brothers, and all his father's household with food, according to the number of their dependents.
13 Now *there was* no bread in all the land; for the famine *was* very severe, so that the land of Egypt and the land of Canaan languished because of the famine.	**13** Now there was no food in all the land, for the famine was very severe, so that the land of Egypt and the land of Canaan languished by reason of the famine.

---

727 See Robert K. Ritner, "Medicine," *OEAE* 2:353.

14 And Joseph gathered up all the money that was found in the land of Egypt and in the land of Canaan, for the grain which they bought; and Joseph brought the money into Pharaoh's house.

15 So when the money failed in the land of Egypt and in the land of Canaan, all the Egyptians came to Joseph and said, "Give us bread, for why should we die in your presence? For the money has failed."

16 Then Joseph said, "Give your livestock, and I will give you *bread* for your livestock, if the money is gone."

17 So they brought their livestock to Joseph, and Joseph gave them bread *in exchange* for the horses, the flocks, the cattle of the herds, and for the donkeys. Thus he fed them with bread *in exchange* for all their livestock that year.

18 When that year had ended, they came to him the next year and said to him, "We will not hide from my lord that our money is gone; my lord also has our herds of livestock. There is nothing left in the sight of my lord but our bodies and our lands.

19 Why should we die before your eyes, both we and our land? Buy us and our land for bread, and we and our land will be servants of Pharaoh; give *us* seed, that we may live and not die, that the land may not be desolate."

20 Then Joseph bought all the land of Egypt for Pharaoh; for every man of the Egyptians sold his field, because the famine was severe upon them. So the land became Pharaoh's.

21 And as for the people, he moved them into the cities, from *one* end of the borders of Egypt to the *other* end.

22 Only the land of the priests he did not buy; for the priests had rations *allotted to them* by Pharaoh, and they ate their rations which Pharaoh gave them; therefore they did not sell their lands.

23 Then Joseph said to the people, "Indeed I have bought you and your land this day for Pharaoh. Look, *here is* seed for you, and you shall sow the land.

24 And it shall come to pass in the harvest that you shall give one-fifth to Pharaoh. Four-fifths shall be your own, as seed for the field and for your food, for those of your households and as food for your little ones."

14 And Joseph gathered up all the money that was found in the land of Egypt and in the land of Canaan, in exchange for the grain that they bought. And Joseph brought the money into Pharaoh's house.

15 And when the money was all spent in the land of Egypt and in the land of Canaan, all the Egyptians came to Joseph and said, "Give us food. Why should we die before your eyes? For our money is gone."

16 And Joseph answered, "Give your livestock, and I will give you food in exchange for your livestock, if your money is gone."

17 So they brought their livestock to Joseph, and Joseph gave them food in exchange for the horses, the flocks, the herds, and the donkeys. He supplied them with food in exchange for all their livestock that year.

18 And when that year was ended, they came to him the following year and said to him, "We will not hide from my lord that our money is all spent. The herds of livestock are my lord's. There is nothing left in the sight of my lord but our bodies and our land.

19 Why should we die before your eyes, both we and our land? Buy us and our land for food, and we with our land will be servants to Pharaoh. And give us seed that we may live and not die, and that the land may not be desolate."

20 So Joseph bought all the land of Egypt for Pharaoh, for all the Egyptians sold their fields, because the famine was severe on them. The land became Pharaoh's.

21 As for the people, he made servants of them from one end of Egypt to the other.

22 Only the land of the priests he did not buy, for the priests had a fixed allowance from Pharaoh and lived on the allowance that Pharaoh gave them; therefore they did not sell their land.

23 Then Joseph said to the people, "Behold, I have this day bought you and your land for Pharaoh. Now here is seed for you, and you shall sow the land.

24 And at the harvests you shall give a fifth to Pharaoh, and four fifths shall be your own, as seed for the field and as food for yourselves and your households, and as food for your little ones."

25 So they said, "You have saved our lives; let us find favor in the sight of my lord, and we will be Pharaoh's servants."

26 And Joseph made it a law over the land of Egypt to this day, *that* Pharaoh should have one-fifth, except for the land of the priests only, *which* did not become Pharaoh's.

25 And they said, "You have saved our lives; may it please my lord, we will be servants to Pharaoh."

26 So Joseph made it a statute concerning the land of Egypt, and it stands to this day, that Pharaoh should have the fifth; the land of the priests alone did not become Pharaoh's.

To his brothers, Joseph taught the spiritual lesson of the God who turns evil into good (45:5). To Pharaoh, Joseph unveiled the real existence of a powerful and compassionate God. That the next focus of interest is the physical welfare of people is not insignificant. The God of creation is not only concerned with the spiritual life of His children, but is also attentive to their physical life. Sharing the good news of the kingdom of God is not enough. We must also care for the physical needs of people. The work of ADRA (Adventist Development and Relief Agency) is as crucial as the preaching and teaching of the Word in churches and seminaries. This principle was strongly affirmed in the life of Jesus, who preached the word (Matt 5:1–12), healed the sick (Matt 15:30), and gave bread to the hungry (Matt 15:36–38). The old rabbinic saying of the Mishnah *'ayn qemakh 'ayn torah* ("no flour, no Torah")[728] also applies here.

47:11–12 In the first stage, Joseph attends to his family. Our parents should receive priority over strangers. Humanitarian work begins here, with our parents and brothers and sisters. In his wisdom, Joseph first provides his family with a home, a physical place to live. They are established **in the best of the land**, an expression that the pharaoh had just used to qualify "the land of Goshen" (47:6). The same land is now called **the land of Rameses** (47:11). Because the city of Rameses was the royal residence of the Ramesside Dynasty (1300–1065 BC), it is unclear whether the appearance of this name (meaning "*Re* has given birth") is due to later scribal updating[729] or is original, considering the testimony of artifacts suggesting that this name already existed during the Hyksos period.[730] Joseph then provides his family with the food they need to survive, ensuring that his help accounts for the number of their families (47:12). Love and goodwill are not enough in humanitarian work. Justice and the rigor of intelligence also ensure that the portions are equal and that the distribution of food is evaluated in proportion to the needs of the people.

47:13–26 In the second stage, Joseph focuses on the needs of the people of Egypt.

47:13 The famine was very severe. The word "famine" is repeated twice in the verse: the first time to note its intensity, and the second time to observe its effect on both the lands of Canaan and Egypt. The gravity of the situation obliges Joseph to take stringent measures, which would not be allowed in ordinary times (1 Sam 8:13–16).[731]

---

728 *'Abot* 3:21.

729 See K. A. Kitchen, "Joseph," *ISBE* 2:1129.

730 Eugene H. Merrill, *Kingdom of Priests: A History of Old Testament Israel* (Grand Rapids: Baker, 1987), 74–75.

731 Vaux observes that the interdiction of this measure by Samuel suggests that the introduction of this practice by Joseph took place before that time. Roland de Vaux, *Early History of Israel* (Philadelphia: Westminster, 1978), 306–307.

47:13–17 When there is no more money (47:15) he exchanges livestock for **bread** (*lekhem*) (a generic word for "food") (47:15, 16, 17). The inclusion of the precious **horses** (47:17) in the deal indicates that even the rich were affected. This measure extends even to the **land of Canaan** (47:13–15), which was at that time under Egyptian control.

47:18–19 In the second year, when nothing is left, the people voluntarily offer their service and their property to Joseph (47:18), that they **may live and not die, that the land may not be desolate** (47:19). The irony is that the people of Egypt have now joined Joseph's brothers as his servants, thus giving his dream a more dramatic and universal character. The young, despised brother who had been sent to serve his older brothers (37:13) and to become the servant of Potiphar (39:1–6) has now become the master who rules over the destiny of his brothers and of all the people of Egypt.

47:20–21 Joseph purchases all the land of Egypt for Pharaoh (47:20) and moves the people from the land to the city to facilitate the distribution of food.

47:22 The land of the priests. Notably, the priests and Joseph's family are the only people who do not need to sell their lands or serve the pharaoh in exchange for the grain provided by the state. The reason for this exception is that Joseph's family has no land to sell and the priests, who were often members of the royal family, had received their lands from Pharaoh. In this extraordinary case, Joseph was related to both groups because he had married the daughter of the priest of On.

47:23–26 Finally, Joseph uses the land, which is now owned by the pharaoh, to institute a tenant arrangement. Joseph distributes seeds to the people and provides them with land to farm; in exchange, they must return one-fifth of their product to the pharaoh, which allows them to keep four-fifths for themselves. This administrative measure was not new in Egypt. This practice of appropriating private land and an imposed tax by the king, including the case for priestly exemption, occurs at all periods from earliest times in Egyptian history. That this case is notably attested during the time that followed the expulsion of the Hyksos, an indication that it had been previously initiated, is intriguing.[732] The ultimate winner of this agrarian program is the pharaoh, who emerges from this experience richer than ever. Pharaoh, who had shown compassion and generosity to Joseph's family, is now blessed, similar to the way in which Potiphar was blessed (39:5), not only because of Joseph, but also because of the blessing he received twice from Jacob (47:7, 10). God's promise to Abraham is once again verified: "I will bless those who bless you" (12:3). Even the people, who seem to be plundered, acknowledge the benefit of Joseph's management: **you have saved our lives** (47:25). The literary form of this report reflects the democratic process and Joseph's profound respect for the people he administers. The narrative alternates with recurring dialogues with the Egyptian population (47:15–16, 18–19, 23–25).[733] This recognition on Egyptian soil resonates with the earlier statement that Joseph cares for the Egyptians as he cared for his family (47:12). Significantly, the word "bread" (*lekem*) occurs in both contexts. It appears first in the context of the salvation of Joseph's family (47:12) and reappears six more times in the context of the salvation of Egypt (47:13, 15–16,[734] 17 [2x], 19). In addition, the term "household" (*bayt*), which concludes Joseph's speech to the Egyptians (47:24), echoes the

---

732 See Kitchen, "Joseph," *NBD* 659.

733 See Mathews, *Genesis: 11:27–50:26*, 855–866.

734 The word is only implied here, as indicated by the word "bread" in italics (NKJV).

same reference to "household" in connection with Joseph's family (47:12). Further-more, the same expression **little ones,** which referred to the family of Jacob (45:19; 46:5), applies now to the family of Egypt (47:24). This commonality of language clearly indicates that Joseph provided for his family and for the people of Egypt with the same sense of ethical duty and efficiency.

FROM EGYPT TO CANAAN (47:27–31)

GEN 47:27–31 NKJV	GEN 47:27–31 ESV
27 So Israel dwelt in the land of Egypt, in the country of Goshen; and they had possessions there and grew and multiplied exceedingly.	**27** Thus Israel settled in the land of Egypt, in the land of Goshen. And they gained possessions in it, and were fruitful and multiplied greatly.
28 And Jacob lived in the land of Egypt seventeen years. So the length of Jacob's life was one hundred and forty-seven years.	**28** And Jacob lived in the land of Egypt seventeen years. So the days of Jacob, the years of his life, were 147 years.
29 When the time drew near that Israel must die, he called his son Joseph and said to him, "Now if I have found favor in your sight, please put your hand under my thigh, and deal kindly and truly with me. Please do not bury me in Egypt,	**29** And when the time drew near that Israel must die, he called his son Joseph and said to him, "If now I have found favor in your sight, put your hand under my thigh and promise to deal kindly and truly with me. Do not bury me in Egypt,
30 but let me lie with my fathers; you shall carry me out of Egypt and bury me in their burial place." And he said, "I will do as you have said."	**30** but let me lie with my fathers. Carry me out of Egypt and bury me in their burying place." He answered, "I will do as you have said."
31 Then he said, "Swear to me." And he swore to him. So Israel bowed himself on the head of the bed.	**31** And he said, "Swear to me"; and he swore to him. Then Israel bowed himself upon the head of his bed.

The author then returns to the destiny of Jacob and his family.

47:27 Israel dwelt … in the country of Goshen. Again, the verb *yashab* "dwell" is used to indicate the intention of a permanent sojourn in Egypt. The language of the verse echoes Joseph's promise to his father (45:10). We hear the same reference to Jacob's children and possessions, yet with intensification. In his earlier statement, Joseph had mentioned "your children, your children's children," and "all that you have" (45:10); now, there is the new acquisition of property and the clan grows and multiplies **exceedingly** (*me'od*) (47:27), language that describes the people of Israel in full maturity, just before the Exodus event (Exod 1:12; cf. Deut 26:5).

47:28 In parallel to the fruitfulness of the people, Jacob's long life is noted. Jacob will live seventeen more years, for a total of 147 years. These last seventeen years of Jacob in Egypt point (and allude) to Joseph's first seventeen years with him in Canaan (37:2).

47:29–31 Given the prospect of returning from Egypt, Jacob asks Joseph to promise not to bury him in Egypt, but in the country of Canaan with his fathers (47:29–30a). Jacob has in mind the cave of Machpelah (23:9), the burial place of Sarah (23:19) and Abraham (25:9), and of Isaac (35:27–29). Furthermore, it is not enough for Jacob that Joseph promises **I will do as you have said** (47:30b). Jacob insists that he swear: **put your hand under my thigh** (47:29). This symbolic gesture (cf. 24:2–4) engages the future and involves, by association, the witnessing presence of the God of life and creation. Joseph's vow now assumes a sacred character. The name of God must be evoked (Deut 6:13) as the guarantee that the vow will be fulfilled. Only after Joseph swears does the old Jacob bow before his son for the first time (47:31). The record of the detail **on the head of the bed** (47:31b) suggests that this scene occurs when Jacob is sick and near death. The reason for Jacob's request has nothing to do with some type of superstitious association with the ancestors, implying belief in the immortality of the soul and the notion that, at death, his soul will join the soul of his deceased relatives. Instead, Jacob's concern to be buried in Canaan is future oriented. Jacob places himself in the perspective of the salvation of his people returning to the Promised Land.

JACOB BLESSES JOSEPH'S SONS (48:1–22)

Jacob's special blessing of Joseph's sons is consistent with Jacob's unique love for Joseph (37:1–11): Jacob does not bless his other grandsons. This unique favor of Jacob to Joseph concludes the cycle of Joseph. Following the introduction about Jacob's and Joseph's preparation to meet each other (48:1–2), the progression of the blessing ceremony is marked by the three-time occurrence of the phrase **Jacob (Israel) said to Joseph** (48:3, 11, 21). First, Jacob elevates the status of his grandsons to that of sons (48:3–7). Jacob then blesses the sons, favoring Joseph's younger son Ephraim over his older son Manasseh (48:8–20). The blessing ceremony ends with Jacob's prospect of the future return to the Promised Land (48:20–22).

48:1–2. JACOB AND JOSEPH HEAR FROM EACH OTHER

GEN 48:1–2 NKJV	GEN 48:1–2 ESV
1 Now it came to pass after these things that Joseph was told, "Indeed your father *is* sick"; and he took with him his two sons, Manasseh and Ephraim.	**1** After this, Joseph was told, "Behold, your father is ill." So he took with him his two sons, Manasseh and Ephraim.
2 And Jacob was told, "Look, your son Joseph is coming to you"; and Israel strengthened himself and sat up on the bed.	**2** And it was told to Jacob, "Your son Joseph has come to you." Then Israel summoned his strength and sat up in bed.

Both Joseph and Jacob receive reports about each other: **Joseph was told** (48:1), **And Jacob was told** (48:2). Each one prepares to meet the other based on the report they hear about the other. When Joseph "hears" about the dying condition of his father, Joseph takes his two sons to his father that he may bless them (48:1). Likewise, when Jacob "hears" about the coming of Joseph, he strengthens himself and sits up on his bed (48:2). The blessing ceremony is conducted in connection with the preceding events, against the prospective backdrop of Jacob's death (47:29–31). The phrase **after these things** (48:1) situates the events chronologically "after" the preceding scene. The report that Jacob is **sick**, points back to the condition of the old Jacob who is approaching death (47:28–29). The information that Jacob **sat up on the bed** (48:2) points back to Jacob's previous significant movement, bowing on the head of the bed (47:31).

48:3–7. FROM GRANDSONS TO SONS

GEN 48:3–7 NKJV	GEN 48:3–7 ESV
3 Then Jacob said to Joseph: "God Almighty appeared to me at Luz in the land of Canaan and blessed me,	**3** And Jacob said to Joseph, "God Almighty appeared to me at Luz in the land of Canaan and blessed me,
4 and said to me, 'Behold, I will make you fruitful and multiply you, and I will make of you a multitude of people, and give this land to your descendants after you *as* an everlasting possession.'	**4** and said to me, 'Behold, I will make you fruitful and multiply you, and I will make of you a company of peoples and will give this land to your offspring after you for an everlasting possession.'
5 And now your two sons, Ephraim and Manasseh, who were born to you in the land of Egypt before I came to you in Egypt, *are* mine; as Reuben and Simeon, they shall be mine.	**5** And now your two sons, who were born to you in the land of Egypt before I came to you in Egypt, are mine; Ephraim and Manasseh shall be mine, as Reuben and Simeon are.
6 Your offspring whom you beget after them shall be yours; they will be called by the name of their brothers in their inheritance.	**6** And the children that you fathered after them shall be yours. They shall be called by the name of their brothers in their inheritance.
7 But as for me, when I came from Padan, Rachel died beside me in the land of Canaan on the way, when *there was* but a little distance to go to Ephrath; and I buried her there on the way to Ephrath (that is, Bethlehem)."	**7** As for me, when I came from Paddan, to my sorrow Rachel died in the land of Canaan on the way, when there was still some distance to go to Ephrath, and I buried her there on the way to Ephrath (that is, Bethlehem)."

48:3–4 As Jacob approaches death, he remembers his previous encounter with God. The language of his reminiscence suggests that he is thinking of the second vision, which he received at Luz/Bethel when he was returning from Padan Aram (35:1–15). The same expressions describe the nature of the experience: **God appeared to me** (48:3; cf. 35:9), **blessed me** (48:3; cf. 35:9). The place is similarly identified as **Luz in the land of Canaan** (48:3; cf. 35:6). God is also referred to as **God Almighty** (48:3; cf. 35:11). Jacob repeats the same words of the promise he had heard then: **fruitful … multiply … multitude of nations** (48:4; cf. 35:11), **give the land** (48:4; cf. 35:12). Only the qualification **everlasting possession** (48:4) belongs to another context that is the covenant with Abraham (17:8). Within the present context of sickness (48:1) and forthcoming death (48:21), this hope of the "everlasting possession" of the Promised Land strikes in the midst of trouble and is a reminder of a luminous eternity precisely in the dark moment of pain.

48:5 The small word *we'atah* **and now** marks Jacob's intention to turn to the present reality. Jacob knows that Joseph has come to visit him with his two sons Manasseh and Ephraim (48:1–2). He applies, then, the first lesson of the promise of fruitfulness he heard at Luz to the destiny of Joseph's two sons. Each one of Joseph's two sons is elevated to the status of Jacob's sons, **as Reuben and Simeon**, who are Jacob's first sons, and hence of tribal ancestors. Joseph's fruitfulness amounts, then, to the fruitfulness of two sons. This is why Jacob begins with Ephraim, not simply because he anticipates his next move, but because the name "Ephraim" (from the root *prh* "fruitful") conveys the idea of "fruitfulness." This emphasis will be retained in biblical tradition: the blessing of Moses will count Ephraim and Manasseh as two tribes (Deut 33:17), omitting Simeon; and the apocalyptic vision of Ezekiel will allow two portions to Joseph (Ezek 47:13), whereas the tribe of Levi receives no portion (Ezek 44:28). Historically, however, Ephraim and Manasseh will still be counted under Joseph (Num 26:28; Deut 33:17; Josh 17:17). Most significantly, Jacob's blessing will still retain Joseph (without the mention of Ephraim and Manasseh) as the tribal ancestor (49:22–26).

48:6 Jacob specifies that this privileged status is limited to only these two sons of Joseph, who were born while Jacob was disconnected from him. This measure may be explained as a way of compensating for Jacob's loss and as a precaution to ensure a fair distribution of the land inheritance among the sons of Jacob. All of Joseph's following sons will be considered strictly as the sons of Joseph. This is the only biblical passage that refers to these other sons of Joseph who will, in the future, be incorporated into the tribes of Manasseh and Ephraim.

48:7 Jacob returns to the chronicle of his return from Padan Aram, the same time he had evoked previously.

Rachel died beside me. Jacob now emotionally recalls the death of his wife Rachel. The Hebrew phrase *metah 'alay* "died beside me" literally means "died upon me." This idiomatic expression means that Rachel's death had a profound effect on Jacob (cf. 42:36).[735] The event of Rachel's death is recorded immediately after the report of his vision at Luz/Bethel (35:9, 16, 19–20). Rachel died and was buried at the end of Jacob's journey, within the confines of the Promised Land. Once again, Jacob's emphasis is on **the land of Canaan**. For the people of the Exodus, Rachel's tomb will serve as a sign of the first possession of the land by Jacob (35:20). This evocation not only reinforces his request to be buried there, but is also an implicit reminder to Ephraim and Manasseh that their future belongs to that land where their grandmother is buried.

48:8–20. EPHRAIM BEFORE MANASSEH

GEN 49:8–20 NKJV	GEN 48:8–20 ESV
8 Then Israel saw Joseph's sons, and said, "Who *are* these?"	**8** When Israel saw Joseph's sons, he said, "Who are these?"
9 And Joseph said to his father, "They *are* my sons, whom God has given me in this *place*." And he said, "Please bring them to me, and I will bless them."	**9** Joseph said to his father, "They are my sons, whom God has given me here." And he said, "Bring them to me, please, that I may bless them."
10 Now the eyes of Israel were dim with age, *so that* he could not see. Then Joseph brought them near him, and he kissed them and embraced them.	**10** Now the eyes of Israel were dim with age, so that he could not see. So Joseph brought them near him, and he kissed them and embraced them.
11 And Israel said to Joseph, "I had not thought to see your face; but in fact, God has also shown me your offspring!"	**11** And Israel said to Joseph, "I never expected to see your face; and behold, God has let me see your offspring also."
12 So Joseph brought them from beside his knees, and he bowed down with his face to the earth.	**12** Then Joseph removed them from his knees, and he bowed himself with his face to the earth.

---

735 The same idiomatic expression *'alay* "upon me" is used in this verse to refer to the particular effect the event had on Jacob, more than anyone else: "these things happen to me" (TNK, NRSV).

13 And Joseph took them both, Ephraim with his right hand toward Israel's left hand, and Manasseh with his left hand toward Israel's right hand, and brought *them* near him.

14 Then Israel stretched out his right hand and laid *it* on Ephraim's head, who *was* the younger, and his left hand on Manasseh's head, guiding his hands knowingly, for Manasseh *was* the firstborn.

15 And he blessed Joseph, and said: "God, before whom my fathers Abraham and Isaac walked, the God who has fed me all my life long to this day,

16 the Angel who has redeemed me from all evil, bless the lads; let my name be named upon them, and the name of my fathers Abraham and Isaac; and let them grow into a multitude in the midst of the earth."

17 Now when Joseph saw that his father laid his right hand on the head of Ephraim, it displeased him; so he took hold of his father's hand to remove it from Ephraim's head to Manasseh's head.

18 And Joseph said to his father, "Not so, my father, for this *one is* the firstborn; put your right hand on his head."

19 But his father refused and said, "I know, my son, I know. He also shall become a people, and he also shall be great; but truly his younger brother shall be greater than he, and his descendants shall become a multitude of nations."

20 So he blessed them that day, saying, "By you Israel will bless, saying, 'May God make you as Ephraim and as Manasseh!'" And thus he set Ephraim before Manasseh.

13 And Joseph took them both, Ephraim in his right hand toward Israel's left hand, and Manasseh in his left hand toward Israel's right hand, and brought them near him.

14 And Israel stretched out his right hand and laid it on the head of Ephraim, who was the younger, and his left hand on the head of Manasseh, crossing his hands (for Manasseh was the firstborn).

15 And he blessed Joseph and said, "The God before whom my fathers Abraham and Isaac walked, the God who has been my shepherd all my life long to this day,

16 the angel who has redeemed me from all evil, bless the boys; and in them let my name be carried on, and the name of my fathers Abraham and Isaac; and let them grow into a multitude in the midst of the earth."

17 When Joseph saw that his father laid his right hand on the head of Ephraim, it displeased him, and he took his father's hand to move it from Ephraim's head to Manasseh's head.

18 And Joseph said to his father, "Not this way, my father; since this one is the firstborn, put your right hand on his head."

19 But his father refused and said, "I know, my son, I know. He also shall become a people, and he also shall be great. Nevertheless, his younger brother shall be greater than he, and his offspring shall become a multitude of nations."

20 So he blessed them that day, saying, "By you Israel will pronounce blessings, saying, 'God make you as Ephraim and as Manasseh.'" Thus he put Ephraim before Manasseh.

48:8–10   Joseph's two sons, who had thus far been merely implied in the conversation, now come to the front of the scene. **Israel saw Joseph's sons** (48:8). Joseph responds, emphasizing that God is the one who gave him these sons **in this place** (48:9). Joseph's pointing to the land of Egypt is the last geographic reference of the series. Note that the references to Egypt and to Canaan are given alternatively (48:3, 7; cf. 48:5, 9). Joseph refers to Egypt, without even naming the place: *bazeh* (lit. trans.: "in this"; cf. ESV: "here"). Joseph's manner of implicitly referring to Egypt suggests his embarrassment regarding Jacob's insistence on "the land of Canaan." Egypt has now lost its name and is reduced to a vague, unidentified place; only Canaan is to be retained. Joseph must have understood Jacob's message. Jacob is now willing to bless Joseph's sons: **please bring them to me, and I will bless them** (48:9).

48:10 **The eyes of Israel were dim with age, so that he could not see** (48:10a).

This information introduces the next scene of Jacob kissing and embracing Joseph's two sons (48:10b). Joseph's maneuver and Jacob's response recalls the blessing scenario of Isaac. On both occasions, the father is visually handicapped, and in both cases, he needs to touch and kiss the son(s) he is about to bless in order to ensure that he will properly bless the one he has in mind (27:26–27).

48:11 Jacob refers to his visual sense: **I had not thought to see your face.** The verb *ra'ah* "see" reappears in its causative form (*hiphil*) in the verb *her'ah* (**has shown**). God is the agent of this miracle: He is the One who caused him to see the sons (*zera'* "seed") of Joseph. Jacob implicitly indicates to Joseph that he has seen his sons, just as he has been able to see Joseph again. Israel now knows who is who and is ready to bless.

48:12–14 Joseph understands this message and bows down to the earth, thereby expressing his gratefulness, just as Jacob did when Joseph had responded positively to his request to be buried in Canaan (47:31). Joseph moves his sons forward, ensuring that Manasseh the elder will come near Jacob's right hand, whereas Ephraim, his younger son, will be near Jacob's left hand (48:13). However, Jacob first stretches his **right hand** to reach the younger son, while he places his left hand on the older son. The author explains that Jacob is obliged to cross his arms to do that, commenting on the abnormal operation: **for Manasseh was the firstborn** (48:14). In the Scriptures, the right hand is the hand of strength, glory, and efficient blessing (Pss 110:1; 121:5; Matt 25:33; Rev 1:17). Once again, the principle of the second prevailing over the first is verified (see the commentary on 11:26). Jacob is fully aware of what he is doing. Whether Jacob had known the position of the respective sons through his previous touching or simply guessed his son's maneuver is unclear.

48:15–16 Although Jacob blessed Joseph's two sons, the introduction to the blessing refers only to Joseph: **he blessed Joseph** (48:15). The meaning of this qualification is that Jacob's strong move in favor of Ephraim over Manasseh does not change the value and significance of his blessing. Joseph is still the one who is blessed. The text of the blessing is poetic and profound. It is first a personal testimony about God in history—in the past, the present, and the future. Jacob begins with the past, referring to the fathers Abraham and Isaac who walked before God (48:15). God walks behind them like the shepherd walks behind his sheep, allowing them to walk freely, and yet watching them to make sure they do not fall in the valley of darkness (Ps 23). The allusion to the shepherd is not only suggested through the respective situation of the two partners; the verb *ro'eh*, translated **has fed** (48:15), is the very term that designates the shepherd (4:2; 47:3; Ps 23:1). Jacob does not simply refer to the past. This God is not merely the God of the past, the God of museums or of tradition. This God has cared for him until this day. Jacob identifies this God as the **Angel who has redeemed me from all evil** (48:16). This hints at the experience of Joseph who saw how God had turned evil into good (44:33–34; 45:5), which is the only way to redeem evil. The word "redeem" (*go'el*) that is used here is a technical term in the Mosaic Law that refers to the kinsman who saves his relative from difficulty or danger. This law applies to the repurchase of a field that was sold in time of trouble, to the freeing of an Israelite slave who sold himself in time of poverty (Lev 25:48ff.), or even to the poor widow who is taken as a wife by her next of kin in order to perpetuate seed and ensure the inheritance of the land (Ruth 4:4–6; cf. Deut 25:5–10). All of these cases fit the context of Joseph and the present redemption of land and relatives. The reference to the Angel evokes high moments in Jacob's life; it points to the Angel of God who identified Himself as "the God of Bethel" (31:11, 13) and recalls Jacob's wrestling with God (cf. Hos 12:5) that resulted in an extraordinary blessing (32:29). This is the same God who will **bless the lads** (48:16b). Jacob turns now toward the future and prays that his name Israel be named upon them (48:16c), a prophecy that will be literally fulfilled. The tribes of Manasseh and Ephraim, often identified under the name of Joseph, will make up the greatest part of the northern kingdom under the name of Israel. The promise of their **growth into a multitude** (48:16d) plays on the word "fish" (*dag*), which is associated with the notion of fruitfulness (1:22).

48:17-18 Noticing that his father had **laid his right hand on the head of Ephraim** (48:17), Joseph interferes with Jacob's blessing and displaces Jacob's hand. Joseph, who is **displeased**, verbalizes his frustration in an authoritative command: **not so, my father … put your right hand on his head** (48:18). Joseph believes that his father must have mistakenly placed his hand on the younger son because of his poor sight.

48:19 **But his father refused.** The Hebrew word *ma'an*, translated "refuse," implies a strong reaction, as its association with the verb *marad* "rebel" (Isa 1:20) suggests. Yet, Jacob immediately signals to his son that he knows what he is doing. Twice he repeats **I know**, reaffirming his good disposition toward him, calling him by the affectionate title **my son**. Finally, he reveals that his blessing will be beneficial for both sons, although Ephraim will be more numerous than his brother (cf. Num 1:33, 35; Deut 33:17).

48:20 The fulfillment of this blessing will be so evident that it will become a common proverb, and the reference to Ephraim and Manasseh will be synonymous to great number (Deut 33:17).

48:21–22. THE FATHERLAND

GEN 48:21–22 NKJV	GEN 48:21–22 ESV
21 Then Israel said to Joseph, "Behold, I am dying, but God will be with you and bring you back to the land of your fathers.	**21** Then Israel said to Joseph, "Behold, I am about to die, but God will be with you and will bring you again to the land of your fathers.
22 Moreover I have given to you one portion above your brothers, which I took from the hand of the Amorite with my sword and my bow."	**22** Moreover, I have given to you rather than to your brothers one mountain slope that I took from the hand of the Amorites with my sword and with my bow."

The phrase **Israel said to Joseph** marks the third and final section of Jacob's blessing of Joseph. This conclusion, which combines the expectation of death (48:1–2) and the prospect of the return from Egypt, points to Joseph's vow to Jacob (47:27–31). This echo has, however, one important difference. Whereas the text of Joseph's vow to Jacob limits the prospect of the return from Egypt to the immediate future, Jacob's death and burial, Jacob's blessing of Joseph projects to the far future and concerns the Exodus, the return of Israel to the Promised Land. Thus far, Jacob's addressee was in the singular, even when he was blessing Joseph's two sons. However, he now shifts to the plural: **God will be with you** (masculine plural) **and bring you** (masculine plural) **back to the land of your** (masculine plural) **fathers** (48:21). This change from the singular to the plural indicates that Jacob not only has Joseph in mind, but all of his brothers. Jacob sees the return of all the tribes of Israel, his descendants, to the Promised Land. Jacob then returns to the singular to tell Joseph that he has something special for him, above what he is giving to his other brothers: **I have given to you one portion above your brothers** (48:22). The construction of Jacob's phrase is unclear and has generated various explanations. The Hebrew word for "portion" is *shekhem*, which typically means "shoulder" (9:23; 21:14). The meaning of "portion" for the word *shekhem* "shoulder" is not attested in the Scriptures. However, the word *shekhem* also refers to the city of Shechem. Jacob may well be alluding to the piece of land he had acquired at Shechem (33:19; cf. Josh 24:32), whose ownership was reinforced by his victory over the Amorites, a generic term for the pre-Israelite population in general (15:16). This campaign is implied in the report of his return from Padan Aram (35:5). The allusion to that text would fit our context well, which already contains many allusions to the same passage (48:3–4, 7). Shechem is indeed associated with Joseph's destiny: the place where Joseph's troubles began (37:13) and where his bones will be buried (Josh 24:32). It was also from Shechem that the land was distributed to the tribes of Israel (Josh 24:1). While Jacob is thinking of his death and burial in the country of Canaan (Machpelah), he is also, by association and under prophetic inspiration, thinking of Joseph's death and burial in the country of Canaan (Shechem). The difference between the two burials, however, is that Jacob's burial belongs to the near future, an event that concerns only himself, whereas Joseph's burial belongs to the far future of the Exodus and is associated with the return of all the tribes of Israel to the Promised Land.

5. PROSPECT OF THE PROMISED LAND:
THE PEOPLE OF ISRAEL

`GENESIS 49–50:26`

This last section of Genesis moves beyond the immediate history to another horizon. The hope of the Promised Land marks, more than ever, the last note of Genesis. This hope is articulated in two ways. First, it is present in Jacob's blessing of his twelve sons in the form of prophecies that concern the future destiny of each tribe of Israel (49:1–28). Second, it is beckoned in the here and now in the report of the death and burial of Jacob (49:29–50:21) and Joseph (50:22–26), tangible signs of the future return of Israel.

THE FUTURE OF ISRAEL (49:1–28)

After having gathered his sons (49:1–2). Jacob blesses them one after another, following the chronological order, from Reuben the elder to Benjamin the youngest (49:3–27). The blessings to Judah and Joseph receive special attention; they are the longest sections, and both have messianic overtones. The blessings conclude like a genealogy referring back to the preceding blessings of the sons, who are, then, identified as the twelve tribes of Israel (49:28).

49:1–2. GATHERING OF THE SONS

GEN 49:1–2 NKJV	GEN 49:1–2 ESV
1 And Jacob called his sons and said, "Gather together, that I may tell you what shall befall you in the last days:	**1** Then Jacob called his sons and said, "Gather yourselves together, that I may tell you what shall happen to you in days to come.
2 "Gather together and hear, you sons of Jacob, and listen to Israel your father.	**2** "Assemble and listen, O sons of Jacob, listen to Israel your father.

49:1 Although the conclusion refers to Jacob's discourse as **his own blessing** (49:28), the preface that calls for the gathering of the sons identifies it as a prophecy. Jacob's first words indicate this specific intention: **I may tell you what shall befall you in the last days** (49:1). The Hebrew words *be'akharit hayyamim* "in the last days" is a technical expression that often refers to the coming of the messianic king and the eschatological salvation (Isa 2:2; Dan 10:14). This phrase, which occurs fourteen times in the Hebrew Bible, has been identified as a key to the structure of the entire Pentateuch, "from Genesis 1 to Deuteronomy 34."[736] That it appears in the introduction of the three "major poems" of the Pentateuch is significant, namely, Genesis 49:1, Numbers 24:14, and Deuteronomy 31:29, thus connecting the three texts with each other. "Central to this connection is the identification of the future warrior of Genesis 3:15 with the messianic king of the larger poems."[737] Upon this

---

736 Sailhamer, *The Meaning of the Pentateuch*, 324.
737 Ibid., 37.

literary observation, Sailhamer concludes "that one of the central issues in the message of the Pentateuch is the coming king and His eternal kingdom."[738] The reading of Jacob's blessing, as it moves from his first son Reuben to his last one Benjamin, should therefore be particularly attentive to the prophetic-eschatological dimension.

49:2 Jacob repeats the invitation to **gather together** that he has just extended to his sons in the preface (49:1). This is the third time in the book of Genesis that a blessing is addressed to a group of persons. The first collective blessing is God's blessing of Adam and Eve (1:28). The second is Noah's blessing of his three sons (10:25–27). Jacob's blessing is more related to Noah's blessing in that both are fatherly blessings and even curses, and both contain specific prophecies unveiling the future destiny of the sons. This type of blessing always appears at the beginning of a new era and marks the first steps of humankind. Therefore, the blessing of Israel has a universal scope. Israel is the new Noah and the new Adam. Jacob's blessing differs, however, from the other blessings in that it calls for attention. The verb **hear/listen** (*shema'*) is used twice. The sons are urged to listen to their **father Jacob/Israel**. The filial relation is affirmed in the introduction (49:1) and in the conclusion (49:28), in inclusio, thus marking the boundaries of the literary unit.

49:3–4. REUBEN

GEN 49:3–4 NKJV	GEN 49:3–4 ESV
3 "Reuben, you are my firstborn, my might and the beginning of my strength, the excellency of dignity and the excellency of power.	**3** "Reuben, you are my firstborn, my might, and the firstfruits of my strength, preeminent in dignity and preeminent in power.
4 Unstable as water, you shall not excel, because you went up to your father's bed; then you defiled *it*—he went up to my couch.	**4** Unstable as water, you shall not have preeminence, because you went up to your father's bed; then you defiled it—he went up to my couch!

The first son is characterized by five positive qualities, which are expressed by nouns: **firstborn**, **might**, **beginning of strength**, **excellency of dignity**, and **excellency of power**. These five extraordinary qualities are upset by five negative actions, which are expressed by verbs: **unstable**, **not excel**, **you went up**, **you defiled**, and **he went up**. This symmetry suggests the just retributive reaction to Reuben's action. Jacob refers here to Reuben's sin when he slept with Bilhah, his father's concubine (35:22). At that time, the story simply states that "Israel heard about it." No reproach or punishment is then recorded. Now, we learn that Jacob had kept the incident in mind. The shift from the second person "you went up," which expresses closeness, to the third person "he went up" (49:4), which expresses strangeness, suggests that Jacob is appealing to the testimony of a third party (the other sons?) to judge how grave the situation is. This switch is also a stylistic manner of preparing the way for the next blessing about Simeon and Levi, which is in the third person.[739] This sin will now determine the destiny of the tribe. Jacob's blessing of Reuben has no prophecy. Only one verb signifies his destiny: **you shall not excel** (49:4). The verb *yatar* "excel" echoes the double occurrence of the verb *yatar* "excel" that had characterized him

---

738 Ibid., 37.
739 See Wenham, *Genesis 16–50*, 472.

in the first line (49:3). Reuben was destined for excellence. The word "excellency" is associated with the word "beginning" (*re'shit*), a notion that conveys the idea of primacy; this is the word that introduces the creation story (1:1). Reuben was not merely excellent, he was the best. His action, however, turned his super excellent nature into nonexcellence. An allusion to the creation text may also be present here, to say that the *re'shit* (49:3; cf.1:1) has turned into the waters of negativity (49:4; cf. 1:2). Reuben all but disappeared from national history, so much so that Moses was concerned about the survival of the tribe (Deut 33:6), which did not leave any visible trace. That the tribe of Reuben is not even mentioned in the Mesha inscription,[740] whereas Gad is, is not accidental. A sign of their weakness was their absence in the war against Jabin and Sisera (Judg 5:15–16). Thus, most commentators note that no king, prophet, or any preeminent person ever came from this tribe.[741]

49:5–7. SIMEON AND LEVI

GEN 49:5–7 NKJV	GEN 49:5–7 ESV
5 "Simeon and Levi *are* brothers; instruments of cruelty *are in* their dwelling place.	**5** "Simeon and Levi are brothers; weapons of violence are their swords.
6 Let not my soul enter their council; let not my honor be united to their assembly; for in their anger they slew a man, and in their self-will they hamstrung an ox.	**6** Let my soul come not into their council; O my glory, be not joined to their company. For in their anger they killed men, and in their willfulness they hamstrung oxen.
7 Cursed *be* their anger, for *it is* fierce; and their wrath, for it is cruel! I will divide them in Jacob and scatter them in Israel.	**7** Cursed be their anger, for it is fierce, and their wrath, for it is cruel! I will divide them in Jacob and scatter them in Israel.

Only two brothers are combined in the blessing. This association can be traced to their partnership in the sacking of Shechem (34:25–39). Jacob strongly dissociates himself from this coalition, which he denounces as opposing his **soul** (*nepesh*), the essence of his nature (49:6a), and against his **honor** (*kabod*) and self-respect (49:6b). The main emphasis of the reproach regards anger and violence. The word **anger** (*'af*) is used twice (49:6–7) and is reinforced by its synonym **wrath** (*'ebrah*) (49:7). The idea of "violence" frames the reproach. The word **violence** (*khamas*) appears in the opening of the reproach (49:5 ESV) and its synonym, the word **cruel** (*qashatah*), appears at the end (49:7a). Jacob then continues and refers to the future effect of his curse. Here again, the punishment reverses the sin. The scattering responds to the coming together (49:7b), as occurring in the story of the tower of Babel, where the same word **scatter** (*hefits*) is used (11:9). Jacob, as father, presents himself as the agent of the action, the one possessing the right to distribute his heritage and initiate the dividing and the scattering. Subsequent history confirms Jacob's prophecy. The Simeonites and the Levites are the only two tribes who did not have their own territory. Simeon had to share a "portion" of Judah. The same root *khalaq*, which

---

740 The Mesha Stele was erected by the Moabite king Mesha at Dibon (cf. 2 Kgs 3:4–5), most likely by the third quarter of the ninth century BC (see *ANET*, 320).

741 Jewish tradition (Gen. Rab. 84:19), however, considers Reuben as the ancestor of the prophet Hosea based on the genealogy of the book of Chronicles, which lists the name of Beerah (cf. with Beeri, father of Hosea, according to Hos 1:1) among the descendants of Reuben (1 Chr 5:6).

describes the dividing process (49:7b), significantly reappears in the word "portion" (*kheleq*), which is used in the report of that distribution (Josh 19:9). As for the Levites, they had no portion (Num 18:20), received no inheritance of their land (Num 18:20; cf. 18:24), and were scattered throughout the country in forty-eight cities (Josh 21:41), which were located on both sides of the Jordan River wherever the children of Israel settled (Num 34:1–12). Their condition as wanderers resulted in their needing support, along with the stranger, the widow, and the poor (Deut 14:28–29; 26:12–13). Eventually, this curse became a blessing to Israel, since the Levites became the chaplains and instructors of the Law in Israel (Neh 8:7–9; cf. 2 Chr 17:7–9; 35:3). Their forbiddance of material property reinforced their spiritual connection: "the Lord is their inheritance" (Deut 18:2; Num 18:20). Uprooted from the land, they were bound to transcend nationalistic sentiments; they even resisted the popular movement promoting the worship of the golden calf (Exod 32:25–30).

49:8–12. JUDAH

GEN 49:8–12 NKJV	GEN 49:8–12 ESV
8 "Judah, you *are he* whom your brothers shall praise; your hand *shall be* on the neck of your enemies; your father's children shall bow down before you.	**8** "Judah, your brothers shall praise you; your hand shall be on the neck of your enemies; your father's sons shall bow down before you.
9 Judah *is* a lion's whelp; from the prey, my son, you have gone up. He bows down, he lies down as a lion; and as a lion, who shall rouse him?	**9** Judah is a lion's cub; from the prey, my son, you have gone up. He stooped down; he crouched as a lion and as a lioness; who dares rouse him?
10 The scepter shall not depart from Judah, nor a lawgiver from between his feet, until Shiloh comes; and to Him *shall be* the obedience of the people.	**10** The scepter shall not depart from Judah, nor the ruler's staff from between his feet, until tribute comes to him; and to him shall be the obedience of the peoples.
11 Binding his donkey to the vine, and his donkey's colt to the choice vine, he washed his garments in wine, and his clothes in the blood of grapes.	**11** Binding his foal to the vine and his donkey's colt to the choice vine, he has washed his garments in wine and his vesture in the blood of grapes.
12 His eyes *are* darker than wine, and his teeth whiter than milk.	**12** His eyes are darker than wine, and his teeth whiter than milk.

The blessing to Judah echoes the blessing to Reuben. It begins with the same direct address to the son, **you** (*'atah*) **Judah** (49:8) || **you** (*'atah*) **Reuben** (49:3), and also shares numerous linguistic links with it: **your father** (49:8; cf. 49:4), **my son** (49:9) || **my firstborn** (49:3), **you have gone up/you went up** (*'alitah*) (49:9; cf. 49:4). This repetitive language indicates Jacob's identification of Judah with the firstborn Reuben. The contrast between the two is already suggested in the Hebrew word order of the address. Whereas in the address to Reuben, the "you" follows the word "firstborn" (Reuben, my firstborn, you), in the address to Judah, the "you" immediately follows the name (Judah, you). The intention of this contrast within the parallel of the two addresses is to emphasize the "you," to say to Judah: "you are the one." Judah is the one who Reuben was supposed to be. Similar to the blessing to

Reuben, the blessing to Judah shifts from the second person direct address (49:8) to the third person (49:9–12). However, the shift now carries another intention. Whereas the blessing to Reuben emphasizes the evil characteristic of the action, the shift in the blessing to Judah is intended to exalt Judah's prowess. Jacob's blessing of Judah consists of four messages about Judah's destiny: his supremacy over his brothers (49:8), his power like a lion (49:9), his messianic rulership (49:10), and his wealth (49:11–12).

49:8 The word **praise** is a double wordplay on Judah's name (*yodukha* "they will praise you"; *yehudah* "Judah") and on the word "hand" (*yodukha* "they will praise you"; *yadkha* "your hand"). The name of Judah occurs three times (49:8–10), a rhythm that resonates with the presence of God (Num 6:24–26; Nah 1:2; Isa 6:3; Matt 28:19; 2 Cor 13:14; Rev 1:4). The image of **your hand ... on the neck of your enemies** is a classic expression that signifies victory (cf. Josh 10:24; 2 Sam 22:41). This language recalls the image of the first messianic prophecy that similarly confronts the enemy (*'eybah ... beynekha* "enmity between you" ‖ *'oybeykha* "your enemies") with the One whose heel will "bruise your head" (3:15). This messianic association is, in fact, coherent with the worshipping response of the others who **shall praise ... shall bow down before you** (49:8). This language is striking, as it is typically God who is the object of praise (Pss 92:2; 106:47; etc.). That the very expression *yodukha* "they will praise you," other than this occurrence, is only used in the Psalms and is always used in connection with God, is also significant (Pss 49:18 [19]; 67:3 [4], 5 [6]; 88:10 [11]; 138:4; 145:10). Therefore, this use of the verb "praise" suggests that none but God is in view, and all the more when the verb is reinforced by its association with the verb *hishtakhaweh* "bow down," which refers to the submission to a king (37:10; 1 Kgs 1:31) and ultimately to God (24:26, 52; 1 Sam 1:3; Ps 138:1–2; Neh 9:3).

49:9 Judah is compared to a **lion**. The lion symbolizes majesty and power and often represents kings (Prov 19:12; Dan 7:4, 17) or even God Himself (Hos 13:8). The three Hebrew words for lion (*gur, 'arieh* [2x], *labi'*) are synonyms (cf. Num 24:9) used to intensify the effect of the "lion" imagery and do not refer to several lions or various ages of the lion. The verbs describe the three down and up movements of this single lion. The lion first bounces down to catch the prey and kill it and comes up victorious. The lion then lies down to enjoy his victory; he is now confident and cannot be moved.

Balaam's prophecy uses the same imagery and the same words (*kara'* "bow down," *'ari, labi'* "lion," *mi yeqimenu* "who will arouse him"):

He bows down, he lies down as a lion; and as a lion, who shall rouse him? (49:9)
He bows down, he lies down as a lion; and as a lion, who shall rouse him? (Num 24:9)

In Balaam's prophecy, the pronoun "he" refers to "his king," its most immediate antecedent (Num 24:7), which points back to Jacob's seed (Num 24:5, 7). Later Balaam's prophecy will identify this king as the "star" of Jacob (Num 24:17). In the light of Balaam's prophecy, we understand that, through the image of the lion, it is not the tribe of Judah per se that is in view but rather more specifically the figure of a king coming from Judah (the "seed," the "star" of Jacob). The book of Revelation identifies the "lion of the tribe of Judah" as being Jesus Christ (Rev 5:5).

49:10 The language of this verse (**scepter, lawgiver**) confirms that it is a king rather than a tribe that is the object of the prophecy. This verse is also echoed in Balaam's prophecy:

A scepter (*shevet*) … from (*mi*) Judah, a lawgiver from (*mi*) between his feet (49:10)
A star from (*mi*) Jacob; a scepter (*shevet*) from (*mi*) Israel (Num 24:17)

The "star from Jacob" in Balaam's prophecy corresponds to the "lion of Judah" in Jacob's prophecy. Furthermore, our passage introduces a temporal element in that rulership: **the scepter shall not depart … until Shiloh comes**. The translation of the adverbial conjunction *'ad ki* "until" does not render the exact meaning of the Hebrew. The Hebrew *'ad ki* does not necessarily refer to an end but rather to a fulfillment or to a climax, expressing a superlative (26:13; 41:19). This means that the royalty of Judah will reach its climax with the coming of the Shiloh. The identity of this person is clarified in the next few words: **to him shall be the obedience of the peoples** (ESV). Note that the word "people" is plural in the Hebrew text (*'amim*). The universal scope of this ruler to whom "peoples" owe obedience suggests a figure of messianic and supernatural dimension. From the earliest times, Jewish tradition has identified the Shiloh as the Messiah.[742] The meaning of the Hebrew word **Shiloh** has been debated, and various interpretations have been suggested, including the following ones: it refers to the city of Shiloh; it is derived from the Egyptian word *sr* "prince" or from the Akkadian word *shilu* "prince"; it is the contracted form of the Hebrew phrase *she lo* "that belongs to him," "to whom it belongs" or *shai lo* "tribute to him." These readings are hardly supported by the spelling of the Hebrew word and often require some emendations of the Hebrew original. We have therefore opted for the interpretation that, in our view, takes the most consideration of the Hebrew word and grammatical form: the word "Shiloh" is a name (see its parallel to the name "Judah") that refers to an individual and is related to the words *shalwah* or *shalom* "peace," both being synonyms (Ps 122:7). This interpretation is attested in the most ancient Christian and Jewish sources[743] and has the merit of fitting the context of our passage (49:11), which associates the coming of this ruler with the reign of peace (cf. Isa 9:5–6; Mic 5:5 [4]; Eph 2:14).

49:11–12 The last two verses of Jacob's blessing to Judah are more a poetic association of motifs, which are more suggestive of the character and mission of the Messiah than an exact historical description of his actions. The Hebrew word for **donkey** (*'ayir*) refers generally to the donkey used for riding (Judg 10:4). The donkey evokes peace and humility in contrast to the horse, which evokes war and arrogance (Prov 21:31; Ps 147:10). The same association of kingship and lowliness is used by Zechariah to describe the "lowly" Davidic king who will ride on a donkey (Zech 9:9) and will reign over the whole world, "from sea to sea … to the ends of the earth" (Zech 9:10). This is reminiscent of Solomon who rides his father's mule to signify that he is the anointed one, the pretender to the Davidic throne (1 Kgs

---

742 See Qumran: 4Q252. 5; Aramaic Targum: Tg. Onq. on 49:10; Midrash Gen. Rab. 98:5; b. Sanh. 98b; Rashi in Miqraot Gedolot on 49:10.

743 See Adolf Posnanski, *Schiloh: ein Beitrag zur Geschichte der Messiaslehre* (Leipzig: J. C. Hinrichsche Buchhandlung, 1904). For more recent holders of this view, see Joseph Klausner, *The Messianic Idea in Israel: From Its Beginning to the Completion of the Mishnah* (New York: Macmillan, 1955), 29–31; A. Caquot, "La Parole sur Juda dans le Testament lyrique de Jacob (Genèse 49,8–12)," *Sem* 26 (1976): 5–32.

1:38–48). Likewise, Jesus' action to "untie" the donkey and His riding on it points back to that tradition (Mark 11:2–11). The other images of **wine** and **milk** and their respective colors of **red/eyes** and **white/teeth** evoke the abundance of life and the peace and security that will characterize the Promised Land (Num 13:23, 27; Isa 7:21–23; Zech 3:10; Mic 4:4). The eye and the tooth are the two main channels for the enjoyment of life. The term "eye" is often used to evoke desire and lust (Prov 17:24; Eccl 4:8; 2 Pet 2:14), while the term "tooth" signifies predatory power (Job 29:17; Ps 124:6; Dan 7:5). Thus, the loss of a tooth was considered as important as the loss of an eye (Exod 21:24; Lev 24:20; Matt 5:38). The reference to eye and tooth in our context intends, then, to suggest the fullness of life and of complete peace that will characterize the messianic kingdom.

49:13. ZEBULUN

GEN 49:13 NKJV	GEN 49:13 ESV
13 "Zebulun shall dwell by the haven of the sea; he *shall become* a haven for ships, and his border shall adjoin Sidon.	**13** "Zebulun shall dwell at the shore of the sea; he shall become a haven for ships, and his border shall be at Sidon.

That Zebulun (sixth son of Leah) is listed here before Issachar (fifth son of Leah) is strange. This priority reflects his preeminence over his brother in the course of future history. The tribe of Zebulun played a critical role in the campaigns of the Judges. The courageous army who fought by the Wadi Kishon was, in large part, composed of the men of Zebulun (Judg 4:6, 10). Deborah praised them for their courage and heroism (Judg 5:18). Zebulun also contributes the greatest contingent to the army of David (1 Chr 12:34 [33]). Many from Zebulun made the pilgrimage to celebrate Hezekiah's Passover in Jerusalem (2 Chr 30:10–11). Although this preeminence of Zebulun is implicit only in its location in the list of sons, it is noteworthy that the blessing is limited to geographical considerations because Zebulun was settled more securely than all the other tribes. Unlike many of his brothers who "dwelt among the Canaanites" (Judg 1:32), in the case of Zebulun, "the Canaanites dwelt among them" (Judg 1:30). The name "Zebulun"—from the root *zabal*, which means "to dwell" (30:20) and again in its synonym *shakan* "to dwell"—alludes to this dwelling security. The verb *shakan*, which implies a temporary residence (14:13; Job 18:15) in **the haven of the sea**, suggests, however, that although Zebulun was not directly open to the sea (Josh 19:10–16), the tribe had some access to it and had thus become **a haven for ships**, an allusion to its commercial activity with the exterior. The reference to Sidon reinforces this business aptitude as this city held a dominant trade position on the Phoenician littoral, to the extent that it was called "Greater Sidon" (Josh 11:8; 19:28), and the name "Sidon" became a general term for Phoenicia (1 Kgs 16:31). An Egyptian story from the eleventh century BC, "The Journey of Wen Amon to Phoenicia," mentions that Sidon had fifty ships in commercial contact with Egypt.[744]

---

744 *ANET*, 27.

49:14–15. ISSACHAR

GEN 49:14–15 NKJV	GEN 49:14–15 ESV
14 "Issachar is a strong donkey, lying down between two burdens;	**14** "Issachar is a strong donkey, crouching between the sheepfolds.
15 he saw that rest *was* good, and that the land *was* pleasant; he bowed his shoulder to bear *a burden*, and became a band of slaves.	**15** He saw that a resting place was good, and that the land was pleasant, so he bowed his shoulder to bear, and became a servant at forced labor.

The ninth son of Jacob and the fifth of Leah, Issachar was typically associated with Zebulun (30:18–20; Deut 33:18; Num 1:28–31), an indication of the close ties between the two tribes, whose varied expertise made them complementary to each other. Whereas Zebulun was the business tribe, Issachar was the agricultural tribe. Jacob's blessing alludes to this capacity in its metaphoric language. The **strong donkey** (49:14), an animal that was used in agricultural operations (Deut 22:10; Isa 30:24), evokes the hard physical work that is required in the tilling of the land. The vocabulary of the blessing is in line with this allusion. The Hebrew word *khamor* is the common word for "donkey," which is used for agricultural work (Deut 22:10). The association of **shoulder** (*shekhem*) and **bear** (*sabal*), which appears in parallel to the "yoke" of the plow (Isa 9:4 [3]; 14:25), suggests an agricultural setting. The Hebrew idiomatic expression *lemas 'obed*, translated **band of slaves** or "forced labor" (ESV), may well preserve the old meaning of "laborer," which later assumed overtones of forced servitude (Josh 16:10; 1 Kgs 9:21). This is also the sense that has been retained by the Septuagint, which translates *georgos* as "farmer."[745] The construction of the sentences commenting on the goodness of rest and the pleasantness of the land is patterned after the sentences reporting God's seven-time appreciation in response to His own work of creation: **He saw that … was good … that was pleasant** (49:15; cf. 1:4, 10, 12, 18, 21, 25, 31). Therefore, the rest of this laborer is not due to his laziness but to his hard work, as the preceding imagery of rest suggests: the donkey rests between two burdens, that is, between two tasks (49:14). The reference to "goodness" and "pleasantness" is thus positive, describing the satisfaction of the hard worker for the resulting quality of his work, hence, his name "Issachar," which means "man of reward." Issachar will enjoy the richest land in Israel; most of his territory lay in the fertile plateau sloping down to the Jordan Valley and the valley of Jezreel. Deborah, the famous prophetess and judge, may have come from Issachar (Judg 5:15).

49:16–18. DAN

GEN 49:16–18 NKJV	GEN 49:16–18 ESV
16 "Dan shall judge his people as one of the tribes of Israel.	**16** "Dan shall judge his people as one of the tribes of Israel.
17 Dan shall be a serpent by the way, a viper by the path, that bites the horse's heels so that its rider shall fall backward.	**17** Dan shall be a serpent in the way, a viper by the path, that bites the horse's heels so that his rider falls backward.
18 I have waited for your salvation, O LORD!	**18** I wait for your salvation, O LORD.

---

745 See Joel D. Heck, "Issachar: Slave or Freeman? (Gen. 49:14–15)," *JETS* 29, no. 4 (1986): 385–396.

49:16 This is the fifth son of Jacob and the first son of Bilhah. The puzzling note **as one of the tribes of Israel** (49:16) alludes to its exceptional inclusion, as one of the handmaid tribes, among the tribes of Leah and Rachel. According to the prophetic words, Dan is the only tribe to receive two blessings. The first one is constructed through wordplay: **Dan shall judge** (*dan yadin*) (49:16).

49:17 The second blessing is suggested through a comparison with an animal: **Dan shall be a serpent** (49:17). Both prophecies find their fulfillment in the history of the tribe. The judging capacity refers to the extraordinary role the Danite Samson would play as a judge of Israel (Judg 16:31), who would not merely govern but, more importantly, vindicate and save Israel (Judg 15:7, 18), a specific nuance that was understood in Rachel's response to the birth of Dan (30:6; cf. 2 Sam 19:10 [9]). This also applies to the tribe of Dan, whose northern position (Num 2:25–29; Deut 33:22) exposed it the most to the enemies of Israel. Although it was compared to a leaping lion (Deut 33:22), it was the most vulnerable tribe. The Danite clans were assimilated into the kingdoms of Judah and Israel or intermingled with their neighbors and were finally exiled to Assyria (2 Kgs 15:29). Dan was also the most idolatrous tribe; it was in Dan that the idol of Micah was found (Judg 18:18) and in which Jeroboam chose to erect the golden calves (1 Kgs 12:29–30). This is the only tribe that is not included in the apocalyptic list of the one hundred and forty-four thousand who are sealed from the tribes of Israel (Rev 7:5–8), most likely because of that tribe's reputation for idolatrous worship (1 Kgs 12:29–30; 2 Kgs 10:29). The image of the **serpent**, which strikes by surprise at the **horse's heel**, generally refers to the way in which the tribe of Dan would attack their enemies (Judg 18:7–12) but also to Samson's guerrilla activities (Judg 15:4–5). The old imagery of the serpent that strikes the heel at the risk of being struck by the heel (cf. 3:15) is here evoked. It alludes to the tragic destiny of the tribe of the Danites who exposed themselves and perished; more specifically, it applies to the tragic destiny of the Danite Samson who sacrificed himself and died "with the Philistines" (Judg 16:30). Israeli biblical scholar Nehama Leibowitz refers to the medieval exegete Isaac Arama (1420–1494), who suggests in his commentary *Akedat Yitzhak,* that the image of the snake that bites the heel of the horse so that the rider falls backward "implies that the snake itself will of necessity be killed as well by the horse falling upon it after its hind leg has been bitten, the rider attacking it after he has been thrown by the smitten horse. Similarly, Samson's last exploit involved sacrificing his own life in dying with the Philistines whose death he himself had encompassed."[746] Samson was the only judge of Israel who fell into enemy hands.

49:18 No wonder Jacob marks, at that instant, a spiritual pause. The tragic destiny of Dan and of Samson and the old prophetic scenario involving the serpent striking at the heel become the epitome of a cosmic lesson about the great controversy. All of these prophetic insights inspire Jacob's prayer for the future salvation of Israel. The Hebrew word for "salvation" (*yeshu'ah*) appears here for the first time in the Bible. The association of the two Hebrew words *qawah* "hope," "wait" and *yeshu'ah* "salvation" is rare in the Hebrew Bible and expresses the intensity of hope in salvation (cf. Isa 25:9; 33:2). This is the sole moment in the entire text of Jacob's blessings that Jacob speaks

---

746 Isaac Arama, *Akedat Yitzhak* (ch. 33), quoted in Nehama Leibowitz, *Studies in the Book of Genesis*, trans. Aryeh Newman (Jerusalem: World Zionist Organization, 1972), 550.

and addresses God personally and directly by His historical name *YHWH*: **O Lord!**
Note also that this is the last time that this divine name occurs in the book of Genesis.
This unexpected invocation, with its particular style, in the midst of Jacob's blessings
have made it suspect for many interpreters who have been tempted to question the
authenticity of its inclusion. Yet, its connection to the blessing of Dan and its location
in the center of Jacob's blessings (five before and five after) make it, on the contrary, not
only relevant, but also highly significant. This literary construction, which integrates
a passionate prayer within the prophetic visions, is not unique in the Bible. Daniel
will likewise include a prayer between two prophecies, also concerning the salvation
of Israel (Dan 9:3–19). The prayers of Jacob and Daniel are the only passages in their
respective contexts that refer to God as *YHWH* "the Lord." This spiritual retreat in
the heart of the blessings suggests that Jacob's prophetic words are more than mere
information about the projected history of the tribes of Israel; they have essentially a
spiritual intention in regard to the hope of salvation.

49:19. GAD

GEN 49:19 NKJV	GEN 49:19 ESV
19 "Gad, a troop shall tramp upon him, but he shall triumph at last.	**19** "Raiders shall raid Gad, but he shall raid at their heels.

Similar to Dan, the prophecy of Gad is suggested through sounds. Four of the
six words resonate with the sound *gd*, which means "attack" (Ps 94:21) or "troops"
(1 Chr 7:4). Jacob's blessing of Gad continues the focus on war that was associated
with Dan. Similar to Dan, the Gadites were men of war; they are described as "skillful
in war" (1 Chr 5:18) and "trained for battle" (1 Chr 12:8). Located in Transjordanian
territory in the region of Gilead (Josh 20:8), Gad was, like Dan, exposed to enemies.
Note that Elijah the prophet was a native of Gilead (1 Kgs 17:1). The history of Gad
consists of a succession of wars against the Ammonites (Judg 10–12; Jer 49:1–6),
the Arameans (1 Kgs 22:3), the Assyrians (2 Kgs 15:29), and even the Moabites, as
testified in the stela of Mesha.[747] Here also, the imagery of the "heel" (*'aqeb*) is an
allusion to the cosmic war initiated in Genesis 3:15, again confirming that Jacob has
more in mind here than the local conflict.

49:20. ASHER

GEN 49:20 NKJV	GEN 49:20 ESV
20 "Bread from Asher *shall be* rich, and he shall yield royal dainties.	**20** "Asher's food shall be rich, and he shall yield royal delicacies.

From the somber perspective of war, we shift to a perspective of happiness and
prosperity. The name of Asher (*'asher*) means "happy" (cf. 1 Kgs 10:8). Although
the land of Asher sometimes carried a poor reputation (1 Kgs 9:13), the accent is
definitely on the positive side. As much as Dan and Gad suffered from exposure
at the borders, Asher enjoyed a safe position on the fertile western slopes of the

---

747 See *ANET*, 320.

Galilean highlands, which provided olive trees (Deut 33:24; Josh 19:24–31). A rabbinic tradition reports that the soil of Asher was so rich that it was sufficient to feed the entire country of Israel, even in a sabbatical year.[748] Whereas the two preceding tribes struggled for possession of the Promised Land, Asher fully enjoyed the fruit of the Promised Land. This notion is present in the two lines of the prophecy. The first line qualifies Asher as **rich**. The Hebrew word *shmenah* for **rich** (JPS: "fat") also refers to "oil" and may be an allusion to the abundance of olive trees that grew on the land of Asher. The same term *shemen* is used in the blessing of Moses, where Asher is pictured with his foot deep in the "oil" (*shemen*) (Deut 33:24). The second line refers to **royal dainties**. The Hebrew word *ma'adan* refers to delightful food (Lam 4:5). Yet, beyond the reference to the physical enjoyment of the fruit of Canaan, this imagery may also have a spiritual application. The oil was a fundamental product in worship activities. Jacob used oil at the altar (28:18; 35:14), and later, the oil would become a crucial part of the sanctuary service (Num 35:25; Exod 25:6). The word *ma'adan* "delight" has also been used in a spiritual sense. The book of Proverbs promises "delight [*ma'adan*] to your soul" to the father who corrects his son (Prov 29:17), not to mention the etymological connection between *ma'adan* and *'eden*, allowing a tangential hint to the Garden of Eden, so rich with the fruit of the land (2:16). What may appear as inconceivable is, in fact, attested in the Psalms where the two words *deshen* and *'eden* are associated to suggest God's loving-kindness for those who put their trust in Him: "They are abundantly satisfied with the fullness [*deshen*] of Your house, and You give them drink from the river of Your pleasures [*'eden*]" (Ps 36:8 [9]). The psalm continues and compares these "pleasures" to "the fountain of life" found in God (Ps 36:9 [10]). The word *'asher*, which comprises the name "Asher," testifies to this spiritual allusion. The word *'asher* occurs in the *'ashrey* "blessed" of the Psalms to refer to the blessing of the righteous person (Pss 84:5; 144:15; 145; 115:18). The book of Proverbs associates the word *'ashrey* with the one who has found wisdom (Prov 3:13) and compares this happiness to the enjoyment of the tree of life (Prov 3:18). The book of Daniel uses this word to qualify those who hope in the future kingdom of God: "blessed is he who waits" (Dan 12:12). Jesus follows the same tradition in His beatitudes when He characterizes as "blessed" those who will inherit the kingdom of heaven (Matt 5:3–10). Note that Anna, the New Testament prophetess, belonged to the tribe of Asher (Luke 2:36).

49:21. NAPHTALI

GEN 49:21 NKJV	GEN 49:21 ESV
21 "Naphtali *is* a deer let loose; he uses beautiful words.	**21** "Naphtali is a doe let loose that bears beautiful fawns.

Little is known of this tribe, except for its decisive contribution in the battle against the Canaanites during the time of Deborah, which was led to victory by the Naphtalite Barak (Judg 4:6, 10). Jacob's blessing may allude to that critical operation that determined the establishment of Israel in Canaan (Judg 4:24; 5:31). The comparison to a **deer** is likely an allusion to Barak's swift raid on Sisera (Judg 4:16). The

748 Sipre Deut 355; Menakh. 85b.

same agility is implied in the song of Deborah where the Naphtalites are praised for their fighting "on the heights of the battlefield" (Judg 5:18). Similar to Asher, Naphtali is depicted as happy and peaceful, enjoying the land he has conquered (cf. Deut 33:23). Naphtali occupied the entire west coast of the Sea of Galilee (Josh 19:32–39), a district that Flavius Josephus described as "universally rich and fruitful, and full of the plantations of trees of all sorts."[749] The reference to **goodly words** may refer to Barak's poetic skills when he joined Deborah in singing of this victory (Judg 5:1). The building of the temple of Solomon is notably associated with the expertise of Hiram, who was the son of a widow from the tribe of Naphtali (1 Kgs 7:14).

49:22–26. JOSEPH

GEN 49:22–26 NKJV	GEN 49:22–26 ESV
22 "Joseph *is* a fruitful bough, a fruitful bough by a well; his branches run over the wall.	**22** "Joseph is a fruitful bough, a fruitful bough by a spring; his branches run over the wall.
23 The archers have bitterly grieved him, shot *at him* and hated him.	**23** The archers bitterly attacked him, shot at him, and harassed him severely,
24 But his bow remained in strength, and the arms of his hands were made strong by the hands of the Mighty *God* of Jacob (from there *is* the Shepherd, the Stone of Israel),	**24** yet his bow remained unmoved; his arms were made agile by the hands of the Mighty One of Jacob (from there is the Shepherd, the Stone of Israel),
25 by the God of your father who will help you, and by the Almighty who will bless you *with* blessings of heaven above, blessings of the deep that lies beneath, blessings of the breasts and of the womb.	**25** by the God of your father who will help you, by the Almighty who will bless you with blessings of heaven above, blessings of the deep that crouches beneath, blessings of the breasts and of the womb.
26 The blessings of your father have excelled the blessings of my ancestors, up to the utmost bound of the everlasting hills. They shall be on the head of Joseph, and on the crown of the head of him who was separate from his brothers.	**26** The blessings of your father are mighty beyond the blessings of my parents, up to the bounties of the everlasting hills. May they be on the head of Joseph, and on the brow of him who was set apart from his brothers.

This is the longest blessing of the twelve; the exceptional size of the blessing to Joseph rivals only the blessing to Judah. The name "Joseph" occurs twice, in the beginning (49:22) and at the end of the blessing (49:26), as an inclusio. This double occurrence of the name hints at Joseph's double blessing through his two sons. The prophecy falls in three sections, elaborating on the destiny of Joseph: the branch by the well (49:22), the bows versus the bow (49:23–24), and the multiple blessings (49:25–26).

49:22 The blessing begins with a parable that compares the destiny of Joseph to **a fruitful bough by a well**. The language of the imagery associates two words, "well" (*'ayin*) and "wall" (*shur*), which occur together elsewhere only in the context of Hagar's affliction in the wilderness (16:7). This unique echo suggests that the image of Jacob's blessing alludes to Hagar's situation to signify Joseph's destiny. Similar to Hagar, Joseph was driven from home, and like Hagar, Joseph owes his blessing to

---

749 Flavius Josephus, *Wars of the Jews*, 3.3.2.

his misery. In both conditions, God intervenes and turns the tragedy into a blessing. Hagar gives birth to a son, and Joseph becomes prince in Egypt. The two success stories also hold a paradoxical connection. Hagar's success, the birth of Ishmael, contributes to Joseph's success: it is the Ishmaelites who will take him to Egypt (37:25, 28; 39:1). The "fruitful bough" represents Joseph's fruitfulness. The Hebrew word *porat* "fruitful," which is repeated twice, alludes to Joseph's two sons and plays on the name "Ephraim" to imply that fruitfulness will be fulfilled through Joseph's two sons. The image of the "bough by a well" and its parallel **his branches run over the wall** remind us of the episode when Joseph's brothers "lifted him out of the pit, and sold him to the Ishmaelites" (37:28). The Hebrew verb *tsa'ad* translated "run over" (NIV: "climb over") suggests the idea of "climbing up" or "ascent,"[750] hinting at Joseph's ascent from the well to be sold to the Ishmaelites.

49:23–24 Consistent with the allusion to Ishmael, this reference to **the archers** (49:23) again alludes to Ishmael, who was designed to become an "archer" (21:20) and a threat to his brothers (16:12). The irony of Jacob's blessing is that Ishmael rescues Joseph against his brothers, who are now "the archers." The curse is reversed into a blessing and vice versa: the enemy is the ally and the brother is the enemy. The plural of the "archers" (49:23), representing the crime of Joseph's brothers against Joseph, contrasts with the singular of **his bow** (49:24), representing Joseph as the victim who yet prevailed. The single verb describing Joseph's tranquility, **remained** (*tesheb*), also contrasts with the multiplicity of verbs describing the brothers' agitation: **bitterly grieved … shot … hated** (49:23). The reason for Joseph's strength is that **the arms of his *hands* were made strong by the *hands* of the Mighty**. The echo between the "hands" (of Joseph and of the Mighty) suggests that God's hands are confounded with the shooter's hands. The strength derives from God, who is qualified by three epithets. This divine origin is indicated three times by the preposition *min* (translated either as "from" or "by"). First, in the phrase ***by … the Mighty … of Jacob,*** which refers to God and is an allusion to the Mighty God who fought for him (35:5; cf. Exod 15:16) and with whom he fought (32:24–32); this phrase occurs in connection to *moshi'a* "Savior" and to *go'el* "Redeemer" (Isa 49:26; 60:16). Second, in the expression ***from … the Shepherd, the Stone of Israel***. The "Shepherd" refers to the God who provides and takes care (48:15; Ps 23:1); and the "Stone of Israel" recalls the "stone" Jacob used as a pillow at Bethel (28:11), on which the ladder stood whose top reached to heaven (28:12), and which he erected as a commemorative pillar (28:18; 35:14). Third, in the phrase ***by* the God of your father,** which summarizes Jacob's personal and historical experience with this God.

49:25–26 This last section focuses on "blessing." The word **bless** (*barak*) occurs six times. The first occurrence of *barak* "bless" is the conjugated verb "will bless you" (*wibarekeka*) that introduces the blessings: **by the Almighty who will bless you** (49:25a).[751] The reference to "the Almighty" (*Shaddai*) contains the promise that God will ensure powerful protection and the future fulfillment of

---

750 See its etymology from the Ugaritic *tsagad* "climb," "advance" or from the Arabic *tsa'ida* "climb up" (H. Ringgren, "*ts'd*," *TDOT* 12:421).

751 Most translations have a preposition "by" or "from" or "because," thus reading "by/from/because of the Almighty" (NKJV, NIV, NRSV, ESV, etc.). However, this preposition is absent in the Hebrew text, which uses instead the particle *'et* indicating a new sentence or an emphasis: "as for Shaddai He will bless you" (see *IBHS*, 13, 4c). This reading is reinforced by the literary observation of the passage (regular use of the preposition *min*, and the occurrence of the verb "bless," which looks forward to the next verses about "blessings").

His promise (see the commentary on 17:1; cf. 43:14).

The next three occurrences of the word "bless" come as a noun in the plural **blessings** (*birkot*), which describes the nature of the blessing: **blessings of heaven above, blessings of the deep that lies beneath, blessings of the breasts and of the womb** (49:25bc). The three blessings belong together; they are related through poetic wordplays (assonances): *shamayim* "heaven" resonates with *shaddayim* "breasts," and *tehom* "deep" resonates with *rekhem* "womb." The intention of this poetic association is to relate the cosmic blessing, involving heaven and earth and echoing the language of creation (cf. 1:1–2) to the promise of human fruitfulness. The blessings of "heaven above" and of the "deep beneath" contain the promise of water from heaven and from the springs and rivers, which watered the land and made it fertile. Note also the allusion to the *rekhem* "womb" of Rachel, which had been opened by God to give birth to Joseph (30:22–24). In addition, the use of the word *shaddayim* "breasts" echoes the divine name *Shaddai*, suggesting an unexpected and subtle connection between the Almighty and the promise of birth and fruitfulness. In using the name *'El Shaddai*, Jacob has in mind, then, the future people of Israel, the fulfillment of God's promise (Exod 6:3).

49:26 Jacob concludes with a hyperbolic remark about the ultimate superiority of his blessing, in comparison to the blessing of his ancestors and the blessings granted to his other sons. These blessings surpass the blessing of his ancestors just like **the everlasting hills**, the evergreen mountains that never dry and whose tops are unreachable. These blessings surpass the blessings to his other sons just like the distinctive **crown of the head of him** [Joseph] makes him **separate from his brothers**. The double superiority of that blessing applies to the royal destiny of Joseph, who not only excels above the destiny of his father Jacob, but also sets him apart from his brothers. The word *nazir*, which is associated with Joseph's head, refers to a royal crown, as the related noun *nezer* "crown" suggests (2 Sam 1:10), hence, the meaning "prince" (Deut 33:16; cf. Lam 4:7 JPS, NAB). The word *nazir* refers also to the status of "Nazarite," the one who is set apart and is consecrated. The term *nazir* derives from the root *nazar* "separate" (Lev 22:2; Hos 9:10) and is therefore translated "separate" (RSV). Joseph's preeminence is therefore not in conflict with the blessing of Judah as the royal tribe. Joseph's distinction among his brothers is essentially of a moral and spiritual order.

The superiority of Joseph's blessing over Jacob's ancestors and over his brothers is, however, ambivalent. It anticipates the double separation from the ancestors and from the brothers, and somehow foreshadows the rivalry between the future kingdoms, the southern kingdom of Judah, which included mostly Judah but also Simeon and later Benjamin, and the northern Israelite kingdom, which included mostly the tribe of Joseph and the other tribes and was often referred to as the "house of Joseph" (Amos 5:6; Obad 1:18; Zech 10:6). The separation of the "house of Joseph" was accompanied by the temptation to find another god and erect alternative altars to compete with the religion of Judah and the temple of Jerusalem (1 Kgs 12:25–33). The two kingdoms never reunited, except on a personal level, when people from the Northern Kingdom joined other Jews in their worshipping activities around the temple of Jerusalem and eventually, for some of them, integrated with the tribe of Judah (2 Chr 11:16; 30:11, 18, 21). Israel was destroyed by the Assyrians, and most of the Israelites were either killed or deported (2 Kgs 17:1–23). The tribe of Ephraim, whose name "Ephraim" was also used as a figure of speech for the Northern Kingdom (Ps 60:9; Jer 31:20), became the symbol of apostasy and idolatry (Hos 4:17; 8:9–11; 2 Chr 30:10–11); no wonder this tribe, like Dan, was omitted in the list of the ideal Israel pictured in the book of Revelation (Rev 7:5–8). Thus, the Northern Kingdom and the tribe of Joseph as such disappeared and were assimilated into the Near Eastern nations. Only Judah survived and became the Jewish people. Curiously, this tragic side of the destiny of the descendants of Joseph seems to be blurred in Jacob's prophecy. It is as if Jacob was not able to, or did not wish to, see this other side of his vision; it was only suggested in the veiled terms of the blessing.

Besides these interpretations, which apply this prophecy to the historical destiny of Joseph and his descendants, one may wonder if this blessing does not also carry messianic significance. The importance of this blessing in comparison to the other blessings, surpassing even the blessing of Judah—the very fact that Joseph received a double blessing (cf. 48:8–20), an indication that Jacob considered him the firstborn (cf. Deut 21:17)—may support the messianic interpretation. In fact, many ancient Jewish and early Christian interpreters saw Joseph as a representative of the suffering aspect of the Messiah and a forerunner of the Messiah.[752] It has been suggested on the basis of typological studies that Joseph was a type of Christ. Joseph experienced humiliation and exaltation and suffered in order to bring salvation to his brothers. Christ similarly endured suffering and humiliation for the salvation of the world and was also "exalted" (Phil 2:8–9).[753]

49:27. BENJAMIN

GEN 49:27 NKJV	GEN 49:27 ESV ○
27 "Benjamin is a ravenous wolf; in the morning he shall devour the prey, and at night he shall divide the spoil."	**27** "Benjamin is a ravenous wolf, in the morning devouring the prey and at evening dividing the spoil."

Paradoxically, the destiny of the tribe of Benjamin contrasts with the modest and timid destiny of its progenitor Benjamin, who is now compared to a **ravenous wolf**, tearing his prey and never losing it, keeping it continuously **in the morning … and at night**. At the time of Jacob's blessing, Benjamin's children are still among the "little ones" (46:5). Nothing in Jacob's time could, then, presage this aggressive character of the future tribe. The last note of Jacob's blessings is therefore a hint at their predictive quality. The description of Jacob's prophecy on Benjamin fits the combative character of the tribe and its war activities. Benjamin is notable for its fighting against the great enemy of Israel, Amalek (Exod 17:8–16). Among the main heroes who confronted Amalek, the Bible records the judge Ehud (Judg 3:15); the

---

752 On the Jewish side, see b. Sukkah 52a; for texts on this Messiah in Jewish tradition, see Raphael Patai, *The Messiah Texts* (Detroit: Wayne State University, 1988), 165–170. On the Christian side, see Church Father Irenaeus in William J. Deane, *Pseudepigrapha: An Account of Certain Apocryphal Sacred Writings of the Jews and Early Christians* (Edinburg: T&T Clark, 1891), 165.

753 See Gerard Van Groningen, *Messianic Revelation in the Old Testament* (Grand Rapids: Baker, 1990), 166; cf. Jan A. Sigvartsen, "Messiah Son of Joseph: Genesis 49:22–26" (MA thesis, Berrien Springs, MI: Andrews University, 1998). According to Ellen G. White, "the life of Joseph illustrates the life of Christ" (PP 239).

first king of Israel, Saul (1 Sam 9:1); and Esther's cousin Mordecai (Esth 2:5–7), who were all Benjamites with the reputation of being great warriors. They were characterized as "mighty men of valor—archers" (1 Chr 8:40; 12:2) and "left-handed" stone slingers (Judg 20:16). Other important men from Benjamin include the prophet Jeremiah (Jer 1:1; 32:8) and the apostle Paul (Rom 11:1). Although the territory of Benjamin was smaller than that of most of the other tribes (Josh 18:11–28), and although Benjamin was the youngest son of Jacob, the tribe played a crucial role in the conquest of Canaan. This is partially because its territory was located at a strategic position, controlling the road connecting Transjordan to the west, the road that the Israelites took when they crossed the Jordan. Another intriguing detail may have played a role in Benjamin's aggressive passion in fighting for the land: the memory that its eponym, Benjamin, was the only son of Jacob who was born in Canaan, not far from Bethlehem (35:18–19), a place that later assumed a messianic significance (Mic 5:2). However, the aggressive character of the Benjamites did not always serve them well. Their stubborn insistence to support the criminals of Gibeah (Judg 19:22–30; Judg 20:13), which was part of their territory (Judg 19:14), and their fierce fighting (Judg 20:21, 25) nearly cost the survival of the tribe (Judg 20:35; Judg 21:3).

49:28. CONCLUSION

GEN 49:28 NKJV	GEN 49:28 ESV
28 All these *are* the twelve tribes of Israel, and this *is* what their father spoke to them. And he blessed them; he blessed each one according to his own blessing.	28 All these are the twelve tribes of Israel. This is what their father said to them as he blessed them, blessing each with the blessing suitable to him.

This concludes Jacob's blessing of his sons. Note the stylistic kinship with the conclusion of the creation story (2:4a), which begins and ends the same way:

49:28: *'elleh* ("these") … *berak 'otam* ("he blessed them")
2:4a: *'elleh* ("these") … *behibar'am* ("he created them")

Note also that the three-time repetition of the blessing is reminiscent of the three blessings of creation (1:22, 28; 2:3). This echo between the creation story and Jacob's blessings functions as an inclusio, bridging the introduction and the conclusion of the book of Genesis. This literary parallel also suggests that Jacob's blessings have the same efficiency as God's acts of creation. The future history of Israel that is prophetically recorded here is under God's control.

The twelve tribes of Israel. This is the first biblical mention of the "twelve tribes." Clearly, the future destiny of all of Israel is in view. This note on the wholeness of Israel echoes the introduction of Jacob's blessings when Jacob called his twelve sons to proclaim their future (49:1). The blessings have a corporate function. The verse states and repeats that the blessing applies to them (*'otam*). All the sons and tribes benefit from the same blessing. They are all equal, despite their flaws and iniquities that were noticed and denunciated. Yet, the blessings are not uniform; each one has its particular characteristic adapted to the particular characteristic and destiny of each tribe. The apocalyptic vision of the heavenly Jerusalem reflects the same truth: each tribe has it own gate, and each gate has its own pearl (Rev 21:21). Beyond the ethical lesson of diversity within unity is the hope of a unified Israel in the ideal Promised Land that is underlined here, anticipating all the dreams of the prophets (Ezek 37:19–22; Isa 11:13; Rom 11:25–26; Rev 7:4–11).

JACOB'S DEATH AND BURIAL (49:29–50:21)

Now that Jacob has delivered his prophetic testament concerning the future of his descendants, "the twelve tribes of Israel" in the Promised Land, he wants to ensure that he will be buried in that land and thus be "gathered to his people" (49:29, 33). For that purpose, referring to the previous deaths and burials of his parents, he gives specific instructions to his sons (49:29–33). However, Joseph alone takes charge of his father's burial (50:1–14) and then reassures his worried brothers of his good intentions toward them (50:15–21). The keyword of this passage is the verb *tsawah* "command," "charge." Jacob "commanded" (*wayetsaw*) (49:29 ESV; NKJV: "charged") his sons to bury him in Canaan. Joseph *wayetsaw* "commanded" his servants to embalm his father (50:2). Joseph's brothers "sent" (*wayetsawu*) Joseph and reported that Jacob "commanded" (*tsiwah*) that he forgive his brothers (50:16).

49:29–33. JACOB'S LAST INSTRUCTIONS

GEN 49:29–33 NKJV	GEN 49:29–33 ESV
29 Then he charged them and said to them: "I am to be gathered to my people; bury me with my fathers in the cave that *is* in the field of Ephron the Hittite,	**29** Then he commanded them and said to them, "I am to be gathered to my people; bury me with my fathers in the cave that is in the field of Ephron the Hittite,
30 in the cave that *is* in the field of Machpelah, which *is* before Mamre in the land of Canaan, which Abraham bought with the field of Ephron the Hittite as a possession for a burial place.	**30** in the cave that is in the field at Machpelah, to the east of Mamre, in the land of Canaan, which Abraham bought with the field from Ephron the Hittite to possess as a burying place.
31 There they buried Abraham and Sarah his wife, there they buried Isaac and Rebekah his wife, and there I buried Leah.	**31** There they buried Abraham and Sarah his wife. There they buried Isaac and Rebekah his wife, and there I buried Leah—
32 The field and the cave that *is* there *were* purchased from the sons of Heth."	**32** the field and the cave that is in it were bought from the Hittites."
33 And when Jacob had finished commanding his sons, he drew his feet up into the bed and breathed his last, and was gathered to his people.	**33** When Jacob finished commanding his sons, he drew up his feet into the bed and breathed his last and was gathered to his people.

The phrase **be gathered to my/his people** occurs in the beginning and at the end of the unit, as an inclusio (49:29, 33), a sign of the unit boundaries and an indication of Jacob's main concern. Between these two boundaries, Jacob's arguments to highlight his request are arranged in a chiastic fashion (ABCB₁A₁):

A Jacob commands to his sons: "Gathered to my people" (49:29a)
   B Localization and legalization of the burial (49:29b–30)
      C Parents buried there (49:31)
   B₁ Localization and legalization of the burial (49:32)
A₁ Jacob finished commanding his sons: "Gathered to his people" (49:33)

49:29 This verb *tsawah* "charge," "command," which occurs here and in the conclusion (49:33), carries a religious connotation. The verb often refers to God's commandments (Exod 34:11; Deut 4:40). Jacob's request is of a religious nature. His words must be received by his sons as God's commandments. Jacob's request is not a sentimental, nostalgic desire to join the parents he loves and had lost. Jacob's concern is that he be buried in the Promised Land where his roots and his hopes are. Jacob situates himself as a link between the past patriarchs (Abraham and Isaac) who are buried in the Promised Land and the future people of Israel who will return there.

49:30 The burial site is precisely identified, what it is (**the cave**), to whom it belongs (**Ephron the Hittite**), and where it is (**in the field of Machpelah, which is before Mamre in the land of Canaan**) in order to assure the proper legalization of the operation. The phrase **a possession for a burial place** concludes and climaxes the verse.

49:31 The parallel between the couples **Abraham and Sarah** || **Isaac and Rebekah** implies the next couple: Jacob and Leah, especially since Leah was already buried in the cave of Machpelah (Rachel had been buried on the way to Ephrath, 35:19). This argument is the apex (the center) of the chiasm and therefore the most important one. Since the first *lek leka*, God's first call to Abraham to "go" to the Promised Land (12:1), the three patriarchs and matriarchs are associated with the same burial place in Canaan. Therefore, Jacob's burial marks the point of arrival and the first step in the fulfillment of God's promise.

49:32 The involvement of **the sons of Heth** in the legal contract parallels the reference to their father "Ephron the Hittite" (49:29b–30) and complements it, adding the force of chronology to the argument. The contract does not merely engage the father but also the sons and thus the following generations. Again, the return of Israel to the Promised Land looms on the horizon (cf. 48:21).

49:33 That Jacob expires precisely after he had **finished commanding his sons** suggests that Jacob feels that he has completed his duty and fulfilled his mission. The detail that Jacob draws **his feet up into the bed** indicates that he was, until now, sitting on his bed (48:2). Either Jacob knows that it is time for him to die, or he controls his death. The fact that the verb "he died" is absent does not mean that Jacob did not die. Jacob used that verb previously when referring to his death (48:21). The simple mention that he **breathed his last** implies that Jacob did not resist death and died peacefully (49:33). These details describing Jacob's death suggest a Jacob quite unlike the familiar Jacob, who tried to control or fight, a Jacob who is now at peace.

However, Jacob's peaceful death does not necessarily mean peace for the surviving sons. Jacob's death not only reinforces Joseph's power, who is the one who takes charge of the burial (50:1–14), but also raises concerns in the minds of the ten brothers who fear that Joseph may now take revenge on them (50:15–21).

Although the twelve sons were present around Jacob, the biblical text refers only to Joseph as the one who cares for Jacob's burial (50:1–14). In so doing, Joseph takes the position of the eldest son who is responsible for the burial, an attitude that is in accordance with Jacob's blessing (49:26). Joseph had also been designated to Jacob by God as the one who would "put his hand on your eyes" (46:4). The story of Jacob's burial involves two parts. The first part takes place in Egypt where Joseph mourns; he commands his servants to embalm his father and asks permission of the pharaoh to bury his father in Canaan (50:1–6). The second part takes place in Canaan where Jacob is buried (50:7–14).

50:1–6. JOSEPH MOURNS IN EGYPT

GEN 50:1–6 NKJV	GEN 50:1–6 ESV
1 Then Joseph fell on his father's face, and wept over him, and kissed him.	**1** Then Joseph fell on his father's face and wept over him and kissed him.
2 And Joseph commanded his servants the physicians to embalm his father. So the physicians embalmed Israel.	**2** And Joseph commanded his servants the physicians to embalm his father. So the physicians embalmed Israel.
3 Forty days were required for him, for such are the days required for those who are embalmed; and the Egyptians mourned for him seventy days.	**3** Forty days were required for it, for that is how many are required for embalming. And the Egyptians wept for him seventy days.
4 Now when the days of his mourning were past, Joseph spoke to the household of Pharaoh, saying, "If now I have found favor in your eyes, please speak in the hearing of Pharaoh, saying,	**4** And when the days of weeping for him were past, Joseph spoke to the household of Pharaoh, saying, "If now I have found favor in your eyes, please speak in the ears of Pharaoh, saying,
5 'My father made me swear, saying, "Behold, I am dying; in my grave which I dug for myself in the land of Canaan, there you shall bury me." Now therefore, please let me go up and bury my father, and I will come back.'"	**5** 'My father made me swear, saying, "I am about to die: in my tomb that I hewed out for myself in the land of Canaan, there shall you bury me." Now therefore, let me please go up and bury my father. Then I will return.'"
6 And Pharaoh said, "Go up and bury your father, as he made you swear."	**6** And Pharaoh answered, "Go up, and bury your father, as he made you swear."

50:1–3 Four verbs describe Joseph's reaction to his father's death: **fell … wept … kissed … commanded** (50:1–2). First, he abandons himself to his emotions that progress from devastation to sadness and then to affection. Only when he has reached the last emotion phase, feeling love for his father, does he moves into action. Although Joseph does not share in the religious beliefs of the Egyptians, he complies with their customs of mummification. The entire ceremonial process takes **seventy days** (50:3), which include forty days for the embalming and thirty days for the mourning. The number of seventy days was determined by the astronomical phenomenon of "decans," stars that remained below the horizon for seventy days before rising above the horizon, an allusion to the Egyptian belief of resurrection. However, it is noteworthy that only the custom of embalming is retained. Other

Egyptian funerary rituals, such as the provision of supplies, including food, vessels, clothing, and ornaments; the recitation of spells; and the offering rituals are completely absent in the biblical report. Although the embalming ritual is specifically mentioned, the omission of rituals is likely because of the theological significance associated with these rituals. Whereas the embalming ritual aimed at the preservation of the body, the intention of the other rituals was to ensure the immortality of the spiritual components of the human person. Joseph must have consented to the embalming practice, without the other Egyptian rituals, because he was essentially concerned with the mummification to enable a proper transportation of the corpse during the forthcoming long trip to Canaan. This observation is consistent with the fact that the only professionals involved in the embalming rituals are identified as **physicians**,[754] although the ceremonial event would normally also require the participation of priests; it is as though Joseph was concerned only with the physiological treatment of the mummification without its Egyptian religious component.

50:4–6 Following the time of mourning, Joseph turns to Pharaoh to ask his permission to bury his father in the country of Canaan. Joseph does not address the pharaoh directly but prefers to speak to certain people who belong to the house of Pharaoh. Scholars have speculated that Joseph did so because of his impure condition because of his recent proximity to the dead (Num 19:11, 14, 16) or because he had not yet completed his period of mourning (50:10); Joseph was still unshaven and improperly dressed to approach the king (41:14). A simpler reason is that Joseph wanted to avoid a rejection from the pharaoh in the presence of his courtiers. Joseph wisely laid the groundwork and lobbied to ensure a positive response. From an Egyptian perspective, Joseph's request is unusual and even offensive. The Egyptian west, the place of sunset, was considered the appropriate place to be buried to ensure eternity. However, Joseph wants to bury his father to the east, in Canaan. Thus, Joseph tactfully explains that this request is his father's express demand and that he made him swear that he would bury him **in the land of Canaan** (50:5), for he had already dug his tomb there. Joseph assures the pharaoh that this is not a strategy to leave, and he promises that he **will come back** (50:5). Given all of Joseph's arguments, the pharaoh retains only his promise to his father: **bury your father, as he made you swear** (50:6).

50:7–14. JOSEPH BURIES HIS FATHER IN CANAAN

GEN 50:7–14 NKJV	GEN 50:7–14 ESV
7 So Joseph went up to bury his father; and with him went up all the servants of Pharaoh, the elders of his house, and all the elders of the land of Egypt,	**7** So Joseph went up to bury his father. With him went up all the servants of Pharaoh, the elders of his household, and all the elders of the land of Egypt,
8 as well as all the house of Joseph, his brothers, and his father's house. Only their little ones, their flocks, and their herds they left in the land of Goshen.	**8** as well as all the household of Joseph, his brothers, and his father's household. Only their children, their flocks, and their herds were left in the land of Goshen.
9 And there went up with him both chariots and horsemen, and it was a very great gathering.	**9** And there went up with him both chariots and horsemen. It was a very great company.

---

754 Egyptologist Warburton describes the embalmers as "highly skilled professionals" who "had close associations with doctors" (David A. Warburton, "Mummification," *OEAE* 2:579).

10 Then they came to the threshing floor of Atad, which *is* beyond the Jordan, and they mourned there with a great and very solemn lamentation. He observed seven days of mourning for his father.

11 And when the inhabitants of the land, the Canaanites, saw the mourning at the threshing floor of Atad, they said, "This *is* a deep mourning of the Egyptians." Therefore its name was called Abel Mizraim, which *is* beyond the Jordan.

12 So his sons did for him just as he had commanded them.

13 For his sons carried him to the land of Canaan, and buried him in the cave of the field of Machpelah, before Mamre, which Abraham bought with the field from Ephron the Hittite as property for a burial place.

14 And after he had buried his father, Joseph returned to Egypt, he and his brothers and all who went up with him to bury his father.

10 When they came to the threshing floor of Atad, which is beyond the Jordan, they lamented there with a very great and grievous lamentation, and he made a mourning for his father seven days.

11 When the inhabitants of the land, the Canaanites, saw the mourning on the threshing floor of Atad, they said, "This is a grievous mourning by the Egyptians." Therefore the place was named Abel-mizraim; it is beyond the Jordan.

12 Thus his sons did for him as he had commanded them,

13 for his sons carried him to the land of Canaan and buried him in the cave of the field at Machpelah, to the east of Mamre, which Abraham bought with the field from Ephron the Hittite to possess as a burying place.

14 After he had buried his father, Joseph returned to Egypt with his brothers and all who had gone up with him to bury his father.

50:7–9 Joseph does not go to Canaan alone. Not only does all of his family accompany him, but also high dignitaries from the Egyptian administration. Even a battalion from the Egyptian army joins the troop. The importance of Egyptian involvement signifies the great honor Pharaoh held for the one who saved Egypt, but it also serves as a protection for the procession. This powerful presence may also subtly prevent any attempt on the part of the camp of Joseph (and more importantly Joseph himself) to escape and thus not to return to their Egyptian duties. Interestingly, much of the terminology describing the procession reappears in the Exodus account (Exod 10:7–10, 24; 11:3). These linguistic echoes alert the reader that the trip to Canaan to bury Jacob foreshadows the future journey of Jacob's descendants to the Promised Land.

50:10–11 The journey progresses in two steps. First, the entire cortege stops for an official mourning ceremony (50:10–11). This pause is located precisely at **the threshing floor of Atad, which is beyond the Jordan** (50:10). The expression *be'eber hayyarden* "beyond the Jordan" refers either to the east or to the west side of the Jordan. Considering the viewpoint of the author who is in Egypt, which is west of the Jordan, the place should be on the east side. Furthermore, the use of the same expression "beyond the Jordan" to locate the place *Abel Mizraim* "the mourning of Egypt" in connection to the perspective of the Canaanites (50:11), who live west of the Jordan, confirms this eastern location.

50:12–13 The second step involves only the sons of Jacob, a detail that is repeated twice (50:12–13). The first mention of **his sons** (50:12) refers back to Jacob's command (49:29) to mark the fulfillment of their duty as sons. The second mention of **his sons** (50:13) refers to their movement into the land of Canaan to imply some distance from the Egyptian camp. The Egyptian staff has remained behind, "beyond the Jordan," and did not cross the Jordan. Only **his sons carried him to the land of**

Canaan (50:13). This detail also parallels the future crossing by Israel who will cross the river, leaving the Egyptian army behind them. More significantly, this geographical precision indicates that the sons of Jacob went around the southern end of the Dead Sea and entered Canaan by crossing the Jordan near Jericho. Therefore, the route the procession takes with the bones of Jacob is basically the same as the Exodus route,[755] again pointing to the future return of Israel with the bones of Joseph. Not only are the Egyptians not mentioned in this second step, but Joseph also. Joseph is simply included in "his sons." This is the only part of the unit where the name of Joseph is absent in the narration. This is not only to affirm the corporate entity of Israel, but is especially intentional to again underline the foreshadowing significance of this journey: the twelve sons of Israel crossing the Jordan anticipate the future twelve tribes of Israel crossing the Jordan. This prophetic beckoning is reinforced by the legal argument of the possession of the land, which has been duly bought by Abraham (50:13).

50:14 Again, the attention is directed to Joseph. Despite the preceding emphasis, the burying of **his father** is twice attributed only to him. Even the remainder of the journey is solely under his control and initiative: **Joseph returned** (*hasheb*), as he promised, to Pharaoh (50:5). His brothers merely follow him, like all the others.

50:15–21. JOSEPH REASSURES HIS BROTHERS

GEN 50:15–21 NKJV	GEN 50:15–21 ESV
15 When Joseph's brothers saw that their father was dead, they said, "Perhaps Joseph will hate us, and may actually repay us for all the evil which we did to him."	**15** When Joseph's brothers saw that their father was dead, they said, "It may be that Joseph will hate us and pay us back for all the evil that we did to him."
16 So they sent *messengers* to Joseph, saying, "Before your father died he commanded, saying,	**16** So they sent a message to Joseph, saying, "Your father gave this command before he died,
17 'Thus you shall say to Joseph: "I beg you, please forgive the trespass of your brothers and their sin; for they did evil to you."' Now, please, forgive the trespass of the servants of the God of your father." And Joseph wept when they spoke to him.	**17** 'Say to Joseph, "Please forgive the transgression of your brothers and their sin, because they did evil to you."' And now, please forgive the transgression of the servants of the God of your father." Joseph wept when they spoke to him.
18 Then his brothers also went and fell down before his face, and they said, "Behold, we *are* your servants."	**18** His brothers also came and fell down before him and said, "Behold, we are your servants."
19 Joseph said to them, "Do not be afraid, for *am* I in the place of God?	**19** But Joseph said to them, "Do not fear, for am I in the place of God?
20 But as for you, you meant evil against me; *but* God meant it for good, in order to bring it about as *it is* this day, to save many people alive.	**20** As for you, you meant evil against me, but God meant it for good, to bring it about that many people should be kept alive, as they are today.
21 Now therefore, do not be afraid; I will provide for you and your little ones." And he comforted them and spoke kindly to them.	**21** So do not fear; I will provide for you and your little ones." Thus he comforted them and spoke kindly to them.

---

755 See Hamilton, *Genesis 18–50*, 597; cf. Rüdiger Bartelmus, "Topographie und Theologie: Exegetische und didaktische Anmerkungen zum letzten Kapitel der Genesis (Gen 50:1–14)," *BN* 29 (1985): 35–57.

50:15 The same verb *hasheb* that is used to refer to Joseph's return is now used by Joseph's brothers to describe the reason for their fear, that he will **repay**. The return of Joseph, which is reassuring to Pharaoh, is a threat to Joseph's brothers. The "return" of Joseph means for them that he will "return" the evil they did to him.

50:16-17 Joseph's brothers do not dare to approach Joseph directly (cf. 50:18). They prefer to speak to him through mediators. They place themselves under the protection of a sacred commandment, the one of the dying father: **before your father died he commanded** (50:16). The verb *tsawah* "command," which was used for the father (49:29), is used twice in the same phrase (50:16).[756] The language of the brothers has a strong religious resonance. In addition to the verb *tsawah*, which is related to the divine commandments (Exod 34:11; Deut 4:40; cf. 49:29), the technical expression *nas' 'awon/pesha'* "forgive trespass/sin" is normally connected to God (Num 14:19; Ps 32:1; Isa 33:24). In the Scriptures, forgiveness is essentially an act of God. Thus, human forgiveness is essentially a response to divine forgiveness. Joseph should forgive his brothers because of his father and thus because of God. This is why, as they ask for forgiveness, they refer to **the God of *your* father** (50:17). Note their use of the second personal pronoun, implying his unique personal relation with his father; they do not say "our father" but "your father." This last word, which evokes *his* father, causes Joseph to weep.

50:18 That the brothers **went and fell down before his face** indicates that the brothers are now physically present before Joseph, who has likely invited them to join him. Joseph's brothers are afraid, for their father is no longer alive to intervene on their behalf. They therefore propose to him to become his slaves in order to save their lives. Again, the scenario of the brothers bowing before Joseph and their willingness to serve him is reminiscent of Joseph's dream, which they had mocked.

50:19-21 Joseph again reassures his brothers that he intends no harm to them. Three times Joseph acknowledges God's works of salvation (50:20, 24-25) and thus concludes his series of seven declarations (cf. 45:5, 7-9). His words **do not be afraid** (50:19) are the same words God used to reassure Abraham of his future (15:1). To relieve the tension, Joseph places himself on the same human level: **am I in the place of God?** (50:19), thus restoring his connection with them. Jacob had used the same phrase with Rachel, who had complained of not having children (30:2). However, in the case of Jacob, these words were an expression of his anger, with a veiled accusation directed toward Rachel who, in his view, should feel guilty about her barrenness. In the case of Joseph, the same words express his love toward his brothers and are meant to discharge them from any worry. This sudden and explicit reference to God is appropriate in this context, not only because divine forgiveness is involved in human forgiveness (see above), but also because they **meant evil ... God meant it for good** (50:20). What they did, which they rightly acknowledge as "evil" (50:15), was designed **to save many people alive** (50:20). Joseph does not merely content himself with granting forgiveness to his brothers, he takes away their feeling of guilt, since their evil action turned out to be good. They can now face Joseph and confront the future. Joseph reassures them with the same words that involve the future, **do not be afraid** (50:21; cf. 50:19), and concludes with the promise that he

---

756 The first occurrence of the verb *tsawah* refers to the brothers' quest to Joseph (NKJV: "sent"); its second occurrence refers to the father's command (NKJV: "commanded").

will provide for them and their children. Only when he informs them regarding the concrete reality of their future do his words become tender; he comforts them and speaks to their hearts. Good sentiments do not precede or replace an action; they follow them and are therefore well received and responded to.

JOSEPH'S DEATH AND BURIAL (50:22–26)

GEN 50:22–26 NKJV	GEN 50:20–26 ESV
22 So Joseph dwelt in Egypt, he and his father's household. And Joseph lived one hundred and ten years.	**22** So Joseph remained in Egypt, he and his father's house. Joseph lived 110 years.
23 Joseph saw Ephraim's children to the third *generation*. The children of Machir, the son of Manasseh, were also brought up on Joseph's knees.	**23** And Joseph saw Ephraim's children of the third generation. The children also of Machir the son of Manasseh were counted as Joseph's own.
24 And Joseph said to his brethren, "I am dying; but God will surely visit you, and bring you out of this land to the land of which He swore to Abraham, to Isaac, and to Jacob."	**24** And Joseph said to his brothers, "I am about to die, but God will visit you and bring you up out of this land to the land that he swore to Abraham, to Isaac, and to Jacob."
25 Then Joseph took an oath from the children of Israel, saying, "God will surely visit you, and you shall carry up my bones from here."	**25** Then Joseph made the sons of Israel swear, saying, "God will surely visit you, and you shall carry up my bones from here."
26 So Joseph died, *being* one hundred and ten years old; and they embalmed him, and he was put in a coffin in Egypt.	**26** So Joseph died, being 110 years old. They embalmed him, and he was put in a coffin in Egypt.

These five verses conclude the last section of the book of Genesis. This conclusion consists of three parts that revolve around three periods. First, the present: Joseph settles in Egypt and lives a long life (50:22). Second, the immediate future: Joseph sees his children until the third generation (50:23). Third, the distant future, which is the most important and longest part: Joseph prepares for the Promised Land (50:24–26).

50:22 The phrase **so Joseph dwelt** echoes the phrase "Now Jacob (Israel) dwelt" (37:1; 47:27) with the same verbal form (*wayyesheb*). However, there is one important difference between the two dwellings. Whereas Jacob dwells in Canaan, Joseph dwells in Egypt. The echo between the two phrases bridges the two experiences. Joseph dwells in Egypt with the memory of Jacob dwelling in Canaan. Joseph knows that his dwelling in Egypt is not ideal. His place should be in Canaan where his father had dwelt and where he had recently buried him. Joseph is in exile. This last occurrence of the verb "dwell" in the phrase "so Joseph dwelt" also echoes the first usage of that verb in the Scriptures, referring to Cain who "dwelt in the land of Nod" (4:16). This echo with Cain, who dwells in Nod, awakens another echo: Joseph is in exile thinking of Canaan, whereas Cain is in exile thinking of the Garden of Eden (4:16b). Joseph assumes his exiled condition and focuses on the present.

Joseph lived one hundred and ten years. A lifespan of 110 years was considered to be the ideal life duration in ancient Egypt[757] and testifies to Joseph's enjoyment of the present life in Egypt. The same number was applied to famous sages such as Djedi, Ptahhotep, Amenhotep son Hapu, and many others from the time of the Old Kingdom (3000–2700 BC). However, the Egyptian significance of this number does not mean that it is a symbolic number. Joseph is not the only one to be graced with such a long life. Joshua also lived 110 years (Josh 24:29).

50:23 Joseph lives long enough to see his grandchildren and great-grandchildren. Ephraim's children are indicated **to the third generation**. Great-grandchildren from Machir, the son of Manasseh, are brought up on his knees. This precision, which is absent for Ephraim, suggests that Joseph prefers his firstborn (48:18). Interestingly, this gateway to the future is also paralleled in the two "dwelling" passages of Jacob and Cain. In both texts, the "dwelling" is followed by a genealogy that elaborates the future of the children (4:17–24; cf. 37:2–11).

50:24 This is the first and only time in the last unit that Joseph speaks: **I am dying** (50:24a). Joseph thinks of his death. Unlike Jacob, who talked to his children as he was about to die (48:21), Joseph talks to his brothers much earlier.[758] This is because it was necessary for Joseph to have this conversation while all his brothers were still alive. Because Joseph and Benjamin were the youngest sons, Joseph knew that he would likely outlive his brothers. Joseph does not simply anticipate his future death—he thinks of the future of the Exodus, the return to the Promised Land. Joseph bases his hope on the memory that God **swore to Abraham, to Isaac, and to Jacob** (50:24b). This is the first time that this classic phrase, associating the three patriarchs, is used in the Scriptures (cf. Exod 3:6).

50:25 The oath that Joseph asks his brothers to take concerning the carrying up of his bones to the Promised Land echoes the oath that God took to the three patriarchs (50:24b) and the oath that he took to bury his father (47:31). The use of the same verb *shaba'* "take an oath" connects the return of the twelve tribes of Israel from Egypt, carrying the bones of Joseph, with the divine promise. Furthermore, this is Joseph's seventh acknowledgment of the work of God's salvation on behalf of His people. The book of Genesis ends with a series of seven works of God, echoing the seven works of the creation story.

50:26 This last verse of the unit (and of the entire book of Genesis) echoes its first verse: **Joseph died … one hundred and ten years** ‖ "Joseph lived one hundred and ten years" (50:22). The text specifies **they embalmed him**. Joseph and Jacob are the only two persons that the Bible records as having been mummified according to the Egyptian ritual. Is it a coincidence that both mentions of embalming, which implied the belief in the recovery of eternal life, are situated in the perspective of the Promised Land? Whereas the text mentions a grave for Jacob but no coffin, for Joseph, the text mentions a **coffin** but no grave. Curiously, no biblical record of a grave where the bones of Joseph were buried or preserved in Egypt is mentioned. Joseph was embalmed, and yet he is not buried because of the hope of the Promised Land. Strangely, Joseph does not command to have his bones buried at his death. He wants his bones to be carried to Canaan only in the context of a universal return,

---

757 See J. M. A. Janssen, "On the Ideal Lifetime of the Egyptians," *OMRO* 31 (1950): 33–43.

758 A little linguistic detail accounts for this difference. Whereas the report of Jacob's preparation uses the adverb *hinneh* "behold," which indicates the immediate future, it is absent in the report of Joseph's preparation.

with all the people of Israel. In the meantime, he is **put in a coffin in Egypt**. The Hebrew uses the definite article *ba'aron,* meaning literally "in *the* coffin," thus stressing the significance of this coffin without a grave. Thus, the book of Genesis ends the same way in which the whole Pentateuch ends—with death, yet without a grave (Deut 34:6), and in the perspective of the Promised Land (Deut 34:1–4). The book of Genesis, similar to the entire Pentateuch, begins with creation and the Garden of Eden (1–2) and ends with the prospect of the Promised Land and the hope of the resurrection of the dead (Deut 34:6; cf. Judg 9). This literary coincidence is not accidental; indeed, this pattern of association is carried over in biblical tradition (Heb 11:1) and affects the structure of several books of the Bible (see, for instance, Isa 1:2; 66:22–23; Eccl 1:1–11; 12:14; Dan 1:12; 12:13; John 1:1–10; 21:22–23) and even the canonical structure of the entire Bible (1–2; Rev 22:20; cf. Mal 4:5).[759]

In a coffin in Egypt. The last two words of the book of Genesis *ba'aron bemitsrayim* (lit. trans.: "in the coffin in Egypt") interestingly echo its first two words *bere'shit bara'* "in the beginning created." In both cases, the two words begin with the same explosive sound "*be*." In addition, the two phrases resonate with each other through the play of common assonances and grammatical parallels (*bara'* ‖ *ba'aron* and *bere'shit* ‖ *bemitsrayim*), thus forming a chiastic structure that relates the two phrases:

*bere'shit **b**ara'* "in the beginning created" (1:1)

X

*ba'aron **b**emitsrayim* "in the coffin in Egypt" (50:26)

This poetic and phonetic link between the first two words and the last two words of Genesis reinforces our previous observation of the echo between the beginning and end of the book of Genesis and suggests a crucial spiritual lesson: beyond the Mosaic hope in the return to the Promised Land lies another hope, more universal and more existential, our hope in the return to Eden and the original creation of the heavens and earth (Isa 65:17–25; Rev 21:1–4).

---

759 See Westermann who noticed this canonical structure and concluded its significance in regard to "the center of the Bible's message" (Westermann, *Beginning and End in the Bible*, 1, 33, 37).

SELECTED ANNOTATED BIBLIOGRAPHY
SUGGESTIONS FOR FURTHER READING OR CONSULTATION

The works listed below contain valuable information for those wishing to dig deeper into the biblical text. They are written with a wide variety of presuppositions about God and Scripture. The list also suggests significant and relevant contributions on Genesis by Seventh-day Adventist writers. The annotations below are designed to assist you in selecting and evaluating what you will read. The Editors

COMMENTARIES ON GENESIS

Arnold, Bill. *Encountering the Book of Genesis.* Grand Rapids: Baker, 1998. Evangelical. A practical introduction (textbook style) for college students. Discusses basic theological questions (creation, sin, etc.) and introductory issues (textual criticism, documentary hypothesis).

Borgman, Paul. *Genesis: The Story We Haven't Heard.* Downers Grove: IVP, 2001. Evangelical. The author, a professor of English, approaches the book of Genesis as a whole, with literary sensitivity, showing the interconnections of its theological themes and weaving the richness of human experience with the presence of a God who is still relevant to our present life.

Calvin, Jean. *Genesis.* Wheaton: Crossway Books, 2001. In this translation of the Franco-Swiss Reformer's commentary, attention is given to the plain reading of the text as well as to pastoral and theological insights.

Cassuto, Umberto. *A Commentary on the Book of Genesis.* 2 vols. English ed. Jerusalem: Magnes Press, Hebrew University, 1961–1964. A critical discussion of documentary hypothesis. Incorporates ANE and rabbinic literature.

Hamilton, Victor P. *The Book of Genesis.* NICOT. 2 vols. Grand Rapids: Eerdmans, 1990, 1995. Evangelical. Attention is given to ANE backgrounds (linguistic and cultural) as well as New Testament appropriations of the texts.

Longman, Tremper, III. *How to Read Genesis.* Downers Grove: IVP, 2005. Evangelical. A practical introduction for the layperson, clearly presenting the larger picture of Genesis. Attention to civilizations and cultures contemporary to the biblical world is provided.

Luther, Martin. *Luther's Works: Lectures on Genesis.* 8 vols. St. Louis: Concordia, 1958–1966. Translation of the German Reformer's commentary. Attention is given to the literal sense of the text and Christological applications. The focus is on traditional Lutheran doctrines.

Mathews, Kenneth A. *Genesis.* NAC. 2 vols. Nashville: Broadman & Holman, 1996,

2005. Evangelical. A high view of Scripture is assumed with intellectual rigor. A theological and exegetical emphasis is provided with detailed commentary, including a thorough discussion of critical views.

Rashi. *Genesis*. Vol. 1 of *The Torah With Rashi's Commentary*. Brooklyn: Mesorah Publications, 1999. This English translation of the great medieval rabbi's commentary on Genesis conveys the traditional Jewish interpretation of the book of Genesis.

Sarna, Nahum. *Genesis*. JPS Torah Commentary 1. Philadelphia: Jewish Publication Society, 1989. Critical moderate. Incorporates rabbinic interpretations.

Turner, Laurence A. *Genesis Readings: A New Biblical Commentary*. Sheffield: Sheffield Academic Press, 2000. Reads Genesis as a coherent whole using a narrative approach, with special attention to the dynamic of plot and characters and their interconnections, noting its ironies and surprises.

Waltke, Bruce K., and Cathi J. Fredericks. *Genesis: A Commentary*. Grand Rapids: Zondervan, 2001. Evangelical. Provides attention to literary techniques and theological lessons.

Walton, John. *Genesis*. NIVAC. Grand Rapids: Zondervan, 2001. Evangelical. An insightful exposition in connection to the ANE world in view of its contemporary significance. However, the author's personal interpretation of biblical ideas is often adopted at the expense of the original intention of the biblical text.

Wenham, Gordon. *Genesis*. WBC. 2 vols. Waco: Word, 1987; Dallas: Word, 1994. Critical moderate. Attention to matters of form, structure, historical setting, and history of interpretation.

Westermann, Claus. *Genesis: A Commentary*. 3 vols. Translated by John J. Scullion. Minneapolis: Augsburg, 1984–1986. Critical. Focuses on theological interpretation.

White, Ellen G. *Patriarchs and Prophets*. Nampa: Pacific Press, 2005. Edifying and inspired exposition of the stories of the Pentateuch. Attention to life lessons and the significance of the history of salvation.

MONOGRAPHS AND ARTICLES ON GENESIS

Alter, Robert. *The Art of Biblical Narrative*. New York: Basic Books, 1981. Valuable use of literary techniques in the Genesis accounts, yet to be read with circumspection as the author is not committed to their historicity.

Andreasen, Niels-Erik. "Town and Country in the Old Testament." *Encounter* 42

(1981): 259–275. A study of the ambivalent status of the city in the Old Testament. Against the generally accepted opinion that the Old Testament is antiurban, this author suggests that the biblical city is not negative and is, on the contrary, ambivalent. This insight is essentially drawn from Genesis (4:17; 11:1–9; 13:12; 14:1ff.; 18–19) and confirmed in the conquest, Psalms, Wisdom texts, and Prophets.

Azevedo, Joaquim. "At the Door of Paradise: A Contextual Interpretation of Gen 4:7." *BN* 100 (1999): 45–59. Against the ANE background and in light of its immediate context, this author suggests a ritual environment of the text, in parallel with the imagery of the sanctuary. For instance, the word *khatta't* "sin" should refer to the atoning sacrifice that stands as a solution to Cain's confusion.

Baldwin, John Templeton, ed. *Creation, Catastrophe, and Calvary: Why a Global Flood Is Vital to the Doctrine of Atonement.* Hagerstown, MD: Review and Herald, 2000. In-depth biblical and geological essays, which to a greater or lesser degree, indicate the dependence between creation, the flood, and the cross. Demonstrates how evolutionary theory is inconsistent with the Christian doctrine of atonement.

Ball, Bryan W., ed. *In the Beginning: Science and Scripture Confirm Creation.* Nampa: Pacific Press, 2012. These essays are written by Adventist biblical scholars and scientists in defense of the biblical teaching of creation. The biblical perspective includes R. Davidson (on Genesis 1:1, the "when" of creation), L. Turner (theological reading of Genesis 1), P. Petersen (biblical theology and doctrine of creation), and S. Thompson (Genesis text in the New Testament). The scientific perspective involves T. Standish (scientific evidence for intelligent design), A. Roth (the Genesis flood confirmed by geological data), J. C. Walton (assessing and challenging neo-Darwinian evolution), and J. Gibson (critical survey on the theory of evolution).

Brand, Leonard. *Faith, Reason & Earth History: A Paradigm of Earth and Biological Origins by Intelligent Design.* 2nd ed. Berrien Springs, MI: Andrews University Press, 2009. Presents a paradigm in which much of the geologic column and its fossil record may appropriately be explained as the Genesis flood. Affirms "the integrity of the scientific process while maintaining a context of faith."

Cairus, Aecio E. "Protection and Reward: The Significance of Ancient Midrashic Expositions on Genesis 15:1–6." PhD diss., Andrews University, 1988. Draws exegetical lessons from midrashic interpretations of Genesis 15:1–6 for an enhanced understanding of key terms of the passage ("protection," "reward," "offspring," "trust," and "righteousness").

Cole, Ross. "The Sabbath and Genesis 2:1–3." *AUSS* 41, no. 1 (2003): 5–12. Refutes the arguments supporting the idea that the Sabbath of the Genesis creation account does not imply observance, and demonstrates on an exegetical and literary basis that, on the contrary, it does.

Davidson, Richard M. "Back to the Beginning: Genesis 1–3 and the Theological Center of Scripture." Pages 5–29 in *Christ, Salvation, and the Eschaton: Essays in Honor of Hans K. LaRondelle.* Edited by D. Heinz, J. Moskala, and P. M. van Bemmelen. Berrien Springs, MI: Andrews University, 2009. Explores the sanctuary/temple references in Genesis 1–3 and contends that they provide a key for biblical theology and the research for its center.

_____. "Earth's First Sanctuary: Genesis 1–3 and Parallel Creation Accounts." *AUSS* 53, no. 1 (2015): 65–89. A detailed examination (forty lines) of the biblical evidence that supports the idea of the Garden of Eden as the original sanctuary.

_____. "The Genesis Account of Origins." Pages 59–129 in *The Genesis Creation Account and Its Reverberations in the Old Testament.* Edited by Gerald A. Klingbeil. Berrien Springs, MI: Andrews University Press, 2015.

_____. "The Genesis Flood Narrative: Crucial Issues in the Current Debate." *AUSS* 42, no. 1 (2004): 49–77. Discusses the various interpretations of the biblical flood story and provides significant literary evidence from the biblical text to support the literal, historical, and global flood.

_____. "Shame and Honor in the Beginning: A Study of Genesis 4." Pages 44–76 in *Shame and Honor: Presenting Biblical Themes in Shame and Honor Contexts.* Edited by Bruce L. Bauer. Berrien Springs, MI: Andrews University, 2014. A discussion of the social and moral values of "shame and honor" from an anthropological perspective applied to the Old Testament, with special focus on the crime of Cain in Genesis 4.

_____. "The Theology of Sexuality in the Beginning: Genesis 1–2." *AUSS* 26, no. 1 (1988): 5–24.

_____. "The Theology of Sexuality in the Beginning: Genesis 3." *AUSS* 26, no. 2 (1988): 121–131. Both articles analyze the high points of creation with concentration on the implication on the man and woman's relationship, finding no support for any hierarchical view of the sexes.

Davidson, Richard M., and Randall W. Younker. "The Myths of the Solid Heavenly Dome: Another Look at the Hebrew *raqia'.*" *AUSS* 49, no. 1 (2011): 125–147. A linguistic and literary refutation of the view that the Hebrews believed in a flat earth and a solid vaulted heaven.

Davidson Schafer, Rahel. "The 'Kinds' of Genesis 1: What Is the Meaning of *Mîn?*" *JATS* 14, no. 1 (2003): 86–100. An analysis of the use of the Hebrew word *mîn* "kind" in 1:1–25 and in the contexts of Genesis, Leviticus, and Deuteronomy suggests that the word refers to a broad concept of categorization, allowing for microevolution.

Doukhan, Jacques B. "The Center of the *'Aqedah*: A Study of the Literary Structure of Genesis 22:1–19." *AUSS* 31, no. 1 (1993): 17–28.

_____. *The Genesis Creation Story: Its Literary Structure.* Andrews University Seminary Doctoral Dissertation Series. Berrien Springs, MI: Andrews University Press, 1978. Attention is given to the literary structure of the Genesis creation account (1:1–2:4a) in connection to its parallel text (2:4b–24) to show its unity and theological significance.

_____. *On the Way to Emmaus: Five Messianic Prophecies Explained*. Clarksville: Messianic Jewish Publishers, 2012. Covers a large field of biblical texts from Genesis onward to Isaiah and Daniel. Argues and demonstrates that messianic texts carry original messianic intention.

Gage, Warren A. *The Gospel of Genesis: Studies in Protology and Eschatology*. Winona Lake: Carpenter Books, 1984. Evangelical. Creative attention to literary patterns and keywords. Insightful and theological.

Garrett, Duane, A. *Rethinking Genesis: The Sources and Authorship of the First Book of the Pentateuch*. Grand Rapids: Baker, 1991. Evangelical. A careful discussion of critical issues in the book of Genesis (documentary hypothesis, Mosaic authorship, structure of Genesis).

Hasel, Gerhard F. "The Genealogies of Gen 5 and 11 and Their Alleged Background." *AUSS* 16 (1978): 361–374. By comparing the genealogies of Genesis 5 and 11 with Mesopotamian texts, this author concludes, based on his observation (e.g., names, longevity of reigns, antediluvians, beginning and end of respective documents), that a significant lack of agreement exists between the two sources, which belong to different types of literature, with different functions and philosophical purposes.

_____. "The Meaning of 'Let Us' in Gen 1:26." *AUSS* 13 (1972): 58–66. Following a survey of various interpretations of the plural form of the verb (e.g., Trinitarian, plural of majesty, of deliberation), this author argues for the plural of fullness involving a plurality of persons.

_____. "The Polemic Nature of the Genesis Cosmology." *EvQ* 46 (1974): 81–102. Shows the polemic intention of the Genesis creation account against its Near Eastern background, focusing on *tehom* "deep," *tannim* "large water creatures," and the creation by word.

_____. "The Significance of the Cosmology in Genesis 1 in Relation to ANE Parallels." *AUSS* 10 (1972): 1–20. This close examination of similarities and differences of crucial terms and motifs between Genesis 1 and ANE cosmologies (such as *tehom-Tiamat*, luminaries, creation of man) indicates that Genesis 1 is basically different and sharply antimythological, with a strong polemic intention based on a specific Hebrew understanding of reality.

Hoffmeier, James K. *Israel in Egypt: The Evidence for the Authenticity of the Exodus Tradition*. New York: Oxford University Press, 1996. Defends the plausibility of the biblical stories (esp. Joseph) based on archaeological evidence in Egypt.

Klingbeil, Gerald A., ed. *The Genesis Creation Account and Its Reverberations in the Old Testament*. A collection of essays discussing issues of interpretation and theology in the Genesis creation account (R. Davidson: the first line of creation; J. Doukhan: the absence of death in creation; K. and M. Hasel: polemic against ANE cosmology; R. Davidson and R. W. Younker: the heavenly dome). Other articles explore the impact of creation in the Old Testament (R. Davidson: Ps 104; P. Gregor: the Pentateuch; M. Klingbeil: the Prophets; A. M. Rodríguez: Wisdom; A. Muran: Psalms).

Moskala, Jiří. "Dietary Laws of Leviticus 11 and Creation." Pages 17–28 in *Creation and Hope, Essays in Honor of Jacques B. Doukhan*. Edited by Jiří Moskala. Berrien Springs: Old Testament Department, Andrews University, 2000. Examines the literary and linguistic links between key terms of the dietary list of Leviticus 11 and Genesis 1 and establishes that "creation is the umbrella" of the legislation of clean and unclean animals and food.

_____. "A Fresh Look at Two Genesis Accounts: Contradictions?" *AUSS* 49, no. 1 (2011): 45–65. Examines the differences and contrasts between the two creation stories and observes their complementarity, while addressing various issues of apparent contradictions between them.

_____. "Interpretation of *bereshit* in the Context of Genesis 1:1–3." *AUSS* 49, no. 1 (2011): 33–44. A comprehensive overview of the diverse translations and interpretations of the first word of Genesis 1, followed by a stylistic analysis of the sequence of thoughts in Genesis 1:1–3; emphasis on the historical and not liturgical intention of the text, even though it leads to worship.

_____. "Toward Trinitarian Thinking in the Hebrew Scriptures." *JATS* 21, no. 1 (2010): 245–275. In this comprehensive yet nuanced study, the author discusses key passages of the Old Testament (including Genesis texts such as 1:1–3, 26; 3:22; 11:7; 18:1–2; 32:14) pointing to the idea of Trinity.

Ojewole, Afolarin O. "The Seed in Genesis 3:15: An Exegetical and Intertextual Study." PhD diss., Andrews University, 2002. Analyzes exegetically and intertextually the meaning of the word *zera'* "seed" in Genesis 3:15 and establishes, based on the syntax, that it refers to a single individual and has messianic intention.

Ostring, Elisabeth. "The Theology of Human Work as Found in the Genesis Narrative, Compared With the Co-Creationist Theology of Human Work." PhD diss., Avondale College of Higher Education, 2015. Using a narrative literary approach, the author analyzes the theology of work in the book of Genesis ("blessed relational") and compares it to current theologies of work.

Ouro, Roberto. "The Earth of Genesis 1:2: Abiotic or Chaotic? Part III." *AUSS* 38, no. 1 (2000): 59–67. Last part of a series on Genesis 1:2. Based on his linguistic and literary study of the text, compared with the ANE and in light of its parallel with Genesis 2:5, the author establishes that the description of the pre-creation suggests a state without vegetation and uninhabited by humans and animals ("abiotic").

Pritchard, James B., ed. *Ancient Near Eastern Texts Relating to the Old Testament*. Princeton: Princeton University Press, 1969. Contains translations of the most important ANE texts, which are relevant for understanding the Old Testament (parallels and contemporary), with introductions and notes. Comprehensive.

Regalado, Ferdinand O. "The Creation Account in Genesis 1: Our World Only or the Universe?" *JATS* 13, no. 2 (2002): 108–120. Based on a systematic contextual analysis of its specific expressions (e.g., "in the beginning," "heavens and earth") and considering the Hebrew view of the world, this author concludes that the creation account (chapter 1) refers only to this world.

Roth, Ariel A. *Origins: Linking Science and Scripture*. Hagerstown, MD: Review and Herald, 1998. An introduction to the study of the intersection of religion and science written by a scientist, showing how much science supports Scripture. Covers challenging topics in biology, paleontology, and geology. Tone is constructive and respectful, not polemic nor apologetic.

_____. *Science Discovers God: Seven Convincing Lines of Evidence for His Existence*. Hagerstown, MD: Review and Herald, 2008. A survey of how some aspects of science point to the existence of God. Analyzes the fine-tuning of the universe, the origin and complexity of life, the issue of time, scientific paradigms, and limitations of science.

Sailhamer, John H. *The Pentateuch as Narrative: A Biblical-Theological Commentary*. Grand Rapids: Zondervan, 1992. Evangelical. Treatment of literary techniques of the Pentateuch with special attention to its eschatological and messianic purpose.

Sigvartsen, Jan A. "Messiah Son of Joseph: Genesis 49:22–26." MA thesis, Andrews University, 1998. A discussion of the messianic view of Joseph from a typological perspective, and a thorough review of the interpretation of Joseph as a type of the Messiah in traditional Jewish and early Christian sources.

Stefanovic, Zdravko. "The Great Reversal: Thematic Links Between Genesis 2 and 3." *AUSS* 32, no. 1 (1994): 47–56. An attentive study of chapter 2 and 3 discloses a carefully crafted chiastic structure. Genesis 3 contains a reversed order of similar elements found in Genesis 2, testifying to the literary unity of the stories and to the theological lesson of the disruption of sin.

Turner, Laurence A. *Back to the Present: Encountering Genesis in the 21st Century*. Granthan, England: Autumn House, 2004. From his narrative reading of the text, the author infers lessons on the significance of key literary features of the book of Genesis and on the reality of the person of God with whom we can relate.

Warning, Wilfried. "Terminological Patterns and Genesis 38." *AUSS* 38, no. 2 (2000): 293–305. A search of terminological patterns in Genesis 38 (*natan, ba', shem*) and in similar interlinking major parts of Genesis (*bagad, sur, kasah, natah, bagad*) enlightens the pivotal role of Judah among his brothers and suggests an interesting network of related theological ideas.

Younker, Randall W. *God's Creation: Exploring the Genesis Story.* Nampa, ID: Pacific Press, 1999. A Seventh-day Adventist perspective on the book of Genesis with special emphasis on the historicity of chapters 1–11, creation week, relationship between Genesis 1 and 2, the fall and its consequences, Sabbath, and re-creation.

Zinke, E. Edward. "A Theology of the Sabbath." *JATS* 2, no. 2 (1991): 145–149. Discusses the crucial role of the Sabbath in regard to foundational theological truths (salvation, eschatology) but also as a part of the personal life (relationship with God, joy, and faithfulness) and as the essence of the entire Christian experience.